Instructor's Notes and Solutions Manual

Mathematics *for* High School Teachers

An Advanced Perspective

Usiskin • Peressini • Marchisotto • Stanley

PEARSON

Prentice Hall

Upper Saddle River, NJ 07458

Editor-in-Chief: Sally Yagan
Supplement Editor: Joanne Wendelken
Assistant Managing Editor: John Matthews
Production Editor: Donna Crilly
Supplement Cover Manager: Paul Gourhan
Supplement Cover Designer: Joanne Alexandris
Manufacturing Buyer: Ilene Kahn

© 2003 by Pearson Education, Inc.
Pearson Education, Inc.
Upper Saddle River, NJ 07458

Printed in the United States of America

10 9 8 7 6 5 4 3 2 1

ISBN 0-13-046154-7

Pearson Education Ltd., *London*
Pearson Education Australia Pty. Ltd., *Sydney*
Pearson Education Singapore, Pte. Ltd.
Pearson Education North Asia Ltd., *Hong Kong*
Pearson Education Canada, Inc., *Toronto*
Pearson Educación de Mexico, S.A. de C.V.
Pearson Education—Japan, *Tokyo*
Pearson Education Malaysia, Pte. Ltd.
Pearson Education, *Upper Saddle River, New Jersey*

CONTENTS

INSTRUCTOR'S NOTES

GENERAL REMARKS

As the preface indicates, these materials are meant for prospective or practicing high school teachers and others interested in a deeper understanding of school mathematics. The materials assume that the student has had calculus and at least one mathematics course beyond calculus in which students were expected to do proofs and algebraic structures were discussed such as linear or abstract) algebra or real analysis. Certain chapters of the book refer to specific background topics such as matrix algebra or groups, but full courses in these topics are not prerequisites for this course. Rather, instructors may fill in the required background if they choose to cover these chapters. These Notes occasionally alert instructors to specific topics that may need to be covered for students with only the minimum prerequisites outlined above.

This book is suitable for upper division undergraduate or graduate mathematics or mathematics education majors who are prospective mathematics teachers or for the professional development of graduate mathematics teachers. Specifically, we believe this to be a suitable book for a number of specialized audiences. As the text for one or two **capstone courses** for preservice high school mathematics teachers, this book can serve as a vehicle helping them to apply what they have learned in the college mathematics courses they have taken to the high school courses they will teach. Many beginning high school teachers are no better prepared mathematically to teach such topics as congruent triangles, factoring and division of polynomials, and decimals as they were when they entered college. This book contains ample material to help such teachers. The same applies to preservice middle school mathematics teachers, but for them the instructor should select sections and problems within sections so that the content parallels middle school concepts.

These materials are not meant to replace any existing course. Yet sections of this book have commonalities with the content of what is presently in abstract or higher algebra courses, college-level geometry courses, and courses devoted to sharpening student abilities in proof or problem solving. It is likely more valuable for future teachers than a course in complex variables, partial differential equations, differential geometry, or a second course in linear algebra.

It is our belief that every student receiving a graduate degree in mathematics education should be familiar with the kind of content covered in this book. At the **graduate level**, a two-course sequence is possible, taking the chapters in order.

Many people may find it useful to use parts of the book in a series of **workshops** not necessarily adding up to a single course. Particularly appropriate for workshops and similar activities are the sections dealing with extended problem analyses. These sections can be introduced by the instructor in a guided discovery way, then discussed with the class, with problems given to be solved before the next workshop.

We caution that these materials are not meant to constitute a course in the methods of teaching mathematics. An important goal of the materials is to have students using the materials engage in the methods of mathematicians and other mathematically proficient people, but these are mathematical methods, not teaching methods. While mathematical methods such as extensions of common problems, or examinations of concepts may suggest certain types of teaching methods in schools, the authors do not wish to be prescriptive here about how these ideas should be translated into the high school classroom. In particular, the authors caution against using these materials or the problems in them with high school students without careful consideration of the backgrounds of the students and adaptation to those backgrounds.

From our experience with many pilots nationwide in a wide variety of settings, we conclude that, under normal conditions, there is enough material in this book for at least a full year (two semesters) of study even if only about 50% of the problems are assigned. Aside from a few exceptions, the chapters are relatively independent and an instructor may choose from them. However, some chapters contain more sophisticated content than others. As a result, there are four reasonably natural sequences that might occupy a semester's work:

Algebra emphasis:	Chapters 1-6
Geometry emphasis:	Chapters 1, 7-11
For less prepared students:	Chapters 1, 3, 4, 7, 8, 10
For better prepared students:	Chapters 1, 2, 5, 6, 9, 11.

Notice that in each sequence we suggest beginning with Chapter 1 so that students are aware of the features of this book and of some of the differences between this course and other mathematics courses they have taken.

If an instructor wishes to skip around, we should note that Chapter 6 is helped by having done Chapters 2 and 5; Chapter 8 is eased by having covered Chapter 7; Chapter 9 and Chapter 10 are relatively independent but each is helped by having done Chapter 8; Chapter 11 is helped by having done Chapter 7. Unlike many college-level mathematics texts, this text does not adhere to a strictly ordered logical sequence, so you may find that some ideas and theorems introduced in one chapter are discussed and proved in a later chapter. But within chapters, instructors are encouraged not to take sections out of order.

We expect students to have technology beyond paper and pencil while studying from these materials. To use Part I, students should have a graphing calculator or computer equivalent, and it does not hurt at times to have available a computer algebra system such as that found on a TI-89, TI-92, Mathematica or Maple. In Part II, some problems ask students to use a dynamic geometry drawing program such as Cabri Geometrié or The Geometer's Sketchpad.

We welcome your comments and suggestions. Please direct them to: Zalman Usiskin, 5835 S. Kimbark, Chicago, IL 60647.

CHAPTER 1 – What Is Meant by "An Advanced Perspective"?

Objectives

After completing Chapter 1, the student should be able to:

- describe the goals of this course and indicate how they differ from those of most other college mathematics courses.

- identify some features of an *extended analysis* of a problem and apply them to a problem such as the average test-grade or scoring title problem.

- identify features of a *concept analysis* and apply them to a concept such as parallelism in geometry.

- provide examples of corresponding properties of addition and multiplication of numbers and the sets on which these properties apply.

Notes

Students enter mathematics courses with preconceptions about what they will cover. They often think that this course will be like other mathematics courses, yet easier because it discusses the mathematics taught in high school. We strongly urge that all classes cover this chapter because it quickly challenges those preconceptions.

Also, we think it advisable that all students read the preface.

Chapter 1 Reading

Because this chapter is likely not to be read before the first day of class, you may wish to use Problem 9 (page 15) as an in-class activity. If you do this, then you may wish to have students keep their books closed. This can easily take an hour or more but can be well worth the time. A detailed exposition of the problem, with commentary for the instructor, is provided in the Solutions.

If you wish to mimic the example of concept analysis, you can start by finding out the views of your students towards parallelism. It is our experience that many students view parallelism only with lines (and planes, if you remind them) and associate parallelism only with non-intersection. You might get varying opinions if you ask your students whether they think rays in opposite directions on different parallel lines are (or should be called) parallel. Or you might do a totally different analysis with a concept of your own choosing.

Still another approach is to run through the problem analysis given in the chapter. In Jane's average test-grade problem, a goal is fixed. In the Shaq-Jordan extension, the goal is for Shaq to beat Jordan's average, which (before the final game of the season) is not known. So the goal for Shaq is variable. This is why the problem gains a variable and why functions are so natural in its analysis.

An alternative to the Shaq-Jordan extension is to extend Jane's problem directly. Suppose Andy has an average of 86 after 2 tests. What does he have to score on his third test in order to have a higher average than Jane after her next test? Analogous to the Shaq-Jordan case, Jane's average after 2 tests is higher than Andy's, but she can score above him on the next test yet still have a lower overall average.

On page 10, where we have written $g^{-1} \circ f(j)$, some people prefer to write $(g^{-1} \circ f)(j)$ to emphasize that the composite function is acting on j. The ambiguity that exists without parentheses allows the expression to be interpreted either as $g^{-1}(f(j))$ or as the equivalent $(g^{-1} \circ f)(j)$.

To discuss the mathematical connections can also take a full hour. Along the way it is nice to present corresponding properties not given in the text.

Chapter 1 Problems

Problems 1-4 relate to the idea of concept analysis; problems 5-9 to problem analysis; and 10-12 to connections.

Problem 1:   We have found that students often differ in their responses. Fortunately, responses here are opinions, neither right nor wrong.

Problem 6d: The situation here seems to many students to be impossible. Jordan comes in with a higher average. How can he outscore Shaq in the last game and still lose the scoring title? The answer is explained by the fact that Shaq has played in fewer games before the last game. So every point Shaq scores in the last game adds more to his average than every point Jordan scores adds to Jordan's average. This circumstance is related to Simpson's Paradox, that there exist eight positive numbers such that
$$\frac{a_1}{b_1} > \frac{c_1}{d_1} \text{ and } \frac{a_2}{b_2} > \frac{c_2}{d_2}, \text{ but } \frac{a_1 + a_2}{b_1 + b_2} < \frac{c_1 + c_2}{d_1 + d_2}.$$

Problem 9:   As noted above, details are given in the Solutions for the instructor who wishes to use this as an in-class activity.

Problem 10 and 12: Because different letters have been employed to stand for variables, some students become very confused.

Problem 11:   Although all pre-college textbooks mention the properties $0a = 0$ for all a and $x^0 = 1$ for all $x \neq 0$, most textbooks do not hint that the properties might correspond.

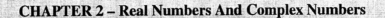

CHAPTER 2 – Real Numbers And Complex Numbers

Objectives

After completing Chapter 2, the student should be able to:

- explain the connection between finite, infinite repeating, and infinite nonrepeating decimals and rational and irrational numbers, and answer questions such as: Why is .999....9... = 1? and What can we say about the period of the decimal representation of the simple fraction a/b in lowest terms? (We do not answer the question of the length of the period, except in a problem.)

- describe the sets of rational, algebraic, transcendental, and irrational numbers and the definitions of special numbers such as π and e.

- summarize the historical evolution of the real and complex numbers.

- explain the arithmetic and geometric properties of the complex numbers and some of their connections to trigonometry and plane geometry.

Notes

The systems of real and complex numbers are discussed in this chapter and again in Chapter 6. In this chapter, we identify the set of real numbers with the set of points on the real line, and the set of complex numbers with the set of points in the complex plane. Our objective is to use these intuitive geometric models to develop the basic algebraic and geometric features of these number systems.

In Unit 6.2, we investigate the real and complex number systems as algebraic systems with the objective of identifying a set of characteristic properties of each of these number systems. Specifically, we describe the real number system as a complete ordered field and the complex number system as the smallest field containing the real numbers as a subfield and also containing an element e such that $e^2 = -1$. This difference in approach explains the wide separation of the two developments in the organization of this book.

Of the sections in this chapter, sections 2.1.1, 2.1.2, 2.2.1, and 2.2.2 are referred to most frequently in the remainder of the book. In particular, our treatment of congruence and similarity transformations in Chapter 7 and 8 uses their representations as transformations of the complex plane. (See also Project 7 for this chapter.)

Introduction

Research done in Israel with the language of probability in Hebrew, Arabic, Russian, and English suggests that it is more difficult for students to learn the mathematical meanings of words when they have everyday meanings in their language than when they do not possess everyday meanings (Tatyana Zaslavsky, Orit Zaslavsky, and Michael Moore, "Language Influences on Prospective Mathematics Teachers' Understanding of Probabilistic Concepts", *Focus on Learning Problems in Mathematics* 23:2 (Spring 2001) and 23:3 (Summer 2001), pp. 23-40). This may account for the difficulty students have with "real", "imaginary", "complex", and many other mathematical terms.

Unit 2.1: The Real Numbers

Section 2.1.1

Most students are likely to be familiar with the meaning and most basic facts about rational and irrational numbers (e.g. rational numbers are those that can be expressed as quotients of integers, periodic decimals are rational numbers, $\sqrt{2}, \pi, e$ are irrational). This section extends this basic knowledge to territory that is likely to be less familiar to students and yet that should be part of any mathematics teacher's background. We recommend assigning most of the problems in this section including Problems 3, 11 and 12.

The Division Algorithm is stated in Section 2.1.1 but its proof is delayed until Chapter 5 because we want to deduce it from the Well-Ordering Property of the natural number system. However, most students find the following "proof" of the Division Algorithm quite convincing: Given two positive integers a and b, the existence of integers q and r such that

$$a = qb + r \quad \text{and} \quad 0 \le r < b$$

can be explained by plotting a and all multiples of b on the number line as in the diagram below

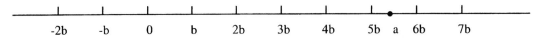

In the diagram, the integer a lies between 5b and 6b so the integers q and r in the Division Algorithm are given by q = 5 and r = a – 5b. In general, the point a either falls on a multiple of b (in which case q is that multiple and r = 0) or it lies between two successive multiples of b, say qb and (q + 1)b (in which case r = a – qb). The existence of q and r in the case in which the integer a is negative can be explained by a similar diagram. The point of the proof of this result presented in Section 5.2.1 is that the Division Algorithm rests on carefully stated properties of the systems of integers and natural numbers rather than the intuitive but relatively imprecise identification of the real number system with the real number line.

The indirect proof of Theorem 2.2 may be a little more complicated than students have previously encountered. The supposition is an "and" statement: *n is a positive integer* and $\sqrt{n}$ *is not an integer,* and $\sqrt{n}$ *is rational.* We show that this supposition leads to a contradiction by proving that the three parts together imply that *n is not an integer*. This gives us a contradiction (n cannot both be a positive integer and not an integer) and shows that the three parts of the supposition cannot be simultaneously true.

Problems 1 and 3: A point to be emphasized is that a number does not have to look like a fraction to be a rational number.

Problem 1d: There are two points of view regarding the integer part and fractional part of a negative number such as -6.75. Under one point of view, the integer part is -7 and the fractional part is 0.25. This first point of view is consistent with the idea that the integer part of any number is the greatest integer less than or equal to that number. A second point of view is that the integer part is -6 and the fractional part is -0.75. This second point of view considers negative numbers as opposites of positive numbers and takes their integer and fractional parts accordingly. Under the first point of view, the function that maps each real number onto its fractional part is periodic. Under the second point of view, that function is symmetric to the y-axis. We have taken the first point of view in our solution but many calculator and computer programs give answers consistent with the second point of view.

Problem 2: Many students may never have used the single-hooked bracket for the greatest integer (floor) function, instead using [x].

Problems 3b-c: This is a brief instance of problem analysis, as done in Chapter 1.

Problem 8: The result surprises many students.

Problem 12c: There are not as many sets as some students at first think.

Section 2.1.2

In the presentation of the decimal representation of real numbers in Section 2.1.2, as with the Division Algorithm, we assume results that we discuss later. For decimal representation, we assume the Nested Interval Property of the real number system and the distribution of the integers among the real numbers (essentially the Archimedean Property) as properties of our number line model of the real numbers. Although these properties are intuitively quite acceptable for the number line model, their deductive basis rests on the completeness of the ordered field of real numbers as discussed in Unit 6.2. We take decimal representation full circle by describing it first on the basis the number line model of the real number system in this chapter. Then, in Unit 6.2, we carefully identify the algebraic properties of the real number system that are used in decimal representation and arrive at the algebraic structure of a complete ordered field as a formal description of the real number system. Finally, at the end of Section 6.2.1, we show how a decimal representation can be assigned to each element of a complete ordered field. This, together with the discussion of decimal representation in Chapter 2, shows that any complete ordered field can be identified with the real number line.

The approach to decimal representation of real numbers discussed in this section results in two possible decimal representations for some real numbers. It is possible to modify the constructions in this section in such a way that each real number has a unique decimal representation. This approach is described in Project 1 for this chapter. Uniqueness of decimal representation is helpful in certain contexts because it sets up a one-one correspondence between the set of real numbers and the set of representing decimals. For example, this correspondence is useful in Unit 6.2 for describing how any complete ordered field can be identified with the real number line, or in describing the Cantor diagonalization process in the proof of

Theorem 2.18. The uniqueness of decimal representation of real numbers has the disadvantage that it forces some choices that are subtle and confusing for students. For example, although each real number then has a unique decimal that represents it, there may be another decimal that determines that real number but does not represent it. For example, in the context of the unique decimal representation discussed in Project 1, both of the decimals 1.0000...0... and .99999..9... *determine* the real number 1, only the decimal 1.0000..0..*represents* it!

In our approach, the (finite or infinite) decimal representation for a negative real number is found by examining the representation of its additive inverse. Thus, for example, $-2\frac{3}{10} = -(2.3) = -(2 + .3) = -2 - .3 = -2 - \frac{3}{10}$. On the other hand, for the Division algorithm, we think of $2\frac{3}{10}$ as $2 + \frac{3}{10}$, but $-2\frac{3}{10}$ as being $-3 + \frac{7}{10}$ because remainders are always positive.

The proof of Theorem 2.4 uses but does not state the Pigeon-Hole Principle, that if b distinct elements are to be distributed among b-1 sets, then at least one set will have two or more objects.

Problem 6:   In their responses, some students may use the detailed description of real number given in this section. Others may use properties of finite sums and extend them to infinite sums.

Section 2.1.3

The information in Table 4 can be motivated and described effectively through the discussion of a selection of examples. The proofs of the results summarized in the table are somewhat technical. Some instructors may wish to take a more informal, descriptive approach to the content of this section based on the discussion of examples and omit some of the formal proofs. We recommend assigning Problems 1 through 8 to encourage students to explore interesting features of periodic decimal representations.

Section 2.1.4

The second part of this section dealing with cardinality of certain sets of real numbers can be omitted without consequence to the material in later chapters. It can also be discussed in connection with one-to-one correspondences in Chapter 3. The critical point to emphasize is that although rational numbers are much more in everyday use than irrational numbers, from the cardinality standpoint almost all numbers are irrational.

Unit 2.2: The Complex Numbers

Many prospective and experienced high school teachers lack familiarity with the use of complex numbers and their applications beyond their use in representing solutions of quadratic and polynomial equations. Section 2.2.1 reviews the basic terminology and arithmetic of complex numbers in preparation for their geometric treatment in Section 2.2.2. In particular, do not ignore the polar forms of complex numbers and their corresponding graphs in polar coordinates.

Section 2.2.1

The subsection of on the migration of polynomial zeros in the complex plane and the related exercises, Problems 4 and 5, are likely to be new and revealing to most students. The point of the example illustrating the migration of the zeros of the quadratic polynomial defined by $y = x^2 + 2x + c$ as c increases from -8 to 2 can be presented very effectivly as a computer animation. The animation can be produced by cycling through a sequence of "split screen" plots indexed by integer values of c ranging from -8 and to +2. For each value of c, one half of the split screen displays the graph of $y = x^2 + 2x + c$, while the other half displays the zeros of that function plotted in the complex plane. For example, in Mathematica, the Table command can be used to create the sequence of plots of the functions $f(x,c) = x^2 + 2x + c$ for integer values of c from -8 to +2 as well as the corresponding sequence of plots of the zeros of $f(x, c)$ in the complex plane. These plots can be combined into a split screen sequence using the GraphicsArray command, and then animated with the Animate Selected Graphics Command. Since the primary inputs for such an animation program are the function $f(x, c)$ and the plot window, the animation program is easily modified to animate the migratory behavior of the zeros of higher degree polynomials. Such animations are fascinating to the students and convey very graphically the dependence of the zeros of polynomials on their coefficients.

Problem 1:   This straightforward exercise may reveal how little some students know about complex numbers.

Section 2.2.2

The content of this section establishes the strong connection that exists between the arithmetic and geometry of complex numbers. This connection is exploited extensively in our treatment of congruence and similarity transformations in Chapters 7 and 8. (See also Project 7 for this chapter.) To illustrate complex number multiplication, you may wish to choose three complex numbers whose graphs are not collinear. Then multiply these numbers by a fixed complex number, say $1 + i$. The triangle formed by the three product points is similar to the triangle formed by the original points. Furthermore, the transformation that maps one triangle onto the other is easily found by writing $1 + i$ as $[\sqrt{2}, 45°]$. The product triangle is the image of the original triangle under the composite of a size transformation of magnitude $\sqrt{2}$ and a rotation of 45°, a spiral similarity (see section 8.2.6).

Your students may be surprised that nth roots of complex numbers are in many ways more easily described than nth roots of real numbers. The connection of nth roots with regular polygons, DeMoivre's Theorem, is testimony to the unity of mathematics.

We recommend assigning Problems 3, 6 and 13 because of their close connection to analytic geometry.

Chapter 2 Projects

Project 5 presents the Cardano-Tartaglia method for solving cubic equations. This method is historically significant and demonstrates that complex numbers are needed even if one is only interested in real solutions of cubic equations.

Project 6 discusses the complex exponential, its properties and some connections to the solution of trigonometric and exponential equations.

CHAPTER 3 – Functions

Objectives

After completing Chapter 3, the student should be able to:

- explain and compare the "rule" and "ordered pair" descriptions of functions and describe the historical evolution of the function concept.

- explain, give examples of, and solve problems involving function-related concepts such as domain, range, inverses, composites and restrictions.

- analyze the behavior of a given real function.

- use the special properties of specific types of real functions including their limit behavior, graphical characteristics and comparative growth rates to analyze their usefulness for modeling data.

- give examples of the broad applicability of the function concept within and outside of mathematics.

- use functions to give deeper analyses of common high school problems such as the box problem, motion problems, or mixture problems.

Notes

The students in this course have been working with functions for a long time. However, it has been our experience that many students have some misconceptions about functions that can limit their ability to use and to teach the concept effectively. Among these common misconceptions are:

Functions are formulas or equations.

Functions are "given" items like dimensions, speeds or costs in math problems; they are not things that you "create" to solve math problems.

Functions, like the natural numbers, triangles, and circles, have always been familiar mathematical objects whose meaning has remained fixed for many centuries.

Functions always involve numbers and, when x appears, it is always a domain value of a function.

Our objective in this chapter is to address these misconceptions and to broaden and deepen the students' understanding of the function concept that they developed in high school and lower division college mathematics courses.

Unit 3.1: The Definitions, Historical Evolution, and Basic Machinery of Functions

Students should be encouraged to read this introduction carefully as it sets up the content of the chapter.

The formula for V on page 67 is found in Problem 1 of Section 3.1.1 and also in Problem 6 of Section 3.2.2.

Section 3.1.1

In high school mathematics, from the first algebra course on, functions and equations play central roles. Yet teachers are not always clear on just what these roles are, and how they relate to each other. One reason for this is that, just a generation ago, functions played a far smaller role than they do today in early high school courses; equations are the central object of study in a traditional beginning algebra course. Another reason is that mathematicians, mathematics educators, and texts themselves are sometimes inconsistent in the way they use terminology relating to functions and equations. This is unfortunate, since functions and equations relate to each other in a beautiful, systematic, and general way, and understanding this can certainly enhance students' and teachers' understanding of mathematics.

We begin by comparing the "rule" description of a function with its description as a set of ordered pairs. We then discuss the different ways of representing functions and the important distinction and relationships between functions and equations that is often blurred in textbooks. The section concludes with a discussion of the historical evolution of the function concept.

Here is some further discussion of how functions and equations are related to each other, and how they are different. Briefly, a function is a mapping from a domain set to a range set, and an equation states a condition on the domain set of a function, a condition that is met by the solutions of the equation.

For example, consider a function of one real variable, which we designate by the mapping notation $x \rightarrow f(x)$. An equation in one unknown based on this function is of the form $f(x) = k$, where k is any real number. Often, we use the value $k = 0$ which gives the "normal form" $f(x) = 0$ of an equation. A simple example is the function $x \rightarrow x^2 - 1$ and the related equation $x^2 - 1 = 0$.

We evaluate a function when we find the unique output value that comes from a given input value in the function's domain. For example, we evaluate the function $x \rightarrow x^2 - 1$ at $x = 7$ by calculating $(7)^2 - 1 = 48$.

We solve an equation based on a function when we find the value(s) of the input that the function maps to a given output. It is in this sense that an equation states a condition on the domain set of a function. For example, the solutions of the equation $x^2 - 1 = 99$ are 10 and -10. Why? In function language, they are solutions because these numbers (and only these) are mapped to the given output 99 by the function $x \rightarrow x^2 - 1$, and so meet the condition stated by the equation.

In short, evaluating a function matches an output to a given input, while solving an equation matches an input (or inputs) to a given output of a function. Notice that we never speak of solving a function or evaluating an equation.

This discussion shows that, although functions and equations are related in a systematic way, each has a different mathematical status. Nevertheless, when we start to talk about representing evaluations of functions and solutions of equations graphically, the very same graph can be interpreted one way in terms of a function and another way in terms of an equation. This can be a source of conceptual and terminological confusion. To sort out the issues, we extend the ideas above to functions of 2 variables and to equations of 2 unknowns based on them.

We do this in the table below. Once the structure of the table becomes apparent, it is clear that the same sort of relationship can be extended to functions of 3 variables and equations of 3 unknowns based on them (see the next page). In fact, the table as a whole gives a systematic framework for thinking about functions of any number n variables, equations of n unknowns, and their relationship. Further, an inspection of the table shows how the same graph can be interpreted one way in terms of a function and another way in terms of an equation. Specifically, the graph of a function of 1 variable and the solutions of an equation in 2 unknowns are both the same sort of object, namely, a curve in the x-y plane. See the rightmost column of row 1b and row 2d.

	mathematical object	its symbolic form	what the object is
1a	a function of 1 variable	$x \rightarrow f(x)$	a mapping $\mathbf{R} \rightarrow \mathbf{R}$
1b	a graph of this function	$\{(x, y): y = f(x)\}$	**a curve in the x-y plane**
1c	an equation in 1 unknown	$f(x) = 0$	a condition on numbers $x \in \mathbf{R}$
1d	solutions of this equation	$\{x: f(x) = 0\}$	a set of points on the x-axis
	functions and equations based on the expression f(x)		
2a	a function of 2 variables	$(x, y) \rightarrow F(x, y)$	a mapping $\mathbf{R}^2 \rightarrow \mathbf{R}$
2b	a graph of this function	$\{(x, y, z): z = F(x, y)\}$	a surface in x-y-z space
2c	an equation in 2 unknowns	$F(x, y) = 0$	a condition on pairs $(x, y) \in \mathbf{R}^2$
2d	solutions of this equation	$\{(x, y): F(x, y) = 0\}$	**a curve in the x-y plane**
	functions and equations based on the expression F(x, y)		

3a	a function of 3 variables	$(x, y, z) \rightarrow G(x, y, z)$	a mapping $\mathbf{R}^3 \rightarrow \mathbf{R}$
3b	a graph of this function	$\{(x, y, z, w): w = G(x, y, z)\}$	a 3-d subset of x-y-z-w space
3c	an equation in 3 unknowns	$G(x, y, z) = 0$	a condition on triples $(x, y, z) \in \mathbf{R}^3$
3d	solutions of this equation	$\{(x, y, z): G(x, y, z) = 0 \}$	a surface in x-y-z space
	functions and equations based on the expression $G(x, y, z)$		

As an example of how a graph can be interpreted one way in terms of a function and another way in terms of an equation, consider the function of two variables defined by $F(x, y) = 4x - y - 8$. The equation $F(x, y) = 0$, which we can write explicitly as $4x - y - 8 = 0$, has as its solution the line in the x-y plane with intercepts $(0, -8)$ and $(2, 0)$. On the other hand, the function of one variable defined by $f(x) = 4x - 8$ has as its graph the very same line.

Related to this discussion is the fact that the x-y plane serves two different kinds of roles. On the one hand, curves in the x-y plane are described by equations of the general form $F(x, y) = 0$, and their geometric properties studied via these equations; this is the traditional subject of elementary analytic geometry. On the other hand, the study of analytic properties of functions of one variable is enhanced by giving them a geometric representation; this is done through their graphs, which are curves in the x-y plane. We might note that functions and their graphs are receiving increased attention in school mathematics in recent years, while analytic geometry receives much less emphasis than it once did.

Problems 2 through 8 are relatively straightforward but useful exercises that probe students' understanding of the function concept.

Problem 1:   Because the function $V = f(d)$ relating the volume V of fuel in a tank to its depth to the depth d of fuel in the tank that is discussed in the chapter introduction is used to illustrate several points in the chapter, we recommend assigning this problem.

Problem 2:   The word "given" is the signal for the domain variable in each part.

Problem 9:   This problem provides a very fine exercise in what some call "parsing" a formula, i.e., determining the meaning of the formula by examining each individual part in relation to the others.

Section 3.1.2

Section 3.1.2 demonstrates how a very concrete "catch-up time" problem typical of those found in beginning algebra textbooks can be generalized and analyzed more deeply and fruitfully by introducing appropriate parameters, equations and functions.

Problems 6 and 7: These problems guide students through similar analyses in different but related problem contexts. Either is appropriate for extended classroom discussion in which students make presentations.

Section 3.1.3

Section 3.1.3 draws on the previous high school and college mathematics background to illustrate the wide variety of ways in which functions are presented and their broad applicability as a tool for organizing and analyzing mathematical problems and concepts. It also presents a careful development of composite and inverse functions that is used extensively in Chapters 4 through 9. None of the problems in this section is particularly difficult so you may wish to assign many of them.

Unit 3.2: Properties of Real Functions

This unit deals with the type of functions that are likely to be the most familiar to students; that is, functions whose domains and ranges are sets of real numbers. Various categories of these functions such as sequences, polynomials, rational functions, exponential and trigonometric functions and their inverses are discussed in detail in calculus and pre-calculus courses. Our objective in this unit and the next is to consider aspects of real functions that are meaningful across these categories and thereby provide a deeper, more unified view of the nature of real functions. Thus, although the functions considered in this section should be familiar to the students, appreciation of the "cross category" character of the results and comments will likely take some time.

Section 3.2.1

Section 3.2.1 describes precisely various categories of real functions and presents systematic procedures and examples of their analysis. The list of ten characteristics on page 91 is by no means definitive. You may wish to modify this list to suit your own taste.

Problems 4-11: These problems require students to carry out analyses similar to those found in the section. We recommend assigning several of these problems, but the instructor should appreciate that each analysis, even if elementary, takes a good deal of time for most students.

Problem 13: Here is an interesting connection to the content on rational and irrational numbers in Chapter 2.

Section 3.2.2

Section 3.2.2 develops those aspects of composite and inverse functions that are special to real functions. The problems in this section require the students to consider carefully less familiar aspects of familiar and important types of real functions.

Problem 6: This problem builds on Problem 1 of Section 3.1.1.

Problems 8-10: These problems delve into trigonometric functions in ways which may have never before been seen by students even though they are in some school textbooks.

Problem 12:   The derivations of the properties of logarithms are useful for all teachers to know.

Problem 13:   This property of logarithms is likely not to be known to students yet it is quite easy. You might ask students to supply values of x, b, and c that allow the property to be easily checked (e.g., x = 1,000,000; b = 10; c = 100).

Section 3.2.3

In Section 3.2.2, we asked when a function has an inverse and found that a sufficient condition for a function to have an inverse is it is 1-1. In this section, we ask when a function is 1-1 and find that a sufficient condition is that it be strictly monotone. We discuss monotonicity, asymptotes and end behavior more carefully and systematically than is typical for calculus courses.

Problem 7:   In the first printing, there is an error. The second D should be f(D).

Problem 12:   This problem generalizes Problem 11.

Problem 13:   We do not expect students to use mathematical induction here.

Section 3.2.4

The content on orders of growth of real functions, which relates the various categories of functions in terms of their growth rates, is likely to be entirely new content for most students. Although the statement of Theorem 3.14 is rather formidable, the proofs of most of the parts are straightforward applications of L'Hopital's Rule (Theorem 3.13).

Problems 4-12: These problems cover the various parts of Theorem 3.14. It is likely best to assign some but not all of them.

Section 3.3: Problems Involving Real Functions

The first three sections of this unit continue the study of cross-category properties of real functions by finding ways of recognizing a real function's type (e.g. linear, exponential, polynomial) from its values at equally spaced points, and then using such information to fit real functions to data. The fourth section concludes our discussion of real functions with an extended analysis of the familiar Box Problem (i.e. finding the dimensions of the open box of maximum volume that can be constructed from a given rectangular sheet of cardboard).

Although the content of this unit is not referred to frequently in subsequent chapters of the book, we believe that it provides teachers with a deeper understanding and appreciation of the various categories of functions that are studied in high school mathematics, and their use in modeling real data.

Section 3.3.1

This section shows that linear and exponential functions can be distinguished by their growth rates and applies this distinction to construct functions that can be used to extrapolate and interpolate data.

Problems 1-3: If this section is covered, we recommend assigning at least one of these problems.

Section 3.3.2

Here we show that polynomials of degree n are determined by constant nth-differences and uses this description as a basis for fitting data wit polynomial functions.

Problems 1-3: If this section is covered, we again recommend assigning at least one of these problems.

Section 3.3.3

The extended analysis of the box problem here is independent of specific results in earlier sections of this unit. It could also be presented after Section 3.2.1. It illustrates the power of careful algebraic and graphical analysis of real functions and the introduction of parameters in problems for which the initial data is entirely numerical.

Problems 1 and 3: These problems ask the student to carry out analyses of problems quite similar to the box problem.

Chapter 3 Projects

Project 3: This is a natural extension of the discussion in Section 3.3.1 and uses calculus to characterize linear and exponential functions in terms of their instantaneous growth and percentage growth rates.

Project 4: The Lagrange Interpolation Formula provides an alternative approach to data fitting with polynomial functions discussed in Section 3.3.2. The Lagrange Interpolation Formula has an interesting analog in number theory – the Chinese Remainder Theorem on the solution of linear congruences – that is discussed in Section 6.1.3.

Project 6: This project guides the student through a proof that the two standard limit definitions of the base e of the natural logarithm are equal; i.e., that $e = \lim_{n \to \infty} \left(1 + \frac{1}{n}\right)^n = \sum_{n=0}^{\infty} \frac{1}{n!}$.

CHAPTER 4 – Equations

Objectives

After completing Chapter 4, the student should be able to:

- explain, contrast, compare and give examples in the context of high school mathematics of terminology such as: equality and equivalence; non-equivalent and equivalent equations, equivalence relations, and identities.

- explain in terms of group and field properties the steps in the solution of the following types of equations:

$$a \bullet x = b \qquad a + x = b \qquad a \bullet x + b = c \bullet x + d.$$

- describe the historical evolution of the solution of general quadratic, cubic and quartic polynomial equations.

- utilize equations and functions to analyze problems such as the average speed problem.

- show how theorems from algebra and analysis justify familiar procedures for solving equations and inequalities.

- provide examples of the use of arithmetic and harmonic means.

- analyze solution processes to equations and inequalities in terms of function language and general properties of functions.

Notes

Students enrolled in this course already have considerable experience working with equality and inequality, and equations and inequalities in a wide variety of contexts. However, nearly all of this experience has been acquired in very specific contexts with a primary emphasis on solution procedures tailored to the given context. As a result, most students know how to "solve" or "simplify" equations and inequalities, but are unable to explain the mathematical principles that underlie the procedures they apply in a given mathematical context or to see and understand similarities between procedures applied in different contexts.

Students may be familiar with such mathematical principles and theorems from upper division college courses in analysis and abstract algebra. However, it is often the case that the connection between these principles and theorems and the solution procedures of high school mathematics are not explained in sufficient detail to prepare an individual to teach this material in a manner that is likely to result in real understanding by his or her students

The purpose of this chapter is to discuss the concepts and mathematical principles that underlie instances of equality and inequality as well as methods for solving equations and inequalities within high school mathematics. We demonstrate the wide diversity of instances of equality in the context in high school mathematics, investigate the concepts and principles that are common to all solution procedures for equations and inequalities in high school mathematics, and explain apparent similarities between such procedures in different contexts.

Unit 4.1: The Concept of Equation

This unit explores mathematical ideas related to equality and equations and discusses the logical principles involved in solving equations or systems of equations. The illustrative examples and problems are drawn mostly from familiar contexts in high school mathematics.

Section 4.1.1

The error of adding all numbers in a problem, discussed in the subsection "The equal sign", has been found by many researchers. If there are students in your class who are working with students younger than 5th grade, you might ask them to try the problem out with those students.

In the discussion of isomorphism, we intentionally provide two interpretations of isomorphic structures. The authors cannot find a logical reason to prefer one over the other. In some contexts isomorphic structures can be viewed as different but equivalent, while in other contexts they can be viewed as the same structure.

The problems in this section are not unlike problems found in some higher algebra texts.

Problem 8:   This problem shows that positive and negative integers can be viewed as ordered pairs of positive integers. Here, for any positive integer a, the class of all ordered pairs equivalent to $(a + 1,1)$ can be thought of as a, and the class of all ordered pairs equivalent to $(1,a + 1)$ can be thought of as -a. For example, -3 is the equivalence class $\{(1, 4), (2, 5), (3, 6), (4, 7), ...\}$. This construction is analogous to the way that positive rational numbers are constructed as equivalence classes of positive integers. (In the first printing, there is an error in the last line of the left column. The $\times$ should be a $\bullet$ (for multiplication).

Section 4.1.2

The language of "sentence", "open sentence", and "compound sentence", as used here is more common in school mathematics textbooks than in college-level texts. It may be helpful to discuss with students the nature of the analogy between the idea of *sentence* as commonly understood in English and the idea of *sentence* as discussed here.

Problem 6:   There may be disagreement regarding the appropriate domains in parts **a** and **b**. Discussion of the reasons to prefer one domain over another gets at the heart of the issues in selecting a domain. This is a main reason for the problem. And then part **c** brings forth a negative value of t that has meaning in the situation but may not have been considered in either parts **a** or **b**.

Problem 10:   While this book was in press, postal rates increased to 37 cents for the first ounce and 23 cents for each additional ounce. You may wish to use the current rates in place of those given.

Problem 19:   We recommend allowing students latitude (e.g., elliptical eyes, shaded regions, etc.).

Unit 4.2: Algebraic Structures and Solving Equations

This unit treats the solution of linear equations from the point of view of algebraic structures. Consequently, students with some background in abstract algebra are likely to find this unit relatively straightforward, while those lacking this background may have some difficulty appreciating the references of group and field structures and concepts.

All of the problems illustrating group and field structures in this unit are based on the familiar operations of addition and multiplication on sets of numbers and 2×2 matrices. We do this to keep the discussion of group and field structures in familiar territory. Other examples of groups and fields are discussed in Chapter 6, 7 and 8. The purpose of this discussion of such algebraic structures in this course is to make connections between high school content and the content of abstract algebra courses that the students have taken or will take in the future. For this reason we do not undertake a systematic development of the properties of groups and fields.

Section 4.2.1

Sections 4.2.1 and 4.2.2 demonstrate how the algebraic structures of groups and fields support and explain the familiar methods for solving linear equations in a single variable in which the domain of the variable is either a group or field of numbers or 2×2 matrices.

Problems 3 and 4:   These problems are especially useful for exploring the connection between algebraic structure and standard methods for solving equations.

Section 4.2.2

Problems 1, 2, 3, 7 and 8:   These problems also connect algebraic structures and standard equation-solving methods.

Section 4.2.3

The solution of quadratic equations and higher degree polynomial equations are important topics in high school algebra. Section 4.2.3 presents an in-depth look at the solution of such equations including a sketch of their history and a detailed discussion of Viete's Theorem expressing the coefficients of quadratic equations in terms of its roots.

Problem 7:   This problem extends Viete's Theorem to cubic polynomials.

Unit 4.3 The Solving Process

This unit considers several methods for solving equations and inequalities that are likely to be familiar to students from their calculus and pre-calculus background but that are often not carefully justified in those courses. The "advanced perspective" developed in this unit shows how these familiar methods derive from properties of functions and the logic of statements.

Section 4.3.1

The procedures of adding to or multiplying both sides of an equation by an algebraic expression are considered here. These procedures are so familiar that students take them for granted. Moreover, the importance of the domain of the variable is often ignored. The characterization of an equation in one variable to be solved as $f(x) = g(x)$ may be new for some students. The problem set is relatively short and straightforward. We recommend assigning most of these problems to assure that the students will get enough practice with the idea of this section.

Section 4.3.2

This section extends and generalizes the preceding one by conceptualizing "doing the same thing to both sides of an equation" as applying a particular function to both sides of an equation. The process highlights the significance of the existence or nonexistence of an inverse for such a function. We recommend assigning most of the problems.

Section 4.3.3

Section 4.3.3 applies the ideas Sections 4.3.1 and 4.3.2 to solving inequalities. The first part of the section should be familiar to students, but still should be read carefully. Beginning with the subsection "Solving $f(x) < g(x)$", the content is likely to be unfamiliar. It may surprise students that the monotonicity of a function comes into play. The process of Example 1 may be known to students from prior courses.

Section 4.3.4

Section 4.3.4 demonstrates how a careful analysis of the equations and inequalities that arise in the solution of a generalized version of a standard algebra problem on average speeds leads to an interesting and surprising connection between the average speed and the harmonic mean of the velocities.

Problem 11:   There is an error in the first printing. The exponent 2 in ax^2 is missing.

Problem 15:   This problem provides the student with an excellent opportunity to carry out an extended analysis of an interesting problem related to the average speeds problem considered in the section.

Chapter 4 Projects

Projects 4 and 5 on the exact solution of cubic and quartic equations are closely related to Project 5 of Chapter 2.

CHAPTER 5 – Integers and Polynomials

Objectives

After completing Chapter 5, the student should be able to:

- apply proof by mathematical induction and recursively defined sequences in a wide variety of contexts.

- explain how mathematical induction and recursion are based on the structure of the natural number system.

- describe and explain the basic divisibility concepts and results for integers, including the Division and Euclidean Algorithms, prime factorization and the distribution of prime numbers and base representation of natural numbers.

- use linear equations with integer solutions (i.e., linear Diophantine equations) to model problems and describe the complete set of integer solutions systematically.

- illustrate a variety of analogies between the divisibility properties of integers and polynomials and explain these analogies in terms of the algebraic properties of the systems of integers and polynomials.

Notes

The ordering and placement of the three chapters of this book devoted to number systems: Chapter 2 on the real and complex numbers systems, Chapter 5 on integers and polynomials, and Chapter 6 on number system structures, may seem odd to the instructor. A "natural" order in terms of inclusion would be: Natural numbers→Integers→Rational Numbers→Real Numbers→Complex Numbers, and finally number-like algebraic systems such as the systems of polynomials and modular arithmetic. Our ordering and placement of these topics evolved from considerations related to the way number systems are taught in high school and their many connections to other central topics in high school mathematics. We began with the real number line and the real numbers because of their importance in high school, and discussed the rational and irrational numbers in that context. This led naturally to discussion of the complex number plane and complex numbers in Chapter 2, a topic that we feel is often presented in a very shallow way at the high school level, and so we presented a deeper and more detailed level. In that setting, the natural numbers and integers are special rational numbers that serve as tick marks on the real number line.

In this chapter, we investigate the systems of natural numbers and integers from a more intrinsic point of view. This viewpoint reveals the intimate connection between the system of natural numbers and mathematical induction and recursion, between the systems of integers and polynomials, and between the integers and modular arithmetic. Along the way, we also take a deeper look at standard topics concerning multiples and number bases, and we explore the correspondences to these concepts for polynomials. Thus, although Unit 5.1 and all but the last section of Unit 5.2 are devoted to the study of properties of natural numbers and integers, much of the "bang" of the chapter comes from Section 5.2.5 and Unit 5.3, where many of those properties are seen to have analogues in properties of polynomials.

Unit 5.1: Natural Numbers, Induction, and Recursion

The focus of this unit is on mathematical induction, its application in a variety of contexts, and its roots in the system of natural numbers. Although most students have used mathematical induction in previous high school and college mathematics courses to prove formulas or statements about natural numbers, few of them may realize that this method of proof is based on the structure of the natural number system, and few of them may have seen it used as a tool for mathematical investigation as it is presented here.

Section 5.1.1

This section is an introduction to recursively defined sequences and mathematical induction centered around a careful analysis of the famous Tower of Hanoi problem. This analysis leads quite naturally to a recursive description of the problem and to the use of mathematical induction as a means of verifying its explicit solution.

Problem 5:   This problem provides an excellent counterpart to the Tower of Hanoi problem because it can also be solved through exploration of cases, a recursive formulation based on these cases, and conjecture and verification of the conjecture through mathematical induction.

Section 5.1.2

Proof by mathematical induction and its basis in the Peano Axioms for the system of natural numbers are discussed in this section. A variety of applications of mathematical induction are given in the problems.

Problems 1-12: We recommend assigning most of these applications of mathematical induction because they review typical applications of mathematical induction found in high school and lower division college texts.

Problems 13-16: These problems help to deepen a student's understanding of mathematical induction and its connection to the well-ordering property. You might also ask the students to do one or two of Problems 1-12 with the well-ordering property instead of mathematical induction.

Section 5.1.3

Here we apply mathematics induction to the analysis of recursively-defined sequences. The Fibonacci sequence may be the only recursively-defined sequence familiar to the students, but its importance and many properties make it a rich source of potential problems.

The second example in this section demonstrates how familiar "laws of exponents" can be proved with mathematical induction. Often textbooks state such general results on the basis of a few sample cases without proof and often without mention of any need for proof.

Problems 1-8, 11-13: These involve the Fibonacci or similar sequences.

Problems 9 and 10: These involve proofs of the "laws of exponents" using mathematical induction.

Problem 18: There is an error in the first printing. Replace $2u_{n+1} + u_{n+2}$ by $2u_n + u_{n+1}$.

Problem 20b: There is an error in the first printing. Switch P2 and P1.

Problem 22: There is an error in the first printing. Insert "and $(k + 1) \bullet n$ to be $k \bullet n + n$" before the period of the last sentence in the box.

Section 5.1.4

In this section, we use the main tools of the unit, exploration, recursion, and mathematical induction, to carry out an extended analysis of counting the number of regions determined by n points on a line, n lines in a plane, and n planes in space. We strongly recommend assigning at least two or three of Problems 2 through 7 so that your students will have the opportunity to carry out similar analyses in related contexts. Simply reading and believing the given extended analysis is not sufficient for understanding the analysis process.

Problem 1: Conway and Guy show that c_n is the sum of the first five elements in the nth row of Pascal's triangle.

Unit 5.2: Divisibility Properties of the Integers

In this unit, students study algorithmic procedures for computing the greatest common factor and least common multiple, for long division, and for the prime factorization of integers. Then in Unit 5.3 the corresponding algorithms are developed and examined for polynomials. In both contexts, the algorithms are presented through examples and are used for calculation and simplification. In this unit, we also investigate other topics related to divisibility, such as the identification and distribution of prime numbers and the description of integer solution of linear Diophantine equations. Although most students will be quite familiar with the ideas and algorithms we discuss, it is likely that they will need time and work to assimilate the precise and formal treatment of these topics here. The worthwhile outcomes of this effort for high school teachers will be a broader knowledge of the divisibility issues that are considered in the high school mathematics curriculum, a deeper understanding of the divisibility analogies between integers and polynomials, and some new approaches to the solution of problems in which integer solutions are required.

Section 5.2.1

The integer division and rational number division described in this section are comparable to polynomial division and rational expression division in Section 5.3.1. Interested students might read ahead.

Problems 4-6: These are straightforward applications of the Division Algorithm.

Problem 7: This problem provides a simple proof of the Division Algorithm based on the greatest integer function. We did not use that proof in the text because the definition of the greatest integer function reflects a relatively deep property of the real number system, the Archimedean property, that is not discussed in detail until Unit 6.2.

Section 5.2.2

In Example 1 we have modified the customary notation for integers that requires commas because the commas make it difficult to read the ordered pair. The detail of Example 1 and the Euclidean Algorithm may cause students to miss the basic idea, namely, that to find a greatest common factor of two positive integers a and b we subtract one from the other and then subtract differences from the smaller number until it is the case that we reach zero. When we reach zero, the last difference subtracted must have been the greatest common factor.

Problems 2 and 5: Problem 5 requires that students have done Problem 2. They show an important property of least common multiples and greatest common factors.

Problem 4:   This problem is quite easy and would be even easier if the extraneous information $p_1 + q_1 = p_2 + q_2$ were not included. Students may think there is an error in the book because they do not use some given information, but we have purposely included a problem with too much information.

Section 5.2.3

To solve a specific stamp problem we are led to the solution of the general linear Diophantine equation. A practical advantage of knowing the solution is that it determines the lattice points on the graph of the equation and thus allows easy graphing.

The problem of finding Pythagorean triples, introduced as an example of a Diophantine equation, is discussed in Section 5.2.4 and its problems.

Problem 6:   The periodicity inherent in the solution to the general linear Diophantine equation (from one solution you can add multiples of coefficients to determine all others) means that the distance from a line to the nearest lattice point is also a periodic function. Consequently, however close a line gets to a lattice point in one cycle will be the closest it gets to a lattice point in any cycle.

Problems 8-12: These problems show the power of knowing the solution to the general linear Diophantine equation. We recommend assigning several of these problems. High school students find Pythagorean triples interesting and teachers find them to be very useful for constructing examples and problems. However, most students and teachers know few examples beyond {3, 4, 5} and perhaps {5, 12, 13}. We also recommend assigning several of Problems 12 through 19 to broaden their experience in this regard.

Section 5.2.4

This section contains several very well-known theorems, but students may never have seen a proof. Euclid's classic proof of the infinitude of primes (Theorem 5.11) is something that students should be able to replicate.

Students tend to think that there are only a few Pythagorean triples ({3, 4, 5}, {5, 12, 13}, and their multiples). They may be surprised to learn that there are infinitely many different primitive triples.

Problems 5-9: These problems provide interesting information on the distribution of prime numbers that is accessible even to young high school students.

Problems 12-19: These problems deal with aspects of Pythagorean triples.

Section 5.2.5

In the pilot studies of this book, we found that some students who were mathematics majors had never before studied bases other than base 10.

Unit 5.3: Divisibility Properties of Polynomials

It is fortunate that, for the most part, the language that is used for divisibility with polynomials mimics that used for divisibility with integers. Thus the analogies between polynomials and integers identified in this unit are, for the most part, quite evident. Still, they may be unfamiliar to students.

Section 5.3.1

In the polynomial long divisions displayed in this book, we have aligned the quotient to the left. This alignment makes it easy to identify the multiplications that are performed as part of the algorithm. For instance, in the first polynomial long division example, we place the x^2 in the quotient above the x^4 in the dividend because x^2 in the quotient times x^2 in the divisor yields x^4. Some people place the x^2 in the quotient above the equal power $2x^2$ in the dividend, a placement that more closely mimics the traditional long division layout for whole numbers and decimals.

Problems 1 and 2: These problems, like the example in the subsection "Polynomial division vs. rational expression division", illustrate how polynomial division can be used to determine the behavior for large $|x|$ of a rational function of x. This is an application of polynomial division with a graphical interpretation unlike the other standard applications to simplifying or finding zeros of polynomial functions.

Section 5.3.2

Although prime factorization over fields with monic polynomial factors is emphasized in abstract algebra courses, factorization over the integers is stressed in high school texts. The subsection 'Prime factorization' addresses this difference in viewpoint. Problems 1 through 6 help to clarify this point.

Chapter 5 Projects

Project 1 outlines how the Peano Axioms can be used to derive some of the basic properties of addition and multiplication for the system **N** of natural numbers. The project makes substantial use of mathematical induction.

Most high school teachers and many students know the statement of Fermat's Last Theorem primarily because of the notoriety associated with the result when it was finally proved by Andrew Wiles in 1997. However, few teachers and students may have realized that special cases of the result are relatively easy to prove. Project 6 guides the student through the interesting special case when the exponent n in $x^n + y^n = z^n$ is a multiple of 4.

CHAPTER 6 – Number System Structures

Objectives

After completing Chapter 6 the student should be able to:

- tell what it means for the system of real numbers to be completely described algebraically as a complete ordered field.

- define, distinguish, and give examples of fields that are or are not ordered and/or Archimedean.

- tell what it means for the system of complex numbers to be completely described as a field containing the system of real numbers and an element e such that $e^2 = -1$.

- articulate the similarities and differences among the algebraic structures of the various number systems of school mathematics (natural numbers, integers, rational numbers, real numbers and complex numbers).

- explain modular arithmetic as a number system and apply this system to problems and contexts relevant to high school mathematics.

Notes

The discussion of the real and complex number systems in Chapter 2 is based on their respective familiar geometric models: the number line and the complex plane. In contrast, this chapter studies the real and complex number systems and related systems from an algebraic viewpoint. The objective is to obtain algebraic characterizations of the real and complex number systems and to discuss other related examples of algebraic systems that share some but not all of their properties. The emphasis of the chapter is on examples and sample results rather than a complete development of these algebraic systems as might be done in courses in abstract algebra and analysis.

The development in this chapter presumes that the reader is familiar with the content of Chapter 2 and Chapter 5. Students with no background in abstract algebra or analysis should find this chapter to be good preparation for complete courses in such subjects, while those who have taken such courses are likely to find connections with high school mathematics that may not have been discussed there.

Unit 6.1: The Systems of Modular Arithmetic

The goals in this introduction to modular arithmetic are modest. In Section 6.1.1 we develop enough of the language and properties of modular arithmetic to show the applications to integer division and properties of divisibility. In Section 6.1.2 we apply modular arithmetic to the construction and deciphering of codes. In Section 6.1.3, we apply modular arithmetic to the solution of some Diophantine equations.

Section 6.1.1

Students who have taken a course in abstract algebra or number theory are likely to be familiar with the content of Section 6.1.1. For students without this background, we recommend assigning all or most of the first 11 problems because they are relatively straightforward and help students to become comfortable with the concepts introduced in the section.

Problem 13:   The divisibility tests for 3, 9 and 11 are among the most important applications of modular arithmetic to school mathematics content.

Problem 14a: You can extend this problem by asking students to prove that the square of an odd integer is congruent to 1 modulo 8.

Section 6.1.2

These applications to calendars and cryptography are often not covered in courses in abstract algebra and number theory but are found in some textbook and supplementary materials for high school students. The historical connection to Julius Caesar may not be appreciated by students unfamiliar with world history (or Shakespeare), so you may find it useful to indicate who Caesar was.

Problems 1 and 2: We recommend assigning at least one of these problems. You also may wish to ask students to pick a date of their own choosing and use the formula to determine the day of the week.

Problems 3 and 4: We recommend assigning at least one of these problems.

Section 6.1.3

Even students who have taken a course in number theory and have encountered the Chinese Remainder Theorem there are not likely to have seen its connection with the Lagrange Interpolation Formula. Our discussion continues the analogies described in Chapter 5 between integers and polynomials.

The most elementary method for fitting a polynomial
$$p_n(x) = a_n x^n + a_{n-1} x^{n-1} + \ldots + a_1 x + a_0$$
to n+1 data points $(x_0, y_0), (x_1, y_1), \ldots, (x_{n-1}, y_{n-1}), (x_n, y_n)$ is to solve the system of n + 1 linear equations
$$p_n(x_k) = y_k \text{ for } 0 \leq k \leq n$$
for the n + 1 unknowns $a_n, a_{n-1}, \ldots, a_1, a_0$, as we did in our discussion of the Method of Finite Differences in Section 3.3.2. By contrast, the Lagrange Interpolation Formula expresses the polynomial $p_n(x)$ as the sum of n + 1 monomials such that the kth monomial summand has the value y_k at x_k and the value 0 at all x_j for $j \neq k$ (see Project 4 of Chapter 3 for details). This representation turns out to be identical to a Chinese Remainder Theorem solution of the system of polynomial congruences
$$p(x) \equiv y_k \text{Mod}(x - x_k) \text{ for } 0 \leq k \leq n,$$
where two polynomials $q_1(x)$ and $q_2(x)$ are defined to be congruent modulo $x - x_k$ if and only if $x - x_k$ is a factor of $q_1(x) - q_2(x)$.

An important application of the Chinese Remainder Theorem to computer arithmetic is discussed in Project 3 for this chapter.

Problem 2:   This problem is a "game" version of the coconut problem in the section that students (or teachers!) can perform in front of a class.

Problem 4:   This is perhaps the most famous form of the coconut problem.

Unit 6.2: Number Fields

Although we describe the difference in the approach between Chapter 2 and this chapter at several points in the development, we encourage you to reinforce this difference in specific situations. For example, if we identify the real numbers as points in order on a number line as we do in Chapter 2, then it is apparent that each real number is either an integer or lies between consecutive integers. However, if we start with the view that the real numbers are a complete ordered field, then the property that for each positive real number x there is an integer n such that $n \le x < n + 1$ must follow from properties of a complete ordered field. We may take one of these views as intuitive and from it develop the other. The relevance of this property for teachers is that it is basic to the definitions of the decimal representation of a real number and the greatest integer function. So, if a teacher wishes to connect intuition with theory, the teacher needs to be aware both of the number line and the complex plane as visual models for the systems of real and complex numbers and also understand the algebraic structures of these systems as well.

Students with little or no background in abstract algebra are likely to find this material difficult even though the field content is presented primarily through examples. For such students, we recommend working through the examples and assigned problems in detail with their active participation.

Section 6.2.1

Some students will find the formal derivation the familiar properties of the order relation < for real numbers in Theorems 6.6 through 6.9 for ordered fields to be challenging because they cannot use properties of < they have known for many years. The development is significant because the underlying order axioms **O-1** through **O-4** seem very modest when compared with their many consequences stated in these theorems. Emphasize that the *organization* or *ordering* of items to be proved from axioms is very important to the proof process.

Problem 1:   This problem relates the content of this section to that of Section 6.1.1.

Problems 2 and 3: For students who are encountering fields for the first time, we recommend assigning Problem 2 rather than Problem 3

Problems 5 and 6: For students who are encountering fields for the first time, we recommend assigning Problem 6 rather than Problem 5.

Section 6.2.2

Emphasize the four statements of the summary on pages 269-70. As a test of understanding, students should be able to indicate why <**Q**, +, •> is a field, an ordered field, and an Archimedean ordered field, and why it is not a complete ordered field.

Section 6.2.3

You might wish to connect this section with earlier work in the book. In Section 4.2.2, we identified the field $<S, +, \bullet>$ with the existence of a unique solution to any equation $a \bullet x + b = c$, where the coefficients a, b, and c are in S. If S contains all the integers, then S must contain all the rationals.

Now suppose we replace the linear equation $a \bullet x + b = c$ with polynomial equations of degree n. If S is to include the integers and the solutions to all these equations, then S must contain all the algebraic numbers. This suggests that the set of allowable coefficients is typically a proper subset of the set of possible solutions. For instance, if we allow coefficients of the polynomial equation to be any real numbers, then solutions can be any complex number.

The Fundamental Theorem of Algebra indicates that the set of complex numbers breaks the pattern. Specifically, we can allow coefficients of a polynomial equation to be any complex numbers, and all solutions will be complex numbers. No larger set is needed.

Problems 3 and 4: We think all teachers should encounter these properties of polynomial equations.

PART II
GEOMETRY WITH CONNECTIONS
TO ALGEBRA AND ANALYSIS

Chapters 7-10 constitute an intense study of the main geometric relations and functions of high school mathematics. Although these chapters can be covered independently of earlier chapters, we continue to make connections with earlier chapters in order to reinforce the many ways in which algebra and geometry support each other. Our goal for Part II, in addition to making such connections, is to expose students to the many faces of and different approaches to Euclidean geometry – revealed through its history, and by examining the properties of the concepts and relations that characterize it. Such investigations should give students a good basis for understanding and appreciating what characterizes Euclidean geometry, and should prepare them for its axiomatic treatment in Chapter 11.

Our approaches in Part II are different from traditional treatments in a variety of ways that will become clear as you work through the text. For example, instead of coupling similarity and congruence, we pair similarity with distance. Our discussion of the measurement functions of Euclidean geometry – one, two, and three dimensional – is directed toward enabling the student to understand the mathematical bases for and the relationships between the familiar distance, area, and volume formulas. Angle measure is introduced both in relation to rotations and within the context of trigonometry. The latter is genetically and historically developed in a way that is perhaps new to your students.

Our experience, as well as the results of pilot-testing earlier versions of this book, indicate that:
1) Undergraduate students in this course who have not taken a college-level course in Euclidean geometry will be familiar with the concept of congruence for triangles, circles, line segments, and angles from their high school background. However, their understanding of the concept is likely to be rather informal and imprecise, and their grasp of the tools used to establish the congruence of two geometric figures may be limited to the application of the SAS and other congruence criteria for triangles or to such tests as the congruence of alternate interior angles for a pair of parallel lines cut by a transversal. They are not likely to have any global perspective of plane geometry or the role of congruence in plane geometry such as are presented here.
2) Practicing high school teachers enrolled in this course are likely to be quite familiar with the content and presentation of high school geometry but their views of how geometric concepts and figures are defined and how proofs are written may be unnecessarily rigid. This rigidity may be the result of their being familiar with only one approach to Euclidean geometry. For this reason, we present multiple approaches.
3) Both groups tend to view high school geometry as quite separate from the other courses in high school mathematics in content and teaching style. In some schools, the teaching of geometry is left to the "specialists" and avoided entirely by some teachers. Euclidean geometry, even at the college level, often appears to members of both groups to be irrelevant to other college-level courses taken by high school mathematics teachers. We try to dispel that notion here.

CHAPTER 7 – Congruence

Objectives

After completing Chapter 7 the student should be able to:

- provide alternate definitions for various geometric figures and indicate reasons for preferring one definition over another.

- summarize the historical evolution of the concept of congruence in Euclidean geometry from Euclid to the present time.

- give synthetic, coordinate, and complex number descriptions of congruence transformations of the plane.

- deduce the main triangle congruence theorems of Euclidean plane geometry (SSS, ASA, SAS, etc.) and the properties of symmetric figures using transformations.

- describe rotations, translations, and glide reflections as composites of reflections and indicate why there are no other congruence transformations.

- be able to apply congruence to the analysis of geometric figures, equation and function graphs and the symmetry of figures.

- subject a given type of geometric figure to in-depth analysis.

Notes

We study congruence first because of its importance in the logical derivation of properties of figures, because of its significance in the history of western geometry, and because multiple approaches to congruence exist in today's schoolbooks. The last of these reasons can be disquieting to students who have been led to believe that the way they were taught congruence is the only elementary way to approach the subject. We choose to define congruence in terms of transformations, and in this chapter we demonstrate the benefits of doing so. This sets the stage for definitions of symmetry in Unit 7.3 and of similarity in Chapter 8 in terms of transformations, and provides the opportunity for comparative analyses of these relations.

Unit 7.1: Euclid and Congruence

Unit 7.1 is especially important to set the stage for what follows. It begins with a look at Euclid's *Elements* and the different approaches to his geometry that are discussed in Part II. We make a special effort to help the student understand Euclid's method of deductively developing geometry – both with respect to the power of deductive reasoning and the dangers inherent in careless applications of it. We recommend that you take the time to thoroughly discuss the sections on the use of diagrams and the importance of correct definitions, and assign many of the problems in these sections. With respect to Chapter 7, in particular, an understanding of the different types of definitions of congruence is important.

Section 7.1.1

You might wish to emphasize the difference between *Euclid's geometry* and *Euclidean geometry*. Some writers (unwisely, in our opinion) convey the impression that approaches to Euclidean geometry that involve coordinates, transformations, or vectors are not Euclidean geometry, when they are more accurately not Euclid's geometry.

A title to Table 1 on page 276 might be: "Various perspectives to Euclidean geometry". The availability of a variety both of synthetic and analytic approaches with any of these perspectives means that are quite a number of mathematical ways to examine Euclidean geometry.

Students are unlikely to have seen the three-part *tour de force* by Heath on Euclid's *Elements*. Having that text available can help students to see that the lists of definitions, postulates, and common notions are found together in Euclid's Book I, while the list of propositions had to be compiled by going through Euclid's development.

Problems 1-4: These problems are designed to get students to read through the lists of definitions, postulates, common notions, and propositions.

Problems 5-7: It is impossible to define all terms without avoiding circularity. The purpose of these problems is to show that, even were there not that difficulty, to define primitive terms is not particularly helpful because the terms that are used in the definitions are themselves hazy.

Section 7.1.2

This section discusses the need for care in deduction. The examples that are given demonstrate the danger of using inadequate drawings and explain why, to most mathematicians today, rigorous arguments need to be independent of drawings. A rigorous approach to solving these difficulties can be found in our later discussion of betweenness in Section 11.1.2.

A student may wonder if the given solution to the problem of covering a checkerboard with dominoes does not violate the proscription in the rest of the section regarding the use of figures. It does not because checkerboards of given dimensions are all similar. So if an argument works for one checkerboard, it will work for them all.

Problem 2: Some students view proof more as demonstrating the validity of propositions that one believes are true, while others view proof more as demonstrating the validity of propositions that do not seem to be true. This question can stimulate a discussion of these two perspectives.

Section 7.1.3

Some instructors have covered this section while discussing earlier chapters. We place the section here because, in school mathematics, the nature of definitions is more likely to be studied in geometry than in any other mathematics course, and because of its connection to the next section.

At the time of the publication of this book, a fine source for the evolution of definitions can be found at http://members.aol.com/jeff570/mathword.html. You need not be an aol member to access the site.

Problems 8 and 9: Except in Chapter 11, we use the second definitions of trapezoid and isosceles trapezoid in this book.

Problem 17: There is an error in the first printing. The reference should be to page 293.

Section 7.1.4

Here we define congruence in terms of transformations. Ironically, this definition can be viewed as closer to Euclid's conception of the idea than the definitions given by those who tried to put Euclidean geometry on a rigorous basis a century ago. In school mathematics, the two main advantages of the transformation definition are its applicability to all types of figures and its power in deducing theorems. We show the latter in Units 7.3 and 7.4. The main advantages for later mathematics are the natural connections of transformations with many important concepts: functions, vectors, matrices, complex numbers, and groups. We preview some of these ideas in the problems for this section and discuss some of these connections in more detail in Unit 7.2.

Problems 1 and 2: You might wish to compare transformation proofs with the traditional proofs requested here.

Problem 8: The description of orientation in this section is informal; this problem provides for a precise mathematical definition.

Unit 7.2: The Congruence Transformations

This unit examines the four kinds of congruence transformations, first individually, and then in consort as a group with composition. We examine this group in this unit, synthetically and analytically, in the Euclidean, Cartesian, and Argand (complex number) planes. From synthetic and/or analytic definitions. the basic properties of the transformations and analytic formulas for the images of points are derived. We end the unit with proofs of powerful theorems about congruent graphs that have applications beyond two-dimensional Euclidean geometry.

Section 7.2.1

A synthetic and an analytic definition of *translation* are presented, both in terms of vectors, and the connection to addition of complex numbers is made. This last connection is important for the analytic descriptions of the other transformations in terms of complex numbers.

Problem 4: You might relate this problem to the discussion of the word "parallel" in Chapter 1. Here is a use of the word "parallel" in which parallel objects can intersect.

Section 7.2.2

Here we start with a synthetic definition of rotation and move quickly to an analytic formula for the rotation of 90° or $\frac{\pi}{2}$ about the origin, and then to a formula for the rotation of ϕ about the origin. By referring back to the connection between rotations and complex numbers made in Chapter 2, we are able to obtain an analytic formula for the rotation image of a point about any point as center in the complex plane. The simplicity of the description using complex numbers comes as a surprise to many students but exemplifies the intimate connection between geometry, trigonometry, and complex numbers.

Problem 1c: The images in parts **a** and **b** are not only congruent, but translation images of each other.

Problems 5-7: These problems show that formulas for R_ϕ for some values of ϕ do not require trigonometry either for their derivation or their delineation.

Problem 8:   Some people use the term "check" only for what we call a "sure check".

Problem 13:   This result generalizes to vertices of a regular n-gon.

Section 7.2.3

Here we use a synthetic definition of reflections to derive analytic formulas for reflections over certain lines containing the origin. Then we show that the composite of two reflections over intersecting lines is a rotation (Theorem 7.9a) and use that theorem to derive a formula for the refection image of a point over any line containing the origin. Last, we use this result to obtain a complex number formula for the reflection image of a point over any line in the complex (or coordinate) plane.

That rotations and translations can be considered as composites of reflections (Theorems 7.9a and 7.9b) is one of the beautiful results in the theory of congruence transformations. And because of this result, some treatments of congruence transformations begin with reflections.

Problem 13:   The answer runs counter to the intuition of many people.

Section 7.2.4

Glide reflections are often overlooked in school treatments of transformations because they seem to be composites of other transformations with no individual integrity. However, they are seen as necessary when we want to identify all congruence transformations, as we do in Section 7.2.5. Here we give a synthetic definition and use that definition and the results of prior sections to obtain a formula using complex numbers for the image of a point under any glide reflection in the plane.

Section 7.2.5

A careful and detailed exposition of this section may be needed. Here transformations are treated as objects to be manipulated algebraically. That type of manipulation may be difficult for students who are studying transformations for the first time and think of them only as functions relating preimage to image.

The major theorem of the section is Theorem 7.17. You might demonstrate its proof by drawing a reasonably complicated figure on an overhead projector transparency. Project the figure onto a chalkboard or whiteboard (not onto a screen) and trace the projection image. Now move the transparency, possibly turning it over. Then move the projector but keep it at the same distance from the board. Trace the new projection image. The two tracings will be congruent and related by one of the four types of isometries.

Section 7.2.6

For most students, a graph is a representation not able to be described rigorously, and graphing is a process that is not associated with any theorems. Through this book, we take the position that a graph in $\mathbf{R}^2$ is a set of points. This approach enables us to treat graphs as we would any other geometric figures. One of the nice consequences of this view is the extremely useful set of theorems about graphing found in this section.

Problems 2 and 3: These problems show that descriptions of graphs derived by other means can be seen as special cases of the Graph Translation Theorem.

Problem 4:   We can use the word "congruent" here only because the definition of congruence using transformations applies to all figures.

Problem 6:   Because of the Graph Translation Theorem, this nonintuitive result has eseentially a one-step proof.

Unit 7.3: Symmetry

The goal of this unit is to expose and apply the fundamental relationship that exists between congruence and symmetry. We define symmetry by means of transformations, and then use the results established in Unit 7.2 to prove the familiar symmetric properties of common geometric figures. Students may be familiar with these properties, but many may not have seen such proofs. They may also be unfamiliar with the use of geometrical arguments to deduce properties of curves, such as the conic sections, that they have encountered only algebraically.

Section 7.3.1

In this section we deduce the reflection-symmetry of many of the figures of high school geometry and algebra, and apply that symmetry (rather than congruent triangles) to derive properties of the figures. This approach parallels one's intuition as to why figures have properties (e.g., why the diagonals of a rhombus are perpendicular). Perhaps there are cultures on other worlds in which symmetry is the basic building block from which geometry results are obtained.

Problem 9:   Here we use the term "kite" as we often do for all polygons in discussions of area, in the more general reference to the region enclosed by the polygon.

Section 7.3.2

It would be mathematically incomplete to stop at reflection symmetry. This section mentions the corresponding symmetries for the other congruence transformations. Two examples are highlighted: the parallelogram, with rotation but not reflection symmetry; and the sine wave, with symmetry under all four types of isometries, and identities corresponding to each symmetry.

Problem 13:   You should expect students to detail the symmetry by giving equations for lines of symmetry and coordinates of points of symmetry, etc. Part **a** is necessary for part **e**.

Unit 7.4: Traditional Congruence Revisited

A variety of approaches to congruence are found in today's school texts. Some books assume the SAS, SSS, and ASA triangle congruence propositions. Some assume SAS and state SSS and ASA as theorems and may or may not give proofs. At least one uses the approach found in this unit, to deduce these propositions as theorems. Section 7.4.2 shows a concept analysis that encourages students to examine special properties of a geometric figure. The unit ends with powerful theorems about congruence that can be viewed as a culmination of the results about Euclidean congruence.

Section 7.4.1

Here we use the general definition of congruence in terms of transformations to establish the sufficient conditions for congruence of special figures – segments, angles, and triangles. A nice feature of this section is the opportunity to explore different congruence proofs of the same theorem. Students should be encouraged to reflect on the different proofs and express opinions about which are most appealing to them, and why. The SsA Theorem at the end of the section is a theorem about triangle congruence that is not found in Euclid's *Elements*, and will likely be new to the students. A nice connection between this theorem and the Law of Sines is discussed in Section 9.1.2.

Problem 1, 2, and 5: These problems require students to go through the steps of the proofs of corresponding theorems in the section.

Problem 8:   This problem shows how the SsA Theorem can explain in advance how many solutions to expect when solving a triangle given two sides and a nonincluded angle.

Section 7.4.2

This section is especially important to assist students with geometric reasoning. Emphasize that the list of aspects of the figure to be examined is not fixed. The more geometry a person knows, the longer the list might be.

Problem 1:   If other definitions of trapezoid and isosceles trapezoid are used (see part **d** here and Problems 7 and 8 in Section 7.1.3), then the network of the hierarchy is not topologically equivalent. Nor is it as easy to see how the properties of the different types intuitively relate to each other. You might wish to examine the symmetry, diagonals, sides, or angles of quadrilaterals, and identify their properties with the nodes of this network. For example, figures in D (isosceles trapezoids) possess reflection symmetry and figures in E (parallelograms) possess rotation symmetry, so figures in G and H must possess both.

Problems 6-8 and 13: We urge assigning one or more of these problems to give students an opportunity to do their own analysis of a geometric figure. You may wish to ask less-prepared students to analyze one or more of the standard quadrilaterals identified in Problem 1.

Section 7.4.3

Theorems 7.43 and 7.44 are direct consequences of the existence of only four types of isometries. Figures 85 and 86 purposely show figures more complicated than triangles in order to emphasize the generality of the theorems.

Problem 1:   A coordinate proof of Theorem 7.41 is relatively easy when right $\triangle ABC$ is in standard position. You might ask students for a proof when right triangle ABC is located anywhere on the coordinate plane. This requires the determination of reasonable vertices for the triangle, a difficult concept for some students.

Chapter 7 Projects

Projects 2 and 3 take the complex number description of transformations further than we do in the text. This approach has the advantage of algebraic elegance and simplicity but has the disadvantage of masking the underlying geometry unless care is taken to keep the geometry in the forefront. They are excellent projects for a group of capable students. The simplicity of these descriptions extends to similarity transformations, discussed in Chapter 8.

CHAPTER 8 – Distance and Similarity

Objectives

After completing Chapter 8 the student should be able to:

- illustrate with examples the meaning of the mathematical concept of distance in E^2, $\mathbf{R}^2$, E^3, and $\mathbf{R}^3$, and on a sphere, and apply this concept to the solution of minimum distance problems.

- apply the basic properties of similarity to the analysis of geometric figures and the graphs of functions and relations.

- compare and contrast the basic properties of similarity transformations and congruence transformations.

- be able to use similarity and similarity transformations to develop theorems of Euclidean geometry.

- to describe and relate geometrical pictures and situations involving arithmetic, geometric and harmonic means.

- To apply similarity to analyze and solve problems such as the Receding Telephone Poles Problem.

Notes

Chapter 8 is a natural extension of Chapter 7. Similarity can be defined in terms of ratios of distances, and we build on this relationship in Chapter 8. To this end, we begin by first examining the idea of distance, and what is at the basis of any definition of it.

Unit 8.1: Distance

In this unit, we explore distance in several different contexts. In Section 8.1.1, we reflect on how contexts affect what distance means and show several different kinds of distance functions. By distance we tend to mean "shortest distance", and so we are led naturally into Section 8.1.2, where we examine problems of finding the minimum distance between two points given certain conditions. In both of these sections the idea of "equidistance" arises, an idea explored in the locus problems of Section 8.1.3. In Section 8.1.4, we revert back to the idea of Section 8.1.1 and discuss distance and shortest distance on the surface of a sphere.

Section 8.1.1

Euclidean and taxicab distance are introduced in this section, and comparisons between them are made. The Hamming distance in data transmission helps provide students with an understanding of distance outside of the context of geometry. A definition of a distance function establishes the properties of distance illustrated by these types of distance. In Chapter 10, we establish similar criteria for area and volume functions.

Problem 1:   In the weeks before publication of these materials, one of the authors encountered a situation where a major airline charged more for a specific single round trip A to B to A than for a triangle A to B to C to A even though the leg from B to C included a stop at A and thus included all the flights of the single round trip and more. Specifics of this kind of example are sought here.

Problem 2:   Students may remember such a formula from their study of geometry in school.

Problem 12:   The endpoints of this finite semicircle model of R can be thought of as $-\infty$ and $+\infty$, two "ideal points" attached to the real number system R, at a chordal distance of π from one another. For some students, this characterization takes some of the mystery out of the meaning of the symbols $-\infty$ and $+\infty$.

Section 8.1.2

Geometric distance is typically calculated as the length of the shortest path between two points. This leads us first to explore the shortest distance between a point and various different point sets. Although Theorems 8.1 and 8.2 are often taken for granted in textbooks at the high school and beginning college level, we believe that it is important for teachers to realize that these intuitive results can be proved with a little care. Then we deduce solutions to three relatively well-known minimal path problems: Hero's problem, Fermat's problem, and Fagnano's problem. Each solution is elegant and involves transformations, reinforcing ideas of Chapter 7. A geometry drawing program can be used to support the solution of each of these problems very effectively. The constructions for the Fermat point and the Fagnano triangle are stated in italics following the solutions of these problems.

Problems 1 and 2: The answers to these questions may help students to understand why perpendicularity and the relationship between a radius and a tangent to a circle at a point are so important.

Problem 6a: The angles of incidence and reflection are traditionally measured from the perpendicular (or normal) to the surface, but many construe the equality of the angles to mean the equality of the complementary angles formed by the path and the surface.

Problem 12:   These are actual cities and students should use maps in an atlas or on the internet to help answer the question.

Section 8.1.3

The set of points satisfying certain conditions is a powerful idea that used to be given more importance in school geometry than it has today. Do not assume that students have heard of the word "locus" even if they are familiar with the ideas of the propositions on page 375.

This section treats two problems of finding the locus of points at a given distance from a given set. The first is the familiar dog-on-a-leash problem, a locus problem which is given an extended analysis like that given to the box problem and catch-up problem in Chapter 3. Six problems give students the opportunity to apply, generalize and extend this problem. You should try to assign as many of them as you can.

Another locus problem, dealing with the distance from a rectangle, closes the section.

Problems 1-6: These relate to the dog-on-a-leash problem.

Problems 8 and 9: These relate to the problem of finding the locus of points at a given distance from a given rectangle.

Section 8.1.4

Some hand-held devices are able to communicate with GPS (global positioning satellites) and thus determine latitude and longitude. By entering the latitude and longitude of one's destination, the distance of the device from the destination can be calculated. This calculation uses the Spherical Law of Cosines (Theorem 8.6) or an equivalent. This "law" is a reasonably straightforward application of the law of cosines for the plane.

Figure 18 is not drawn to scale, so students may not realize that $\angle DCO$ is a right angle.

You may have to stress that spherical trigonometry uses the same sines and cosines as plane trigonometry. Some students may think that because a spherical angle is constituted of arcs, so the trigonometric functions of that angle are somehow different.

Problems 5b and 5c: Emphasize that although a particular proof might collapse, there might be other proofs that do not collapse. Thus the collapse of a first proof might not signify that the theorem does not hold more generally.

Problem 9: The intuition of many people is that flying "due east" on a circle of latitude from one place to another would be the shortest distance. They may be surprised to see that the answer to part **a** is smaller than the answer to parts **b** or **c**.

Problem 11: Students interested in learning more about spherical trigonometry might be encouraged to check an old trigonometry textbook out of the library. Trigonometry texts before 1940 routinely discussed spherical trigonometry in some detail.

Unit 8.2: Similar Figures

This unit makes substantial use of the material in Unit 7.2 on congruence transformations. In fact, a course segment on geometric transformations can be based on Units 7.2 and 8.2 covered successively (with only minimal references to Unit 7.1), perhaps followed by selected sections from Unit 7.3, 7.4 and 8.3. In this unit, we define similarity, as we defined congruence, by means of transformations. Then we apply the definition to three kinds of figures: graphs, polygons, and arcs. Arcs play an important role in a set of theorems that we combine into one general theorem. Finally, we catalog similarity transformations in a way similar to the catalog for congruence transformations.

The book *Geometric Transformations II*, by I.M. Yaglom, contains some of the theory of this unit and many problems not presented here.

Section 8.2.1

After noting that Euclidean geometry can be described as the science that studies those properties of geometric figures that are not changed by similarity transformations, we carefully describe and define similar figures. The analogies between the definitions of congruent figures and similar figures should be discussed. One way is to copy the identical parts of the definitions with spaces where they differ, and then discuss the differences. The Fundamental Property of Similarity, stated on page 386, might be viewed as a theorem, but it follows so immediately from the definition that we view it as restating the defining criterion for similar figures.

In the theory of similar figures, Theorem 8.11 is especially important because it demonstrates the relationship between a size change and any similarity and explains why many properties of similarity transformations can be derived from the properties of size changes. Theorem 8.11 is applied in Section 8.2.2 in deducing sufficient conditions for two triangles to be similar.

Problem 12b: Although the entire theory of similarity can be developed using only size changes of positive magnitude, it is sometimes quite elegant to consider negative magnitudes, as this application shows.

Section 8.2.2

The generality of the definition of similarity via transformations is illustrated in this consideration of similarities of graphs on the Cartesian plane. Theorem 8.12 about size change is comparable to theorems in Section 7.2.6 for translations and reflections, and has important applications about the graphs of functions. The specific application to change of units covers a topic usually ignored in mathematics classes.

Problems 1, 3-6, 8 and 9: These problems each treat the idea of determining the limitations of a class of figures if all members of the class are to be similar, or if they are to be homothetic.

Section 8.2.3

The three parts of Theorem 8.13 are found in virtually all school geometry texts, but typically without proof. Transformations allow the proofs to be rather elegant. In contrast, Theorems 8.14 and 8.15 are not typically found in schoolbooks in the forms in which they are stated here. Theorem 8.15 becomes the focus of attention in Section 8.1.5.

Problem 2:   This problem is trivial for some students while deceptively difficult for others.

Problems 11-14: These problems can be enhanced considerably through use of a geometry drawing program.

Section 8.2.4

The similarity of arcs is important in the study of trigonometry, particularly in treatments in which the trigonometric functions sine and cosine are defined in terms of arc lengths or arc measures. Such a treatment is found in Section 9.2.1.

The key idea to emphasize is that similar arcs have the same *measure* (in radians or degrees) but do not have the same length. Instead, their lengths are proportional to the radii of the corresponding circles.

Section 8.2.5

Theorem 8.18 is like Theorems 4.9 and 4.11 about the solution of equations and inequalities in that it combines propositions that students usually learn as separate and not closely-related statements. As with those theorems, it demonstrates an essential unity and consistency to the mathematical results to which it refers.

The notion of a "complete angle", found in the restatement of Theorem 8.18, is ours. We do not know of another source that states the general theorem in this way (though it would not surprise us to find such a source).

Problem 5: The two parts of this problem provide alternate proofs of theorems usually derived directly from the fact that the sum of the measures of the interior angles of a triangle is 180°.

Section 8.2.6

The crux of this section is found in Table 1 on page 414. Listed there are the four types of similarity transformations and their corresponding special cases (when the ratio of similarity is 1) in the catalog of isometries.

The simplicity of Theorems and 8.22 and 8.24 is startling. Its existence demonstrates once again that complex numbers and Euclidean geometry are related in fundamental ways.

Problem 3: The first printing of the text has an error. The point A should be the center of each of the seven spiral similarities. The points C, B, and the consecutive images B', B", ... lie on a logarithmic (or equiangular) spiral. In the complex plane, if the original triangle is placed so that $A = 0$, $C = 1$, and $B = 1 + i$, then $B' = (1+i)^2$, and the nth image of B is $(1+i)^{n-1}$.

Problem 8: The transformation may only be a dilative reflection, but its relative rarity in relationships in elementary geometry causes students to have great difficulty in determining corresponding sides in the similar triangles that result.

Unit 8.3: Distances within Figures

Except for Section 8.2.5, the preceding unit has concerned itself with ratios of corresponding distances between figures. Here we turn our attention to ratios in an individual figure to demonstrate a few applications of the power of similarity.

Section 8.3.1

We show many instances of figures in which one length is the geometric mean of two other lengths, justifying the name *geometric mean*. They are derived from one of two basic figures. First is the existence of a geometric mean in the lengths of a tangent, secant, and the external part of the secant to a circle from a point. Second are the many geometric means in the lengths of sides of a right triangle and the segments formed by the altitude to the hypotenuse. In Section 10.1.5, geometric means recur in the quadrature of the rectangle.

The second part of this section shows an example of a harmonic mean (first mentioned in Section 4.3.4) in a figure that combines the two basic figures just mentioned. We are able, using this figure, to show that the positive geometric mean of two different positive numbers is greater than their harmonic mean and less than their arithmetic mean. Together these ideas show once again the remarkable relationships between algebra and geometry.

Theorem 8.28 does not require $a < b$, only that $a \neq b$ and that they are both positive.

Problems 11 and 12: These problems are designed to give students practice in the symbolism for arithmetic means as well as to show instances of these means they may not have realized.

Section 8.3.2

Section 8.3.2 connects two concepts of Euclidean geometry that some students may see as unrelated: similarity and parallelism. Theorem 8.29 establishes a fundamental result that enables the proofs of the other two theorems in the section. The section concludes with an extended analysis of an interesting application of these latter two theorems to the perspective drawing of equally-spaced telephone poles.

Problems 7-9: Problem 7 is necessary for Problem 8, whose ideas in turn are utilized in Problem 9.

Chapter 8 Projects

Project 5: Bezier curves are used in graphical programs to create smooth curves. For example, the Pen Tool in the computer animation program Flash implements the construction of Bezier curves determined by control points set by the user.

Project 6: The content of this project used to be rather standard in school geometry books but now is not always found in them. The triangle centers discussed in this project and in Project 7 do not begin to exhaust the catalog of such points that have been investigated by geometry researchers. The companion web site for this book has a link to Clark Kimberling's Encyclopedia of Triangle Centers, which is a very well organized and maintained resource for information on this subject.

CHAPTER 9 – Trigonometry

Objectives

After completing Chapter 9 the student should be able to:

- outline the development of trigonometry over time, indicating its major applications and connections to other parts of mathematics.

- describe the basis in similarity for the six trigonometric ratios and their interconnections, and be able to apply them to solve a wide variety of indirect measurement problems.

- explain how the trigonometric functions extend the trigonometric ratios to real functions.

- apply the trigonometric functions to analyze and solve problems involving periodic phenomenon (e.g., the length of daylight) and parametric description of curves (e.g., ellipses and cycloids).

- derive trigonometric identities and apply them to develop properties of numbers and functions and in the solution of problems.

Notes

In this chapter, we follow the customary school practice of treating trigonometry in two rather different ways. At first the discussion is centered around angles, arcs, segments, and triangles, and the applications are primarily to problems of determination of unknown distances and angles. In the second unit, the discussion shifts to the trigonometric functions as real functions and the applications are to situations exhibiting periodicity. The final unit touches on the most important properties of the sine and cosine functions, independent of these applications.

Unit 9.1: Angle Measure and the Trigonometric Ratios

This unit takes students from the establishment of units for angle measure and arc length through the solution of triangles. All students should have studied the basics of this content, but many will not have encountered the underlying theory, applications, or history.

Section 9.1.1

The proportion of Theorem 9.1 can be rewritten as the equality between the ratio of lengths of two circular arcs with the same measure and the ratio of the radii of their circles. This statement is closely related to, and also follows from Theorem 8.17, that the ratio of the lengths of two similar arcs equals the ratio of lengths of their chords. In Theorem 9.1, let $r_1 = 1$ so that the first arc is on a unit circle. Then the length L_1 of the first arc in radians also equals the radian measure θ of that arc. Then, since the second arc has the same measure θ, we have $L_2 = \theta \cdot r_2$, which with the subscripts dropped becomes Theorem 9.2.

We have mentioned elsewhere in these notes that many students have great difficulty with unit conversions. Some of the problems provide practice in this important skill.

Problem 4:   Some calculators do these conversions automatically. When using a calculator, the problem then becomes how to know that the answer is correct.

Problem 5:   The use of minutes and seconds both as units of time and units of angle and arc measure makes this problem confusing for many students. You might wish to capitalize the units for one or the other to distinguish them.

Section 9.1.2

Theorem 9.4 is a restatement of the proportion of Theorem 8.17. Aside from the historical comments, the content of this section should have been encountered by students in their precalculus mathematics studies.

Problem 3b: You might wish to have students draw a unit circle with an inscribed $\triangle ABC$, measure the side lengths, and see how close those lengths are to the sines of A, B, and C.

Problem 6:   This problem asks for one of the standard proofs of the Law of Cosines.

Section 9.1.3

This section begins with the basic right triangle trigonometry problem of finding an unknown height using the tangent. It proceeds through a series of problems, each with weaker conditions than the previous, and thus each requiring a little more work for its solution. The fourth problem involves given information such as would be available to a surveyor trying to use triangulation.

Problems 1-5: These problems are variants or generalizations of problems in the section.

Unit 9.2: The Trigonometric Functions and Their Connections

In Unit 9.1, the sine and cosine are functions of angles or arcs with measures between 0 and π radians. In this unit we extend the notions first to functions of real numbers, then to functions of complex numbers. Then we provide some history and some applications to periodic phenomena.

Section 9.2.1

To extend the sine and cosine to represent functions of real numbers, we seek an interpretation of sine and cosine that is consistent with the original domain but that includes the new domain. The most common interpretation identifies the cosine and sine as the first and second coordinates of points on the unit circle. With the wrapping function definition of the sine and cosine, (cos t, sin t) is the image of the point (1, t) when the line x = 1 is wrapped around the circle in the manner described in the section. With the definition of the sine and cosine using rotations, (cos t, sin t) is the image of (1, 0) under a rotation of magnitude t. In either interpretation, t can be any real number and we can quickly obtain the identity $\cos t = \cos(-t)$, the periodic nature of the function through $\cos t = \cos(t + 2\pi)$, and specific values such as $\cos \pi = -1$. To extend the sine and cosine to represent functions of complex numbers, we again seek an

Section 9.2.2

Most of this section is devoted to one problem, modeling the length of daylight over a year. The goal is to closely estimate L(d), the length of day d of a year. Example 1 shows that the function is a sine wave. Example 2 uses actual data to determine the parameters of the sine wave. The remainder of the section is devoted to parametric equations of curves using sine and cosine functions. Three types of curves are described: circles, ellipses, and cycloids.

Problem 7: Another set of parametric equations is x = acosh ø and y = bsinh ø, where cosh and sinh are the hyperbolic cosine and sine satisfying cosh $\varnothing = \frac{1}{2}(e^\varnothing + e^{-\varnothing})$ and sinh $\varnothing = \frac{1}{2}(e^\varnothing - e^{-\varnothing})$. You could substitute these parametric equations for the ones given in the problem.

Problem 8b: There is an error in the first printing. s(x) = 1 if $2k\pi < x < (2k+1)\pi$ and s(x) = -1 if $(2k+1)\pi < x \le 2(k+1)\pi$. Graphs closer to the graph of the square wave function can be obtained by including more terms of the sequence $s_n = \frac{1}{2n-1}(\sin(2n-1)x)$.

Section 9.2.3

The history of trigonometric functions presented here is more extensive than corresponding histories of most of the other mathematical ideas in this book. Our reason is simple: the history is interesting and involves mathematicians from many parts of the world. It provides testimony to the universality of mathematics. The problems here include three of the most famous applications in the history of trigonometry.

Problem 3c: Such errors plagued all astronomical measurements before the invention of the telescope in the early 17th century.

Problem 4c: Assume the error could be in either direction.

Unit 9.3: Properties of the Sine and Cosine Functions

The first section of this unit discuss identities that are based on the identities for sin(x + y) and cos (x + y), the *sine or cosine of a sum*. The second section discusses a problem in mechanical vibrations that leads to an expression involving the *sum of a sine and/or cosine*. The last section explains why the second derivative of the sine function (and also the cosine function) is the opposite of that function.

Section 9.3.1

This section reviews and extends identities students should have seen in their precalculus work. We use the formula for a rotation image (Theorem 9.9) to derive the sum and difference formulas for the sine and cosine (Theorems 9.10a and 9.10b). In many treatments the reverse order is used. Our order displays the wonderfully elegant derivation that shows that the sum formulas can be interpreted as angle addition in matrix form. The problems include many important trigonometric identities.

Problem 4g: You may wish to alert students to use mathematical induction.

Problem 6d: As an example of a pattern that does not persist, consider the following:

$$\sin 30° = \frac{1}{2} = \frac{\sqrt{1}}{2}$$

$$\sin 45° = \frac{\sqrt{2}}{2}$$

$$\sin 60° = \frac{\sqrt{3}}{2}$$

all of which satisfy $\sin 15n° = \frac{\sqrt{n-1}}{2}$, but the pattern does not continue. You might ask students whether the pattern is true for *any* other values of n. (No.)

Problem 8: In the 16th century (before the invention of logarithms), algorithms for multiplication like those learned by students today in 3rd and 4th grade were not widely known.

Section 9.3.2

In contrast to Section 9.3.1, the identities in this section are not customarily studied in school mathematics. In school treatments, phase shift and amplitude are often viewed as theoretical phenomena and their origin as descriptors of waves is lost. Theorem 9.11 and its application to mechanical vibration in Example 3 can help students to see how phase shift and amplitude derive from a real problem.

Problems 4-6: These problems can be used to determine whether students understand one of the main ideas of the section.

Section 9.3.3

When an object is in circular motion at a constant speed, its velocity at any point on the circle is in the direction of the tangent to the circle at that point, and the magnitude of its acceleration is constant and directed towards the center of the circle. From these principles, we deduce that the coordinates of points on the circle must be of the form (Rcos t, Rsin t), where R is the radius of the circle. Theorems 9.12a and 9.12b state this result in vector language. This provides another justification for calling the sine and cosine "circular" functions.

Chapter 9 Projects

Project 2: This project is an extended analysis of Regiomontanus's problem.

Project 4: Parts **i-l** are not usually considered to be identities, since there is no variable. But they are proved just as identities are, since the values of the various sines and cosines do not need to be found. Students may enjoy finding equivalent identities to these that show other patterns. For instance, part **j** is equivalent to $\sin 10° \cdot \sin 30° \cdot \sin 50° \cdot \sin 70° = \frac{1}{16}$, and part **k** is equivalent to $\sin 6° \cdot \sin 42° \cdot \sin 78° \cdot \sin 114° = \frac{1}{16}$.

CHAPTER 10 – Area and Volume

Objectives

After completing Chapter 10 the student should be able to:

- explain how the axioms for area and volume enable formulas for the area and volume of some geometric figures to be obtained.

- know and be able to derive area formulas for a variety of plane figures, including the various kinds of quadrilaterals, triangles (including Hero's Formula and the ASA and SAS formulas), regular polygons, circles, and ellipses.

- analyze synthetically and analytically minimum area problems, such as the line through a given point minimizing area problem and isoperimetric problems.

- explain how a square can be constructed whose area equals the area of a given rectangle, triangle, or other polygon.

- know and be able to derive surface area and volume formulas for a variety of solid figures, including parallelepipeds, prisms, pyramids, cylinders, cones, and spheres.

- understand the Fundamental Theorem of Similarity and its implications for the structure of area and volume formulas.

Notes

Chapter 10 continues the discussion of Euclidean measure begun in Chapter 7. The goal here, as there, is to help students understand there is an underlying theory of one-, two- and three-dimensional measures that supports the formulas they learned in high school. In this chapter we explore area and volume in parallel ways that emanate from formal definitions of these measures analogous to that given for distance in Chapter 7. In doing so, we show similarities and differences in their construction, and explain what is possible (or not) relative to their development. We also connect the different ways that area and volume are treated in geometry and calculus courses. Throughout the development, we provide algebraic and both synthetic and analytic geometric proofs of theorems to reinforce the connections between algebra and geometry and to demonstrate the possibilities of different approaches.

Unit 10.1: Area

In schoolwork through calculus, area usually begins and ends with formulas. Occasionally students see how one formula leads to another, but for the most part they do not encounter a broad look at the concept of area. Here we offer such a look, working from a definition of an area function that assumes only the area of a square. We cut and rearrange squares and their parts into rectangles, triangles, and other figures and are able to obtain the area of a circle and under a curve. Then we reverse the process and examine whether figures can be cut and rearranged into squares and, if so, how this can be done. In a last section, we touch on the relationship of area to probability.

Section 10.1.1

In Section 10.1.1, we define area, and indicate the assumptions on which the definition rests. We then use the definition to build the familiar formulas for areas of figures bounded by line segments, beginning with the area of a square. Table 1 can be used as a flow chart to show the development. We also introduce perimeter and establish several theorems about area in relation to it.

Theorem 10.2 is an isoperimetric problem of the type discussed further in Section 10.3.2. Theorem 10.4 is found in many schoolbooks only in the special case where the quadrilateral is a rhombus. Theorem 10.6 is especially useful for its applications to the area of triangles in Section 10.1.2 and to the area of circles in Section 10.1.4.

Problem 8:   The solution depends on proving that the length of the median of a trapezoid is the arithmetic mean of the lengths of its two bases. This provides a geometric picture of an arithmetic mean akin to pictures shown in Section 8.3.1.

Problem 13:   The nonconvex hexagon ABGEID is a figure known as a *gnomon*. In general, a gnomon is a figure that, when affixed to a given polygon, produces a new polygon that is similar to the original. In this case, polygons ABCD and EGCI are similar.

Problems 16 and 17:   These nice formulas are typically not encountered by students because area is studied before trigonometry.

Section 10.1.2

Many students are aware of only the formula $A = \frac{1}{2}bh$ and at most one other formula (Hero's Formula) for the area of a triangle. Even then it is unlikely they have seen a proof of Hero's Formula. The goal of this section is to show how different pieces of given information can be put together to determine the area of a triangle. Hero's Formula requires knowing the lengths of the triangle's sides (SSS), and Theorems 10.8 and 10.9 do the same when SAS or ASA are known. The problems afford possibilities to develop additional area formulas for triangles, as well as for other figures.

Problem 5:   This problem is a special case of the Fundamental Theorem of Similarity discussed in Section 10.3.3.

Problem 7:   Surely this is one of the most wonderful area formulas. You might want to show students how it holds for all rectangles.

Problem 13:   The first printing has an error. The reference to Problem 10 should be to Problem 11.

Section 10.1.3

This section exhibits an extended analysis of a minimum area problem from a precalculus text. In generalizing this problem the discussion moves from analytic results to geometric ones with some powerful results. Although a discussion is likely to take a good deal of time, the involvement of various equations for a line, area formulas, calculus, and the interplay of algebra and geometry will likely make the time well spent. The problems build on the results of this extended analysis.

Problem 5:   The first printing has an error. Change 23f to 23e.

Section 10.1.4

This section moves the discussion to considerations of areas of figures bounded by curves, building on the results of ancient mathematicians and showing the connections to the methods of calculus. To make this move, the definition of an area function needs to be extended to provide for the area of figures bounded by curves. The familiar area formula for a circle (Theorem 10.10) is then seen to be an extension of the area formula for polygons inscribed in a circle (Theorem 10.6).

The history of the attempts to approximate π by rational numbers and to obtain more and more numbers in its decimal expansion is fascinating even to people not particularly interested in mathematics. We strongly recommend alerting students to the references at the end of the chapter for further reading.

Problem 5:   The use of transformations affords an elegant derivation of the formula $A = \pi ab$ for the area of an ellipse with semimajor axis a and semiminor axis b.

Problem 7:   The existence of harmonic and geometric mean relationships among the perimeters of inscribed and circumscribed regular polygons of n sides and 2n sides is not well known. By giving steps in the proof, we enable students to recreate a full proof.

Section 10.1.5

The proof of Theorem 10.13 suggests strongly that the Greeks needed the Pythagorean Theorem in their theory of area. Consequently, we are led to conjecture that the problem of quadrature led the Greeks to prefer an area proof of the Pythagorean Theorem to the ostensibly simpler proof using similar triangles (see the discussion in Section 8.3.1 after Theorem 8.27).

Problem 5:   You may wish to ask students for other ways to estimate the area of a circle knowing the areas of inscribed and circumscribed polygons whose areas are relatively easily found.

Section 10.1.6

This brief discussion of area and probability is designed to show that areas can stand for quantities that are not areas. Students should know this fact from calculus, but it is often the case that students encounter applications of derivatives but not integrals. The connection with probability leads us to discuss Monte Carlo methods and the more general problem of finding areas of irregularly shaped regions.

Problem 4: Remind students that with 100 points there is no way to have an approximation to π that is correct beyond the second decimal place.

Problem 6: Figure 44 shows the size of the quarter but may mislead some students. The requested probability is that the coin cover a lattice point, not that it land so as not to cover any lattice points (though the two probabilities are obviously related).

Unit 10.2: Volume

The discussion of volume proceeds analogously to the discussion of area. We begin with a definition that gives us only the volume of a cube (rather than the area of a square). From this formula we are able to derive formulas for the volumes of many polyhedra. With the inclusion of Cavalieri's principle to enable treatment of curved surfaces, formulas for the volumes of cones, cylinders, and spheres can be deduced.

Section 10.2.1

The first three defining properties for volume are analogous to those for area. The fourth property, Cavalieri's Principle, can be viewed as analogous to the fourth property for area in that it enables us to deal with a class of figures not covered by the first three properties. Both properties help in determining areas of figures with curved boundaries.

Cavalieri's Principle may be new to students and should be carefully discussed. You may wish to point out how calculus generalizes this principle.

Problems 5 and 6: These are designed to help students to understand Cavalieri's Principle.

Section 10.2.2

This section develops the familiar formulas for volume, proceeding in a way analogous to the sequence for area in Section 10.1.1. We proceed from cubes to right rectangular parallelepipeds (boxes) to prisms to tetrahedra to pyramids. While this material is found in some school texts, few provide the detail we have here and many high school classes never reach this content.

The proof of Theorem 10.14, using the lemma that precedes it, is ours. While it seems far-fetched that no one else has derived Theorem 10.14 from the volume of a cube, we do not know of another source.

Problem 1: Students will have to estimate the average volume of a human. You might point out that an upper estimate is sufficient for this problem.

Section 10.2.3

Prisms and cylinders are cylindric solids, and the use of Cavalieri's Principle to obtain the volume of one from the volume of the other is straightforward. Even though pyramids and cones are conic solids, the derivation of the volume of a cone from the volume of a pyramid is somewhat trickier but still involves a basic application of Cavalieri's Principle. The volume of a sphere can be obtained by putting together pyramids in a way analogous to putting together triangles to obtain the area of a circle.

Problem 4a: This result is counter to the intuition of many.

Problem 6:   Since all pyramids and prisms are prismatoids, you might wish to show or have students show how the volume formulas for pyramids and prisms are special cases of this formula.

Unit 10.3: Relationships among Area, Volume, and Dimension

Several ideas that connect area and volume are brought together in this unit. The results here may be new to students, or may explain patterns or coincidences they have noticed, but could not explain.

Section 10.3.1

This section demonstrates that the surface areas of many common three-dimensional figures, including cones, cylinders, prisms, and pyramids, are calculated in the same way as two-dimensional areas. The sphere is an exception since its surface cannot be rolled flat, but the formula for its volume can be used to obtain a formula for its surface area. This section includes an interesting discussion of relationships between the formulas for the boundary (circumference and surface area) and the capacity (area and volume, respectively) of circles and spheres.

Problem 4:   Usually we have presented the special case first and then asked students to generalize it. Here the generalization is first.

Problem 5a: You might ask students why they think the relationship between A' and P does not hold here, while it does hold for a circle.

Section 10.3.2

Given the long history and interesting applications of problems dealing with figures that have the same area, it is somewhat depressing that some young students cannot distinguish area from perimeter. This shows the danger of learning ideas without context. The two theorems of this section are the major theorems of the subject in two and three dimensions. The corollaries present the results of the theorems in algebraic terms. The proof for the two-dimensional isoperimetric inequality (Theorem 10.23) involves several ingenious arguments.

Problems 1 and 2: These problems provide specific examples supporting Theorem 10.23.

Problem 3:   In general, the "closer" a polygon with fixed perimeter is to a regular polygon, the greater its area.

Problem 10:   Calculus is expected to be used here.

Section 10.3.3

This section discusses what happens to area and volume under similarity transformations. Theorem 10.25 summarizes the consequence, providing valuable insights into the structure of area and volume formulas. A consequence is that real objects of a certain shape that need to support themselves can only be

The section concludes with two theorems specifying the structure of area and volume formulas for sets of similar figures.

Problem 2:   Many people believe that 158 lb is too low to be the middle suggested healthy weight for a 6-foot person. The range of healthy weights given in *The World Almanac and Book of Facts 2002* is 140 lb to 177 lb.

Problem 9:   This formula seems simpler than the formula for the volume of a sphere in terms of its radius.

Section 10.3.4

One way that mathematics grows is when a concept thought to be applicable only in certain contexts is found to have broader applicability. For example, exponents were limited to whole numbers before their application in logarithms and to problems of growth were discovered. Over the past century the concept of dimension had been studied and generalized by various mathematicians, but the pivotal person who popularized the idea is Benoit Mandlebrot. Mandlebrot's book *Fractals: Form, Chance, and Dimension* synthesized the works of many who came before him by explaining why fractional-dimensional objects were reasonable and by showing how many physical features of Earth's surface and other objects could be modeled by these objects. The idea of the length of a coastline is taken from that book, as is the discussion of the Koch curve. In the former case, the modeling is approximate; in the later case the modeling is exact.

Problem 1b: In the first printing, the requirement that $n \geq 2$ in the formula for $\alpha(S_{n+1})$ is missing.

Chapter 10 Projects

The projects cover a wide range of topics, including: the famous unsolved problems of antiquity and related problems (Projects 3, 5, 7, and 8); areas of regions not usually encountered in high school (Projects 1, and 4); extended problems involving volume (Projects 6 and 9), and historically important developments (Projects 2 and 10).

CHAPTER 11 – Axiomatics and Euclidean Geometry

Objectives

After completing Chapter 11 the student should be able to:

- describe the historical evolution and the origins of the axiomatic approach to geometry and the power as well as the limitations of the axioms in Euclid's *Elements*.

- identify and use the axioms for incidence and betweenness in Euclidean geometry and their consequences, and show examples of other geometries that satisfy these axioms.

- apply the congruence axioms and explain why they, together with the incidence and betweenness axioms, are not sufficient to define Euclidean geometry.

- explain the roles of the continuity and parallel axioms in Euclidean geometry, including the identification of properties dependent on, or equivalent to them.

- explain why the Cartesian coordinate system is a model of the axiom system constructed for Euclidean geometry in the text, and use it to deduce theorems of Euclidean geometry.

- explain what is meant by a categorical set of axioms for a mathematical system, and what that specifically means for Euclidean geometry.

Notes

In the preceding chapters, students have opportunities to examine properties of the figures and relations characteristic of Euclidean geometry. In this chapter, we provide an axiomatic foundation to support these properties. In Chapter 7 we note that a definition of Euclidean geometry can be given in terms of its fundamental group of congruent transformations. In Unit 11.1, we provide a definition of Euclidean geometry in terms of its axioms. The discussions in Chapter 7 regarding deductive reasoning and definitions are especially important for this development, so you may want to review Unit 7.1 before you begin this chapter. In Unit 11.2, our definition of Euclidean geometry is verified by examining the Cartesian model of its axioms.

Unit 11.1: Constructing Euclidean Geometry

Unlike many axiomatic treatments which give a list of axioms at the beginning (as Euclid did), our approach introduces sets of axioms, and discusses their consequences before introducing new ones. We purposefully do not incorporate diagrams, as we intend that the students will develop them. Our goal is to help the students understand what the axioms provide for, and equally as important, what they do not. In discussions that follow the statements of the axioms, we include questions and comments intended to encourage the students to reflect on what properties the axioms guarantee.

We assume *point* and *line* as undefined objects, and *on* (incidence), *between*, and *congruent* as undefined relations. The properties of these objects and relations are then revealed through the axioms, which are written in terms of them. As we collect axioms in the construction of our system, we continually revisit the question of whether or not we have achieved a definition of Euclidean geometry. We rely on the fact that the students are familiar with Euclidean geometry and the nature of its objects and relations. Here we want students to determine when precisely they have amassed a sufficient set of axioms to achieve a definition.

Section 11.1.1

In Section 11.1.1 a first group of four axioms for Euclidean geometry is introduced. We demonstrate, using models of finite incidence geometries, that these four axioms are not sufficient for a definition of Euclidean geometry. Try to assign many problems from this section, because working in the environment of finite incidence geometries can give students a good sense of how to derive results from axioms and the necessity of doing so.

Problems 1 and 12: These problems give students opportunities to create their own models of incidence geometries and should help to give them an appreciation for the power of axioms as well as their limitations.

Section 11.1.2

The results in Section 11.1.1 show that the incidence axioms alone are not sufficient for a definition of Euclidean geometry. In particular, the need for an infinite number of points on a line motivates the introduction of the betweenness axioms in Section 11.1.2. These axioms enable us to define *segment*, and the fact that they do so should not be lost on the students. That is, students should understand that in an axiomatic development of a theory, definitions are only possible within the bounds of the properties of figures and relations established by the axioms.

In the first printing, the statement of the Corollary to Theorem 11.3 is in error. It has two parts and should read (1): If A-B-C and B-C-D, then A-B-D and A-C-D. (2): If A-B-D and B-C-D, then A-B-C and A-C-D.

The model of hyperbolic geometry introduced here shows that the incidence and betweenness axioms are not sufficient to define Euclidean geometry. Since triangle congruence is equivalent to triangle similarity in hyperbolic geometry, while it is not in Euclidean geometry, we are motivated to next explore the properties of our third and last undefined relation – congruence.

Section 11.1.3

Congruence is revisited here from an axiomatic point of view. Segment congruence and angle congruence are treated separately, making evident the many analogies between their congruence axioms. Triangle congruence (Axiom C-7) is then described in terms of segment and angle congruence. Definitions of such relations as *greater than* in terms of congruence rather than in terms of measurement may be new to your students. The discussion following the definition of *circle* is a bit subtle and we suggest you review it with students. In Section 11.1.5, we revisit the existence of a circle containing three given non-collinear points. This section concludes with an axiom of continuity (D-1), which we motivate by illustrating a famous defect in Euclid's proof of a theorem.

Problems 2 and 5: These problems provide practice in finding definitions without involving numbers for terms that students have probably always seen defined in terms of numerical relationships.

Problem 7: In the first printing, the reference to C-6 is in error. It should be C-7.

Section 11.1.4

The parallel postulate is the most famous (infamous?) of all of Euclid's postulates, and one which he evidently delayed as long as he could in his development in the *Elements*. We look here at some of the many Euclidean theorems that can be proven without the parallel postulate, not only to pay homage to Euclid, but to reveal the role the postulate plays in the construction of Euclidean geometry. Students may have seen some of these theorems (such as the existence of a unique midpoint of a segment) proved using the parallel postulate. But proofs can demonstrate that the parallel postulate is not necessary to deduce them.

In the first printing, there is an error in the statement of Theorem 11.10. Replace $\overline{AC} \cong \overline{DF}$ by $\angle ACB \cong \angle DFE$.

Problems 5-7: Stress this subtle difference between what we can prove and what we cannot. We can prove, without the parallel postulate or an equivalent statement, that given a point P and a line ℓ, there is *at least one* line parallel to ℓ through P. We cannot prove that given a point P and a line ℓ, there is *exactly one* line parallel to ℓ through P. That is, we can prove existence but not uniqueness.

Section 11.1.5

This section explores the parallel postulate and statements equivalent to it. In this development, the parallel postulate is the final axiom needed for our axiomatic definition of Euclidean geometry. The reason the parallel postulate is stated last is the richness of hyperbolic geometry, which satisfies all the postulates except that its parallel postulate allows more than one line to be parallel to a given line through a given point.

Problems 1-4: Proofs of equivalence of statements are often difficult for students, partly because they may have trouble sorting out what is given from what they need to prove.

Problem 6: In the first printing, the second-to-last sentence is extraneous and should be deleted.

Unit 11.2: The Cartesian Model for Euclidean Geometry

In Unit 11.2 we revisit the familiar Cartesian plane, helping students understand (perhaps for the first time) its relationship to Euclidean geometry.

Section 11.2.1

We can show that the Cartesian plane is a model of Euclidean geometry by proving that all sixteen axioms we used to define Euclidean geometry are satisfied in the Cartesian plane. In this section, demonstrations are given for all the incidence axioms and for the parallel postulate.

Problem 4:   In algebra, the existence of this line is taken for granted. The development in this section shows the reason we can do so: The Cartesian plane, with the usual algebraic descriptions of lines and points, incorporates Euclidean geometry.

Section 11.2.2

In order to justify the use of coordinates to deduce theorems in Euclidean geometry, we must show that Euclidean geometry, as we have defined it with the axioms of this chapter, is *categorical*. This means that any theorem proved in the model will be a theorem in Euclidean geometry. The synthetic and analytic proofs of Theorem 11.20 give students an opportunity to compare a proof based on axioms with one that emanates from the Cartesian model.

Problems 1 and 4: Some students may have done these proofs as high school students.

Chapter 11 Projects

Project 1f: Here "two lines" means "two distinct lines".

SOLUTIONS

GENERAL REMARKS

Because the problems are such an integral part of this book, the authors have endeavored to provide a complete set of solutions. The solutions are intended for the instructor, not the student. Nevertheless, the solutions are not here to serve merely as an instructor's guide for getting to the problem's correct answer. They are also intended as a model for how students should be thinking about the problem. For this reason, many solutions are written out in great detail, with explicit statements of the theorems and carefully drawn graphs and figures.

Since one of the book's main goals is to have students explore mathematical problems from different perspectives, the authors have tried to provide solutions reflecting a range of algebraic, geometrical, and computational approaches. In general, solutions utilize the definitions, theorems, and techniques introduced in the preceding sections. There is, of course, the possibility of correct solutions different from the ones given. For a problem where it is deemed highly likely that students will have a different solution, we label ours as a "sample solution". For a problem where the answer is of a more discursive or open-ended nature, we make no attempt to provide a sample answer. Instead, for such problems we note "Answers will vary."

As a problem-solving aid, we generally encourage the use of technology, whether in the form of geometry drawing programs, symbolic calculator systems, or graphing calculators and computer graphing programs. In many cases, it is clear from the statement of the problem what type of technology could be employed. We believe that it is important to discuss what makes a use of technology for a specific topic appropriate or inappropriate, since high school teachers encounter the same issues in their classes. But the instructor should not be concerned about the simplistic use of or excessive need of technology for the book. Very few problems can be solved by a simple mechanical use of technology, and most are solvable with no appeal to it.

CHAPTER 1 – What Is Meant by "An Advanced Perspective"?

1. Answers will vary. There are no right or wrong answers. We give here what some students have said.
    a. equidistant; go in the same direction
    b. equidistant
    c. do not intersect; go in the same direction
    d. do not intersect
    e. go in the same direction
    f. do not intersect

2. For Leibniz' definition of parallel curves, see Figure 4 and the accompanying discussion. Consider a line segment S perpendicular to a line L in 3-space and bisected by L. If S moves along L and at the same time rotates around it, each end will trace out a helix. By Leibniz' definition, each helix is parallel to L. Thus as a consequence of this definition of parallel in 3-space, we have a situation where a curve is parallel to a straight line

3. a. The diagram below shows rays R_1, R_2, ..., R_k from point P intersecting lines L_a and L_b. Line L_a cuts off segments on the rays of lengths a_1, a_2, ..., a_k, while lines L_a and L_b together cut off segments on the rays of lengths b_1, b_2, ..., b_k. The hypothesis of the given statement is that lines L_a and L_b are parallel. The conclusion is that these segments are proportional: that is, for some constant r we have $b_i = r \cdot a_i$ for i = 1, 2, ..., k.

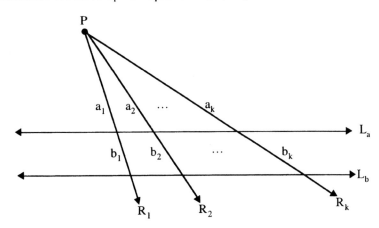

    b. The diagram below shows rays R_1, R_2, ... , R_k, R_{k+1} from point P intersecting lines L_a and L_b. The rays cut off segments on L_a of lengths a_1, a_2,..., a_k and segments on L_b of lengths we designate b_1, b_2, ..., b_k. The hypothesis of the given statement is that lines L_a and L_b are parallel. The conclusion is that these segments are proportional: that is, for some constant r we have $b_i = r \cdot a_i$ for i = 1, 2, ..., k.

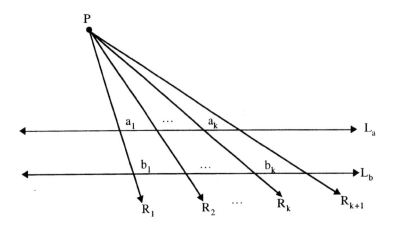

c. The statement for part **a** is true. To prove it, construct another ray R_0 from P perpendicular to L_a and L_b. Let d_a and d_b be the distances of these lines from P. See the diagram below.

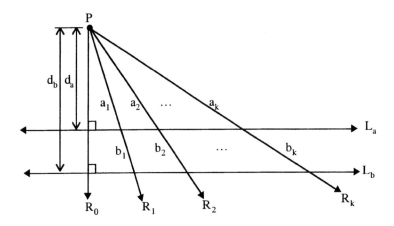

By similar triangles, $\dfrac{b_1 + a_1}{a_1} = \dfrac{d_b}{d_a}$. Subtracting 1 from each side yields $\dfrac{b_1}{a_1} = \dfrac{d_b - d_a}{d_a}$. The same method shows that $\dfrac{b_i}{a_i} = \dfrac{d_b - d_a}{d_a}$ for all i. Let $r = \dfrac{d_b - d_a}{d_a}$ Then r is the constant of proportionality relating the paired segments b_i and a_i such that $b_i = r \bullet a_i$ for i = 1, 2, ..., k. The statement for part **b** is also true. To prove it, construct the same ray R_0 from P perpendicular to L_a and L_b. Let d_a and d_b be the distances of these lines from P. See the diagram below.

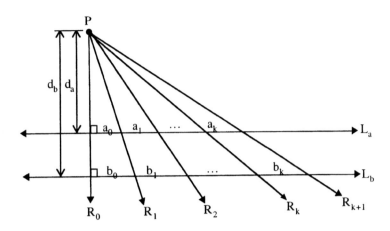

By similar triangles, $\frac{b_0}{a_0} = \frac{d_b}{d_a}$ and $\frac{b_0 + b_1}{a_0 + a_1} = \frac{d_b}{d_a}$. Combining these results gives $\frac{b_1}{a_1} = \frac{d_b}{d_a}$. The same method shows that $\frac{b_i}{a_i} = \frac{d_b}{d_a}$ for all i. Let $r = \frac{d_b}{d_a}$. Then r is the constant of proportionality relating the paired segments b_i and a_i such that $b_i = r \cdot a_i$ for i = 1, 2, …, k.

4. Let |a| be the absolute value of the real number a.

a. Algebraic definition: |a| = a if a ≥ 0; |a| = -a if a < 0.
An alternative, equivalent definition is $|a| = \sqrt{a^2}$.
Geometric definition: |a| is the distance on the number line of a from 0.

b. Sample: |a| ≥ 0 and |a| = 0 if and only if a = 0 is easily understood with either algebraic or geometric definition; |a| + |b| ≥ |a + b| is easily understood from the geometric definition.

c. The graph of f(x) = |x| is a right angle. One side is the ray y = x for x ≥ 0, and the other side is the ray y = -x for x < 0.

d. The absolute value function is multiplicative since |x • y| = |x| • |y|, but it is not additive since, for example, |-1 + 1| ≠ |-1| + |1|.

e. Based on the answer to part **a**, we can consider these possible definitions of absolute value for a complex number z:
– Geometric definition of absolute value: The absolute value of z is written |z| and is defined as the distance in the complex plane of a from (0, 0). This is reasonable; it says that the absolute value of every complex number is a positive real number, and |z| = 0 if and only if z = 0. (Note: |z| is called the modulus of z.)
– Algebraic definition of absolute value: Since the concept of positive and negative does not apply in general to complex numbers, the first definition of part **a** is of no use. Moreover, defining the absolute value as $|z| = \sqrt{z^2}$ is not good, since $\sqrt{z^2}$ might not be real. For example, $\sqrt{i^2} = i$. But if we write z in its real and imaginary parts as z = x + iy, then we can define |z| as $|z| = \sqrt{x^2 + y^2}$. By the Pythagorean Theorem, this is equivalent to the geometric definition.

f. For a vector $\mathbf{x} = (x_1, x_2, …, x_n)$ we can generalize the last definition in part **e** and define $|\mathbf{x}| = \sqrt{x_1^2 + x_2^2 + … + x_n^2}$. This represents the distance from $\mathbf{x}$ to the origin.

g. A weight bobbing up and down on a spring at a frequency f cycles per second with a total path length of 2R will be at a distance $|R\sin(2\pi ft)|$ from the equilibrium point at any time t seconds after it passes the neutral point.

5.   a.   To say that Jane has an average of G after 4 tests means that $G = \frac{s_1 + s_2 + s_3 + s_4}{4}$.

Let x be the score she needs on the 5th test to have an average of H. Then

$H = \frac{s_1 + s_2 + s_3 + s_4 + x}{5}$. Hence $x = 5H - (s_1 + s_2 + s_3 + s_4) = 5H - 4G$.

   b.   Generalizing directly from the solution of part **a** we see that the required score is $(n + 1)H - nG$.

   c.   To say that Jane has an average of H after n + m tests means that

$H = \frac{s_1 + s_2 + ... + s_n + s_{n+1} + s_{n+2} + ... + s_{n+m}}{n + m}$.

Multiplying both sides by n + m gives

$(n + m)H = (s_1 + s_2 + ... + s_n) + (s_{n+1} + s_{n+2} + ... + s_{n+m})$.

Dividing by nm gives

$(\frac{n+m}{nm})H = \frac{G}{m} + \frac{K}{n}$,

where K is the average on the (n + 1)st to the (n + m)th test:

$K = \frac{s_{n+1} + s_{n+2} + ... + s_{n+m}}{m}$.

Writing K in terms of G, H, n, and m gives

$K = \frac{(n + m)H - nG}{m}$.

(This is a weighted average of H and G.)

   d.   Sample: Typical high school students are probably most comfortable with (a), since the formulas are all "closed" (they have a definite number, 4, of terms). Next in difficulty might be (b); they might not see that the solution for (b) can be obtained directly from the work in (a) by generalizing 4 to n. Finally, (c) might be hardest, largely because of the "ellipsis" and the use of subscript notation in $s_1 + s_2 + ... + s_n + s_{n+1} + s_{n+2} + ... + s_{n+m}$.

6.   a.   Write the equation as $41s - 30j = 1084$.

By trial we find one integer solution: $s = 44, j = 24$. This means that 41 $(44) - 30(24) = 1084$. By adding and subtracting the product $41 \cdot 30$ we get other solutions as follows:

Since $1084 = 41(44 + 30) - 30(24 + 41) = 41(74) - 30(65)$, $s = 74, j = 65$ is another integer solution.

Since $1084 = 41(74 + 30) - 30(65 + 41) = 41(104) - 30(106)$, $s = 104, j = 106$ is another integer solution. In general, the positive integer solutions are $(j, s) = (24 + 41n, 44 + 30n)$ for $n = 0, 1, 2, ...$.

   b.   The equation can be written $s = \frac{30}{41}j + \frac{1084}{41}$. The s-intercept $\frac{1084}{41} \approx 26.44$ represents the number of points Shaq needs to score if Jordan scores no points, if their averages are to be the same. (In other words, if Jordan plays and scores 0 points, then if Shaq scores 26 points he still loses, but if he scores 27 points he wins.) The slope $\frac{30}{41} \approx 0.73$ represents the number of further points Shaq needs to score for every point Jordan scores, if their averages are to be the same.

   c.   The equation can be written $j = \frac{41}{30}s - \frac{1084}{30}$. The j-intercept $-\frac{1084}{30} \approx -36.13$ represents the number of points Jordan needs to score if Shaq scores no points, if their averages are to be the same. Since the number is negative, it has no direct meaning in this context. (If penalties were given by subtracting points from the score, Jordan could have a penalty of 36 points and still beat Shaq if Shaq scored no points, but if he had a penalty of 37 points he would lose, even if Shaq scored no points.) The slope $\frac{41}{30} \approx 1.37$ represents the number of points Jordan needs to score for every point Shaq scores, if their averages are to be the same.

   d.   Solve the system $j - 1 = s$ (Jordan just beats Shaq) and $s = \frac{30}{41}j + \frac{1084}{41}$ (from 4b). This shows that if Jordan scores 103 points and Shaq scores 102 points, Shaq will win the season title, even though he had a lower average going into the final game and scored fewer points in the final game. (This is a case of Simpson's Paradox.)

7. a. Formulas for these functions are $f(j) = \dfrac{J + j}{n_J}$ and $g(s) = \dfrac{S + s}{n_S}$.

    b. The intercept $\dfrac{J}{n_J}$ of $f(j)$ is Jordan's average going into the final game. The slope $\dfrac{1}{n_J}$ is the amount by which Jordan's average increases for every point he scores in the final game. The intercept $\dfrac{S}{n_S}$ of $g(s)$ is Shaq's average going into the final game. The slope $\dfrac{1}{n_S}$ is the amount by which Shaq's average increases for every point he scores in the final game.

    c. Equating the function values $\dfrac{S + s}{n_S} = \dfrac{J + j}{n_J}$ amounts to stating a condition under which Jordan and Shaq have identical season averages. Solving for s gives s as the following function $F(j)$ of j:

    $$F(j) = s = \frac{n_S}{n_J} \bullet j + (\frac{J}{n_J} \bullet n_S - S).$$

    The interpretation is that if Jordan scores j points in the final game, Shaq must score $s = F(j)$ points if he is to have the same final average. Since the number of points scored in a game must be a non-negative integer, to be meaningful the values of $F(j)$ must be rounded up or down to an integer, and with them the corresponding values of j. The intercept $(\dfrac{J}{n_J} \bullet n_S - S)$, if positive, is the number of points Shaq would have to score to tie Jordan if Jordan played in the final game and scored no points. Structurally it is the difference between the number $\dfrac{J}{n_J} \bullet n_S$ of points someone would score in a season with Jordan's average and Shaq's number of games and the number S of points Shaq scored in the season up to the last game. The slope $\dfrac{n_S}{n_J}$ is the number of points Shaq has to score for every point Jordan scores if their season averages are to be the same. Solving for j gives $j = \dfrac{n_J}{n_S} \bullet s + (\dfrac{S}{n_S} \bullet n_J - J)$. A similar interpretation holds for this case.

8. a. If P is Sosa's season average for the next m years, then $450 + m \bullet P = 755$. Hence $P = \dfrac{755 - 450}{m} = \dfrac{305}{m}$.

    b. Sample: In general, if R is the record lifetime total and N is a player's current total then the required average P per year for playing m more years and matching the record is $P = \dfrac{R - N}{m}$.

9. *The following solution is more complete than could be expected of students. It is meant to serve as another example of what an "extended analysis" of a problem means, to supplement the Shaq-Jordan problem in the text. It can be used as notes for a class activity based on this problem.*

    a. There are many ways to arrive at an answer, some very simple, others not so. We illustrate such a solution here.
        Suppose there are 100 units of substance to start off. It is divided this way:
        water: 99 units   non-water: 1 unit.
        Let p be the unknown proportion of water that evaporates. Then a proportion $1 - p$ of the water remains. After the evaporation we have
        water: $99(1 - p)$ units   non-water: 1 unit.
        The fact that the water is 98% of the total now can be represented in the equation
        $$99(1 - p) = 0.98 (1 + 99(1 - p)).$$
        Solving equation (3) for p gives $p = 0.505050... $.

This is a surprising result. More than half the water has to evaporate to get a drop of just 1% in the water content. Surely there is a little mystery here.

b.   Students' answers will vary. There are two main reasons this problem is a classic. First, there is a "trap" that many people fall into. There is a tendency to say that getting the percentage of water to drop by 1% must mean that 1% of the water has to evaporate. This is not right, and so the person giving the problem can say "Gotcha!" or something similar. The other reason is that the correct answer, getting the percentage of water to drop by 1% means that more than 50% of the water has to evaporate, is very surprising at first. It seems counter intuitive. *The point that might be made in class is that it is incomplete to leave the problem at this stage. If we are curious we will want to see clearly just why this surprising situation occurs. This we will get to in the later parts of this problem.*

c.   Suppose the original substance consists of 99 units of water and 1 unit of a dissolved solute. After the evaporation, 98% of the total is water, but there is still 1 unit of dissolved solute. This 1 unit must therefore represent 2% of the total. If 2% of the substance is 1 unit, then each 1% of the substance is now half a unit. So the 98% which is water must comprise 49 units. This means that 99 – 49 = 50 units of water have evaporated. As a proportion, this 50 units of evaporated water is $\frac{50}{99}$ of the original amount of water. The fraction $\frac{50}{99}$ is about 50.5%.

Another numerical approach works directly with the percentages of the dissolved solute, not the water. Since the substance is going from 1% solute to 2% solute, the proportion of solute is exactly doubled. But this means the total amount of the substance must be exactly cut in half. (Why?) So an original 100 units of substance becomes 50 units. Of this, 49 units are water, since the 1 unit of solute is unchanged. So 50 units of water have evaporated, which as a proportion is $\frac{50}{99}$ of the original amount of water.

So there are a variety of ways to obtain the answer to the problem, but their methods do not offer much insight into the situation.

d.   *We don't usually think of "diagrams" as being used in mathematical reasoning, but they can be quite powerful tools, paralleling and complementing concrete numerical approaches.*
Consider these diagrams, which represent schematic before and after pictures of the situation.

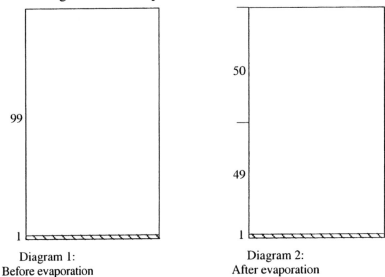

Diagram 1:
Before evaporation

Diagram 2:
After evaporation

In Diagram 1, the cross-hatched portion represents the 1% solute and the rest is the 99% water. In Diagram 2, the cross hatched portion representing the solute must be the same size, but now must be 2% of the whole, meaning that the water is 49% of the whole. The top half (shaded) thus represents the water that must have evaporated. We see that what has evaporated is *exactly half* of the original total substance, and more than half of the original water. In fact, inspecting this diagram, we can see that $\frac{50}{99}$ of the water must have evaporated. This is just what was found above.

The above diagrams are not the only ones that can be used. The diagrams below also show that exactly half the substance has evaporated, and more than half the water.

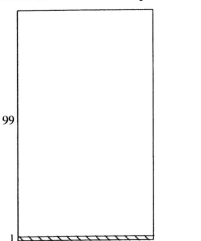 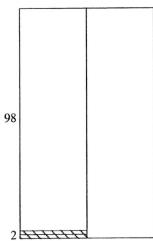

e. *Although algebra is not needed to solve the problem as stated, use of algebra lets us abstract from the particular numbers 99 and 98 to reach a more general result. This is essential to get beyond viewing this problem as an interesting curiosity.*

Introduce the following parameters.

Let   p   = the proportion of water at the start (= 0.99),
      p'   = the proportion of water at the end   (= 0.98),
      q   = the proportion of water that has evaporated (the unknown).

To solve the problem we need to express q symbolically in terms of p and p'. To do this it is very helpful to introduce these "absolute" quantities.

Let   W   = the number of units of water at the start,
      W' = the number of units of water after evaporation,
      S   = the number of units of solute present.

(We have used lowercase letters for proportions, uppercase for absolute amounts. Further, primed symbols represent the situation after the evaporation.) Express the proportional amounts in terms of the absolute quantities.

$$p = \frac{W}{W+S} \qquad p' = \frac{W'}{W'+S} \qquad q = \frac{W-W'}{W} = 1 - \frac{W'}{W}$$

This yields 3 equations involving 6 quantities. Of these, 2 are considered as known (p and p'), which leaves 4 unknowns. Having 3 equations and 4 unknowns might seem to be a difficulty until we realize that to find q (which is what the problem asks for) we don't need to know W *and* W', but only their *ratio*, and in that ratio the quantity S cancels. To see this, solve the left two equations for W and W'.

$$W = \frac{p}{1-p}S \qquad\qquad W' = \frac{p'}{1-p'}S$$

Substituting these values of W and W' into the formula for q above,

$$q = 1 - \frac{p'(1-p)}{p(1-p')} = \frac{p-p'}{p(1-p')}.$$

This last formula expresses the unknown portion q of the water that has evaporated in terms of the given initial and final percentages of water p and p'. It is, in a sense, a fully general answer to the problem. However, it is not particularly revealing about why such a small drop in water percentage requires such a large roportion of water evaporation. To get more insight, we need to carry the analysis further.

f. Fix the relationship between p and p'.

$$p - p' = 0.01.$$

Now substitute in the formula for q, and get q as a function of p alone:

$$q(p) = \frac{.01}{p(1.01 - p)}.$$

This function expresses the proportion q(p) of water that has evaporated in terms of the proportion p of water in the original substance. Notice that q is the reciprocal of a quadratic function $f(p) = p(1.01 - p)$. The quadratic function has zeros at $p = 0$ and $p = 1.01$. Hence its reciprocal q has vertical asymptotes at these same points. (The physical nature of the situation requires that $0 < p < 1$, so the poles of q at the values $p = 0$ and $p = 1.01$ are not a problem.) Here is a graph of the function q.

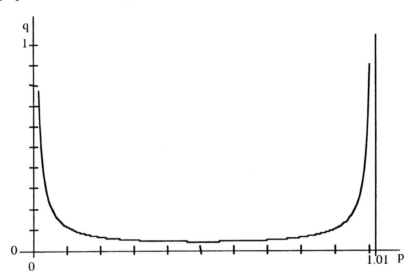

This graph shows nicely what is going on in this problem. The graph is quite steep at the right-hand end, for values of p close to 1. This means that to obtain even a *small* decrease in p (the portion of water in the whole), we need a very *large* value of q (the portion of the water content that evaporates). Put differently, for certain values of p, the portion q of water that evaporates is extremely "sensitive" to the percentage p of water in the substance: a small change in p is associated with a large change in q.

g. Let the fixed amount of solute S = 1 unit. Then

$$p(W) = \frac{W}{W + 1} = \frac{1}{1 + \frac{1}{W}}.$$

This function is graphed here.

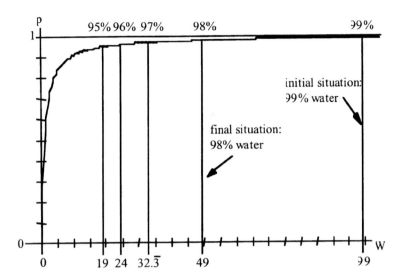

The initial situation, p = 0.99, is represented by the vertical line at W = 99, since p(99) = 0.99. The final situation, p = 0.98, is represented by the vertical line at W = 49, since p(49) = 0.98. Drops of p from 99% to 97%, 96%, and 95% are also indicated on the graph. The surprising result of the original problem is here explained by the very flat nature of the graph for p as p approaches 1. It takes a lot of added units of water to make p go up by just 1%.

h.   *Students will tend to answer this question in a brief way. Here is a detailed response that might be given by an instructor.*

We have taken as our starting point a type of problem often given in a high school setting and have gone beyond the initial analysis that is required to find the numerical answer $\frac{50}{99}$ to the problem. Instead of a single number, our "extended analysis" gives a function that models the situation and gives a mathematical explanation for the surprising answer to the problem. Particular numbers can be obtained by evaluating this function at particular values. An alternative analysis gives another function that explains the situation in a different way.

Here are two features of this extended analysis to emphasize:

(a)   A deeper analysis is achieved by using general "parameters" instead of specific numbers in the statement of the problem.

(b)   Knowing when to be less general by looking at an appropriate type of special case is sometimes the key to achieving useful results.

These principles operate hand in hand: it takes practice or trial and error to arrive at a choice of parameters that help us to best express what is going on in a situation, a choice that allows us to be general enough but not too general. In the evaporation problem the appropriate special case came with the realization that this problem is really about what happens with a *fixed small* drop in water content, not about arbitrary drops. This is captured in the specific relationship p – p' = .01. The problem and its analysis involve this use of mathematics:

•   Seeing several different methods for solving a problem side by side to show the advantage of each (numerical reasoning, diagrams, algebra, functions).

•   Showing how a general mathematical solution to the problem in terms of functions explains why the answer to the problem is surprising.

•   Seeing how to provide a result that is appropriately general but not so general that the impact of the original situation is lost.

•   Seeing an application of quadratic functions in which it is the reciprocal of a quadratic that is needed.

10. a. This is a multiplicative property. It can also be written as $x^m \cdot x^{-n} = x^{m-n}$.
The corresponding additive property is found by replacing exponentiation by multiplication and multiplication by addition. It is the following case of the distributive property:
$mx - nx = (m - n)x$.

   b. This is an additive property, the distributive rule (for distributing multiplication over addition). The corresponding multiplicative property is found by replacing addition by multiplication and multiplication by exponentiation: $a^{b+c} = a^b \cdot a^c$.

   c. This is a multiplicative property. It can also be written as $p^{1/n} \cdot q^{1/n} = (p \cdot q)^{1/n}$. The corresponding additive property is found by replacing exponentiation by multiplication and multiplication by addition. It is a rule for adding fractions with the same denominator:
$\frac{p}{n} + \frac{q}{n} = \frac{p+q}{n}$.

   d. This is a multiplicative property. It can also be written as $G(p, q) = (p \cdot q)^{1/2}$. The corresponding additive property is found by replacing exponentiation by multiplication and multiplication by addition. It is the definition of arithmetic mean: $A(p, q) = \frac{p+q}{2}$.

   e. This is an additive property. It is one case of the general definition: Subtracting a quantity is equivalent to adding the opposite of the quantity. The corresponding multiplicative property is found by replacing addition by multiplication and subtraction by division: $\dfrac{\frac{p}{q}}{\frac{r}{s}} = \frac{p}{q} \cdot \frac{r}{s}$.

   This is a general definition for dividing one fraction by another: Dividing by a quantity is equivalent to multiplying by the inverse of the quantity.

   f. This is a property of multiplication and powers. The corresponding property of addition and multiples is: $(5a + b + 4c) - (a + b + 6c) = 4a - 2c = 4a + -2c$.

11. $x^m \cdot x^n = x^{(m+n)}$, for all nonzero x, and m and n nonnegative integers. Thus
$x^m \cdot x^0 = x^{(m+0)}$.
Since 0 is the additive identity,
$x^m \cdot x^0 = x^m$
So x^0 is the multiplicative identity. So $x^0 = 1$.

12. a. This is an additive property of all real numbers. The corresponding multiplicative properties are found by replacing addition by multiplication and are true when all numbers are positive:
$x < y \Rightarrow zx < zy$.

   b. This is also an additive property about the pivot 0. The corresponding multiplicative property is
$x > 1$ and $y > 1 \Rightarrow xy > 1$.

   c. This is also an additive property about the pivot 0. The corresponding multiplicative property requires that the numbers be positive: $x < 1$ and $y < 1 \Rightarrow xy < 1$.

   d. This is a property of multiples. The corresponding multiplicative property is about powers and uses 1 as a pivot but keeps the operator m the same: If $x > 1$ and $m < 0$, then $x^m < 1$.

   e. There are two ways to interpret this property. One is as a multiplicative property. The corresponding additive property is more general, since it requires no restriction on n: If $x < y$ then $x - n < y - n$. The other is as a property of multiples. The corresponding multiplicative property is: If $x < y$ and $n > 0$, then $x^{1/n} < y^{1/n}$.

CHAPTER 2 – Real Numbers And Complex Numbers

Section 2.1.1

1.   a. $3.14159 = \frac{314159}{100000}$; int. pt. = 3; frac. pt. = $\frac{14159}{100000}$

     b. $\frac{35709.22}{47.6} = \frac{7501963975}{1000000}$; int. pt. = 750; frac. pt. = $\frac{1963975}{1000000}$

     c. $\log_{10}\sqrt[3]{100} = \log_{10}(100)^{1/3} = \frac{1}{3}\log_{10}100 = \frac{2}{3}$; int. pt. = 0; frac. pt. = $\frac{2}{3}$

     d. $-6\frac{3}{4} = \frac{-27}{4}$; int. pt. = 6; frac. pt. = $\frac{3}{4}$ (some prefer int. pt. = -6, frac. pt. = $\frac{-3}{4}$; others prefer int. pt. = -7, frac. pt. = $\frac{1}{4}$.)

2.   a.   Let $x = \frac{9}{10}$. Then $\left\lfloor x + \frac{1}{10} \right\rfloor = 1$ and $\lfloor x \rfloor = \left\lfloor \frac{9}{10} \right\rfloor = 0$.

     b.   Let $x = \frac{9}{10}$ and $y = \frac{1}{10}$. Then $\lfloor x + y \rfloor = 1$ and $\lfloor x \rfloor + \lfloor y \rfloor = 0$.

     c.   Let $x = 1$ and $y = \frac{1}{10}$. Then $\lfloor x - y \rfloor = 0$ and $\lfloor x \rfloor - \lfloor y \rfloor = 1$.

3.   a.   Work from the inside out. Suppose $8 - 2\sqrt{7} = (a + b\sqrt{7})^2$. Then $2ab = -2$ and $a^2 + 7b^2 = 8$. There are two solutions to this quadratic system, $(a, b) = (1, -1)$ and $(a, b) = (-1, 1)$, from which $a + b\sqrt{7} = 1 - \sqrt{7}$ or $a + b\sqrt{7} = -1 + \sqrt{7}$. Since $\sqrt{8 - 2\sqrt{7}}$ is positive, $\sqrt{8 - 2\sqrt{7}} = -1 + \sqrt{7}$. Consequently, $\sqrt{3 + \sqrt{7} - \sqrt{8 - 2\sqrt{7}}} = \sqrt{3 + \sqrt{7} - (-1 + \sqrt{7})} = \sqrt{4} = 2$.

     b.   Sample: $(5 + \sqrt{2})^2 = 27 + 10\sqrt{2}$, so $\sqrt{4 - \sqrt{2} + \sqrt{27 + 10\sqrt{2}}} = \sqrt{4 - \sqrt{2} + (5 + \sqrt{2})} = 3$.

     c.   Again work from the inside out. Start with a positive expression of the form $a + b\sqrt{c}$, where a, b, and c are integers and $c > 0$. Square it to get $a^2 + cb^2 + 2ab\sqrt{c}$. Then pick d so that $a + d$ is a perfect square. Consequently, $\sqrt{d - b\sqrt{c} + \sqrt{a^2 + cb^2 + 2ab\sqrt{c}}}$ will be an integer.

4.   a.   Let p and q be the two rational numbers. Since they are rational, there exist integers a, b, c, and d with $p = \frac{a}{b}$ and $q = \frac{c}{d}$, and $b \neq 0$ and $d \neq 0$. Then $p - q = \frac{a}{b} - \frac{c}{d} = \frac{ad - bc}{bd}$. Since products and differences of integers are integers, both $ad - bc$ and bd are integers, and because neither b nor d is 0, $bd \neq 0$. Thus $p - q$ is the quotient of two integers and is rational.

     b.   Let p and q be the two rational numbers. Then there exist integers a, b, c, and d with $p = \frac{a}{b}$ and $q = \frac{c}{d}$, and $b \neq 0$ and $d \neq 0$. Then $pq = \frac{a}{b} \cdot \frac{c}{d} = \frac{ac}{bd}$. Because the product of two integers is an integer, and $bd \neq 0$ since $b \neq 0$ and $d \neq 0$, it follows that pq is a rational number.

     c.   Let p and q be the two nonzero rational numbers. Then there exist nonzero integers a, b, c, and d with $p = \frac{a}{b}$ and $q = \frac{c}{d}$. Because $p \div q = \frac{a}{b} \div \frac{c}{d} = \frac{ad}{bc}$, and the product of nonzero integers is a nonzero integer, it follows that the quotient of p and q is a nonzero rational number.

5.   a.   No. For example, if $a = 2$ and $b = \frac{1}{2}$, then a and b are rational numbers but $2^{1/2} = \sqrt{2}$ is not a rational number.

     b.   No. For example, e and ln 10 are irrational, but $e^{\ln 10} = 1$ is a rational number.

6. No. Assume that there exists a rational number such that $\sqrt{25} = \frac{a}{b}$. Then by squaring both sides, $25 = \frac{a^2}{b^2}$, from which $25b^2 = a^2$. Now factor a and b into primes. $25b^2$ is not the product of an odd number of primes because $25 = 5 \cdot 5$. So both sides are factors of even numbers of primes and the proof breaks down.

7. Suppose that then there exists a rational number $\frac{a}{b}$ in lowest terms such that $\sqrt[n]{p} = \frac{a}{b}$. Taking the nth-power of both sides , we obtain $p = \frac{a^n}{b^n}$ from which $pb^n = a^n$. Now if we factor a and b into primes, pb^n and a^n will be the products of primes. Suppose a has j prime factors and b has k prime factors, and the prime factors of a are different from those of b because the fraction is in lowest terms. Then pb^n has $nk + 1$ prime factors and a^n has nj prime factors. These cannot be equal when j and k are integers. By the Fundamental Theorem of Arithmetic, two different prime factorizations of pb^n are impossible, so the supposition must be false and $\sqrt[n]{p}$ is irrational.

8. Proof: If ΔRST is a right triangle with right angle at S, and if r, s, and t are the opposite side lengths, then $s^2 = r^2 + t^2$. Therefore, if $a = r^2, b = t^2$, it follows that $r = \sqrt{a}, t = \sqrt{b}$, and $s = \sqrt{a+b}$.

9. a. The proof is indirect. Suppose s – v is a rational number r. Then $v = s - r$ is rational because the difference of rational numbers is rational. This contradicts the given information, indicating that the supposition is false. Therefore, s – v   must be irrational.

    b. The proof is indirect. If sv is a rational number r, then $v = \frac{r}{s}$ must be rational because the quotient and product of rational numbers is rational. This contradicts the assumption that v is irrational so sv must be irrational.

    c. If $\frac{s}{v}$ is a rational number r, then $v = \frac{s}{r}$ is rational because the quotient of rational numbers is rational. Therefore, $\frac{s}{v}$ must be irrational.

10. a. Sample: $\sqrt{2} + -\sqrt{2} = 0$ b. Sample: $\frac{\sqrt{2}}{-\sqrt{2}} = -1$

11. a. Since the set of integers is closed under multiplication and subtraction, if a, b, and c are integers, then $b^2 - 4ac$ is an integer. But we are given that $\sqrt{b^2 - 4ac}$ is not an integer. So, by Theorem 2.2, $\sqrt{b^2 - 4ac}$ is irrational. By Theorem 2.3, then, $\frac{-b \pm \sqrt{b^2 - 4ac}}{2a}$ is irrational.

    b. Sample: Take $a = 1, b = 5$, and $c = 2$ to conclude that the roots $\frac{-5 \pm \sqrt{17}}{2}$ of $x^2 + 5x + 2 = 0$ are irrational.

12. a. $\sqrt{27} + \sqrt{48} = 3\sqrt{3} + 4\sqrt{3} = 7\sqrt{3} = \sqrt{147}$
    b. Sample: $\sqrt{50} + \sqrt{18} = 5\sqrt{2} + 3\sqrt{2} = 8\sqrt{2} = \sqrt{128}$
    c. p, q, and r must be of the form na^2, nb^2, and nc^2, where n is not a perfect square, a, b, and c are different integers, $a + b = c$, and $nc^2 < 100$. Assume without loss of generality that $a < b$. If $n = 2$, then $c \leq 7$, so $(a, b) = (1, 2), (1, 3), (1, 4), (1, 5), (1, 6), (2, 3), (2, 4), (2, 5)$, and $(3, 4)$. These are the nine possibilities from the multiples of $\sqrt{2}$. For example, $(1, 2)$ gives the possibility $1\sqrt{2} + 2\sqrt{2} = 3\sqrt{2}$, or $\sqrt{2} + \sqrt{8} = \sqrt{18}$.

If n = 3, then c ≤ 5, so (a, b) = (1, 2), (1, 3), (1, 4), or (2, 3).

If n = 5 or n = 6, then c ≤ 4, so (a, b) = (1, 2) or (1, 3).

If n = 7, n = 8, or n = 10, then c ≤ 3, so (a, b) = (1, 2).

This yields a total of 20 possibilities.

13.   a.   The only perfect squares between 1 and 9 are 1, 4, and 9. So, by Theorem 2.2, the other 7 square roots are irrational.

       b.   Only k of the integers between 1 and k^2 will be perfect squares. Thus the probability that n is a perfect square is $\frac{k}{k^2} = \frac{1}{k}$. By Theorem 2.2, if n is not a perfect square, $\sqrt{n}$ is irrational. The probability that n is not a perfect square is $1 - \frac{1}{k} = \frac{k-1}{k}$.

Section 2.1.2

1.   Using long division, $\frac{21}{20} = 1.05$ and $\frac{20}{21} = .\overline{952380}$. A different decimal representation for $\frac{21}{20}$ is $1.04\overline{9}$.

2.   a.   By definition, if x is represented by the finite decimal $D.d_1d_2...d_k$, then $x = D + \frac{d_1}{10} + ... + \frac{d_k}{10^k}$. So x can also be represented by the infinite decimal $D.d_1d_2...d_k0000...$, since

$$D + \frac{d_1}{10} + ... + \frac{d_k}{10^k} + \frac{d_{k+1}}{10^{k+1}} + ... + \frac{d_{k+j}}{10^{k+j}} \leq \frac{a}{b} \leq D + \frac{d_1}{10} + ... + \frac{d_k}{10^k} + \frac{d_{k+1}}{10^{k+1}} + ... + \frac{d_{k+j}}{10^{k+j}} + \frac{1}{10^{k+j}} \text{ for all}$$

$j \geq 1$, provided $d_{k+j} = 0$ for all $j \geq 1$.

       b. $D.d_1d_2...(d_k - 1)99999...$

3.   a.   The decimal representation of π, to 5 decimal places, is 3.14159. By definition, then, the decimal representation of –π, to 5 decimal places, is –3.14159. Thus the first six digits of -π are D = 3, $d_1 = 1$, $d_2 = 4$, $d_3 = 1$, $d_4 = 5$, and $d_5 = 9$.

       b.   The decimal representation for –π is constructed by first constructing π using the intervals $I_1 = [3.1, 3.2]$, $I_2 = [3.14, 3.15]$, $I_3 = [3.141, 3.142]$, $I_4 = [3.1415, 3.1416]$, $I_5 = [3.14159, 3.14160]$, $I_6 = [3.141592, 3.141593]$.

(It is also possible to use the intervals $I_1 = [-3.2, -3.1]$, $I_2 = [-3.15, -3.14]$, etc.

4.   Since $4 < 7 < 9$, $2 < \sqrt{7} < 3$ and D = 2.

$$2 + \frac{d_1}{10} \leq \sqrt{7} \leq 2.1 + \frac{d_1}{10} \Rightarrow (2 + \frac{d_1}{10})^2 \leq 7 \leq (2.1 + \frac{d_1}{10})^2 \Rightarrow (20 + d_1)^2 \leq 700 \leq (21 + d_1)^2 \Rightarrow d_1 = 6$$

$$2.6 + \frac{d_2}{100} \leq \sqrt{7} \leq 2.61 + \frac{d_2}{100} \Rightarrow (2.6 + \frac{d_2}{100})^2 \leq 7 \leq (2.61 + \frac{d_2}{100})^2 \Rightarrow (260 + d_2)^2 \leq 70000$$

$$\leq (261 + d_2)^2 \Rightarrow d_2 = 4$$

$$2.64 + \frac{d_3}{1000} \leq \sqrt{7} \leq 2.641 + \frac{d_3}{1000} \Rightarrow (2.64 + \frac{d_3}{1000})^2 \leq 7 \leq (2.641 + \frac{d_3}{1000})^2 \Rightarrow (2640 + d_3)^2$$

$$\leq 7000000 \leq (2641 + d_3)^2 \Rightarrow d_3 = 5$$

Thus $2.645 \leq \sqrt{7} \leq 2.646$.

5.   a. $817 = 22(37) + 3$, $30 = 0 \bullet 37 + 30$, $300 = 8(37) + 4$, $40 = 1(37) + 3$, repeat;

$$\frac{817}{37} = 22 + \frac{0}{10} + \frac{8}{10^2} + \frac{1}{10^3} + \frac{0}{10^4} + \frac{8}{10^5} + \frac{1}{10^6} + ... = 22.\overline{081}$$

b. $60 = 2(25) + 10$, $100 = 4(25) + 0$; $\frac{6}{25} = \frac{2}{10} + \frac{4}{10^2} = .24$

c. $46 = 3(12) + 10$, $100 = 8(12) + 4$, $40 = 3(12) + 4$, repeat; $\frac{46}{12} = 3 + \frac{8}{10} + \frac{3}{10^2} + \ldots = 3.8\overline{3}$

6. Argument 1:

$n = .99999\ldots$

$10n = 10 \bullet .99999\ldots$	Multiplication Property of Equality
$= 9.99999\ldots$	Multiplying by 10 moves decimal one place to the right
$10n - n = 9.99999\ldots - .99999\ldots$	Addition Property of Equality
$9n = 9$	Distributive Property and subtraction
$n = 1$	Multiplication Property of Equality

Argument 2:

$\frac{1}{3} = 0.333333\ldots$

$3 \bullet \frac{1}{3} = 3 \bullet 0.333333\ldots$	Multiplication Property of Equality
$1 = .99999\ldots$	Multiplication

Argument 3:

$\frac{4}{9} = 0.44444\ldots$ and $\frac{5}{9} = 0.55555\ldots$

$\frac{4}{9} + \frac{5}{9} = 0.44444\ldots + 0.55555\ldots$	Addition Property of Equality
$1 = 0.99999\ldots$	Addition

Argument 4:

$.99999\ldots = \frac{9}{10} + \frac{9}{10^2} + \ldots + \frac{9}{10^n} + \ldots$	Definition of decimal
$= \frac{9}{10}\left(1 + \frac{1}{10} + \frac{1}{10^2} + \ldots + \frac{1}{10^{n-1}} + \ldots\right)$	Distributive Property
$= \frac{9}{10}\left(\dfrac{1}{1 - \frac{1}{10}}\right)$	Sum of a geometric series with $\lvert r \rvert < 1$
$= \frac{9}{10} \bullet \frac{10}{9} = 1$	Multiplication

7. Long division applied to $a = \frac{p}{q}$ involves the following steps. First, the Division Algorithm is applied to p and q. This yields unique integers D and r_1 such that $p = Dq + r_1$, where $0 \le r_1 < q$. Since $\frac{p}{q} = D + \frac{r_1}{q}$ and $0 \le \frac{r_1}{q} < 1$, D must be the greatest integer less than or equal to a, i.e., $D = \lfloor a \rfloor$. If $a - D = \frac{r_1}{q} = x_1$, then $0 \le x_1 < 1$ and $0 \le 10x_1 < 10$. The second step in the long division process is to perform the subtraction $p - Dq = r_1$. The third step is to apply the Division Algorithm to $10r_1$ and q. This yields integers d_1 and r_2 such that $10r_1 = d_1q + r_2$, where $0 \le r_2 < q$. As above, $0 \le \frac{r_2}{q} < 1$ implies $d_1 = \left\lfloor \frac{10r_1}{q} \right\rfloor = \lfloor 10x_1 \rfloor$. Then $d_1 \le 10x_1 < d_1 + 1$ and $D + \frac{d_1}{10} \le a < D + \frac{d_1}{10} + \frac{1}{10}$.

The long division process continues by applying the second and third steps recursively until $r_{k+1} = 0$: subtracting gives $r_k - d_k q = r_{k+1}$, and the Division Algorithm applied to $10r_{k+1}$ and q gives integers d_{k+1} and r_{k+2} such that $10r_{k+1} = d_{k+1}q + r_{k+2}$, where $0 \le r_{k+2} < q$. If $x_k = \frac{r_k}{q}$, then $x_{k+1} = 10x_k - d_k$, and since

$0 \le \frac{r_{k+2}}{q} < 1$, $d_{k+1} = \left\lfloor \frac{10r_{k+1}}{q} \right\rfloor = \lfloor 10x_{k+1} \rfloor$. Thus the long division algorithm produces the process for finding the decimal equivalent of a real number.

8. Basis step: Let $D = \lfloor x \rfloor$ and $x_1 = x - D$. Since $x > 0$, $0 \le x_1 < 1$ and $0 \le 10x_1 < 10$. Let $d_1 = \lfloor 10x_1 \rfloor$.

Then $d_1 \le 10x_1 < d_1 + 1$, which is equivalent to $D + \frac{d_1}{10} \le x < D + \frac{d_1}{10} + \frac{1}{10}$. Thus $0 \le d_j \le 9$ and

$D + \frac{d_1}{10} \le x < D + \frac{d_1}{10} + \frac{1}{10^j}$ is true for $j = 1$. Inductive step: Assume for any natural number j there

exist integers $d_1, \ldots, d_j$, where $0 \le d_i \le 9$ and $D + \frac{d_1}{10} + \ldots + \frac{d_j}{10^j} \le x < D + \frac{d_1}{10} + \ldots + \frac{d_j}{10^j} + \frac{1}{10^j}$. Then

$0 \le x - (D + \frac{d_1}{10} + \ldots + \frac{d_j}{10^j}) < \frac{1}{10^j}$, or $0 \le 10^{j+1}(x - (D + \frac{d_1}{10} + \ldots + \frac{d_j}{10^j})) < 10$. Let

$d_{j+1} = \left\lfloor 10^{j+1}(x - D + \frac{d_1}{10} + \ldots + \frac{d_j}{10^j}) \right\rfloor$. Then d_{j+1} is an integer such that $0 \le d_{j+1} \le 9$

and $d_{j+1} \le 10^{j+1}(x - (D + \frac{d_1}{10} + \ldots + \frac{d_j}{10^j})) < d_{j+1} + 1$, or equivalently,

$D + \frac{d_1}{10} + \ldots + \frac{d_{j+1}}{10^{j+1}} \le x < D + \frac{d_1}{10} + \ldots + \frac{d_{j+1}}{10^{j+1}} + \frac{1}{10^{j+1}}$. Thus, by the Principle of Mathematical Induction,

for every natural number k there is an integer d_k such that $0 \le d_k \le 9$ and

$D + \frac{d_1}{10} + \ldots + \frac{d_k}{10^k} \le x < D + \frac{d_1}{10} + \ldots + \frac{d_k}{10^k} + \frac{1}{10^k}$.

Section 2.1.3

1. *A computer or calculator program will be extremely helpful in finding the periods of the decimal representations for those fractions marked with a *.*

Terminating Decimals (Theorem 2.6): $\frac{1}{20} = \frac{1}{2^2 5}$ (2 decimal places), $\frac{1}{25} = \frac{1}{5^2}$ (2 decimal places), $\frac{1}{32} = \frac{1}{2^5}$ (5

decimal places), $\frac{1}{40} = \frac{1}{2^3 5}$ (3 decimal places);

Simple-Periodic Decimals (Theorems 2.7, 2.8): $\frac{1}{17} * = \frac{588235294117647}{10^{16} - 1}$ (p = 16),

$\frac{1}{19} * = \frac{52631578947368421}{10^{18} - 1}$ (p = 18), $\frac{1}{21} = \frac{47619}{10^6 - 1}$ (p = 6), $\frac{1}{23} * = \frac{4347826086956521739 13}{10^{22} - 1}$ (p = 22),

$\frac{1}{27} = \frac{37}{999}$ (p = 3), $\frac{1}{29} * = \frac{3448275862068965517241 37931}{10^{28} - 1}$ (p = 28), $\frac{1}{31} * = \frac{322580645 16129}{10^{15} - 1}$ (p = 15),

$\frac{1}{33} = \frac{3}{99}$ (p = 2), $\frac{1}{37} = \frac{27}{999}$ (p = 3), $\frac{1}{39} = \frac{25641}{10^6 - 1}$ (p = 6), $\frac{1}{41} = \frac{2439}{10^5 - 1}$ (p = 5)

Delayed-Periodic Decimals (Theorems 2.9, 2.10): $\frac{1}{18} = \frac{5}{10(10 - 1)}$ (delay = 1, p = 1), $\frac{1}{22} = \frac{45}{10(10^2 - 1)}$

(delay = 1, p = 2), $\frac{1}{24} = \frac{375}{10^3(10 - 1)}$ (delay = 3, p = 1), $\frac{1}{26} = \frac{384615}{10(10^6 - 1)}$ (delay = 1, p = 6), $\frac{1}{28} = \frac{3571425}{10^2(10^6 - 1)}$

(delay = 2, p = 6), $\frac{1}{30} = \frac{3}{10(10-1)}$ (delay = 1, p = 1), $\frac{1}{34}* = \frac{2941176470588235}{10(10^{16}-1)}$ (delay = 1, p = 16),

$\frac{1}{35} = \frac{285714}{10(10^6-1)}$ (delay = 1, p = 6), $\frac{1}{36} = \frac{25}{10^2(10-1)}$ (delay =1, p = 1), $\frac{1}{38}* = \frac{263157894736842105}{10(10^{18}-1)}$

(delay = 1, p = 18)

2. Since m and n are relatively prime positive integers and m < n, if $n = 2^r \cdot 5^s$, then, by Theorem 2.6, $\frac{m}{n}$ is

    represented by a terminating decimal, and if n has no factors equal to 2 or 5, then, by Theorem 2.8, $\frac{m}{n}$ is

    represented by a simple-periodic decimal. Otherwise, the decimal representation of $\frac{m}{n}$ is delayed-

    periodic. Thus the behavior of the decimal representation of $\frac{m}{n}$ is dependent only on n.

3. a. Suppose for $\frac{1}{19}$, a calculator displays only the first 6 decimal digits 0.052631 (we assume that the

        calculator does not round up the result in the last decimal place). The remaining 12 digits can be

        found by using two applications of the Division Algorithm. First, $1 \times 10^6 = 19 \cdot 52631 + r_1$. So

        $r_1 = 11$. Then the calculator can be used to compute $\frac{11}{19}$, which yields 0.578947. The long

        Division Algorithm is then applied a second time: $11 \times 10^6 = 19 \cdot 578947 + r_2$. So $r_2 = 7$. Then

        the calculator can be used to compute $\frac{7}{19}$, which yields 0.368421. Observe that applying the

        Division Algorithm a third time, $7 \times 10^6 = 19 \cdot 368421 + r_3$, gives $r_3 = 1$, so that the entire process

        will repeat itself. Thus we can "piece together" our previous results to obtain
        $\frac{1}{19} = \frac{52631}{10^6} + \frac{578947}{10^{12}} + \frac{368421}{10^{18}} + \ldots = 0.\overline{052631578947368421}$.

    b. $0.\overline{169014084507042253521126760563380 28}$

4. a. For $\frac{1}{k}$ to be simple-periodic with a period of 1, $\frac{1}{k} = \frac{M}{9}$, or kM = 9, for prime k and positive integer

        M. Thus k is a prime factor of 9. Since the only prime factor of 9 is 3, k = 3.

    b. For $\frac{1}{k}$ to be simple-periodic with a period of 2, $\frac{1}{k} = \frac{M}{99}$, or kM = 99, for prime k and positive

        integer M. Thus k is a prime factor of 99. Since the only prime factor of 99 that is not a prime

        factor of $10^p - 1$ for p < 2 is 11, k = 11.

    c. For $\frac{1}{k}$ to be simple-periodic with a period of 3, $\frac{1}{k} = \frac{M}{999}$, or kM = 999, for prime k and positive

        integer M. Thus k is a prime factor of 999. Since the only prime factor of 999 that is not a prime

        factor of $10^p - 1$ for p < 3 is 37, k = 37.

    d. For $\frac{1}{k}$ to be simple-periodic with a period of 4, $\frac{1}{k} = \frac{M}{9999}$, or kM = 9999, for prime k and positive

        integer M. Thus k is a prime factor of 9999. Since the only prime factor of 9999 that is not a

        prime factor of $10^p - 1$ for p < 34 is 101, k = 101.

    e. For $\frac{1}{k}$ to be simple-periodic with a period of 5, $\frac{1}{k} = \frac{M}{99999}$, or kM = 99999, for prime k and

        positive integer M. Thus k is a prime factor of 99999. Since the only prime factors of 99999 that

        are not prime factors of $10^p - 1$ for p < 5 are 41 and 271, k = 41 or k = 271.

    f. For $\frac{1}{k}$ to be simple-periodic with a period of 6, $\frac{1}{k} = \frac{M}{999999}$, or kM = 999999, for prime k and positive integer M. Thus k is a prime factor of 999999. Since the only prime factors of 999999 that are not prime factors of $10^p - 1$ for p < 6 are 7 and 13, k = 13 or k = 7.

5. a. For $\frac{1}{k}$ to be simple-periodic with a period of 1, $\frac{1}{k} = \frac{M}{9}$ for positive integers k and M, or kM = 9. Thus k = 3 or k = 9.

   b. For $\frac{1}{k}$ to be simple-periodic with a period of 2, $\frac{1}{k} = \frac{M}{99}$ for positive integers k and M, or kM = 99. Thus k = 11 or k = 33 or k = 99.

   c. For $\frac{1}{k}$ to be simple-periodic with a period of 2, $\frac{1}{k} = \frac{M}{999}$ for positive integers k and M, or kM = 999. Thus k = 27, k = 37, k = 111, k = 333, or k = 999.

6. a. $\frac{1}{27} = .\overline{037}$, $\frac{1}{37} = .\overline{027}$

   b. The relationship occurs because 27 • 37 = 999. So $\frac{1}{27} = \frac{37}{999}$ and $\frac{1}{37} = \frac{27}{999}$. An example of a similar relationship can be found by factoring 99999 = 369 • 271. So $\frac{1}{271} = \frac{369}{99999} = .\overline{00369}$ and $\frac{1}{369} = \frac{271}{99999} = .\overline{00271}$.

7. $10^1 - 1 = 9 = 3^2$; $10^2 - 1 = 99 = 3^2 \cdot 11$; $10^3 - 1 = 999 = 3^3 \cdot 37$;
   $10^4 - 1 = 9999 = 3^2 \cdot 11 \cdot 101$; $10^5 - 1 = 99999 = 3^2 \cdot 41 \cdot 271$;
   $10^6 - 1 = 999999 = 3^3 \cdot 7 \cdot 11 \cdot 13 \cdot 37$; $10^7 - 1 = 9999999 = 3^2 \cdot 239 \cdot 4649$;

   For a fraction $\frac{m}{n}$ in reduced form, only these factors can appear as factors of the denominator for the decimal representation to be simple-periodic. Thus these factors fully determine whether the decimal representation is simple-periodic up to period 7.

8. $\frac{3}{7} = .\overline{428571}$, $\frac{4}{7} = .\overline{571428}$, $\frac{5}{7} = .\overline{714285}$, $\frac{6}{7} = .\overline{857142}$. This behavior is not exhibited by all primes (consider, for example, $\frac{1}{3}$ or $\frac{1}{11}$).

9. If $x = \frac{M}{10^t} < 1$, then $M < 10^t$. Since M is a positive integer, we can let $M = d_1 10^{t-1} + d_2 10^{t-2} + \ldots + d_t 10^0$, where $0 \le d_j \le 9$ and, since M is not divisible by 10, $d_t \ne 0$. Then $\frac{M}{10^t} = \frac{d_1}{10} + \frac{d_2}{10^2} + \ldots + \frac{d_t}{10^t} = 0.d_1 d_2 d_3 \ldots d_t$, where $d_t \ne 0$. This is the definition of a terminating (finite) decimal.

10. Assume that $\frac{m}{n}$ is a reduced rational number with a simple-periodic decimal representation with period p. Then, by what was shown in the statement of the problem, $\frac{m}{n} = \frac{q}{10^{\phi(n)} - 1} = 0.\overline{d_1 d_2 \ldots d_p}$, for some $q \in \mathbf{Z}$. But this implies that $q = 10^{\phi(n)} \cdot 0.\overline{d_1 d_2 \ldots d_p} - 0.\overline{d_1 d_2 \ldots d_p}$. Since $\phi(n)$ must be a multiple of p for q to be an integer, p divides $\phi(n)$.

11. a. The denominator, 21, has no factors which are integer powers of 2 or 5. Therefore, by Theorem 2.8, the decimal representation of $\frac{1}{21}$ must be simple-periodic.

    b. There are 20 natural numbers less than 21; 8 of these (3, 6, 7, 9, 12, 14, 15, and 18) have factors in common with 21, so $\phi(n) = 20 - 8 = 12$. By the result of Problem 9, p must divide 12.

c. By Theorem 2.7, $\frac{1}{21} = \frac{M}{10^P - 1}$, where M is a positive integer, so $21M = 10^P - 1$. By part **b**, p = 2, 3, 4, 6 or 12 (p cannot equal 1 since $10^1 - 1 = 9$ and $9 < 21M$). Thus 21 must divide 99, 999, 9999, 999999, or 999999999999.

d. A calculator check will show that 21 does not divide 99, 999, or 99999. However, $21 \cdot 47619 = 999999$. Therefore $\frac{1}{21} = \frac{47619}{10^6 - 1}$ and, by Theorem 2.7, $\frac{1}{21}$ has period 6.

e. $\frac{1}{21} = 0.\overline{047619}$ confirms that the period is 6.

12. Suppose that N is a number between 0 and 1 that can be represented in the form $N = \frac{M}{10^t(10^P - 1)}$, where M, p, t $\in \mathbf{Z}^+$, and p and t are as small as possible. By the Division Algorithm, $M = A(10^P - 1) + B$, for integers A and B, where $0 < B < 10^P - 1$. Thus $N = \frac{A}{10^t} + 10^{-t}\frac{B}{10^P - 1}$. Since p and t are as small as possible, by Theorems 2.5 and 2.7, $\frac{A}{10^t} = 0.d_1 d_2 ... d_t$ and $\frac{B}{10^P - 1} = 0.\overline{d_1' d_2' ... d_p'}$, respectively. So,

$N = \frac{A}{10^t} + 10^{-t}\frac{B}{10^P - 1} = 0.d_1 d_2 ... d_t + 0.\underbrace{0...0}_{t\ zeros}\overline{d_1' d_2' ... d_p'} = 0.d_1 d_2 ... d_t\overline{d_1' d_2' ... d_p'}$; that is, N has a delayed-periodic decimal representation with period p and t digits before the start of the period.

13. ($\Rightarrow$) Let $\frac{m}{n}$ be a rational number between 0 and 1 that is in lowest terms. Suppose that $\frac{m}{n}$ has a delayed-periodic decimal representation with a period p that starts t digits after the decimal point. Then, by Theorem 2.9, $\frac{m}{n} = 0.d_1 d_2 ... d_t\overline{d_{t+1} ... d_{t+p}} = \frac{M}{10^t(10^P - 1)}$, where p and t are as small as possible. So, $m \cdot 10^t(10^P - 1) = m \cdot 2^t 5^t(10^P - 1) = nM$. Since n cannot divide m, n divides $2^t 5^t(10^P - 1)$ and so, $n = 2^r \cdot 5^s \cdot q$, where q divides $10^P - 1$ and is relatively prime to 2 and 5, r and s are not both 0, and t is the largest of r and s.

($\Leftarrow$) Now, suppose that $n = 2^r \cdot 5^s \cdot q$, where q is relatively prime to 2 and 5, r and s are not both 0, and t is the largest of r and s. So, $\frac{m}{n} = \frac{m}{2^r 5^s q}$. Without loss of generality, assume $t = r > s$. Then, $\frac{m}{n} = \frac{5^{r-s} m}{10^t q}$. Since q is relatively prime to 2 and 5, it is relatively prime to 10, and so, by Euler's Theorem (see Problem 10), q divides $10^{\phi(q)} - 1$. Thus $10^{\phi(q)} - 1 = qk$, for some $k \in \mathbf{Z}^+$, and $\frac{m}{n} = \frac{5^{r-s} m}{10^t q} = \frac{5^{r-s} mk}{10^t(10^{\phi(q)} - 1)}$.

By Theorem 2.9, then, $\frac{m}{n}$ has a delayed-periodic decimal representation that starts t digits after the decimal point.

Section 2.1.4

1. a. Sample rational: -86.5; sample irrational: $-50\sqrt{3}$

   b. Sample rational: -.000042; sample irrational: $-\frac{\sqrt{17}}{100000}$

   c. Sample rational: 3.14; sample irrational: $\pi - \frac{1}{2^8}$

   d. Sample rational: .0099999; sample irrational: $\frac{.01 + \sin(.01)}{2}$

2. Let q be an integer such that $q > \frac{\sqrt{2}}{x}$ and $q > \frac{\sqrt{2}}{y-x}$. Then $0 < \frac{\sqrt{2}}{q} < x$ and $0 < \frac{\sqrt{2}}{q} < y - x$. It follows that $1 < \frac{x}{\sqrt{2}/q}$. Theorem 2.11 implies that there is an integer $p > 2$ such that $p > \frac{x}{\sqrt{2}/q} \geq p - 1$. From this, $p(\frac{\sqrt{2}}{q}) > x \geq (p-1)(\frac{\sqrt{2}}{q})$. That is, $s = \frac{p\sqrt{2}}{q} > x$. We claim that $s < y$. Suppose to the contrary that $\frac{p\sqrt{2}}{q} \geq y$. Then $\frac{p\sqrt{2}}{q} \geq y > x \geq \frac{(p-1)\sqrt{2}}{q}$, so $y - x < \frac{p\sqrt{2}}{q} - \frac{(p-1)\sqrt{2}}{q} = \frac{\sqrt{2}}{q}$, which contradicts the fact that $y - x > \frac{\sqrt{2}}{q}$. This proves that $s = \frac{p\sqrt{2}}{q}$ is in the interval (x, y), and since a nonzero rational number multiplied by an irrational number is irrational, s is irrational.

3. Let the rational number $r = \frac{m}{n}$, where $m, n \in \mathbf{Z}$ and $n \neq 0$. Then r is a root of the polynomial $p(x) = nx - m$. Thus r is algebraic.

4. Let the rational number $r = \frac{m}{n}$, where $m, n \in \mathbf{Z}$ and $n \neq 0$. Then $\sqrt[k]{r}$ is a root of the polynomial $p(x) = nx^k - m$. Thus $\sqrt[k]{r}$ is algebraic.

5. a. $-\sqrt{12}$ is a solution of the quadratic polynomial $x^2 - 12 = 0$ and is algebraic.

   b. Assume $1 + \sqrt{3}$ is the solution of a quadratic $x^2 + bx + c = 0$. So $(1 + \sqrt{3})^2 + b(1 + \sqrt{3}) + c = 0$. This gives rise to the two equations $4 + b + c = 0$ and $2\sqrt{3} + b\sqrt{3} = 0$. So $b = -2$ and $c = -2$. Thus $1 + \sqrt{3}$ is a solution of the quadratic polynomial $x^2 + -2x + -2 = 0$ and is algebraic.

   c. Let $y = \sqrt{2} + \sqrt{3}$. Then $y^2 = 5 + 2\sqrt{6}$. Assume y^2 is the solution of a quadratic $x^2 + bx + c = 0$. So $(5 + 2\sqrt{6})^2 + b(5 + 2\sqrt{6}) + c = 0$. This gives rise to the two equations $49 + 5b + c = 0$ and $20\sqrt{6} + 2b\sqrt{6} = 0$. So $b = -10$ and $c = 1$. So y^2 is a solution to the quadratic $x^2 + -10x + 1 = 0$ and y is a solution to the polynomial $x^4 + -10x^2 + 1 = 0$. Therefore $\sqrt{2} + \sqrt{3}$ is algebraic.

   d. Assume $1 - \sqrt[3]{5}$ is the solution of a cubic of the form $x^3 + bx^2 + cx + d = 0$. So $(1 - \sqrt[3]{5})^3 + b(1 - \sqrt[3]{5})^2 + c(1 - \sqrt[3]{5}) + d = 0$. This gives rise to the three equations $-4 + b + c + d = 0$, $-3\sqrt[3]{5} - 2b\sqrt[3]{5} - c\sqrt[3]{5} = 0$, and $3\sqrt[3]{5^2} + b\sqrt[3]{5} = 0$. So $b = -3$, $c = 3$, and $d = 4$. Thus $1 - \sqrt[3]{5}$ is a solution of the cubic polynomial $x^3 + -3x^2 + 3x + 4 = 0$ and is algebraic.

6. The set $\mathbf{R}$ of real numbers is the union of the set of algebraic numbers and the set of transcendental numbers. By Theorem 2.17, the set of algebraic numbers is countably infinite. Suppose the set of transcendental numbers were also countably infinite. Then $\mathbf{R}$ would also be countably infinite, which contradicts Corollary 1 of Theorem 2.18. Thus the set of transcendental numbers is not countably infinite.

7. Sample: positive, negative, and zero

8. a. Let $f: \mathbf{Z} \to \mathbf{E}$ be the 1-1 function $f(x) = 2x$. Thus there exists a 1-1 correspondence between the set of integers and the set of even integers.

   b. Let $f: \{x: x \in (a, b)\} \to \{y: y \in (c, d)\}$ be the 1-1 function $f(x) = \frac{d-c}{b-a}x + c - \frac{d-c}{b-a}a$. Thus there exists a 1-1 correspondence between these two intervals and so they have the same cardinality.

9. Since $\mathbf{Z}^+$ and $\mathbf{Q}^+$ are countably infinite, $\mathbf{Z}^-$ and $\mathbf{Q}^-$ must also be countably infinite (they are related by the 1-1 correspondence f: $\mathbf{Q}^+ \rightarrow \mathbf{Q}^-$ given by f(x) = -x). Thus 1-1 correspondences between the sets $\mathbf{Z}^+$ and $\mathbf{Q}^+$ and between the sets $\mathbf{Z}^-$ and $\mathbf{Q}^-$ can be established. Combining these correspondences with the 1-1 correspondence g: {0}$\rightarrow$ {0} gives a 1-1 correspondence between $\mathbf{Z} = \mathbf{Z}^+ \cup \mathbf{Z}^- \cup \{0\}$ and $\mathbf{Q} = \mathbf{Q}^+ \cup \mathbf{Q}^- \cup \{0\}$. Thus $\mathbf{Q}$ has the same cardinality as $\mathbf{Z}$, which was shown to be countably infinite.

10. First, by letting f: $\{x: x \in \mathbf{Q}^+\} \rightarrow \{y: y \in (0, 1) \cap \mathbf{Q}\}$ be the 1-1 function $f(x) = \frac{x}{x+1}$, we can establish that there exists a 1-1 correspondence between $\mathbf{Q}^+$ and the set of rational numbers in the interval (0, 1). Thus the set of rational numbers in the interval (0, 1) is countably infinite. Similarly, the set of rational numbers in the interval $(n - 1, n)$, where $n \in \mathbf{N}$, is countably infinite. Now, if $S = S_1 \cup S_2 \cup S_3 \ldots$ represents a countable union of countably infinite sets, we can let the elements of S_k correspond to the elements of $\mathbf{N}$, for k = 1, and correspond to the elements of the set of rational numbers in the interval $(k - 2, k - 1)$, for each $k \geq 2$. Since $\mathbf{Q}^+$ is simply the union of $\mathbf{N}$ and the set of rational numbers in all intervals $(n - 1, n)$, where $n \in \mathbf{N}$, S has the same cardinality as $\mathbf{Q}^+$ and is thus countably infinite.

11. Let f: $\{x: x \in \mathbf{Q}^+ \cup \{0\}\} \rightarrow \{y: y \in [0, \frac{\varepsilon}{2}) \cap \mathbf{Q}\}$ be the 1-1 function $f(x) = \frac{\varepsilon}{2}\left(\frac{x}{x+1}\right)$ and let g: $\{x: x \in \mathbf{Q}^-\} \rightarrow \{y: y \in (-\frac{\varepsilon}{2}, 0) \cap \mathbf{Q}\}$ be the 1-1 function $f(x) = \frac{\varepsilon}{2}\left(\frac{x}{1-x}\right)$. Then $f \cup g$ is the 1-1 function that maps $\mathbf{Q}$ onto the set of rational numbers in the interval $(-\frac{\varepsilon}{2}, \frac{\varepsilon}{2})$, which has total length ε.

Section 2.2.1

1. a. $z = (-5, 2)$; $r = \sqrt{(-5)^2 + 2^2} = \sqrt{29}$, $\tan \theta = -\frac{2}{5}$, $\theta \approx 158.20°$,

        $z \approx \sqrt{29} \cos 158.20° + \sqrt{29}\, i \sin 158.20°$; $z \approx [\sqrt{29}, 158.20°]$, Re(z) = -5, Im(z) = 2, $|z| = \sqrt{29}$

    b. $z = 3\cos 235° + 3i \sin 235°$; $x = 3\cos 235° \approx -1.72$, $y = 3\sin 235° \approx -2.46$, $z \approx -1.72 + -2.46i$;

        $z \approx (-1.72, -2.46)$, Re(z) $\approx$ -1.72, Im(z) $\approx$ -2.46, $|z| = 3$

    c. $z = [.5, \frac{\pi}{5}]$; $x = .5\cos \frac{\pi}{5} \approx .405$, $y = .5\sin \frac{\pi}{5} \approx .294$, $z \approx .405 + .294i$; $z \approx (.405, .294)$,

        Re(z) $\approx$ .405, Im(z) = .294, $|z| = .5$

    d. $z = 12 - 2i$; $r = \sqrt{12^2 + (-2)^2} = \sqrt{148}$, $\tan \theta = -\frac{2}{12}$, $\theta \approx -9.46°$,

        $z \approx \sqrt{148} \cos (-9.46°) + \sqrt{148}\, i \sin (-9.46°)$; $z \approx [\sqrt{148}, -9.46°]$, Re(z) = 12, Im(z) = -2,

        $|z| = \sqrt{148}$

    e. $z = \frac{4+i}{4-i} \cdot \frac{4+i}{4+i} = \frac{15}{17} + \frac{8}{17}i$; $z = (\frac{15}{17}, \frac{8}{17})$; $r = \sqrt{\left(\frac{15}{17}\right)^2 + \left(\frac{8}{17}\right)^2} = 1$, $\tan \theta = \frac{8}{15}$, $\theta \approx 28.07°$,

        $z \approx \cos 28.07° + i \sin 28.07°$; $z \approx [1, 28.07°]$, Re(z) = $\frac{15}{17}$, Im(z) = $\frac{8}{17}$, $|z| = 1$

f. $z = i^{430} = i^2 = -1$; $z = (-1, 0)$; $r = 1$, $\theta = \pi$, $z = \cos \pi + i \sin \pi$; $z = [1, \pi]$, $\text{Re}(z) = -1$, $\text{Im}(z) = 0$,

$|z| = 1$

2.   Let $z = a + bi$. Then $\bar{z} = a - bi$.

a. $\dfrac{z + \bar{z}}{2} = \dfrac{(a + bi) + (a - bi)}{2} = \dfrac{2a}{2} = a = \text{Re}[z]$

b. $\dfrac{z - \bar{z}}{2i} = \dfrac{(a + bi) - (a - bi)}{2i} = \dfrac{2bi}{2i} = b = \text{Im}[z]$

3. $x = r'\cos \theta' = (-r)\cos(\theta + \pi(2n + 1)) = (-r)(-\cos \theta) = r \cos \theta$

$y = r'\sin \theta' = (-r)\sin(\theta + \pi(2n + 1)) = (-r)(-\sin \theta) = r \sin \theta$

4. $S_b = \left\{ \dfrac{-b \pm \sqrt{b^2 - 8}}{2} \right\}$ is the solution set of $x^2 + bx + 2 = 0$. When $b > 2\sqrt{2}$, the solution set consists of

two points on the real axis which are symmetric to the point $\dfrac{-b}{2}$ and whose distances from this point

increase as b increases. When $b < -2\sqrt{2}$, the solution set consists of two points on the real axis which

are symmetric to the point $\dfrac{-b}{2}$ and whose distances from this point increase as b decreases. When

$b = \pm 2\sqrt{2}$, the solution set consists of just the real point $\dfrac{-b}{2}$. When $|b| < 2\sqrt{2}$, S_b consists of two

points symmetric to the real axis on the vertical line through $\dfrac{-b}{2}$. The distance between these points

increases as $|b|$ decreases.

5.   The complex zeros of $p_c(x) = 4x^4 + 8x^3 - 3x^2 - 9x + c$ are displayed in the table and the complex plane

below. Arrows in the graph show how the zeros move as the value of c increases from -4 to 6.

Solutions to $4x^4 + 8x^3 - 3x^2 - 9x = -c$; exact values in bold

c	x_1	x_2	x_3	x_4
-4	-1.922	-.603 − .312i	-.603 + .312i	1.128
-2	-1.813	**-1.000**	-0.258	1.071
0	**-1.500**	**-1.500**	**0.000**	**1.000**
2	-1.560 − .343i	-1.560 + .343i	0.217	0.904
4	-1.607 − .463i	-1.607 + .463i	0.500	0.714
6	-1.647 − .546i	-1.647 + .546i	.647 − .284i	.647 + .284i

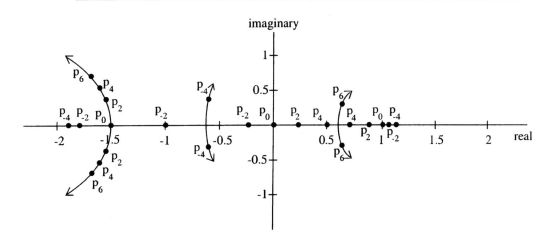

6.   a.   the equatorial circle of the Riemann sphere

       b.   the great circle passing through the South Pole with the North Pole removed in the plane containing the real axis

       c.   the great circle passing through the South Pole with the North Pole removed in the plane containing the imaginary axis

       d.   the great circle passing through the South Pole with the North Pole removed in the plane containing the given line

       e.   the circle with the north pole removed, obtained by the intersection of Riemann sphere with the plane containing both the north pole and the given straight line.

7.   On the Riemann sphere, $\bar{z}$ is the reflection image of z over the plane containing the real axis and passing through the North Pole.

Section 2.2.2

1.   a. $z_1 + z_2 = -2 + 8i + -2 - 8i = -4$; $z_1 - z_2 = -2 + 8i - (-2 - 8i) = 16i$;

$$z_1 z_2 = (-2 + 8i)(-2 - 8i) = 4 + 16i - 16i - 64i^2 = 4 + 64 = 68;$$

$$\frac{z_1}{z_2} = \frac{-2 + 8i}{-2 - 8i} = \frac{-2 + 8i}{-2 - 8i} \cdot \frac{-2 + 8i}{-2 + 8i} = \frac{4 - 16i - 16i - 64}{68} = \frac{-60 - 32i}{68} = -\frac{15}{17} - \frac{8}{17}i$$

       b. $z_1 = \frac{1}{2} + \frac{\sqrt{3}}{2}i$, $z_2 = 1$; $z_1 + z_2 = \frac{1}{2} + \frac{\sqrt{3}}{2}i + 1 = \frac{3}{2} + \frac{\sqrt{3}}{2}i$;

$$z_1 - z_2 = \frac{1}{2} + \frac{\sqrt{3}}{2}i - 1 = -\frac{1}{2} + \frac{\sqrt{3}}{2}i;\quad z_1 z_2 = (\frac{1}{2} + \frac{\sqrt{3}}{2}i)1 = \frac{1}{2} + \frac{\sqrt{3}}{2}i;$$

$$\frac{z_1}{z_2} = \frac{1}{2} + \frac{\sqrt{3}}{2}i$$

       c. $z_1 = [3, 225°] = 3(\cos \frac{5\pi}{4} + i \sin \frac{5\pi}{4}) = -\frac{3\sqrt{2}}{2} + -\frac{3\sqrt{2}}{2}i$,

$$z_2 = 7(\cos \frac{5\pi}{3} + i \sin \frac{5\pi}{3}) = \frac{7}{2} + \frac{-7\sqrt{3}}{2}i;$$

$$z_1 + z_2 = -\frac{3\sqrt{2}}{2} + -\frac{3\sqrt{2}}{2}i + \frac{7}{2} + \frac{-7\sqrt{3}}{2}i = \frac{7 - 3\sqrt{2}}{2} + \frac{-7\sqrt{3} - 3\sqrt{2}}{2}i;$$

$$z_1 - z_2 = -\frac{3\sqrt{2}}{2} + -\frac{3\sqrt{2}}{2}i - (\frac{7}{2} + \frac{-7\sqrt{3}}{2}i) = \frac{-7 - 3\sqrt{2}}{2} + \frac{7\sqrt{3} - 3\sqrt{2}}{2}i;$$

$$z_1 z_2 = 21(\cos(\frac{5\pi}{4} + \frac{5\pi}{3}) + i \sin(\frac{5\pi}{4} + \frac{5\pi}{3})) = 21(\cos \frac{35\pi}{12} + i \sin \frac{35\pi}{12}) = [21, \frac{35\pi}{12}];$$

$$\frac{z_1}{z_2} = \frac{3}{7}(\cos(\frac{5\pi}{4} - \frac{5\pi}{3}) + i \sin(\frac{5\pi}{4} - \frac{5\pi}{3})) = \frac{3}{7}(\cos \frac{-5\pi}{12} + i \sin \frac{-5\pi}{12}) = [\frac{3}{7}, \frac{-5\pi}{12}]$$

       d. $z_1 = \frac{-1 + \sqrt{1 - 4}}{2} = -\frac{1}{2} + \frac{\sqrt{3}}{2}i$, $z_2 = \frac{-1 - \sqrt{1 - 4}}{2} = -\frac{1}{2} - \frac{\sqrt{3}}{2}i$;

$$z_1 + z_2 = -\frac{1}{2} + \frac{\sqrt{3}}{2}i + -\frac{1}{2} - \frac{\sqrt{3}}{2}i = -1;$$

$$z_1 - z_2 = -\frac{1}{2} + \frac{\sqrt{3}}{2}i - (-\frac{1}{2} - \frac{\sqrt{3}}{2}i) = \sqrt{3}i;$$

$$z_1 z_2 = (-\frac{1}{2} + \frac{\sqrt{3}}{2}i)(-\frac{1}{2} - \frac{\sqrt{3}}{2}i) = \frac{1}{4} + \frac{3}{4} = 1;$$

$$\frac{z_1}{z_2} = \frac{-1+\sqrt{3}i}{-1-\sqrt{3}i} = \frac{-1+\sqrt{3}i}{-1-\sqrt{3}i}\frac{-1+\sqrt{3}i}{-1+\sqrt{3}i} = \frac{1-2\sqrt{3}i-3}{4} = -\frac{1}{2} - \frac{\sqrt{3}}{2}i$$

2. The points $0, z_1, z_2, z_1 + z_2$ are vertices of a parallelogram. $|z_1|$ and $|z_2|$ are the lengths of the parallelogram's sides while $|z_1 + z_2|$ and $|z_1 - z_2|$ are the lengths of the parallelogram's diagonals.

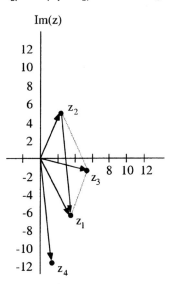

3. Since $|z_1| = |z_2| = |z_3|$, z_1, z_2 and z_3 can be thought of as three points lying on a circle in the complex plane with center O. The quantity $\mathrm{Arg}(\frac{z_2}{z_1}) = \theta_2 - \theta_1 = \theta$ is the angle between vectors extending from the origin to the points z_2 and z_1. The quantities $z_3 - z_2$ and $z_3 - z_1$ are the vectors extending from z_2 to z_3 and z_1 to z_3, respectively, and the quantity $\mathrm{Arg}(\frac{z_3 - z_2}{z_3 - z_1}) = \phi_2 - \phi_1 = \phi$ is the angle between these vectors. Thus the relationship $\mathrm{Arg}(\frac{z_3 - z_2}{z_3 - z_1}) = \frac{1}{2}\mathrm{Arg}(\frac{z_2}{z_1})$ is equivalent to the statement from Euclidean geometry that the measure of an inscribed angle is one-half the measure of its intercepted arc.

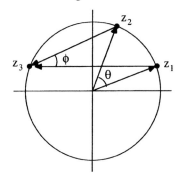

4. Let $z = x + iy$. $|x + iy - 2i| = |x + (y - 2)i| = 6$. So $(x + (y - 2)i)(x - (y - 2)i) = 36$ or $x^2 + (y - 2)^2 = 36$. Thus the set of points z describes a circle with radius 6 and center $(0, 2)$.

5. a. $\overline{z_1 + z_2} = \overline{z_1} + \overline{z_2}$. Let $z_1 = a_1 + b_1i$ and $z_2 = a_2 + b_2i$. Then $\overline{z_1 + z_2} = (a_1 + a_2) - (b_1 + b_2)i = a_1 - b_1i + a_2 - b_2i = \overline{z_1} + \overline{z_2}$.

b. $\overline{z_1 z_2} = \overline{z_1}\,\overline{z_2}$. Let $z_1 = a_1 + b_1 i$ and $z_2 = a_2 + b_2 i$. Then
$\overline{z_1 z_2} = \overline{(a_1 + b_1 i)(a_2 + b_2 i)} = (a_1 a_2 - b_1 b_2) - (a_1 b_2 + b_1 a_2)i =$
$(a_1 - b_1 i)(a_2 - b_2 i) = \overline{z_1}\,\overline{z_2}$

c. $\overline{\left(\dfrac{z_1}{z_2}\right)} = \dfrac{\overline{z_1}}{\overline{z_2}}$. By part **b**,
$\overline{\left(\dfrac{z_1}{z_2}\right)} = \overline{z_1 \dfrac{1}{z_2}} = \overline{z_1}\,\overline{\left(\dfrac{1}{z_2}\right)}$. Letting $z_2 = a_2 + b_2 i$, $\overline{\left(\dfrac{1}{z_2}\right)} = \overline{\left(\dfrac{1}{a_2 + b_2 i}\right)} = \overline{\left(\dfrac{a_2 - b_2 i}{a_2^2 + b_2^2}\right)} = \dfrac{a_2 + b_2 i}{a_2^2 + b_2^2} = \dfrac{1}{\overline{z_2}}$.

d. $\overline{z^1} = \overline{z} = (\overline{z})^1$ and $\overline{z^{n+1}} = \overline{z \cdot z^n} = \overline{z} \cdot \overline{z^n}$ (by part **b**) $= \overline{z} \cdot (\overline{z})^n$ (by inductive hypothesis)
$= (\overline{z})^{n+1}$, so true for all n.

6. Since z_1, z_2, and z_3 are on the unit circle, they can be written $z_1 = \cos\theta_1 + i\sin\theta_1$, $z_2 = \cos\theta_2 + i\sin\theta_2$, and $z_3 = \cos\theta_3 + i\sin\theta_3$. The equation $z_1 + z_2 + z_3 = 0$ then yields the two independent equations $\cos\theta_1 + \cos\theta_2 + \cos\theta_3 = 0$ and $\sin\theta_1 + \sin\theta_2 + \sin\theta_3 = 0$. These can be rearranged to $\cos\theta_1 + \cos\theta_2 = -\cos\theta_3$ and $\sin\theta_1 + \sin\theta_2 = -\sin\theta_3$, which when squared and added give the equation
$\cos^2\theta_1 + \cos^2\theta_2 + 2\cos\theta_1\cos\theta_2 + \sin^2\theta_1 + \sin^2\theta_2 + 2\sin\theta_1\sin\theta_2 = \cos^2\theta_3 + \sin^2\theta_3$
$= 1 + 1 + 2(\cos\theta_1\cos\theta_2 + \sin\theta_1\sin\theta_2) = 1$

So $\cos\theta_1\cos\theta_2 + \sin\theta_1\sin\theta_2 = -\dfrac{1}{2}$, which is equivalent to $\cos(\theta_2 - \theta_1) = -\dfrac{1}{2}$.

Thus $\theta_2 - \theta_1$, the angle between the points z_2 and z_1 on the unit circle, is $\dfrac{2\pi}{3}$. In a similar manner it can be shown that the angle between z_3 and z_2 is $\dfrac{2\pi}{3}$. Thus z_1, z_2, and z_3 lie at the vertices of an equilateral triangle.

7. Let $z = x + iy$, $z_1 = x_1 + iy_1$, and $z_2 = x_2 + iy_2$. Then
$|z - z_1| + |z - z_2| = \sqrt{(x - x_1)^2 + (y - y_1)^2} + \sqrt{(x - x_2)^2 + (y - y_2)^2}$,
which is the sum of the distances from the point $z = (x, y)$ to the points $z_1 = (x_1, y_1)$ and $z_2 = (x_2, y_2)$ in the complex plane. So the solution set to the equation
$|z - z_1| + |z - z_2| = c$ will be the set of all points z in the complex plane such that the sum of the distances from z to z_1 and from z to z_2 equals the constant c. This solution set describes an ellipse.

8. Let $z_1 = r_1 e^{i\theta_1}$ and $z_2 = r_2 e^{i\theta_2}$. Then $z_1 z_2 = r_1 r_2 e^{i(\theta_1 + \theta_2)}$ and $\dfrac{z_1}{z_2} = \dfrac{r_1}{r_2} e^{i(\theta_1 - \theta_2)}$.

Proof:

$\begin{aligned}
z_1 z_2 &= (r_1 e^{i\theta_1})(r_2 e^{i\theta_2}) \\
&= r_1 r_2 e^{i\theta_1} e^{i\theta_2} && \text{Associative and Commutative Properties of Multiplication} \\
&= r_1 r_2 e^{i\theta_1 + i\theta_2} && \text{Product of Powers Property} \\
&= r_1 r_2 e^{i(\theta_1 + \theta_2)} && \text{Distributive Property}
\end{aligned}$

$\dfrac{z_1}{z_2} = \dfrac{r_1 e^{i\theta_1}}{r_2 e^{i\theta_2}}$

$$= \frac{r_1}{r_2} e^{i\theta_1 - i\theta_2} \qquad \text{Quotient of Powers Property}$$

$$= \frac{r_1}{r_2} e^{i(\theta_1 - \theta_2)} \qquad \text{Distributive Property}$$

9.   Basis step: $z^1 = r^1(\cos(1\theta) + i \sin(1\theta))$. Inductive step: Assume $z^k = r^k(\cos(k\theta) + i \sin(k\theta))$. Then
z^{k+1}

$= z^k \bullet z$

$= r^k(\cos(k\theta) + i \sin(k\theta)) \bullet r(\cos(\theta) + i \sin(\theta))$

$= r^{k+1}(\cos(k\theta)\cos(\theta) - \sin(k\theta)\sin(\theta) + (\sin(\theta)\cos(k\theta) + \sin(k\theta)\cos(\theta))i)$

$= r^{k+1}(\cos(k\theta + \theta) + i \sin(k\theta + \theta))$

$= r^{k+1}(\cos((k+1)\theta) + i \sin((k+1)\theta))$

Thus $z^n = r^n(\cos(n\theta) + i \sin(n\theta))$ for all natural numbers n.

10.   a. $O(z) = \{z^1 = [1, \frac{3\pi}{5}],\ z^2 = [1, \frac{6\pi}{5}],\ z^3 = [1, \frac{9\pi}{5}],\ z^4 = [1, \frac{12\pi}{5}],\ z^5 = [1, 3\pi],\ z^6 = [1, \frac{18\pi}{5}],$
$z^7 = [1, \frac{21\pi}{5}],\ z^8 = [1, \frac{24\pi}{5}],\ z^9 = [1, \frac{27\pi}{5}],\ z^{10} = [1, 6\pi] = [1, 0]\}$

   b. $O(z) = \{[1, n]\colon\ n \in \mathbf{N}\}$

   c.   If θ is a rational multiple of π, then $\theta = \frac{p}{q}\pi$ for some integers p and q. Since
$z^{2q} = [1, 2p\pi] = \cos 2p\pi + i \sin 2p\pi = 1$, so $z^{2q+1} = z^{2q} \bullet z = z$ and $z^{2q+n} = z^{2q} \bullet z^n = z^n$. Hence there will be at most 2q elements in $O(z)$.

   d.   i.   For the orbit of z to be a finite set, $z^q = z^k$ for positive integers q and k, where $q > k$. Thus $z^{q-k} = 1$. This would imply that the point 1 is in the orbit of z, which is not possible (see ii).

          ii.   For the point 1 to be in the orbit of z, $z^q = 1$. This implies, $q\theta = 2\pi m$ for positive integers q and m. For $\theta = 1$ radian, then, $q = 2\pi m$. However, since π is irrational, there are no integers q and m that would make this equality hold.

          iii.   One can find natural numbers p and q such that $\frac{p}{q} \approx 2\pi$. Thus $p \approx 2\pi q$ and
$z^p = [1, 1]^p = [1, p] \approx [1, 2\pi q] = [1, 0]$.

11.   Let $z = [r, \theta]$ be an nth root of $a = [|\,a\,|, \mathrm{Arg}(a) + 2\pi k]$, where k is any integer. Then by Theorem 2.22,
$z^n = [r^n, n\theta] = [|\,a\,|, \mathrm{Arg}(a) + 2\pi k]$. So $r = \sqrt[n]{|a|}$ and $\theta = \frac{\mathrm{Arg}(a) + 2\pi k}{n}$. Thus there will be an nth root
$z_k = [\sqrt[n]{|a|}, \frac{\mathrm{Arg}(a)}{n} + \frac{2\pi k}{n}]$ for any integer k. But since the sine and cosine functions are periodic with period 2π, there are only n distinct complex roots for $k = 0, 1, 2, \ldots, n - 1$.

12.   Since $a = 1 + \sqrt{3}$, $|\,a\,| = 1 + \sqrt{3}$ and $\mathrm{Arg}(a) = 0$. From DeMoivre's Theorem, the four roots are
$$z_0 = \sqrt[4]{1 + \sqrt{3}}\left(\cos\left(\frac{0 \bullet 2\pi}{4}\right) + i\sin\left(\frac{0 \bullet 2\pi}{4}\right)\right) = \sqrt[4]{1 + \sqrt{3}}$$
$$z_1 = \sqrt[4]{1 + \sqrt{3}}\left(\cos\left(\frac{1 \bullet 2\pi}{4}\right) + i\sin\left(\frac{1 \bullet 2\pi}{4}\right)\right) = \sqrt[4]{1 + \sqrt{3}}\,i$$
$$z_2 = \sqrt[4]{1 + \sqrt{3}}\left(\cos\left(\frac{2 \bullet 2\pi}{4}\right) + i\sin\left(\frac{2 \bullet 2\pi}{4}\right)\right) = -\sqrt[4]{1 + \sqrt{3}}$$
$$z_3 = \sqrt[4]{1 + \sqrt{3}}\left(\cos\left(\frac{3 \bullet 2\pi}{4}\right) + i\sin\left(\frac{3 \bullet 2\pi}{4}\right)\right) = -\sqrt[4]{1 + \sqrt{3}}\,i$$

These four points lie at the vertices of a square, with z_0 and z_2 on the real axis and z_1 and z_3 on the imaginary axis.

13. $|1| = 1$ and $\text{Arg}(1) = 0$. By DeMoivre's Theorem, the seven roots are

$$z_0 = \cos\left(\frac{0 \cdot 2\pi}{7}\right) + i\sin\left(\frac{0 \cdot 2\pi}{7}\right) = 1$$

$$z_1 = \cos\left(\frac{1 \cdot 2\pi}{7}\right) + i\sin\left(\frac{1 \cdot 2\pi}{7}\right) \approx .62 + .78i$$

$$z_2 = \cos\left(\frac{2 \cdot 2\pi}{7}\right) + i\sin\left(\frac{2 \cdot 2\pi}{7}\right) \approx -.22 + .97i$$

$$z_3 = \cos\left(\frac{3 \cdot 2\pi}{7}\right) + i\sin\left(\frac{3 \cdot 2\pi}{7}\right) \approx -.90 + .43i$$

$$z_4 = \cos\left(\frac{4 \cdot 2\pi}{7}\right) + i\sin\left(\frac{4 \cdot 2\pi}{7}\right) \approx -.90 + -.43i$$

$$z_5 = \cos\left(\frac{5 \cdot 2\pi}{7}\right) + i\sin\left(\frac{5 \cdot 2\pi}{7}\right) \approx -.22 + -.97i$$

$$z_6 = \cos\left(\frac{6 \cdot 2\pi}{7}\right) + i\sin\left(\frac{6 \cdot 2\pi}{7}\right) \approx .62 + -.78i$$

These seven roots lie at the vertices of a regular heptagon inscribed in the unit circle. The real axis is one heptagon's symmetry axes.

14.   a. $\cos(3\theta) + i\sin(3\theta) = (\cos\theta + i\sin\theta)^3$

       $= \cos^3\theta + 3i\cos^2\theta\sin\theta - 3\cos\theta\sin^2\theta - i\sin^3\theta$

       So $\cos(3\theta) = \cos^3\theta - 3\cos\theta\sin^2\theta$ and $\sin(3\theta) = 3\cos^2\theta\sin\theta - \sin^3\theta$.

  b. $\sin^2\theta = 1 - \cos^2\theta$. So $\cos(2\theta) = \cos^2\theta - \sin^2\theta = 2\cos^2\theta - 1$ and

       $\cos(3\theta) = \cos^3\theta - 3\cos\theta\sin^2\theta = \cos^3\theta - 3\cos\theta(1 - \cos^2\theta) = 4\cos^3\theta - 3\cos\theta$.

  c.   By Mathematical Induction, $\cos(n\theta) + i\sin(n\theta) = (\cos\theta + i\sin\theta)^n$ for all n (Theorem 2.22 and Problem 8), and, using the Binomial Theorem,

$$(\cos\theta + i\sin\theta)^n = \sum_{i=0}^{n}\binom{n}{i}(\cos\theta)^{n-i}(i\sin\theta)^i = \cos^n\theta + in\cos^{n-1}\theta\sin\theta - \binom{n}{2}\cos^{n-2}\theta\sin^2\theta$$

$$-i\binom{n}{3}\cos^{n-3}\theta\sin^3\theta + \binom{n}{4}\cos^{n-4}\theta\sin^4\theta + \ldots + n\cos\theta(i\sin\theta)^{n-1} + (i\sin\theta)^n$$

Thus, for n even,

$$\cos(n\theta) = \cos^n\theta - \binom{n}{2}\cos^{n-2}\theta\sin^2\theta + \binom{n}{4}\cos^{n-4}\theta\sin^4\theta + \ldots \pm \sin^n\theta$$

and, for n odd,

$$\cos(n\theta) = \cos^n\theta - \binom{n}{2}\cos^{n-2}\theta\sin^2\theta + \binom{n}{4}\cos^{n-4}\theta\sin^4\theta + \ldots \pm n\cos\theta\sin^{n-1}\theta.$$

Since $\cos(n\theta)$ will only contain even powers of $\sin\theta$, each $\sin^2\theta$ can be replaced by $1 - \cos^2\theta$ and $\cos(n\theta)$ can be written in terms of $\cos\theta$ for all natural numbers n.

15.   z has exactly n distinct complex nth roots: $z_k = \sqrt[n]{r}\, e^{i(\theta + 2k\pi)/n}$ for $k = 0, 1, \ldots, n - 1$.

CHAPTER 3 – Functions

Section 3.1.1

1. We wish to show that the depth of fuel in a cylindrical tank determines the volume of the fuel according to the formula $V(d) = \ell(\pi r^2 - r^2\cos^{-1}(\frac{d-r}{r}) + (d-r)\sqrt{2dr - d^2})$. There are two cases to consider: case (1) $d \geq r$ (i.e., the tank is more than half full), and case (2) $d < r$ (i.e., the tank is less than half full).

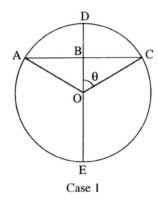

Case 1

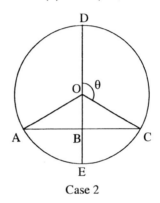

Case 2

Case (1): We know that $AO = r$, $CO = r$, and $BO = (d-r)$, where $d = BE$. By the Pythagorean Theorem, we find that $BC = \sqrt{r^2 - (d-r)^2}$, which simplifies to $BC = \sqrt{2dr - d^2}$.
The volume of fuel in the tank is $\ell \bullet$ (area of region AECBA), where ℓ is the length of the tank. The area of the region AECBA is $\pi r^2 - 2$(area of sector ODC) + area of $\triangle OAC$. Let $\angle DOC = \theta$, as labeled above. The area of sector $DOC = \frac{\theta}{2\pi}\pi r^2 = \frac{1}{2}\theta r^2$. The area of $\triangle OAC = \frac{1}{2}BO \bullet AC$
$= \frac{1}{2}(d-r)(2\sqrt{2dr - d^2}) = (d-r)\sqrt{2dr - d^2}$. Thus the area of region AECBA
$= \pi r^2 - 2(\frac{1}{2}\theta r^2) + (d-r)\sqrt{2dr - d^2}$ and the volume of the fuel in the tank is
$V(d) = \ell(\pi r^2 - \theta r^2 + (d-r)\sqrt{2dr - d^2})$. For $d \geq r$, $0 \leq \theta \leq \frac{\pi}{2}$ and $\cos\theta = \frac{BO}{r} = \frac{d-r}{r}$. Thus,
$V(d) = \ell(\pi r^2 - r^2\cos^{-1}(\frac{d-r}{r}) + (d-r)\sqrt{2dr - d^2})$ as desired.
Case (2): The area of the region AECBA is $\pi r^2 - 2$(area of sector ODC) – area of $\triangle OAC$. However, now $BO = (r-d)$, so $V(d) = \pi r^2 - \theta r^2 + (d-r)\sqrt{2dr - d^2}$. For $d < r$, $\frac{\pi}{2} < \theta \leq \pi$ and
$\cos\theta = \cos(\pi - m\angle BOC) = -\cos(m\angle BOC) = -\frac{BO}{r} = \frac{d-r}{r}$. Thus, again,
$V(d) = \ell(\pi r^2 - r^2\cos^{-1}(\frac{d-r}{r}) + (d-r)\sqrt{2dr - d^2})$.

2. a. A is the set of all circles C in the plane. B is the set of all triangles T in the plane. The relationship stated is not a function f: $A \to B$ because any three points on a given circle will determine an inscribed triangle. A given circle C does not determine a unique triangle T.

    b. A is the set of all triangles T in the plane. B is the set of all circles C in the plane. The relationship stated is a function f: $A \to B$. The vertices of a given triangle T are the three points that determine a unique circumscribed circle C.

c.   A is the set of all triangles in the plane. B is the set of all nonnegative real numbers. The relationship stated describes a function f: $A \to B$, since a given triangle contains a constant area α.

d.   A is the set of all ellipses E in the plane. B is the set of all pairs of points $\{p, q\}$ in the plane. The relationship stated describes a function f: $A \to B$, since a given ellipse has constant major and minor axes and a fixed center – these values determine the location of the foci.

3. a.   Samples: $y = 2x^3 - 4x^2 + 7$, $f(\theta) = \tan(\theta)$, f: $t \to -3t + 7$

b.   With the domain limited to integers, functions like $y = |x| + 2$ or f: $x \to x^2 + 2$ will work.

c.   Samples: $y = x^2 + k$, $g(x) = |x| + k$

d.   Sample: $y = (\frac{a-b}{2})\sin x + (\frac{a+b}{2})$

e.   Sample: $y = \frac{1}{\sqrt{x-2}} + 1$

4. a.   The empty set $\emptyset$ is the only function from an empty set A to a set B. Notice that the empty set satisfies the definition of a function. It is a subset of $\emptyset \times B = \emptyset$ and it is vacuously true that every $a \in A = \emptyset$ appears once and only once as the first element of an ordered pair in $\emptyset$.

b.   If B is the empty set and A is a nonempty set, then there are no subsets of $A \times \emptyset = \emptyset$ such that every $a \in A$ appears once and only once as the first element of an ordered pair.

5. a.   Every one of the x elements in A can be matched with y possible elements in B. Therefore, there are y^x possible functions.

b.   The answer to part a fails only if sets A and B are both empty. Notice that if $x = 0$ (i.e., A is the empty set) and $y > 0$ (B is nonempty), then there is still one function from A to B, namely, the empty set.

6.   A = set of all pairs of points $\{(x_1, y_1), (x_2, y_2)\}$ in $\mathbf{R}^2$. (Or, A = the set $\mathbf{R}^2 \times \mathbf{R}^2$.)
B = the set of real numbers d: $d \geq 0$
Thus, the formula for distance between (x_1, y_1) and (x_2, y_2) can be written d: $\{(x_1, y_1), (x_2, y_2)\} \to \sqrt{(x_1 - x_2)^2 + (y_1 - y_2)^2}$.

7. a.   {(A, 2), (B, 2), (C, 2), (D, 3), (E ,3), (F, 3), (G, 4), (H, 4), (I, 4), (J, 5), (K, 5), (L, 5), (M, 6), (N, 6), (O, 6), (P, 7), (R, 7), (S, 7), (T, 8), (U, 8), (V, 8), (W, 9), (X, 9), (Y, 9)}

b.   This correspondence is a function, because each element of the domain (i.e., each letter of the alphabet other than Q and Z) appears as the first element in no more than one ordered pair. In other words, a letter used as an input will always yield the same output.

8.

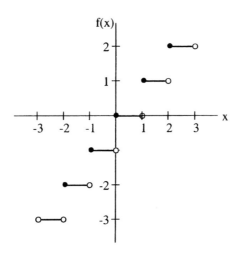

Depending on the grapher used, the calculator plot would not show clearly that the left endpoints on the steps are inclusive and the right endpoints are exclusive. Some graphing calculators attach each right endpoint to the left endpoint above it, resulting in a graph that appears to have vertical segments or asymptote-like features.

9.   a.   Since m > 1, m! must include the factor 2, and m! is always an even positive integer. With m!x as a positive even integer, $\cos(m!\pi x)$ can be written in the form $\cos(2k\pi)$, which is 1 for any integer k. So $(\cos(m!\pi x))^n = 1^n = 1$ when x is an integer.

      b.   We have x, a rational number with denominator q. Assuming $m \geq 2q$, we are guaranteed that m! has a factor of 2, to make m! even, and a separate factor q, making m!x integral. Thus m!x is an even integer and once again $\cos(m!\pi x) = 1$. So $(\cos(m!\pi x))^n = 1^n = 1$.

      c.   If x is irrational, there is no m for which the product m!x is integral, so $\cos(m!\pi x)$ lies somewhere between -1 and 1. Thus $(\cos(m!\pi x))^n$ approaches zero as n increases and $\lim_{n \to \infty}(\cos(m!\pi x))^n = 0$.

      d.   What we have implied is that as $m \to \infty$, an m! will emerge which, when multiplied by any rational number x, will yield an integral product m!x. This will occur when m = 2q (q being the denominator of x), if not at a value of m smaller than 2q. When this integral product m!x is reached, $\cos(m!x\pi)$ will equal 1. An irrational x will never allow m!x to be integral, thus $-1 < \cos(m!x\pi) < 1$ and, when raised to higher and higher powers, this cosine value approaches zero. The order of the limits is important, since taking the m limit first leads to a divergent sequence for irrational x. This formula, then, describes the Dirichlet function, for which any rational input is mapped to the value 1 and any irrational input is mapped to the value 0.

Section 3.1.2

1.   a.   Solving the equation $v(t + h) = wt$ for t yields $t = \frac{v}{w - v}h$. So the catch-up time is related to the delay by an equation of the form $t = kh$, where $k = \frac{v}{w - v}$.

b.   Dividing the numerator and denominator of k by v, the constant of proportionality can be rewritten as $k = \dfrac{1}{\frac{w}{v} - 1}$. If $\alpha = \frac{w}{v}$, then $t = \dfrac{1}{\alpha - 1}h$.

2.   The first derivative of f(w) is $f'(w) = -\dfrac{150}{(w - 50)^2}$. Evaluating this at w = 75 gives

$f'(75) = -\dfrac{150}{(75 - 50)^2} \approx -\dfrac{1}{4}$. Thus at 75 mph, the change in catch-up time is approximately $-\dfrac{1}{4}$ hr for

each 1 mph increase in speed. The second derivative of f(w) is $f''(w) = \dfrac{300}{(w - 50)^3}$. Evaluating this at

w = 75 gives $f''(75) = \dfrac{300}{(75 - 50)^3} \approx \dfrac{1}{50}$. So at or near 75 mph, the value of $-\dfrac{1}{4}$ hr changes by about $\dfrac{1}{50}$ hr

for each 1 mph increase in speed. If the catch-up speed increases from 75 to 80 mph, then the catch-up

time goes from 6 hrs to 5 hrs, an average change of $-\dfrac{1}{5}$ mph for each 1 mph above 75 mph. If the

catch-up speed decreases from 75 to 70 mph, then the catch-up time goes from 6 hrs to 7.5 hrs, an

average change of $\dfrac{3}{10}$ mph for each 1 mph below 75 mph.

3.   a.   Given the catch-up time is given by $t = \dfrac{3}{\frac{w}{50} - 1}$, the catch-up distance is given by

$d = g(w) = wt = \dfrac{3w}{\frac{w}{50} - 1} = \dfrac{3}{\frac{1}{50} - \frac{1}{w}}$.

$50 \le x \le 100,$ x-scale = 10
$0 \le y \le 2000,$ y-scale = 200

b. $d = \dfrac{h}{\frac{1}{v} - \frac{1}{w}}$

4.   One possible way of proceeding is this: Using a dynamic geometry program, construct the graph of Figure 8 as a geometric figure with line A fixed and line B pivoting about the origin. Then ask the program to calculate the distance from the origin to the projection of the intersections of lines A and B onto the x-axis. Finally, ask the program to graph this distance as a function of the slope of line B. The resulting graph will be essentially that of Figure 7.

5.   a.   Let v represent the speed of person A, w the speed of person B, d the distance between them, and t the time it will take to meet. Then vt = d − wt. Solving for t yields $t = \dfrac{d}{v + w}$.

b.   If we assume person A starts at position x = 0, then, since x = vt, the location of the meeting place will be given by $x = \dfrac{dv}{v + w}$.

6.   a.   If the wind speed is 0, the time for the round trip is $\frac{2000}{400} = 5$ h. If there is a wind $w > 0$, the average plane speed is less than 400, since more time is spent at speed $400 - w$ than at speed $400 + w$. Thus the total time is more than 5 hours, and so the round trip time increases with wind speed. As the wind speed approaches 400 km/h, the time for the trip approaches infinity. In summary, the graph increases from $t = 5$ h and has a vertical asymptote at $w = 400$ km/h.

     b.   The time for the outbound leg of the trip is $t_1 = \frac{1000}{400 - w}$. The time for the return trip is $t_2 = \frac{1000}{400 + w}$. So the total time, as a function of w, is $t = t_1 + t_2 = f(w)$ $= \frac{1000}{400 - w} + \frac{1000}{400 + w} = \frac{800000}{160000 - w^2}$. For $t = f(50) = \frac{800000}{160000 - 50^2} \approx 5.08$ h. With no wind, the total trip time is $f(0) = \frac{800000}{160000} = 5$ h. This supports the conclusion that a wind will prolong the trip.

     c.   Let d be the distance of the one-way trip, and w and v be the speeds of the plane and wind, respectively. If t_1 is the one-way trip time with the wind and t_2 the one-way trip time against the wind, then $t_1 = \frac{d}{v - w}$ and $t_2 = \frac{d}{v + w}$. So the total trip time $t = t_1 + t_2 = \frac{d}{v + w} + \frac{d}{v - w} = \frac{2dv}{v^2 - w^2}$

     d.   With a zero wind speed, the total trip time would be $t_0 = \frac{2d}{v}$. With a nonzero wind speed, the total trip time can be expressed as $t = \frac{\frac{2d}{v}}{1 - \frac{w^2}{v^2}}$, or $t = \frac{t_0}{1 - \frac{w^2}{v^2}}$. This equation also appears in Einstein's theory of special relativity as the Lorenz transformation of the time coordinate. In relativity theory, if t_0 is the time as measured in a reference frame moving with a speed w, then the time as measured in a stationary reference frame is given by the equation $t = \frac{t_0}{1 - \frac{w^2}{v^2}}$, where $v = c$, the speed of light in a vacuum. This equation reveals the phenomenon known as time dilation in special relativity.

     e. $g(w) = \frac{1000}{400 - w}$ and $h(w) = \frac{1000}{400 + w}$. $f(w) = g(w) + h(w)$

     f.   Letting $r = \frac{w^2}{v^2}$, the total time for the round trip flight is given by $t = \frac{1}{1 - r^2}t_0$, where t_0 is the round trip time with a zero wind speed. For this equation to apply to the physical situation, r must be in the range $0 \leq r < 1$. That is, the wind speed must be less than the plane speed, or else the plane will never reach its destination on the outbound leg of the trip (the plane is being blown backwards). Since $0 \leq r < 1$, $\frac{1}{1 - r^2} > 1$. So $t \geq t_0$.

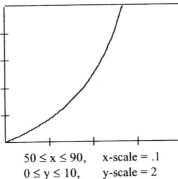

$0 \le x \le 1,$ x-scale = .2
$0 \le y \le 10,$ y-scale = 2

7. a. $5(\frac{50}{100}) + \frac{90}{100}y = (5 + y)(\frac{80}{100}) \Rightarrow 2.5 + \frac{90}{100}y = 4 + \frac{80}{100}y \Rightarrow .1y = 1.5 \Rightarrow y = 15$ oz.

    b. $5(\frac{50}{100}) + \frac{90}{100}y = (5 + y)(\frac{x}{100}) \Rightarrow 2.5 + \frac{90}{100}y = 5\frac{x}{100} + \frac{x}{100}y \Rightarrow y(\frac{90}{100} - \frac{x}{100}) = 5\frac{x}{100} - 2.5$

    $\Rightarrow y = \frac{5x - 250}{90 - x}.$

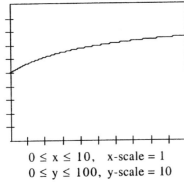

$50 \le x \le 90,$ x-scale = .1
$0 \le y \le 10,$ y-scale = 2

(The graph is the part of a hyperbola with asymptotes x = 90 and y = -5 that is above the x-axis.)
In order to get a solution that is x% alcohol, you need to add y ounces of 90% solution to the
initial 5 ounces of 50% solution. The closer x is to 90, the more solution you need.

    c.   Solving the equation in part **b** for x yields $x = \frac{250 + 90y}{5 + y}.$

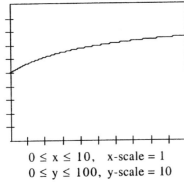

$0 \le x \le 10,$ x-scale = 1
$0 \le y \le 100,$ y-scale = 10

(The graph is still part of a hyperbola with asymptotes x = 90 and y = -5.)
As more and more of the 90% solution is added to the initial 5 ounces of 50% solution, the
resulting solution asymptotically approaches 90% alcohol.

d. Replacing 90% by A in part **a** and solving for y yields $y = \dfrac{150}{A - 80}$.

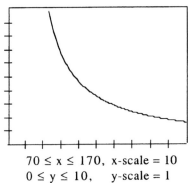

$70 \leq x \leq 170$, x-scale = 10
$0 \leq y \leq 10$, y-scale = 1

(The graph is the part of a hyperbola with asymptotes A = 90 and y = 0.)
This graph shows that as the strength of the solution that is being added to the 5 ounces of 50% solution increases, the amount that you need to add to get an 80% solution decreases, until only 7.5 ounces of the maximum strength 100% alcohol is needed. As the strength of the added solution decreases towards 80%, the amount that you have to add increases without bound. Thus $.8 < A \leq 1$.

e. Replacing 5 by G in part **a** and solving for y yields y = 3G.
This graph shows that there is a linear relationship between the amount of the original solution and the amount of 90% solution that has to be added to produce an 80% solution. That is, as the amount of 50% solution changes, the amount of 90% solution needed also changes, but the ratio of 90% solution to 50% solution in the final solution remains constant at 3:1.

Section 3.1.3

1.

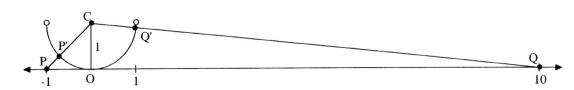

a. Since $\tan(\angle PCO) = -1$, $f(-1) = \angle PCO = -\dfrac{\pi}{4}$. Since $\tan(\angle QCO) = 10$, $f(10) \approx 1.471$.

b. In general, $\tan(\angle PCO) = \dfrac{x}{1}$, so $\angle PCO = f(x) = \tan^{-1}(x)$.

c. The function $f(x) = \tan^{-1}(x)$ is continuous over its entire domain.

2. a. By changing the function in Problem 1 to $f(x) = \dfrac{b-a}{\pi}\tan^{-1}(x) + \dfrac{b+a}{2}$, a 1-1 correspondence can be created between **R** and any open interval (a, b). Thus any interval (a, b) has the same cardinality as **R**.

b. Let $x \in (a, b)$ and $y \in (c, d)$, then a 1-1 correspondence between these two intervals can be given by $y = \dfrac{d-c}{b-a}x + c - \dfrac{d-c}{b-a}a$.

3.   Given $x_1 \neq x_2$, x_1, $x_2 \in A$. Suppose $f(x_1) = f(x_2)$. Then $g(f(x_1)) = g(f(x_2))$ and $I_A(x_1) = I_A(x_2)$, so $x_1 = x_2$. This contradicts our given premise $x_1 \neq x_2$. Since $x_1 \neq x_2$ implies $f(x_1) \neq f(x_2)$, f is one-to-one. To show $g = f^{-1}$, we must show that $g(y) = x$ when $f(x) = y$. Given $f(x) = y$, we have $g(f(x)) = g(y)$ and $I_A(x) = g(y)$, so $x = g(y)$. Thus for every point $(x, y) \in f$, $(y, x) \in g$ and $g = f^{-1}$ by definition.

4.   a.   An even integer will contain a factor of 2, and the square of an even integer will contain not one, but two factors of 2. Therefore, the square of an even integer will also be even, and an integer (since integers are closed under multiplication). Thus the set **E** is closed under the operation of squaring.

      b.   An odd integer contains no factor of 2, and the square of an odd integer will not contain any factors of 2 either. Therefore, the square of an odd integer will also be odd, and an integer (since integers are closed under multiplication). Thus the set **O** is closed under the operation of squaring.

      c.   A prime integer has factors of only 1 and itself, but the square of a prime number p will have the factors 1, p, and p^2. Thus, the square of a prime integer is not prime, and the set **P** is not closed under the operation of squaring.

      d.   A composite integer is made up of prime factors multiplied together. The square of a composite integer would contain each of these prime factors twice, resulting in another composite integer. Thus the set **C** is closed under the operation of squaring.

5.   a.   If x and y are limited to the set of positive integers, we can say that the greatest common divisor function $\gcd\{x, y\}$ is a binary operation which maps $\mathbf{Z}^+ \times \mathbf{Z}^+ \to \mathbf{Z}^+$.

      b.   Given x and y from the set of real numbers, we can say that the function $\max\{x, y\}$ is a binary operation which maps $\mathbf{R} \times \mathbf{R} \to \mathbf{R}$.

6.   Let the operations of multiplication by k and division by k be expressed $M(x) = kx$ and $D(x) = \frac{x}{k}$, for all $x \in \mathbf{R}$ and $k \in \mathbf{R} - \{0\}$. Then $M \circ D(x) = k(\frac{x}{k}) = \frac{kx}{k} = x$, so $M \circ D(x) = I(x)$, the identity function, and $D \circ M(x) = (\frac{kx}{k}) = \frac{kx}{k} = x$, so $D \circ M(x) = I(x)$, the identity function. Thus, the operations of multiplication and division by k are inverse operations.

7.   Let $r(a) = \frac{1}{a}$ and $s(a) = a^2$. Then, $(r \circ s)(a) = (s \circ r)(a) = \frac{1}{a^2}$. Thus, the operations r and s commute. That is, the order of composition doesn't affect the outcome. Let $n(a) = -a$. Then, $(n \circ s)(a) = -(a^2) = -a^2$ and $(s \circ n)(a) = (-a)^2 = a^2$. Since these are not equal for $a \neq 0$, we know that $(n \circ s)(a) \neq (s \circ n)(a)$ and the operations n and s do not commute.

8.   a.   P is commutative, since $P(x, y) = 2x + 2y = P(y, x) = 2y + 2x$.

      b. $(x\,P\,y)\,P\,z = 2(2x + 2y) + 2z = 4x + 4y + 2z$
            $x\,P\,(y\,P\,z) = 2x + 2(2y + 2z) = 2x + 4y + 4z$
            So, in general, $(x\,P\,y)\,P\,z \neq x\,P\,(y\,P\,z)$. Therefore, P is not associative.

      c.   P can be used to calculate the perimeter of a parallelogram with length x and width y. The commutativity property of P is equivalent to the property that the perimeter of a parallelogram does not change when the length and width are interchanged.

9.   a.   A is commutative since multiplication is commutative.

        b.   A is associative since multiplication is associative.

        c.   A can be used to calculate the area of a rectangle with length x and width y. The commutativity property of A is equivalent to the property that the area of a rectangle does not change when the length and width are interchanged.

10.   a.   There are n^2 possible argument combinations for a given binary operation on $S \times S$. For each of these combinations, there are n possible results. Thus there are $n^{(n^2)}$ possible binary operations on $S \times S$.

        b.   For a commutative binary operation, interchanging the arguments produces the same result. Thus there are only $C(n, 2) + n = \frac{n^2}{2} + \frac{n}{2}$ independent argument combinations. For each of these, there are n possible results. Thus there are $n^{\frac{(n^2 + n)}{2}}$ possible commutative binary operations on $S \times S$.

11.   a.   We can say that $P(n, r) = P(r, n)$ in the trivial case where $n = r$, but in cases where $n > r$, $P(n, r)$ is defined but $P(r, n)$ is not, since factorial is not defined for negative arguments. Thus, P is not commutative in all meaningful cases.

        b. $P(n, r)$ is defined as $\frac{n!}{(n - r)!}$, which can also be written $n(n - 1)(n - 2)(n - 3) \bullet ... \bullet (n - r + 1)$. This is the product of natural numbers, so it will also be a natural number, since the operation of multiplication is closed under the set $\mathbf{N}$. So P is closed on $\mathbf{N}$.

12.   a.   We can say that $C(n, r) = C(r, n)$ in the trivial case where $n = r$, but in cases where $n > r$, $C(n, r)$ is defined but $C(r, n)$ is not, since factorial is not defined for negative arguments. Thus, C is not commutative in all meaningful cases.

        b.   For $n \geq r$, C must be closed on $\mathbf{N}$ because the number of combinations of n objects taken r at a time must be a natural number.

13.   a.   If we only allow $x, y \in \mathbf{R}^+$, we are looking at a positive real number raised to a positive exponent. The result of this operation can only be a positive real number, thus exponentiation is a binary operation on $\mathbf{R}^+$.

        b.   p is not a binary operation on $\mathbf{R} \times \mathbf{R}$ because it is possible to raise a real-number base to a real-number exponent, with a nonreal result. Two examples: $p(0, -2)$ (which is undefined because of division by zero) and $p(-4, \frac{1}{2})$ (which is imaginary, the square root of a negative number).

        c.   Most calculators will return a result of -2 for $p(-8, \frac{1}{3})$. For $p(-8, \frac{2}{6})$, most calculators will reduce $\frac{2}{6}$ to $\frac{1}{3}$ and give a result of -2. However, some calculators calculate $x^{\frac{m}{n}}$ to be $\sqrt[n]{x^m}$ and then the result will be 2.

        d.   The answer to part **c** is an example of what might happen if a binary function is not well defined. If, for example, $p(x, y)$ is defined as $\sqrt[n]{x^m}$ when $y = \frac{m}{n}$, it is really a ternary operation masquerading as a binary one.

14.   a.   Both X and P have five elements, which means that the subsets can be counted: there will be $_5C_1$ subsets with one element, $_5C_2$ subsets with two elements, and so on. The total number of subsets,

in each case, will be: $_5C_0 + {}_5C_1 + {}_5C_2 + {}_5C_3 + {}_5C_4 + {}_5C_5 = 1 + 5 + 10 + 10 + 5 + 1 = 32$

b. Define the function $f : P(X) \to D(2310)$ by:

$f(\{\}) = 1; f(\{a\}) = 2; f(\{b\}) = 3; f(\{c\}) = 5; f(\{d\}) = 7; f(\{e\}) = 11$ and for any set $C \subseteq P(X)$, $f(C)$ is given by $\prod_{x_i \in C} f(\{x_i\})$. For example, if $C = \{a, b, e\}$, then

$f(C) = f(\{a\}) \cdot f(\{b\}) \cdot f(\{e\}) = 66$.

We need to show that f is 1-1 and onto. Let A and B be two subsets of X such that $A \neq B$. Since $A \neq B$, there exists at least one element x such that $x \in A$ and $x \notin B$ or element $y \in B$ and $y \notin A$. Without loss of generality, assume $x \in A$ and $x \notin B$. So $f(\{x\})$ is a factor of $f(A) = \prod_{x_i \in A} f(\{x_i\})$,

but $f(\{x\})$ is not a factor of $f(B) = \prod_{y_j \in B} f(\{y_j\})$, since $f(\{y_j\})$ is prime for all j, $f(\{x\})$ is prime, and

$f(\{x\})$ is not among the $f(\{y_j\})$. So $f(A) \neq f(B)$ and f is 1-1.

To show that f is onto, let $n \in D(2310)$. Then n is some product of the numbers 1, 2, 3, 5, 7, or 11, with each number other than 1 taken at most once. Let C be the subset of P(X) containing the elements x_i such that $f(\{x_i\})$ equals some number in the prime factorization of n. Then $f(C) = n$ and f is onto.

The function f has the property that $f(A \cup B) = \text{lcm}(f(A), f(B))$:

$\text{lcm}(f(A), f(B)) = \text{lcm}(\prod_{x_i \in A} f(\{x_i\}), \prod_{y_j \in A} f(\{y_j\}))$.

Because the $f(\{x_i\})$ and $f(\{y_j\})$ are all prime,

$\text{lcm}(\prod_{x_i \in A} f(\{x_i\}), \prod_{y_j \in A} f(\{y_j\})) = \prod_{z_k \in (A \cup B)} f(\{z_k\}) = f(A \cup B)$.

The function f has the property that $f(A \cap B) = \gcd(f(A), f(B))$:

$\gcd(f(A), f(B)) = \gcd(\prod_{x_i \in A} f(\{x_i\}), \prod_{y_j \in A} f(\{y_j\}))$.

Because the $f(\{x_i\})$ and $f(\{y_j\})$ are all prime,

$\gcd(\prod_{x_i \in A} f(\{x_i\}), \prod_{y_j \in B} f(\{y_j\})) = \prod_{z_k \in (A \cap B)} f(\{z_k\}) = f(A \cap B)$.

15. a. We can show that $\times$ is a binary operation on S_4 by demonstrating that S_4 is closed under $\times$:

In each case, the product of two elements of S_4 is itself an element of S_4. Thus, the set is closed under the operation $\times$.

A set together with an operation must satisfy four criteria in order to be a group:

1. S_4 must be closed under the operation $\times$ — we showed closure above.

2. The elements of S_4 must follow associative laws. We know that multiplication of complex numbers is associative generally, so it is also associative for the elements of our set.

3. There must exist an identity element e, such that $e \times a = a \times e = a$ for all $a \in S_4$. We see from our multiplications above that 1 serves this purpose. Thus, an identity element exists.

4. Each element $a \in S_4$ must have an inverse element $b \in S_4$, such that $a \times b = b \times a = 1$. Examining our multiplications above, we see that 1 is its own inverse, -1 is its own inverse, and i and $-i$ are inverses for each other. Thus, for each element, an inverse exists.

Since $\langle S_4, \times \rangle$ satisfies these four criteria, it is a group.

b. Let the function h: $\mathbf{Z} \to S_4$ be defined by $h(n) = i^n$ for each $n \in \mathbf{Z}$. h is onto since $1 = h(0)$, $i = h(1)$, $-1 = h(2)$, and $-i = h(3)$. For $n \geq 4$, $h(n) = h(n \bmod(4))$. Since $\mathbf{Z}$ is closed under addition, for a, $b \in \mathbf{Z}$, $a + b \in \mathbf{Z}$ and $h(a + b) = i^{a+b} = i^a \times i^b = h(a) \times h(b)$. Also, $h(-n) = i^{-n} = (h(n))^{-1}$, since $i^{-n} \times i^n = 1$.

Section 3.2.1

1. a. not a real function (domain is not a subset of **R**)
    b. not a real function (fails vertical line test)
    c. not a real function (domain and range not subsets of **R**)
    d. real function
    e. real function
    f. real function

2. a. Changing to $m < 0$ calls for the following adjustments in the analysis:
      6. f(x) is decreasing on the entire domain.
      7. $f(x) \to -\infty$ as $x \to \infty$ and $f(x) \to \infty$ as $x \to -\infty$.

    b. Changing to $m = 0$ calls for the following adjustments in the analysis:
      3. The range of f(x) is $\{b\}$.
      4. There are no zeros unless $b = 0$, in which case every point (x, f(x)) is a solution to $f(x) = 0$.
      5. For a constant function, every point is a relative maximum and a relative minimum.
      6. f is neither increasing nor decreasing, since it is constant on the entire domain.
      7. $f(x) \to b$ as $x \to \pm\infty$.
      8. f is still continuous and differentiable, with $f' = m = 0$. But $\int f(x)dx = bx + C$.
      9. The graph of f is a horizontal line, which is reflection-symmetric to itself and to every vertical line.
      10. f is a model for constant value. It does not have the same applications as other linear models, since $f(x) = b$ cannot represent variability in f.

3. a. There are singularities at every $x = \frac{\pi}{2} + k\pi$, with k an integer. These singularities are essential.

    b. There is a singularity at $t = 1$. It is removable; g(t) is defined and continuous for all $t \in \mathbf{R}$ if $g(1) = 2$.

    c. There are singularities at $a = 2$ and $a = -\frac{4}{3}$. These singularities are essential.

    d. j(y) is continuous over the set of real numbers with no singularities.

4.   Let g be this function.
   1.   The domain of g is **R**.
   2.   g has no singularities.
   3.   The range of g is $[-\frac{b^2}{4a}, \infty)$.
   4.   g has zeros at $x = 0$ and $x = -\frac{b}{a}$.
   5.   g has one minimum at $(-\frac{b}{2a}, -\frac{b^2}{4a})$
   6.   g(x) is decreasing for $x < -\frac{b}{2a}$ and increasing for $x > -\frac{b}{2a}$.
   7. $g(x) \to \infty$ as $x \to \pm\infty$.
   8.   g is continuous and differentiable with g'(x) = 2ax + b and $\int g(x)dx = \frac{a}{3}x^3 + \frac{b}{2}x^2 + C$. Its power series is g(x) itself.
   9.   The graph of g is a parabola opening upwards; g is not periodic; the graph of g is symmetrical with respect to the vertical line $x = -\frac{b}{a}$.
   10. Quadratic functions can model objects moving under a constant nonzero acceleration, such as those subject to a constant gravitational force. (When such a model is graphed, using time and height or distance as variables, the resulting parabola can be misleading for students, as it appears to be a picture of vertical and horizontal displacement.)

5.   Let E be this function.
   1.   The domain of E is **R**.
   2.   E has no singularities or vertical asymptotes.
   3.   The range of E is **R**$^+$.
   4.   E has no x-axis intercepts.
   5.   E has no maximum value. It approaches a minimum value y = 0.
   6.   E is everywhere increasing.
   7. $E(x) \to \infty$ as $x \to \infty$, and $E(x) \to 0$ as $x \to -\infty$.
   8.   E is continuous and differentiable with derivative $y' = 5000(\ln 1.06)1.06^x$. The antiderivative of y is $\int y dx = \frac{5000}{\ln 1.06}1.06^x$. The power series for $e^x = 1 + x + \frac{x^2}{2!} + \frac{x^3}{3!} + ...$, and $1.06^x = e^{x \ln 1.06}$. Thus the power series for this function is $5000(1 + x \ln 1.06 + \frac{(x \ln 1.06)^2}{2!} + \frac{(x \ln 1.06)^3}{3!} + ...)$.
   9.   The function E represents exponential, or geometric, growth. As x increases by a constant difference, E(x) increases by a constant factor. The graph of E is not periodic or symmetrical.
   10. The function $E(x) = 5000(1.06^x)$ represents exponential growth of 6% per unit x, with initial condition E(0) = 5000. For instance, it could model an initial investment of $5000 accruing simple interest at a rate of 6% per year. Another example is a model of 6% yearly growth in a town of 5000 people.

6.   1.   The domain is **R**.
   2.   Singularities and vertical asymptotes: none
   3.   The range is **R**.
   4.   f has zeros at $x = \frac{5}{4}$ and $x = 0$.

5. There are no global maxima or minima, but f has a relative minimum at (0, 0).
6. f is everywhere increasing.
7. End behavior: as x → ∞, f(x) → ∞ and as x → - ∞, f(x) → - ∞.
8. This function is continuous and differentiable everywhere except at x = 0. The derivatives can be defined piecewise: $f'(x) = \begin{cases} 2x, & x \geq 0 \\ 4, & x < 0 \end{cases}$. An antiderivative formula can be defined piecewise as well, with $\int f(x)\,dx = \begin{cases} \frac{1}{3}x^3 + C, & x \geq 0 \\ 2x^2 + 5x + C', & x < 0 \end{cases}$. These antiderivative formulas can be used to calculate definite integrals if the upper and lower parameters are both negative or both positive. Definite integrals which have one positive and one negative parameter must be broken up into two integrals at x = 0, since the two parts of the integrals have different antiderivatives. f(x) is polynomial in both parts, so its power series would be f(x) itself.
9. f is not symmetrical or periodic.
10. The function f could model the kinematics of an object that is subject to no force before time 0, and then is subject to a nonzero constant force after time 0.

7.
1. Domain: the set of all nonzero real numbers.
2. Singularities: f has an essential singularity at x = 0.
3. Range: {1, −1}
4. f has no x intercepts.
5. The maximum value of f(x) is 1, and occurs at all positive x. The minimum value of f(x) is –1, and occurs at all negative x.
6. f(x) is constant everywhere over its domain.
7. End behavior: as x → ∞, f(x) → 1 and as x → - ∞, f(x) → -1.
8. f is continuous everywhere except at x = 0. It is not differentiable at x = 0, but everywhere else, f '(x) = 0. An antiderivative formula can be defined piecewise as well, with $\int f(x)\,dx = \begin{cases} x + C, & x > 0 \\ -x + C', & x < 0 \end{cases}$. These antiderivative formulas can be used to calculate definite integrals if the upper and lower parameters are both negative or both positive. Definite integrals which have one positive and one negative parameter must be broken up into two integrals at x = 0, since the two parts of the integrals have different antiderivatives. f(x) is polynomial in both parts, so its power series would be f(x) itself, but restricted to the domains either x < 0 or x > 0.
9. f is symmetric with respect to the point (0, 0). It is not periodic.
10. f could be used to model situations that are binary in nature.

8. Let this function be g.
1. The domain of g is **R**.
2. There are no singularities or asymptotes - the function is defined everywhere on **R**.
3. The range of g is **R**.
4. There are zeros at every $t = \frac{1}{2}\tan^{-1}(\frac{4}{3}) + k\pi, k \in \mathbf{I}$.
5. Relative minima occur at every $t = \frac{1}{2}\tan^{-1}(-\frac{52}{61}) + k\pi$, when k is an even integer. Relative maxima occur at every $t = \frac{1}{2}\tan^{-1}(-\frac{52}{61}) + k\pi$, when k is an odd integer.

6. The function g is increasing on every interval $(\frac{1}{2}\tan^{-1}(-\frac{52}{61}) + k\pi, \frac{1}{2}\tan^{-1}(-\frac{52}{61}) + (k+1)\pi)$, with k an even integer. When k is an odd integer, the same interval describes areas where the function is decreasing. (Basically, the function is increasing on every interval where the left endpoint is a minimum and the right endpoint is the next maximum, and vice versa for decreasing intervals.)

7. The function $g \to 0$ as $t \to \infty$. As $t \to -\infty$, y oscillates with increasing magnitude.

8. g is continuous and differentiable, with $y' = e^{-0.125t}(6.5\cos(2t) + 7.625\sin(2t))$ and $\int y\,dt = \frac{-8}{257}e^{-.125t}(44\cos(2t) + 67\sin(2t)) + C$. The power series expansion is given by
$$a_0 + a_1 t + \frac{a_2 t^2}{2!} + \frac{a_3 t^3}{3!} + \ldots + \frac{a_n t^n}{n!} + \ldots, \text{ where } a_n \text{ is given by}$$
$$\begin{bmatrix} a_n \\ b_n \end{bmatrix} = \begin{bmatrix} -k & C \\ -C & -k \end{bmatrix}^n \begin{bmatrix} A \\ B \end{bmatrix} = \begin{bmatrix} -.125 & 2 \\ -2 & -.125 \end{bmatrix}^n \begin{bmatrix} -4 \\ 3 \end{bmatrix}.$$

9. g is not periodic, although it has zeros, maxima, and minima at regular intervals. It is not symmetrical. This function has two components: the trigonometric wave $-4\cos(2t) + 3\sin(2t)$ and the damping factor $e^{-0.125t}$. It oscillates over the t-axis, finally converging to the t-axis as t increases.

10. This formula is a model for a damped periodic function. Some examples could be: a sound wave with decreasing amplitude, resulting in decreasing volume of sound, or the height of ripples in water moving outward from a source of turbulence.

9. The sequence $\{g_n\}$ is equivalent to the function with rule $g(n) = 3(0.5^n)$, where $n \in \{0, 1, 2, 3, \ldots\}$.
   1. The domain is the set of nonnegative integers.
   2. $\{g_n\}$ asymptotically approaches the line $g = 0$ from above.
   3. The range is the infinite set $\{1, 1.5, 0.75, \ldots, 3(0.5^n), \ldots\}$.
   4. The sequence has no zeros.
   5. The sequence has a maximum of 1. It has no minimum value, but it has a greatest lower bound of 0.
   6. The sequence is decreasing on the entire domain.
   7. $g_n \to 0$ as $n \to \infty$.
   8. g is discontinuous and nondifferentiable.
   9. The graph of g is exponentially decreasing.
   10. g is a geometric sequence. It can model situations of exponential decay, where g_n represents the quantity of a substance that remains after n half-lives.

10. The sequence $\{a_n\}$ is equivalent to the function $a(n) = 4n + 3$, where $n \in \{0, 1, 2, 3, \ldots\}$.
    1. The domain is the set of nonnegative integers.
    2. $\{a_n\}$ asymptotically approaches the line $g = 0$ from above.
    3. The range is the infinite set $\{3, 7, 11, \ldots, 4n + 3, \ldots\}$.
    4. The sequence has no zeros.
    5. The sequence has no minimum of 3 and no maximum value.
    6. The sequence is increasing on the entire domain.
    7. $a_n \to \infty$ as $n \to \infty$.
    8. a is discontinuous and nondifferentiable.

9. The graph of a is increasing.

10. a is an arithmetic sequence. It can model situations in which there is a constant increase at regular intervals.

11. The sequence $\{s_n\}$ is equivalent to the function $s(n) = 2^n + 9$, where $n \in \{0, 1, 2, 3, \ldots\}$.

    1. The domain is the set of nonnegative integers.

    2. $\{s_n\}$ has no asymptotes.

    3. The range is the infinite set $\{10, 11, 13, \ldots, 2^n + 9, \ldots\}$.

    4. The sequence has no zeros.

    5. The sequence has a minimum of 10 and no maximum value.

    6. The sequence is increasing on the entire domain.

    7. $s_n \to \infty$ as $n \to \infty$.

    8. s is discontinuous and nondifferentiable.

    9. The graph of s is exponentially increasing.

12. a. Subtracting P_n from both sides of the recurrence relation $P_{n+1} = 1.15 P_n - \dfrac{0.15}{20000} P_n^2$ gives

$P_{n+1} - P_n = 0.15 P_n - \dfrac{0.15}{20000} P_n^2$. Factoring out $0.15 P_n$ yields $P_{n+1} - P_n = 0.15 P_n (1 - \dfrac{P_n}{20000})$.

    b. The population can be given explicitly by $P_n = 2500(1.15^n)$. After 25 years, there will be about 82,000 animals. After 50 years, there will be about 2,700,000 animals.

    c. For values of $P_n \ll 20{,}000$, the quantity $1 - \dfrac{P_n}{20000} \approx 1$, so $P_{n+1} - P_n \approx 0.15 P_n$. As P_n approaches 20,000, the quantity $1 - \dfrac{P_n}{20000}$ approaches 0, so $P_{n+1} - P_n \approx 0$. In other words, the population will not be able to exceed 20,000 animals.

13. a. $x^2 = \dfrac{5 + \sqrt{5}}{8}$ and $x^4 = \dfrac{15 + 5\sqrt{5}}{32}$. $16x^4 - 20x^2 + 5 = \dfrac{15 + 5\sqrt{5}}{2} - \dfrac{25 + 5\sqrt{5}}{2} + 5 = 0$.

    b. If $r = \dfrac{m}{k}$ is a rational root of $16x^4 - 20x^2 + 5$, then, by the Rational Root Test, m is a factor of 5 and k is a factor of 16. Thus the possible values for r are $\dfrac{5}{16}, -\dfrac{5}{16}, \dfrac{1}{16}, -\dfrac{1}{16}, \dfrac{5}{8}, -\dfrac{5}{8}, \dfrac{1}{8}, -\dfrac{1}{8}, \dfrac{5}{4}, -\dfrac{5}{4}, \dfrac{1}{4}, -\dfrac{1}{4}, \dfrac{5}{2}, -\dfrac{5}{2}, \dfrac{1}{2}, -\dfrac{1}{2}, 5, -5, 1,$ or -1.

    c. $x = \sqrt{\dfrac{5 + \sqrt{5}}{8}} \approx 0.951$. Since none of the possible rational roots listed in part **b** has a decimal equivalent equal to x, and x is a root of the polynomial, x must be irrational.

    d. Assume $a + \sqrt{b} = \sqrt{\dfrac{5 + \sqrt{5}}{8}}$, where a and b are rational. If $b = 0$, then $a = \sqrt{\dfrac{5 + \sqrt{5}}{8}}$, which was shown to be irrational in parts **a-c**. If $a = 0$, then $b = \dfrac{5 + \sqrt{5}}{8}$, which, by Theorems 2.2 and 2.3, is irrational. So $a \neq 0$ and $b \neq 0$.

$a + \sqrt{b} = \sqrt{\dfrac{5 + \sqrt{5}}{8}} \Rightarrow (a + \sqrt{b})^2 = a^2 + b + 2a\sqrt{b} = \dfrac{5 + \sqrt{5}}{8}$

$\Rightarrow a^2 + b - \dfrac{5}{8} = \dfrac{\sqrt{5}}{8} - 2a\sqrt{b}$

$$\Rightarrow (a^2 + b - \tfrac{5}{8})^2 = (\tfrac{\sqrt{5}}{8} - 2a\sqrt{b})^2 = \tfrac{5}{64} + 4a^2b - \tfrac{a}{2}\sqrt{5b}$$

$$\Rightarrow -2((\tfrac{\sqrt{5}}{8} - 2a\sqrt{b})^2 - (\tfrac{5}{64} + 4a^2b)) = a\sqrt{5b}$$

By Theorem 2.1, the left-hand side of this equation is rational. Since $a \neq 0$ and $b \neq 0$, in order for $a\sqrt{5b}$ to be rational, $b = 5r^2$, for some positive rational number r. Thus $a^2 + b - \tfrac{5}{8} = \tfrac{\sqrt{5}}{8} - 2ar\sqrt{5} = (\tfrac{1}{8} - 2ar)\sqrt{5}$. Since $\sqrt{5}$ is irrational but $a^2 + b - \tfrac{5}{8}$ and $\tfrac{1}{8} - 2ar$ are rational, the only way this equation can hold is if $a^2 + b - \tfrac{5}{8} = 0$ and $\tfrac{1}{8} - 2ar = 0$. This implies $a^2 + b = \tfrac{5}{8}$ and $2a\sqrt{b} = \tfrac{\sqrt{5}}{8}$. Solving these two equations for a yields the quartic polynomial $256a^4 - 160a^2 + 5 = 0$, which has the solutions $a = \pm\sqrt{\dfrac{5 - 2\sqrt{5}}{16}}$ and $a = \pm\sqrt{\dfrac{5 + 2\sqrt{5}}{16}}$. Applying the procedure of parts **a-c**, these solutions can be shown to be irrational, thus contradicting the assumption that a is rational.

Section 3.2.2

1. a. $(f \circ g)(x) = \sin^2 x$. The domain of this function is **R**, and the range is $[0, 1]$.
    b. $(g \circ f)(x) = \sin(x^2)$. The domain of this function is **R**, and the range is $[-1, 1]$.

2. a. $(f \circ g)(x) = \sqrt{x^2 - 7}$. The domain is all real numbers $x \geq \sqrt{7}$ or $x \leq -\sqrt{7}$. The range is the set of nonnegative real numbers.
    b. $(g \circ f)(x) = x - 7$. The domain is all real numbers $x \geq 3$ and the range is all real numbers $y \geq -4$.

3. As x approaches zero from the left, we have:

    $$x \to 0^-$$
    $$-\tfrac{1}{x} \to +\infty$$
    $$e^{-1/x} \to +\infty$$
    $$1 + e^{-1/x} \to +\infty$$
    $$\frac{1}{1 + e^{-1/x}} \to 0^+$$

    As x approaches zero from the right, we have:

    $$x \to 0^+$$
    $$-\tfrac{1}{x} \to -\infty$$
    $$e^{-1/x} \to 0^+$$
    $$1 + e^{-1/x} \to 1^+$$
    $$\frac{1}{1 + e^{-1/x}} \to 1^-$$

4. a. Since f is 1-1, for $x_1, x_2 \in A$, if $x_1 \neq x_2$, then $f(x_1) \neq f(x_2)$. Since g is 1-1, for $y_1, y_2 \in B$, if $y_1 \neq y_2$, then $g(y_1) \neq g(y_2)$. Thus if $x_1 \neq x_2$, $g(f(x_1)) \neq g(f(x_2))$ and $g \circ f$ is 1-1. Since g is onto, for each z

in C, there exists a y in B, such that $g(y) = z$. Since f is onto, for each y in B, there exists an x in A such that $f(x) = y$. Thus for each z in C there exists an x in A such that $g(f(x)) = z$ and $g \circ f$ is onto.

b. If g is not 1-1, there exist y_1 and y_2 in B such that $y_1 \neq y_2$ and $g(y_1) = g(y_2)$. Since f is onto, there exist x_1 and x_2 in A such that $f(x_1) = y_1$ and $f(x_2) = y_2$. So $g(f(x_1)) = g(f(x_2))$ and $g \circ f$ is not 1-1. For all $x \in A$, $f(x) \in B$. Since g is not onto, there exists a z in C such that $g(y) \neq z$ for all y in B. Thus $g(f(x)) \neq z$ for all x in A and $g \circ f$ is not onto.

c. If f is not 1-1, there exist x_1 and x_2 in A such that $x_1 \neq x_2$ and $f(x_1) = f(x_2)$. So $g(f(x_1)) = g(f(x_2))$ and $g \circ f$ is not 1-1. Since g is 1-1 and onto, for every z in C there is a unique y in B such that $g(y) = z$. But since f is not onto, there exists a y in B such that $f(x) \neq y$ for all x in A. Thus there exists a z in C such that $g(f(x)) \neq z$ for all x in A and $g \circ f$ is not onto.

5. Let $a = x^2 - 3$. Then $a - \frac{1}{a} = 0 \Rightarrow a \neq 0$, so $x \neq \pm\sqrt{3}$.

$a - \frac{1}{a} = 0 \Leftrightarrow a = \frac{1}{a} \Leftrightarrow a = \pm 1 \Leftrightarrow a = 1$ or $a = -1$

$\Leftrightarrow x^2 - 3 = 1$ or $x^2 - 3 = -1$

$\Leftrightarrow x^2 = 4$ or $\Leftrightarrow x^2 = 2$

$\Leftrightarrow x = \pm 2$ or $x = \pm\sqrt{2}$

6. a. The following explanation is based on properties of the physical situation described by the function. Given a value d for depth of fuel, there is only one value V for volume that could correspond. Thus V^{-1} is clearly a function, which means that V has an inverse. As an alternate explanation, consider the fact that V must be everywhere increasing on its natural domain (the volume of fuel would never decrease as the depth is increasing!). Since V is monotonic, it must be invertible.

b. There are three significant points on the graph, representing the states when the tank is empty $(0, 0)$, half-full $(r, \frac{1}{2}\pi r^2 \ell)$, and full $(2r, \pi r^2 \ell)$. Before the halfway point, the graph of V(d) is concave up, because each successive cross-section of the tank is larger in area than the last, thus V is growing at an increasing rate. After the halfway point, the opposite relationship occurs, so the graph is concave down. The volume will be increasing most rapidly at the halfway point, and the graph is also symmetrical about this point $(r, \frac{1}{2}\pi r^2 \ell)$.

7. a. The domain of f is $\mathbf{R} - \{\frac{-d}{c}\}$ The range of f is $\mathbf{R} - \{\frac{a}{c}\}$ except in some special cases. If $a = mc$ and $b = md$, then the range of f is $\{m\}$. Also, if $c = 0$, the range of f is $\mathbf{R}$.

b. <u>Part 1: f(x) is one-to-one $\Rightarrow ad - bc \neq 0$</u>

Given that f(x) is one-to-one, we wish to show that $ad - bc \neq 0$.

Instead, assume that $ad - bc = 0$ so $\frac{a}{b} = \frac{c}{d}$.

Thus $f(x) = \frac{ax + b}{cx + d} = \frac{\frac{b}{b}(ax + b)}{\frac{d}{d}(cx + d)} = \frac{b(\frac{a}{b}x + 1)}{d(\frac{c}{d}x + 1)} = \frac{b}{d}$, a constant. Since a constant function is not one-to-one, this contradicts our given premise and disproves that $ad - bc = 0$.

Thus, if f(x) is one-to-one, then $ad - bc \neq 0$.

<u>Part 2: $ad - bc \neq 0 \Rightarrow$ f(x) is one-to-one</u>

Given $ad - bc \neq 0$, assume that f(x) is not one-to-one. Then for some x_1 and x_2, $x_1 \neq x_2$ and $f(x_1) = f(x_2)$. So we have $\dfrac{ax_1 + b}{cx_1 + d} = \dfrac{ax_2 + b}{cx_2 + d}$, which simplifies to $bc(x_2 - x_1) = ad(x_2 - x_1)$. Since $x_1 \neq x_2$, we may divide by $(x_2 - x_1)$, leaving $bc = ad$ and $ad - bc = 0$. This directly contradicts our given premise that $ad - bc \neq 0$, disproving our assumption that f(x) is not one-to-one.

c. $f(x) = y = \dfrac{ax + b}{cx + d}$

$ax + b = cxy + dy$

$ax - cxy = dy - b$

$x(a - cy) = dy - b$

$x = \dfrac{dy - b}{a - cy}$, so $f^{-1}(x) = \dfrac{dx - b}{a - cx}$

d. Given $a = -d$, we have:

$f(x) = \dfrac{ax + b}{cx + d} = \dfrac{-dx + b}{cx + d} = -\dfrac{-dx - b}{cx + d}$ and

$f^{-1}(x) = \dfrac{dx - b}{a - cx} = \dfrac{dx - b}{a - cx} = -\dfrac{dx - b}{cx + d}$, showing algebraically that, given $a = -d$, $f^{-1} = f$.

8. a. i. The sine function is not 1-1 on the interval $\{x: 0 \leq x \leq \pi\}$.

ii. The cosine function is not 1-1 on the interval $\{x: -\frac{\pi}{2} \leq x \leq \frac{\pi}{2}\}$.

iii. The cosine function is not 1-1 on the interval $\{x: -\pi \leq x \leq \pi\}$.

iv. The domain of the inverse tangent function would only include nonnegative real numbers.

b. $\{x: 0 \leq x \leq \pi\}$; Note that the $\cos^{-1}$ function is decreasing on this domain.

c. $\{x: -\frac{\pi}{2} < x < \frac{\pi}{2}\}$

9. a. $\cos^{-1}(\cos(6\pi)) = 0$

b. $\sin(\sin^{-1}(0.5)) = 0.5$

c. $\tan(\cot^{-1}(\sqrt{3})) = \dfrac{\sqrt{3}}{3} \approx 0.5774$

10. a. domain: $\mathbf{R}$, range: $\{y: -\frac{\pi}{2} \leq y \leq \frac{\pi}{2}\}$

b. domain: $\{x: -1 \leq x \leq 1\}$, range: $\{y: -1 \leq y \leq 1\}$, $f(x) = x$

c. domain: $\{x: -1 \leq x \leq 1\}$, range: $\{y: 0 \leq y \leq 1\}$, $f(x) = \sqrt{1 - x^2}$

d. domain: $\{x: -1 < x < 1\}$, range: $\{y: -\infty < y < \infty\}$, $f(x) = \dfrac{x}{\sqrt{1 - x^2}}$

e. domain: $\{x: -1 \leq x < 0 \text{ or } 0 < x \leq 1\}$, range: $\{y: y \leq -1 \text{ or } 1 \leq y\}$, $f(x) = \dfrac{1}{x}$

f. domain: $\{x: x \leq -1 \text{ or } 1 \leq x\}$, range: $\mathbf{R}$, $f(x) = \dfrac{|x|}{x}\sqrt{x^2 - 1}$

11. arcsecant: domain $= (-\infty, -1] \cup [1, \infty)$; range $= [0, \pi] - \{\frac{\pi}{2}\}$

The secant function is limited so that each element in the range is represented exactly once, the acute angles between 0 and $\frac{\pi}{2}$ are included, and the domain corresponds to the restriction of cosine for the arccosine function.

arccosecant: domain = $(-\infty, -1] \cup [1, \infty)$; range = $[-\frac{\pi}{2}, \frac{\pi}{2}] - \{0\}$

The cosecant function is limited so that each element in the range is represented exactly once, the acute angles between 0 and $\frac{\pi}{2}$ are included, and the domain corresponds to the restriction of sine for the arcsine function.

arccotangent: domain = $\mathbf{R}$; range = $[0, \pi]$

The cotangent function is limited so each element of the range is represented exactly once, and the acute angles between 0 and $\frac{\pi}{2}$ are included. The domain restrictions in cotangent do not correspond to the domain restrictions in tangent, presumably to preserve continuity in cotangent and arccotangent.

12. Let $y_1 = \exp_b(x_1)$ and $y_2 = \exp_b(x_2)$. So $x_1 = \log_b(y_1)$ and $x_2 = \log_b(y_2)$.

(2) Product of Powers $\Rightarrow$ Logarithm of a Product

$\exp_b(x_1) \bullet \exp_b(x_2) = \exp_b(x_1 + x_2) \Rightarrow \log_b(\exp_b(x_1) \bullet \exp_b(x_2)) = \log_b(\exp_b(x_1 + x_2))$
$= \log_b(y_1 y_2) = x_1 + x_2 = \log_b(y_1) + \log_b(y_2)$

(3) Quotient of a Power $\Rightarrow$ Logarithm of a Quotient

$\dfrac{\exp_b(x_1)}{\exp_b(x_2)} = \exp_b(x_1 - x_2) \Rightarrow \log_b\left(\dfrac{\exp_b(x_1)}{\exp_b(x_2)}\right) = \log_b(\exp_b(x_1 - x_2)) = \log_b(\dfrac{y_1}{y_2}) = x_1 - x_2$
$= \log_b(y_1) - \log_b(y_2)$

(4) Power of a Power $\Rightarrow$ Logarithm of a Power

$\left(\exp_b(x_1)\right)^{x_2} = \exp_b(x_1 x_2) \Leftrightarrow \log_b\left(\left(\exp_b(x_1)\right)^{x_2}\right) = \log_b(\exp_b(x_1 x_2))$
$= \log_b(y_1^{x_2}) = x_1 x_2 = x_2 \log_b(y_1)$

13. $\log_b(x) + \log_c(x) = \dfrac{\log_x(x)}{\log_x(b)} + \dfrac{\log_x(x)}{\log_x(c)}$ Change of Base Property

$= \dfrac{1}{\log_x(b)} + \dfrac{1}{\log_x(c)}$ $\log_x(x) = 1$; Definition of logarithm

$= \dfrac{\log_x(b) + \log_x(c)}{\log_x(b) \bullet \log_x(c)}$ Addition of fractions

$= \dfrac{\log_x(bc)}{\log_x(b) \bullet \log_x(c)}$ Logarithm of a Product Property

14. If b is even, $f(-x) = (-x)^b = x^b = f(x)$, so f is not 1-1 and hence does not have an inverse over the domain $\mathbf{R}$. If b is odd, $f(-x) = (-x)^b = -(x)^b = -f(x)$. So f is 1-1 and has an inverse over the domain $\mathbf{R}$.

15. a. A function f: $S \to C$ can be defined geometrically as follows: For any point p on the square, draw the ray connecting the origin to p. This ray will intersect the circle's circumference at a unique point q. Likewise, we can describe f^{-1}: $C \to S$ by taking any point q on the circle, drawing the radius with q as its endpoint. This radius will intersect the square at a unique point p.

b. For f: $S \to C$, given the point (a, b) on the square, draw the line segment connecting (a, b) to the origin, intersecting the point (c, d) on the circle. The line segment is a subset of the line $y = \dfrac{b}{a} x$.

This equation can be solved simultaneously with the circle's equation $x^2 + y^2 = 4$. Thus the coordinates of the point (c, d) can be written $(\pm\dfrac{2a}{\sqrt{a^2+b^2}}, \pm\dfrac{2b}{\sqrt{a^2+b^2}})$.

Section 3.2.3

1. Let $x, y \in S$ such that $x \neq y$. Then either $x < y$ or $y < x$. Suppose f_s is strictly increasing. If $x < y$, then $f_s(x) < f_s(y)$, and if $y < x$, $f_s(y) < f_s(x)$. So $f_s(y) \neq f_s(x)$. Similarly, suppose f_s is strictly decreasing. If $x < y$, then $f_s(y) < f_s(x)$, and if $y < x$, $f_s(x) < f_s(y)$. So $f_s(y) \neq f_s(x)$. Thus f_s is one-to-one.

    Since the function's domain is a subset of itself, the Corollary follows immediately from the theorem.

2. For all $x, y \in \mathbf{R}$, if $0 < x < y$, then $\frac{1}{x} > \frac{1}{y}$. However, for all $x, y \in \mathbf{R}$, if $x < 0$ and $0 < y$, then $\frac{1}{y} > \frac{1}{x}$. So f is neither strictly increasing nor strictly decreasing on the set of real numbers.

3. Sample: Consider the function $f(x) = x^3$. This function is strictly increasing on the open interval $(-\infty, \infty)$, but $f'(x) = 0$ at $x = 0$.

4. Let $x, y \in \mathbf{R}$ and $x < y$. Since $f(y) - f(x) = a(y-h)^2 + k - (a(x-h)^2 + k) = a(y^2 - x^2 - 2yh + 2xh)$ $= a(y-x)((y+x) - 2h)$, $y - x > 0$, and $a > 0$, the sign of $f(y) - f(x)$ depends only on the sign of $(y+x) - 2h$. If $x, y \in [h, \infty)$, then $y > x \geq h$ and $y + x > 2h$. Thus $(y-x)(a(y+x) - 2ah) > 0$. So $f(x) < f(y)$ and f is strictly increasing on $[h, \infty)$. Similarly, if $x, y \in (-\infty, h]$, then $x < y \leq h$ and $y + x < 2h$. Thus $(y-x)(a(y+x) - 2ah) < 0$. So $f(y) < f(x)$ and f is strictly decreasing on $(-\infty, h]$.

5. The graph of f is a parabola symmetric to the vertical line $x = -\frac{b}{2a}$ passing through its vertex. Thus the largest domains over which f is 1-1, and hence has an inverse, are $(-\infty, -\frac{b}{2a}]$ and $[-\frac{b}{2a}, \infty)$. If the coefficient a is positive (negative), then f^{-1} is strictly decreasing (increasing) over $(-\infty, -\frac{b}{2a}]$ and strictly increasing (decreasing) over $[-\frac{b}{2a}, \infty)$.

6. Let $x, y \in \mathbf{R}$ and $0 < x < y$. From the properties of logarithms $f(y) - f(x) = \ln y - \ln x = \ln \frac{y}{x}$ and for $\frac{y}{x} > 1$, $\ln \frac{y}{x} > 0$. Therefore, $f(y) > f(x)$ and f is strictly increasing on its domain.

7. a. Suppose f is strictly increasing, but f^{-1} is not strictly increasing. Then for some $x, y \in f(D)$, $x < y$ implies $f^{-1}(y) \leq f^{-1}(x)$. However, since f is strictly increasing, $f(f^{-1}(y)) \leq f(f^{-1}(x))$. This implies $y \leq x$, which is a contradiction.

    b. Replacing "increasing" by "decreasing" in all places and $\leq$ by $\geq$ in the first occurrences in part **a** will produce a solution for part **b**.

8. When $f(x) = x^3$, $f^{-1}(x) = x^{1/3}$, so $(f^{-1})'(x) = \frac{1}{3}x^{-2/3}$. Thus $(f^{-1})'(f(x)) = \frac{1}{3}(x^3)^{-2/3} = \frac{1}{3}x^{-2}$. Also, $f'(x) = 3x^2$, so $\frac{1}{f'(x)} = \frac{1}{3}x^{-2}$. Thus $(f^{-1})'(f(x)) = \frac{1}{f'(x)}$ in this case.

9. From Section 3.2.2, the lines tangent to the graphs of $f(x)$ and $f^{-1}(x)$ at the points (x_0, y_0) and (y_0, x_0), respectively, are inverse functions. Let $y = mx + b$ be the equation of the line tangent to $f(x)$ at (x_0, y_0). The inverse of this is $y = \frac{1}{m}x - b$, and is the equation of the line tangent to $f^{-1}(x)$ at (y_0, x_0). We know that the slope of the line tangent to $f(x)$ at (x_0, y_0) is $f'(x_0) = m$ and the slope of the tangent to $f^{-1}(x)$ at (y_0, x_0) is $(f^{-1})'(y_0) = (f^{-1})'(f(x_0)) = \frac{1}{m} = \frac{1}{f'(x_0)}$ for all x_0.

10. a.

0	1	2	3	4	5	6	7	8	9
0.00	0.84	5.66	16.05	32.00	52.56	76.37	101.97	128.00	153.25
10	11	12	13	14	15	16	17	18	19
176.78	197.85	216.00	230.93	242.54	250.85	256.00	258.21	257.74	254.90
20	21	22	23	24	25	26	27	28	29
250.00	243.36	235.29	226.08	216.00	205.30	194.19	182.87	171.50	160.22

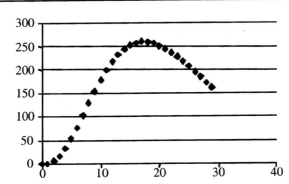

   b. From the table, it is apparent that $\{s_n\}$ is monotone increasing for $n = 0$ to $n = 17$ and monotone decreasing for $n = 17$ to $n = 29$. Since exponential functions have higher growth rates than polynomial functions (see Section 3.2.4), the sequence will remain monotone decreasing for $n \geq 17$.

11. a. For the sequence defined by $s_0 = 1$ and $s_{n+1} = \frac{1}{8}(3s_n + 6)$ for $n \geq 0$ we see that $s_1 = \frac{9}{8}$ and $s_2 = \frac{75}{64}$, so the sequence appears to be increasing. To show that s is strictly increasing we have to show that $s_n < s_{n+1}$ for all n. $s_n < s_{n+1} \Rightarrow s_n < \frac{1}{8}(3s_n + 6) \Rightarrow s_n < \frac{6}{5}$, so if we can show that $s_n < \frac{6}{5}$ for all n, then s is a strictly increasing sequence. Using induction with the base cases above, suppose that $s_k < \frac{6}{5}$ for some k. Then $s_{k+1} = \frac{1}{8}(3s_k + 6) < \frac{1}{8}(3(\frac{6}{5}) + 6) = \frac{48}{40} = \frac{6}{5}$, so $s_k < \frac{6}{5} \Rightarrow s_{k+1} < \frac{6}{5}$ and by the principle of mathematical induction, $s_n < \frac{6}{5}$ for all n, so the sequence s is strictly increasing.

   b. For the sequence defined by $s_0 = 1$ and $s_{n+1} = \frac{1}{8}(3s_n + 5)$ for $n \geq 0$ we see that $s_1 = 1$, $s_2 = 1$ and

$s_3 = 1$. Since for all n, $s_n = s_{n+1} = 1$, this sequence is not strictly monotonic. It is, however, both monotone increasing and monotone decreasing, since for any $j < k$, $s_j \le s_k$ and $s_j \ge s_k$ hold.

12. For the sequence defined by $s_0 = 1$ and $s_{n+1} = as_n + b$ for $n \ge 0$ to be strictly increasing we need to have $s_{n+1} > s_n$ for all n. $s_{n+1} > s_n \Rightarrow as_n + b > s_n \Rightarrow s_n(a-1) > -b \Rightarrow s_n > \frac{-b}{a-1}$ when $a > 1$ and $s_n < \frac{-b}{a-1}$ when $a < 1$. Therefore $s_{n+1} > s_n$ whenever $s_n > \frac{-b}{a-1}$ when $a > 1$, and $s_{n+1} > s_n$ whenever $s_n < \frac{-b}{a-1}$ when $a < 1$. We have shown when $s_{n+1} > s_n$, so now we need to show, via induction, that for all n, $s_n > \frac{-b}{a-1}$ when $a > 1$ and $s_n < \frac{-b}{a-1}$ when $a < 1$, which implies that $s_{n+1} > s_n$ for all n, i.e., that the sequence is strictly increasing. Since $s_0 = 1$, we must have $1 > \frac{-b}{a-1}$ when $a > 1$ and $1 < \frac{-b}{a-1}$ when $a < 1$ in order to establish a basis case for the induction proof. In each of these cases the condition on a and b is that $a + b > 1$, since both a and b are positive. With the basis case established (with the condition that $a + b > 1$), we can suppose that $s_k > \frac{-b}{a-1}$ when $a > 1$ and $s_k < \frac{-b}{a-1}$ when $a < 1$. Then, when $a > 1$, $s_{k+1} = as_k + b > a(\frac{-b}{a-1}) + b = \frac{-ab + ab - b}{a-1} = \frac{-b}{a-1}$, so $s_k > \frac{-b}{a-1}$ when $a > 1$ $\Rightarrow s_{k+1} > \frac{-b}{a-1}$ when $a > 1$. When $a < 1$, then $s_{k+1} = as_k + b < a(\frac{-b}{a-1}) + b = \frac{-ab + ab - b}{a-1} = \frac{-b}{a-1}$, so $s_k < \frac{-b}{a-1}$ when $a < 1 \Rightarrow s_{k+1} < \frac{-b}{a-1}$ when $a < 1$. Therefore, by the principle of mathematical induction, s_n is a strictly increasing sequence when $a + b > 1$. A similar proof shows that when $a + b < 1$, s_n is a strictly decreasing sequence.

13. $\frac{1}{p!} > \frac{1}{2^{p-1}}$ for all integers $p > 2$ is equivalent to $\frac{p!}{2^{p-1}} > 1$ for all integers $p > 2$.

$\frac{p!}{2^{p-1}} = \frac{p(p-1)(p-2)\cdots(3)(2)}{\underbrace{2 \bullet 2 \bullet 2 \bullet \cdots \bullet 2}_{p-1 \text{ times}}}$. Since the numerator and the denominator each have $p - 1$ terms, and every term in the numerator except one is greater than every term in the denominator, $\frac{p!}{2^{p-1}} > 1$ for all integers $p > 2 \Rightarrow \frac{1}{p!} > \frac{1}{2^{p-1}}$ for all integers $p > 2$.

Section 3.2.4

1. a. The function $f(x) = x^{-7}$ has no zeroes, a vertical asymptote at $x = 0$, and approaches 0 as x goes to $\pm \infty$.

   b. The function $g(x) = \frac{4}{x^8}$ has no real zeroes, a vertical asymptote at $x = 0$, and approaches 0 as x goes to $\pm \infty$.

   c. The function $h(x) = 2 \bullet 3^{x+2}$ has no zeroes or vertical asymptotes, approaches zero as x goes to $-\infty$ and approaches $+\infty$ as x goes to $+\infty$.

   d. The function $k(t) = \frac{2t - 5}{7t + 1}$ has a zero at $t = \frac{5}{2}$, a vertical asymptote at $t = -\frac{1}{7}$, and approaches $\frac{2}{7}$

as t goes to $\pm \infty$.

e. For $g(u) = \dfrac{(u-1)(u-2)^2(u-3)^3}{(u-1)^3(u-2)^2(u-3)}$, let $g*(u) = \dfrac{(u-3)^2}{(u-1)^2}$. The function $g(u)$ has no zeroes since at all of the possible zeroes ($u = 1$, $u = 2$, and $u = 3$), it is undefined. It has a vertical asymptote at $u = 1$, but nowhere else since $\lim\limits_{u \to 2} g*(u) = 1$ and $\lim\limits_{u \to 3} g*(u) = 0$. As u goes to positive or negative infinity, $g(u)$ approaches 1 since both the numerator and denominator of the function are sixth degree polynomials with a leading coefficient of 1.

f. The function $v(x) = 6 \ln(x + 3)$ has a zero when $x + 3 = 1$, i.e., when $x = -2$. It has a vertical asymptote at $x = -3$ and as x goes to positive infinity, so does $v(x)$. $v(x)$ is undefined for all $x \le -3$.

g. The function $w(t) = \dfrac{9t^2 - 4}{3t - 2} = \dfrac{(3t + 2)(3t - 2)}{3t - 2}$ has a zero at $t = -\frac{2}{3}$, no vertical asymptotes (although it is undefined at $t = \frac{2}{3}$), approaches $+\infty$ as x goes to $+\infty$ and approaches $-\infty$ as x goes to $-\infty$.

h. The function $r(x) = \dfrac{x^3 - 8x^2 + 4x - 32}{x^5 - 1} = \dfrac{(x - 8)(x^2 + 4)}{x^5 - 1}$ has one real zero at $x = 8$, a vertical asymptote at $x = 1$ and approaches zero as x goes to $\pm \infty$.

2. $\cot x = \dfrac{\cos x}{\sin x}$ and since there is no value of x where $\sin x = \cos x = 0$, the cotangent function has an asymptote whenever $\sin x = 0$, i.e., when $x = 0 + k\pi$, where k is an integer. The inverse cotangent function has no vertical asymptotes and no zeros, but $\cot^{-1} x$ approaches 0 as x goes to $\pm \infty$.

3. For the sequence defined by $s_1 = 100$ and $s_{n+1} = \frac{1}{2}(s_n + \frac{1}{3})$, let $L = \lim\limits_{n \to \infty} s_n$. Then $L = \lim\limits_{n \to \infty} s_{n+1} = \lim\limits_{n \to \infty} \frac{1}{2}(s_n + \frac{1}{3}) = \frac{1}{2} \lim\limits_{n \to \infty} s_n + \frac{1}{6} = \frac{1}{2}L + \frac{1}{6} \Rightarrow \frac{1}{2}L = \frac{1}{6} \Rightarrow L = \frac{1}{3}$. (This limit does not depend on the initial term in the sequence.)

4. For fixed positive c and b, the sequence $s_n = \dfrac{n!}{cb^n}$, formed by dividing a factorial by an exponential, diverges to infinity. This can be seen by the ratio test. More informally, note that for $n > b$, the sequence is increasing because each new term of the sequence is formed from the previous term by multiplying by a factor $\frac{n}{b}$, which is greater than 1. Further, as n increases, this factor increases, and this implies that the graph of the sequence is concave up. An increasing positive concave up function must diverge to plus infinity.

5. Let $g(x) = a_g(b_g)^x$ and $h(x) = a_h(b_h)^x$ where a_g, $a_h > 0$. If $b_g = b_h > 1$, then $\lim\limits_{x \to \infty} \dfrac{a_g(b_g)^x}{a_h(b_h)^x} = \dfrac{a_g}{a_h}$, so g and h have the same order of growth when $b_g = b_h > 1$. If $b_g > b_h > 1$, then $\lim\limits_{x \to \infty} \dfrac{a_g(b_g)^x}{a_h(b_h)^x} = \dfrac{a_g}{a_h} \lim\limits_{x \to \infty} \left(\dfrac{b_g}{b_h}\right)^x = \infty$

since $\dfrac{b_g}{b_h} > 1$, so g has a higher order of growth than h when $b_g > b_h > 1$.

6. Let $g(x) = cb^x$ with $c > 0$ and $b > 1$ and let $h(x) = a_n x^n + \ldots + a_0$ with $a_n > 0$. Then each of the first $n - 1$ derivatives of $h(x)$ is a polynomial with a positive leading coefficient, so each will approach $+\infty$ as x goes to $+\infty$, and the kth derivative of $g(x)$ will be $c(\ln b)^k b^x$, which also approaches $+\infty$ as x goes to $+\infty$. Then, applying L'Hôpital's Rule n times, $\lim\limits_{x \to \infty} \dfrac{g(x)}{h(x)} = \lim\limits_{x \to \infty} \dfrac{g^n(x)}{h^n(x)} = \lim\limits_{x \to \infty} \dfrac{c(\ln b)b^x}{n! a_n} = \infty$, so g has a higher order of growth than h.

7. Let $g(x) = a_m x^m + \ldots + a_0$ and let $h(x) = a_n x^n + \ldots + a_0$. Then $\lim\limits_{x \to \infty} \dfrac{g(x)}{h(x)} = \lim\limits_{x \to \infty} \dfrac{a_m x^m}{a_n x^n} = \dfrac{a_m}{a_n} \lim\limits_{x \to \infty} x^{m-n}$

$= \dfrac{a_m}{a_n}$ if $m = n$ and ∞ if $m > n$. Therefore, if $m = n$, then g and h have the same order of growth and if $m > n$, then g has a higher order of growth than h.

8. a. Let $g(x) = 3x^3 + 2x + 1$ and $h(x) = \log_{10}(x)$. Then, using L'Hôpital's Rule,
$\lim\limits_{x \to \infty} \dfrac{g(x)}{h(x)} = \lim\limits_{x \to \infty} \dfrac{g'(x)}{h'(x)} = \lim\limits_{x \to \infty} \dfrac{3x^2 + 2}{\frac{1}{x}\log_{10} e} = \infty$, so g(x) has a higher growth rate than h(x).

   b. Let g(x) be any polynomial function with a positive leading coefficient and let $h(x) = \log_b(x)$ where $b > 1$. Then, applying L'Hôpital's Rule,
$\lim\limits_{x \to \infty} \dfrac{g(x)}{h(x)} = \lim\limits_{x \to \infty} \dfrac{g'(x)}{h'(x)} = \lim\limits_{x \to \infty} \dfrac{g'(x)}{\frac{1}{x}\log_b e} = \dfrac{1}{\log_{10} e} \lim\limits_{x \to \infty} x g'(x) = \infty$, since xg'(x) is a polynomial with a positive leading coefficient. So g has a higher growth rate than h.

9. $\lim\limits_{n \to \infty} \dfrac{a_m x^m + \ldots + a_1 x + a_0}{x^{\frac{1}{n}}} = \lim\limits_{n \to \infty} \dfrac{a_m x^m}{x^{\frac{1}{n}}} = \lim\limits_{n \to \infty} a_m x^{(m - \frac{1}{n})} = \infty$, since $a_m > 0$, $m \geq 1$, and $0 < \dfrac{1}{n} < 1$.

   Therefore, the polynomial function dominates the nth root function and so it has a higher growth rate.

10. Let $f(x) = \sqrt[m]{x}$ and $g(x) = \sqrt[n]{x}$. Then $\lim\limits_{x \to \infty} \dfrac{f(x)}{g(x)} = \lim\limits_{x \to \infty} \dfrac{\sqrt[m]{x}}{\sqrt[n]{x}} = \lim\limits_{x \to \infty} x^{(\frac{1}{m} - \frac{1}{n})}$, so f(x) has a higher growth rate then g(x) when $\dfrac{1}{m} > \dfrac{1}{n}$, i.e., when $m < n$, and f(x) and g(x) have the same growth rate when m = n.

11. Let $f(x) = \sqrt[n]{x}$ and $g(x) = \log_b(x)$. Then, using L'Hôpital's rule, $\lim\limits_{x \to \infty} \dfrac{f(x)}{g(x)} = \lim\limits_{x \to \infty} \dfrac{f'(x)}{g'(x)} = \lim\limits_{x \to \infty} \dfrac{\frac{1}{n} x^{-(\frac{n-1}{n})}}{\frac{1}{x} \ln b}$

$= \dfrac{1}{n \ln b} \lim\limits_{x \to \infty} x^{(\frac{1}{n})} = \infty$, so any nth root function has a higher growth rate than any logarithmic function.

12. Let $g(x) = \log_{b_g}(x)$ and $h(x) = \log_{b_h}(x)$. Then, using the change of base property for logarithms,
$\log_{b_h}(x) = \dfrac{\log_{b_g}(x)}{\log_{b_g}(b_h)} \Rightarrow \log_{b_g}(b_h) = \dfrac{\log_{b_g}(x)}{\log_{b_h}(x)} = \dfrac{g(x)}{h(x)}$, so for all x, $\dfrac{g(x)}{h(x)}$ is a positive constant which

implies that g(x) and h(x) are positive multiples and have the same order of growth.

13. a. The order of growth of the function f: $x \to x^{5/2}$ falls between the orders of growth of polynomials of degree 2 and 3.

    b. For rational power functions $f(x) = ax^m$ with $a > 0$ and $m \geq 0$, larger values of m have higher orders of growth.

14. We already know that of the functions discussed in the chapter and the problems that the logarithmic function has the smallest order of growth and log(log x) appears to have an even smaller order of growth. Let $f(x) = \log(\log x)$ and $g(x) = \log x$. Then, using L'Hôpital's rule,

$$\lim_{x \to \infty} \frac{g(x)}{f(x)} = \lim_{x \to \infty} \frac{g'(x)}{f'(x)} = \lim_{x \to \infty} \frac{\frac{1}{x} \ln 10}{(\frac{1}{\log x} \ln 10)(\frac{1}{x} \ln 10)} = \frac{1}{\ln 10} \lim_{x \to \infty} \log x = \infty$$, so $f(x) = \log(\log x)$ does have a

smaller order of growth than a logarithmic function, and therefore a smaller order of growth than any of the other functions discussed in the chapter.

Section 3.3.1

1. a. California: A linear model with equation $y = 4.5 \times 10^5 x - 3 \times 10^7$ fits the data for years 1940 to 1990 with a correlation coefficient of 0.998. Oregon: A linear model with equation $y = 3.5 \times 10^4 x - 2 \times 10^6$ fits the data for years 1950 to 1990 with a correlation coefficient of 0.990. Another linear model with equation $y = 1.6 \times 10^4 x - 3.6 \times 10^5$ fits the data for years 1900 to 1940 with a correlation coefficient of 0.990. Washington: A linear model with equation $y = 4.5 \times 10^4 x - 2 \times 10^6$ fits the data for years 1900 to 1990 with a correlation coefficient of 0.980.

    b. California: An exponential function with equation $y = 2.0 \times 10^5 e^{0.04x}$ fits the data well for years 1850 to 1970. Oregon: An exponential model does not appear to fit the data well for any of the intervals. Washington: An exponential model does not appear to fit the data well for any of the intervals.

    c. An exponential model appears suitable for the California population data up until about 1970, at which time it levels off and a linear model becomes more suitable. The population data for Oregon and Washington are best described with linear or piecewise linear functions.

2. a. The first differences alternate between 2.2 and 2.1, so no exact linear function can be found for f(x) when values in f are rounded to the nearest tenth. The line of best fit is $y \approx 2.15x + 1.2214$, which has a correlation coefficient $r \approx .9998$.

    b. Because all the first differences equal 2, an exact linear model can be found: $y = 2x + 2$.

    c. Rounding the original f values to the nearest tenth makes it impossible to match an exact linear model; this has to do with the fact that the first differences in f are $\Delta f = 2.15$, a value which has significant digits into the hundredths. Rounding the f values to the nearest tenth means that, in some cases, the difference will be rounded to 2.2, and in other cases, to 2.1. This problem is resolved when we round to the nearest integer, since the f-value difference 2.15 rounds to 2.0 for the given set of points. This is why we can fit a linear model to the set of points rounded to the nearest integer, but not to the nearest tenth. It is interesting to note that if the point (9, 20.58) were included in the set (which fits in the original linear model), rounding the f-values to the nearest integer will no longer yield constant differences.

3. a. Linear functions fit the data well for the following intervals:
    All 1900-1940: $y = 0.409x + 46.62$; $R = 0.994$
    All 1950-1990: $y = 0.184x + 58.68$; $R = 0.988$
    All 1900-1990: $y = 0.3258x + 48.518$; $R = 0.983$
    Male 1900-1940: $y = 0.387x + 45.7$; $R = 0.992$

Male 1950-1990: y = 0.158x + 57.16; R = 0.966
Male 1900-1990: y = 0.29x + 47.78; R = 0.978
Female 1900-1940: y = 0.436x + 47.58; R = 0.989
Female 1950-1990: y = 0.198x + 61.18; R = 0.995
Female 1900-1990: y = 0.3608x + 49.435; R = 0.983

b. Exponential functions do not appear to fit the data well for any of the intervals.

c. The data seem to be best modeled by linear or piecewise linear functions.

4. Sample:

T(c) = 4c + 1

5. a. The number of toothpicks needed for the first car is n. The subsequent c – 1 cars are each formed from a "defective" polygon requiring n – 1 toothpicks. Thus
T(n, c) = n + (c –1)(n – 1) = (n – 1)c + 1.

b. For a train having c cars, there will be c – 1 common sides. The two end cars will each have n – 1 noncommon sides, and the c – 2 other cars will have n – 2 noncommon sides. Thus
T(n, c) = c – 1 + 2(n – 1) + (c – 2)(n – 2) = (n – 1)c + 1.

c.

n	c	T(n, c)	n	c	T(n, c)
3	1	3	6	2	11
4	1	4	4	4	13
3	2	5	5	3	13
5	1	5	7	2	13
6	1	6	4	5	16
3	3	7	6	3	16
4	2	7	5	4	17
7	1	7	7	3	19
3	4	9	5	5	21
5	2	9	6	4	21
4	3	10	7	4	25
3	5	11	6	5	26
			7	5	31

6. a. The income for Company A is the first difference A(t + 1) – A(t) = 500,000.

The income for Company B is the first quotient $\frac{B(t + 1)}{B(t)} = 1.15$, which is 100% + 15% growth.

b. Company B's net income will eventually surpass Company A's, because Company A's income is growing at a fixed rate of change, while Company B's income is growing at an increasing rate of change.

Let t = 0 in the year 2000. Then:
A(t) = 5,000,000 + 500,000t
B(t) = 2,000,000(1.15)^t

A(t) and B(t) coincide when t ≈ 12.29 and A(t) = B(t) = $11,150,000. So the income of Company B will surpass that of Company A sometime during the year 2012.

7. Part (a): Suppose f is an exponential function defined by $f(x) = f(0)b^x$. Then $f(x + 1) = f(0)b^{x+1}$. So

$$\frac{f(x+1)}{f(x)} = \frac{f(0)b^{x+1}}{f(0)b^x} = b.$$

Part (b): We wish to show that if f has the property that, for all real numbers x, $\frac{f(x+1)}{f(x)} = b$ for a

positive real number b, then the exponential function G, defined by $G(x) = f(0)b^x$ agrees with f at all nonnegative integers n. We use induction on n. Note that $G(0) = f(0)b^0 = f(0)$, so the conclusion holds

for n = 0. Assume that for some nonnegative integer k, $G(k) = f(k)$. Then, because $\frac{f(k+1)}{f(k)} = b$, it

follows that $G(k + 1) = f(0)b^{k+1} = f(0)b^k \cdot b = G(k) \cdot b = f(k) \cdot b = f(k + 1)$. In the last step, we have used the assumed property of f. We have shown that $G(k) = f(k)$ implies $G(k + 1) = f(k + 1)$. Therefore, by the Principle of Mathematical Induction, $G(n) = f(n)$ for all nonnegative integers n.

8. a. We wish to show that $\Theta g(a) = \frac{g(a+1)}{g(a)} = 2$ for all a.

$$\frac{g(a+1)}{g(a)} = \frac{2^{(a+1)+\sin(2\pi a + 2\pi)}}{2^{a+\sin(2\pi a)}} = \frac{2^a 2^1 2^{\sin(2\pi a + 2\pi)}}{2^a 2^{\sin(2\pi a)}}$$

Since the sine function has period 2π, $\sin(2\pi a + 2\pi) = \sin(2\pi a)$ and so $\frac{g(a+1)}{g(a)} = \frac{2^a 2^1}{2^a} = 2$.

Thus we have shown that $\Theta g(a) = 2$ for all $a \in \mathbf{R}$. However, one property of an exponential function $f(x)$ $a \cdot b^x$ is that $f(x + m) = b^m \cdot f(x)$ for any values x and x + m in the domain. Here, $g(0) = 2^{0 + \sin(0)} = 1$, and $g(\frac{1}{4}) = 2^{1/4 + \sin(\pi/2)} = 2^{5/4}$. If this function were exponential, we would

expect to see that $g(\frac{1}{4}) = 2^{1/4}g(0) = 2^{1/4}$. Additionally, we see that $g(x) = 2^{x+\sin(2\pi x)}$ can be written $g(x) = 2^x \cdot 2^{\sin(2\pi x)}$, which cannot be written in the form $a \cdot b^x$, a standard form for an exponential function.

    b. The periodicity of the sine function.

9. Let $\{a_n\}$ be an exponential sequence with constant ratio r. Then $\frac{a_{n+1}}{a_n} = r$ for all $n \geq 1$. By the Logarithm

of a Quotient Property, $\log\left(\frac{a_{n+1}}{a_n}\right) = \log a_{n+1} - \log a_n = \log r$ for all $n \geq 0$. Thus $\{\log a_n\}$ is a linear

sequence with constant difference $\log r$.

10. The Corollary follows from Theorem 3.16 by letting the function $g: \mathbf{N} \to \mathbf{R}$ be the function $f: \mathbf{R} \to \mathbf{R}$ of Theorem 3.16 restricted to the domain of nonnegative integers.

Section 3.3.2

1. a.

n	3	4	5	6	7	8	9	10	11
d(n)	0	2	5	9	14	20	27	35	44
$\Delta d(n)$	2	3	4	5	6	7	8	9	
$\Delta^2 d(n)$	1	1	1	1	1	1	1		

The calculations in this table show that d(n) can be fitted with a polynomial of degree 2, $d(n) = an^2 + bn + c$. Then, since $d(3) = a(3)^2 + b(3) + c = 9a + 3b + c = 0$, $d(4) = a(4)^2 + b(4) + c = 16a + 4b + c = 2$, and $d(5) = a(5)^2 + b(5) + c = 25a + 5b + c = 5$, $d(4) - d(3) = 7a + b = 2$, $d(5) - d(4) = 9a + b = 3$, and $(d(5) - d(4)) - (d(4) - d(3)) = 2a = 1$.

Thus $a = \frac{1}{2}$, $b = 2 - 7a = -\frac{3}{2}$, and $c = -9a - 3b = 0$. Therefore, a polynomial of degree 2 that fits d(n) is $d(n) = \frac{1}{2}n^2 - \frac{3}{2}n$.

b.　A diagonal of a polygon connects nonadjacent vertices. For each of the n vertices of a polygon, there are n − 3 nonadjacent vertices to which it can be connected. But this will connect each diagonal twice. Thus there are $\frac{1}{2}n(n - 3) = \frac{1}{2}n^2 - \frac{3}{2}n$ diagonals.

2.　Since $S(n) = \sum_{k=1}^{n} k^4$, we have the following table of successive differences:

n	1	2	3	4	5	6	7
S(n)	1	17	98	354	979	2275	4674
$\Delta S(n)$	16	81	256	625	1296	2401	
$\Delta^2 S(n)$	65	175	369	671	1105		
$\Delta^3 S(n)$	110	194	302	434			
$\Delta^4 S(n)$	84	108	132				
$\Delta^5 S(n)$	24	24					

The calculations in this table show that S(n) can be fitted with a polynomial of degree 5, $f(x) = ax^5 + bx^4 + cx^3 + dx^2 + ex + f$. Then, since $f(1) = a(1)^5 + b(1)^4 + c(1)^3 + d(1)^2 + e(1) + f = 17$
$f(2) = a(2)^5 + b(2)^4 + c(2)^3 + d(2)^2 + e(2) + f = 98$
$f(3) = a(3)^5 + b(3)^4 + c(3)^3 + d(3)^2 + e(3) + f = 354$
$f(4) = a(4)^5 + b(4)^4 + c(4)^3 + d(4)^2 + e(4) + f = 979$
$f(5) = a(5)^5 + b(5)^4 + c(5)^3 + d(5)^2 + e(5) + f = 2275$
$f(6) = a(6)^5 + b(6)^4 + c(6)^3 + d(6)^2 + e(6) + f = 4676$, we have

$$\begin{bmatrix} 1 & 1 & 1 & 1 & 1 & 1 \\ 32 & 16 & 8 & 4 & 2 & 1 \\ 243 & 81 & 27 & 9 & 3 & 1 \\ 1024 & 256 & 64 & 16 & 4 & 1 \\ 3125 & 625 & 125 & 25 & 5 & 1 \\ 7776 & 1296 & 216 & 36 & 6 & 1 \end{bmatrix} \bullet \begin{bmatrix} a \\ b \\ c \\ d \\ e \\ f \end{bmatrix} = \begin{bmatrix} 1 \\ 17 \\ 98 \\ 354 \\ 979 \\ 2275 \end{bmatrix} \Rightarrow \begin{bmatrix} a \\ b \\ c \\ d \\ e \\ f \end{bmatrix} = \begin{bmatrix} \frac{1}{5} \\ \frac{1}{2} \\ \frac{1}{3} \\ 0 \\ -\frac{1}{30} \\ 0 \end{bmatrix}.$$

The polynomial of degree 5 that fits S(n) is $f(x) = \frac{1}{5}x^5 + \frac{1}{2}x^4 + \frac{1}{3}x^3 - \frac{1}{30}x$
$= \frac{6x^5 + 15x^4 + 10x^3 - x}{30} = \frac{x(x + 1)(2x + 1)(3x^2 + 3x - 1)}{30}$.

3.　a.　If x is the number of years after 1900, then the fourth degree polynomial
$P(x) \approx -1.42 \times 10^{-4}x^4 + 5.42 \times 10^{-2}x^3 - 7.25x^2 + 409x - 7722$ fits the five given data points.

b. The polynomial wiggle problem presents itself if the data is extrapolated well into the future. The function P(x) will increase until about the year 2043 and then it will sharply decrease, reaching 0 around the year 2068.

c. The fifth degree polynomial
$P(x) \approx -5.26 \times 10^{-6} x^5 + 1.66 \times 10^{-3} x^4 - 1.96 \times 10^{-1} x^3 + 9.91 x^2 - 173x + 81$ fits the six data points including (1900, 81). However, interpolating using this function yields negative population values for years 1901 to 1935.

4. a. $(x + 1)^{(n)} = (x + 1)(x)(x - 1) \cdot \ldots \cdot (x + 1 - n + 1) = (x + 1)x^{(n-1)}$
    $x^{(n)} = (x)(x - 1) \cdot \ldots \cdot (x - n + 1) = (x - n + 1)x^{(n-1)}$
    $\Delta x^{(n)} = (x + 1)^{(n)} - x^{(n)} = (x + 1)x^{(n-1)} - (x - n + 1)x^{(n-1)} = nx^{(n-1)}$

    b. Let $p(x) = b_n x^{(n)} + b_{n-1} x^{(n-1)} + \ldots + b_1 x^{(1)} + b_0$.
    $\Delta p(x) = b_n(x - 1)^{(n)} + b_{n-1}(x - 1)^{(n-1)} + \ldots + b_1(x - 1)^{(1)} + b_0 - (b_n x^{(n)} + b_{n-1} x^{(n-1)} + \ldots$
    $\qquad + b_1 x^{(1)} + b_0)$
    $\qquad = b_n \Delta x^{(n)} + b_{n-1} \Delta x^{(n-1)} + \ldots + b_1 \Delta x^{(1)}$
    By part **a**, $\Delta p(x) = b_n n x^{(n-1)} + b_{n-1}(n - 1)x^{(n-2)} + \ldots + 2b_2 x^{(1)} + b_1$

    c. Suppose $p(x) = a_n x^n + a_{n-1} x^{n-1} + \ldots + a_1 x^1 + a_0 = b_n x^{(n)} + b_{n-1} x^{(n-1)} + \ldots + b_1 x^{(1)} + b_0$.
    For $i > 0$, x is a factor of $x^{(i)}$, so
    $p(x) = x(b_n(x - 1)^{(n-1)} + b_{n-1}(x - 1)^{(n-2)} + \ldots + b_2(x - 1)^{(1)} + b_1) + b_0 = xq_1(x) + b_0$,
    where $q_1(x) = b_n(x - 1)^{(n-1)} + b_{n-1}(x - 1)^{(n-2)} + \ldots + b_2(x - 1)^{(1)} + b_1$.
    Similarly, for $i > 0$, $(x - 1)$ is a factor of $(x - 1)^{(i)}$, so
    $q_1(x) = (x - 1)(b_n(x - 2)^{(n-2)} + b_{n-1}(x - 2)^{(n-3)} + \ldots + b_3(x - 2)^{(1)} + b_2) + b_1 = (x - 1)q_2(x) + b_1$,
    where $q_2(x) = b_n(x - 2)^{(n-2)} + b_{n-1}(x - 2)^{(n-3)} + \ldots + b_3(x - 2)^{(1)} + b_2$, and so on.

    d. The coefficients of the factorial form of the polynomial can be computed by performing successive synthetic divisions of the coefficients of p(x) by 0, 1, 2, 3, …, n. That is, defining $q_0(x) = p(x)$, compute each remainder (the coefficients b_i) and the quotient coefficients of $q_{i+1}(x)$ by performing a synthetic division using the coefficients of the polynomial $q_i(x)$ and the integer i, for i = 0, 1, 2, 3, …, n.

    e. $p(x) = 5x^{(4)} + 28x^{(3)} + 41x^{(2)} + 31x^{(1)} + -31$

Section 3.3.3

1. a. If we assume we already know that the area maximizing shape for a closed rectangular pen with fixed perimeter is a square, there is a simple way to see that the area maximizing shape for an open rectangular pen with fixed perimeter P is half a square: start with perimeter 2P, form the square that maximizes the area, and cut it in half. Otherwise, we can find the maximum value of this function usin techniques from calculus, or properties of quadratic functions. Let the fixed length of fencing be L. Then the dimensions of the pen can be described as follows:

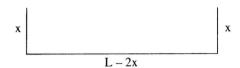

The area of this pen is $A(x) = x(L - 2x) = Lx - 2x^2$. To determine the maximum value of $A(x)$ without calculus, note that $A(x)$ is a quadratic with a leading coefficient that is negative. Thus, the vertex of the parabola that is the graph of A will yield the maximum value. The x-coordinate of the vertex is $-\dfrac{L}{-2 \bullet 2} = \dfrac{1}{4}L$. This means that the pen has dimensions as follows:

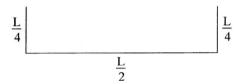

This is half of a square with sides of length $\dfrac{L}{2}$.

Using calculus, we can find the maximum of $A(x)$ by finding the value of x at which its derivative is 0. Since $A'(x) = L - 4x$, $A'(x) = 0$ when $L - 4x = 0$, or $\dfrac{L}{4} = x$. We can confirm that this is a maximum by checking that $A'(x)$ is positive to the left of $\dfrac{L}{4} = x$ and negative to the right of $\dfrac{L}{4} = x$.

b.   Part **a** shows that for a fixed perimeter the shape of a rectangular pen with one side open that maximizes the area is half a square. This might tempt us to conjecture the following answer to the box problem: The shape of an open rectangular box that maximizes the volume is half a cube. However, the analogy is not complete. All of the surface area of the rectangular cardboard is not used in forming the box (since the cut out corners are not used), while all the perimeter is used in the fence problem.

But if we consider the following analogous problem, we do indeed get an analogous answer. That is, for a fixed surface area, the shape of an open rectangular box (with that surface area) that maximizes the volume is in fact half a cube. This can be seen by a simple argument analogous to the one in the beginning of part **a**, if we let ourselves assume that the volume maximizing shape of a closed box with given surface area is a cube.

2. $$\lim_{L \to \infty} \frac{L + 1 - \sqrt{(L+1)^2 - 3L}}{6} = \lim_{L \to \infty} \frac{L + 1 - \sqrt{(L+1)^2 - 3L}}{6} \bullet \frac{L + 1 + \sqrt{(L+1)^2 - 3L}}{L + 1 + \sqrt{(L+1)^2 - 3L}}$$

$$= \lim_{L \to \infty} \frac{3L}{6(L + 1 + \sqrt{(L+1)^2 - 3L})} = \lim_{L \to \infty} \frac{3}{6(1 + \frac{1}{L} + \sqrt{\frac{(L+1)^2}{L^2} - \frac{3}{L^2}})}$$

$$= \frac{3}{6(1 + 0 + \sqrt{1 - 0})} = \frac{1}{4}$$

3.   a.   The volume of the box V as a function of the height of the box x is given by
$V(x) = \pi(R - x)^2 x = \pi(R^2 x - 2Rx^2 + 3x^3)$, where R is the initial radius of the given circle.
Maximizing this function by taking the derivative and setting equal to 0 yields $x = \dfrac{R}{3}$.

b.   The volume of the box V as a function of the length x cut from each end of a side of the triangle is given by $V(x) = \frac{\sqrt{3}}{4}(S-2x)^2 \frac{\sqrt{3}}{3}x = \frac{1}{4}(S^2x - 4Sx^2 + 4x^3)$, where S is the initial length of a side of the triangle. Maximizing this function by taking the derivative and setting equal to 0 yields $x = \frac{S}{6}$. The height will be $\frac{\sqrt{3}}{3}x = \frac{\sqrt{3}}{3}\frac{S}{6} = \frac{S\sqrt{3}}{18}$. Thus, the ratio of the height to the new side length is $\frac{\frac{S\sqrt{3}}{18}}{\frac{2}{3}S} = \frac{\sqrt{3}}{12}$.

4. If each small square in Figure 34 is one square unit, there is a total of 36 square units. Removing one square unit from each corner gives us a total of 32 square units. When we fold the sides up to make a box, each side will be 4 square units and the total "wall" area will be 16 square units. The base of the box will be 4×4 square units, so the base area will also be 16 square units. Thus, removing one square unit from each corner (this being 1/6 the side of the original square) yields the maximum volume.

5. Assume the rectangle has length and a and width b. Then the border area of this rectangle is $2a + 2b - 4$ and the interior area would be $(a-2)(b-2)$. Setting border area equal to interior area, $b = \frac{4a - 8}{a - 4}$. Testing (a, b) pairs shows that the ordered pairs where a and b are integers are (5, 12), (6, 8), (8, 6), and (12, 5). These are the only integer values, because as either one of the variables approaches ∞, the other approaches 4. Thus there are no pairs with integer values unless $a > 4$ and $b > 4$.

6. a. The distance from the point (-1, 3) to a point on the line $y = 4x - 1$ is given by $s = \sqrt{(-1-x)^2 + (3-y)^2} = \sqrt{(-1-x)^2 + (3-(4x-1))^2} = \sqrt{17x^2 - 30x + 17}$. We can find the point on $y = 4x - 1$ that minimizes s by solving $\frac{d}{dx}s(x) = 0$ for x. However, instead of minimizing s, we can simplify the algebra by minimizing $s^2 = 17x^2 - 30x + 17$. Solving $\frac{d}{dx}s^2(x) = 34x - 30 = 0$ yields $x = \frac{15}{17}$ and $y = 4(\frac{15}{17}) - 1 = \frac{43}{17}$.

    b. In general, the distance from a point (x_0, y_0) to the line $y = mx + b$ is given by $s(x) = \sqrt{(x_0 - x)^2 + (y_0 - (mx + b))^2}$. Solving $\frac{d}{dx}s^2(x) = 2(m^2 + 1)x - 2(x_0 + (y_0 - b)m) = 0$ yields $x = \frac{x_0 + m(y_0 - b)}{m^2 + 1}$ and $y = mx + b = \frac{mx_0 + m^2 y_0 + b}{m^2 + 1}$.

    Here is a completely different way of generalizing this problem. It gives a way of seeing why the formulas for x and y derived above for the point (x, y) on a line closest to a given point (x_0, y_0) have the form they do.

    Consider the diagram, where we define the angle α by $\alpha = \arctan m$.

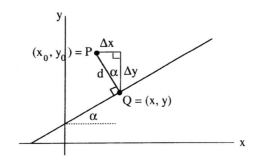

The "directed" distance from a point (x_0, y_0) to the line $y = mx + b$ is given by the following formula, which can be derived fairly easily: $d = \dfrac{y_0 - (mx_0 + b)}{\sqrt{1 + m^2}}$.

The formula gives a positive value of d for points above the line, and a negative one for points below. The directed distances $\Delta x = x - x_0$ and $\Delta y = y - y_0$ are given as

$$\Delta x = d\sin\alpha = d\frac{m}{\sqrt{1 + m^2}} = \frac{m(y_0 - (mx_0 + b))}{1 + m^2} \text{ and}$$

$$\Delta y = -d\cos\alpha = d\frac{-1}{\sqrt{1 + m^2}} = \frac{(mx_0 + b) - y_0}{1 + m^2}.$$

Finally, x and y can be given in terms of x_0 and y_0:

$$x = x_0 + \Delta x = x_0 + \frac{m(y_0 - (mx_0 + b))}{1 + m^2} \text{ and}$$

$$y = y_0 + \Delta y = y_0 + \frac{(mx_0 + b) - y_0}{1 + m^2}.$$

It can be checked that these are the same formulas as derived earlier with calculus.

CHAPTER 4 – Equations

Section 4.1.1

1. {{b}, {a, b}}

2. Sample: (a, b, c) = ((a, b), c) = $\left\{\{\{a\},\{a,b\}\},\{\{\{a\},\{a,b\}\},c\}\right\}$

3. ($\Rightarrow$) Assume that (a, b) = (c, d). Then, by the definition of ordered pair,
    {{a}, {a, b}} = {{c}, {c, d}} $\Rightarrow$ {a} = {c} and {a, b} = {c, d} since equality between sets
    means that each set contains the same elements and {a} $\neq$ {c, d}. {a} = {c} $\Rightarrow$ a = c by the
    definition of equality of sets. a = c and {a, b} = {c, d} $\Rightarrow$ b = d also by the definition of equality
    of sets.
    ($\Leftarrow$) Assume that a = c and b = d. Then {a} = {c} and {a, b} = {c, d} $\Rightarrow$ {{a}, {a, b}}
    = {{c}, {c, d}} by the definition of equality of sets and (a, b) = (c, d) by the definition of
    ordered pair.

4. a. Sample: Consider the relation S "shares a side with" defined on all polygons in a plane. Let A, B,
        C, D, and E be distinct points. For all A, B, and C, $\triangle$ABC S $\triangle$ABC, so S is reflexive. And if
        $\triangle$ABC S $\triangle$ABD, then $\triangle$ABD S $\triangle$ABC, so S is symmetric. But S is not transitive, for though
        $\triangle$ABC S $\triangle$ABD and $\triangle$ABD S $\triangle$BDE, $\triangle$ABC does not share a side with $\triangle$BDE. (See also
        Problem 5.)

    b. Sample: Consider the relation "$\neq$" on the set {1}. This relation is the empty set. Thus it is
        vacuously true that the relation is both symmetric and transitive, since for all x, y, z $\in$ {1}, if
        (x, y) $\in$ "$\neq$", then (y, x) $\in$ "$\neq$" and if (x, y) and (y, z) $\in$ "$\neq$", (x, z) $\in$ "$\neq$". But the relation is
        not reflexive, since (1, 1) $\notin$ "$\neq$".

    c. Sample: Consider the relation "$\geq$" on **R**. The relation is reflexive: For all x, x $\geq$ x. The relation is
        transitive: for all x, y, z, if x $\geq$ y and y $\geq$ z, then x $\geq$ z. But it is not symmetric: 3 $\geq$ 2, but 2 $\geq$ 3.
        (See also Problem 6.)

5. No. It is not transitive. Example: 100 is close to 104 and 104 is close to 108 but 100 is not close to
    108.

6. The relation $\Rightarrow$ is reflexive and transitive but not symmetric; therefore it is not an equivalence relation.
    Proof:
    Reflexive: The statement p $\Rightarrow$ p is true for all p.
    Transitive: The statement [if p $\Rightarrow$ q and q $\Rightarrow$ r, then p $\Rightarrow$ r] is true for all p, q and r.
    But not symmetric: The statement [if p $\Rightarrow$ q, then q $\Rightarrow$ p] is *not* necessarily
    true for all p and q. (Let p be false and q be true.)

7.   a. $(a, b) + (c, d) = (a + b, c + d)$; $(a, b) \cdot (c, d) = (ac - bd, ad + bc)$
     b.   Answers will vary.

8.   (A geometric characterization of S) Two points are equivalent in S if and only if they lie on the same line with slope 1. In the first printing, $\times$ is used for $\cdot$ in the definition of $\cdot$.

     a. $(a_1, b_1) \equiv (a_2, b_2)$ and $(c_1, d_1) \equiv (c_2, d_2)$
          $\Rightarrow a_1 + b_2 = b_1 + a_2$ and $c_1 + d_2 = d_1 + c_2$
          Adding these last two equations together yields
          $\Rightarrow (a_1 + b_2) + (c_1 + d_2) = (b_1 + a_2) + (d_1 + c_2)$
          $\Rightarrow (a_1 + c_1) + (b_2 + d_2) = (b_1 + d_1) + (a_2 + c_2)$
          $\Rightarrow (a_1 + c_1, b_1 + d_1) \equiv (a_2 + c_2, b_2 + d_2)$
          $\Rightarrow (a_1, b_1) + (c_1, d_1) \equiv (a_2, b_2) + (c_2, d_2)$.

     b. $(a_1, b_1) \equiv (a_2, b_2)$ and $(c_1, d_1) \equiv (c_2, d_2)$
          $\Rightarrow a_1 + b_2 = b_1 + a_2$ and $c_1 + d_2 = d_1 + c_2$
          $\Rightarrow a_1 - b_1 = a_2 - b_2$ and $c_1 - d_1 = c_2 - d_2$
          Multiplying the last two equations together yields
          $\Rightarrow (a_1 c_1 + b_1 d_1) - (a_1 d_1 + b_1 c_1) = (a_2 c_2 + b_2 d_2) - (a_2 d_2 + b_2 c_2)$
          $\Rightarrow (a_1 c_1 + b_1 d_1) + (a_2 d_2 + b_2 c_2) = (a_2 c_2 + b_2 d_2) + (a_1 d_1 + b_1 c_1)$
          $\Rightarrow (a_1 c_1 + b_1 d_1, a_1 d_1 + b_1 c_1) \equiv (a_2 c_2 + b_2 d_2, a_2 d_2 + b_2 c_2)$
          $\Rightarrow (a_1, b_1) \cdot (c_1, d_1) \equiv (a_2, b_2) \cdot (c_2, d_2)$

     c. $(a, b) \cdot ((c, d) + (e, f)) = (a, b) \cdot (c + e, d + f)$
          $= (a(c + e) + b(d + f), a(d + f) + b(c + e))$
          $= (ac + ae + bd + bf, ad + af + bc + be)$
          $= ((ac + bd) + (ae + bf), (ad + bc) + (af + be))$
          $= (ac + bd, ad + bc) + (ae + bf, af + be)$
          $= (a, b) \cdot (c, d) + (a, b) \cdot (e, f)$

     d.   Let the function $T: S \to \mathbf{Z}$ be defined such that $T((a, b)) = a - b$. First we show that T is 1-1.
          $T((a, b)) = T((c, d)) \Rightarrow a - b = c - d \Rightarrow a + d = c + b \Rightarrow (a, b) \equiv (c, d)$
          Now we show that T preserves the operations + and $\cdot$.
          $T((a, b) + (c, d)) = T((a + c, b + d)) = a + c - (b + d) = a - b + c - d$
          $= T((a, b)) + T((c, d))$
          $T((a, b) \cdot (c, d)) = T((ac + bd, ad + bc)) = ac + bd - (ad + bc) = (a - b)(c - d)$
          $= T((a, b)) \cdot T((c, d))$

9.   System (d) is not isomorphic to the others. Each of the other systems has only one element, other than the identity element, that is its own inverse. In system (a) this element is -1, in (b) it is f, and in (c) it is a rotation of magnitude 180°. System (d) has three elements that are their own inverses: s, t, and u.

Section 4.1.2

1.   a.   true
     b.   false
     c. $(x + 10)^2 = x^2 + 100$ when $x = 0$; $(x + 10)^2 \neq x^2 + 100$ when $x = 1$.

2.   a.   true
     b.   false
     c. $\sin y = \cos y \bullet \tan y$ when $y = 0$ or $y = \frac{\pi}{4}$; when $y = \frac{\pi}{2}$, $\sin y = 1$ while $\cos y \bullet \tan y$ is undefined.

3.   a.   false
     b.   false
     c. $\frac{10 + 2z}{6 + z} = 2$ has no solution, so it cannot be true as either an existential or a universal statement.

4.   In the set of complex numbers there are eight solutions: $\pm 1, \pm\frac{1}{2}, \pm\sqrt{2}$, and $\pm i$. Consequently, if x is a real number, there are six solutions; if x is a rational number, there are four solutions; if x is an integer, there are two solutions. If x must be positive, then the number of real solutions is cut in half.

5.   The answer is (c) because it is not an identity since it fails for odd r, but then again it is not a false statement since it is true for $r = 1$.

6.   a.   The appropriate domain is the positive integers and half-integers.
     b.   The appropriate domain is the positive real numbers.
     c.   This could mean the value of the account three and a half years ago, or it could mean what present amount will become $5000 in three and a half years.

7.   Equations (b) and (d) are equivalent since they have identical solution sets, namely, $\{5\}$. Equation (a) has no solutions; equation (c) has the solution set $\{-5, 5\}$.

8.   Equations (b) and (d) are equivalent since they have identical solution sets, namely, $\{(A, B): A = \frac{3}{5}B\}$. Equation (a) has the solution set $\{(A, B): A = \frac{5}{3}B\}$; equation (c) has the solution set $\{(A, B): A = \frac{3}{5}B, (A, B) \neq (0, 0)\}$.

9.   (b); $x = \sqrt{9}$ only has the one solution 3.

10.   a.   Examples: (0.2, 33), (1, 33), (1.2, 55), (2, 55), (2.2, 77)

b.

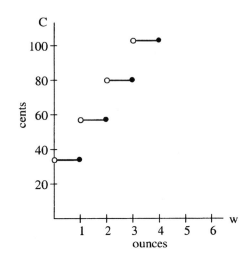

c. The first is a step graph with discontinuities at every integer value; the second is a linear equation. The values of the first are always greater than or equal to the second.

d. They are equivalent, because $\lceil w - 1 \rceil = \lceil w \rceil - 1$ and so
$34 + 23\lceil w - 1 \rceil = 34 + 23(\lceil w \rceil - 1) = 34 + 23\lceil w \rceil - 23 = 11 + 23\lceil w \rceil$. (But $C = 23\lceil w \rceil + 11$ is not equivalent to $\lceil 23w \rceil + 11$.)

11. a. $\left(\sqrt{(x+3)^2 + (y-9)^2} - 4 \right)^2 + \left(\sqrt{(x-2)^2 + (y-5)^2} - 6 \right)^2$

b. The two points of intersection of two circles.

12. a. $(x^2 + y^2 - 25)(|(x-10)^2 + y^2 - 100|) + ((x-10)^2 + y^2 - 100) = 0$

b. Refer to Figure 2. The graph is the union of the interior of the larger circle and the entire smaller circle.

13. a. $(x^2 + y^2 - 25) + ((x-10)^2 + y^2 - 100) = 2x^2 + 2y^2 - 20x - 25 = 0$. This is equivalent to $(x-5)^2 + y^2 = \frac{75}{2}$, which is the equation for a circle with center $(5, 0)$ and radius $\frac{5\sqrt{6}}{2}$. This circle contains points A and B.

b. $(x^2 + y^2 - 25) - ((x-10)^2 + y^2 - 100) = 20x - 25 = 0$. This is equivalent to $x = \frac{5}{4}$, which is the equation for the vertical line containing points A and B.

c. Any linear combination of the equations has a graph containing points A and B. This is because if (x, y) satisfies two equations, then it satisfies their sum, their difference, and any multiple of either.

14. The solution set for
$(x^2 + y^2)^2 - 13(x^2 + y^2) + 36 = 0$ is
the same as for the compound
sentence $x^2 + y^2 = 9$ or $x^2 + y^2 = 4$.
The graph is two concentric circles

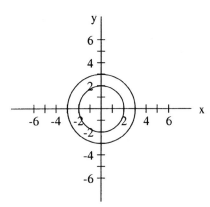

15. In the following solution, d is the distance from (h, k) to (j, m); or, algebraically,
$d = \sqrt{(h - j)^2 + (k - m)^2}$. Assume $d \neq 0$.
   a. The circles will intersect in two points if $r + s > d > |r - s|$.
   b. The circles will intersect in exactly one point if $r + s = d$ or if $|r - s| = d$.
   c. The circles will not intersect if $d > r + s$ or if $d < |r - s|$.

16. Since x = -1 and x = 2 are both solutions to $x^3 = 5x^2 - 2x - 8$, we divide $x^3 - 5x^2 + 2x + 8$ by
$(x + 1)(x - 2) = x^2 - x - 2$. This gives $(x - 4)$ as the quotient, so x = 4 is the remaining solution.

17.

Graph $y = x^3$ and $y = x^2$ as at left. The graph
shows two solutions, x = 0 and x = 1

$-2 \leq x \leq 2$,   x-scale = .4
$-2 \leq y \leq 2$,   y-scale = .4

18. a. The solution set for $3x^2 + 5xy - 2y^2 - 9x + 10y - 12 = 0$ is equivalent to the solution set for the
compound sentence $3x - y + 3 = 0$ or $x + 2y - 4 = 0$, whose graph is a pair of lines.
   b. $Ax^2 + Bxy + Cy^2 + Dx + Ey + F = 0$ will be an equation for a pair of lines if and only if it can
be written as the product of two linear expressions, i.e.,
$Ax^2 + Bxy + Cy^2 + Dx + Ey + F = (ax + by + c)(dx + ey + f)$.
   c. Sample: $(y - x - 1)(y - x) = x^2 - 2xy + y^2 + x - y = 0$
   d. $xy(y - x)(y + x) = y^3x - x^3y = 0$

19. Sample: $[x^2 + y^2 = 200$ or $(x - 10)^2 + (y - 10)^2 = 1$ or $(x + 10)^2 + (y - 10)^2 = 1$ or
$(x^2 + (y - 5)^2 = 200$ and $y < -\frac{1}{5}x$ and $y < \frac{1}{5}x)]$

Section 4.2.1

1. a. $a + (b + -a) = a + (-a + b)$ by the commutative property of addition.
        $a + (-a + b) = (a + -a) + b$ by the associative property of addition.
        $(a + -a) + b = 0 + b = b$ by the inverse and identity properties of addition.
    b. $a * (b * a^{-1}) = a * (a^{-1} * b)$ by the commutative property of multiplication.
        $a * (a^{-1} * b) = (a * a^{-1}) * b$ by the associative property of multiplication.
        $(a * a^{-1}) * b = 1 * b = b$ by the inverse and identity properties of multiplication.

2. $y * a = b$
    $(y * a) * a^{-1} = b * a^{-1}$ by the existence of inverses
    $y * (a * a^{-1}) = b * a^{-1}$ by associativity of *
    $y * 1 = b * a^{-1}$ by definition of inverses
    $y = b * a^{-1}$ by definition of identity element

3. a. yes
    b. no; $2x = 6$
    c. no; $3 + x = 5$
    d. no; $3x = 1$

4. a. yes
    b. no; $7x = 14$
    c. yes
    d. no; $\begin{bmatrix} 0 & 0 \\ 0 & 0 \end{bmatrix} M = \begin{bmatrix} 1 & 0 \\ 0 & 1 \end{bmatrix}$
    e. no; $\sqrt{2} + x = 1 + \sqrt{2}$

Section 4.2.2

1. a. $2x + 0 = 0x + 1$
    b. $\sqrt{4}x + \sqrt{0} = \sqrt{0}x + \sqrt{1}$
    c. $1ix + 0i = 0ix + 1i$
    d. $2^0 x + 2^0 = 2^2$

2. Let $S = \{ m + n\sqrt{2} : m, n \in \mathbf{Q}\}$. Properties of associativity, commutativity and distributivity will carry over from the field $\langle R, +, \rangle$. Since $0 = 0 + 0\sqrt{2}$ and $1 = 1 + 0\sqrt{2}$, $0, 1 \in S$. Let $a + b\sqrt{2}$, $c + d\sqrt{2} \in S$.
    $(a + b\sqrt{2}) + (c + d\sqrt{2}) = (a + c) + (b + d)\sqrt{2}$
    Since $(a + c), (b + d) \in \mathbf{Q}$, $(a + c) + (b + d)\sqrt{2} \in S$. So S is closed under addition.
    $(a + b\sqrt{2})(c + d\sqrt{2}) = (ac + 2bd) + (ad + bc)\sqrt{2}$
    Since $(ac + 2bd), (ad + bc) \in \mathbf{Q}$, $(ac + 2bd) + (ad + bc)\sqrt{2} \in S$. So S is closed under multiplication.
    For $m, n \in \mathbf{Q}$, $-m, -n \in \mathbf{Q}$. So if $x = m + n\sqrt{2} \in S$, $-m + -n\sqrt{2} = -(m + n\sqrt{2}) = -x \in S$.
    Let $x = m + n\sqrt{2} \in S$. Then $\dfrac{1}{x} = \dfrac{1}{m + n\sqrt{2}} = \dfrac{m - n\sqrt{2}}{m^2 - 2n} = \dfrac{m}{m^2 - 2n} - \dfrac{n}{m^2 - 2n}\sqrt{2}$

3. $(3 + 4\sqrt{2})x + (5 - 6\sqrt{2}) = (2 + \sqrt{2})x + 4\sqrt{2}$
    $\Rightarrow (2 + 3\sqrt{2})x = -5 + 10\sqrt{2}$
    $\Rightarrow x = \dfrac{-5 + 10\sqrt{2}}{2 + 3\sqrt{2}} = \dfrac{10 - 5\sqrt{2}}{2}$

4. The set is not closed under multiplication. Consider, for example, $\sqrt{2} \cdot \sqrt{3} = \sqrt{6}$. There is no number of the form $a + b\sqrt{2} + c\sqrt{3}$, with a, b, and c rational, equal to $\sqrt{6}$.

5. a. $P(n) = 30000 + 1500n$; $Q(n) = 30000 + 1750n$; $R(n) = 28000 + 1750n$

   b. $P(n) = R(n)$
   $30000 + 1500n = 28000 + 1750n$
   $2000 = 250n$
   $n = 8$ years

   c. $P(n) = Q(n)$
   $30000 + 1500n = 30000 + 1750n$
   $1500n = 1750n$
   $n = 0$

   d. $Q(n) = R(n)$
   $30000 + 1750n = 28000 + 1750n$
   $2000 = 0n$
   no solution

   e. $T(n) = S_T + nE_T$; $U(n) = S_U + nE_U$

   $T(n) = U(n)$
   $S_T + nE_T = S_U + nE_U$
   $S_T - S_U = nE_U - nE_T$
   $n = \dfrac{S_T - S_U}{E_U - E_T}$

6. $\left(\begin{bmatrix} a & b \\ c & d \end{bmatrix} \cdot \begin{bmatrix} e & f \\ g & h \end{bmatrix} \right) \cdot \begin{bmatrix} w & x \\ y & z \end{bmatrix} =$

$\begin{bmatrix} (ae + bg)w + (af + bh)y & (ae + bg)x + (af + bh)z \\ (ce + dg)w + (cf + dh)y & (ce + dg)x + (cf + dh)z \end{bmatrix} =$

$\begin{bmatrix} a(ew + fy) + b(gw + hy) & a(ex + fz) + b(gx + hz) \\ c(ew + fy) + d(gw + hy) & c(ex + fz) + b(gx + hz) \end{bmatrix} =$

$\begin{bmatrix} a & b \\ c & d \end{bmatrix} \cdot \left(\begin{bmatrix} e & f \\ g & h \end{bmatrix} \begin{bmatrix} w & x \\ y & z \end{bmatrix} \right)$

7. a. Assuming c, d, and $ad - bc \neq 0$, we can solve these systems using multiplication and addition.

   $(wa + xc) + -\dfrac{c}{d}(wb + xd) = 1$

   $wa - \dfrac{c}{d}wb = 1$

   $w\dfrac{ad - bc}{d} = 1$

   $w = \dfrac{d}{ad - bc}$

   $x = \dfrac{1 - wa}{c} = \dfrac{1}{c} - \dfrac{a}{c}\dfrac{d}{ad - bc} = \dfrac{-b}{ad - bc}$

   $(ya + zc) + -\dfrac{c}{d}(yb + zd) = -\dfrac{c}{d}$

   $ya - \dfrac{c}{d}yb = -\dfrac{c}{d}$

$$y \frac{ad - bc}{d} = -\frac{c}{d}$$

$$y = \frac{-c}{ad - bc}$$

$$z = -\frac{ya}{c} = \frac{a}{ad - bc}$$

b. In matrix notation, the systems in part **a** can be represented by

$\begin{bmatrix} w & x \\ y & z \end{bmatrix} \begin{bmatrix} a & b \\ c & d \end{bmatrix} = \begin{bmatrix} 1 & 0 \\ 0 & 1 \end{bmatrix}$. Solving for $\begin{bmatrix} w & x \\ y & z \end{bmatrix}$ yields

$\begin{bmatrix} w & x \\ y & z \end{bmatrix} = \begin{bmatrix} 1 & 0 \\ 0 & 1 \end{bmatrix} \begin{bmatrix} a & b \\ c & d \end{bmatrix}^{-1}$ and since $\begin{bmatrix} 1 & 0 \\ 0 & 1 \end{bmatrix}$ is the identity matrix,

$\begin{bmatrix} w & x \\ y & z \end{bmatrix} = \begin{bmatrix} a & b \\ c & d \end{bmatrix}^{-1} = \frac{1}{ad - bc} \begin{bmatrix} d & -b \\ -c & a \end{bmatrix} = \begin{bmatrix} \dfrac{d}{ad - bc} & \dfrac{-b}{ad - bc} \\ \dfrac{-c}{ad - bc} & \dfrac{a}{ad - bc} \end{bmatrix}$, provided

$ad - bc \neq 0$.

8. a. $\begin{bmatrix} 2 & -5 \\ 4 & -15 \end{bmatrix} \begin{bmatrix} x \\ y \end{bmatrix} = \begin{bmatrix} 11 \\ -4 \end{bmatrix}$

$\begin{bmatrix} 2 & -5 \\ 4 & -15 \end{bmatrix}^{-1} \begin{bmatrix} 2 & -5 \\ 4 & -15 \end{bmatrix} \begin{bmatrix} x \\ y \end{bmatrix} = \begin{bmatrix} 2 & -5 \\ 4 & -15 \end{bmatrix}^{-1} \begin{bmatrix} 11 \\ -4 \end{bmatrix}$

$\begin{bmatrix} x \\ y \end{bmatrix} = \begin{bmatrix} 2 & -5 \\ 4 & -15 \end{bmatrix}^{-1} \begin{bmatrix} 11 \\ -4 \end{bmatrix}$

$\begin{bmatrix} x \\ y \end{bmatrix} = \frac{1}{-10} \begin{bmatrix} -15 & 5 \\ -4 & 2 \end{bmatrix} \begin{bmatrix} 11 \\ -4 \end{bmatrix} = \begin{bmatrix} 18.5 \\ 5.2 \end{bmatrix}$

b. $\begin{bmatrix} a & b \\ c & d \end{bmatrix} \begin{bmatrix} x \\ y \end{bmatrix} = \begin{bmatrix} e \\ f \end{bmatrix}$

$\begin{bmatrix} x \\ y \end{bmatrix} = \begin{bmatrix} a & b \\ c & d \end{bmatrix}^{-1} \begin{bmatrix} e \\ f \end{bmatrix}$

$\begin{bmatrix} x \\ y \end{bmatrix} = \frac{1}{ad - bc} \begin{bmatrix} d & -b \\ -c & a \end{bmatrix} \begin{bmatrix} e \\ f \end{bmatrix} = \begin{bmatrix} \dfrac{de - bf}{ad - bc} \\ \dfrac{af - ce}{ad - bc} \end{bmatrix}$

9. They are equal.

Section 4.2.3

1. a. $x + y = -10$ and $xy = 5$

$\Rightarrow x(-10 - x) = 5$

$\Rightarrow x^2 + 10x + 5 = 0$

$\Rightarrow x = \frac{-10 \pm \sqrt{10^2 - 4(5)(1)}}{2(1)} = -5 \pm 2\sqrt{5}$

b. $x + y = 1$ and $xy = 1$

$\Rightarrow x(1 - x) = 1$

$$\Rightarrow x^2 - x + 1 = 0$$

$$\Rightarrow x = \frac{1 \pm \sqrt{(-1)^2 - 4(1)(1)}}{2(1)} = \frac{1 \pm \sqrt{3}i}{2}$$

c. $xy = 60$ and $2x + 2y = 200$

$$\Rightarrow x(100 - x) = 60$$

$$\Rightarrow x^2 - 100x + 60 = 0$$

$$\Rightarrow x = \frac{100 \pm \sqrt{(-100)^2 - 4(60)(1)}}{2(1)}$$

$x \approx 99.400$ cm and $y \approx 0.604$ cm

2.   If m and n are distinct solutions to $ax^2 + bx + c = 0$, then they are distinct solutions to $x^2 + \frac{b}{a}x + \frac{c}{a} = 0$. By Theorem 4.5, $m + n = -\frac{b}{a}$ and $mn = \frac{c}{a}$. Conversely, $m + n = -\frac{b}{a}$ and $mn = \frac{c}{a}$ implies that $m(-\frac{b}{a} - m) = \frac{c}{a}$, or $m^2 + \frac{b}{a}m + \frac{c}{a} = 0$. So m is a solution to the quadratic equation $ax^2 + bx + c = 0$. Solving these two equations for n yields the same result.

3.   a.   Let $k = 2b$. Then $x^2 + 2bx + c = x^2 + kx + c$. By Theorem 4.6(a),

$$x = -\frac{k}{2} \pm \sqrt{\frac{k^2}{4} - c} = -\frac{2b}{2} \pm \sqrt{\frac{(2b)^2}{4} - c} = -b \pm \sqrt{b^2 - c}.$$

   b. $ax^2 + bx + c = 0 \Leftrightarrow x^2 + \frac{b}{a}x + \frac{c}{a} = 0$. By Theorem 4.6(a),

$$x^2 + \frac{b}{a}x + \frac{c}{a} = 0 \Leftrightarrow \frac{-\frac{b}{a}}{2} \pm \sqrt{\frac{\left(-\frac{b}{a}\right)^2}{4} - \frac{c}{a}} = \frac{-b \pm \sqrt{b^2 - 4ac}}{2a}.$$

4. $xy = 18$ and $x + y = k \Rightarrow x(k - x) = 18 \Leftrightarrow x^2 - kx + 18 = 0$. Thus $x = \frac{k \pm \sqrt{k^2 - 4(18)}}{2}$. If $k^2 < 4(18)$, then the discriminant is negative and the quadratic equation has no real solutions. Thus if $-2\sqrt{18} < k < 2\sqrt{18}$, the line and the hyperbola will not intersect.

5. $\frac{-b + \sqrt{b^2 - 4ac}}{2a} - \frac{-b - \sqrt{b^2 - 4ac}}{2a} = \frac{\sqrt{b^2 - 4ac}}{a}$

6.   Let $m = \frac{-b + \sqrt{b^2 - 4ac}}{2a}$ and $n = \frac{-b - \sqrt{b^2 - 4ac}}{2a}$.

   a. $m^2 + n^2 = \frac{b^2 + (b^2 - 4ac) - 2b\sqrt{b^2 - 4ac}}{4a^2} + \frac{b^2 + (b^2 - 4ac) + 2b\sqrt{b^2 - 4ac}}{4a^2}$

$= \frac{4b^2 - 8ac}{4a^2} = \frac{b^2 - 2ac}{a^2}$ OR $m^2 + n^2 = (m + n)^2 - 2mn = -\left(\frac{b}{a}\right)^2 - 2\left(\frac{c}{a}\right) = \frac{b^2 - 2ac}{a^2}$

   b. $m^3 + n^3 = (m + n)(m^2 - 2mn + n^2) = \frac{c}{a}(\frac{b^2 - 2ac}{a^2} - 2(\frac{c}{a})) = \frac{c(b^2 - 2ac - 2a^2)}{a^3}$

7.   a-c.   If r_1, r_2, and r_3 are solutions to $ax^3 + bx^2 + cx + d = 0$, then they are solutions to $x^3 + \frac{b}{a}x^2 + \frac{c}{a}x + \frac{d}{a} = 0$. By the Factor Theorem, $x^3 + \frac{b}{a}x^2 + \frac{c}{a}x + \frac{d}{a} = (x - r_1)(x - r_2)(x - r_3) = x^3 - (r_1 + r_2 + r_3)x^2 + (r_1r_2 + r_2r_3 + r_1r_3)x - r_1r_2r_3$. Letting $x = 0$, we can establish that $r_1r_2r_3 = -\frac{d}{a}$. Thus $-(r_1 + r_2 + r_3)x^2 + (r_1r_2 + r_2r_3 + r_1r_3)x = \frac{b}{a}x^2 + \frac{c}{a}x$. By letting

x = 1 and x = -1 and solving the system of equations, we can establish that $r_1 + r_2 + r_3 = -\frac{b}{a}$ and $r_1 r_2 + r_2 r_3 + r_1 r_3 = \frac{c}{a}$.

d. In general, if r_1, r_2, ..., r_n are solutions to the equation
$a_n x^n + a_{n-1} x^{n-1} + ... + a_1 x + a_0 = 0$, then

$$\frac{a_{n-1}}{a_n} = (-1)^{n-1}(r_1 + r_2 + ... + r_n)$$

$$\frac{a_{n-2}}{a_n} = (-1)^n (r_1 r_2 + r_1 r_3 + ... + r_1 r_n + r_2 r_3 + ... + r_2 r_n + ... + r_{n-1} r_n) = \sum_{i=1, j=1, i \neq j}^{i=n, j=n} (-1)^n r_i r_j$$

...

$$\frac{a_1}{a_n} = (-1)^{n-1} \underbrace{r_1 r_2 r_3 ... r_{n-1} + ... + r_1 r_2 r_3 ... r_{n-2} r_n + ... + r_2 r_3 ... r_{n-1} r_n}_{n \text{ terms}} ($$

$$\frac{a_0}{a_n} = (-1)^n r_1 r_2 ... r_n$$

Section 4.3.1

1. a. $\log x = x^2 - 2$ has one real solution at $x \approx 1.47$.

    b. $e^t = 1 + t$ has one real solution at $x = 0$.

    c. $\sin \theta = \frac{\theta}{10}$ has seven real solutions at $x = 0$, $x \approx \pm 2.85$, $x \approx \pm 7.07$, and $x \approx \pm 8.42$.

2. a. There are no solutions in the set of real numbers.

    b. The only solution is y = 5. y cannot be –5 because the log function is not defined for $y \geq \frac{3}{2}$.

    c. No real solution, because, except for the values z = -1 and z = 15 and z < 20, $z + 1 = \sqrt{z - 20}$ and the discriminant of $z^2 + z + 21 = 0$ is negative.

    d. There is no solution because the left-hand side of the equation is either 1 for w ≠ -1 or undefined for w = -1.

3. Step 6 is in error because dividing by x – y is equivalent to dividing by 0.

4. Let a and b be any two real numbers.
    Step 1: 1 = 2   Given
    Step 2: 1(b – a) = 2(b – a)   Multiplication Property of Equality
    Step 3: b – a = 2b – 2a   Distributive Property
    Step 4: (b – a) + (2a – b) = (2b – 2a) + (2a – b) Addition Property of Equality
    Step 5: a = b   Addition

5. Let x, x + 1, x + 2, and x + 3 be four consecutive integers. The product of the first and last integers is $x(x + 3) = x^2 + 3x$. The product of the middle two integers is $(x + 1)(x + 2) = x^2 + 3x + 2$. The equation $x^2 + 3x + 2 = x^2 + 3x$ has no solutions.

6. a. Let x, x + 1, x + 2, and x + 3 be four consecutive integers. The sum of the first and last integers is x + (x + 3) = 2x + 3. The sum of the middle two integers is (x + 1) + (x + 2) = 2x + 3.

    b. Sample: For n consecutive integers, when n is even, the sum of the middle two is always equal to the sum of the first and last. For n consecutive integers, when n is odd, twice the middle integer is equal to the sum of the first and last.

Proof: Consider n consecutive integers x, x + 1,..., x + n – 1. The sum of the first and last integers is x + (x + n – 1) = 2x + (n – 1). For even n, the sum of the middle two integers is $(x + \frac{n-2}{2}) + (x + \frac{n}{2}) = 2x + \frac{2n-2}{2} = 2x + (n - 1)$. For odd n, twice the middle integer is $2(x + \frac{n-1}{2}) = 2x + (n - 1)$.

Section 4.3.2

1. a.   Apply the function f(x) = ln x to each side. This yields $t^2 = 3t$. Subtracting 3t from both sides of the equation and factoring yields t(t – 3) = 0. By the Zero Product Property, t = 0 or t = 3.

    b.   m = ±25; apply the function $f(x) = 5^x$ and then $g(x) = \pm\sqrt{x}$.

    c.   p = ±2; apply the function $f(x) = 5^x$ and then $g(x) = \pm\sqrt{x}$.

    d. $z = \log_6 3 \approx 0.6131$; apply the function $f(x) = \log_6 x$

    e.   Subtracting 12n from both sides of the equation and factoring yields $n(n^{11} - 12) = 0$. By the Zero Product Property, n = 0 or $n^{11} = 12$. Applying the function $f(x) = n^{1/11}$ to both sides of $n^{11} = 12$ yields $n = 12^{1/11}$.

    f.   x = 3; Apply $f(x) = (2x)^y$, followed by $g(x) = \frac{x}{3}$, followed by $h(x) = \log_2 x$, and then $j(x) = x^y$.

2.   ($\Rightarrow$) If f is a 1-1 function, then there is an inverse f^{-1} such that $f^{-1}(f(x)) = x$ for all x in the domain of f. So $x = f^{-1}(f(x)) = f^{-1}(k)$.

     ($\Leftarrow$) If f is a 1-1 function, then there is an inverse f^{-1} such that $f(f^{-1}(y)) = y$ for all x in the domain of f^{-1}. So $k = f(f^{-1}(k)) = f(x)$.

3.   The other solution to $\sin\theta = \frac{\sqrt{3}}{2}$ in the interval $[0, 2\pi)$ is $\frac{2\pi}{3}$. All other solutions can be found by adding integral multiples of 2π to these two solutions, i.e., $\theta = \frac{\pi}{3} + 2n\pi$ and $\theta = \frac{2\pi}{3} + 2n\pi$.

4. a.   In the interval $[0, \pi]$, $v = \cos^{-1} 0.5 = \frac{\pi}{3} \approx 1.047$. In the interval $(\pi, 2\pi)$, $v = \cos^{-1} 0.5 = \frac{5\pi}{3} \approx 5.236$.

    b.   In the interval $[0, 2\pi)$, $w = 3\tan^{-1} 1 = \frac{3\pi}{4} \approx 2.356$.

5. a.   I(x) = 1x + 0. I(f(x)) = 1(ax + b) + 0 = ax + b and f(I(x)) = a(1x + 0) + b = ax + b.

    b. $f^{-1}(x) = \frac{x+4}{5}$

    c.   Let f(x) = 5x – 4 = 12. Then $f^{-1}(f(x)) = \frac{(5x-4)+4}{5}$. So $x = f^{-1}(12) = \frac{16}{5}$.

6.   It has not violated Theorem 4.9, since the theorem only applies when h is a 1-1 function. The function $h(x) = x^3$ is not a 1-1 function when its domain is the set **C**.

7. a.   Solve $155000 = 112000(1 + r)^8$; $r + 1 = (\frac{155000}{112000})^{1/8} \approx 1.041$.

    b.   Solve $2 = (1.06)^x$; ln 2 = x ln 1.06; $x = \frac{\ln 2}{\ln 1.06} \approx 11.9$ years.

    c. $\frac{\ln 2}{\ln 1.02} \approx 35$ years, $\frac{\ln 2}{\ln 1.04} \approx 17.7$ years, $\frac{\ln 2}{\ln 1.08} \approx 9$ years

d. The function $n = f(r) = \dfrac{\ln 2}{\ln\left(1 + \frac{r}{100}\right)}$ gives the number n of years for an amount with an annual

inflation factor of r% to double. The function $n = g(r) = \frac{72}{r}$ is the rule of 72 estimate for n. The

graphs of f and g, which are both drawn below, are very nearly identical.

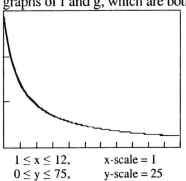

$1 \le x \le 12,$ x-scale = 1
$0 \le y \le 75,$ y-scale = 25

Section 4.3.3

1. The functions A(t) = 15 + .21t and B(t) = 20 + .18t are graphed below over the domain [0, 300]. The
    solution set of the inequality A(t) < B(t) is given by the values of t for which the graph of B(t) is above
    the graph of A(t), namely, $0 \le t < 167$.

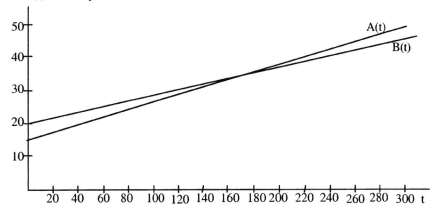

2. a. C(t) = 19.99 + .21t; D(t) = 19.99 + .19t; the inequality 19.99 + .21t < 19.99 + .19t will never be
        true, so company C will never be preferred.

    b. C(t) = 19.99 + .21t; D(t) = 18.99 + .19t; the inequality 19.99 + .21t < 18.99 + .19t will again
        never be true, so company C will never be preferred.

    c. C(t) = 19.99 + .21t; D(t) = 5 + .35t; the inequality 19.99 + .21t < 5 + .35t will be true for
        t > 107.1.

3. $a + b > c > |a - b|$

4. a. $d < |r - s|$ b. $d = |r - s|$ c. $r + s > d > |r - s|$
    d. $d = r + s$ e. $d > r + s$

5. The Triangle Inequality yields the three inequalities y > 10 − x, x + 10 > y and y > x − 10.

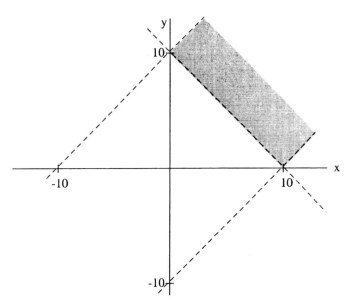

6. h is the function given by h(x) = -x. Since h is a decreasing function, if f(x) < g(x), then, by Theorem 4.11, h(f(x)) > h(g(x)).

7. h is strictly decreasing ⇔ for all a, b, on an interval, a < b ⇒ h(a) > h(b). The ⇒ direction of the theorem follows by substituting f(x) for a and g(x) for b. Now, because h is a decreasing function, it has an inverse h⁻¹ that is decreasing. Think of h(f(x)) and h(g(x)) as being a and b, and h⁻¹ as the decreasing function. Then apply h⁻¹ to both sides.

8. The statement of Theorem 4.11 for the case of a constant function h is that for continuous real functions f and g, with domain D, if h is constant on the intersection of f(D) and g(D), then f(x) < g(x) ⇔ h(f(x)) = h(g(x)). This is not a valid theorem. Although the ⇒ direction is true (since h is a constant function), the ⇐ direction is false. For a counterexample take f = g.

9. The result found in this lesson is $0 \le x \le \frac{1}{5}$. The graph of $y = x^{-3}$ shown below is above the line y = 125 when $0 \le x \le \frac{1}{5}$, so the result checks.

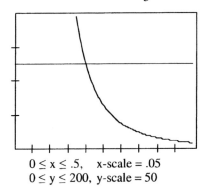

$0 \le x \le .5$, x-scale = .05
$0 \le y \le 200$, y-scale = 50

10. Begin with $\frac{1}{x} < 2$. Apply $h(x) = x^{-1}$ to both sides.

Case 1: $x > 0$

$(\frac{1}{x})^{-1} > 2^{-1}$ The sense of the inequality is reversed.

$x > \frac{1}{2}$ by Theorem 4.11b, since h is decreasing for $x > 0$.

Case 2: $x < 0$

$(\frac{1}{x})^{-1} < 2^{-1}$ The sense of the inequality is kept.

$x < \frac{1}{2}$ by Theorem 4.11a, since h is increasing for $x < 0$.

So the solution is $x < 0$ or $x > \frac{1}{2}$.

11. $0.15 \le (\frac{1}{2})^{\frac{x}{5730}} \le 0.20$

$\ln 0.15 \le (\frac{x}{5730}) \ln \frac{1}{2} \le \ln 0.20$

$5730 \frac{\ln 0.15}{\ln 0.5} \ge x \ge 5730 \frac{\ln 0.20}{\ln 0.5}$

$15682.8 \ge x \ge 13304.6$ years

12. $\sin \theta > \sin 2\theta$

$\sin \theta > 2 \sin \theta \cos \theta$

$\frac{1}{2} > \cos \theta$

$\cos^{-1}(\frac{1}{2}) < \theta$

$\frac{\pi}{3} < \theta < \frac{\pi}{2}$

13. a. $y < -2$ or $y > 1.5$

     b. $-0.25 \le t \le 1$

     c. $(x - 1)^3 < 8$ when $x - 1 < 2$, or $x < 3$.

     d. $-1 - \sqrt{62} \le d \le -1 + \sqrt{62}$

     e. $3^{2^x - 1} < \frac{1}{9} = 3^{-2}$ when $2^x - 1 < -2$, or $2^x < -1$. Since $2^x > 0$ for all x, there are no real solutions.

     f. $y < -1.1$ or $y > -0.9$

     g.   The equality will never hold. The inequality will hold when $(x + a < 0$ and $x + b > 0)$ or when $(x + a > 0$ and $x + b < 0)$. So $-b < x < -a$ or $-a < x < -b$.

     h. $\frac{x^2 + 10x + 25}{x + 5} = \frac{(x + 5)^2}{x + 5} = x + 5$, when $x \ne -5$. $x + 5 > 6 \Rightarrow x > 1$.

14. Since $a > 0$, the graph of $ax^2 + bx + c$ is a parabola that is concave up. This means all solutions to $ax^2 + bx + c < 0$ will lie between the two zeros, i.e., $\frac{-b - \sqrt{b^2 - 4ac}}{2a} < x < \frac{-b + \sqrt{b^2 - 4ac}}{2a}$.

Section 4.3.4

1. $$\cfrac{1}{\frac{1}{2}\left(\frac{1}{x}+\frac{1}{y}\right)} = \frac{1}{2}\left(\frac{1}{x}+\frac{1}{y}\right) = \frac{\frac{1}{x}+\frac{1}{y}}{2}$$

2. $$\frac{2}{\frac{1}{x}+\frac{1}{y}} = \frac{2}{\left(\frac{y+x}{xy}\right)} = \frac{2xy}{y+x}$$

3. $$\lim_{w\to\infty}\frac{2}{\frac{1}{w}+\frac{1}{30}} = \frac{2}{0+\frac{1}{30}} = 60$$

4.
   a. The slope of segment 3 is the arithmetic mean of the slopes of segments 1 and 2.
   b. The slope of segment 3 is the harmonic mean of the slopes of segments 1 and 2.
   c. Figure 14 demonstrates that if an object travels at two different rates for the same amount of time, then the average rate will be the arithmetic mean of the two rates. Figure 15 demonstrates that if an object travels at two different rates over the same distance, then the average rate will be the harmonic mean of the two rates.

5.
   a. Let us use the term "pace" to refer to a speed measured in minutes per mile. The average pace s is the total time in minutes divided by the total distance in miles. Let the one-way distance be d miles. The time out is 6d minutes (since the pace is 6 minutes per mile), and the time back is 12d minutes. Therefore, $s = \frac{6d+12d}{2d} = 9$ minutes per mile.
   b. On a round trip with a pace of p minutes per mile on the way out and q minutes per mile on the way back, the solution in part **a** shows that the average pace is $\frac{pd+qd}{2d} = \frac{p+q}{2}$. This is the *arithmetic* mean of the paces p and q. This differs from round trips with speed measured in the usual units of distance per time, where the average speed is the *harmonic* mean of the individual speeds.

6.
   a. Let us again use the term "pace" to refer to a speed measured in minutes per mile. The average pace s is the total time in minutes divided by the total distance in miles. Let the time of each segment be t minutes. The distance of the first segment is $\frac{t}{6}$ miles (since the pace is 6 minutes per mile), and the distance of the second segment is $\frac{t}{12}$ miles. Therefore, $s = \frac{2t}{\frac{t}{6}+\frac{t}{12}} = 8$ minutes per mile.
   b. On a run of two equal segments with a pace of p minutes per mile on the first segment and q minutes per mile on the second segment, the solution in part **a** shows that the average pace is $\frac{2t}{\frac{t}{p}+\frac{t}{q}}$. This is the *harmonic* mean of the paces p and q. This differs from trips of equal time segments with speed measured in the usual units of distance divided by time, where the average speed is the *arithmetic* mean of the individual speeds.

7. Let $a > b$. Then $\frac{a}{2} > \frac{b}{2}$. Add $\frac{b}{2}$ to both sides. So $\frac{a}{2} + \frac{b}{2} = \frac{a+b}{2} > \frac{b}{2} + \frac{b}{2} = b$. Similarly, adding $\frac{a}{2}$ to both sides yields $\frac{a}{2} + \frac{a}{2} = a > \frac{b}{2} + \frac{a}{2} = \frac{a+b}{2}$. Combining these results, $b < \frac{a+b}{2} < a$.

8. From Problem 7, given $a > b > 0$, $a > \frac{a+b}{2} > b$. Taking the reciprocals, $\frac{1}{a} < \frac{2}{a+b} < \frac{1}{b}$. So $\frac{b}{ab} < \frac{2}{a+b} < \frac{a}{ab}$. Thus $b < \frac{2ab}{a+b} < a$.

9. Let $a > b > 0$. Then $a \bullet a > a \bullet b$. So $a^2 > ab$ or $a > \sqrt{ab}$. Alternatively, $a \bullet b > b \bullet b$. So $ab > b^2$ or $\sqrt{ab} > b$.

10. a. Let $a, b > 0$. Then
$$\sqrt{\frac{1}{\frac{1}{2}\left(\frac{1}{a} + \frac{1}{b}\right)} \cdot \frac{a+b}{2}} = \sqrt{\frac{1}{\frac{1}{2}\left(\frac{a+b}{ab}\right)} \cdot \frac{a+b}{2}} = \sqrt{\frac{2ab}{a+b} \cdot \frac{a+b}{2}} = \sqrt{ab}$$

   b. For $a = b$, the geometric mean, harmonic mean, and arithmetic mean are all equal. For $a, b > 0$ and $a \neq b$, $(a - b)^2 > 0$. So
   $a^2 - 2ab + b^2 > 0$
   $a^2 + 2ab + b^2 > 4ab$
   $(a + b)^2 > 4ab$
   $a + b > \frac{4ab}{a+b}$
   $\frac{a+b}{2} > \frac{2ab}{a+b} = \frac{1}{\frac{1}{2}\left(\frac{1}{a} + \frac{1}{b}\right)}$

   So for two positive numbers the arithmetic mean is greater than the harmonic mean. By part **a** the geometric mean of the two numbers equals the geometric mean of the harmonic mean and arithmetic mean of the two numbers. So the general ordering relationship is arithmetic mean > geometric mean > harmonic mean.

11. In the first printing, the exponent 2 in ax^2 is missing. If the solutions are m and n, then
$$H(m, n) = \frac{2}{\frac{1}{m} + \frac{1}{n}} = \frac{2mn}{m+n} = \frac{2\frac{c}{a}}{-\frac{b}{a}} = \frac{-2c}{b} \text{ (see Theorem 4.5).}$$

12. For all integers $n > 1$, $\frac{1}{n}$ is the harmonic mean of $\frac{1}{n-1}$ and $\frac{1}{n+1}$. More generally, $\frac{1}{n}$ is the harmonic mean of $\frac{1}{n-a}$ and $\frac{1}{n+a}$.

13. a. $\frac{z}{y} = \frac{EA}{d}$
    $\frac{z}{x} = \frac{d - EA}{d} = 1 - \frac{EA}{d}$
    $\frac{z}{x} = 1 - \frac{z}{y}$
    $z = \frac{1}{\frac{1}{x} + \frac{1}{y}}$, so $z = H(x, y)$.

   b. The length of $\overline{EF}$ is dependent only on the lengths of $\overline{AB}$ and $\overline{CD}$. It does not depend on d.

   c. Answers will vary.

14. a. Car A is traveling at a speed $\frac{100}{t_A}$ and car B at a speed $\frac{100}{t_B}$. When the two cars meet after a time t, the sum of their distances traveled will equal 100. Thus $\frac{100}{t_A}t + \frac{100}{t_B}t = 100$, or $t(\frac{1}{t_A} + \frac{1}{t_B}) = 1$. So $t = \dfrac{1}{\frac{1}{t_A} + \frac{1}{t_B}}$. The times are proportional to the distances, so they can be thought of as proxies for the distances.

  b. If person A can do a job in time t_A and person B can do the same job in time t_B, then A will be working at a rate $\frac{1}{t_A}$ jobs per unit time and B at a rate of $\frac{1}{t_B}$ jobs per unit time. Together they would work at a rate of $\frac{1}{t_A} + \frac{1}{t_B}$ jobs per unit time. Thus to complete a job working together would take time $\dfrac{1}{\frac{1}{t_A} + \frac{1}{t_B}}$.

  c. In part **a**, the job can be thought of as traveling the entire 100-mile distance. Car A can do the job in time t_A and car B can do it in time t_B. Together, they can cover the entire distance (do the job) in time $\dfrac{1}{\frac{1}{t_A} + \frac{1}{t_B}}$.

15. a. i. The flaw is in the assumption that $(v_P - v_S)(t_S - t_P)$ equals either $v_P t_P$ or $v_S t_S$, either of which equals the distance from the earthquake epicenter to the seismograph station.

  ii. The difference between the speeds of the two waves, 2.2 $\frac{km}{sec}$, represents the rate at which the faster P-wave is pulling ahead of the slower S-wave. Multiplying this by 15 seconds to get 33 km gives the distance the P-wave is ahead of the S-wave 15 seconds after the earthquake strikes. This time has nothing to do with the given problem, where the 15 seconds refers to the time difference in arrival of the two waves at the seismograph station.

  b. Let $x = 0$ be the position of the seismograph station and $t = 0$ be the time the P-wave arrives at the station. Then the P-wave and S-wave distance vs. time functions are given by the equations $x = 5.6t$ and $x = 3.4t - (3.4)(15)$, respectively. The intersection of the graphs represents the epicenter, and so the distance to the epicenter is the amount this intersection is below the t-axis. Measuring on the graph gives an answer of about 130 km.

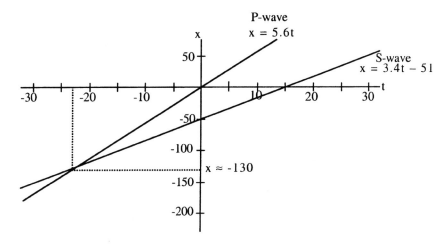

c.   The S and P-waves travel the same distance x to reach the station. Let the P-wave arrive in time t. Then the S-wave arrives in time t + 15. So x = 5.6t = 3.4(t + 15); 2.2t = 51;

$d = 5.6(\frac{51}{2.2}) \approx 129.8$ km.

d. $pt = s(t + d)$; $pt - st = sd$; $t(p - s) = sd$; $t = \frac{sd}{p - s}$; $x = pt = \frac{psd}{p - s} = \frac{sp}{p - s}d = \frac{1}{\frac{1}{s} - \frac{1}{p}}d$

e.   Sample: The harmonic mean of two numbers is symmetric with respect to its arguments since

$H(p, s) = \frac{2}{\frac{1}{p} + \frac{1}{s}} = \frac{2}{\frac{1}{s} + \frac{1}{p}} = H(s, p)$, whereas the harmonic difference is antisymmetric, i.e.,

$D(p, s) = \frac{1}{\frac{1}{p} - \frac{1}{s}} = -\frac{1}{\frac{1}{s} - \frac{1}{p}} = -D(s, p)$. Also, the harmonic mean and harmonic difference differ in

their limits as one argument goes to infinity, i.e., $\lim_{p \to \infty} H(p, s) = 2s$ and $\lim_{s \to \infty} H(p, s) = 2p$, but

$\lim_{p \to \infty} D(p, s) = -s$, and $\lim_{s \to \infty} D(p, s) = p$

f.   i.   For two resistors R_1 and R_2 in parallel, the potential drop across each will be the same ($\Delta V_1 = \Delta V_2 = \Delta V$) and the total current will be the sum of the currents passing through each ($I_{tot} = I_1 + I_2$). The equivalent resistance R_{eq} of the two resistors can then be found by

applying Ohm's Law ($\Delta V = IR$). $I_{tot} = I_1 + I_2 = \frac{\Delta V}{R_1} + \frac{\Delta V}{R_1} = \frac{\Delta V}{R_{eq}}$. So $\frac{1}{R_{eq}} = \frac{1}{R_1} + \frac{1}{R_1}$, or

$R_{eq} = \frac{1}{\frac{1}{R_1} + \frac{1}{R_2}}$. Thus the equivalent resistance of two resistors in parallel is half the

harmonic mean of their resistances.

ii.   For a thin convex lens, a formula relating the focal length f of the lens to the distances from the lens of the object d_0 and image d_i can be derived as follows. A light ray emanating from a point on the object and parallel to the lens's axis of symmetry will be bent so as to pass through the focus on the far side of the lens. A light ray emanating from the same point and passing through the lens's focus on the near side will be bent parallel to the lens's axis on

the far side. From similar triangles, $\frac{d_0 - f}{h_0} = \frac{f}{h_i}$ and $\frac{d_i - f}{h_i} = \frac{f}{h_0}$. So $\frac{d_0 - f}{f} = \frac{f}{d_i - f}$, or

$f = \frac{1}{\frac{1}{d_i} + \frac{1}{d_0}}$. Thus the focal length is half the harmonic mean of the distances from the lens

of the object and its image.

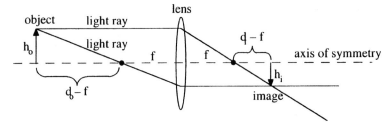

16.   The harmonic mean of n numbers $a_1, a_2, \ldots, a_n$ is $\dfrac{1}{\dfrac{1}{n}\left(\dfrac{1}{a_1} + \dfrac{1}{a_2} + \ldots \dfrac{1}{a_n}\right)}$.

CHAPTER 5 – Integers and Polynomials

1. a. Samples: $a_n = \frac{n^2}{2} - \frac{n}{2} + 2$; 8, 12, 17

   $b_n = F_{n-2}$, where F_n is the nth Fibonacci number; 8, 13, 21

   b. Samples: $a_n = 2^n$; 16, 32, 64

   $b_n = n^2 - n + 2$; 14, 22, 32

   c. Samples: $a_n = 4 + (-1)^{n+1}\left\lceil \frac{n}{2} \right\rceil$; 2, 7, 1

   $b_1 = 5, b_2 = 3, b_n = b_{n-1} + b_{n-2} - 2$ for $n \geq 3$; 7, 11, 16

   d. Samples: $a_n = \frac{n}{1 + 2^{n-1}}$; $\frac{4}{9}, \frac{5}{17}, \frac{6}{33}$

   $b_1 = \frac{1}{2}, b_2 = \frac{2}{3}, b_n = \frac{n}{F_n}$ for $n \geq 3$, where F_n is the nth Fibonacci term; $\frac{1}{2}, \frac{5}{13}, \frac{2}{7}$

2. Transferring 5 disks requires $2^5 - 1 = 31$ moves. Begin by transferring the top 4 disks to another peg. In turn, do that by transferring the top 3 disks to another peg.

Step 1

5	0	0	→	4	1	0	
4	1	0	→	3	1	1	(Top 2 disks from A to C)
3	1	1	→	3	0	2	
3	0	2	→	2	1	2	(Middle disk from A to B)
2	1	2	→	3	1	1	
3	1	1	→	3	2	0	(Top 3 disks at B; bottom
3	2	0	→	2	3	0	two at A)

Step 2

2	3	0	→	1	3	1	
1	3	1	→	1	2	2	
1	2	2	→	2	1	1	
2	1	2	→	3	1	1	
3	1	1	→	3	0	2	
3	0	2	→	2	1	2	
2	1	2	→	1	1	3	
1	1	3	→	1	0	4	(Top 4 disks at C)

Thus, it takes 15 moves to transfer the top 4 disks from A to C. Next, use 1 move to transfer the fifth disk from A to B, and finish by transferring the 4 disks on C to B in 15 moves essentially the same as the 15 moves used to transfer the top 4 disks from A to C. The total number of moves is $15 + 1 + 15 = 31$.

3. a. It takes at least $2^8 - 1 = 255$ moves to transfer 8 disks.

    b. In 7 moves we can transfer 3 disks to C. In the remaining three moves we can move the next largest to B and then move two disks from C onto A and B. So after 10 moves there will be 5 on A, 2 on B and 1 on C.

    c. In 63 moves we can transfer 6 disks to B. Then we move the next largest to C. In 31 moves we can move 5 disks from B to A, then 1 disk from B to C and then in 3 moves 2 disks from A to B and finally one disk from A to C. So after 100 moves there will be 3 on A, 2 on B, and 3 on C.

4. a. $\log_{10}(2^{64} - 1) \approx \log_{10} 2^{64} = 64 \log_{10} 2 \approx 19.3$. So $2^{64} - 1$ has 20 digits.

    b. On the average, a year has about 31,556,926 seconds. Thus it would take approximately 584,554,531,000 years.

5. a. First weighing: Place three of the nine coins on the left pan of the balance and three coins on the right pan. If the counterfeit coin is one of the six coins on the balance, the balance will tilt, with the pan holding the counterfeit coin rising. If the counterfeit coin is one of the three coins not on the balance, the balance will be level.
        Second weighing: From the batch of three coins that includes the counterfeit coin, place one coin on the left pan and one coin on the right pan of the balance. Again, if the counterfeit coin is one of the two coins on the balance, the balance will tilt, with the pan holding the counterfeit coin rising. If the counterfeit coin is the one coin not on the balance, the balance will be level.

    b. Proof by induction: In part **a** we have proved the basis step: for 3^1 coins, only 1 weighing is required. Thus the conjecture is true for n = 1. Now assume that the conjecture is true for k coins: it is possible to identify the counterfeit coin among 3^k coins by using the balance just k times. Since 3^{k+1} coins can be divided into three groups, each containing 3^k coins, place one group of 3^k coins on the left pan and another group of 3^k coins on the right pan of the balance. If the counterfeit coin is one of the $2 \cdot 3^k$ coins on the balance, the balance will tilt, with the pan holding the counterfeit coin rising. If the counterfeit coin is one of the 3^k coins not on the balance, the balance will remain level. Thus, in one use of the balance, the situation involving 3^{k+1} has been reduced to a situation involving 3^k coins. So if k weighings are needed for 3^k coins, k + 1 weighings are needed for 3^{k+1} coins. By the Principle of Mathematical Induction, then, for all natural numbers n, if 3^n coins are identical in appearance, it is possible to identify the counterfeit coin by using a balance just n times.

6. For four posts, if the smallest number of moves to transfer n disks is a_n, then $a_1 = 1$, $a_2 = 3$ and $a_n = 2a_{n-2} + 3$, for n > 2.

Section 5.1.2

1. a. Assume S(k) is true. Then the sum of the first k natural numbers is $\frac{1}{2}n^2 + \frac{1}{2}n + 1000$. Now
        $$S(k + 1) = S(k) + (k + 1) = \frac{1}{2}k^2 + \frac{1}{2}k + 1000 + (k + 1) = \frac{1}{2}(k + 1)^2 + \frac{1}{2}(k + 1) + 1000$$
        $$= S(k + 1).$$

    b. S(n) is not true for n = 1, since S(1) = 1001. (See Problem 13a.)

2. Basis step: Prove true for n = 1: $1^2 = \frac{1(1+1)(2+1)}{6} = \frac{6}{6}$.

Prove that if true for n = k, then true for n = k + 1:

Assume true for n = k. Then

$$1^2 + 2^2 + \ldots + (k+1)^2 = \frac{k(k+1)(2k+1)}{6} + (k+1)^2 = \frac{2k^3 + 9k^2 + 13k + 6}{6}$$
$$= \frac{(k+1)(k+2)(2k+3)}{6}.$$

Therefore true for n = k + 1.

3. Basis step: Prove true for n = 1: $1 \bullet 3 = \frac{1}{3}(4 + 6 - 1)$.

Prove that if true for n = k, then true for n = k + 1:

Assume true for n = k. Then

$$\sum_{i=1}^{k+1}[(2i-1)(2i+1)] = (2k+1)(2k+3) + \sum_{i=1}^{k}[(2i-1)(2i+1)]$$
$$= 4k^2 + 8k + 3 + \frac{1}{3}(4k^3 + 6k^2 - k)$$
$$= \frac{1}{3}(4k^3 + 18k^2 + 23k + 9)$$
$$= \frac{1}{3}(4(k+1)^3 + 6(k+1)^2 - (k+1))$$

Therefore true for n = k + 1.

4. Basis step: Prove true for n = 1: $\frac{1}{1 \bullet 2} = \frac{1}{1+1}$.

Prove that if true for n = k, then true for n = k + 1:

Assume true for n = k. Then

$$\frac{1}{1 \bullet 2} + \frac{1}{2 \bullet 3} + \ldots + \frac{1}{(k+1)(k+2)} = \frac{k}{k+1} + \frac{1}{(k+1)(k+2)}$$
$$= \frac{k(k+2)}{(k+1)(k+2)} + \frac{1}{(k+1)(k+2)}$$
$$= \frac{k^2 + 2k + 1}{(k+1)(k+2)} = \frac{(k+1)(k+1)}{(k+1)(k+2)} = \frac{k+1}{(k+1)+1}$$

Therefore true for n = k + 1.

5. Basis step: Prove true for n = 1: $1(1+1) = 2 = \frac{1(1+1)(1+2)}{3}$.

Prove that if true for n = k, then true for n = k + 1:

Assume true for n = k.

$$\sum_{i=1}^{k+1} i(i+1) = (k+1)(k+2) + \sum_{i=1}^{k} i(i+1)$$
$$= k^2 + 3k + 2 + \frac{k(k+1)(k+2)}{3}$$
$$= \frac{3k^2 + 9k + 6 + k^3 + 3k^2 + 2k}{3} = \frac{k^3 + 6k^2 + 11k + 6}{3}$$
$$= \frac{(k+1)(k+2)(k+3)}{3}$$

Therefore true for n = k + 1.

6. Basis step: Prove true for n = 3. A triangle has $\frac{3(3-3)}{2} = 0$ diagonals.

Prove that if true for n = k, then true for n = k + 1:

Assume true for n = k. A k+1-gon will have one more vertex and therefore (k – 2) + 1 diagonals, one connecting the new vertex to each of k – 2 vertices and one connecting the two neighboring vertices.

Since $\frac{k(k-3)}{2} + (k-1) = \frac{k^2 - k - 2}{2} = \frac{(k+1)(k-2)}{2}$, we have shown the statement true for n = k + 1.

7. Basis step: Prove true for n = 1: For $0 < x < 1$, $0 < x^2 < x < 1$.

Prove that if true for n = k, then true for n = k + 1:

Assume true for n = k: Then $0 < x^{k+1} < x^k < 1$. Multiplying through by x, where $0 < x < 1$, we have $0 < x^{k+2} < x^{k+1} < x < 1$ and therefore true for n = k + 1.

8. Basis step: Prove true for n = 4: $2^4 = 16 < 4! = 24$.

Prove that if true for n = k, then true for n = k + 1:

Assume true for n = k: Then $2^k < k!$. Multiplying through by 2, we have $2(2^k) = 2^{k+1} < k! \cdot 2 < k!(k+1) = (k+1)!$ and therefore true for n = k + 1.

9. Let S(n) be the statement that there exists an integer k such that $100^n < n!$ for all integers n > k.

Basis step: We need to show that there is some positive integer k such that $100^k < k!$. Choose k = 20000. Now $100^{20000} = 10^{40000}$. But 20000! has 20000 factors, and 10000 of them are greater than 10000. So $20000! > 10000^{10000} = 10^{4(10000)} = 10^{40000}$. So S(20000) is true.

Inductive step. Suppose S(k) is true for some k ≥ 100. Then $100^k < k!$. Now $100^{k+1} \le 100^k(k + 1) < (k + 1)!$, so S(k + 1) is true.

Thus, by the principle of mathematical induction, S(n) is true for all n ≥ 20000. This answers the question. So k = 20000 is an integer such that $100^n < n!$ for all integers > k.

10. a. Basis step: Prove true for n = 2: If 2 people are standing in line, beginning with a woman and ending with a man, then a man is standing directly behind a woman.

Prove that if true for n = k then true for n = k + 1:

Assume true for n = k. Consider a line of k + 1 people, beginning with a woman and ending with a man. Remove a person in the middle of the line. Then there is a line of k people with a man standing directly behind a woman. Reinsert the removed person at his or her original position in the line. If the person is not inserted between the woman and the man, then there is still a man standing directly behind a woman. If the person is inserted between the woman and the man, then, if the person is a man, she will be directly behind a woman or, if the person is a woman, he will be directly in front of a man.

b. The proof is essentially the same as part **a**, except that we must first establish that every integer is either even or odd, i.e., for all integers x, either x = 2m (even) or x = 2m + 1 (odd), for some integer m. For nonnegative integers, this can be established by mathematical induction. Let S(n) be the statement: For any integer n ≥ 0, n = 2m or n = 2m + 1, for some integer m. S(0) is true, since 0 = 2(0). Assume S(k) is true for some integer k ≥ 0. If k = 2m, then k + 1 = 2m + 1 and if k = 2m + 1, then k + 1 = (2m + 1) + 1 = 2(m + 1). Thus S(k + 1) is true. By mathematical induction, then, S(n) is true for all $n \geq 0$. Now let $x = -n$ for some $n \geq 0$. Then either $x = -(2m) = 2(-m)$ or $x = -(2m + 1)$ $= 2(-m - 1) + 1$, for some integer m. Thus every integer is either even or odd.

11. We want to show that $\sum_{i=1}^{n} i(i + 1)(i + 2) = \dfrac{n(n + 1)(n + 2)(n + 3)}{4}$.

    Basis step: Prove true for $n = 1$: $1(1 + 1)(1 + 2) = \dfrac{1(1 + 1)(1 + 2)(1 + 3)}{4}$.

    Prove that if true for $n = k$ then true for $n = k + 1$:

    Assume true for $n = k$. Adding the next term to the sum of the first k terms, we get

    $\dfrac{k(k + 1)(k + 2)(k + 3)}{4} + (k + 1)\ (k + 2)\ (k + 3) = \dfrac{(k + 1)(k + 2)(k + 3)(k + 4)}{4}$.

12. Yes. Consider the formula $\dfrac{n(n + 1)}{2} + n(n - 1)(n - 2)\bullet...\bullet(n - 1,000,000)$. This formula equals

    $1 + 2 + 3 +...+ n$ for the first million natural numbers and then fails after that.

13. a. Sample: See Problem 1.

    b. Sample: For all natural numbers n, n = n.

14. $P(k)$ implies $P(k + 1)$ only if $k \geq 2$; otherwise the logic fails: when you remove one, there must be at least two remaining for any comparison to take place. In other words, the inductive step does not begin at the base case.

15. Let T be the set of all n such that $P(n)$ is false. By the well-ordering property, there exists an element k in T which is the smallest. (Note: k is at least 2 because $P(1)$ is true.) So $1 + 2 + 3 +... + k \neq \dfrac{k(k + 1)}{2}$.

    But then subtracting k from both sides we have So $1 + 2 + 3 +... + (k - 1) \neq \dfrac{k(k + 1)}{2} - k$

    $= \dfrac{k^2 - k}{2} = \dfrac{k(k - 1)}{2}$. So $P(k - 1)$ is false as well, which contradicts our assumption that k is the smallest element in T.

16. Let T be the set of all n such that $P(n)$ is false. By the well-ordering property, there exists an element k in T which is the smallest. The element k must be composite (otherwise, k is prime and hence divisible by a prime). So $k = mn$, for natural numbers m and n. But m and n must themselves be members of T, since if either is divisible by a prime, then k is divisible by a prime. This contradicts the assumption that k is the smallest element of T.

17. a. $s_n = (n + 1)! - 1$

    b. $s_1 = 1 \bullet 1! = 1 = (1 + 1)! - 1$; Assume $s_k = (k + 1)! - 1$. $s_{k+1} = s_k + (k + 1)(k + 1)!$

       $= (k + 1)! - 1 + (k + 1)(k + 1)! = (k + 1)!(k + 2) - 1 = (k + 2)! - 2$. By mathematical induction, $s_n = (n + 1)! - 1$ for all natural numbers n.

18. u_1 is odd and, for all $n > 1$, u_n is even. For $k \geq 2$, assume u_k even, i.e., $u_k = 2m$, for some integer m. Then $u_{k+1} = 2u_{k-1} + u_k = 2u_{k-1} + 2m = 2(u_{k-1} + m)$, for some integer m. Thus u_{k+1} is even. By mathematical induction, u_n is even for all $n \geq 2$.

19. a. Suppose there exists $n \in \mathbf{N}$ such that $s(n) = n$. By P1 $n \neq e$, since e is the successor of no element. For all $x \in \mathbf{N}$, if $s(x) = n = s(n)$, then by P2 $x = n$. Thus n is its own predecessor. Let the

set $M = \mathbf{N} - \{n\}$. M contains e and all the successors of e, but $M \neq \mathbf{N}$. This contradicts P3.

b. Suppose there exists a k in $\mathbf{N}$ other than e such that k is the successor of no element. Let M be the set $\mathbf{N} - \{k\}$. As in part **a**, the set M violates M3.

20. a. The subset $M = \{x \in \mathbf{Q}^+: x = \frac{k}{2}$ for some $k \in \mathbf{N}\}$ does not satisfy P-3.

b. P2 true: There is only one element in the set and $s(1) = 1$. P3 true: Let $1 \in M$ and for all $n \in M$, $s(n) \in M$. Then $s(1) = 1 \in M$. So $M = \{1\} = S$. P1 false: $1 = s(1)$.

c. P1 true: $1 \neq s(n)$ for any $n \in S$. P3 true: Let $1 \in M$ and for all $n \in M$, $s(n) \in M$. Then $s(1) = 2 \in M$ and $s(2) = 2 \in M$. So $M = \{1, 2\} = S$. P2 false: $s(1) = s(2) = 2$, but $1 \neq 2$.

21. a. Let the nonempty set be $\mathbf{N}$. Then, by M4, there exists at least one element e_1 in $\mathbf{N}$ such that $e_1 \neq s(n)$ for all $n \in \mathbf{N}$. So there is at least one element that is not the successor of any number. Suppose there exists e_2 in $\mathbf{N}$ such that $e_2 \neq s(n)$ for all $n \in \mathbf{N}$. By M3, $e_1 = e_2$. Thus there is exactly one element that is not the successor of any number.

b. Let M be a subset of $\mathbf{N}$ that contains the number 1 and that contains the number $s(n)$ whenever it contains the number n. Suppose $M \neq \mathbf{N}$. Then $B = \mathbf{N} - M \neq \varnothing$. By M4, B contains b such that $b \neq s(a)$ for all a in B. However, $b \neq 1$ since $1 \in M$. Since, by part **a**, there is exactly one element in $\mathbf{N}$ that has no successor, and that is 1, $b = s(k)$ for some $k \in \mathbf{N}$. But if $k \in \mathbf{N}$ and $k \notin B$, then $k \in M$, which contradicts the premise that $n \in M$ implies $s(n) \in M$. So $M = \mathbf{N}$.

22. a. By definition, $1 \bullet 1 = 1$. Suppose $1 \bullet k = k$ for some k. Then

$$1 \bullet (k + 1) = 1 \bullet k + 1, \qquad \text{by definition}$$
$$= k + 1 \qquad \text{by hypothesis}$$

So, by mathematical induction, $1 \bullet n = n$ for all natural numbers n.

b. From part **a** and definition, $1 \bullet n = n = n \bullet 1$ for all n. Now suppose $k \bullet n = n \bullet k$, for all n and some k. Then

$$n \bullet (k + 1) = n \bullet k + n \qquad \text{by definition}$$
$$= k \bullet n + n \qquad \text{by hypothesis}$$
$$= (k + 1) \bullet n \qquad \text{by definition}$$

c. By the definition, $n \bullet (k + 1) = n \bullet k + n$, for all n and k, so the statement is true for $\ell = 1$. Suppose $n \bullet (k + m) = n \bullet k + n \bullet m$, for all n and k and some m. Then

$$n \bullet (k + (m + 1)) = n \bullet (k + (1 + m)) \qquad \text{commutativity of addition}$$
$$= n \bullet ((k + 1) + m) \qquad \text{associativity of addition}$$
$$= n \bullet (k + 1) + n \bullet m \qquad \text{by hypothesis}$$
$$= (n \bullet k + n) + n \bullet m \qquad \text{by definition}$$
$$= n \bullet k + (n + n \bullet m) \qquad \text{associativity of addition}$$
$$= n \bullet k + (n \bullet m + n) \qquad \text{commutativity of addition}$$
$$= n \bullet k + n \bullet (m + 1) \qquad \text{by definition}$$

Thus, by mathematical induction, $n \bullet (k + \ell) = n \bullet k + n \bullet \ell$, for all n, k and ℓ.

23. a. i. Area(B′C′D′DCBB′) = Area(ABCD) – Area(AB′C′D′)

$$= \left(\frac{(10)(11)}{2}\right)^2 - \left(\frac{(9)(10)}{2}\right)^2 = \frac{10^2(11^2 - 9^2)}{4} = 10^3$$

   ii. Area(B″C″D″D′C′B′B″) = Area(AB′C′D′) – Area(AB″C″D″)

$$= \left(\frac{(9)(10)}{2}\right)^2 - \left(\frac{(8)(9)}{2}\right)^2 = \frac{9^2(10^2 - 8^2)}{4} = 9^3$$

b. The area of square ABCD is $AB^2 = (1 + 2 + \ldots + 9 + 10)^2$, which is equal to the sum of the areas of all the inverted L regions, and part **a** has shown that the area of each inverted L region equals the cube of the length of its shortest side.

c. Basis step: $1^3 = 1^2$.
Inductive step: Assume $1^3 + 2^3 + \ldots + k^3 = (1 + 2 + \ldots + k)^2$. Then
$(1 + 2 + \ldots + k + (k + 1))^2 = (1 + 2 + \ldots + k)^2 +$
$2(k + 1)(1 + 2 + \ldots + k) + (k + 1)^2$
$= 1^3 + 2^3 + \ldots + k^3 + 2(k + 1)\frac{k(k+1)}{2} + (k + 1)^2$
$= 1^3 + 2^3 + \ldots + k^3 + k(k + 1)^2 + (k + 1)^2$
$= 1^3 + 2^3 + \ldots + k^3 + (k + 1)^3$.
Thus, by the Principle of Mathematical Induction, $1^3 + 2^3 + \ldots + n^3 = (1 + 2 + \ldots + n)^2$ is true for all natural numbers n.

24. a. $\frac{a}{b} = \sqrt{2} \Rightarrow \frac{a^2}{b^2} = 2 \Rightarrow \frac{a}{b} = \frac{2b}{a} \Rightarrow \frac{a}{b} + 1 = \frac{2b}{a} + 1$

$\Rightarrow \frac{a+b}{b} = \frac{2b+a}{a} \Rightarrow \frac{a}{b} = \frac{2b+a}{a+b}$

b. $S_1 = \frac{7}{5} = 1.4$, $S_2 = \frac{17}{12} = 1.41\overline{6}$, $S_3 = \frac{41}{29} \approx 1.4379$, $S_4 = \frac{99}{70} \approx 1.414286$,

$S_5 = \frac{239}{169} \approx 1.414201$

c. The proof has two parts. We first show that $\frac{a}{b}$ and $\frac{a+2b}{a+b}$ are on different sides of $\sqrt{2}$. Suppose

$\frac{a}{b} > \sqrt{2}$. Then $\frac{a+2b}{a+b} = 1 + \frac{b}{a+b} = 1 + \frac{1}{\frac{a}{b}+1} < 1 + \frac{1}{\sqrt{2}+1}$ (because we are making the

denominator smaller by substituting $\sqrt{2}$ for $\frac{a}{b}$), and the right side equals $\sqrt{2}$. Similarly, if

$\frac{a}{b} < \sqrt{2}$, then $\frac{a+2b}{a+b} > \sqrt{2}$.

Now we are ready to prove the desired result. Again, there are two possibilities according to whether $\frac{a}{b} > \sqrt{2}$ or $\frac{a}{b} < \sqrt{2}$. Suppose $\frac{a}{b} > \sqrt{2}$. Then, from the first part, $\frac{a+2b}{a+b} < \sqrt{2}$ and we wish to show that

$$\sqrt{2} - \frac{a+2b}{a+b} < \frac{a}{b} - \sqrt{2}.$$

From the above, this is equivalent to

$$\sqrt{2} - (1 + \frac{1}{\frac{a}{b}+1}) < \frac{a}{b} - \sqrt{2}.$$

Let $x = \frac{a}{b}$. We now wish to show that

$$\sqrt{2} - (1 + \frac{1}{x+1}) < x - \sqrt{2},$$

which is equivalent to the inequality

$$x + 1 + \frac{1}{x+1} - 2\sqrt{2} > 0.$$

Now let $y = x + 1$ (to make solving the quadratic a little easier). We now have

$$y + \frac{1}{y} - 2\sqrt{2} > 0,$$

which is equivalent to

$$y^2 - 2\sqrt{2}\,y + 1 > 0.$$

Solving this inequality, we find

$$y < \sqrt{2} - 1 \qquad \text{or} \qquad y > \sqrt{2} + 1.$$

That is, $\qquad x + 1 < \sqrt{2} - 1 \qquad$ or $\qquad x > \sqrt{2}$

$$x < \sqrt{2} - 2 \qquad\qquad \text{or} \qquad x > \sqrt{2}.$$

These steps are all reversible. Thus, when $x = \frac{a}{b} > \sqrt{2}$, then

$\sqrt{2} - \frac{a+2b}{a+b} < \frac{a}{b} - \sqrt{2}$, which was to be shown. The other part of the proof is when $\frac{a}{b} < \sqrt{2}$.

Then we need to show

$$\frac{a+2b}{a+b} - \sqrt{2} < \sqrt{2} - \frac{a}{b}.$$

The proof of this part is similar.

Section 5.1.3

1. a. Sample: $a_1 = 2$, $a_{n+1} = a_n + 2$ for all $n \geq 1$

    b. Sample: $a_1 = 0$, $a_{n+1} = a_n + 2$ for all $n \geq 1$

2. a. $F_n = F_{n-1} + F_{n-2} = (F_{n-2} + F_{n-3}) + F_{n-2} = 2F_{n-2} + F_{n-3}$

    b. $F_n = 2F_{n-2} + F_{n-3} = 2(2\,F_{n-4} + F_{n-5}) + (F_{n-4} + F_{n-5}) = 5F_{n-4} + 3F_{n-5}$

    c. $F_n^{\,2} - F_{n-1}^{\,2} = (F_n + F_{n-1})(F_n - F_{n-1})$

    $F_n + F_{n-1} = F_{n+1}$, $F_n - F_{n-1} = F_{n-2}$

    $F_n^{\,2} - F_{n-1}^{\,2} = F_{n+1} \cdot F_{n-2}$

3. a. $n = 2$, $F_2^{\,2} - F_3 \cdot F_1 = 1^2 - 2 \cdot 1 = -1$; $n = 3$, $F_3^{\,2} - F_4 \cdot F_2 = 2^2 - 3 \cdot 1 = 1$;

    $n = 4$, $F_4^{\,2} - F_5 \cdot F_3 = 3^2 - 5 \cdot 2 = -1$; $n = 5$, $F_5^{\,2} - F_6 \cdot F_4 = 5^2 - 8 \cdot 3 = 1$;

    for all $n > 1$, $F_n^{\,2} - F_{n+1} \cdot F_{n-1} = (-1)^{n+1}$.

    b. Basis step: $F_2^{\,2} - F_3 \cdot F_1 = 1^2 - 2 \cdot 1 = (-1)^3$.

    Inductive step: Assume $F_k^{\,2} - F_{k+1} \cdot F_{k-1} = (-1)^{k+1}$.

    $F_{k+1}^{\,2} - F_{k+2} \cdot F_k = F_{k+1} \cdot (F_k + F_{k-1}) - (F_{k+1} + F_k)F_k = F_{k+1} \cdot F_{k-1} - F_k^{\,2}$

    $\qquad\qquad = -(F_k^{\,2} - F_{k+1} \cdot F_{k-1}) = (-1)(-1)^{k+1} = (-1)^{(k+1)+1}$

    Thus, by mathematical induction, $F_n^{\,2} - F_{n+1} \cdot F_{n-1} = (-1)^{n+1}$ for all $n > 1$.

    c. $n = 3$, $F_3^{\,2} - F_5 \cdot F_1 = 2^2 - 5 \cdot 1 = -1$; $n = 4$, $F_4^{\,2} - F_6 \cdot F_2 = 3^2 - 8 \cdot 1 = 1$;

    $n = 5$, $F_5^{\,2} - F_7 \cdot F_3 = 5^2 - 13 \cdot 2 = -1$; $n = 6$, $F_6^{\,2} - F_8 \cdot F_4 = 8^2 - 21 \cdot 3 = 1$;

    for all $n > 2$, $F_n^{\,2} - F_{n+2} \cdot F_{n-2} = (-1)^n$.

    Proof

    Basis step: $F_3^{\,2} - F_5 \cdot F_1 = 2^2 - 5 \cdot 1 = -1$.

Inductive step: Assume $F_k^2 - F_{k+2} \bullet F_{k-2} = (-1)^k$.

$F_{k+1}^2 - F_{k+3} \bullet F_{k-1} = (F_k + F_{k-1})F_{k+1} - (F_{k+2} + F_{k+1})F_{k-1} = F_k \bullet F_{k+1} - F_{k+2} \bullet F_{k-1}$

$\qquad = (F_{k-1} + F_{k-2})(F_{k+2} - F_k) - F_{k+2} \bullet F_{k-1}$

$\qquad = F_{k+2} \bullet F_{k-2} - F_k \bullet F_{k-1} - F_k \bullet F_{k-2}$

$\qquad = F_{k+2} \bullet F_{k-2} - F_k(F_{k-1} + F_{k-2}) = F_{k+2} \bullet F_{k-2} - F_k^2$

$\qquad = -(F_k^2 - F_{k+2} \bullet F_{k-2}) = -1(-1)^k = (-1)^{k+1}$

Thus, by mathematical induction, $F_n^2 - F_{n+2} \bullet F_{n-2} = (-1)^n$ for all $n > 2$.

d. $n = 4$, $F_4^2 - F_7 \bullet F_1 = 3^2 - 13 \bullet 1 = -4$; $n = 5$, $F_5^2 - F_8 \bullet F_2 = 5^2 - 21 \bullet 1 = 4$;

$n = 6$, $F_6^2 - F_9 \bullet F_3 = 8^2 - 34 \bullet 2 = -4$; $n = 7$, $F_7^2 - F_{10} \bullet F_4 = 13^2 - 55 \bullet 3 = 4$;

for all $n > 3$, $F_n^2 - F_{n+3} \bullet F_{n-3} = 4(-1)^{n+1}$.

Proof

Basis step: $F_4^2 - F_7 \bullet F_1 = 3^2 - 13 \bullet 1 = -4$.

Inductive step: Assume $F_k^2 - F_{k+3} \bullet F_{k-3} = 4(-1)^{k+1}$.

$F_{k+1}^2 - F_{k+4} \bullet F_{k-2} = F_{k+1}^2 - (F_{k+3} + F_{k+2})(F_{k-1} - F_{k-3})$

$\qquad = F_{k+1}^2 + F_{k+3} \bullet F_{k-3} + F_{k+2} \bullet F_{k-3} - F_{k+3} \bullet F_{k-1} - F_{k+2} \bullet F_{k-1}$

$\qquad = F_{k+1}^2 + F_{k+3} \bullet F_{k-3} + F_{k+2}(F_{k-1} - F_{k-2}) - (F_{k+1} + F_{k+2})F_{k-1} - F_{k+2} \bullet F_{k-1}$

$\qquad = F_{k+1}^2 + F_{k+3} \bullet F_{k-3} - F_{k+2} \bullet F_{k-2} - F_{k+1} \bullet F_{k-1} - F_{k+2} \bullet F_{k-1}$

$\qquad = F_k^2 + F_{k+3} \bullet F_{k-3} - F_{k+2} \bullet F_{k-2} - F_{k+1} \bullet F_{k-1}$ $\qquad$ (Problem 1c)

$\qquad = F_k^2 + F_{k+3} \bullet F_{k-3} - (F_k + F_{k+1})(F_k - F_{k-1}) - F_{k+1} \bullet F_{k-1}$

$\qquad = F_{k+3} \bullet F_{k-3} + F_k \bullet F_{k-1} - F_{k+1} \bullet F_k$

$\qquad = F_{k+3} \bullet F_{k-3} + F_k(F_{k-1} - F_{k+1})$

$\qquad = F_{k+3} \bullet F_{k-3} - F_k^2$

$\qquad = -(F_k^2 - F_{k+3} \bullet F_{k-3}) = 4(-1)^{(k+1)+1}$

Thus, by mathematical induction, $F_n^2 - F_{n+3} \bullet F_{n-3} = 4(-1)^{n+1}$ for all $n > 3$.

4. $F_{n+3} \bullet F_{n+2} - F_{n+1} \bullet F_n = F_{n+1}^2 + F_{n+2}^2$

Basis step: $F_4 \bullet F_3 - F_2 \bullet F_1 = 3 \bullet 2 - 1 \bullet 1 = 5 = F_2^2 + F_3^2 = 1^2 + 2^2$.

Inductive step: Assume $F_{k+3} \bullet F_{k+2} - F_{k+1} \bullet F_k = F_{k+1}^2 + F_{k+2}^2$.

$F_{k+4} \bullet F_{k+3} - F_{k+2} \bullet F_{k+1} = (F_{k+3} + F_{k+2})F_{k+3} - (F_{k+1} + F_k)F_{k+1}$

$= F_{k+3}^2 + F_{k+2} \bullet F_{k+3} - F_{k+1}^2 - F_{k+1} \bullet F_k = F_{k+3}^2 - F_{k+1}^2 + F_{k+1}^2 + F_{k+2}^2 = F_{k+3}^2 + F_{k+2}^2$

Thus, by the mathematical induction, $F_{n+3} \bullet F_{n+2} - F_{n+1} \bullet F_n = F_{n+1}^2 + F_{n+2}^2$ for all natural numbers n.

5. a. $Q(1) = 1$, $Q(2) = 2$, $Q(3) = 6$, $Q(4) = 15$, $Q(5) = 40$, $Q(6) = 104$

b. $Q(n) = F_n \bullet F_{n+1}$

c. Basis step: $Q(1) = F_1 \bullet F_2 = 1 \bullet 1 = 1$.

Assume true for k. So $Q(k) = F_k \bullet F_{k+1}$.

$Q(k + 1) = Q(k) + F_{k+1}^2 = F_k \bullet F_{k+1} + F_{k+1}^2 = F_{k+1}(F_k + F_{k+1}) = F_{k+1} \bullet F_{k+2}$

Therefore $Q(n) = F_n \bullet F_{n+1}$ is true for all n.

6. a. 1, 3, 4, 7, 11, 18, 29, 47, 76, 123

b. The Lucas numbers will share those properties of the Fibonacci numbers that depend only on the recurrence relation and not on the initial values. Thus Lucas numbers will have all the properties in Problems 1 and 3.

7. Basis step: The probability the 2 heads will occur in two tosses is $\frac{1}{4} = 1 - \frac{F_4}{2^2} = 1 - \frac{3}{4}$.

Inductive step: Assume that if a fair coin is tossed j times, where $0 < j \le k$, the probability that somewhere two consecutive tosses will be heads is $1 - \frac{F_{j+2}}{2^j}$. This implies that the probability that two consecutive heads do not appear is $P(j) = \frac{F_{j+2}}{2^j}$. Suppose a coin is tossed k times. Then there are 2^k possible outcomes. Let N(k) be the number of these outcomes in which no two consecutive heads appear. Then $P(k) = \frac{N(k)}{2^k}$. Further, let H(k) and T(k) be the number of these no consecutive heads outcomes in which the kth toss is heads or tails, respectively. So $H(k) + T(k) = N(k)$. Now in k + 1 tosses of a coin there will be a total of 2^{k+1} possible outcomes, and, of these, $N(k + 1) = H(k + 1) + T(k + 1)$ will be the number of outcomes in which no two consecutive heads appear. There will be no consecutive heads in k + 1 tosses only if there were no consecutive heads after k tosses and the outcome for the k + 1st toss is as follows: the toss can land tails if the kth toss landed either heads or tails, so $T(k + 1) = H(k) + T(k)$; the toss can land heads only if the kth toss landed tails, so $H(k + 1) = T(k)$. Thus

$$N(k + 1) = T(k) + T(k) + H(k)$$
$$= T(k) + N(k)$$
$$= T(k - 1) + H(k - 1) + N(k)$$
$$= N(k - 1) + N(k)$$

Thus $P(k + 1) = \frac{N(k + 1)}{2^{k+1}} = \frac{N(k - 1) + N(k)}{2^{k+1}}$.

By the inductive hypothesis, $P(j) = \frac{N(j)}{2^j} = \frac{F_{j+2}}{2^j}$ for $1 < j \le k$, so $N(k) = F_{k+2}$ and $N(k - 1) = F_{k+1}$.

Therefore, $P(k + 1) = \frac{F_{k+1} + F_{k+2}}{2^{k+1}}$

$$= \frac{F_{k+3}}{2^{k+1}}$$

Thus the probability that consecutive heads will not appear in n tosses is $P(n) = \frac{F_n}{2^n}$ and the probability that two consecutive heads will appear in n tosses is $1 - P(n) = 1 - \frac{F_n}{2^n}$.

8. Basis step: u_1 and u_2 are odd.

Inductive step: For $k \ge 2$, assume u_k odd, i.e., $u_k = 2m + 1$, for some integer m. Then $u_{k+1} = 2u_{k-1} + u_k = 2u_{k-1} + (2m + 1) = 2(u_{k-1} + m) + 1$, for some integer m. Thus u_{k+1} is odd. By mathematical induction, u_n is odd for all $n \ge 2$.

9. Basis step: $(x^m)^1 = x^m$.

Inductive step: Suppose $(x^m)^k = x^{mk}$ for some natural number k. Then

$(x^m)^{k+1} = (x^m)^k(x^m)$ product of powers property

$= (x^{mk})(x^m)$ by hypothesis

$= x^{mk + m}$ product of powers property

$= x^{m(k+1)}$.   Distributive property

Thus $(x^m)^n = x^{mn}$ for all natural numbers m and n.

10.   Basis step: $(xy)^1 = xy = x^1 y^1$.

Inductive step: Suppose $(xy)^k = x^k y^k$ for some natural number k. Then

$$\begin{aligned}(xy)^{k+1} &= (xy)^k(xy) &&\text{product of powers property}\\ &= x^k y^k (xy) &&\text{by hypothesis}\\ &= (x^k x)(y^k y) &&\text{associative and commutative properties of mult.}\\ &= x^{k+1} y^{k+1}. &&\text{product of powers property}\end{aligned}$$

Thus $(xy)^m = x^m y^m$ for all natural numbers m.

11. $x_n = 2^n + 1$

Basis step: $x_0 = 2^0 + 1 = 3$.

Inductive step: Assume $x_k = 2^k + 1$.

$$\begin{aligned}x_{k+1} &= 3x_k - 2x_{k-1}\\ &= 3(2^k + 1) - 2(2^{k-1} + 1)\\ &= 3(2^k) + 3 - 2^k - 2\\ &= 2(2^k) + 1 = 2^{k+1} + 1\end{aligned}$$

Thus $x_n = 2^n + 1$ for all natural numbers n.

12.   a. $P(n) = \frac{n+1}{2n}$. Inductive proof: Basis step: $(1 - \frac{1}{2^2}) = \frac{3}{4}$. Inductive step: Assume

$P(k) = \frac{k+1}{2k}$. Then $P(k+1) = (1 - \frac{1}{(k+1)^2})P(k) = \frac{(k+1)^2 - 1}{(k+1)^2} \bullet \frac{k+1}{2k}$

$= \frac{k^2 + 2k}{(k+1)} \bullet \frac{1}{2k} = \frac{k+2}{2(k+1)}$.

Thus, by mathematical Induction, $P(n) = \frac{n+1}{2n}$ for all natural numbers n greater than 1.

b. $P(n) = (1 - \frac{1}{2})(1 - \frac{1}{3})...(1 - \frac{1}{n})(1 + \frac{1}{2})(1 + \frac{1}{3})...(1 + \frac{1}{n})$

$= (\frac{1}{2} \frac{2}{3} ... \frac{n-1}{n})(\frac{3}{2} \frac{4}{3} ... \frac{n+1}{n}) = \frac{1}{n} \frac{n+1}{2} = \frac{n+1}{2n}$

Mathematical induction must still be used to prove $\frac{1}{2} \frac{2}{3} ... \frac{n-1}{n} = \frac{1}{n}$ and $\frac{3}{2} \frac{4}{3} ... \frac{n+1}{n} = \frac{n+1}{2}$.

13.   a.   The kth term in the nth row of Pascal's Triangle, is given by $a_{n,k} = \binom{n}{k}$, where $n \geq 0$ and

$0 \leq k \leq n$. Since for $n > 0$ and $0 < k < n + 1$, $a_{n+1,k} = a_{n,k-1} + a_{n,k}$, $\binom{n+1}{k} = \binom{n}{k-1} + \binom{n}{k}$.

b.   Basis step: $(a + b)^1 = \sum_{k=0}^{1} \binom{1}{k} a^{1-k} b^k = a^1 b^0 + a^0 b^1 = a + b$.

Inductive step: Assume $(a + b)^j = \sum_{k=0}^{j} \binom{j}{k} a^{j-k} b^k$.

$$\begin{aligned}(a + b)^{j+1} &= (a + b)(a + b)^j\\ &= (a + b) \sum_{k=0}^{j} \binom{j}{k} a^{j-k} b^k\end{aligned}$$

$$= \sum_{k=0}^{j} \binom{j}{k} a^{j-k+1} b^k + \sum_{k=0}^{j} \binom{j}{k} a^{j-k} b^{k+1}$$

$$= \binom{j}{0} a^{j+1} + \binom{j}{1} a^j b + \ldots + \binom{j}{j} ab^j + \binom{j}{0} a^j b + \binom{j}{1} a^{j-1} b^2 + \ldots + \binom{j}{j} b^{j+1}$$

$$= \binom{j}{0} a^{j+1} + \left(\binom{j}{1} + \binom{j}{0} \right) a^j b + \ldots + \left(\binom{j}{j} + \binom{j}{j-1} \right) ab^j + \binom{j}{j} b^{j+1}$$

$$= \binom{j+1}{0} a^{j+1} + \binom{j+1}{1} a^j b + \ldots + \binom{j+1}{j} ab^j + \binom{j+1}{j+1} b^{j+1}$$

$$= \sum_{k=0}^{j+1} \binom{j+1}{k} a^{j+1-k} b^k$$

Thus $(a+b)^n = \sum_{k=0}^{n} \binom{n}{k} a^{n-k} b^k$ is true for all natural numbers n.

Section 5.1.4

1. a.

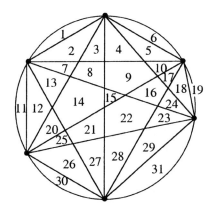

 b.

n	1	2	3	4	5	6
c_n	1	2	4	8	16	31
first differences	1	2	4	8	15	
second differences	1	2	4	7		
third differences	1	2	3			
fourth differences	1	1				

$c_n = an^4 + bn^3 + cn^2 + dn + e$
$c_2 = 16a + 8b + 4c + 2d + e = 2$
$c_3 = 81a + 27b + 9c + 3d + e = 4$
$c_4 = 256a + 64b + 16c + 4d + e = 8$
$c_5 = 625a + 125b + 25c + 5d + e = 16$
$c_6 = 1296a + 216b + 36c + 6d + e = 31$

$$\begin{bmatrix} 16 & 8 & 4 & 2 & 1 \\ 81 & 27 & 9 & 3 & 1 \\ 256 & 64 & 16 & 4 & 1 \\ 625 & 125 & 25 & 5 & 1 \\ 1296 & 216 & 36 & 6 & 1 \end{bmatrix}\begin{bmatrix} a \\ b \\ c \\ d \\ e \end{bmatrix} = \begin{bmatrix} 2 \\ 4 \\ 8 \\ 16 \\ 31 \end{bmatrix}; \quad \begin{bmatrix} a \\ b \\ c \\ d \\ e \end{bmatrix} = \begin{bmatrix} 16 & 8 & 4 & 2 & 1 \\ 81 & 27 & 9 & 3 & 1 \\ 256 & 64 & 16 & 4 & 1 \\ 625 & 125 & 25 & 5 & 1 \\ 1296 & 216 & 36 & 6 & 1 \end{bmatrix}^{-1}\begin{bmatrix} 2 \\ 4 \\ 8 \\ 16 \\ 31 \end{bmatrix};$$

$$\begin{bmatrix} a \\ b \\ c \\ d \\ e \end{bmatrix} = \begin{bmatrix} \frac{1}{24} \\ -\frac{1}{4} \\ \frac{23}{24} \\ -\frac{3}{4} \\ 1 \end{bmatrix}; c_n = \frac{1}{24}n^4 - \frac{1}{4}n^3 + \frac{23}{24}n^2 + 1; c_7 = 57, c_8 = 99$$

c. The function $C(n) = 2^{n-1}$ increases at a much greater rate for large n.

2. $P(n) = \frac{n^2 - n}{2}$; One line has no points of intersection and $P(1) = \frac{1^2 - 1}{2} = 0$. Assume true for k distinct

lines: $P(k) = \frac{k^2 - k}{2}$. One more line can intersect the other k lines in at most k new points. Thus

$k + \frac{k^2 - k}{2} = \frac{k^2 + k}{2} = \frac{(k+1)^2 - (k+1)}{2} = P(k+1)$.

3. $P(n) = n + 1$; Basis step: One line forms two regions, so $P(1) = 2$. Inductive step: Assume $P(k) = k + 1$ true, i.e., k parallel lines form $k + 1$ regions. Adding a parallel line will split one region into two new regions. Thus $P(k + 1) = k + 2$. By induction, then, $P(n) = n + 1$ for all natural numbers n.

4. $C(n) = 2n$; Basis step: One line forms two regions, so $C(1) = 2$. Inductive step: Assume $C(k) = 2k$ true, i.e., k concurrent lines form 2k regions. Adding a concurrent line will add two new regions. Thus $C(k + 1) = 2k + 2 = 2(k + 1)$. By induction, then, $C(n) = 2n$ for all natural numbers n.

5. Basis step: One line forms two adjacent regions, which can be colored with just two colors. Inductive step: Assume the regions formed by k lines can be colored with just two colors in such a way that any two adjacent regions are colored differently. Now lay down another line. On one side of the new line, switch all the colors to the opposite color; on the other side, leave all the colors the same.

6. The first plane divides space into two regions. Suppose $n - 1$ planes intersecting in a common point form $f(n - 1)$ regions of space. Now consider the nth intersecting plane. This plane will intersect all previous $n - 1$ planes in $n - 1$ distinct concurrent lines. By Problem 5, these $n - 1$ concurrent lines will form $2(n - 1)$ regions in the nth plane. These $2(n - 1)$ regions in the plane will in turn form $2(n - 1)$ new regions of space. So for n intersecting planes, there are $f(n - 1) + 2(n - 1)$ regions of space. Thus, $f(n)$ can be defined recursively as

$f(1) = 2$

$f(n) = f(n - 1) + 2(n - 1)$, for $n > 1$,

or explicitly as

$f(n) = 2((n - 1) + (n - 2) + \ldots + 1 + 1) = 2\left(\frac{n(n-1)}{2} + 1\right) = n^2 - n + 2$.

7. The point P will be one vertex of the triangle, while the other vertices will be 2 of the m points on the line. There are $\binom{m}{2} = \frac{m!}{2!(m-2)!}$ ways to choose 2 points from among m, so $\frac{m!}{2!(m-2)!}$ triangles can be formed.

8. At most $(m+1)(n+1)$ regions will be formed. First consider point P_1 between A and B. The segment $\overline{CP_1}$ will divide $\triangle ABC$ into 2 regions. Now consider k points between A and B and assume these points connected to point C form $k+1$ regions in the triangle. The point P_{k+1} must be between two of the other $k+2$ points on $\overline{AB}$. Let these points be P_i and P_{i+1}. The segment $\overline{CP_{k+1}}$ splits the region $\triangle CP_iP_{i+1}$ into two regions $\triangle CP_iP_{k+1}$ and $\triangle CP_{k+1}P_{i+1}$. Thus there are now $k+1+1 = k+2$ regions. By mathematical induction on k, m points between A and B and connected to C will split $\triangle ABC$ into $m+1$ regions. Now suppose m points between A and B and connected to C have split $\triangle ABC$ into $m+1$ regions. Consider point Q_1 between B and C. The segment $\overline{AQ_1}$ will divide the $m+1$ regions into $2(m+1)$ regions. Now assume j points between B and C and connected to point A form $(j+1)(m+1)$ regions in the triangle. The point Q_{j+1} must be between two of the other $j+2$ points on $\overline{BC}$. Let these points be Q_i and Q_{i+1}. The segment $\overline{AQ_{j+1}}$ splits each of the $m+1$ regions inside $\triangle AQ_iQ_{i+1}$ into two regions. Thus there are now $(j+1)(m+1) + (m+1) = (j+2)(m+1)$ regions. By mathematical induction on j, n points between B and C and connected to A will split the $m+1$ regions of $\triangle ABC$ into $(n+1)(m+1)$ regions.

Section 5.2.1

1. a. $q = 5842, r = 15$ b. $q = 5842, r = 16$
    c. $q = 5842, r = 17$ d. $q = -5843, r = 64$
    e. $q = -5843, r = 63$ f. $q = -5843, r = 62$

2. a. $q = 0, r = 0$ b. $q = -3, r = 0$ c. $q = 0, r = 9$

3. By the Division Algorithm, any integer n can be written $n = 1000k_1 + r$, where k_1 and r are integers and $0 \le r < 1000$. If r is divisible by 8, then $r = 8k_2$, where k_2 is an integer. So $n = 1000k_1 + 8k_2 = 8(125k_1 + k_2) = 8k$, for some integer $k = 125k_1 + k_2$. So n is divisible by 8.

4. a. An even integer is one that can be expressed as 2k for some integer k. An odd integer is one that can be expressed as $2k + 1$ for some integer k. By the Division Algorithm, for any integer n, there are unique integers k and r such that $n = 2k + r$, where $0 \le r < 2$. Thus any integer n can be written as either 2k or $2k + 1$.
    b. Let the even numbers be $2k_1$ and $2k_2$. Now the set of integers is closed under addition, subtraction and multiplication, so $k_1 + k_2$, $k_1 - k_2$, and k_1k_2 are integers. Therefore, $2k_1 + 2k_2 = 2(k_1 + k_2)$ is even, $2k_1 - 2k_2 = 2(k_1 - k_2)$ is even, and $2k_1 \cdot 2k_2 = 4k_1k_2$ is even.
    c. The sum of any two odd integers is even: $(2k_1 + 1) + (2k_2 + 1) = 2(k_1 + k_2 + 1) = 2k$. The difference of any two odd integers is even: $(2k_1 + 1) - (2k_2 + 1) = 2(k_1 - k_2) = 2k$. The product of any two odd integers is odd:
    $(2k_1 + 1)(2k_2 + 1) = 4k_1k_2 + 2(k_1 + k_2) + 1 = 2(2k_1k_2 + k_1 + k_2) + 1 = 2k + 1$.

5. By the Division Algorithm, for any integer n, there are unique integers k and r such that $n = 3k + r$, where $0 \le r < 3$. So $n = 3k$ or $n = 3k + 1$ or $n = 3k + 2$.

6. By the Division Algorithm, any integer n can be written $m = kn + r$, where k and r are integers and $0 \le r < n$. If $r = 0$, then $m = kn$ and (a) holds. Otherwise, $0 < r < n$. Since $r > 0$, $m = kn + r > kn$. Since $r < n$, $m = kn + r < kn + n = (k + 1)n$. So $kn < m < (k + 1)n$, which is (b).

7. Let $q = \left\lfloor \frac{a}{b} \right\rfloor$ and $r = a - b\left\lfloor \frac{a}{b} \right\rfloor$. Then $bq + r = b\left\lfloor \frac{a}{b} \right\rfloor + a - b\left\lfloor \frac{a}{b} \right\rfloor = a$. By definition $\left\lfloor \frac{a}{b} \right\rfloor$ is an integer.

   From the definition of greatest integer function, $\frac{a}{b} - 1 < \left\lfloor \frac{a}{b} \right\rfloor \le \frac{a}{b}$. Multiplying through by -b and then adding a yields $b > a - b\left\lfloor \frac{a}{b} \right\rfloor \ge 0$.

8. a. The procedure stops when $R < b$. Since R starts at a and is decreased by b each iteration, the procedure will stop after n iterations if $a - bn < b$. So the procedure must stop when $n > \frac{a}{b} - 1$.

   For a given value of a, since $b > 0$, the procedure will have the maximum number of iterations when $b = 1$. Thus the maximum number of iterations is $n = a - 1$.

   b. From the recursive definitions of R and Q,
   $R_0 = a$, $R_n = R_{n-1} - b$
   $Q_0 = 0$, and $Q_n = Q_{n-1} + 1$,
   R and Q can be shown to have explicit rules $R_n = a - nb$ and $Q_n = n$, and thus $R_n = a - Q_n b$.
   When the procedure stops, $q = Q_n$ and $r = R_n < b$, so $r = a - qb$ or $a = bq + r$.

   c. Here is a program written in C++.

```
#include <iostream>

using std::cout;
using std::cin;
using std::endl;

int main()
{
    int a, b, q, r;

    cout << "Input a and b:" << endl;
    cin >> a >> b;

    r = a;
    q = 0;
    while (r >= b){
        r = r - b;
        q++;
    }

    cout << "q = " << q << "; r = " << r << endl;

    return 0;
}
```

9. a. From the supposition, $3(q_2 - q_1) + r_2 - r_1 = 0 \Rightarrow r_2 - r_1 = 3(q_1 - q_2)$ and $0 \le r_1 < r_2 < 3 \Rightarrow 0 < r_2 - r_1 < 3 - r_1 < 3$. So $r_2 - r_1$ is both a positive integer less than 3, but also a positive integer multiple of 3. But since the least positive integer multiple of 3 is 3, this leads to a

contradiction.

b. Since, from the supposition, $b(q_2 - q_1) + r_2 - r_1 = 0 \Rightarrow r_2 - r_1 = b(q_1 - q_2)$ and $b \neq 0$,

$r_2 - r_1 = 0 \Leftrightarrow q_1 - q_2 = 0$. This implies $r_2 \neq r_1 \Leftrightarrow q_1 \neq q_2$.

c. i. If $0 \leq r_1 < r_2 < b$, then $0 < r_2 - r_1 < b - r_1 < b$.

ii. $b(q_2 - q_1) + r_2 - r_1 = 0 \Rightarrow r_2 - r_1 = b(q_1 - q_2)$. $q_1 - q_2$ is an integer, so $r_2 - r_1$ is an integer multiple of b.

The smallest positive integer multiple of b is b. Thus $r_2 - r_1$ cannot be both a positive integer less than b and an integer multiple of b. So r_2 cannot be greater than r_1. The same reasoning will show that r_1 cannot be greater than r_2. Thus there can be at most one representation $a = bq + r$ with $0 \leq r < b$.

Section 5.2.2

1. $470141 = 97(4841) + 564$; $4841 = 8(564) + 329$; $564 = 1(329) + 235$; $329 = 1(235) + 94$; $235 = 2(94) + 47$; $94 = 2(47) + 0$; $\gcf(470141, 4841) = 47$

2. a. $\gcf(180, 504) = 2^2 \cdot 3^2$; $\lcm(180, 504) = 2^3 \cdot 3^2 \cdot 5 \cdot 7 = 27720$

   b. i. p^n iv. p^m

   ii. $(pq)^n$ v. $(pq)^m$

   iii. $p^n q^n$ vi. $p^m q^m$

3. Example: 6 and 35.

4. Because p_1, p_2, q_1 and q_2 are distinct primes, the numerator and denominator of $\dfrac{p_1 q_1}{p_2 q_2}$ will have no common factors, and thus $\dfrac{p_1 q_1}{p_2 q_2}$ must be in lowest terms. The condition $p_1 + q_1 = p_2 + q_2$ is not relevant information.

5. a. Finding common denominators in order to add and subtract fractions.

   b. $36 \cdot 2520 = 90720$ and $180 \cdot 504 = 90720$; $\gcf(p^n, p^m) \cdot \lcm(p^n, p^m) = p^n p^m$;
   $\lcm((pq)^n, (pq)^m) = (pq)^m$, $\gcf((pq)^n, (pq)^m) \cdot \lcm((pq)^n, (pq)^m) = (pq)^n (pq)^m$;
   $\lcm(p^n q^m, p^m q^n) = p^m q^m$, $\gcf(p^n q^m, p^m q^n) \cdot \lcm(p^n q^m, p^m q^n) = p^n q^n p^m q^m = p^n q^m p^m q^n$

   c. We first show that $ab = q \cdot \lcm(a, b)$, where q is an integer. By the Division Algorithm, we know that $ab = \lcm(a, b)q + r$, where q and r are integers and $0 \leq r < \lcm(a, b)$. Suppose $r \neq 0$.

   Then, since a and b are both divisors of ab, a and b are both divisors of r. So r is a common multiple of a and b that is less than $\lcm(a, b)$. This contradicts the fact that $\lcm(a, b)$ is the least common multiple of a and b. Hence $r = 0$ and $ab = q \cdot \lcm(a, b)$ for some integer q. We now show that if $ab = dm$, d is a common divisor of a and b if and only if m is a common multiple of a and b. First let $m = cm(a, b) = k_1 a = k_2 b$, where k_1 and k_2 are positive integers. Thus $ab = dk_1 a = dk_2 b$, or $b = dk_1$ and $a = dk_2$. So d must be a common divisor of a and b. Now consider $d = cd(a, b)$. So $a = k_3 d$ and $b = k_4 d$, where k_3 and k_4 are integers. Then $ab = md = k_3 bd = k_4 ad$. So $m = k_3 b = k_4 a$ is a common multiple of a and b. So, for $ab = dm$, $d = cd(a, b) \Leftrightarrow m = cm(a, b)$. Given the reciprocal relationship between d and m, if m is lcm(a, b), then d is gcf(a, b). Thus if ab = q • lcm(a, b), q = gcf(a, b).

d. If a and b are relatively prime, then gcf(a, b) = 1 and so, by part **c**, lcm(a, b) = ab.

6. a. Calendar Round = lcm(365, 260) = 18980 days

   b. 18980 days = 52 Haab years

   c. 18980 days = 73 Tzolkin years

7. a. a = 15, b = 24; a < b? True; x = 15, a = 24, b = 15; $r = 24 - 15 \lfloor \frac{24}{15} \rfloor = 9; 9 = 0$? False; a = 15, b = 9; $r = 15 - 9 \lfloor \frac{15}{9} \rfloor = 6; 6 = 0$? False; a = 9, b = 6; $r = 9 - 6 \lfloor \frac{9}{6} \rfloor = 3; 3 = 0$? False; a = 6, b = 3; $r = 6 - 3 \lfloor \frac{6}{3} \rfloor = 0; 0 = 0$? True; gcf = 3

   b. Here is a program written in C++.

```
#include <iostream>

using std::cout;
using std::cin;
using std::endl;

int main()
{
    int a, b, r, x;

    cout << "Input two numbers a and b: ";
    cin >> a >> b;

    if (a < b){x = a; a = b; b = x;}

    r = a - (a/b) * b;

    while (r != 0){a = b; b = r; r = a - (a/b) * b;}

    cout << "gcf = " << b << endl;

    return 0;
}
```

8. a. Basis step: 3 | 3 then 2 | F_3. Since $F_3 = 2$, this is true.
   Inductive step: Suppose 3 | k implies 2 | F_k for some k. If 3 | k, the next integer that is divisible by 3 is k + 3. $F_{k+3} = F_{k+1} + F_{k+2} = 2F_{k+1} + F_k$. By the inductive hypothesis, 2 | F_k, so 2 | ($2F_{k+1} + F_k$). Thus 3 | (k + 3) implies 2 | F_{k+3}. Therefore 3 | n implies 2 | F_n for all n.

   b. Basis step: 4 | 4 then 3 | F_4. Since $F_4 = 3$, this is true.
   Inductive step: Suppose 4 | k implies 3 | F_k for some k. If 4 | k, the next integer that is divisible by 3 is k + 4. $F_{k+4} = F_{k+3} + F_{k+2} = 3F_{k+1} + 2F_k$. By the inductive hypothesis, 3 | F_k, so 3 | ($3F_{k+1} + 2F_k$). Thus 4 | (k + 4) implies 3 | F_{k+4}. Therefore 4 | n implies 3 | F_n for all n.

9. Proof by Induction
   Basis step: Since $F_3 = 2$ and $F_2 = 1$, the Euclidean Algorithm requires 1 step (2 = 2(1) + 0) to conclude that gcf(F_3, F_2) = 1.

   Inductive step: Suppose that it requires k steps of the Euclidean Algorithm to conclude that gcf(F_{k+2}, F_{k+1}) = 1. To find gcf(F_{k+3}, F_{k+2}), the first step of the Euclidean Algorithm is $F_{k+3} = q_1 F_{k+2} + r_1$. But, by the definition of the Fibonacci sequence, $F_{k+3} = F_{k+2} + F_{k+1}$, where

$F_{k+1} < F_{k+2}$. So, by the Division Algorithm, $F_{k+3} = q_1 F_{k+2} + r_1$, where $q_1 = 1$ and $r_1 = F_{k+1}$. By Theorem 5.4, $\gcf(F_{k+3}, F_{k+2}) = \gcf(F_{k+2}, F_{k+1})$. However, by the inductive hypothesis, $\gcf(F_{k+2}, F_{k+1})$ can be shown to equal 1 in k steps of the Euclidean Algorithm. Thus it takes k + 1 steps of the Euclidean Algorithm to conclude $\gcf(F_{k+3}, F_{k+2}) = 1$. By the Principle of Mathematical Induction, then, it takes n steps of the Euclidean Algorithm to conclude $\gcf(F_{n+2}, F_{n+1}) = 1$, for all natural numbers n.

10.   a.   Let $a = r_0$ and $b = r_1$, $a > b$, be the smallest positive integers for which the Euclidean Algorithm stops in n steps. Given that $r_0 > r_1$ in the first step of the algorithm, $q_1 > 0$ and $r_1 > r_2$. Similarly, in each subsequent step, $r_{k-1} > r_k$, so $q_k > 0$. Now, working backwards, consider the final step of the algorithm. Since r_0 and r_1 are relatively prime, $r_n = \gcf(r_0, r_1) = 1$. From this,

$r_{n-1} = q_n$

$r_{n-2} = q_n q_{n-1} + 1$

$r_{n-3} = (q_n q_{n-1} + 1)q_{n-2} + q_n$

$r_{n-4} = ((q_n q_{n-1} + 1)q_{n-2} + q_n)q_{n-3} + q_n q_{n-1} + 1$ and so on.

Since r_1 and r_0 will depend in this manner on the q_k values, and since no q_k can equal 0, all q_k must be 1 to ensure that r_1 and r_0 have minimum values.

b.   For $q_k = 1$, the relation $r_{k-2} = r_{k-1} q_{k-1} + r_k$ becomes $r_{k-2} = r_{k-1} + r_k$, which is just the recursion relation for the Fibonacci sequence. Since $r_{n+1} = 0$ and $r_n = F_n = 1$, each $r_k = F_{n+1-k}$. So $a = r_0 = F_{n+1}$ and $b = r_1 = F_n$.

Section 5.2.3

1.   Because $\gcf(15, 6) = 3$, the set of all postage amounts less than 500 cents that can be paid with 6 cent and 15 cent stamps is 6 cents and $12 + 3n$ cents, for any integer $0 \leq n < 166$.

2.   There are no solutions.

3. $\gcf(77, 112) = 7$; Since 7 does not divide 39, $77x + 112y = 39$ has no solutions over the set of integers, and thus its graph has no lattice points.

4.   a.   By Theorem 5.8, if (x_1, y_1) is a lattice point on the graph of $Ax + By = C$, then so is $(x_1 - \frac{mB}{\gcf(A,B)}, y_1 + \frac{mA}{\gcf(A,B)})$ for any integer m. Let $m = \gcf(A, B)$. Then $(x_1 - B, y_1 + A)$ is a lattice point on the graph.

b.   Sample: (-1, -7)

c.   Sample: $(-1 - (-3), -7 + 10) = (2, 10)$

5. $\gcf(1470, 119) = 7$; $S = \{k: k = 7n, n \in \mathbf{Z}\}$

6.   Consider the oblique line with equation $y = -x + \frac{1}{2}$. This equation can be rewritten $2x + 2y = 1$. Because $\gcf(2, 2) = 2$ and 2 does not divide 1, the graph has no lattice points. It can also be seen that the closest this line ever approaches to a lattice point is $\frac{\sqrt{2}}{4}$. So the statement is false.

7.   It has already been shown that for any positive integers a and b the equation $ax + by = \gcf(a, b)$ has solutions if the Euclidean algorithm for (a, b) terminates in three or fewer steps. Proceeding inductively, suppose the equation has solutions whenever the Euclidean algorithm for (a, b) terminates in k steps,

and suppose the Euclidean algorithm for (a', b') terminates in $k + 1$ steps. Apply the first step of the Euclidean algorithm to get r and q such that $a' = b'q + r$ (where $0 \leq r < b$ and assuming $a' \geq b'$). Then the Euclidean algorithm applied to (b', r) terminates in k steps, so by the inductive assumption the equation $b'x' + ry' = \text{gcf}(b', r)$ has solutions. But

$$b'x' + ry' = b'x' + (a' - b'q)y'$$
$$= a'y' + b'(x' - qy')$$
$$= \text{gcf}(b', r)$$
$$= \text{gcf}(a', b'),$$

so $a'x + b'y = \text{gcf}(a', b')$ has solutions $x = y'$, $y = x' - qy'$.

8.   a.   The final positions in the Track problem can be represented as the set of all integers z such that $z = 15x + 6y$, where x and y are integers. Since -27 is divisible by $\text{gcf}(15, 6) = 3$, the equation $-27 = 15x + 6y$ has integer solutions. Once solution is, let $x = 1$ (1 move of 15 units to the right) and $y = -7$ (7 moves of 6 units to the left).

   b.   Since 88 is not divisible by $\text{gcf}(15, 6) = 3$, by Theorem 5.8 there are no integer solutions to the equation $88 = 15x + 6y$.

   c.   If S is the set of positions you can never end up at, then
   $S = \{z \mid z = 3k + 1 \text{ or } z = 3k + 2 \text{ for all integers } k\}$.

9.   a.   Sample: $13A - 8B = 1$ has the integer solution $A = 5$, $B = 8$.

   b.   Sample: $8B - 13A = 1$ has the integer solution $A = 3$, $B = 5$.

10.   a.   The stacks have the same height when $101A = 23B$. Finding the smallest values of A and B for which this is true is equivalent to finding $\text{lcm}(101, 23)$, which is 2323. A diagram shows a stack of 23 of the 101 mm ingots and 101 of the 23 mm ingots.

   b.   In general, $\text{lcm}(p, q) = \dfrac{pq}{\text{gcf}(p,q)}$ (see Problem 5 of Section 5.2.2).

   c.   If p and q are relatively prime, then $\text{gcf}(p, q) = 1$ so $\text{lcm}(p, q) = pq$.

11.   This problem can be modeled by the Diophantine equation $12x - 7y = d$. Since $\text{gcf}(12, 7) = 1$, there exist integer solutions for any integer value of d. One solution is $(3d, 5d)$. By Theorem 5.8, the set of all integer solutions is given by $(3d + 7m, 5d + 12m)$.

12.   This problem can be modeled by the Diophantine equation $c = 3x + 5y$. Since $\text{gcf}(3, 5) = 1$, there exist integer solutions for any integer value of c. A positive value of x or y represents a weight placed on the pan not holding weight c. A negative value of x or y represents a weight placed on the pan holding weight c.

13.   a.   Working backwards:
   $$1 = r_1 - r_2q_3$$
   $$= (m - nq_1) - (n - r_1q_2)q_3$$
   $$= (m - nq_1) - (n - (m - nq_1)q_2)q_3$$
   $$= m - nq_1 - nq_3 + mq_2q_3 - nq_1q_2q_3$$
   $$= m(1 + q_2q_3) - n(q_1 + q_3 + q_1q_2q_3)$$
   So $x = 1 + q_2q_3$ and $y = -(q_1 + q_3 + q_1q_2q_3)$.

b.   For m = 210 and n = 17, $q_1 = 12$, $r_1 = 6$, $q_2 = 2$, $r_2 = 5$, $q_3 = 1$, $r_3 = 1$. x = 1 + 2•1 = 3, y = 12 + 1 + 12•2•1 = 37.

Section 5.2.4

1. $1062347 = 11 • 13 • 17 • 19 • 23$; $775489 = 11^2 • 13 • 17 • 29$; gcf(1062347, 775489) = 11 • 13 • 17 = 2431

2.   Basis step: S(2) is true since 2 is prime.
Inductive step: Suppose any integer q with $2 \leq q \leq k$ is either prime or the product of prime numbers. k + 1 is either prime or can be factored such that $k + 1 = q_1q_2$, where $2 \leq q_1 \leq k$ and $2 \leq q_2 \leq k$. By the inductive supposition, q_1 and q_2 are either prime or the products of primes. So k + 1 is either prime or the product of primes. Thus S(n) is true for all $n \geq 2$.

3.   Consider the recursively defined infinite sequence of intervals (3, 6), (6, 720), ..., $(n_k, n_k!)$, where $n_{k+1} = n_k!$ By Theorem 5.10, there exists a prime number p_k in each one of these intervals and since these intervals are non-overlapping, $p_k \neq p_{k+1}$. So there must be infinitely many prime numbers.

4.   a.   Let $p = 4k_1 + 1$ and $q = 4k_2 + 1$. Then
$$pq = (4k_1 + 1)(4k_2 + 1)$$
$$= 16k_1k_2 + 4k_1 + 4k_2 + 1$$
$$= 4(4k_1k_2 + k_1 + k_2) + 1$$
Let $k = 4k_1k_2 + k_1 + k_2$. So pq = 4k + 1.

b.   The only other factors of 9, 21, 33, and 77 are 3, 7, and 11. Since 3, 7, 11 $\notin$ M, 9, 21, 33 and 77 must be M-prime. But 9 • 77 = 693 = 21 • 33. So 693 can be factored into M-primes in two ways.

5.   a.   Samples:
10 < 17 < 20
100 < 101 < 200
500 < 997 < 1000
b.   Sample: $k > \frac{5}{3}$
c.   Answers will vary.

6.   Suppose you wish to create a string of consecutive composite numbers. Let k = P(1)P(2)P(3)...P(n), where P(i) is the ith prime number. Then k + 2 through k + P(n) + 1 will be P(n) consecutive composite numbers. Since there is no upper bound to P(n), there is no upper bound to the number of consecutive composite numbers.

7.   a.   P(1)P(2)...P(n) + 1 is either prime number P(k) or has a prime factor P(k), for some k > n. Since $n < n + 1 \leq k$, $P(n + 1) \leq P(k)$.

b.   Basis step: $P(1) = 2 \leq 2^{(2^1)} = 4$.
Inductive step: Suppose for some k and for all $1 \leq j \leq k$, $P(j) \leq 2^{(2^j)}$.
$P(k + 1) \leq [P(1)P(2)...P(k)] + 1$

$$\leq 2^{(2^1)}2^{(2^2)}...2^{(2^k)} + 1 = 2^{(2^1+2^2+...+2^k)} + 1 = 2^{(2^{k+1}-2)} + 1$$
$$\leq 2^2 2^{(2^{k+1}-2)} = 2^{(2^{k+1})}$$

So $P(n) \leq 2^{(2^n)}$ for all positive integers n.

8.   a.   This is a restatement of the Division Algorithm for b = 4.

      b.   In forms (i) and (iii) n is divisible by 2.

      c.   See the solution to Problem 4a.

      d.   This follows immediately by mathematical induction.

      e.   q cannot be prime since, by hypothesis, there are only m primes. Therefore q must be composite. By part **b**, any factor n of q must be of form (ii) or (iv). By part **d**, however, if all prime factors of q were of form (ii), then, q would be of form (ii). Thus, since q is of form (iv), it must have at least one prime factor of form (iv).

9.   a. $q_1 = 2, q_2 = 3, q_3 = 7, q_4 = 43$

      b. $q_5 = 1807 = 13 \cdot 139$ is not prime.

      c. $q_{n+1} = q_1q_2...q_n + 1$ can be shown by induction.

         Basis step: $q_2 = q_1 + 1 = 1 + 1 = 2$.

         Inductive step: Suppose $q_k = q_1q_2...q_{k-1} + 1$. Then

$$q_{k+1} = q_k^2 - q_k + 1$$
$$= q_k(q_k - 1) + 1$$
$$= q_k(q_1q_2...q_{k-1} + 1 - 1) + 1$$
$$= q_1q_2...q_{k-1}q_k + 1$$

         Thus $q_{n+1} = q_1q_2...q_n + 1$ is true for all natural numbers n.

         Either q_{n+1} is prime or q_{n+1} has a prime factor p. If p were also a factor of some q_k when $1 \leq k \leq n$, then p would be a factor $q_{n+1} - q_1q_2...q_n$, which is not possible since $q_{n+1} - q_1q_2...q_n = 1$.

      d.   Since each q_n is either prime or has a unique prime factor, there must be infinitely many prime numbers.

10. $360 = 2^3 \cdot 3^2 \cdot 5$ has 6 prime factors; $360^2 = 2^6 \cdot 3^4 \cdot 5^2$ has 12 prime factors; $360^3 = 2^9 \cdot 3^6 \cdot 5^3$ has 18 prime factors; $360^n = 2^{3n} \cdot 3^{2n} \cdot 5^n$ has 6n prime factors

11.   a. $2940 = 2^2 \cdot 3 \cdot 5 \cdot 7^2$; $3150 = 2 \cdot 3^2 \cdot 5^2 \cdot 7$; gcf(m, n) = $2 \cdot 3 \cdot 5 \cdot 7 = 210$; lcm(m, n) = $2^2 \cdot 3^2 \cdot 5^2 \cdot 7^2 = 210^2 = 44100$

      b.   The gcf(m, n) is the product of the lower power of each prime number factor of both m and n. The lcm(m, n) is the product of the higher power of each prime number factor of both m and n.

12.   (3, 4, 5); (5, 12, 13); (15, 8, 17); (7, 24, 25); (21, 20, 29); (35, 12, 37); (9, 40, 41); (27, 36, 45)

13.   Let (a, b, c) be a Pythagorean triple. Then $a^2 + b^2 = c^2$ and, for any natural number k, $k^2(a^2 + b^2) = k^2c^2$. So $(ka)^2 + (kb)^2 = (kc)^2$. Since ka, kb, kc are all natural numbers, (ka, kb, kc) is a Pythagorean triple.

14.   a.   If a and b are both even, then c is even and (a, b, c) won't be primitive. If a and b are both odd, then a^2 and b^2 are both of the form 4k + 1 and so $a^2 + b^2$ must be of the form 4k + 2. If c^2 is of the form 4k + 2, however, it cannot be a perfect square (it can only have one factor of 2).

      b.   If a is even and b is odd, then a^2 is even and b^2 is odd. An odd number added to an even number is odd. Thus c^2 is odd and c is odd.

c. $(c + b) + (c - b) = v^2 + u^2; 2c = v^2 + u^2; c = \dfrac{v^2 + u^2}{2}$

$(c + b) - (c - b) = v^2 - u^2; 2b = v^2 - u^2; b = \dfrac{v^2 - u^2}{2}$

15. The following is a C++ program.

```
#include <iostream>

using std::cin;
using std::cout;
using std::endl;

int main()
{
    int u, v, a, b, c;

    cout << "Input two odd numbers u and v, with v > u." << endl;
    cin >> u >> v;
    while (u >= v){
        cout << "The second number must be
                greater than the first." << endl;
        cout << "Reinput the two numbers." << endl;
        cin >> u >> v;

        while (u % 2 == 0 || v % 2 == 0){
            cout << "Both numbers must be odd." << endl;
            cout << "Reinput the two numbers." << endl;
            cin >> u >> v;
        }

    }

    a = u * v;
    b = (v * v - u * u)/2;
    c = (v * v + u * u)/2;

    cout << "The primitive Pythagorean triples are" << endl;
    cout << "a = " << a << endl;
    cout << "b = " << b << endl;
    cout << "c = " << c << endl;

    return 0;
}
```

16. a. The relation generates Pythagorean triples for all odd values of m.

b. No; the relation cannot generate Pythagorean triples such as (15, 8, 17), where the smallest value is even.

17. We prove the contrapositive. Since $p \mid x$ and $p \mid y$ implies $p \mid z^2 = x^2 + y^2$, and $p \mid z^2$ implies $p \mid z$, if $gcf(x, y) \neq 1$, then (x, y, z) has a common factor and is not primitive. Similarly, if $p \mid x$ and $p \mid (x^2 + y^2)$, then $p \mid y$, and if $gcf(x, z) \neq 1$, then (x, y, z) has a common factor and is not primitive. The case $gcf(y, z) \neq 1$ is similar to $gcf(x, z) \neq 1$.

18. $|ad - be|^2 + (ae + bd)^2 = a^2d^2 + b^2e^2 - 2adbe + a^2e^2 + b^2d^2 + 2aebd = a^2(d^2 + e^2) + b^2(e^2 + d^2) = (a^2 + b^2)f^2 = c^2f^2$

19. a. $(x_1, y_1, z_1) = (3, 4, 5); 3^2 + 4^2 = 5^2$
   $(x_2, y_2, z_2) = (20, 21, 29); 20^2 + 21^2 = 29^2$
   $(x_3, y_3, z_3) = (119, 120, 169); 119^2 + 120^2 = 169^2$
   $(x_4, y_4, z_4) = (696, 697, 985); 696^2 + 697^2 = 985^2$

   b. Basis step: Shown in part **a**.
   Inductive step: Suppose true for (x_k, y_k, z_k). Then $z_k{}^2 - (x_k{}^2 + y_k{}^2) = 0$.
   From the recursive definitions of x_n, y_n, and z_n:
   $(x_{k+1}, y_{k+1}, z_{k+1}) = (3x_k + 2z_k + 1, 3x_k + 2z_k + 2, 4x_k + 3z_k + 2)$
   $x_{k+1}{}^2 = 9x_k{}^2 + 12x_k z_k + 6x_k + 4z_k{}^2 + 4z_k + 1$
   $y_{k+1}{}^2 = 9x_k{}^2 + 12x_k z_k + 12x_k + 4z_k{}^2 + 8z_k + 4$
   $z_{k+1}{}^2 = 16x_k{}^2 + 24x_k z_k + 16x_k + 9z_k{}^2 + 12z_k + 4$
   So $z_{k+1}{}^2 - (x_{k+1}{}^2 + y_{k+1}{}^2) = z_k{}^2 - (2x_k{}^2 + 2x_k + 1)$
   Since $y_k = x_k + 1$, $z_k{}^2 = x_k{}^2 + y_k{}^2 = 2x_k{}^2 + 2x_k + 1$.
   Thus $z_{k+1}{}^2 - (x_{k+1}{}^2 + y_{k+1}{}^2) = z_k{}^2 - (x_k{}^2 + y_k{}^2) = 0$
   Thus, by mathematical induction, $x_n{}^2 + y_n{}^2 = z_n{}^2$ for all natural numbers n.

20. a. 41, 43, 47, 53, 61, 71, 83, 97, 113, 131, 151, 173, 197, 223, 251, 281, 313, 347, 383, 421, 461, 503, 547, 593, 641, 691, 743, 797, 853, 911, 971, 1033, 1097, 1163, 1231, 1301, 1373, 1447, 1523, 1601 are all prime.

   b. Because x is divisible by 41, $x^2 - x + 41$ is necessarily divisible by 41.

21. For all integers a, n > 1, $a^n - 1 = (a - 1)(a^{n-1} + a^{n-2} + \ldots + a^n + 1)$. So if $a \neq 2$, then $a^n - 1$ must be composite.

22. a. 1, 3, 7, 15, 31, 63, 127, 255, 511, 1023, 2047, 4095

   b. We prove the contrapositive. Suppose m = rs, where r and s are positive integers. Then
   $2^m - 1 = 2^{rs} - 1$
   $\qquad\quad = (2^s - 1)(2^{s(r-1)} + 2^{s(r-2)} + \ldots + 2^s + 1)$.

   So if m is composite, then $M_m = 2^m - 1$ is also composite.

   c. 11 is prime but $2^{11} - 1 = 2047 = 23 \bullet 89$.

23. a. The positive factors of $2^{m-1}M_m$ are 1, 2, 4, ..., 2^{m-1} and $M_m, 2M_m, 4M_m, \ldots,$ $2^{m-1}M_m$. Summing these we get
   $1 + 2 + 4 + \ldots + 2^{m-1} + M_m(1 + 2 + 4 + \ldots + 2^{m-1}) = (2^m - 1)(1 + M_m)$
   $= (2^m - 1)(1 + 2^m - 1) = 2^m(2^m - 1) = 2^m M_m = 2(2^{m-1}M_m)$

   b. Sample: $2^{11}(M_{12}) = 2^{11} \bullet 4095 = 8386560$

Section 5.2.5

1. $421 = 140 \bullet 3 + 1; 140 = 46 \bullet 3 + 2; 46 = 15 \bullet 3 + 1; 15 = 5 \bullet 3 + 0; 5 = 1 \bullet 3 + 2; 1 = 0 \bullet 3 + 1;$
   $421 = (120121)_3$

2. $x + y = 1120_8; x - y = 376_8; xy = 213477_8$

3. a. $3b^3 + 8b^2 + 4$

    b. $f(10) = 3804$; $f(16) = 14340$

    c. $1, 2, 3, 4, 5, 6, 7$

4. a. $1 = 1$, $2 = (1)3 + (-1)$, $3 = (1)3 + 0$, $4 = (1)3 + 1$, $5 = (1)3^2 + (-1)3 + (-1)$,

      $6 = (1)3^2 + (-1)3 + 0$, $7 = (1)3^2 + (-1)3 + 1$, $8 = (1)3^2 + (0)3 + (-1)$, $9 = (1)3^2 + (0)3 + 0$,

      $10 = (1)3^2 + (0)3 + 1$, $11 = (1)3^2 + (1)3 + (-1)$,

      $12 = (1)3^2 + (1)3 + 0$, $13 = (1)3^2 + (1)3 + 1$, $14 = (1)3^3 + (-1)3^2 + (-1)3 + (-1)$,

      $15 = (1)3^3 + (-1)3^2 + (-1)3 + 0$, $16 = (1)3^3 + (-1)3^2 + (-1)3 + 1$,

      $17 = (1)3^3 + (-1)3^2 + (0)3 + (-1)$, $18 = (1)3^3 + (-1)3^2 + (0)3 + 0$,

      $19 = (1)3^3 + (-1)3^2 + (0)3 + 1$, $20 = (1)3^3 + (-1)3^2 + (1)3 + (-1)$,

      $21 = (1)3^3 + (-1)3^2 + (1)3 + 0$, $22 = (1)3^3 + (-1)3^2 + (1)3 + 1$,

      $23 = (1)3^3 + (0)3^2 + (-1)3 + (-1)$, $24 = (1)3^3 + (0)3^2 + (-1)3 + 0$,

      $25 = (1)3^3 + (0)3^2 + (-1)3 + 1$, $26 = (1)3^3 + (0)3^2 + (0)3 + (-1)$,

      $27 = (1)3^3 + (0)3^2 + (0)3 + 0$, $28 = (1)3^3 + (0)3^2 + (0)3 + 1$,

      $29 = (1)3^3 + (0)3^2 + (1)3 + (-1)$, $30 = (1)3^3 + (0)3^2 + (1)3 + 0$

    b. $421 = 140 \cdot 3 + 1$; $140 = 47 \cdot 3 - 1$; $47 = 16 \cdot 3 - 1$; $16 = 5 \cdot 3 + 1$;

      $5 = 2 \cdot 3 - 1$; $2 = 1 \cdot 3 - 1$; $1 = 0 \cdot 3 + 1$;

      $421 = (1)3^6 + (-1)3^5 + (-1)3^4 + (1)3^3 + (-1)3^2 + (-1)3 + 1$

    c. By the Division Algorithm, any integer $n = 3k$, $3k + 1$, or $3k + 2$. If $n = 3k + 2$, then

      $n = 3(k + 1) - 1$, so $n = 3k' - 1$.

    d. Successively apply the (*) algorithm to an integer n to obtain a decreasing series of non-negative

      quotients until a zero is reached:

      $n = 3q_0 + a_0$ where $a_0 = -1, 0, 1$ and $n > q_0$

      $q_0 = 3q_1 + a_1$ where $a_1 = -1, 0, 1$ and $q_0 > q_1$

      $q_1 = 3q_2 + a_2$ where $a_2 = -1, 0, 1$ and $q_1 > q_2$

      $\vdots$

      $q_{k-2} = 3q_{k-1} + a_{k-1}$ where $a_{k-1} = -1, 0, 1$ and $q_{k-2} > q_{k-1}$

      $q_{k-1} = 3(0) + a_k$ where $a_k = -1, 0, 1$

      The balanced ternary representation of n is obtained by beginning with the first equation in the

      preceding list and successively substituting the subsequent numbers of the list as follows:

      $n = 3q_0 + a_0 = 3(3q_1 + a_1) + a_0 = 3^2q_1 + 3a_1 + a_0 = 3^2(3q_2 + a_2) + 3a_1 + a_0$

      $= 3^3q_2 + 3^2a_2 + 3a_1 + a_0$

      $\vdots$

      $= 3^{k-1}q_{k-2} + a_{k-2}3^{k-2} + \ldots + a_13 + a_0$

      $= 3^{k-1}(3q_{k-1} + a_{k-1}) + a_{k-2}3^{k-2} + \ldots + a_13 + a_0$

      $= 3^kq_{k-1} + a_{k-1}3^{k-1} + a_{k-2}3^{k-2} + \ldots + a_13 + a_0$

      $= a_k3^k + a_{k-1}3^{k-1} + a_{k-2}3^{k-2} + \ldots + a_13 + a_0$

      To show uniqueness, suppose to the contrary that for some positive integer n, there is a second

      representation

      $n = c_m3^m + c_{m-1}3^{m-1} + \ldots + c_13 + c_0$

      where the coefficients c_i are integers with $c_m \neq 0$ and $c_i = -1, 0, 1$. We can assume $m = k$. Then

      $0 = (a_k - c_k)3^k + (a_{k-1} - c_{k-1})3^{k-1} + \ldots + (a_1 - c_1)3 + (a_0 - c_0)$

where at least one of the coefficients $(a_i - c_i)$ is nonzero. Let j be the smallest integer such that $a_j - c_j \neq 0$. Then

$$(a_k - c_k)3^k + (a_{k-1} - c_{k-1})3^{k-1} + \ldots + (a_1 - c_1)3^{j+1} = -(a_j - c_j)3^j$$
$$(a_k - c_k)3^{k-j} + (a_{k-1} - c_{k-1})3^{k-j-1} + \ldots + (a_1 - c_1)3 = -(a_j - c_j)$$

The left side of the last equation is divisible by 3, but the right side of the equation can only be -2, -1, 1, or 2, which leads to a contradiction. Thus the representation is unique.

5. a. $10^x = 2^{1000}$; $x = 1000 \log 2 \approx 301$, so there are 302 digits

    b. 1001 digits

    c. $2^{1000} = 2(8)^{333}$, so there are 334 digits

    d. $2^{1000} = 16^{250}$, so there are 251 digits

6. $\left\lceil \dfrac{k}{3} \right\rceil$; Every three digits in base 2 represents a factor of 8, or 1 digit in base 8.

7. a. For $k > 0$, $10^k = 9(10^{k-1} + 10^{k-2} + \ldots + 10 + 1) + 1$, so
    $$a_k 10^k + a_{k-1} 10^{k-1} + \ldots + a_1 10 + a_0$$
    $$= a_k(9(10^{k-1} + 10^{k-2} + \ldots + 10 + 1) + 1) +$$
    $$a_{k-1}(9(10^{k-2} + 10^{k-3} + \ldots + 10 + 1) + 1) + \ldots + a_1(9 + 1) + a_0$$
    $$= 9a_k(10^{k-1} + 10^{k-2} + \ldots + 10 + 1) + 9a_{k-1}(10^{k-2} + 10^{k-3} + \ldots + 10 + 1) + \ldots$$
    $$+ 9a_1 + (a_k + a_{k-1} + \ldots + a_1 + a_0).$$
    Thus 9 divides $a_k 10^k + a_{k-1} 10^{k-1} + \ldots + a_1 10 + a_0$ iff 9 divides
    $a_k + a_{k-1} + \ldots + a_1 + a_0$.

    b. For $k > 0$, $b^k = (b - 1)(b^{k-1} + b^{k-2} + \ldots + b + 1) + 1$, so
    $$a_k b^k + a_{k-1} b^{k-1} + \ldots + a_1 b + a_0$$
    $$= a_k((b - 1)(b^{k-1} + b^{k-2} + \ldots + b + 1) + 1) +$$
    $$a_{k-1}((b - 1)(b^{k-2} + b^{k-3} + \ldots + b + 1) + 1) + \ldots + a_1((b - 1) + 1) + a_0$$
    $$= a_k(b - 1)(b^{k-1} + b^{k-2} + \ldots + b + 1) + a_{k-1}(b - 1)(b^{k-2} + b^{k-3} + \ldots + b + 1) + \ldots$$
    $$+ a_1(b - 1) + (a_k + a_{k-1} + \ldots + a_1 + a_0).$$
    Thus $(b - 1)$ divides $a_k b^k + a_{k-1} b^{k-1} + \ldots + a_1 b + a_0$ iff $(b - 1)$ divides
    $a_k + a_{k-1} + \ldots + a_1 + a_0$.

8. a. For $k > 0$, $10^k = 11(10^{k-1} - 10^{k-2} + \ldots \pm 10^1 \mp 1) \pm 1$, so
    $$a_k 10^k + a_{k-1} 10^{k-1} + \ldots + a_1 10 + a_0$$
    $$= a_k(11(10^{k-1} - 10^{k-2} + \ldots \pm 10 \mp 1) \pm 1) +$$
    $$a_{k-1}(11(10^{k-2} - 10^{k-3} + \ldots \mp 10 \pm 1) \mp 1) + \ldots + a_1(11 - 1) + a_0$$
    $$= 11a_k(10^{k-1} - 10^{k-2} + \ldots \pm 10 \mp 1) + 11a_{k-1}(10^{k-2} - 10^{k-3} + \ldots \mp 10 \pm 1) + \ldots$$
    $$+ 11a_1 + (\pm a_k \mp a_{k-1} \pm \ldots - a_1 + a_0),$$
    where a_k is positive for k even and negative for k odd. Thus 11 divides
    $a_k 10^k + a_{k-1} 10^{k-1} + \ldots + a_1 10 + a_0$ iff 11 divides $\pm a_k \mp a_{k-1} \pm \ldots - a_1 + a_0$.

    b. For $k > 0$, $b^k = (b + 1)(b^{k-1} - b^{k-2} + \ldots \pm b^1 \mp 1) \pm 1$, so
    $$a_k b^k + a_{k-1} b^{k-1} + \ldots + a_1 b + a_0$$
    $$= a_k((b + 1)(b^{k-1} - b^{k-2} + \ldots \pm b \mp 1) \pm 1) +$$
    $$a_{k-1}((b + 1)(b^{k-2} - b^{k-3} + \ldots \mp b \pm 1) \mp 1) + \ldots + a_1((b + 1) - 1) + a_0$$

$$= a_k(b+1)(b^{k-1} - b^{k-2} + \ldots \pm b \mp 1) + a_{k-1}(b+1)(b^{k-2} - b^{k-3} + \ldots \mp b \pm 1) + \ldots$$
$$+ a_1(b+1) + (\pm a_k \mp a_{k-1} \pm \ldots - a_1 + a_0),$$

where a_k is positive for k even and negative for k odd. Thus $(b+1)$ divides $a_k b^k + a_{k-1}b^{k-1} + \ldots + a_1 b + a_0$ iff $(b+1)$ divides $\pm a_k \mp a_{k-1} \pm \ldots - a_1 + a_0$.

9. Let $a_2 b^2 + a_1 b + a_0$ be a 3-digit number in base b. Reversing the digits gives $a_0 b^2 + a_1 b + a_2$ and subtracting yields $(a_2 - a_0)b^2 - (a_2 - a_0) = (a_2 - a_0)(b^2 - 1)$
$= (a_2 - a_0)(b+1)(b-1)$. So the difference is divisible by both $b-1$ and $b+1$.

10. a. $365 = -36(-10) + 5$, $-36 = 4(-10) + 4$, $4 = 0(-10) + 4$; $365 = (445)_{-10}$

b. For any integer $b \neq 0$, every integer n has a unique representation of the form
$$n = a_k b^k + a_{k-1}b^{k-1} + \ldots + a_1 b + a_0$$
where the coefficients a_i are integers with $a_k \neq 0$ and $0 \leq a_i < |b|$ for all i.

Modifications to proof: Change the Division Algorithm to
$n = q_0 b + a_0$ where $0 \leq a_0 < |b|$ and $|n| > |q_0|$
$q_0 = q_1 b + a_1$ where $0 \leq a_1 < |b|$ and $|q_0| > |q_1|$
$q_1 = q_2 b + a_2$ where $0 \leq a_2 < |b|$ and $|q_1| > |q_2|$
$\vdots$
$q_{k-2} = q_{k-1}b + a_{k-1}$ where $0 \leq a_{k-1} < |b|$ and $|q_{k-2}| > |q_{k-1}|$
$q_{k-1} = 0b + a_k$ where $0 \leq a_k < |b|$

11. a. $1000 = (1111101000)_2 = (1750)_8 = (3E8)_{16}$
b. $10^{100} = 16^x$; $100 = x \log 16$; $x \approx 83.05$; 84 digits
c. $10^{100} = 8^x$; $100 = x \log 8$; $x \approx 110.73$; 111 digits

12. a. $15 = (1111)_2$, $9 = (101)_2$, $(1111)_2 + (101)_2 = (11000)_2 = 24$
b. i. $15 = (0001\ 0101)_{BCD}$, $9 = (1001)_{BCD}$, $24 = (0010\ 0100)_{BCD}$
ii. $(1010)_{BCD}$, $(1011)_{BCD}$, $(1100)_{BCD}$, $(1101)_{BCD}$, $(1110)_{BCD}$, $(1111)_{BCD}$
c. i. $(0001\ 0101)_{BCD} + (1001)_{BCD} = (0001\ 1110)_{BCD}$,
$(0001\ 1110)_{BCD} + (0110)_{BCD} = (0010\ 0100)_{BCD}$;
ii. The procedure works because $(0110)_{BCD}$ (decimal 6) is the twos-complement of $(1010)_{BCD}$ (decimal 10); i.e., $(0110)_{BCD} + (1010)_{BCD} = (0000)_{BCD}$ plus a carry bit of 1. Since the sum of two BCD strings of length 4 cannot exceed $(1001)_{BCD}$ (decimal 9), adding $(0110)_{BCD}$ when the sum is $(1010)_{BCD}$ or higher gives a resultant BCD string equal to the sum minus decimal 10 and adds a carry bit to the next higher order BCD string.

Section 5.3.1

1. a. $2x^3 + 3x^2 - 4x - 7 = (x^2 + 1)(2x + 3) + (-6x - 10)$; $q(x) = 2x + 3$;
$r(x) = -6x - 10$
b. From part **a**, $f(x) = \frac{a(x)}{b(x)} = 2x + 3 + \frac{(-6x - 10)}{x^2 + 1}$. For large $|x|$, the fractional part approaches 0 and the graph of f approaches the line $2x + 3$.

2. a. $5x^4 - 1 = (10x^2 + 2)(\frac{1}{2}x^2 - \frac{1}{10}) + -\frac{4}{5}$; $q(x) = \frac{1}{2}x^2 - \frac{1}{10}$; $r(x) = -\frac{4}{5}$

    b. From part **a**, $f(x) = \frac{a(x)}{b(x)} = \frac{1}{2}x^2 - \frac{1}{10} + \frac{-\frac{4}{5}}{10x^2 + 2}$. For large $|x|$, the fractional part approaches 0

    and the graph of f approaches the parabola $\frac{1}{2}x^2 - \frac{1}{10}$.

3. a. $p(x) = x^4 - x^2 - 2 = (x^2 - 2)(x^2 + 1)$
    b. $p(x) = x^4 - x^2 - 2 = (x^2 - 2)(x^2 + 1)$
    c. $p(x) = x^4 - x^2 - 2 = (x^2 - 2)(x^2 + 1) = (x + \sqrt{2})(x - \sqrt{2})(x^2 + 1)$
    d. $p(x) = x^4 - x^2 - 2 = (x^2 - 2)(x^2 + 1) = (x + \sqrt{2})(x - \sqrt{2})(x + i)(x - i)$

4. a. $2\left(\frac{3}{2}\right)^3 - 3\left(\frac{3}{2}\right)^2 - 4\left(\frac{3}{2}\right) + 6 = \frac{27}{4} - \frac{27}{4} - 6 + 6 = 0$

    b. $p(x) = (x - \frac{3}{2})(2x^2 - 4) = (x - \frac{3}{2})(\sqrt{2}x + 2)(\sqrt{2}x - 2)$

5. a. Let $a(x) = x^n - c^n$, where n is a positive integer. $a(x)$ is a polynomial of degree ≥ 1 and $a(c) = 0$.
    Thus, by Theorem 5.18, $x - c$ is a factor of $a(x)$.

    b. Let $a(x) = x^n + c^n$, where n is an odd positive integer. $a(x)$ is a polynomial of degree ≥ 1.
    Since $(-c)^n = -(c^n)$ for odd n, $a(-c) = 0$. Thus, by Theorem 5.18, $x - (-c) = x + c$ is a factor of $a(x)$.

6. a. $x^{12} + 2x^6 + 1 = (x^6 + 1)^2$; $1000002000001 = 10^{12} + 2 \cdot 10^6 + 1 = (10^6 + 1)^2$
    b. $\underbrace{1000...0}_{50\,zeros}2\underbrace{000...0}_{50\,zeros}1 = 10^{102} + 2 \cdot 10^{51} + 1 = (10^{51} + 1)^2 = \underbrace{1000...0}_{50\,zeros}1^2$

    c. Sample: $x^7 + x^6 + x^5 + x^4 + x^3 + x^2 + x + 1 = \frac{x^8 - 1}{x - 1} = (x^4 + 1)(x^2 + 1)(x + 1)$;

    $11111111 = 10^7 + 10^6 + 10^5 + 10^4 + 10^3 + 10^2 + 10 + 1 = \frac{10^8 - 1}{10 - 1} = 10001 \cdot 101 \cdot 11$

    d. Sample: $x^{62} + x^{61} + ... + x + 1 = \frac{x^{63} - 1}{x - 1} = \frac{(x^{21})^3 - 1^3}{x - 1} = \frac{(x^{21} - 1)(x^{42} + x^{21} + 1)}{x - 1}$

    $= \frac{(x^7 - 1)(x^{14} + x^7 + 1)(x^{42} + x^{21} + 1)}{x - 1}$

    $= (x^6 + x^5 + ... + x + 1)(x^{14} + x^7 + 1)(x^{42} + x^{21} + 1)$

    $\underbrace{111...1}_{63\,ones} = 10^{62} + 10^{61} + ... + 10 + 1$

    $= (10^6 + 10^5 + ... + 10 + 1)(10^{42} + 10^{21} + 1) =$
    $= 1111111 \cdot 100000010000001 \cdot \underbrace{100..00}_{20\,zeros}\underbrace{100..00}_{20\,zeros}1$

    e. $ax^3 + a = a(x^3 + 1) = a(x + 1)(x^2 - x + 1)$
    $827827 = 8(10^5) + 2(10^4) + 7(10^3) + 8(10^2) + 2(10) + 7 = (8 \cdot 10^2 + 2 \cdot 10 + 7)(10^3 + 1)$
    $= 827 \cdot 11 \cdot 91 = 827 \cdot 11 \cdot 13 \cdot 7$

    f. $123x^{15} + 123x^{12} + 123x^9 + 123x^6 + 123x^3 + 123$
    $= 123(x^{15} + x^{12} + x^9 + x^6 + x^3 + 1)$
    $123(10)^{15} + 123(10)^{12} + 123(10)^9 + 123(10)^6 + 123(10)^3 + 123$
    $= 123 \cdot 1000000001 \cdot 1001001$

7. a. Let $a(x) = a_n x^n + a_{n-1}x^{n-1} + ... + a_1 x + a_0$, where $a_n > 0$ and $a_k \geq 0$ for $0 \leq k < n$. Suppose $c > 0$.
    Then $a_n c^n > 0$ and $a_k c^k \geq 0$ for $0 \leq k < n$. So $a(c) = a_n c^n + a_{n-1}c^{n-1} + ... + a_1 c + a_0 > 0$, and c cannot

be a solution.

b. $a(x) = a_n x^n + a_{n-1} x^{n-1} + \ldots + a_1 x + a_0$, where $a_k \geq 0$ for all even values of k and $a_k \leq 0$ for all odd values of k.

8. Let $y = x - 1$. Then $x^9 - 1 = (y + 1)^9 - 1$. By the Binomial Theorem,
$(y + 1)^9 - 1 = y^9 + 9y^8 + 36y^7 + 84y^6 + 126y^5 + 126y^4 + 84y^3 + 36y^2 + 9y + 1 - 1$
$= (x - 1)^9 + 9(x - 1)^8 + 36(x - 1)^7 + 84(x - 1)^6 + 126(x - 1)^5$
$+ 126(x - 1)^4 + 84(x - 1)^3 + 36(x - 1)^2 + 9(x - 1)$

Section 5.3.2

1. a. Applying the substitution $y = x^2$, the polynomial $8x^4 + 2x^2 - 1$ becomes $8y^2 + 2y - 1$. Solving the equation $8y^2 + 2y - 1 = 0$ by the Quadratic Formula yields the solutions $y = \frac{1}{4}$ and $y = -\frac{1}{2}$. So $x = \pm\frac{1}{2}$ and $x = \pm\frac{\sqrt{2}}{2}i$ are solutions to $8x^4 + 2x^2 - 1 = 0$. By Theorem 5.18, then, a prime factorization in $\mathbf{C[x]}$ is $(2x - 1)(2x + 1)(\sqrt{2}x - i)(\sqrt{2}x + i)$. In $\mathbf{R[x]}$, $\mathbf{Q[x]}$, and $\mathbf{Z[x]}$ a prime factorization is $(2x - 1)(2x + 1)(2x^2 + 1)$.

   b. The prime factorization into monic polynomials is $8(x + \frac{1}{2})(x - \frac{1}{2})(x + \frac{\sqrt{2}}{2}i)(x - \frac{\sqrt{2}}{2}i)$ in $\mathbf{C[x]}$, and $8(x + \frac{1}{2})(x - \frac{1}{2})(x^2 + \frac{1}{2})$ in $\mathbf{R[x]}$ and $\mathbf{Q[x]}$.

2. Using the Euclidean Algorithm for Polynomials, we get successive remainders of $x^4 + 2x^3 + 2x^2 + 2x + 1$, $x^3 + x$, $x^2 + 1$, and 0. So $x^2 + 1$ is the greatest common divisor.

3. In $\mathbf{R[x]}$, $9x^4 + 440x^2 - 49 = (9x^2 - 1)(x^2 + 49) = (3x + 1)(3x - 1)(x^2 + 49)$.
   In $\mathbf{C[x]}$, $9x^4 + 440x^2 - 49 = (9x^2 - 1)(x^2 + 49) = (3x + 1)(3x - 1)(x + 7i)(x - 7i)$.

4. In $\mathbf{R[x]}$, $x^{106} - x^{100} = x^{100}(x^6 - 1) = x^{100}(x + 1)(x^2 - x + 1)(x - 1)(x^2 + x + 1)$.
   In $\mathbf{C[x]}$, $x^{106} - x^{100} = x^{100}(x^6 - 1) = x^{100}(x + 1)(x^2 - x + 1)(x - 1)(x^2 + x + 1)$
   $= x^{100}(x + 1)(x - 1)(x - \frac{1 + \sqrt{3}i}{2})(x - \frac{1 - \sqrt{3}i}{2})(x - \frac{-1 + \sqrt{3}i}{2})(x - \frac{-1 - \sqrt{3}i}{2})$.

5. a. In $\mathbf{R[x]}$ and $\mathbf{C[x]}$, $ax^2 + bx + c = (x - \frac{-b + \sqrt{b^2 - 4ac}}{2a})(x - \frac{-b - \sqrt{b^2 - 4ac}}{2a})$.

   b. In $\mathbf{R[x]}$, if $b^2 - 4ac < 0$, then $ax^2 + bx + c$ is already prime.
   In $\mathbf{C[x]}$, $ax^2 + bx + c = (x - \frac{-b + i\sqrt{4ac - b^2}}{2a})(x - \frac{-b - i\sqrt{4ac - b^2}}{2a})$.

6. a. $x^{12} - 1 = (x - 1)(x^{11} + x^{10} + x^9 + x^8 + x^7 + x^6 + x^5 + x^4 + x^3 + x^2 + x + 1)$
   $= (x - 1)(x + 1)(x^{10} + x^8 + x^6 + x^4 + x^2 + 1)$
   $= (x - 1)(x + 1)(x^2 + 1)(x^8 + x^4 + 1)$
   $= (x - 1)(x + 1)(x^2 + 1)(x^4 + x^2 + 1)(x^4 - x^2 + 1)$
   $= (x - 1)(x + 1)(x^2 + 1)(x^2 + x + 1)(x^2 - x + 1)(x^4 - x^2 + 1)$

   b. $x^{12} - 1 = (x^6 - 1)(x^6 + 1)$
   $= (x^3 + 1)(x^3 - 1)(x^2 + 1)(x^4 - x^2 + 1)$
   $= (x + 1)(x^2 - x + 1)(x - 1)(x^2 + x + 1)(x^2 + 1)(x^4 - x^2 + 1)$

c. $x^{12} - 1 = (x^4 - 1)(x^8 + x^4 + 1)$
$\qquad = (x^2 + 1)(x^2 - 1)(x^4 + x^2 + 1)(x^4 - x^2 + 1)$
$\qquad = (x - 1)(x + 1)(x^2 + 1)(x^2 + x + 1)(x^2 - x + 1)(x^4 - x^2 + 1)$

d. $x^{12} - 1 = (x^2 - 1)(x^{10} + x^8 + x^6 + x^4 + x^2 + 1)$
$\qquad = (x - 1)(x + 1)(x^2 + 1)(x^8 + x^4 + 1)$
$\qquad = (x - 1)(x + 1)(x^2 + 1)(x^4 + x^2 + 1)(x^4 - x^2 + 1)$
$\qquad = (x - 1)(x + 1)(x^2 + 1)(x^2 + x + 1)(x^2 - x + 1)(x^4 - x^2 + 1)$

7. By the Euclidean Algorithm,
$a(x) = b(x) \bullet (x - 2) + 6x^2 + 3$
$b(x) = (6x^2 + 3) \bullet \frac{1}{3}(x + 1)$
So $\gcd(a(x), b(x)) = 6x^2 + 3$.
$6x^2 + 3 = (2x^4 - 2x^3 + 3x^2 - x + 1)(1) + (2x^3 + 2x^2 + x + 1)(-x + 2)$

8. Since $r(x) = a(x) - b(x)q(x)$, any factor of $a(x)$ and $b(x)$ is also a factor of $r(x)$. So any greatest common factor of $a(x)$ and $b(x)$ will also be a factor of $r(x)$. So, from the definition of gcf, $\gcd(a(x), b(x)) \le \gcd(b(x), r(x))$. Since $a(x) = b(x)q(x) + r(x)$, any factor of $b(x)$ and $r(x)$ will also be a factor of $a(x)$. So $\gcd(b(x), r(x)) \le \gcd(a(x), b(x))$. Thus $\gcd(a(x), b(x)) = \gcd(b(x), r(x))$.

CHAPTER 6 – Number System Structures

Section 6.1.1

1. The congruence class 0 Mod(2) is the set of even integers; the congruence class 1 Mod(2) is the set of odd integers.

2. $0* \supset \{300, 600, 900\}$, $1* \supset \{100, 400, 700, 1000\}$, $2* \supset \{200, 500, 800\}$

3. a. $3783 \equiv 0 \ Mod(13)$

   b. $-578 \equiv 7 \ Mod(13)$

   c. By Fermat's Little Theorem, $16^{12} \equiv 1 \ Mod(13)$. By the Corollary to Theorem 6.2, $(16^{12})^{11} = 16^{132} \equiv 1 \ Mod(13)$. Since $16^6 \equiv 1 \ Mod(13)$, $16^6 \cdot 16^{132} = 16^{138} \equiv 1 \ Mod(13)$.

4. a. Yes, because 3 is relatively prime to 10, by Theorem 6.1 the set S_3 is a complete system of residues.

   b. Yes; $10 \equiv 0 \ Mod(10)$, $11 \equiv 1 \ Mod(10)$, $12 \equiv 2 \ Mod(10)$, $13 \equiv 3 \ Mod(10)$, and $14 \equiv 4 \ Mod(10)$

   c. No; $10 \equiv 0 \ Mod(10)$, $12 \equiv 2 \ Mod(10)$, $14 \equiv 4 \ Mod(10)$, $16 \equiv 6 \ Mod(10)$, and $18 \equiv 8 \ Mod(10)$

   d. Yes; $111 \equiv 1 \ Mod(10)$; $-7 \equiv 3 \ Mod(10)$; $-5 \equiv 5 \ Mod(10)$; $-4 \equiv 6 \ Mod(10)$; $87 \equiv 7 \ Mod(10)$; $138 \equiv 8 \ Mod(10)$; $19 \equiv 9 \ Mod(10)$

5. a. 0

   b. 7

   c. 1

   d. False; $2 \cdot 6 \equiv 0 \ Mod(12)$, yet $2 \not\equiv 0 \ Mod(12)$ and $6 \not\equiv 0 \ Mod(12)$.

6. a. 0

   b. 6

   c. 1

   d. True; Since $ab \equiv 0 \ Mod(11)$ implies $ab = 11k$, for some integer k, either a or b must have a factor of 11. So either $a \equiv 0 \ Mod(11)$ or $b \equiv 0 \ Mod(11)$.

7. Since $a \equiv b \ Mod(m)$ and $c \equiv d \ Mod(m)$, there exist integers k and j with $a - b = jm$ and $c - d = km$. Then $c(a - b) = jmc$ and $b(c - d) = kmb$, so $c(a - b) + b(c - d) = ac - bd$ $= (jc + kb)m$. Since $(jc + kb)$ is an integer, $ac \equiv bd \ Mod(m)$.

8. Proof by induction: Basis step: $a^1 \equiv b^1 \ Mod(m)$, by hypothesis. Inductive step: Assume $a^k \equiv b^k \ Mod(m)$. By Theorem 6.2, $a^k \cdot a = a^{k+1} \equiv b^k \cdot b = b^{k+1} \ Mod(m)$. Thus, by mathematical induction, $a^p \equiv b^p \ Mod(m)$ for all positive integers p.

9. Reflexive Property: $a \equiv a \, \text{Mod}(m)$ since $a - a = 0 = 0 \cdot m$. Symmetric Property: If $a \equiv b \, \text{Mod}(m)$, then $a - b = km$, for some integer k. So $b - a = -km$ and $b \equiv a \, \text{Mod}(m)$. Transitive Property: If $a \equiv b \, \text{Mod}(m)$, and $b \equiv c \, \text{Mod}(m)$, then $a - b = km$ and $b - c = jm$, for some integers k and j. Then $(a - b) + (b - c) = a - c = km + jm = m(k + j)$. So $a \equiv c \, \text{Mod}(m)$.

10. a. $7^2 \equiv 1 \, \text{Mod}(16)$, $(7^2)^{157} = 7^{314} \equiv 1^{157} \, \text{Mod}(16)$, so $7 \cdot 7^{314} = 7^{315} \equiv 7 \, \text{Mod}(16)$

    b. $17 \equiv 1 \, \text{Mod}(16)$, $17^{315} \equiv 1^{315} \, \text{Mod}(16)$

    c. $13^4 \equiv 1 \, \text{Mod}(16)$, $(13^4)^{78} = 13^{312} \equiv 1 \, \text{Mod}(16)$,
        $13^{312} \cdot 13^3 = 13^{315} \equiv 13^3 \cdot 1 \, \text{Mod}(16)$, $13^{315} \equiv 5 \, \text{Mod}(16)$

    d. $14^4 \equiv 0 \, \text{Mod}(16)$, $14^4 \cdot 14^{311} = 14^{315} \equiv 0 \cdot 14^{311} \, \text{Mod}(16) \equiv 0 \, \text{Mod}(16)$

    e. Sample: In terms of the number of steps, the order of difficulty, from least to most difficult, is b, d, a, c.

11. Since $5 \equiv -1 \, \text{Mod}(6)$, $5^{100} \equiv (-1)^{100} = 1 \, \text{Mod}(6)$. So the remainder when 5^{100} is divided by 6 is 1.

12. m is of the form $p_1 p_2 \ldots p_k$, where the p_i are distinct primes. Suppose m is of the form $p_1 p_2 \ldots p_k$ and, for some x, $x^2 \equiv 0 \, \text{Mod}(m)$. Then all p_i^2 will be factors of x^2, so all p_i will be factors of x and $x \equiv 0 \, \text{Mod}(m)$. Suppose m is not of the form $p_1 p_2 \ldots p_k$; that is, m is of the form $p_1^{t_1} p_2^{t_2} \ldots p_k^{t_k}$, where at least one $t_i \geq 2$. Without loss of generality, assume $t_1 \geq 2$ and let $x = p_1^{t_1 - 1} p_2^{t_2} \ldots p_k^{t_k}$. Then $x^2 = p_1^{2(t_1 - 1)} p_2^{2t_2} \ldots p_k^{2t_k}$. Since $2(t_1 - 1) \geq t_1$ for all $t_1 \geq 2$, $x^2 \equiv 0 \, \text{Mod}(m)$. However, $p_1^{t_1 - 1} p_2^{t_2} \ldots p_k^{t_k} < p_1^{t_1} p_2^{t_2} \ldots p_k^{t_k}$, so $x \not\equiv 0 \, \text{Mod}(m)$.

13. a. Since $10 \equiv 1 \, \text{Mod}(9)$, $10^j \equiv 1 \, \text{Mod}(9)$ and, for any digit a_j, $a_j 10^j \equiv a_j \, \text{Mod}(9)$. Also by Theorem 6.2, $a_j 10^j + a_i 10^i \equiv a_j + a_i \, \text{Mod}(9)$, so
        $a_k 10^k + a_{k-1} 10^{k-1} + \ldots + a_1 10 + a_0 \equiv a_k + a_{k-1} + \ldots + a_1 + a_0 \, \text{Mod}(9)$. Thus
        $a_k 10^k + a_{k-1} 10^{k-1} + \ldots + a_1 10 + a_0 \equiv 0 \, \text{Mod}(9)$ if and only if
        $a_k + a_{k-1} + \ldots + a_1 + a_0 \equiv 0 \, \text{Mod}(9)$. The same argument applies for $\text{Mod}(3)$.

    b. Since $10 \equiv -1 \, \text{Mod}(11)$, $10^j \equiv 1 \, \text{Mod}(11)$, for j even, and $10^j \equiv -1 \, \text{Mod}(11)$, for j odd. Thus, for any digit a_j, $a_j 10^j \equiv a_j \, \text{Mod}(11)$, for j even, and $a_j 10^j \equiv -a_j \, \text{Mod}(11)$, for j odd. So for k even
        $a_k 10^k + a_{k-1} 10^{k-1} + \ldots + a_1 10 + a_0 \equiv a_k - a_{k-1} + \ldots - a_1 + a_0 \, \text{Mod}(11)$, and for k odd
        $a_k 10^k + a_{k-1} 10^{k-1} + \ldots + a_1 10 + a_0 \equiv -a_k + a_{k-1} - \ldots - a_1 + a_0 \, \text{Mod}(11)$. Thus
        $a_k 10^k + a_{k-1} 10^{k-1} + \ldots + a_1 10 + a_0 \equiv 0 \, \text{Mod}(11)$ if and only if $a_k - a_{k-1} + \ldots - a_1 + a_0 \equiv 0 \, \text{Mod}(11)$
        or $-a_k + a_{k-1} - \ldots - a_1 + a_0 \equiv 0 \, \text{Mod}(11)$.

14. a. By the Division Algorithm, any integer $m = 4k$, $4k + 1$, $4k + 2$, or $4k + 3$. If $m = 4k$, then $m^2 = 16k^2 = 4(4k^2)$. So $m^2 \equiv 0 \, \text{Mod}(4)$.
        If $m = 4k + 1$, then $m^2 = 16k^2 + 8k + 1 = 4(4k^2 + 2k) + 1$. So $m^2 \equiv 1 \, \text{Mod}(4)$.
        If $m = 4k + 2$, then $m^2 = 16k^2 + 16k + 4 = 4(4k^2 + 4k + 1)$. So $m^2 \equiv 0 \, \text{Mod}(4)$.
        And if $m = 4k + 3$, then $m^2 = 16k^2 + 24k + 9 = 4(4k^2 + 6k + 2) + 1$. So $m^2 \equiv 1 \, \text{Mod}(4)$.

b. By part **a**, x^2 and y^2 are congruent to either 0 Mod(4) or 1 Mod(4). So $x^2 + y^2$ is congruent to either 0 Mod(4), 1 Mod(4), or 2 Mod(4). Since $z \equiv 3$ Mod(4), $x^2 + y^2$ cannot equal z.

15. a ≡ b Mod(1) if and only if b – a is an integer.
   a. Sample: 0.24, -0.76, 29.24
   b. Sample: $\frac{8}{5}$, $-\frac{2}{5}$, $\frac{28}{5}$
   c. π + n where n is an integer
   d. 0.11
   e. False; $\frac{1}{4} \cdot 4 \equiv \frac{1}{2} \cdot 4$ Mod(1), yet $\frac{1}{4} \not\equiv \frac{1}{2}$ Mod(1)

16. a. sin x = sin y whenever x – y is divisible by 2π, so if x ≡ y Mod (2π), then sin x = sin y.
   b. tan x = tan y when x – y is divisible by π, so if x ≡ y Mod (π), then tan x = tan y.
   c. $x - \lfloor x \rfloor = y - \lfloor y \rfloor$ when x – y is an integer, so if x ≡ y Mod (1), then $x - \lfloor x \rfloor = y - \lfloor y \rfloor$.

Section 6.1.2

1. $12 + 2 \cdot 4 + \left\lfloor \frac{3(4+1)}{5} \right\rfloor + 1861 + \left\lfloor \frac{1861}{4} \right\rfloor - \left\lfloor \frac{1861}{100} \right\rfloor + \left\lfloor \frac{1861}{400} \right\rfloor + 2 = 2337$;

   2337 Mod(7) = 6; Friday

2. a. Sample: For February 3, 1959, m = 14, d = 3, and y = 1958. w ≡ 3 Mod(7). So February 3, 1959, the "day the music died," was a Tuesday.
   b. Sample: For October 29, 1929, m = 10, d = 29, and y = 1929. w ≡ 3 Mod(7). So October 29, 1929, "Black Tuesday," was a Tuesday.
   c. They both fall on a Monday.
   d. The expression d will add the number of days from the beginning of the month. Since $365y \equiv y$ Mod(7), the expression y will add 1 day for each year. The expression $\left\lfloor \frac{y}{4} \right\rfloor$ will add an extra day if y is a leap year, and the expression $- \left\lfloor \frac{y}{100} \right\rfloor + \left\lfloor \frac{y}{400} \right\rfloor$ will ensure that a leap day is not added for centesimal years, unless divisible by 400.
   e. Every whole month between March 1 and month m adds a minimum of 30 days. Since $30 \equiv 2$ Mod(7), each elapsed month shifts the day of the week by a minimum of 2 days. The expression + 2m adds an extra 2 days for each elapsed month. For each elapsed month having 31 days, an extra day needs to be added. The expression $+ \left\lfloor \frac{3m}{5} \right\rfloor$ would ensure that a whole day is added at $\frac{5}{3}$ month intervals, thus at months 4, 5, 7, 9, 10, 12, and 14. By changing the expression to $+ \left\lfloor \frac{3(m+1)}{5} \right\rfloor$, the extra day is added at months 3, 4, 6, 8, 9, 11, 13, and 14, which, with the exception of March, are the months that follow months with 31 days. The expression + 2 adjusts the formula so that March 1 of a given year corresponds to the correct day of the week

3.   Sample: Using the affine code C ≡ (9T + 3) Mod(26), the plaintext "JANE DOE" corresponds to the ciphertext 06 03 16 13 04 25 13 or "GDQNEZN."

4.   If m | 26, then m would not produce a complete system of residues modulo 26, which means that there would be fewer cipher letters than original letters. For example, if m = 2, then the only possible cipher letters are 0 + b, 2 + b, 4 + b, … , 24 + b, of which there are only 13.

Section 6.1.3

1.   a.   Because 5, 7 and 9 are relatively prime, Theorem 6.5 can be used. We have m = 315 and the congruence equations $63b_1 \equiv 1$ Mod(5), $45b_2 \equiv 1$ Mod(7), and $35b_3 \equiv 1$ Mod(9) have solutions. $b_1 = 2$, $b_2 = 5$, and $b_3 = 8$. Thus x ≡ 1(2)(63) + 5(5)(45) + 6(8)(35) Mod(315) ≡ 96 Mod(315). So all integer solutions are given by x = 96 + 315n, where n is an integer. 96 is the smallest positive integer solution.

      b.   By Theorem 6.3, if 2x ≡ 1 ≡ 6 Mod(5), then x ≡ 3 Mod(5), and if 3x ≡ 4 ≡ 18 Mod(7), then x ≡ 6 Mod(7). Because 4, 5, and 7 are relatively prime, Theorem 6.5 can be used. We have m = 140 and $35b_1 \equiv 1$ Mod(4), $28b_2 \equiv 1$ Mod(5), and $20b_3 \equiv 1$ Mod(7) have solutions $b_1 = 3$, $b_2 = 2$, and $b_3 = 6$. So x ≡ 3(3)(35) + 3(2)(28) + 6(6)(20) Mod(140) ≡ 83 Mod(140). All integer solutions are given by x = 83 + 140n, where n is an integer. 83 is the smallest positive integer solution.

2.   Finding the remainder when N is divided by 3, 5, and 7 is equivalent to solving the system of congruences N ≡ R_3 Mod(3), N ≡ R_5 Mod(5), and N ≡ R_7 Mod(7). Since 3, 5, and 7 are relatively prime, the Chinese Remainder Theorem can be used to find the solution. here m = 105 and the congruence equations are $35b_1 \equiv 1$ Mod(3), $21b_2 \equiv 1$ Mod(5), and $15b_3 \equiv 1$ Mod(7). So $b_1 = 2$, $b_2 = 1$, and $b_3 = 1$. The solution is then the smallest positive value of K such that K ≡ R_3(2)(35) + R_5(1)(25) + R_7(1)(15) Mod(105).

3.   Let B be the number of dollar bills. The three situations give rise to the system of congruences B ≡ 3 Mod(17), B ≡ 10 Mod(16), and B ≡ 0 Mod(15). 4. Since 17, 16, and 15 are relatively prime, the Chinese Remainder Theorem can be used to find the solution. Here m = 4080 and the congruence equations are $240b_1 \equiv 1$ Mod(17), $255b_2 \equiv 1$ Mod(16), and $272b_3 \equiv 1$ Mod(15). So $b_1 = 9$, $b_2 = 15$, and $b_3 = 8$. The solution is then the smallest positive value of B such that B ≡ 3(9)(240) + 10(15)(255) + 0(8)(272) Mod(4080) ≡ 3930 Mod(4080). Thus $3930 is the least amount of money in the sack.

4.   We can start from the bottom and work our way up. Let x be the number of coconuts that are left for the fifth sailor to find. We know that x is divisible by 4, since the fourth sailor took her portion after dividing by 5. We also know that x – 1 is divisible by 5. This leads to the system of congruences x ≡ 0 Mod(4) and x ≡ 1 Mod(5). Applying the Chinese Remainder Theorem, which can be done since 4 and 5 are relatively prime, x ≡ 16 Mod(20), or x = 16 + 20j, for some nonnegative integer j. The number of

coconuts left by the third sailor for the fourth sailor must then be $\frac{5}{4}x + 1 = 21 + 25j$. This number must also be divisible by 4, so $21 + 25j \equiv 0 \ \text{Mod}(4)$, or $j \equiv 3 \ \text{Mod}(4)$. Thus $j = 3 + 4k$, for some nonnegative integer k. The number of coconuts left by the second sailor for the third sailor must be $\frac{5}{4}(21 + 25(3 + 4k)) + 1 = 121 + 125k$. Again, this number is divisible by 4, so $121 + 125k \equiv 0 \ \text{Mod}(4)$, or $k \equiv 3 \ \text{Mod}(4)$. Thus $k = 3 + 4m$, for some nonnegative integer m. The number of coconuts left by the first sailor for the second sailor must be $\frac{5}{4}(121 + 125(3 + 4m)) + 1 = 621 + 625m$. Again, this number is divisible by 4, so $621 + 625m \equiv 0 \ \text{Mod}(4)$, or $m \equiv 3 \ \text{Mod}(4)$. Thus $m = 3 + 4n$, for some nonnegative integer n. So the number of coconuts left for the second sailor to find is of the form $621 + 625(3 + 4n) = 2496 + 2500n$. Thus the original number of coconuts is $\frac{5}{4}(2496 + 2500n) + 1$. The smallest number of coconuts, which occurs when n = 0, is then 3121.

5. The system of congruences is $p(x) \equiv 1 \ \text{Mod}(x + 1)$, $p(x) \equiv 0 \ \text{Mod}(x)$, and $p(x) \equiv 1 \ \text{Mod}(x - 1)$. This gives $m(x) = x(x + 1)(x - 1) = x^3 - x$ and $b_1 x(x - 1) \equiv 1 \ \text{Mod}(x + 1)$, $b_2(x + 1)(x - 1) \equiv 1 \ \text{Mod}(x)$, and $b_3(x + 1)x \equiv 1 \ \text{Mod}(x - 1)$. So $b_1 = \frac{1}{2}$, $b_2 = 1$, and $b_3 = \frac{1}{2}$. By the Chinese Remainder Theorem, $p(x) \equiv 1(\frac{1}{2})(x^2 - x) + 0(1)(x^2 - 1) + 1(\frac{1}{2})(x^2 + x) \ \text{Mod}(x^3 - x)$, or $p(x) \equiv x^2 \ \text{Mod}(x^3 - x)$. So $p(x) = x^2 + k(x^3 - x)$, where k is any integer.

6. a. Let $x = a - b$. Since $a \equiv b \ \text{Mod}(m_1)$ and $a \equiv b \ \text{Mod}(m_2)$, x is divisible by m_1 and m_2. Thus x is a common multiple of m_1 and m_2. All common multiples of m_1 and m_2 are divisible by the $\text{lcm}(m_1, m_2)$. Therefore x is divisible by $\text{lcm}(m_1, m_2)$ and $a \equiv b \ \text{Mod}(\text{lcm}(m_1, m_2))$.

   b. By part **a**, the statement is true for n = 2. Now assume the statement is true for $m_1, m_2, \ldots, m_k$, that is, $a \equiv b \ \text{Mod}(m_1)$, $a \equiv b \ \text{Mod}(m_2)$, ..., $a \equiv b \ \text{Mod}(m_k)$ implies $a \equiv b \ \text{Mod}(\text{lcm}(m_1, m_2, \ldots, m_k))$. If $a \equiv b \ \text{Mod}(m_{k+1})$, then, by part **a**, $a \equiv b \ \text{Mod}(\text{lcm}(m_{k+1}, \text{lcm}(m_1, m_2, \ldots, m_k)))$. But $\text{lcm}(m_{k+1}, \text{lcm}(m_1, m_2, \ldots, m_k)) = \text{lcm}(m_1, m_2, \ldots, m_k, m_{k+1})$. So $a \equiv b \ \text{Mod}(\text{lcm}(m_1, m_2, \ldots, m_k, m_{k+1}))$. By the principle of mathematical induction, then, the statement is true for all natural numbers n > 1.

   c. By Theorem 6.2, if $a_1 \equiv b_1 \ \text{Mod}(m)$ and $a_2 \equiv b_2 \ \text{Mod}(m)$, then $a_1 + a_2 \equiv b_1 + b_2 \ \text{Mod}(m)$. Now assume $a_1 \equiv b_1 \ \text{Mod}(m)$, $a_2 \equiv b_2 \ \text{Mod}(m)$, ..., $a_k \equiv b_k \ \text{Mod}(m)$ implies $a_1 + a_2 + \ldots + a_k \equiv b_1 + b_2 + \ldots + b_k \ \text{Mod}(m)$. If $a_{k+1} \equiv b_{k+1} \ \text{Mod}(m)$, then, by Theorem 6.2, $(a_1 + a_2 + \ldots + a_k) + a_{k+1} \equiv (b_1 + b_2 + \ldots + b_k) + b_{k+1} \ \text{Mod}(m)$. By the principle of mathematical induction, then, the statement is true for all natural numbers n > 1.

Section 6.2.1

1. The operations + and × are commutative and associative:

$a* + b* = (a + b)* = (b + a)* = b* + a*$

$(a* + b*) + c* = (a + b)* + c* = ((a + b) + c)* = (a + (b + c))* = a* + (b + c)*$
$= a* + (b* + c*)$

$a* \times b* = (a \times b)* = (b \times a)* = b* \times a*$

$(a* \times b*) \times c* = (a \times b)* \times c* = ((a \times b) \times c)* = (a \times (b \times c))* = a* \times (b \times c)*$

$= a* \times (b* \times c*)$

Distributive property: $a* \times (b* + c*) = a* \times (b + c)* = (a \times (b + c))*$

$= (a \times b + a \times c)* = (a \times b)* + (a \times c)* = a* \times b* + a* \times c*$

$0*$ is the additive identity: $a* + 0* = (a + 0)* = a*$

$1*$ is the multiplicative identity: $a* \times 1* = (a \times 1)* = a*$

Additive inverse: If $a* \in \mathbf{Z_p}$, then $-(a*) = (-a)*$ since $a* + (-a)* = (a + -a)* = 0*$

Multiplicative inverse: Suppose $a* \in \mathbf{Z_p}$ and $a* \neq 0*$. Since p is prime, $a*$ and p are relatively prime and therefore, by Theorem 6.1, the set $S_a = \{0, a, 2a, 3a, \ldots, (p-1)a\}$ is a complete system of residues modulo p. Thus for some $b \in S_a$, $(b \times a)* = 1*$ then $(a*)^{-1} = (-a)*$

2.   a. $0 = 0 + 0\sqrt{n}$ and $1 = 1 + 0\sqrt{n}$ for any positive integer n.

      b.   Let $x = a + b\sqrt{n}$ and $y = c + d\sqrt{n}$ be elements of $\mathbf{Q}\sqrt{n}$, for some integer n. Then $x + y = a + b\sqrt{n} + c + d\sqrt{n} = (a + c) + (b + d)\sqrt{n}$. Since $\mathbf{Q}$ is closed under addition, $a + c$ and $b + d$ are both rational. Thus $x + y \in \mathbf{Q}\sqrt{n}$.

$$xy = (a + b\sqrt{n})(c + d\sqrt{n})$$
$$= ac + bc\sqrt{n} + ad\sqrt{n} + bdn$$
$$= (ac + bdn) + (bc + ad)\sqrt{n}$$

        Since $\mathbf{Q}$ is closed under multiplication, $ac + bdn$ and $bc + ad$ are both rational. Thus $xy \in \mathbf{Q}\sqrt{n}$.

      c. $\mathbf{Q}\sqrt{n} \subset \mathbf{R}$. By part a, 0 and 1, the additive and multiplicative identities, exist in $\mathbf{Q}\sqrt{n}$. By part b, $\mathbf{Q}\sqrt{n}$ is closed under addition and multiplication. The commutative, associative, and distributive properties of + and • all carry over from the field $\langle \mathbf{R}, +, \bullet \rangle$. Suppose $x = a + b\sqrt{n} \in \mathbf{Q}\sqrt{n}$. Then $-x = -a + -b\sqrt{n} \in \mathbf{Q}\sqrt{n}$, since the opposite of a rational number is rational. Also $x^{-1} = \frac{a}{a^2 - nb^2} + \frac{-b\sqrt{n}}{a^2 - nb^2}$. Because $a, b, n \in \mathbf{Q}$, $\frac{a}{a^2 - nb^2}$ and $\frac{-b}{a^2 - nb^2}$ are rational. Because n is an integer that is not a perfect square and $a, b \in \mathbf{Q}$, $a^2 \neq nb^2$. So $a^2 - nb^2 \neq 0$. Thus for all $x \in \mathbf{Q}\sqrt{n}$, $x^{-1} \in \mathbf{Q}\sqrt{n}$. $\mathbf{Q}\sqrt{n}$ therefore satisfies all the conditions of a field

      d.   Assume $\sqrt{3} \in \mathbf{Q}\sqrt{2}$. Then for some $a, b \in \mathbf{Q}$, $\sqrt{3} = a + b\sqrt{2}$. This implies $3 = (a + b\sqrt{2})^2 = a^2 + 2ab\sqrt{2} + 2b^2$. Thus $\sqrt{2} = \frac{3 - a^2 - 2b^2}{2ab}$. The right-hand side of this equation is rational, but the left-hand side is not, which is a contradiction. So $\sqrt{3} \notin \mathbf{Q}\sqrt{2}$.

3.   Commutativity of addition:

$$(r_1 + r_2)(x) = \frac{p_1(x)q_2(x) + p_2(x)q_1(x)}{q_1(x)q_2(x)} = \frac{p_2(x)q_1(x) + p_1(x)q_2(x)}{q_2(x)q_1(x)} = (r_2 + r_1)(x)$$

Associativity of addition:

$$(r_3 + (r_1 + r_2))(x) = \frac{p_3 q_1(x)q_2(x) + (p_1(x)q_2(x) + p_2(x)q_1(x))q_3(x)}{q_3(x)q_1(x)q_2(x)}$$
$$= \frac{p_3 q_1(x)q_2(x) + p_1(x)q_2(x)q_3(x) + p_2(x)q_1(x)q_3(x)}{q_3(x)q_1(x)q_2(x)}$$

$$= \frac{(p_3 q_1(x) + p_1(x)q_3(x))q_2(x) + p_2(x)q_1(x)q_3(x)}{q_3(x)q_1(x)q_2(x)}$$

$$= ((r_3 + r_1) + r_2)(x)$$

Commutativity of multiplication:

$$(r_1 \bullet r_2)(x) = \frac{p_1(x)p_2(x)}{q_1(x)q_2(x)} = \frac{p_2(x)p_1(x)}{q_2(x)q_1(x)} = (r_2 \times r_1)(x)$$

Associativity of multiplication:

$$(r_3 \bullet (r_1 \bullet r_2))(x) = \frac{p_3(x)(p_1(x)p_2(x))}{q_3(x)(q_1(x)q_2(x))} = \frac{(p_3(x)p_1(x))p_2(x)}{(q_3(x)q_1(x))q_2(x)} = ((r_3 \bullet r_1) \bullet r_2)(x)$$

Distributivity of multiplication over addition:

$$(r_3 \bullet (r_1 + r_2))(x) = \frac{p_3(x)(p_1(x)q_2(x) + p_2(x)q_1(x))}{q_3(x)(q_1(x)q_2(x))}$$

$$= \frac{p_3(x)p_1(x)q_2(x) + p_3(x)p_2(x)q_1(x)}{q_3(x)q_1(x)q_2(x)}$$

$$= \frac{p_3(x)p_1(x)q_2(x)q_3(x) + p_3(x)p_2(x)q_1(x)q_3(x)}{q_3(x)q_1(x)q_3(x)q_2(x)}$$

$$= ((r_3 \bullet r_1) + (r_3 \bullet r_2))(x)$$

For all x, let $I_A(x) = 0$ and $I_M(x) = 1$. Then $(r + I_A)(x) = r(x)$ and $(r \times I_M)(x) = r(x)$.

If $r(x) = \frac{p(x)}{q(x)}$, let $-r(x) = \frac{-p(x)}{q(x)}$. Then $(r + -r)(x) = \frac{p(x)q(x) + -p(x)q(x)}{q(x)q(x)} = I_A(x)$.

If $r(x) = \frac{p(x)}{q(x)}$, where $p(x) \neq 0$, let $r^{-1}(x) = \frac{q(x)}{p(x)}$. Then $(r \bullet r^{-1})(x) = \frac{p(x)}{q(x)} \frac{q(x)}{p(x)} = I_A(x)$.

4.   a.   Let $-x \in F$ be negative. Then $-x < 0 \Rightarrow x + (-x) < x + 0 \Rightarrow 0 < x \Rightarrow x$ is positive.

     b.   Let $x, y \in F$ be positive. Then, by O-3 and O-2, $0 < y = 0 + y < x + y$. Also, by O-4 and O-2, $0 < y \Rightarrow 0 \bullet y < x \bullet y$.

     c.   If x is positive, then x^2 is positive from part **b**.
If x is negative, then -x is positive from part **a**, and so $0 < (-x)^2 = x^2$ by algebraic properties of a field.

     d.   Because $1 \neq 0$, and $1^2 = 1$, it follows from part **c** that $0 < 1$.

5.   Any ordered field **F** must contain an isomorphic (for <) copy N* of the set **N** of natural numbers. For each positive integer n, define n* recursively as follows: $1^* = 1$, the multiplicative identity of **F**. Given that n* has been defined, define $(n + 1)^* = n^* + 1^*$. Then, for each positive integer k and n, $n^* < (n + k)^*$ by induction on k. Because **N** is infinite, so is N*.

6.   Parts (b) and (c) of Theorem 6.6 would be violated since $(1 + 2i)(1 + 2i) = -3 + 4i$, i.e., a positive times a positive would not be positive. Part (d) would be violated since the definition would imply that $1 = 1 + 0i$, the multiplicative identity, is not positive.

7.   Basis step: For $0 < x$, $1x = x$. So S(n) is true for n = 1.
Inductive step: Assume true for k. Then for $0 < x$, $0 < kx$. By O-3, $0 + x < kx + x$. By A-3 and D, $x < (k + 1)x$. Since $0 < x$ and $x < (k + 1)x$, by O-2, $0 < (k + 1)x$. So nx is positive for all natural numbers n.

8. Suppose $0 < x$ and $x^{-1} < 0$. By O-4, $x^{-1} \bullet x < 0 \bullet x$. So $1 < 0$. This contradicts Theorem 6.6(d).

9. Let $x, y < 0$. By Property D, $x \bullet 0 = x(y + -y) = xy + x(-y) = 0$. So $xy = -(x(-y))$. By Theorem 6.6(a), if $y < 0$, then $0 < -y$. By Theorem 6.9(a), $x(-y) < 0$. By Theorem 6.6(a), $0 < -(x(-y))$. Thus the product of two negatives is positive.

Section 6.2.2

1. P1: $e = 1$ since $1 = s(0) \in$ N*, but $0 \notin$ N*. P2: Because F is a field and N* is a subset of F, for any elements $a, b \in$ N*, $a + 1 = b + 1 \Rightarrow a = b$. P3: The definition of M is precisely the definition of N*, so M = N*.

2. $n \bullet \frac{a}{b} > \frac{c}{d} \Leftrightarrow n > \frac{bc}{ad}$

3. $\langle \mathbf{Q}\sqrt{n}, +, \bullet, < \rangle$ is a subfield of $\langle \mathbf{R}, +, \bullet, < \rangle$ and any subfield of $\langle \mathbf{R}, +, \bullet, < \rangle$ will contain N*. Thus for any $x \in \mathbf{Q}\sqrt{n}$ there is a positive integer $k \in \mathbf{Q}\sqrt{n}$ such that $x < k$. To see that $\langle \mathbf{Q}\sqrt{n}, +, \bullet, < \rangle$ is not complete, consider the subset $\{x \in \mathbf{Q}\sqrt{n} : x > \pi\}$. This subset is bounded below by π, but since $\pi \notin \{x \in \mathbf{Q}\sqrt{n} : x > \pi\}$, the subset has no greatest lower bound.

4. Suppose $\{a_k\} = \{1, 1.4, 1.41, 1.414, ...\}$ is the increasing sequence of decimal approximations to the square root of 2. Then $\{[a_k, 2]\}$ is a sequence of nested intervals in $\mathbf{Q}$ whose intersection is $\{r \in \mathbf{Q}: \sqrt{2} < r \le 2\}$, which is not a closed interval in $\mathbf{Q}$.

5. The solution is similar to that of Problem 3 of Section 6.2.1. Keeping in mind that the set of rational numbers, $\mathbf{Q}$, is itself a field under the operations of addition and multiplication, the set of polynomials with rational number coefficients will be closed under addition and multiplication.

6. Let $f(\frac{a}{b}) = \frac{h(a)}{h(b)}$. This mapping is an isomorphism. For example, we can show that it is one-to-one. Suppose $f(\frac{a}{b}) = f(\frac{c}{d})$, where $a, b, c, d \in \mathbf{Q}$. Then $\frac{h(a)}{h(b)} = \frac{h(c)}{h(d)}$, which, since F is a field, implies $h(a)h(d) = h(b)h(c)$. Since h is itself an isomorphism, $h^{-1}(h(a)h(d)) = h^{-1}(h(b)h(c))$ and so $ad = bc$. Thus $\frac{a}{b} = \frac{c}{d}$. In a similar manner, the other properties of the isomorphism can be shown to hold.

7. a. Let $1a = a$ and $na = (n-1)a + a$, for $n > 1$. Let $a^1 = a$ and $a^n = a^{n-1} \bullet a$, for $n > 1$. Assume $a > 0$. Then $1a = a > 0$. Assume $ka > 0$. Then $(k + 1)a = ka + a$, by the recursive definition, and $ka + a > 0$, by the inductive hypothesis and Theorem 6.6b. By the principle of mathematical induction, $na > 0$ for all natural numbers n. Similarly, $a^1 = a > 0$. Assume $a^k > 0$. Then $a^{k+1} = a^k \bullet a$, by the recursive definition, and $a^k \bullet a > 0$, by the inductive hypothesis and Theorem 6.6b. By the principle of mathematical induction, $a^n > 0$ for all natural numbers n.

   b. $\frac{a}{b} = a \bullet \frac{1}{b}$. Since b is negative, $\frac{1}{b}$ must also be negative. Otherwise, if $\frac{1}{b}$ were positive, then, by Theorem 6.9(a), $b \bullet \frac{1}{b}$ would be negative. But $b \bullet \frac{1}{b} = 1$, which, by Theorem 6.6(d) is positive. So $\frac{1}{b}$ is negative. Therefore, since a and $\frac{1}{b}$ are both negative, by Theorem 6.9(b), $\frac{a}{b}$ is positive.

8. Since the polynomial q_c of degree 0 is just the real number c, the rational expression $r_c = \dfrac{q_c(x)}{q_1(x)} = c$.

    Thus the function g: $\mathbf{R} \to \mathbf{K(x)}$ is just the identity mapping. The identity mapping is 1-1 and onto, and so g is an isomorphism.

Section 6.2.3

1. a. Using the quadratic formula, $x = \dfrac{-i \pm \sqrt{(-i)^2 - 4(1+i)(1-i)}}{2(1+i)}$, so $x = \dfrac{1+i}{2}$ or

        $x = -1 - i$. Thus $p(x) = (x - \dfrac{1+i}{2})(x - (-1-i))$.

    b. $p(x) = 0 \Rightarrow x^8 = 1$. Using De Moivre's Theorem, $x = \cos\dfrac{2\pi k}{8} + i\sin\dfrac{2\pi k}{8}$, for $k = 0,\ldots, 7$. Thus,

        the solution set is $\{1, \dfrac{\sqrt{2}}{2} + \dfrac{\sqrt{2}}{2}i, i, -\dfrac{\sqrt{2}}{2} + \dfrac{\sqrt{2}}{2}i, -1, \dfrac{\sqrt{2}}{2} - \dfrac{\sqrt{2}}{2}i, -i, -\dfrac{\sqrt{2}}{2} - \dfrac{\sqrt{2}}{2}i\}$ and

        $p(x) = (x - 1)(x - -1)(x - i)(x - -i)(x - (\dfrac{\sqrt{2}}{2} + \dfrac{\sqrt{2}}{2}i))(x - (-\dfrac{\sqrt{2}}{2} + \dfrac{\sqrt{2}}{2}i))$

        $\bullet \; (x - (\dfrac{\sqrt{2}}{2} - \dfrac{\sqrt{2}}{2}i))(x - (-\dfrac{\sqrt{2}}{2} - \dfrac{\sqrt{2}}{2}i))$

    c. $p(x) = 0 \Rightarrow x^3 = -1$. Using De Moivre's Theorem, $x = \cos\dfrac{\pi + 2\pi k}{3} + i\sin\dfrac{\pi + 2\pi k}{3}$, for $k = 0, 1, 2$.

        Thus the solution set is $\{-1, \dfrac{1 \pm \sqrt{3}i}{2}\}$ and $p(x) = (x - -1)(x - \dfrac{1 + \sqrt{3}i}{2})(x - \dfrac{1 - \sqrt{3}i}{2})$.

2. The multiplicative identity e would be $1 + i$, since $(x + iy)(1 + i) = x + iy$. However, any number of the form x or iy would then not have an inverse.

3. a. The proof uses the following facts: For any real number x, $\bar{x} = x$. For any complex number x, $(\bar{x})^n = \overline{(x^n)}$. For any complex numbers x and y, $\bar{x}\,\bar{y} = \overline{(xy)}$ and $\bar{x} + \bar{y} = \overline{(x + y)}$. Let
        $p(x) = a_n x^n + a_{n-1}x^{n-1} + \ldots + a_1 x + a_0$ and let $p(c) = 0$. Then
        $p(\bar{c}) = a_n(\bar{c})^n + a_{n-1}(\bar{c})^{n-1} + \ldots + a_1(\bar{c}) + a_0$
        $\qquad = \overline{a_n}\,(\bar{c})^n + \overline{a_{n-1}}(\bar{c})^{n-1} + \ldots + \overline{a_1}(\bar{c}) + \overline{a_0}$
        $\qquad = \overline{a_n c^n} + \overline{a_{n-1}c^{n-1}} + \ldots + \overline{a_1 c} + \overline{a_0}$
        $\qquad = \overline{(a_n c^n + a_{n-1}c^{n-1} + \ldots + a_1 c + a_0)}$
        $\qquad = \bar{0} = 0$

    b. Since $p(x)$ has real coefficients, then by part **a**, if c is a solution of $p(x)$ so is $\bar{c}$. Thus, by Theorem 6.15, $(x - c)$ and $(x - \bar{c})$ are factors of $p(x)$. If all of the solutions were nonreal, then $(x - c)$ and $(x - \bar{c})$ would be distinct and there would be an even number of linear factors. This   would imply the degree of $p(x)$ is even.

    c. Let $p(x) = a_n x^n + a_{n-2}x^{n-2} + \ldots + a_0$, where n is even and all $a_j > 0$. Then, for any real number c, $p(c) = a_n c^n + a_{n-2}c^{n-2} + \ldots + a_0$ and since each $a_j c^j > 0$, $p(c) > 0$

4. $p(x) = a(x^3 + \dfrac{b}{a}x^2 + \dfrac{c}{a}x + \dfrac{d}{a}) = a(x - r_1)(x - r_2)(x - r_3)$
    $= a(x^3 - (r_1 + r_2 + r_3)x^2 + (r_1 r_2 + r_1 r_3 + r_2 r_3)x - r_1 r_2 r_3)$

$\frac{b}{a} = -(r_1 + r_2 + r_3)$, $\frac{c}{a} = (r_1r_2 + r_1r_3 + r_2r_3)$, and $\frac{d}{a} = - r_1r_2r_3$

If r_1, r_2, r_3, and r_4 are roots of the fourth degree polynomial $p(x) = ax^4 + bx^3 + cx^2 + dx + e$, then

$\frac{b}{a} = -(r_1 + r_2 + r_3 + r_4)$, $\frac{c}{a} = (r_1r_2 + r_1r_3 + r_2r_3 + r_1r_4 + r_2r_4 + r_3r_4)$,

$\frac{d}{a} = -(r_1r_2r_3 + r_1r_2r_4 + r_1r_3r_4 + r_2r_3r_4)$, and $\frac{e}{a} = r_1r_2r_3r_4$.

5. Since $1 + i$ is a zero of $p(x)$, then so is $1 - i$. Thus $p(x) = (x - (1 + i))(x - (1 - i)) \bullet q(x)$
    $= (x^2 - 2x + 2) \bullet q(x)$. Dividing the polynomials gives $q(x) = x^2 - 2x - 1$. Using the quadratic formula
    to find the zeros of $q(x)$ gives $x = 1 \pm \sqrt{2}$. Thus $p(x)$ has the additional zeros $1 \pm \sqrt{2}$ and the complete
    factorization
    $p(x) = (x - (1 + i))(x - (1 - i))(x - (1 + \sqrt{2}))(x - (1 - \sqrt{2}))$.

6. Let r and s be zeros of quadratic polynomials with rational coefficients. Then $r = a + b\sqrt{c}$ and
    $s = d + e\sqrt{f}$, where a, b, c, d, e, and f are all rational, and r + s is of the form $A + B\sqrt{C} + D\sqrt{E}$, where
    again A, B, C, D, and E are all rational. We need to show that this is the zero of some polynomial with
    rational coefficients, or equivalently, that $(x - (A + B\sqrt{C} + D\sqrt{E}))$ is a factor of some polynomial
    with rational coefficients. We can show this by building a polynomial with
    $(x - (A + B\sqrt{C} + D\sqrt{E}))$ as a factor:
    $(x - (A + B\sqrt{C} + D\sqrt{E}))(x - (A - B\sqrt{C} - D\sqrt{E}))$
    $= x^2 - 2Ax + A^2 - (B\sqrt{C} + D\sqrt{E})^2 = x^2 - 2Ax + A^2 - B^2C - D^2E - BD\sqrt{CE}$.
    If we let $A^2 - B^2C - D^2E = F$, then we have $x^2 - 2Ax + F - BD\sqrt{CE}$. Then
    $(x^2 - 2Ax + F - BD\sqrt{CE})(x^2 - 2Ax + F + BD\sqrt{CE})$
    $= x^4 - 4Ax^3 + (4A + 2F)x^2 - 4AFx + F^2 - B^2D^2CE$, a fourth degree polynomial with rational
    coefficients and $(x - (A + B\sqrt{C} + D\sqrt{E}))$ as a factor.

CHAPTER 7 – Congruence

Section 7.1.1

1. a. Euclid uses the term "line" to denote any one-dimensional curve or a "straight line," depending on the context, Euclid's "straight line" is a modern "line". Euclid's "finite straight line" is today's "line segment."

   b. Yes. Euclid's use of the phrase "a plane figure contained by one line" suggests that a circle includes its interior.

   c. The "extremities" of a line would be its endpoints; the "extremities" of a surface would be its boundary. Euclid's Definition 13 also suggests that the term "extremity" corresponds to the more modern term "boundary."

   d. No. Euclid's definition restricts an isosceles triangle to a triangle that has "two of its sides *alone* equal."

   e. Euclid's quadrilateral definitions are not inclusive: a square is neither an oblong (rectangle) nor a rhombus. Squares, rectangles and rhombuses are not rhomboids (parallelograms). Trapezia include all quadrilaterals other than these, so include quadrilaterals with no parallel sides.

2.

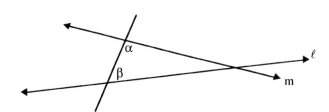

   Suppose coplanar lines ℓ and m are cut by a transversal. If the sum of the measures of the interior angles α and β on one side of the transversal is less than 180°, then the lines will intersect on that side of the transversal.

3. 1. Transitive Property of Equality: If a = b and b = c, then a = c.
   2. Addition Property of Equality: If a = b, then a + c = b + c.
   3. Addition Property of Equality: If a = b, then a + -c = b + -c.
      or Subtraction Property of Equality; If a = b, then a – c = b – c.

4. a. Construction Propositions: 1-3, 7, 9-12, 22-23, 31, 45-46
   b. Triangle Congruence Propositions: 4 (SAS), 8 (SSS), 26 (ASA, AAS)
   c. Pythagorean Theorem: Proposition 47
   d. Sum of the angle measures of a triangle is 180°: Proposition 32.
   e. In Propositions 35-45, Euclid uses the word "equal" to mean "equal in area."

5. Answers will vary.

6. Sample: Definition 4 and, perhaps, Definition 2 ensure that a line is not circular.

7. Answers will vary.

8.   Answers will vary.

Section 7.1.2

1.   A nonoverlapping covering using m 1×2 dominoes must have m white and m black squares. Because $n^2 - 2 = 2m$, n must be even. However, for any n, odd or even, two contiguous edges of an $n \times n$ checkerboard always have $2n - 1$ squares, an odd number, so the two opposite corners will always be the same color. So, if n is even, a checkerboard with opposite corners removed will have $\frac{n^2}{2}$ of one color, but only $\frac{n^2}{2} - 2$ of the other color. Therefore there is no way to cover by 1×2 dominoes an $n \times n$ checkerboard with opposite corners removed.

2.   a.   Answers will vary.
        b.   Answers will vary.

3.   (1) Proposition 9; (2) Propositions 10 and 11, Postulate 5; (3) Proposition 12; (4) Proposition 12; (5) Postulate 4; (6) Common Notion 4; (7) Proposition 26; (8) Proposition 26; (9) Proposition 16; (10) Proposition 4; (11) Common Notion 3

4.   (1) and (2) Proposition 8; (3) and (4) Proposition 4; (5) Proposition 5.

5.   The fallacy lies in the assumption that $\overline{CD}$ will intersect the two circles at two different points. In fact, $\overline{CD}$ will intersect both circles at point A. Thus no triangle BEF will be formed.

6.   The statement that $\overline{AD} \cong \overline{BC}$ is not properly justified, since the equality of opposite sides is not directly implied by the definition of a parallelogram. We can show that it is true, however, using the following argument: It has already been shown that $\angle ADB \cong \angle DBC$, and, by similar reasoning, $\angle ABD \cong \angle CDB$. Since $\overline{BD} \cong \overline{BD}$, by ASA, $\triangle DAB \cong \triangle BCD$. Thus $\overline{AD} \cong \overline{BC}$, since corresponding parts of congruent triangles are congruent.

7.   Answers will vary.

Section 7.1.3

1.   Sample (i):
        a.   Definition 1: Human life begins at conception. Definition 2: Human life begins when the fetus is viable outside the mother.
        b.   Commonly understood terms: conception, fetus, mother, outside. Words purposely left undefined: viable.
        c.   Definition 1 could be used to argue that an abortion at any stage of pregnancy should be considered an illegal act of murder, whereas Definition 2 could be used to argue that an early term abortion should be considered a legal and ethical act.

2.   a.   Meaning part: If a polygon is a dodecagon, then it has 12 sides. Sufficient condition part: If a polygon has 12 sides, then it is a dodecagon.

c.

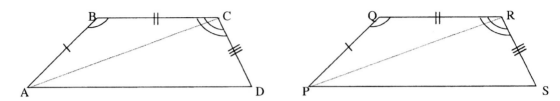

Proof: In quadrilaterals ABCD and PQRS, let $\overline{AB} \cong \overline{PQ}$, $\overline{BC} \cong \overline{QR}$, $\overline{CD} \cong \overline{RS}$, $\angle ABC \cong \angle PQR$, and $\angle BCD \cong \angle QRS$. Then, by the SAS Triangle Congruence Theorem, $\triangle ABC \cong \triangle PQR$, and $\overline{AC} \cong \overline{PR}$, $\angle BCA \cong \angle QRP$, and $\angle BAC \cong \angle QPR$. Since $\angle BCD \cong \angle QRS$ and $\angle BCA \cong \angle QRP$, $\angle ACD \cong \angle PRS$. Again, by SAS, $\triangle ACD \cong \triangle PRS$, and $\overline{AD} \cong \overline{PS}$, $\angle CDA \cong \angle RSP$, and $\angle DAC \cong \angle SPR$. Since $\angle DAC \cong \angle SPR$ and $\angle BAC \cong \angle QPR$, $\angle DAB \cong \angle SPQ$. So, by the given definition, the quadrilaterals are congruent.

3.   a. $d(T(x_2, y_2), T(x_1, y_1)) = \sqrt{((x_2 + 5) - (x_1 + 5))^2 + (y_2 - y_1)^2}$
$= \sqrt{(x_2 - x_1)^2 + (y_2 - y_1)^2} = d((x_2, y_2), (x_1, y_1))$

       b. $T^{-1} = (x - 5, y)$

4.   a.   Distance-preserving:
$d(T(x_2, y_2), T(x_1, y_1)) = \sqrt{((x_2 + 4) - (x_1 + 4))^2 + ((y_2 - 10) - (y_1 - 10))^2}$
$= \sqrt{(x_2 - x_1)^2 + (y_2 - y_1)^2} = d((x_2, y_2), (x_1, y_1))$

       b.   Not distance-preserving: $d(T(1, 0), T(0, 0)) = \sqrt{(4 - 0)^2 + (0 - 0)^2} = 4 \neq d((1, 0), (0, 0)) = 1$

       c.   Not distance-preserving: $d(T(1, 0), T(0, 0)) = \sqrt{(5 - 4)^2 + (-9 - -10)^2} = \sqrt{2} \neq d((1, 0), (0, 0)) = 1$

5.   Let S and T be two isometries and P and Q be any two points of the plane. If $P' = S(P)$ and $Q' = S(Q)$, then $P'Q' = PQ$, since S preserves distance. If $P'' = T(P')$ and $Q'' = T(Q')$, then $P''Q'' = P'Q' = PQ$, since T preserves distance. Thus the composite of S and T is distance-preserving and an isometry.

6.   a.   Suppose C is a point on $\overleftrightarrow{AB}$. Without loss of generality, assume C is between A and B. Let T be an isometry such that $T(A) = A'$, $T(B) = B'$, and $T(C) = C'$. If C is between A and B, then $AC + CB = AB$. Since T is distance-preserving, $AC = A'C'$, $CB = C'B'$, and $AB = A'B'$. Thus $A'C' + C'B' = A'B'$ and C' is between A' and B'. By the triangle inequality, the equality $A'C' + C'B' = A'B'$ can only hold if C' is collinear with A' and B'. So collinear points map to collinear points. Suppose D' is a point on line $\overleftrightarrow{A'B'}$. If $D' = A'$, then $D = A$, so D is on $\overleftrightarrow{AB}$. Similarly, if $D' = B'$, then $D = B$, so D is on $\overleftrightarrow{AB}$. If D' is between A' and B', then $A'D' + D'B' = A'B'$, and since isometries preserve distance, $A'D' = AD$, $D'B' = DB$, and $A'B' = AB$. So $AD + DB = AB$. Thus D is between A and B, so D is on line $\overleftrightarrow{AB}$. In a similar fashion, we can show that if A' is between D' and B', or if B' is between D' and A', then D has to be on line $\overleftrightarrow{AB}$. Thus, in all possible locations for D' on $\overleftrightarrow{A'B'}$, D is on $\overleftrightarrow{AB}$. This shows that the image of $\overleftrightarrow{AB}$ is the entire line $\overleftrightarrow{A'B'}$.

       b.   Let T be an isometry such that $T(A) = A'$ and $T(B) = B'$. Consider points on $\overrightarrow{AB}$. If C is a point

11. a.

Partition of
natural numbers

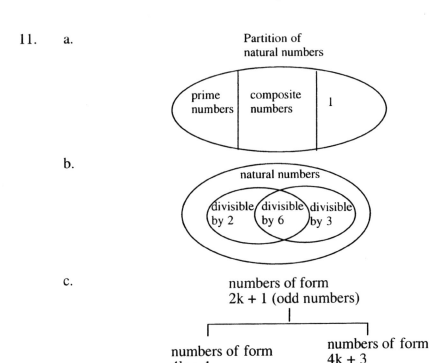

b.

c.

numbers of form
2k + 1 (odd numbers)

numbers of form
4k + 1

numbers of form
4k + 3

12. Sample: polygons-quadrilaterals-parallelograms-rectangles-squares; A quadrilateral is a square with exactly 4 sides. A parallelogram is a quadrilateral with 2 pairs of parallel sides. A rectangle is a parallelogram with a right angle. A square is a rectangle with 2 adjacent congruent sides.

13. A parallelogram either has a single right angle or it doesn't. If it has a single right angle, then it is a rectangle. If it doesn't and its adjacent sides are of equal length, then it is a rhombus. If it doesn't have a right angle and its adjacent sides are of unequal length, then it is a rhomboid. Thus rectangles, rhombi, and rhomboids form a partition of the set of parallelograms.

14. a. Euclid forms two different partitions of the set of trilateral figures. In one the set is partitioned into equilateral, isosceles, and scalene triangles. In the other, it is partitioned into right-angled, obtuse-angled, and acute-angled triangles. Euclid's definitions also contains the following nest: figures-rectilineal figures-quadrilateral figures-trapezia.
     b. Euclid seems to prefer partitions.

15. Let the L_n be the set of least residues modulo n, i.e., $L_n = \{0, 1, 2, 3, ..., n-1\}$. By the Division Algorithm, any integer k is congruent modulo n to exactly one of the elements of L_n. Thus the congruence sets modulo n partition the integers into n sets.

16.

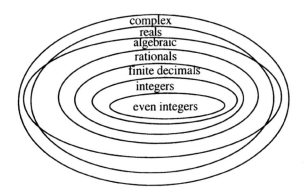

17.   Definition 1: An integer g is the gcd(a, b) if and only if g is the largest integer that is a divisor of a and b.
Definition 2: An integer g is the gcd(a, b) if and only if (i) g divides both a and b and (ii) for any integer d that divides a and b, then d divides g.

Let g be the gcd(a, b) according to Definition 1. Let w = as + bt be the least positive linear combination of a and b. We can show that w is a divisor of a and b. If w is not a divisor of a, then, by the Division Algorithm, a = wq + r, where 0 < r < w. Thus 0 < r = a – wq = a – (as + bt)q = a(1 – sq) + b(-tq) < w, which contradicts the assumption that w is the least positive linear combination of a and b. Similarly, we can show that w is a divisor of b. So, by Definition 1, w ≤ g. But, since g divides a and b, g divides w and g ≤ w. Thus g = w. Therefore, since g = as + bt, any common divisor of a and b will also divide g.

Let g be the gcd(a, b) according to Definition 2 and let d be some integer that also divides both a and b. By Definition 2, d must divide g, so g ≥ d. Thus g is the greatest integer that divides a and b.

Section 7.1.4

1.   a.   By the definition of congruent circles, if two circles are congruent, then their radii are congruent. By the definition of congruent segments, the circles' radii have the same length. Since the area of a circle is given by $A = \pi r^2$, and is dependent only on the length of a circle's radius, the two circles will have the same area.

     b.   If two circles have the same area, then, since $r = \sqrt{\frac{A}{\pi}}$, they will have radii of the same length.

          Thus, by the definition of congruent segment, the circles' radii will be congruent. By the definition of congruent circles, then, the circles will be congruent.

2.   Sample Definition: Two quadrilaterals are congruent if and only if there is a correspondence between their vertices such that the four pairs of corresponding sides have the same length and the four corresponding angles have the same measure.

     a.   True. Since they are both rectangles, all angles are 90° and thus all corresponding angles have the same measure. Since opposite sides are congruent in a rectangle, all four corresponding sides of the two rectangles will have the same length.

     b.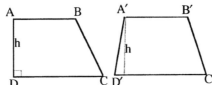

          False. Consider trapezoid ABCD with m∠ADC = 90°. We can construct trapezoid A′B′C′D′, with the same height h, AB = A′B′, DC = D′C′, but with no right angle. By the definition, the quadrilaterals are not congruent.

c.

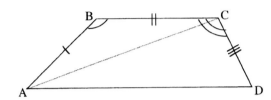 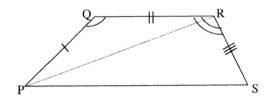

Proof: In quadrilaterals ABCD and PQRS, let $\overline{AB} \cong \overline{PQ}$, $\overline{BC} \cong \overline{QR}$, $\overline{CD} \cong \overline{RS}$, $\angle ABC \cong \angle PQR$, and $\angle BCD \cong \angle QRS$. Then, by the SAS Triangle Congruence Theorem, $\triangle ABC \cong \triangle PQR$, and $\overline{AC} \cong \overline{PR}$, $\angle BCA \cong \angle QRP$, and $\angle BAC \cong \angle QPR$. Since $\angle BCD \cong \angle QRS$ and $\angle BCA \cong \angle QRP$, $\angle ACD \cong \angle PRS$. Again, by SAS, $\triangle ACD \cong \triangle PRS$, and $\overline{AD} \cong \overline{PS}$, $\angle CDA \cong \angle RSP$, and $\angle DAC \cong \angle SPR$. Since $\angle DAC \cong \angle SPR$ and $\angle BAC \cong \angle QPR$, $\angle DAB \cong \angle SPQ$. So, by the given definition, the quadrilaterals are congruent.

3.   a. $d(T(x_2, y_2), T(x_1, y_1)) = \sqrt{((x_2 + 5) - (x_1 + 5))^2 + (y_2 - y_1)^2}$
            $= \sqrt{(x_2 - x_1)^2 + (y_2 - y_1)^2} = d((x_2, y_2), (x_1, y_1))$

   b. $T^{-1} = (x - 5, y)$

4.   a.   Distance-preserving:
       $d(T(x_2, y_2), T(x_1, y_1)) = \sqrt{((x_2 + 4) - (x_1 + 4))^2 + ((y_2 - 10) - (y_1 - 10))^2}$
            $= \sqrt{(x_2 - x_1)^2 + (y_2 - y_1)^2} = d((x_2, y_2), (x_1, y_1))$

   b.   Not distance-preserving: $d(T(1, 0), T(0, 0)) = \sqrt{(4-0)^2 + (0-0)^2} = 4 \neq d((1, 0), (0, 0)) = 1$

   c.   Not distance-preserving: $d(T(1, 0), T(0, 0)) = \sqrt{(5-4)^2 + (-9 - -10)^2} = \sqrt{2} \neq d((1, 0), (0, 0)) = 1$

5.   Let S and T be two isometries and P and Q be any two points of the plane. If $P' = S(P)$ and $Q' = S(Q)$, then $P'Q' = PQ$, since S preserves distance. If $P'' = T(P')$ and $Q'' = T(Q')$, then $P''Q'' = P'Q' = PQ$, since T preserves distance. Thus the composite of S and T is distance-preserving and an isometry.

6.   a.   Suppose C is a point on $\overleftrightarrow{AB}$. Without loss of generality, assume C is between A and B. Let T be an isometry such that $T(A) = A'$, $T(B) = B'$, and $T(C) = C'$. If C is between A and B, then $AC + CB = AB$. Since T is distance-preserving, $AC = A'C'$, $CB = C'B'$, and $AB = A'B'$. Thus $A'C' + C'B' = A'B'$ and C' is between A' and B'. By the triangle inequality, the equality $A'C' + C'B' = A'B'$ can only hold if C' is collinear with A' and B'. So collinear points map to collinear points. Suppose D' is a point on line $\overleftrightarrow{A'B'}$. If $D' = A'$, then $D = A$, so D is on $\overleftrightarrow{AB}$. Similarly, if $D' = B'$, then $D = B$, so D is on $\overleftrightarrow{AB}$. If D' is between A' and B', then $A'D' + D'B' = A'B'$, and since isometries preserve distance, $A'D' = AD$, $D'B' = DB$, and $A'B' = AB$. So $AD + DB = AB$. Thus D is between A and B, so D is on line $\overleftrightarrow{AB}$. In a similar fashion, we can show that if A' is between D' and B', or if B' is between D' and A', then D has to be on line $\overleftrightarrow{AB}$. Thus, in all possible locations for D' on $\overleftrightarrow{A'B'}$, D is on $\overleftrightarrow{AB}$. This shows that the image of $\overleftrightarrow{AB}$ is the entire line $\overleftrightarrow{A'B'}$.

   b.   Let T be an isometry such that $T(A) = A'$ and $T(B) = B'$. Consider points on $\overrightarrow{AB}$. If C is a point on $\overleftrightarrow{AB}$ we know from part **a** that T(C) = C' will be on $\overleftrightarrow{A'B'}$. If C is between A and B, then AC + CB = AB. Since T is distance-preserving, AC = A'C', CB = B'B', and AB = A'B'. Thus A'C' + C'B' = A'B' and C' is between A' and B'. So the image of segment $\overline{AB}$ under isometry T is segment $\overline{A'B'}$. Similarly, if B is between A and C, then AB + BC = AC. Since T is distance-preserving, AB = A'B', BC = B'C', and AC = A'C'. Thus A'B' + B'C' = A'C' and B' is between A' and C'. Every point on $\overrightarrow{A'B'}$ is an image of a point on $\overrightarrow{AB}$ by an argument like that given in part **a**. Thus the image of a ray under an isometry is a ray.

c. If T is an isometry and $\overrightarrow{BA}$ and $\overrightarrow{BC}$ are rays, by part **b**, $T(\overrightarrow{BA}) = \overrightarrow{B'A'}$ and $T(\overrightarrow{BC}) = \overrightarrow{B'C'}$. So $T(\angle ABC) = T(\overrightarrow{BA} \cup \overrightarrow{BC}) = T(\overrightarrow{BA}) \cup T(\overrightarrow{BC}) = \overrightarrow{B'A'} \cup \overrightarrow{B'C'} = \angle A'B'C'$. Thus the image of an angle under an isometry is an angle.

7. Let Q = T(P). Since Q is the midpoint of $\overline{PC}$, QC = $\frac{1}{2}$PC. Thus T is not distance-preserving and not an isometry.

8. a. Letting $\overrightarrow{AC}$ be the vector from point A to point C and $\overrightarrow{AB}$ the vector from point A to point C, then $z_C - z_A = \overrightarrow{AC} = be^{i\theta}$ and $z_B - z_A = \overrightarrow{AB} = ce^{i\varphi}$ and

$\frac{z_C - z_A}{z_B - z_A} = \frac{be^{i\theta}}{ce^{i\varphi}} = \frac{b}{c}e^{i(\theta - \varphi)} = \frac{b}{c}(\cos(\theta - \varphi) + i\sin(\theta - \varphi))$. So $\text{Im}(\frac{z_C - z_A}{z_B - z_A})$

$= \frac{b}{c}\sin(\theta - \varphi)$. Since A = $|\theta - \varphi|$, $\text{Im}(\frac{z_C - z_A}{z_B - z_A}) = \frac{b}{c}\sin A$, when $\theta > \varphi$ (C is to the left of the

directed line from A to B), and $\text{Im}(\frac{z_C - z_A}{z_B - z_A}) = -\frac{b}{c}\sin A$, when $\theta < \varphi$ (C is to the right of the

directed line from A to B).

b. From part **a**, C will be to the left of the directed line segment from A to B (defined to be a

counterclockwise orientation) if and only if $\text{Im}(\frac{z_C - z_A}{z_B - z_A}) > 0$.

c. $\text{Im}(\frac{z_C - z_A}{z_B - z_A}) = \text{Im}(\frac{z_C - z_A}{z_B - z_A}\frac{\overline{z_B - z_A}}{\overline{z_B - z_A}})$. From part **a**, $z_B - z_A = ce^{i\varphi}$, so

$(z_B - z_A)(\overline{z_B - z_A}) = c^2$. Also $\overline{(z_B - z_A)} = \overline{z_B} - \overline{z_A}$. So $\text{Im}(\frac{z_C - z_A}{z_B - z_A})$

$= \frac{1}{c^2}\text{Im}((z_B - z_A)(\overline{z_B} - \overline{z_A}))$.

d. $(z_C - z_A)(\overline{z_B} - \overline{z_A}) = z_C\overline{z_B} + |z_A|^2 - z_C\overline{z_A} - z_A\overline{z_B}$
$= x_Cx_B + y_Cy_B - ix_Cy_B + ix_By_C + y_B^2 + x_A^2 + y_A^2 - (x_Cx_A - ix_Cy_A$
$+ ix_Ay_C + y_Cy_A) - (x_Bx_A + ix_By_A - ix_Ay_B + y_By_A)$. So $\text{Im}((z_B - z_A)(\overline{z_B} - \overline{z_A}))$

$= -x_Cy_B + x_By_C + x_Cy_A - x_Ay_C - x_By_A + x_Ay_B$, which equals $\begin{vmatrix} x_A & x_B & x_C \\ y_A & y_B & y_C \\ 1 & 1 & 1 \end{vmatrix}$.

e. A triangle in the coordinate plane has a counterclockwise orientation if and only if the determinant

of $\begin{bmatrix} x_A & x_B & x_C \\ y_A & y_B & y_C \\ 1 & 1 & 1 \end{bmatrix}$ is positive.

Section 7.2.1

1.   a. $T_{2,-5}(A) = (-2, 2)$, $T_{2,-5}(B) = (3, -5)$, $T_{2,-5}(C) = (7, 1)$

    b. $2 + -5i$

2.   a. $T_z(w) = 3 + 5i + 1 + 2i = 4 + 7i$; $T_{z+\bar{z}}(w) = 3 + 5i + (1 + 2i + 1 - 2i) = 5 + 5i$;

        $T_{z-\bar{z}}(w) = 3 + 5i + (1 + 2i - (1 - 2i)) = 3 + 9i$

    b.   For any complex number $z = x + iy$, $z + \bar{z} = 2x$ and $z - \bar{z} = 2iy$. So $T_{z+\bar{z}}$ has only a horizontal component and $T_{z-\bar{z}}$ has only a vertical component.

3.   a.   magnitude $= \sqrt{2^2 + (-5)^2} = \sqrt{29}$

    b. $\sqrt{((x + h) - x)^2 + ((y + k) - y)^2} = \sqrt{h^2 + k^2}$

    c. $|z| = \sqrt{z\bar{z}} = \sqrt{(x + yi)(x - yi)} = \sqrt{x^2 + y^2}$

    d.   Let T_a and T_b be translations by vectors **a** and **b**, respectively. Then $|a|$ and $|b|$ are the magnitudes of translations T_a and T_b, and $|a + b|$ is the magnitude of the composite translation $T_b \circ T_a$. If **a** and **b** are not parallel, then vectors **a**, **b**, and **a + b** form three sides of a triangle. Since the sum of the lengths of two sides of a triangle is always greater than third, $|a| + |b| > |a + b|$.

4.   a. $h_1 k_2 = h_2 k_1$

    b. $Arg(z_1) = Arg(z_2) + n\pi$ for some integer n.

5.   a.   Since $T(A) = B$, let $T_{\overrightarrow{AB}}$ be the translation specified by the directed line segment $\overrightarrow{AB}$. From the synthetic definition of a translation, if C is not on $\overleftrightarrow{AB}$, then D is the point such that BACD is a parallelogram. Since opposite sides of a parallelogram are congruent, AC = BD and T is distance-preserving. If C is on $\overleftrightarrow{AB}$, then, from the definition, D is the point such that BD = AC, so, again, T is distance-preserving.

    b.   Any translation is of the form $T_{h,k}(x, y) = (x + h, y + k)$. Let $A = (x_1, y_1)$ and $C = (x_2, y_2)$. Then $B = T_{h,k}(A) = (x_1 + h, y_1 + k)$ and $D = T_{h,k}(C) = (x_2 + h, y_2 + k)$. Thus

$$BD = \sqrt{((x_2 + h) - (x_1 + h))^2 + ((y_2 + k) - (y_1 + k))^2} = \sqrt{(x_2 - x_1)^2 + (y_2 - y_1)^2} = AC.$$

    c.   Sample: Since a translation moves all points in a particular direction by the same distance, the *relative* positions of all points will be invariant. Thus, under a translation, the orientation of any triangle will be fixed and the isometry will be direct.

Section 7.2.2

1.   a.   Answers will vary.

    b.   Answers will vary.

    c.   The images can be shown to be congruent by SAS congruence.

    d.   Sample: If β_1 and β_2 are the images of α under two rotations with the same magnitude, then $\beta_2 \approx \beta_1$.

2.   a. $R_{c,k+360n}$, for any integer n   b. $R_{c,k+2n\pi}$ for any integer n

3.   a. $0 + 2n\pi$ b. $-\frac{\pi}{4} + 2n\pi$

4.   Suppose a line passing through the origin has equation $y = mx$ and contains the point (a, b), which is on neither the x- nor y-axis. Then $m = \frac{b}{a}$. The line perpendicular to $y = mx$ and passing through the origin will then contain $R_{90°}(a, b)$, which is the point $(-b, a)$, and will have equation $y = m'x$, where $m' = -\frac{a}{b}$. Thus $mm' = -1$.

5.   a. $R_{180°}(x, y) = R_{90°} \circ R_{90°}(x, y) = R_{90°}(-y, x) = (-x, -y)$
              $R_{270°}(x, y) = R_{90°} \circ R_{180°}(x, y) = R_{90°}(-x, -y) = (y, -x)$

    b. $R_{180°} \circ R_{180°}(x, y) = R_{180°}(-x, -y) = (x, y)$;
              $R_{90°} \circ R_{270°}(x, y) = R_{90°}(y, -x) = (x, y)$

6.   a. $y = -x$; $x^2 + (-x)^2 = 1$; $2x^2 = 1$; $x = \pm\frac{\sqrt{2}}{2}$; $\{(\frac{\sqrt{2}}{2}, -\frac{\sqrt{2}}{2}), (-\frac{\sqrt{2}}{2}, \frac{\sqrt{2}}{2})\}$

    b. $\frac{3\pi}{4}, \frac{7\pi}{4}$

7. $R_{5\pi/6}(x, y) = (x \cos \frac{5\pi}{6} - y \sin \frac{5\pi}{6}, x \sin \frac{5\pi}{6} + y \cos \frac{5\pi}{6}) = (-\frac{1}{2}x - \frac{\sqrt{3}}{2}y, \frac{\sqrt{3}}{2}x + -\frac{1}{2}y)$

    Check: By synthetic geometry, the image of the point $(\frac{1}{2}, \frac{\sqrt{3}}{2})$ is $(-1, 0)$. By the formula, the image is

    $(-\frac{1}{2} \cdot \frac{1}{2} - \frac{\sqrt{3}}{2} \cdot \frac{\sqrt{3}}{2}, \frac{\sqrt{3}}{2} \cdot \frac{1}{2} + -\frac{1}{2} \cdot \frac{\sqrt{3}}{2}) = (-1, 0)$.

8.   a.

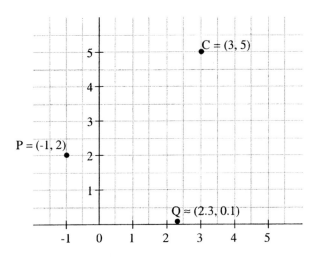

    b. $PC = \sqrt{(-1-3)^2 + (2-5)^2} = 5$; $QC = \sqrt{\left(\left(3 - \frac{\sqrt{2}}{2}\right) - 3\right)^2 + \left(\left(5 - \frac{7\sqrt{2}}{2}\right) - 5\right)^2}$

           $= \sqrt{\frac{1}{2} + \frac{49}{2}} = 5$

    c.   Neither check confirms that the angle of rotation is $\frac{\pi}{4}$.

9. a. $p = 2 + 5i, q = -1 + 4i, r = 6, c = i, z_{40°} = \cos 40° + i\sin 40° \approx .77 + .64i$;

$p - c = 2 + 4i, q - c = -1 + 3i, r - c = 6 - i$;

$p' = z_{40°}(p - c) + c = 2\cos 40° - 4\sin 40° + (4\cos 40° + 2\sin 40° + 1)i$

$\approx -1.0 + 5.3i$,

$q' = z_{40°}(q - c) + c = -\cos 40° - 3\sin 40° + (3\cos 40° - \sin 40° + 1)i \approx -2.7 + 2.7i$,

$r' = z_{40°}(r - c) + c = 6\cos 40° + \sin 40° + (-\cos 40° + 6\sin 40° + 1)i \approx 5.2 + 4.1i$

b. $PQ = \sqrt{(2--1)^2 + (5-4)^2} = \sqrt{10}$; $QR = \sqrt{(-1-6)^2 + (4-0)^2} = \sqrt{53}$;

$PR = \sqrt{(2-6)^2 + (5-0)^2} = \sqrt{41}$; $P'Q' = |p' - q'|$

$= |3\cos 40° - \sin 40° + (\cos 40° + 3\sin 40°)i|$

$= \sqrt{(3\cos 40° - \sin 40°)^2 + (\cos 40° + 3\sin 40°)^2} = \sqrt{10(\cos^2 40° + \sin^2 40°)}$

$= \sqrt{10}$; $Q'R' = |q' - r'| = |-7\cos 40° - 4\sin 40° + (4\cos 40° - 7\sin 40°)i|$

$= \sqrt{(-7\cos 40° - 4\sin 40°)^2 + (4\cos 40° - 7\sin 40°)^2}$

$= \sqrt{53(\cos^2 40° + \sin^2 40°)} = \sqrt{53}$; $P'R' = |p' - r'|$

$= |-4\cos 40° - 5\sin 40° + (5\cos 40° - 4\sin 40°)i|$

$= \sqrt{(-4\cos 40° - 5\sin 40°)^2 + (5\cos 40° - 4\sin 40°)^2}$

$= \sqrt{41(\cos^2 40° + \sin^2 40°)} = \sqrt{41}$; By SSS congruence ΔPQR and $\Delta P'Q'R'$ are congruent.

10. a. Consider the rotation $R_{C,\varphi}$ applied to any two points P and Q such that $P' = R_{C,\varphi}(P)$ and $Q' = R_{C,\varphi}(Q)$. From the definition of rotation, $PC = P'C, QC = Q'C$, and $m\angle PCP' = m\angle QCQ' = |\varphi|$, so $m\angle PCQ = m\angle P'CQ'$. By SAS congruence, then, $\Delta P'CQ'$ and ΔPCQ are congruent and $P'Q' = PQ$. Thus $R_{C,\varphi}$ is distance-preserving and it is an isometry.

b. Let $(x_1', y_1') = R_\varphi(x_1, y_1)$ and $(x_2', y_2') = R_\varphi(x_2, y_2)$. Then $d((x_2', y_2'), (x_1', y_1'))$

$= \sqrt{((x_2 - x_1)\cos\varphi - (y_2 - y_1)\sin\varphi)^2 + ((x_2 - x_1)\sin\varphi + (y_2 - y_1)\cos\varphi)^2}$

$= \sqrt{(x_2 - x_1)^2(\cos^2\varphi + \sin^2\varphi) + (y_2 - y_1)^2(\cos^2\varphi + \sin^2\varphi)}$

$= \sqrt{(x_2 - x_1)^2 + (y_2 - y_1)^2} = d((x_2, y_2), (x_1, y_1))$. Thus the rotation R_φ is an isometry.

11. $\overline{z_\varphi} = \overline{\cos\varphi + i\sin\varphi} = \cos\varphi - i\sin\varphi = \cos(-\varphi) + i\sin(-\varphi) = z_{-\varphi}$

12. $R_{c,\varphi}(x, y) = (\cos\varphi + i\sin\varphi)(x + iy - (a + bi)) + (a + bi)$

$= (\cos\varphi + i\sin\varphi)((x - a) + i(y - b)) + (a + bi)$

$= (x - a)\cos\varphi - (y - b)\sin\varphi + a + i((x - a)\sin\varphi + (y - b)\cos\varphi + b)$

So $R_{c,\varphi}(x, y) = ((x - a)\cos\varphi - (y - b)\sin\varphi + a, (x - a)\sin\varphi + (y - b)\cos\varphi + b)$.

13. a. First, observe that $w = z_{2\pi/3}$. Because the set of all rotations in the plane under the operation of composition is isomorphic to the set of complex numbers on the unit circle under the operation of multiplication, the complex number w^3 corresponds to the rotation $R_{2\pi/3} \circ R_{2\pi/3} \circ R_{2\pi/3} \equiv R_0$. R_0 is

the identity transformation, so $w^3 = 1$.

b. $3k = 2n\pi$ for integer n; $z_{\pi/3} = \cos\frac{4\pi}{3} + i\sin\frac{4\pi}{3}$

c.   Let $\triangle ABC$ be an equilateral triangle inscribed in the unit circle. Then $c = \cos\varphi + i\sin\varphi$, for some angle φ. Points A and B are images of C under rotations about the origin of magnitudes $\frac{4\pi}{3}$ and $\frac{2\pi}{3}$, respectively. So $a = z_{4\pi/3}c$ and $b = z_{2\pi/3}c$. Therefore, $aw^2 + bw + c = z_{4\pi/3}a + z_{2\pi/3}b + c$

$= z_{4\pi/3}(z_{4\pi/3}c) + z_{2\pi/3}(z_{2\pi/3}c) + c = z_{8\pi/3}c + z_{4\pi/3}c + c$

$= (z_{8\pi/3} + z_{4\pi/3} + 1)c = (z_{2\pi/3} + z_{4\pi/3} + 1)c$

$= (\cos\frac{2\pi}{3} + i\sin\frac{2\pi}{3} + \cos\frac{4\pi}{3} + i\sin\frac{4\pi}{3} + 1)c = 0$

Now, suppose $\triangle A'B'C'$ is an equilateral triangle not inscribed in the unit circle. If P is the center of this triangle, then, $a' = ra + p$, $b' = rb + p$, and $c' = rc + p$, where a, b, and c are complex numbers representing the vertices of some equilateral triangle inscribed in the unit circle. Thus $a'w^2 + b'w + c'$

$= (ra + p)w^2 + (rb + p)w + (rc + p) = r(aw^2 + bw + c) + p(w^2 + w + 1)$

$= r(0) + p(0) = 0$.

Section 7.2.3

1.   a.   By Theorem 7.7(b), $r_{y\text{-axis}}(x, y) = (-x, y)$, so $M = \begin{bmatrix} -1 & 0 \\ 0 & 1 \end{bmatrix}$.

      b.   By Theorem 7.7(c), $r_{x=y}(x, y) = (y, x)$, so $M = \begin{bmatrix} 0 & 1 \\ 1 & 0 \end{bmatrix}$.

      c. $r_{y=-x}(x, y) = (-y, -x) = r_{y\text{-axis}}(r_{x\text{-axis}}(r_{y=x}(x, y)))$, so $M = \begin{bmatrix} 0 & -1 \\ -1 & 0 \end{bmatrix}$.

2.   Case (1): Since $A = A'$ and $B = B'$, $AB = A'B'$. Case (2): Since A is on m, $A = A'$. Since B is not on m, m is the perpendicular bisector of $\overline{BB'}$. Let m intersect $\overline{BB'}$ at point Q. Then $BQ = B'Q$. If $Q = A$, then $AB = A'B'$. If $Q \neq A$, then $\overline{BQ} \cong \overline{B'Q}$, $\overline{AQ} \cong \overline{A'Q}$, and $\angle AQB \cong \angle A'QB'$, since they are both right angles. By SAS, $\triangle AQB \cong \triangle A'QB'$. So $\overline{AB} \cong \overline{A'B'}$ and $AB = A'B'$. Case (3): Let m intersect $\overline{AA'}$ at point Q and $\overline{BB'}$ at point P. If $Q = P$, then $AB = |AQ - BQ| = |A'Q - B'Q| = A'B'$. If $Q \neq P$, then, by SAS, $\triangle AQP \cong \triangle A'QP$. Thus $\overline{AP} \cong \overline{A'P}$ and $\angle QPA \cong \angle QPA'$. Since $\overline{AP} \cong \overline{A'P}$, $\overline{BP} \cong \overline{B'P}$, and $\angle APB \cong \angle A'PB'$, by SAS, $\triangle APB \cong \triangle A'PB'$ and $\overline{AB} \cong \overline{A'B'}$. So $AB = A'B'$. Case (4): Let m intersect $\overline{AA'}$ at point Q, $\overline{BB'}$ at point P, and $\overline{AB}$ at point R. If $Q = P$, then $AB = AQ + BQ = A'Q + B'Q = A'B'$. If $Q \neq P$, then, by SAS, $\triangle AQR \cong \triangle A'QR$ and $\triangle BPR \cong \triangle B'PR$. So $\overline{AR} \cong \overline{A'R}$ and $\overline{BR} \cong \overline{B'R}$. Thus $AR = A'R$ and $BR = B'R$. Since R is between A and B and R is between A' and B', $AB = AR + BR = A'R + B'R = A'B'$.

3.   Let A, B, and C be three noncollinear points that determine $\angle BAC$. By the corollaries to Theorem 7.8, under a reflection the image of a triangle is a triangle. So $r_m(\triangle ABC) = \triangle A'B'C'$. Since, by Theorem 7.8,

reflections preserve distance, by SSS, $\triangle ABC \cong \triangle A'B'C'$ and $\angle BAC \cong \angle B'A'C'$. Thus $m\angle BAC = m\angle B'A'C'$.

4. By the Two-Reflection Theorem for Rotations, $r_{90°} = r_{y=x} \circ r_{x\text{-axis}}$, and $r_{y=x} \circ r_{x\text{-axis}}(x, y) = r_{y=x}(x, -y) = (-y, x)$.

5. Both Theorems apply. The composite transformation under the Two-Reflection Theorem for Rotations yields the identity rotation. The composite transformation under the Two-Reflection Theorem for Translations yields the identity translation.

6.   a.   Sample: m: $x = -1$; n: $x = 1.5$
     b.   Sample: m: $y = x - x_0 + y_0$; n: $y = -x + x_0 + y_0$
     c.   Sample: m: $y = 0$; n: $y = \tan(20°)x$
     d.   Sample: m: $y = -\frac{3}{4}x$; n: $y = -\frac{3}{4}x + \frac{25}{8}$

7. The transformation is a composite of two reflections in parallel planes. Suppose r_{front} and r_{back} represent the reflections in the mirrors in front and in back of you, respectively. Since these mirrors are parallel, the composite reflection $r_{front} \circ r_{back}$ will form an image of the back of your head that has been translated a distance equal to twice the distance between the mirrors, in the direction from back to front.

8. $Q = r_b(P)$; $U = r_a(P)$; $T = r_a(Q) = r_a \circ r_b(P)$; $R = r_b(U) = r_b \circ r_a(P)$; $S = r_a(R) = r_a \circ r_b(U) = r_a \circ (r_b \circ r_a(P))$

9.   a.   If lines k and ℓ intersect at O, then points A, B, and C cannot be collinear. Since O is on line k, it is equidistant from points A and B and since it is on line ℓ it is equidistant from points B and C. Thus O is equidistant from three noncollinear points A, B, and C and is the center of a circle containing all three points.

     b.   By Theorem 7.9(a), $r_\ell \circ r_k$ is a rotation with center O and twice the measure of the directed angle from k to ℓ. Twice the measure of this angle equals $m\angle AOC$, since $\triangle AOB$ and $\triangle BOC$ are both isosceles, and $m\angle AOC = m\,\overset{\frown}{AC}$, since O is the center of the circle.

     c.   Let $s = m\,\overset{\frown}{AC}$. Then s is the magnitude of the rotation $r_\ell \circ r_k$ because $r_\ell \circ r_k(A) = C$ and ℓ and k intersect at the center of the circle of this arc. Now the angle between ℓ and k is $\angle CBA$, and the magnitude of the rotation $r_\ell \circ r_k$ (by the Two-Reflection Theorem for Rotations) is $2m\angle CBA$. Thus $2m\angle CBA = m\,\overset{\frown}{AC}$, and so the measure of the inscribed angle is half the measure of the intercepted arc.

10.   a.   The lines are parallel, so the transformation is a translation. The distance between two parallel lines $y = mx + b_1$ and $y = mx + b_2$ is given by $(b_2 - b_1)\frac{\sqrt{m^2 + 1}}{m^2 + 1}$, so the translation has magnitude $8\frac{\sqrt{10}}{10}$ and is in the direction from m to n.

     b.   Lines u and v can be any lines with equations of the form $y = 3x + k$ and $y = 3x + k + 4$.

11. $x = \frac{1-m}{m^2+1}x + \frac{2m}{m^2+1}y$ and $y = \frac{2m}{m^2+1}x - \frac{1-m}{m^2+1}y$. See Problem 12.

12. By Theorem 7.11, $r_\varphi(z) = z_{2\varphi}\bar{z}$. Since $\varphi = \tan^{-1}k$, $z_{2\varphi} = \cos(2\tan^{-1}k) + i\sin(2\tan^{-1}k)$.

We have $\cos(2\tan^{-1}k) = \cos^2(\tan^{-1}k) - \sin^2(\tan^{-1}k) = \dfrac{1-k}{k^2+1}$ and

$\sin(2\tan^{-1}k) = 2\sin(\tan^{-1}k)\cos(\tan^{-1}k) = \dfrac{2k}{k^2+1}$. So, if $z = x + iy$, then

$z' = (\dfrac{1-k}{k^2+1} + i\dfrac{2k}{k^2+1})(x - iy) = \dfrac{1-k}{k^2+1}x + \dfrac{2k}{k^2+1}y + i(\dfrac{2k}{k^2+1}x - \dfrac{1-k}{k^2+1}y)$.

13.

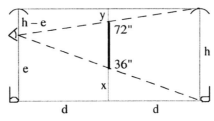

a. Since the person's reflection image will appear a distance d behind the mirror, we have $\dfrac{e}{2d} = \dfrac{x}{d}$, where x is the distance from the ground to the point in the mirror where the person must look to see his feet. Thus, $e = 2x$. So if $36'' \le x \le 72''$, then $72'' \le e \le 144''$.

b. Similarly, we have $\dfrac{h-e}{2d} = \dfrac{y}{d}$, where y is the distance from the top of the head to the point in the mirror where the person must look to see the top of his head. Thus, $y = \dfrac{h-e}{2}$. So if $36'' \le h - y \le 72''$, then $72'' \le h + e \le 144''$. However, since $72'' \le e \le 144''$ and $h > e$, there are no values of h and e for which the person can see the image of his entire front in the mirror.

c. Part **a** demonstrates that x, the point in the mirror in which the shoes are visible, will always be $\dfrac{e}{2}$. Therefore standing closer to the mirror neither increases nor decreases the ability to see your feet in a mirror.

12. By Theorem 7.11, $r_\varphi(z) = z_{2\varphi}\bar{z}$. Since $\varphi = \tan^{-1}k$, $z_{2\varphi} = \cos(2\tan^{-1}k) + i\sin(2\tan^{-1}k)$.

We have $\cos(2\tan^{-1}k) = \cos^2(\tan^{-1}k) - \sin^2(\tan^{-1}k) = \dfrac{1-k}{k^2+1}$ and

$\sin(2\tan^{-1}k) = 2\sin(\tan^{-1}k)\cos(\tan^{-1}k) = \dfrac{2k}{k^2+1}$. So, if $z = x + iy$, then

$z' = (\dfrac{1-k}{k^2+1} + i\dfrac{2k}{k^2+1})(x - iy) = \dfrac{1-k}{k^2+1}x + \dfrac{2k}{k^2+1}y + i(\dfrac{2k}{k^2+1}x - \dfrac{1-k}{k^2+1}y)$.

Section 7.2.4

1. a. $r_{y\text{-axis}} \circ T_{0,-3}(x, y) = r_{y\text{-axis}}(x + 0, y + -3) = (-x, y + -3)$

b. Sample:

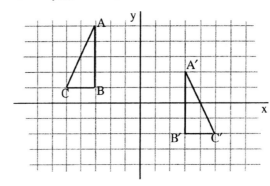

2. a. The translation $T_{0,0}$ is parallel to every line m. So the reflection $r_m = r_m \circ T_{0,0} = T_{0,0} \circ r_m$ can be thought of as a glide reflection with a translation of magnitude 0.

    b. A translation preserves orientation, while a glide reflection does not.

3. a. $r_{y=3x} \circ T_{2,6}(z) = r_{y=3x}(z + 2 + 6i) = (\overline{z + 2 + 6i})(\frac{1-3^2}{1+3^2} + \frac{2 \bullet 3}{1+3^2}i)$

    $= (\bar{z} + 2 - 6i)(\frac{1-3^2}{1+3^2} + \frac{2 \bullet 3}{1+3^2}i)$

    $= (\bar{z} + 2 - 6i)(-.8 + .6i) = \bar{z}(-.8 + .6i) + (2 + 6i)$

    b. $z = x + iy$, $\bar{z} = x - iy$, $z' = (x - iy + 2 - 6i)(-.8 + .6i)$

    $= (x - iy)(-.8 + .6i) + (2 + 6i) = (-.8x + .6y + 2) + (.6x + .8y + 6)i$

    $(x', y') = (-.8x + .6y + 2, .6x + .8y + 6)$

    c. Applying Theorem 7.14,

    $r_{y=3x-5} \circ T_{2,6}(z) = r_{y=3x-5}(z + 2 + 6i)$

    $= (\overline{z + 2 + 6i - -5i})(\frac{1-3^2}{1+3^2} + i\frac{2 \bullet 3}{1+3^2}) + -5i$

    $= (\bar{z} + 2 - 11i)(-.8 + .6i) + -5i = \bar{z}(-.8 + .6i) + (5 + 10i) + -5i$

    $= \bar{z}(-.8 + .6i) + (5 + 5i)$.

    So $(x', y') = (-.8x + .6y + 5, .6x + .8y + 5)$.

    d. Since $r_{y=3x-5} \circ T_{2,6} = T_{2,6} \circ r_{y=3x-5}$, we can apply the reflection first. The line perpendicular to $y = 3x - 5$ and passing through a point (a, b) has equation $y = -\frac{1}{3}(x - a) + b$. If (a_r, b_r) is the reflection image of (a, b) over the line $y = 3x - 5$, then the lines $y = -\frac{1}{3}(x - a) + b$ and $y = 3x - 5$ intersect at the point $(x_0, y_0) = (\frac{a+3b+15}{10}, \frac{3a+9b-5}{10}) = (\frac{a+a_r}{2}, \frac{b+b_r}{2})$. Thus $(a_r, b_r) = (2x_0 - a, 2y_0 - b) = (\frac{-4a+3b+15}{5}, \frac{3a+4b-5}{5})$. The translation image when $T_{2,6}$ is applied to the point (a_r, b_r) is $(\frac{-4a+3b+15}{5} + 2, \frac{3a+4b-5}{5} + 6) = (-.8a + .6b + 5, .6a + .8b + 5)$.

4. By Theorem 7.14, $g_{m,b}(x + iy) = z_{2\varphi}(\overline{(x+iy) - (x_0 + iy_0)}) + x_0 + iy_0 + h + ik$, where

    $z_{2\varphi} = \cos(2\tan^{-1}\frac{k}{h}) + i\sin(2\tan^{-1}\frac{k}{h})$. So

    $g_{m,b}(x + iy) = (\cos(2\tan^{-1}\frac{k}{h}) + i\sin(2\tan^{-1}\frac{k}{h}))(x - x_0 - i(y - y_0)) + x_0 + iy_0 + h + ik$

    $= (x - x_0)\cos(2\tan^{-1}\frac{k}{h}) + (y - y_0)\sin(2\tan^{-1}\frac{k}{h}) + x_0 + h + i((x - x_0)\sin(2\tan^{-1}\frac{k}{h}) - (y - y_0)\cos(2\tan^{-1}\frac{k}{h})$

    $+ y_0 + k)$. Finally, $\cos(2\tan^{-1}\frac{k}{h}) = \cos^2(\tan^{-1}\frac{k}{h}) - \sin^2(\tan^{-1}\frac{k}{h}) = \frac{h^2 - k^2}{h^2 + k^2}$ and

    $\sin(2\tan^{-1}\frac{k}{h}) = 2\sin(\tan^{-1}\frac{k}{h})\cos(\tan^{-1}\frac{k}{h}) = \frac{2hk}{h^2 + k^2}$. Thus $x' = (x - x_0)\frac{h^2 - k^2}{h^2 + k^2} + (y - y_0)\frac{2hk}{h^2 + k^2} + x_0 + h$

    and $y' = (x - x_0)\frac{2hk}{h^2 + k^2} - (y - y_0)\frac{h^2 - k^2}{h^2 + k^2} + y_0 + k$.

5. G is the glide reflection $r_{y=x} \circ T_{1,1}$.

6. a. i. For $\varphi \neq 2n\pi$, where n is an integer, the only fixed point is C. For $\varphi = 2n\pi$, all points in the plane are fixed.

ii.   For $b \neq 0$, there are no fixed points. For $b = 0$, all points are fixed.

iii.   All points on m are fixed.

b. $G(a, b)$ has a fixed point z if and only if $G(a, b)(z) = z$, or $a\bar{z} + b = z$. Multiplying both sides by $\bar{a}$ yields $\bar{a}a\bar{z} + \bar{a}b = \bar{a}z$. But $\bar{a}a = 1$. So $\bar{z} + \bar{a}b = \bar{a}z$. Taking the complex conjugate of both sides of $a\bar{z} + b = z$ yields $\bar{a}z + \bar{b} = \bar{z}$. Substituting for $\bar{z}$ gives $\bar{a}z + \bar{b} + \bar{a}b = \bar{a}z$. Finally, subtracting $\bar{a}z$ from both sides yields $\bar{b} + \bar{a}b = 0$. Taking the complex conjugate yields $a\bar{b} + b = 0$.

c. $a(\overline{z - \frac{b}{2}}) + \frac{b}{2} = a\bar{z} - \frac{a\bar{b}}{2} + \frac{b}{2} = a\bar{z} - \frac{a\bar{b}}{2} + b - \frac{b}{2}$

$= a\bar{z} - \frac{a\bar{b} + b}{2} + b = a\bar{z} + b$

d.   From part **b**, if $G(a, b)$ has fixed points, then $a\bar{b} + b = 0$. From part **c**, if $a\bar{b} + b = 0$, then $G(a, b) = a(\overline{z - \frac{b}{2}}) + \frac{b}{2}$. Since $|a| = 1$, $a = \cos 2\varphi + i \sin 2\varphi$, for some angle φ. By Theorem 7.14, $G(a, b)$ is a reflection over the line containing point $\frac{b}{2}$ and making an angle φ with the positive ray of the real axis.

e.   The only isometries with no fixed points are translations and glide reflections. Because $G(a, b) = a\bar{z} + b$, where $|a| = 1$, by Theorem 7.13, $G(a, b) = T_b \circ r_\varphi$. Therefore, $G(a, b)$ is a glide reflection.

Section 7.2.5

1.   a.   translations, rotations

b.   reflections, glide reflections

c.   reflections, glide reflections

2.   any even n

3.   a. z must be parallel to w, x, and y. The directed distance from y to z must be equal to the directed distance from w to x.

b. z must contain the point of concurrency of w, x, and y. The measure of the angle from y to z must equal the measure of the angle from w to x.

4.   Suppose $(r_d \circ r_c) \circ (r_b \circ r_a)$ is the composite of a translation following a rotation. Translate lines c and d so that line c' is concurrent with lines a and b. So $(r_d \circ r_c) \circ (r_b \circ r_a) = (r_{d'} \circ r_{c'}) \circ (r_b \circ r_a)$. By the associativity of composition, $(r_{d'} \circ r_{c'}) \circ (r_b \circ r_a) = r_{d'} \circ (r_{c'} \circ r_b \circ r_a)$. Since lines a, b, and c' are concurrent, $r_{c'} \circ r_b \circ r_a$ is a single reflection. Finally, the composition of two reflections is either a translation or a rotation.

5.

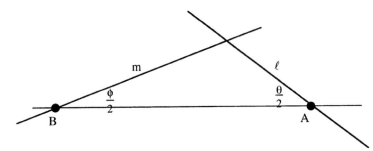

Let the rotations be $R_{A,\theta}$ and $R_{B,\phi}$. $R_{A,\theta}$ is the composite of two reflections over lines intersecting at A with acute angle $\frac{\theta}{2}$ between them. Choose the lines so that the *second* reflecting line is $\overleftrightarrow{AB}$. Similarly, $R_{B,\phi}$ is the composite of two reflections over lines intersecting at B with acute angle $\frac{\phi}{2}$ between them. Choose these lines so that the *first* reflecting line is $\overleftrightarrow{AB}$.

$$R_{B,\phi} \circ R_{A,\theta} = (r_m \circ r_{\overleftrightarrow{AB}}) \circ (r_{\overleftrightarrow{AB}} \circ r_\ell)$$
$$= r_m \circ (r_{\overleftrightarrow{AB}} \circ r_{\overleftrightarrow{AB}}) \circ r_\ell$$
$$= r_m \circ I \circ r_\ell$$

The composite is a translation iff $\ell \parallel m$. Now $\theta + \phi \equiv 0 \, \text{Mod}(2\pi) \Rightarrow \theta + \phi = 2\pi \Rightarrow \frac{\theta}{2} + \frac{\phi}{2} = \pi$ $\Rightarrow \ell \parallel m$. Otherwise, the lines ℓ and m intersect and the composite is a rotation.

6. a. Let $R_{(5,0),80°} = r_c \circ r_{\text{x-axis}}$, where line c has a slope of $\tan 40°$. Then $R_{(5,0),80°} \circ r_{\text{x-axis}} = r_c \circ r_{\text{x-axis}} \circ r_{\text{x-axis}} = r_c$. So the composite transformation is a single reflection.

    b. Let $T_{7,1} = r_b \circ r_a$, where lines a and b both have slope -7. Then $T_{7,1} \circ r_{y=x} = r_b \circ r_a \circ r_{y=x}$. Since lines a and b are parallel to each other but are not parallel to the line $y = x$, the three lines must have at least two points of intersection. Thus the transformation is a glide reflection.

    c. Let $R_{75°} = r_{\text{x-axis}} \circ r_a$ and $R_{(10,0),75°} = r_d \circ r_{\text{x-axis}}$, where lines a and d have slopes $\tan{-37.5°}$ and $\tan 37.5°$, respectively. Then $R_{(10,0),75°} \circ R_{75°} = (r_d \circ r_{\text{x-axis}}) \circ (r_{\text{x-axis}} \circ r_a) = r_d \circ r_a$. Since lines a and d intersect, the composite transformation is a rotation.

    d. Let $R_{90°} = r_{\text{x-axis}} \circ r_{y=-x}$ and $T_{\pi,0} = r_{y=\pi/2} \circ r_{\text{x-axis}}$. Then $T_{\pi,0} \circ R_{90°} = (r_{y=\pi/2} \circ r_{\text{x-axis}}) \circ (r_{\text{x-axis}} \circ r_{y=-x}) = r_{y=\pi/2} \circ r_{y=-x}$. Since these two reflecting lines intersect, $T_{\pi,0} \circ R_{90°}$ is a rotation.

7. If the centers A and B coincide, then the composite is the identity transformation. If A and B do not coincide, then the composite is a translation with a magnitude equal to twice the distance between the centers.

8. Answers will vary.

9. By Theorem 7.8, if a transformation is a reflection, then it is distance-preserving. The composite of any number of distance-preserving transformations is still distance-preserving. By Theorem 7.19, if a transformation is distance-preserving it is the composite of reflections. Thus the set of all composites of reflections is identical to the set of all distance-preserving transformations. By Theorem 7.16, any composite of four reflections is either a translation or a rotation. By Theorems 7.9(a) and 7.9(b), any translation or rotation can be decomposed into a composite of two reflections. So any composite of four or more reflections is also a composite of one, two, or three reflections. Thus the set of all composites of reflections is identical to the set of all composites of three or fewer reflections. By Theorems 7.9(a) and 7.9(b), any rotation or translation is the composite of two reflections. Thus the set of all composites of reflections, rotations, and translations is identical to the set of all reflections.

Finally, by definition, the set of all distance-preserving transformations is identical to the set of all congruence transformations and the set of all isometries.

Section 7.2.6

1. a. One lattice point is (20, 20). Since $\gcd(61, 39) = 1$, by Theorem 5.8, the set of all solutions is given by $(20 - 39m, 20 + 61m)$ for all integers m. So a second lattice point is (-19, 81).

    b. If (x_0, y_0) is a lattice point of $61x + 39y = 2000$, then $(x_0 - 14, y_0 + 167)$ is a lattice point of $61(x + 14) + 39(x - 167) = 2000$. Thus, using the points of part **a**, (6, 187) and (-33, 248) are two lattice points.

2. The graph of $y = mx + b$ can be generated by applying the vertical translation $T_{0,b}$ to the graph of $y = mx$. The line $y = mx$ contains (0, 0) and has slope m. Translating this line using $T_{0,b}$,

3. a. the circle of radius r and center (0, 0); the circle of radius r and center (h, k)

    b. the interior of the circle of radius r and center (0, 0); the interior of the circle of radius r and center (h, k)

    c. a v-shaped graph with vertex at (0, 0) symmetric to the y-axis; a congruent v-shaped graph with vertex at (h, k)

    d. the ellipse with center (0, 0) and endpoints of axes at (a, 0), (0, b), (-a, 0), (0, -b); an ellipse with center (h, k) and endpoints of axes at (a + h, k), (h, b + k), (-a + h, k), (h, -b + k)

    e. a hyperbola with center (0, 0) and vertices at (a, 0) and (-a, 0); a hyperbola with center (h, k) and vertices at (a + h, k) and (-a + h, k)

4. By the Graph Translation Theorem, applying the translation $T_{-\pi/2,0}$ to the graph of $y = \sin x$ yields the same graph as $y = \sin(x - \frac{\pi}{2}) = \cos x$. Since $T_{-\pi/2,0}$ is a congruence transformation, the graphs of $y = \sin x$ and $y = \cos x$ are congruent.

5. Since x has been replaced by $x - h$, by the Graph Translation Theorem, any point (x, y) on the graph of $y = ax^2 - k$ will be translated to (x + h, y) on the graph of $y = a(x - h)^2 - k$. So if $(\pm\sqrt{\frac{k}{a}}, 0)$ are points on $ax^2 - k$, then $(\pm\sqrt{\frac{k}{a}} + h, 0)$ are points on $y = a(x - h)^2 - k$. So the solutions to $a(x - h)^2 - k = 0$ are $\pm\sqrt{\frac{k}{a}} + h$.

6. For any $k > 0$, $\log kx = \log x + \log k$. So the equation $y = \log kx$ can be rewritten $y - \log k = \log x$. By the Graph Translation Theorem, the graph of $y - \log k = \log x$ is the image of $y = \log x$ under the translation $T_{0,\log k}$. Since a $T_{0,\log k}$ is congruence transformation, for any $k > 0$, the graph of $y = \log kx$ is congruent to the graph of $y = \log x$.

7. a. $222 - 0.4n$

    b. In 1999 the record was 222 seconds. This time is reduced on average by 0.4 seconds per year. So $t = 222 - 0.4n$, where n is the number of years since 1999. Since the year Y is related to n by $Y = 1999 + n$, or $n = Y - 1999$, the record time can be given by $t = 222 - 0.4(Y - 1999)$.

8. Since the year Y is related to n by $Y = n + 1999$, then $n = Y - 1999$. So, by substitution, $P = 6(1.013)^{Y - 1999}$.

9. By the Graph Translation Theorem, the graph $t = \dfrac{3}{\frac{w}{50} - 1} = \dfrac{150}{w - 50}$ is the image of the graph of $t = \dfrac{150}{w}$ under the translation $T_{50,0}$. So c = 150.

10. Applying the translation $T_{a,b,c}(x, y, z) = (x + a, y + b, z + c)$ to the given sphere moves its center to (a, b, c) and has the same graph as $(x - a)^2 + (y - b)^2 + (z - c)^2 = r^2$.

11. $\{z: |z - z_0| = k, k \in \mathbf{R}, k > 0\}$

12. If the original graph contained the point $[r_0, \theta_0]$, the new graph will contain the point $[r_0, \theta_0 + \Phi]$. So the graph will be rotated by an angle Φ.

13. a. Let (x', y') be a point on the image graph. For reflection over the x-axis, $x' = x$ and $y' = -y$. Solving these equations for x and y, $x = x'$ and $y = -y'$. Thus, by substitution, the original equation or inequality is replaced by one in x' and $-y'$. After dropping the "primes" in x' and y', the theorem follows.

    b. Let (x', y') be a point on the image graph. For reflection over the line $x = y$, $x' = y$ and $y' = x$. Solving these equations for x and y, $x = y'$ and $y = x'$. Thus, by substitution, the original equation or inequality is replaced by one in which x is replaced by y' and y is replaced by x'. After dropping the "primes" in x' and y', the theorem follows.

14. Let $(x', y') = R_\varphi(x, y)$ be a point on the image graph. Then $(x', y') = (x\cos\varphi - y\sin\varphi, x\sin\varphi + y\cos\varphi)$. We can then solve the system $\begin{cases} x' = x\cos\varphi - y\sin\varphi \\ y' = x\sin\varphi + y\cos\varphi \end{cases}$ for x and y. To solve for x, multiply x' by $\cos\varphi$ and y' by $\sin\varphi$ and then add to get $x'\cos\varphi + y'\sin\varphi = x\cos^2\varphi + x\sin^2\varphi = x$. To solve for y, multiply x' by $\sin\varphi$ and y' by $\cos\varphi$ and then subtract to get $x'\sin\varphi - y'\cos\varphi = -y\sin^2\varphi - x\cos^2\varphi = -y$, or $y = -x'\sin\varphi + y'\cos\varphi$. Substituting $x'\cos\varphi + y'\sin\varphi$ for x and $-x'\sin\varphi + y'\cos\varphi$ for y and dropping the "primes" yields the desired result.

15. Use Theorem 7.23.

    a. Substituting $x\cos 45° + y\sin 45° = \frac{\sqrt{2}}{2}x + \frac{\sqrt{2}}{2}y$ for x and $-x\sin 45° + y\cos 45° = -\frac{\sqrt{2}}{2}x + \frac{\sqrt{2}}{2}y$ for y, yields $(\frac{\sqrt{2}}{2}x + \frac{\sqrt{2}}{2}y)^2 - (-\frac{\sqrt{2}}{2}x + \frac{\sqrt{2}}{2}y)^2 = 1$. Simplifying yields $2xy = 1$, or $xy = \frac{1}{2}$.

    b. Substituting $x\cos 60° + y\sin 60° = \frac{1}{2}x + \frac{\sqrt{3}}{2}y$ for x and $-x\sin 60° + y\cos 60° = -\frac{\sqrt{3}}{2}x + \frac{1}{2}y$ for y, yields $(\frac{1}{2}x + \frac{\sqrt{3}}{2}y)^2 - (-\frac{\sqrt{3}}{2}x + \frac{1}{2}y)^2 = 1$. Simplifying yields $\frac{1}{2}y^2 - \frac{1}{2}x^2 + \sqrt{3}xy = 1$.

    c. Substituting $x\cos 90° + y\sin 90° = y$ for x and $-x\sin 90° + y\cos 90 = -x$ for y, yields $-x = y^2$, or $x = -y^2$.

    d. Substituting $x\cos 45° + y\sin 45° = \frac{\sqrt{2}}{2}x + \frac{\sqrt{2}}{2}y$ for x and $-x\sin 45° + y\cos 45° = -\frac{\sqrt{2}}{2}x + \frac{\sqrt{2}}{2}y$ for y, yields $-\frac{\sqrt{2}}{2}x + \frac{\sqrt{2}}{2}y = (\frac{\sqrt{2}}{2}x + \frac{\sqrt{2}}{2}y)^2$, or $\frac{1}{2}x^2 + \frac{1}{2}y^2 + xy + \frac{\sqrt{2}}{2}x - \frac{\sqrt{2}}{2}y = 0$.

    e. Substituting $x\cos -90° + y\sin -90° = -y$ for x and $-x\sin -90° + y\cos -90° = x$ for y, yields $x = (-y)^2 = y^2$.

f. Substituting $x\cos 90° + y\sin 90° = y$ for x and $-x\sin 90° + y\cos 90° = -x$ for y, yields

$$\frac{y^2}{4} + \frac{(-x)^2}{4} = \frac{y^2}{4} + \frac{x^2}{4} = 1.$$

16. The translation $T_{-\pi/2,0}$ applied to the graph of $y = \tan x$ yields the graph of $y = \dfrac{\sin\left(x + \frac{\pi}{2}\right)}{\cos\left(x + \frac{\pi}{2}\right)} = \dfrac{\cos x}{-\sin x}$. The

graph of $y = \dfrac{\cos x}{-\sin x}$ reflected across the y-axis then has equation $y = \dfrac{\cos{-x}}{-\sin{-x}} = \dfrac{\cos x}{\sin x} = \cot x$. Thus a

composition of a translation and a reflection will map the graph of $y = \tan x$ onto the graph of $y = \cot x$. So the two graphs are congruent.

17. The graph of $g(x) = 1 - e^{-x}$ can be obtained by applying the composite of transformations $T_{0,1} \circ r_{x=0} \circ r_{y=0}$ to the graph of $f(x) = e^x$. Since these transformations are all isometries, the resulting graph is congruent to the original.

18. a. A reflection across a vertical line does not change the y-coordinate, so $y' = y$. The directed distance from the line $x = 3$ to a preimage point (x, y) is $d = x - 3$. So the directed distance from the image point (x', y') to the line $x = 3$ is $x' - 3 = -d = 3 - x$. Hence $x' = 6 - x$. So $(x', y') = (6 - x, y)$.

 b. Sample: Let the relation be a circle centered at $(0, 0)$ with radius 1. This circle has equation $x^2 + y^2 = 1$. The reflection image of the circle over the line $x = 3$ has equation $(6 - x)^2 + y^2 = (x - 6)^2 + y^2 = 1$, which is a circle centered at $(6, 0)$ with radius 1. Thus the preimage is a circle centered 3 units to the left of the reflecting line, while the image is a congruent circle centered 3 units to the right of the reflecting line.

Section 7.3.1

1. If the two circles have different centers and different radii, then there is only one symmetry line, viz., the line joining their centers. If the two circles have different centers and the same radius, then there are two lines of symmetry: the line joining their centers and the perpendicular bisector of this line. If the two circles have the same center, then every line passing through this center is a symmetry line.

2.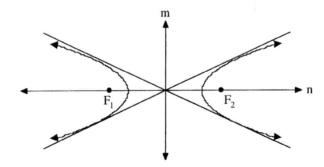

Let n pass through foci F_1 and F_2 of hyperbola H. Let P be any point on H. So $|PF_1 - PF_2| = k$. We wish to show that $P' = r_n(P)$ is on H. Since n contains F_1 and F_2, $r_n(F_1) = F_1$ and $r_n(F_2) = F_2$. Since reflections preserve distance, $P'F_1 = PF_1$ and $P'F_2 = PF_2$. So $|P'F_1 - P'F_2| = |PF_1 - PF_2| = k$. Consequently, P' is on H. Thus $r_n(H) \subset H$, and, by Theorem 7.25, H is symmetric with respect to n.

Now let m be the perpendicular bisector of $\overline{F_1F_2}$, let Q be any point on H, and let $Q' = r_m(Q)$. By the definition of reflection, $r_m(F_1) = F_2$ and $r_m(F_2) = F_1$. Since reflections preserve distance, $Q'F_1 = QF_2$ and $Q'F_2 = QF_1$. So $|Q'F_1 - Q'F_2| = |QF_1 - QF_2| = k$. So Q' is on the hyperbola, and using the same argument as before, from this H is symmetric with respect to m.

3.

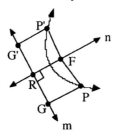

Let n be a line perpendicular to the directrix m that passes through the focus F and let n intersect m at point R. If P is a point on the parabola, then PF = PG, where G is the point of intersection of m and the line perpendicular to m passing through P. Let $P' = r_n(P)$ and $G' = r_n(G)$. Since F is on n, $r_n(F) = F$, and, since reflections are distance preserving, PF = P'F and PG = P'G'. So P'F = P'G'. It remains to be shown that P'G' is the distance from P' to line m. Since R is on n, $r_n(R) = R$. So $r_n(\angle PGR) = \angle P'G'R$. By Corollary 2 to Theorem 7.8, then, $m\angle PGR = m\angle P'G'R$. Thus $\angle P'G'R$ is a right angle. Since G' is on m, P'G' is the distance from P' to line m. Thus for any point P on the parabola, $r_n(P)$ is also on the parabola. So n is a line of symmetry.

4. An equilateral triangle can be viewed as an isosceles triangle with three different vertex angles. So, by Theorem 7.30, an equilateral triangle is symmetric to the three distinct lines bisecting the three vertex angles.

5. Let $\triangle ABC$ be isosceles with AB = AC. Let line m be the bisector of the vertex angle of $\triangle ABC$. Suppose m intersects base $\overline{BC}$ at point Q. By Theorem 7.30, $\triangle ABC$ is symmetric to m, so $r_m(\angle BQA) = \angle CQA$. Because $\angle BQA$ and $\angle CQA$ are both congruent and supplementary, they are right angles. Because m is a line perpendicular to the base that passes through the opposite vertex, it is an altitude of $\triangle ABC$. By symmetry, we also have $r_m(\overline{BQ}) = \overline{CQ}$, which means BQ = CQ. Thus line m is a bisector of $\overline{BC}$. Because m is bisector of a base that passes through the opposite vertex, it is a median of $\triangle ABC$. Finally, because m is both perpendicular to and a bisector of $\overline{BC}$, it is a perpendicular bisector.

6. We know that $r_m(F \cap m) = r_m(F) \cap r_m(m)$. By the definition of reflection, $r_m(m) = m$. So $r_m(F \cap m) = r_m(F) \cap m$. For any $P \in (F \cap m)$, $P \in m$. So $r_m(P) = P$, or $r_m(F \cap m) = F \cap m$. Therefore $F \cap m = r_m(F) \cap m$.

7.

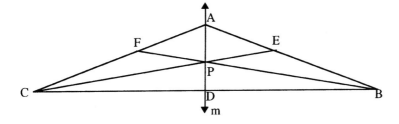

Let $\triangle ABC$ be isosceles with AB = AC. Let line m be the bisector of $\angle CAB$. By the corollary to Theorem 7.29, then, line m is also a median of $\triangle ABC$. By Theorem 7.30, $\triangle ABC$ is symmetric with respect to m. Let $\overline{BF}$ be a median to side $\overline{AC}$. Since F is the midpoint of $\overline{AC}$, E = r_m(F) is the midpoint of $\overline{AD}$. Thus $\overline{CE}$ = $r_m(\overline{BF})$ is the median to side $\overline{AB}$. Let P be the point of intersection of line m and $\overline{BF}$, i.e., P = m ∩ $\overline{BF}$. Let P′ be the point of intersection of line m and $\overline{CE}$, i.e., P′ = m ∩ $\overline{CE}$ = m ∩ $r_m(\overline{BF})$. By Problem 6, m ∩ $\overline{BF}$ = m ∩ $r_m(\overline{BF})$. So P = P′ and the medians are concurrent.

8. As was shown in the text, F must be on the line of symmetry. Also, the line of symmetry is the perpendicular bisector of $\overline{DE}$, so r(D) = E. Thus r($\overline{DF}$) = $\overline{EF}$ and DF = EF.

9.

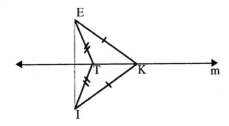

Theorem 7.31 does hold for nonconvex kites. Consider the nonconvex kite KITE. Let line m be the perpendicular bisector of $\overline{EI}$. Since triangles $\triangle ETI$ and $\triangle EKI$ are isosceles, by the corollary to Theorem 7.30, line m is the bisector of vertex angles T and K. By Theorem 7.30, $r_m(\triangle ETI) = \triangle ETI$ and $r_m(\triangle EKI) = \triangle EKI$. So we have

r_m(KITE) = r_m(($\triangle ETI \cup \triangle EKI) - \overline{EI}$)) = ($r_m(\triangle ETI) \cup r_m(\triangle EKI)) - r_m(\overline{EI})$

= ($\triangle ETI \cup \triangle EKI) - \overline{EI}$ = KITE.

10. Let the relation R(x, y) be an equation or inequality describing the set of points.
    a. For its graph to be reflection symmetric with respect to the x-axis, R(x, y) = R(x, -y). So replacing y by -y yields the same equation or inequality.
    b. For its graph to be reflection symmetric with respect to the y-axis, R(x, y) = R(-x, y). So replacing x by -x yields the same equation or inequality.
    c. For its graph to be reflection symmetric with respect to the x-axis, R(x, y) = R(-y, -x). So replacing x by -y and y by -x yields the same equation or inequality.
    d. For its graph to be reflection symmetric with respect to the x-axis, R(10 – k, y) = R(10 + k, y). Letting x = 10 – k, R(x, y) = R(20 – x, y). So replacing x by 20 – x yields the same equation or inequality.
    e. A reflection across the line x + 2y = 5 is equivalent to the transformation $T_{0,5/2} \circ R_{\varphi} \circ r_{y=0} \circ R_{-\varphi} \circ T_{0,-5/2}$, where $\varphi = \tan^{-1} -\frac{1}{2}$. The transformation $R_{\varphi} \circ r_{y=0} \circ R_{-\varphi}$ can be represented by the matrix

$$M = \begin{bmatrix} \cos\varphi & -\sin\varphi \\ \sin\varphi & \cos\varphi \end{bmatrix} \begin{bmatrix} 1 & 0 \\ 0 & -1 \end{bmatrix} \begin{bmatrix} \cos\text{-}\varphi & -\sin\text{-}\varphi \\ \sin\text{-}\varphi & \cos\text{-}\varphi \end{bmatrix} = \begin{bmatrix} \cos^2\varphi - \sin^2\varphi & 2\cos\varphi\sin\varphi \\ 2\cos\varphi\sin\varphi & \sin^2\varphi - \cos^2\varphi \end{bmatrix}$$

$= \begin{bmatrix} \frac{3}{5} & -\frac{4}{5} \\ -\frac{4}{5} & -\frac{3}{5} \end{bmatrix}$. Applying the first translation yields $T_{0,-5/2}(x, y) = (x, y - \frac{5}{2})$. Applying the

transformation represented by M yields $\begin{bmatrix} \frac{3}{5} & -\frac{4}{5} \\ -\frac{4}{5} & -\frac{3}{5} \end{bmatrix}\begin{bmatrix} x \\ y - \frac{5}{2} \end{bmatrix} = \begin{bmatrix} \frac{3}{5}x - \frac{4}{5}y + 2 \\ -\frac{4}{5}x - \frac{3}{5}y + \frac{3}{2} \end{bmatrix}$. Applying the final

translation yields $T_{0,5/2}(\frac{3}{5}x - \frac{4}{5}y + 2, -\frac{4}{5}x - \frac{3}{5}y + \frac{3}{2}) = (\frac{3}{5}x - \frac{4}{5}y + 2, -\frac{4}{5}x - \frac{3}{5}y + 4)$

So replacing x by $\frac{3}{5}x - \frac{4}{5}y + 2$ and y by $-\frac{4}{5}x - \frac{3}{5}y + 4$ yields the same equation or inequality.

f. A reflection across the line y = 4x − 3 is equivalent to the transformation
$T_{0,-3} \circ R_\varphi \circ r_{y=0} \circ R_{-\varphi} \circ T_{0,3}$, where $\varphi = \tan^{-1}4$. The transformation $R_\varphi \circ r_{y=0} \circ R_{-\varphi}$ can be represented

by the matrix $M = \begin{bmatrix} \cos\varphi & -\sin\varphi \\ \sin\varphi & \cos\varphi \end{bmatrix} \begin{bmatrix} 1 & 0 \\ 0 & -1 \end{bmatrix} \begin{bmatrix} \cos\text{-}\varphi & -\sin\text{-}\varphi \\ \sin\text{-}\varphi & \cos\text{-}\varphi \end{bmatrix} = \begin{bmatrix} \cos^2\varphi - \sin^2\varphi & 2\cos\varphi\sin\varphi \\ 2\cos\varphi\sin\varphi & \sin^2\varphi - \cos^2\varphi \end{bmatrix}$

$= \begin{bmatrix} -\frac{15}{17} & \frac{8}{17} \\ \frac{8}{17} & \frac{15}{17} \end{bmatrix}$. Applying the first translation yields $T_{0,-3}(x, y) = (x, y + 3)$. Applying the

transformation represented by M yields $\begin{bmatrix} -\frac{15}{17} & \frac{8}{17} \\ \frac{8}{17} & \frac{15}{17} \end{bmatrix}\begin{bmatrix} x \\ y + 3 \end{bmatrix} = \begin{bmatrix} -\frac{15}{17}x + \frac{8}{17}y + \frac{24}{17} \\ \frac{8}{17}x + \frac{15}{17}y + \frac{45}{17} \end{bmatrix}$. Applying the final

translation yields $T_{0,-3}(-\frac{15}{17}x + \frac{8}{17}y + \frac{24}{17}, \frac{8}{17}x + \frac{15}{17}y + \frac{45}{17}) = (-\frac{15}{17}x + \frac{8}{17}y + \frac{24}{17}, \frac{8}{17}x + \frac{15}{17}y$

$- \frac{6}{17})$. So replacing x by $-\frac{15}{17}x + \frac{8}{17}y + \frac{24}{17}$ and y by $\frac{8}{17}x + \frac{15}{17}y - \frac{6}{17}$ yields the same inequality.

11. By performing the translation $T_{h,k}$, where $h = \frac{b}{2a} = 1$ and $k = -\frac{b^2}{4a} + c = -13$, the graph of
$y = 3x^2 + 6x - 10$ can be mapped onto a congruent graph of the form $y' = 3x^2$. Since $y'(x) = 3x^2$ is an
even function, its graph is reflection-symmetric with respect to the line x = 0. Hence the graph of the
function $y = 3x^2 + 6x - 10$ is reflection-symmetric with respect to the line x = -1.

12. First, the identity element is a member of the set since I(F) = F. Suppose S_1, S_2, and S_3 are any three
elements in the set. Since $S_1(S_2(F)) = S_1(F) = F$, the set is closed under the operation of composition,.
The inverse of any element of the set is also in the set, since $F = I(F) = S_1^{-1}(S_1(F)) = S_1^{-1}(F)$. Finally,
the operation of composition is associative.

13. a. $y \in f(A \cup B) \Leftrightarrow$ for some $x \in A \cup B$, $y = f(x) \Leftrightarrow$ for some $x \in A$ or $x \in B$,
    $y = f(x) \Leftrightarrow y \in f(A)$ or $y \in f(B) \Leftrightarrow y \in f(A) \cup f(B)$. So $f(A \cup B) = f(A) \cup f(B)$.

    b. $y \in f(A \cap B) \Rightarrow y = f(x)$, for some $x \in A \cap B \Rightarrow y = f(x)$, for some $x \in A$ and
    $x \in B \Rightarrow y \in f(A)$ and $y \in f(B) \Rightarrow y \in f(A) \cap f(B)$; $y \in f(A) \cap f(B) \Rightarrow y \in f(A)$ and
    $y \in f(B) \Rightarrow y = f(x_1)$ and $y = f(x_2)$, for some $x_1 \in A$ and $x_2 \in B \Rightarrow$ (since f is 1-1, $x_1 = x_2$) for
    some $x_1 \in A \cap B$, $y = f(x_1) \Rightarrow y \in f(A \cap B)$. So $f(A) \cap f(B) = f(A \cap B)$.

Section 7.3.2

1. Sample:

2. Most crossword puzzles have 2-fold rotation symmetry.

3. An equilateral triangle is symmetric with respect to each of its three perpendicular bisectors (see Problem 4 of 6.3.1). The angle between any two of these symmetry lines is 60°, so the composition of two reflections is a rotation of 120°. Thus an equilateral triangle has 3-fold rotation symmetry.

4. Since a square is both a kite and a rectangle, it has a symmetry line containing one pair of vertices and a symmetry line that is the bisector of one pair of sides. The angle between these two symmetry lines is 45°, so the composition of these two reflections is a rotation of 90°. Thus a square has 4-fold rotation symmetry.

5. Suppose a quadrilateral ABCD has rotational symmetry. Then there is a rotation with nonzero magnitude such that either $R(\overline{AB}) = \overline{BC}$, $R(\overline{AB}) = \overline{CD}$, or $R(\overline{AB}) = \overline{DA}$. If $R(\overline{AB}) = \overline{BC}$, then $R(\overline{BC}) = \overline{CD}$, $R(\overline{CD}) = \overline{DA}$, and $R(\overline{DA}) = \overline{AB}$. Since R is an isometry, all four sides of the quadrilateral are congruent. Thus ABCD is a rhombus, which means ABCD is a parallelogram. Similarly, if $R(\overline{AB}) = \overline{DA}$, then ABCD is a rhombus. If $R(\overline{AB}) = \overline{CD}$, then $R(\overline{BC}) = \overline{DA}$. Thus opposite sides of the quadrilateral are congruent, and the quadrilateral is a parallelogram.

6. a. Many light bulbs are reflection-symmetric with respect to any plane passing through the bulb's center and base. Therefore they also have rotation symmetry. The rotation symmetry allows light to radiate equally in all directions.

    b. Viewed from above, many bathtubs have the same symmetry as a rectangle. The 2-fold rotation symmetry allows a person to lie in the bath in either direction.

    c. Many doorknobs have the same symmetry as light bulbs in part **a**. The rotation symmetry allows the knob to turned from any angle.

    d. Viewed from above, a 4-sided card table has the same symmetry as a square. The 4-fold rotation symmetry gives each of 4 players equal access to the table.

7. a. $T(x, y) = (x + 1, y + 1)$
    b. $\sqrt{((x+1) - x)^2 + ((y+1) - y)^2} = \sqrt{2}$

8. Sample: Translation symmetry: If (x, y) is on the graph, so is $(x + 4\pi, y)$. So $\sin(x + 4\pi) = \sin x$. Rotation symmetry about $(\pi, 0)$: If (x, y) is on the graph, so is $(2\pi - x, -y)$. So $-\sin x = \sin(2\pi - x)$. Reflection symmetry over $x = \frac{3\pi}{2}$: If (x, y) is on the graph, so is $(3\pi - x, y)$. So $\sin(3\pi - x) = \sin x$.
    Glide reflection symmetry: If (x, y) is on the graph, so is $(x - \pi, -y)$. So $\sin(x - \pi) = -\sin x$.

9. a. $\sin(n\pi + -x) = -\sin(n\pi + x)$, for all integers n

    b. $\sin((2n + 1)\frac{\pi}{2} + x) = \sin((2n + 1)\frac{\pi}{2} + -x)$, for all integers n

    c. $-\sin x = \sin(x + (2n + 1)\pi)$, for all integers n

10. Translation symmetry: When (x, y) is on the graph, so is (x + 2π, y). Thus $\cos(x + 2\pi) = \cos x$. Rotation symmetry about $(\frac{\pi}{2}, 0)$: When $(\frac{\pi}{2} + x, y)$ is on the graph, so is $(\frac{\pi}{2} - x, -y)$. Thus $\cos(\frac{\pi}{2} + x) = -\cos(\frac{\pi}{2} - x)$. Reflection symmetry over the line x = 0: When (x, y) is on the graph, so is (-x, y). Thus $\cos x = \cos -x$. Glide reflection symmetry: When (x, y) is on the graph, so is (x + π, -y). Thus $\cos(x - \pi) = -\cos x$.

11. Translation symmetry: When (x, y) is on the graph, so is (x + π, y). Thus $\tan(x - \pi) = \tan x$. Rotation symmetry about the point (0, 0): When (x, y) is on the graph, so is (-x, -y). Thus $\tan -x = -\tan x$. The tangent function has no reflection or glide reflection symmetry.

12. Because $\csc x = \frac{1}{\sin x}$, the cosecant function has the same symmetries as the sine function. See pp. 342-3.

13. a. 2-fold rotation symmetry about the point (0, 0)

    b. 2-fold rotation symmetry about the point (a, c)

    c. 2-fold rotation symmetry about the points (2nπ, 0) and translation symmetry

    d. reflection symmetry about the line $-\frac{b}{2a}$

    e. By performing the translation $T_{h,k}$, where $h = \frac{b}{3a}$ and $k = -\frac{2b^3}{27a^2} + \frac{cb}{3a} - d$, the graph of $k(x) = ax^3 + bx^2 + cx + d$ can be mapped onto a congruent graph of the form $k'(x) = ex^3 + fx$. Since $k'(x) = ex^3 + fx$ is an odd function, its graph has 2-fold rotation symmetry about the point (0, 0). Hence the graph of the function $k(x) = ax^3 + bx^2 + cx + d$ has 2-fold rotation symmetry about the point $(-\frac{b}{3a}, \frac{2b^3}{27a^2} - \frac{cb}{3a} + d)$.

Section 7.4.1

1.

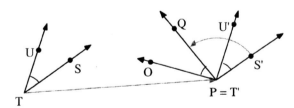

Let A be the translation associated with the vector $\overline{TP}$. This translation maps ∠STU onto angle ∠S′T′U′ = ∠S′PU′ of the same measure. Let R be the rotation with center P and magnitude m∠S′PQ. Because m∠STU = m∠QPO = m∠S′T′U′, R(∠S′T′U′) = ∠QPO. Thus R ∘ A(∠STU) = ∠QPO, and so ∠STU ≅ ∠QPO.

2.

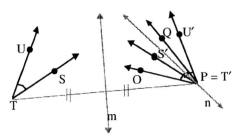

Let m be the perpendicular bisector of $\overline{TP}$. Then r_m maps $\angle STU$ onto angle $\angle S'T'U' = \angle S'PU'$ of the same measure. Let n be the bisector of $\angle S'PQ$. By Theorem 7.30, $r_n(\overrightarrow{PS'}) = \overrightarrow{PQ}$. Because $m\angle S'T'U' = m\angle QPO$, line n will also be the bisector of $\angle OPU'$. Thus $r_n(\overrightarrow{PU'}) = \overrightarrow{PO}$. So $r_n(\angle S'PU') = \angle QPO$. Thus $r_n \circ r_m(\angle STU) = \angle QPO$, and so $\angle STU \cong \angle QPO$.

3.   Line n is the bisector of $\angle ZXC'$.

4.   Proof 3: Consider $\triangle ABC$ and $\triangle XYZ$ with $\overline{AB} \cong \overline{XY}$, $\angle CAB \cong \angle ZYX$, and $\angle ABC \cong \angle XYZ$. Because $\overline{AB} \cong \overline{XY}$, there is a congruence transformation T that maps $\overline{AB}$ onto $\overline{XY}$ such that T(A) = X and T(B) = Y. Apply T to $\triangle ABC$. There are two possible cases: (1) T(C) and Z are on the same side of $T(\overleftrightarrow{AB})$, or (2) T(C) and Z are on opposite sides of $T(\overleftrightarrow{AB})$. Case (1): Because T(A) = X and T(B) = Y, $T(\overrightarrow{AB}) = \overrightarrow{XY}$ and $T(\overrightarrow{BA}) = \overrightarrow{YX}$. Because $T(\angle CAB) \cong \angle ZYX$ and $T(\angle ABC) \cong \angle XYZ$, $T(\overrightarrow{AC}) = \overrightarrow{XZ}$ and $T(\overrightarrow{BC}) = \overrightarrow{YZ}$. And since two distinct lines can intersect in at most one point, T(C) = Z. Thus $T(\triangle ABC) = \triangle XYZ$. Case (2): If T(C) and Z are on opposite sides of $T(\overleftrightarrow{AB})$, then reflect $T(\triangle ABC)$ over $\overleftrightarrow{AB}$. Then the same argument can be made for $r \circ T(\triangle ABC)$ that was made for $T(\triangle ABC)$ in case (1).

5.   Label the triangles $\triangle ABC$ and $\triangle DEF$. ($\triangle ABC$ counterclockwise with A at left; $\triangle DEF$ clockwise with D at right). Let ℓ be $\overleftrightarrow{AB}$. Let m be the perpendicular bisector of $\overline{AD}$. Let $\triangle A''B''C'' = r_m \circ r_\ell(\triangle ABC)$. Then if n is the perpendicular bisector of $\overline{B''E}$, $r_n \circ r_m \circ r_\ell(\triangle ABC) = \triangle DEF$.

6.   This is an instance of the so-called ambiguous case of SSA. From the Law of Cosines, $10^2 + x^2 - 2 \cdot 10 \cdot x \cos 30° = 6^2$, where x is the length of $\overline{BC}$. Simplifying yields $x^2 - 10\sqrt{3}x + 64 = 0$. Solving for x yields $x = 5\sqrt{3} \pm \sqrt{11}$. So $BC \approx 12$ or $BC \approx 5.3$. From the Law of Sines, $\frac{6}{\sin 30°} = \frac{10}{\sin\theta}$, where $\theta = m\angle BCA$. Solving for θ yields $\sin^{-1}\theta = \frac{5}{6}$. So $m\angle BCA \approx 56.4°$ or $m\angle BCA \approx 123.6°$. Finally, $m\angle BAC = 180° - (m\angle BCA + m\angle ABC)$. So $m\angle BAC \approx 93.6°$ or $m\angle BAC \approx 26.4°$.

7.   a.   When $XZ < XY$, $\overrightarrow{ZY}$ intersects the circle in exactly one point, so r(B') is necessarily equal to Y. If $XZ > XY$, then $\overrightarrow{ZY}$ would intersect the circle in two points. If this were the case, r(B') would not necessarily equal Y.

       b.   The argument would still work if $XZ = XY$. Even though $\overrightarrow{ZY}$ would intersect the circle at two points, one of the points can be excluded, since it lies on $\overleftrightarrow{XZ}$ and thus violates the condition that points X, Y, and Z form a triangle.

8.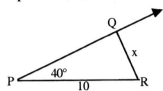

   a. No triangle is possible when x is less than value it has when $\overline{RQ} \perp \overrightarrow{PQ}$, or $x < 10\sin 40° \approx 6.4$.

   b. By the SsA Congruence Theorem, if $x = 10\sin 40°$ or if $x \geq 10$, then all possible triangles are congruent.

   c. Following from part **b**, if $10\sin 40° < x < 10$, then there exist non-congruent triangles.

   d. For a given value of x in the range $10\sin 40° < x < 10$, there exist two non-congruent triangles, one in which $\angle R$ is acute and one in which $\angle R$ is obtuse.

9. The assertion is false. Consider the following counterexample. As long as x > y, the quadrilaterals are not congruent.

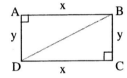 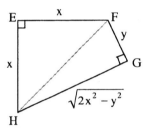

Section 7.4.2

1. a. A = cyclic quadrilaterals, B = trapezoids, C = kites, D = isosceles trapezoids, E = parallelograms, F = rhombi, G = rectangles, H = squares

   b.

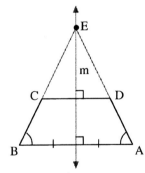 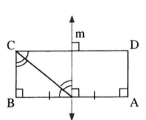

   Let isosceles trapezoid ABCD have bases $\overline{AB}$ and $\overline{CD}$, and let base angles $\angle DAB \cong \angle CBA$ be acute. Since $\overleftrightarrow{AD}$ and $\overleftrightarrow{BC}$ are not parallel, they will meet at some point E, to form isosceles $\triangle AEB$. Since $\overline{DC} \text{//} \overline{AB}$, by the Parallel Postulate, $\angle EDC \cong \angle DAB$ and $\angle ECD \cong \angle CBA$. So

∠EDC ≅ ∠ECD and ΔDEC is also isosceles. Let line m be the bisector of ∠AEB. By Theorem 7.29, ΔAEB and ΔDEC are both symmetric to line m. Thus r_m(A) = B and r_m(D) = C and ABCD is symmetric to m. Since trapezoids can include parallelograms, we must also consider the case when ∠DAB and ∠CBA are congruent to a right angle. Since $\overline{DC} // \overline{AB}$, by the Parallel Postulate, ∠DCB and ∠CDA are also right angles. We can show, by ASA congruence, that if line m is the perpendicular bisector of $\overline{AB}$, then it is also the perpendicular bisector of $\overline{CD}$. Thus m is a symmetry line of isosceles trapezoid ABCD.

   c.   Squares and rectangles are special types of isosceles trapezoids. So they must also have a symmetry line. Moreover, since squares and rectangles are isosceles trapezoids with either pair of opposite sides as bases, they must have at least two lines of symmetry.

   d.

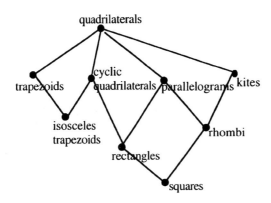

If *trapezoid* is defined to be a quadrilateral with exactly one pair of parallel sides, then the quadrilateral hierarchy would look like the tree above, and rectangles and squares would no longer be considered special types of isosceles trapezoids.

2.   No, it is not possible. If adjacent triangles are congruent, then the trapezoid is a square. If top and bottom triangles are congruent, then the trapezoid is a parallelogram. If the side triangles are congruent, then the trapezoid is either a parallelogram or an isosceles trapezoid.

3.   a.   The perpendicular bisector of a side of a cyclic quadrilateral contains all the points in the plane that are equidistant from the two endpoints of that side. Since the center of the circle is equidistant from all the points on the circle, it must lie on the perpendicular bisectors of all four of the quadrilateral's sides. Thus the perpendicular bisectors are all concurrent at the circle's center.

   b.   Consider a cyclic quadrilateral ABCD inscribed in a circle. The inscribed angle ∠ADC has half the measure of arc $\overset{\frown}{ABC}$ and the opposite inscribed angle ∠ABC has half the measure of arc $\overset{\frown}{ADC}$. Since m $\overset{\frown}{ABC}$ + m $\overset{\frown}{ADC}$ = 2π, ∠ADC + m∠ABC = π. Thus opposite angles in a cyclic quadrilateral are supplementary.

   c.   Due to the reflection symmetry of an isosceles trapezoid, the top and bottom bases share the same perpendicular bisector, which intersects the perpendicular bisectors of the other two sides at a common point. This point is then equidistant from the trapezoid's four vertices and so these vertices lie on a common circle.

   d.   We prove the contrapositive of the statement. Consider a noncyclic quadrilateral ABCD.

Three points determine a unique circle, so let vertices A, B, and C lie on circle O. However, because the quadrilateral is noncyclic, vertex D does not lie on circle O. So either vertex D lies inside circle O or it lies outside circle O. Suppose it lies inside the circle. Extend side $\overline{CD}$ so that it intersects circle O at point E. Quadrilateral ABCE is cyclic, so by part **b**, ∠AEC is supplementary to ∠ABC. By the Exterior Angle Theorem, m∠ADC > ∠AEC. So ∠ADC cannot be supplementary to ∠ABC. A similar argument can be used if vertex D lies outside circle O.

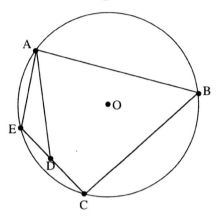

4. Let the cyclic quadrilateral be rectangle ABCD. Then AC = BD, AB = CD, and BC = AD. From Ptolemy's Theorem, AC • AC = BC • BC + AB • AB, which is the Pythagorean Theorem.

5. b. For a rectangle, a = c and b = d, so
$$\frac{\sqrt{(ab + cd)(ac + bd)(ad + bc)}}{4R} = \frac{\sqrt{(2ab)(a^2 + b^2)(2ab)}}{4R} = ab\frac{\sqrt{a^2 + b^2}}{2R}.$$ The diagonal of a rectangle inscribed in a circle is also a diameter of the circle, so $\sqrt{a^2 + b^2} = 2R$. Thus the area of a rectangle is ab.

6. a.

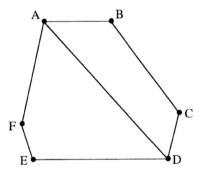

Sample: Opposite angles are congruent. Consider parallexagon ABCDEF. Since $\overleftrightarrow{AB} /\!/ \overleftrightarrow{ED}$ and $\overleftrightarrow{AF} /\!/ \overleftrightarrow{CD}$, by the Parallel Postulate, ∠BAD ≅ ∠ADE and ∠FAD ≅ ∠ADC. Thus ∠FAB ≅ ∠EDC.

b.

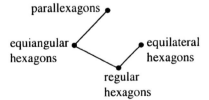

7. a. If z is the side opposite the 60° angle, then from the Law of Cosines, $z^2 = x^2 + y^2 - xy$.

   b. Sample: The area A of the triangle is given by $A = \frac{\sqrt{3}}{4}xy$.

8. a. If z is the side opposite the 120° angle, then from the Law of Cosines, $z^2 = x^2 + y^2 + xy$.

   b. Sample: The area A of the triangle is given by $A = \frac{\sqrt{3}}{4}xy$.

9. By symmetry and the fact that $m\angle\alpha = m\angle\beta$, the quadrilateral has four equal sides. The quadrilateral also has four right angles.

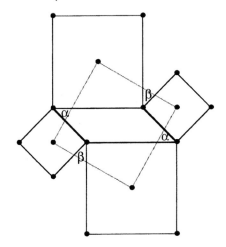

10. a. Napoleon's Theorem states the following: The three centroids of the equilateral triangles formed from the sides of any $\triangle ABC$ are at the vertices of an equilateral triangle, $\triangle C_1C_2C_3$.

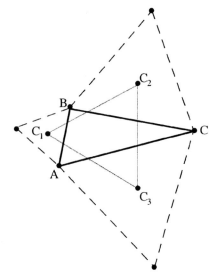

   b. For any $\triangle ABC$, the line m that connects the triangle's centroid G to the triangle's circumcenter O is the triangle's Euler line m. The triangle's orthocenter, nine-point center, and DeLongchamps point all fall on the Euler line in such a way that when you vary $\triangle ABC$, the relative distances between these points and G and O remain the same.

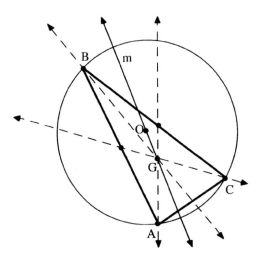

c.   Form the three escribed circles of any ΔABC. These are the circles tangent to one side of the triangle and to the extensions of the other two sides. Let these circles be tangent to the triangle at points E, F, and G. Then the segments $\overline{AG}$, $\overline{BE}$, and $\overline{CF}$ coincide at the Nagel point N of the triangle.

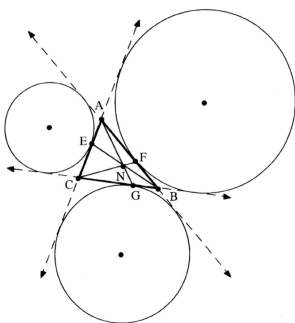

11.   Answers will vary.

12.   Answers will vary.

13.   Answers will vary.

Section 7.4.3

1.   Consider a right triangle with vertices $(0, 0)$, $(a, 0)$, and $(0, b)$. The hypotenuse of the triangle has equation $y = -\frac{b}{a}x + b$. The perpendicular bisector of one side of the triangle has equation $y = \frac{b}{2}$.

Solving the system $\begin{cases} y = -\frac{b}{a}x + b \\ y = \frac{b}{2} \end{cases}$ to find the point of intersection yields $(\frac{a}{2}, \frac{b}{2})$, which is the midpoint

of the hypotenuse.

2. Sample: Any line parallel to the base of a triangle and bisecting one side, bisects the other side.
Proof: Let line m be parallel to base $\overline{BC}$ and bisect $\overline{AB}$ of $\triangle ABC$. Construct the altitude $\overline{AD}$ from vertex A to $\overleftrightarrow{BC}$. Since m is parallel to $\overleftrightarrow{BC}$ and $\overline{AD}$ is perpendicular to $\overleftrightarrow{BC}$, m is perpendicular to $\overline{AD}$. Because there is a unique line that is perpendicular to a given line and that contains a given point, if m contains the midpoint of hypotenuse of $\triangle ABD$ and is perpendicular to leg $\overline{AD}$, by Theorem 7.41, m is the perpendicular bisector of leg $\overline{AD}$. Since m is the perpendicular bisector of $\overline{AD}$, by Theorem 7.41, m bisects hypotenuse $\overline{AC}$ of $\triangle ACD$.

3. Viewed as rotation images of each other, the image of point A = (0, 0) is A′ = (0, 3) and the image of B = (2, 4) is B′ = (4, 1). The center of rotation is the intersection of the perpendicular bisectors of $\overline{AA'}$ and $\overline{BB'}$. The line $\overleftrightarrow{AA'}$ is given by equation x = 0 and the midpoint of $\overline{AA'}$ is $(0, \frac{3}{2})$. The line $\overleftrightarrow{BB'}$ is given by equation $y = -\frac{3}{2}x + 7$ and the midpoint of $\overline{BB'}$ is $(3, \frac{5}{2})$. So the equations for the perpendicular bisectors of $\overline{AA'}$ and $\overline{BB'}$ are $y = \frac{3}{2}$ and $y = \frac{2}{3}x + \frac{1}{2}$, respectively. The center of rotation is thus $(\frac{3}{2}, \frac{3}{2})$.

4. Answers will vary.

5. Point D is the image of B, E is the image of C, and F is the image of A. The glide reflecting line is the line passing through the midpoints of all segments connecting corresponding points on $\triangle ABC$ and $\triangle DEF$. The midpoint of $\overline{DB}$ is $(\frac{11}{2}, 0)$ and the midpoint of $\overline{EC}$ is $(\frac{23}{2}, 6)$. The equation for the glide reflecting line is thus $y = x - \frac{11}{2}$.

CHAPTER 8 – Distance and Similarity

Section 8.1.1

1. Answers will vary. See the Instructor's Notes for one type of example.

2. $d_E = |x_1 - x_2|$

3. Let $P = (x_1, y_1)$, $Q = (x_2, y_2)$, and $R = (x_3, y_3)$. Then
    $d_T(P, Q) = |x_1 - x_2| + |y_1 - y_2|$.
    D1: Since both $|x_1 - x_2|$ and $|y_1 - y_2| \geq 0$, $d_T(P, Q) \geq 0$
    D2: Since $|x_1 - x_2| + |y_1 - y_2| = 0$ iff $|x_1 - x_2| = 0$ and $|y_1 - y_2| = 0$ iff
    $x_1 - x_2 = 0$ and $y_1 - y_2 = 0$ iff $x_1 = x_2$ and $y_1 = y_2$, $d_T(P, Q) = 0$ iff $P = Q$.
    D3: Since $|x_1 - x_2| = |x_2 - x_1|$ and $|y_1 - y_2| = |y_2 - y_1|$,
    $d_T(P, Q) = |x_1 - x_2| + |y_1 - y_2| = |x_2 - x_1| + |y_2 - y_1| = d_T(Q, P)$.
    D4: Since $|x_1 - x_2| + |x_2 - x_3| \geq |(x_1 - x_2) + (x_2 - x_3)| = |x_1 - x_3|$ and
    $|y_1 - y_2| + |y_2 - y_3| \geq |(y_1 - y_2) + (y_2 - y_3)| = |y_1 - y_3|$,
    $d_T(P, Q) + d_T(Q, R) = |x_1 - x_2| + |y_1 - y_2| + |x_2 - x_3| + |y_2 - y_3|$
    $= |x_1 - x_2| + |x_2 - x_3| + |y_1 - y_2| + |y_2 - y_3| \geq |x_1 - x_3| + |y_1 - y_3| = d_T(P, R)$.

4. Sample: With the taxicab metric, the set of points equidistant from the two points $(0, 0)$ and $(1, 1)$ is
    given by $|x| + |y| = |x - 1| + |y - 1|$. If $x \leq 0$, then $|y| = 1 + |y - 1|$, which has $y \geq 1$ as solutions. If
    $x \geq 1$, then $|y| = |y - 1| - 1$, which has $y \leq 0$ as solutions. If $0 < x < 1$, then $x + |y| = -(x - 1) + |y - 1|$,
    or $2x + |y| = 1 + |y - 1|$, which has the solutions of $x + y = 1$ for $0 < x < 1$ and $0 < y < 1$.

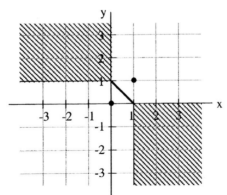

This shape is quite different from the shape of the set of points equidistant (under the taxicab metric)
from $(0, 0)$ and $(1, 0)$. Points (x, y) in that set satisfy $|x| + |y| = |x - 1| + |y|$, which implies that
$|x| = |x - 1|$, whose only solution is $x = 0.5$. Thus the set of points equidistant from $(0, 0)$ and $(1, 0)$
under the taxicab metric is the line $x = 0.5$, the same set of equidistant points under the Euclidean
metric.

5. Given points $P = (x_1, y_1)$ and $Q = (x_1, y_2)$, $d_T(P, Q) = |y_2 - y_1| + |x_2 - x_1|$. Let P' and Q' be the images of P and Q, respectively, when rotated about the origin by an angle θ. Then $P' = (x_1\cos\theta - y_1\sin\theta, x_1\sin\theta + y_1\cos\theta)$ and $Q' = (x_1\cos\theta - y_2\sin\theta, x_1\sin\theta + y_2\cos\theta)$. So $d_T(P', Q') = |-y_2\sin\theta + y_1\sin\theta| + |y_2\cos\theta - y_1\cos\theta| = (|\sin\theta| + |\cos\theta|)|y_2 - y_1|$. By the Triangle Inequality, $|\sin\theta| + |\cos\theta| \geq 1$, and $|\sin\theta| + |\cos\theta| = 1$ only when $\theta = n90°$, where n is an integer. So, all rotations other than those that are integer multiples of 90° will increase the taxicab distance of a vertical line segment.

6. a.

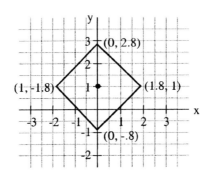

    b. A taxicab circle with center $P = (x, y)$ and radius r will be a Euclidean square with vertices $(x + r, y)$, $(x, y + r)$, $(x - r, y)$, and $(x, y - r)$. The slopes of the sides of the square will alternate between 1 and -1.

7. Sample: The two "taxicab circles" with centers (0, 0) and (1, 1) and radius 1 have the line segment from (1, 0) to (0, 1) in common.

8. a. $d_E(P, Q) = \sqrt[2]{|x_1 - x_2|^2 + |y_1 - y_2|^2}$, $p = 2$; $d_T(P, Q) = |x_1 - x_2|^1 + |y_1 - y_2|^1$, $p = 1$

    b. See Figure 4 in this section.

    c. For $p = 2$, the graph is a circle. As p increases, the graph becomes flatter on the top and bottom, approaching a square with vertices at (1, 1), (1, -1), (-1, -1), and (-1, 1).

    d. For $|x| = 1$ and $|y| < 1$, $\lim_{p\to\infty}(|x|^p + |y|^p) = \lim_{p\to\infty}|x|^p + \lim_{p\to\infty}|y|^p = 1 + 0 = 1$. Similarly, for $|x| < 1$ and $|y| = 1$, $\lim_{p\to\infty}(|x|^p + |y|^p) = \lim_{p\to\infty}|x|^p + \lim_{p\to\infty}|y|^p = 0 + 1 = 1$. For $|x| = 1$ and $|y| = 1$, $\lim_{p\to\infty}(|x|^p + |y|^p) = \lim_{p\to\infty}|x|^p + \lim_{p\to\infty}|y|^p = 1 + 1 = 2$. For $|x| < 1$ and $|y| < 1$, $\lim_{p\to\infty}(|x|^p + |y|^p) = \lim_{p\to\infty}|x|^p + \lim_{p\to\infty}|y|^p = 0 + 0 = 0$. And for $|x| > 1$ and $|y| > 1$, $\lim_{p\to\infty}(|x|^p + |y|^p) = \lim_{p\to\infty}|x|^p + \lim_{p\to\infty}|y|^p = \infty$. Thus $\lim_{p\to\infty}\{(x, y): |x|^p + |y|^p = 1\} = \{(x, y): (|x| = 1$ and $|y| < 1)$ or $(|x| < 1$ and $|y| = 1)\}$.

9. a. Geometrically, $d_M(P, Q)$ gives the length of the longest leg of the right triangle with vertices (x_1, y_1), (x_2, y_2), and (x_1, y_2).

    b. Let $R = (x_3, y_3)$ and, without loss of generality, assume $|x_1 - x_2| \geq |y_1 - y_2|$ and $|y_2 - y_3| \geq |x_2 - x_3|$, so $d_M(P, Q) = |x_1 - x_2|$ and $d_M(Q, R) = |y_2 - y_3|$. We have already shown (see Problem 8 of 7.1.1) that $|x_1 - x_2|$ satisfies the first three conditions of a metric. We also have $|x_1 - x_2| + |y_2 - y_3| \geq |x_1 - x_2| + |x_2 - x_3|$ and

$|x_1 - x_2| + |y_2 - y_3| \geq |y_1 - y_2| + |y_2 - y_3|$. But (from Problem 8 of 7.11) we know that

$|x_1 - x_2| + |x_2 - x_3| \geq |x_1 - x_3|$ and $|y_1 - y_2| + |y_2 - y_3| \geq |y_1 - y_3|$. So

$|x_1 - x_2| + |y_2 - y_3| \geq \max(|x_1 - x_3|, |y_1 - y_3|)$, or $d_M(P, Q) + d_M(Q, R) \geq d_M(P, R)$.

c.   Without loss of generality, assume $|x_1 - x_2| \geq |y_1 - y_2|$. Then

$$\lim_{p \to \infty} d_p(P, Q) = \lim_{p \to \infty} \sqrt[p]{|x_1 - x_2|^p + |y_1 - y_2|^p} = \lim_{p \to \infty} \sqrt[p]{|x_1 - x_2|^p \left(1 + \frac{|y_1 - y_2|^p}{|x_1 - x_2|^p}\right)}$$

$$= |x_1 - x_2| \lim_{p \to \infty} \sqrt[p]{\left(1 + \frac{|y_1 - y_2|^p}{|x_1 - x_2|^p}\right)}. \text{ Since, for all } p, \; 0 \leq \frac{|y_1 - y_2|^p}{|x_1 - x_2|^p} \leq 1, \; \lim_{p \to \infty} \sqrt[p]{\left(1 + \frac{|y_1 - y_2|^p}{|x_1 - x_2|^p}\right)} = 1. \text{ So}$$

$$|x_1 - x_2| \lim_{p \to \infty} \sqrt[p]{\left(1 + \frac{|y_1 - y_2|^p}{|x_1 - x_2|^p}\right)} = |x_1 - x_2|.$$

10.   Let $P = (a_1 a_2 \ldots a_n)$, $Q = (b_1 b_2 \ldots b_n)$, and $R = (c_1 c_2 \ldots c_n)$, where $a_j, b_j = 0$ or 1. Then
$d_H(P, Q) = |a_1 - b_1| + |a_2 - b_2| + \ldots + |a_n - b_n|$.

D1: Since $|a_j - b_j| \geq 0$ for all $1 \leq j \leq n$, $d_H(P, Q) \geq 0$

D2: Since $|a_1 - b_1| + |a_2 - b_2| + \ldots + |a_n - b_n| = 0$ iff $|a_j - b_j| = 0$ for all $1 \leq j \leq n$ iff

$a_j - b_j = 0$ for all $1 \leq j \leq n$ iff $a_j = b_j$ for all $1 \leq j \leq n$, $d_H(P, Q) = 0$ iff $P = Q$.

D3: Since $|a_j - b_j| = |b_j - a_j|$ for all $1 \leq j \leq n$,

$d_H(P, Q) = |a_1 - b_1| + |a_2 - b_2| + \ldots + |a_n - b_n| = |b_1 - a_1| + |b_2 - a_2| + \ldots + |b_n - a_n| = d_H(Q, P)$.

D4: Since $|a_j - b_j| + |b_j - c_j| \geq |(a_j - b_j) + (b_j - c_j)| = |a_j - c_j|$ for all $1 \leq j \leq n$ (see Problem 8 of 7.1.1),

$d_H(P, Q) + d_H(Q, R)$

$= |a_1 - b_1| + |a_2 - b_2| + \ldots + |a_n - b_n| + |b_1 - c_1| + |b_2 - c_2| + \ldots + |b_n - c_n|$

$= |a_1 - b_1| + |b_1 - c_1| + |a_2 - b_2| + |b_2 - c_2| \ldots + |a_n - b_n| + |b_n - c_n|$

$\geq |a_1 - c_1| + |a_2 - c_2| + \ldots + |a_n - c_n| = d_H(P, R)$.

11.

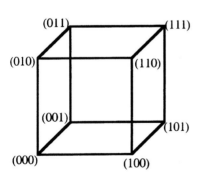

12.   a.   Think of r, s, r′, and s′ as naming points.

D1: $d_C(r, s) \geq 0$ because the length of the chord $\overline{r's'}$ is nonnegative.

D2: $d_C(r, s) = 0 \Leftrightarrow r' = s' \Leftrightarrow r = s$ because the correspondence is 1-1.

D3: $d_C(r, s) = r's' = s'r' = d_C(s, r)$

D4: Let t' be the point corresponding to $(t, 0)$.

$d_C(r, s) + d_C(s, t) \geq d_C(r, t) \Leftrightarrow r's' + s't' \geq r't'$, and the latter holds always because of the triangle inequality in d_E in the plane.

b. Think of r, s, r′, and s′ as naming points. Let the line parallel to $\overleftrightarrow{rs}$ through s′ intersect $\overleftrightarrow{rr'}$ at q. Since $\angle Cr's' \cong \angle Cs'r'$, $\angle s'rr'$ is obtuse. So $r's' < s'q$. By similar triangles, $\dfrac{Cs}{Cs'} = \dfrac{s'q}{sr}$, and since $Cs' < Cs$, then $s'q < sr$. So $r's' < rs$. That is, the chordal distance is always less than the usual distance function.

c. The maximum chordal distance between two points on the x-axis will occur in the limit as one point approaches $(\infty, 0)$ and the other $(-\infty, 0)$. The corresponding points on the semicircle will then approach $(1, 1)$ and $(-1, 1)$, and the length of the chord between these two points is just the length of the semicircle's diameter, 2.

Section 8.1.2

1. a. Let A be a point in the interior of a circle with center O. The shortest distance between A and the circle is the length of the segment $\overline{AP}$, where P is the point of intersection of the circle and the line $\overleftrightarrow{OA}$ such that A is between O and P. The length of $\overline{AP}$ is R – AO, where R is the radius of the circle. If A is at the center of the circle, then every point on the circle is equidistant from A and the shortest distance is R.

Proof: Let A be a point in the interior of circle O, let P be the point on the circle and on the radius passing through A. We want to show that for any other point R on the circle AR > AP. By the Triangle Inequality, we have AO + AR > RO. Since RO = PO, RO = AO + AP. Thus AO + AR > AO + AP. So AR > AP.

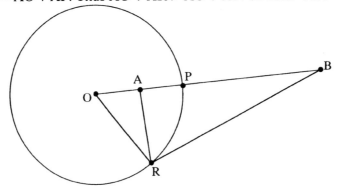

b. Let B be a point in the exterior of a circle with center O. The shortest distance between B and the circle is the length of the segment $\overline{BP}$, where P is the point of intersection of the circle and the line $\overleftrightarrow{OB}$ such that P is between O and B. The length of $\overline{BP}$ is BO – R, where R is the radius of the circle.

Proof: Let B be a point in the exterior of circle O, let P be the point on the circle and on the radius passing through B. We want to show that for any other point R on the circle, BR > BP. By the Triangle Inequality, we have BR + RO > BO. Since RO = PO,

BO = BP + RO. Thus BR + RO > BP + RO. So BR > BP.

c.   Since the point is on the circle, the shortest possible distance is the distance between the point and itself, which is 0.

2.   a.   If A is a point in the interior of a sphere with center O, then the shortest distance between A and the sphere is the length of the segment $\overline{AP}$, where P is the point of intersection of the sphere and the line $\overleftrightarrow{OA}$ such that A is between O and P. If A is at the center of the sphere, then every point on the sphere is equidistant from A and the shortest distance is the radius of the sphere. If B is a point in the exterior of a sphere with center O, then the shortest distance between B and the sphere is the length of the segment $\overline{BP}$, where P is the point of intersection of the sphere and the line $\overleftrightarrow{OB}$ such that P is between O and B.

b.   Given a sphere S with center O and a plane M that does not intersect S, let ℓ be the line perpendicular to M that passes through O. The shortest distance between M and S is the length of the segment $\overline{XY}$, where X is the point of intersection of ℓ and M and Y is the point of intersection of ℓ and S that is between X and O.

c.   Consider two circles with centers A and B. If circle B is interior to circle A, but not concentric with A, then the shortest distance from circle A to circle B is the length of segment $\overline{XY}$, where X and Y are the points of intersection of $\overleftrightarrow{AB}$ with circles B and A, respectively, such that B is between A and X and B is between A and Y. Segment $\overline{XY}$ has length $R_A - (R_B + AB)$.

Proof: Suppose P and Q are points on circles B and A, respectively. Then, from the Triangle Inequality, $PQ + BP \geq BQ$ and $AB + BQ \geq AQ$. We also have AQ = AY, BP = BX, and XY = AY − (BX + AB). So
$PQ \geq BQ − BP = BQ − BX \geq (AQ − AB) − BX = AY − (BX + AB) = XY.$

Thus XY is the shortest distance from circle B to circle A.

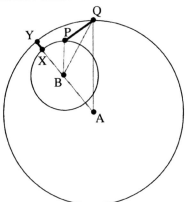

If circle B is exterior to circle A, then the shortest distance from circle A to circle B is the length of segment $\overline{XY}$, where X and Y are the points of intersection of $\overleftrightarrow{AB}$ with circles B and A, respectively, such that X and Y are between B and A.   Segment $\overline{XY}$ has length $AB − (R_A + R_B)$.

Proof: Suppose P and Q are points on circles B and A, respectively. Then, from the Triangle Inequality, $PQ + AQ \geq AP$ and $BP + AP \geq AB$. We also have AQ = AY, BP = BX, and XY = AB − (BX + AY). So

$PQ \geq AP - AQ = AP - AY \geq (AB - AP) - AY = AB - (BX + AY) = XY$.

Thus XY is the shortest distance from circle B to circle A.

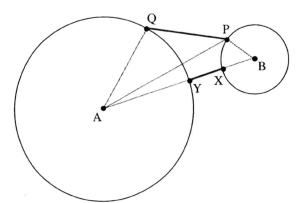

If the two circles are concentric, then the shortest distance is $R_A - R_B$. If the two circles are tangent or intersect at two points, then the shortest distance is 0. The shortest distance between two spheres is the same as for two circles.

3.   By the Pythagorean Theorem, for any other point Q′ on ℓ, the Euclidean distance is given by

$PQ' = \sqrt{(PQ)^2 + (QQ')^2} > \sqrt{PQ^2} = PQ$. Thus PQ is the shortest distance from point P to line ℓ.

4.

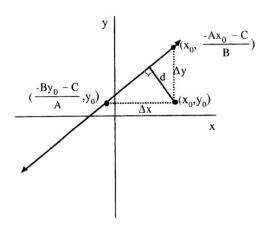

For the case when $A \neq 0$ and $B \neq 0$, the line $Ax + By + C = 0$ will pass through points

$(\frac{-By_0 - C}{A}, y_0)$ and $(x_0, \frac{-Ax_0 - C}{B})$. Then $\Delta x = \left| \frac{-By_0 - C}{A} - x_0 \right| = \left| \frac{Ax_0 + By_0 + C}{A} \right|$ and

$\Delta y = \left| \frac{-Ax_0 - C}{B} - y_0 \right| = \left| \frac{Ax_0 + By_0 + C}{B} \right|$. From similar triangles, $\frac{d}{\Delta y} = \frac{\Delta x}{\sqrt{\Delta x^2 + \Delta y^2}}$. So $d = \frac{\Delta x \Delta y}{\sqrt{\Delta x^2 + \Delta y^2}}$.

Since $\Delta x \Delta y = \frac{\left| Ax_0 + By_0 + C \right|^2}{|AB|}$ and $\sqrt{\Delta x^2 + \Delta y^2} = \frac{\left| Ax_0 + By_0 + C \right|}{|AB|} \sqrt{A^2 + B^2}$, $d = \frac{\left| Ax_0 + By_0 + C \right|}{\sqrt{A^2 + B^2}}$

5.   The reflection image of (8, 5) over the x-axis is (8, -5). The Euclidean distance from (-1, 7) to (8, -5) is

$d_E = \sqrt{(8 - -1)^2 + (-5 - 7)^2} = 15$.

6. a. Let $\overline{BB'}$ intersect ℓ at point E. Then $\triangle BEC \cong \triangle B'EC$. So m$\angle$EC = m$\angle$ECB'. Since $\angle$ECB' and $\angle$C'CA are vertical angles, m$\angle$ECB = m$\angle$C'CA. Since $\overrightarrow{CD} \perp \ell$, m$\angle$ECD = m$\angle$C'CD = 90°. Thus m$\angle$ACD = m$\angle$C'CD – m$\angle$C'CA = m$\angle$ECD – m$\angle$ECB = m$\angle$DCB. The angles of incidence and reflection are therefore of equal measure.

    b. The line connecting A = (0, 4) and B' = (6, -2) has equation y = -x + 4. This intersects the x-axis at (4, 0). Thus C = (4, 0).

7. Answers will vary.

8. Given $\triangle$ABC, we can construct the exterior equilateral triangles $\triangle$ABC', $\triangle$AB'C, and $\triangle$A'BC. The point of intersection of the three lines $\overleftrightarrow{AA'}$, $\overrightarrow{BB'}$, and $\overleftrightarrow{CC'}$ is the Fermat point for $\triangle$ABC.

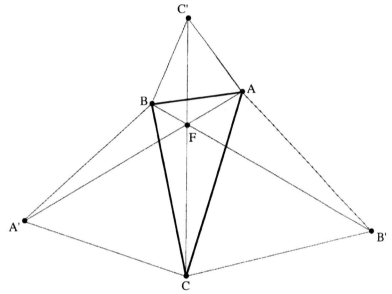

9. a. If m$\angle$ABC > 120°, then m$\angle$ABC + m$\angle$ABC' = m$\angle$ABC + 60° > 180°. Thus $\overline{CC'}$ cannot pass through $\triangle$ABC.

    b. As long as m$\angle$ABC < 120° and m$\angle$BAC < 120°, $\overline{CC'}$ passes through $\triangle$ABC, and as long as m$\angle$BCA < 120°, the circle through A, B, and C' lies inside $\triangle$ABC. Thus, if m$\angle$ABC < 120°, m$\angle$BAC < 120°, and as m$\angle$BCA < 120°, the constructed point P lies inside $\triangle$ABC.

    c. For m$\angle$ABC $\geq$ 120°, the Fermat point is vertex B.

10. Construct external equilateral triangles ACB' and BCA', where B' = $(\frac{3}{2}, \frac{3\sqrt{3}}{2})$ and A' = $(-2\sqrt{3}, 2)$. Then the line $\overleftrightarrow{AA'}$ has equation y = $\frac{-2}{3 + 2\sqrt{3}}$x + $\frac{6}{3 + 2\sqrt{3}}$ and the line $\overleftrightarrow{BB'}$ has equation y = $\frac{-3\sqrt{3} - 8}{3}$x + 4. These lines intersect at the point P = $(\frac{384 - 138\sqrt{3}}{193}, \frac{162 - 16\sqrt{3}}{193})$, which is the Fermat point. The sum of the distances from the three vertices to the Fermat point is given by AP + BP + CP $\approx$ 6.766.

11. From the solution to the Fermat point problem in the section, we know that on each of $\overline{AA'}$, $\overline{BB'}$, and $\overline{CC'}$ there exists a point from which each of the three sides of the triangle subtends a 120° angle. If we can show that only one such point exists (i.e., that the Fermat point is unique), then we will have shown that $\overline{AA'}$, $\overline{BB'}$, and $\overline{CC'}$ are concurrent. Let P be the Fermat point of ΔABC as given by the solution to the problem in the section. Then m∠BPA = m∠APC = m∠BPC = 120°. Assume that there exists another point Q inside ΔABC such that m∠BQA = m∠AQC = m∠BQC = 120° (i. e. that Q is also a Fermat point of ΔABC). Then Q must be either in or on the edge of one of the three triangular regions formed

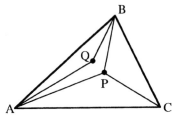

by connecting the vertices of ΔABC to P. Without loss of generality, assume that Q is in ΔAPB. Then m∠PBA > m∠QBA and m∠PAB > m∠QAB. Then

180° = m∠QBA + m∠QAB + m∠BQA = m∠PBA + m∠PAB + m∠BPA

⇒ m∠PBA + m∠PAB + m∠BQA > m∠PBA + m∠PAB + m∠BPA ⇒ m∠BQA > m∠BPA = 120°,

a contradiction. A similar argument produces the same contradiction if Q is on one of the segments from the vertices of ΔABC to P. Thus, since the Fermat point is unique, $\overline{AA'}$, $\overline{BB'}$, and $\overline{CC'}$ are concurrent.

12. a. The Tri-Cities Regional Airport is about 1.5 miles from the Fermat point of the triangle determined by Kingsport, Johnson City, and Bristol. The sum of the distances from the three cities to the airport is about 36.7 miles, whereas the sum of the distances from the three cities to the Fermat point is about 36.6 miles.

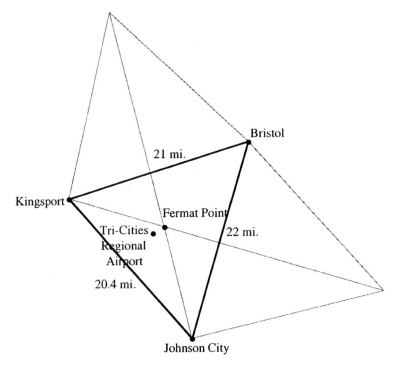

b.   The Tri-City Airport is about 5.4 miles from the Fermat point of the triangle determined by Midland, Bay City, and Saginaw. The sum of the distances from the three cities to the airport is about 30.4 miles, whereas the sum of the distances from the three cities to the Fermat point is about 28.1 miles.

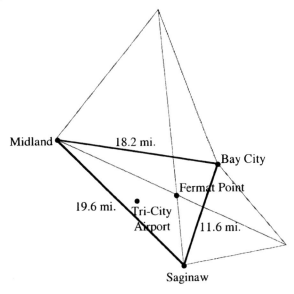

13.   a.   By the definition of Fermat point, PA + PB + PC < AA + AB + AC. Since AA = 0, PA + PB + PC < AB + AC.

b.   Since ABCD is a square AE = BE = CE = DE = $\frac{\sqrt{2}}{2}$s, where s is the length of a side of the square. So AE + BE + CE + DE = $2\sqrt{2}$ s and AB + BC + CD = 3s. Since $3 > 2\sqrt{2}$, So AE + BE + CE + DE < AB + BC + CD.

c.   The diagonals of square ABCD intersect at the midpoint of segment $\overline{EF}$. Let this point be M. By part **a**, EA + ED + EM < AM + DM and FB + FC + FM < BM + CM. Thus EA + ED + EM + FB + FC + FM = EA + ED + FB + FC + EF < AM + DM + BM + CM = AC + BD.

d.   For a rectangle of length ℓ and width w, where $\ell \geq w$, the sum of the lengths of the pictured interior segments is less than the sum of the lengths of the rectangle's diagonals. The shorter length equals $w\sqrt{3} + \ell$, whereas the length of the diagonals is $2\sqrt{\ell^2 + w^2}$.

14.   Answers will vary.

15.   If angle A is obtuse, then the implicit assumption that $\overleftrightarrow{U'}\overrightarrow{U''}$ intersects $\triangle ABC$ is false.

16.   Consider $\triangle ABC$ with altitudes $\overline{AD}$, $\overline{BE}$, and $\overline{CF}$. By Theorem 8.1, the shortest distance from A to $\overleftrightarrow{BC}$ is $\overline{AD}$, the shortest distance from B to $\overleftrightarrow{AC}$ is $\overline{BE}$, and the shortest distance from C to $\overleftrightarrow{AB}$ is $\overline{CF}$. Since a triangle can have at most one right angle, if $\triangle ABC$ is a right triangle, without loss of generality, let $\angle ACB$ be the right angle. Thus AD ≤ AC, CF ≤ CB, and BE < BA. Therefore AD + CF + BE < AC + BC + AB.

17.   Consider quadrilateral ABCD with point P the point of intersection of diagonals $\overline{AC}$ and $\overline{BD}$. The sum of the distances from P to the four vertices is PA + PC + PB + PD = AC + BD. Now consider a second point P′ in the interior of the quadrilateral. By the Triangle Inequality, P′A + P′C ≥ AC and P′B + P′D ≥ BD, where P′A + P′C = AC if and only if P′ is on $\overline{AC}$ and P′B + P′B = BD if and only if P′ is on $\overline{BD}$. So the sum of the distances from P′ to the four vertices is

P′A + P′C + P′B + P′D ≥ AC + BD,

where

P′A + P′C + P′B + P′D = AC + BD

if and only if P′ = P.

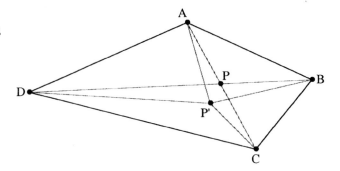

18.   a.   An equation for $\overleftrightarrow{AC}$ is y = x + 2. So an equation for the line perpendicular to $\overleftrightarrow{AC}$ that passes point B is y = -x + 2. These two lines intersect at D = (0, 2). An equation for $\overleftrightarrow{BC}$ is y = -3x + 6. So an equation for the line perpendicular to $\overleftrightarrow{BC}$ that passes through point A is y = $\frac{1}{3}$ + $\frac{2}{3}$. These two lines intersect at E = ($\frac{8}{5}$, $\frac{6}{5}$). The foot of the perpendicular to $\overleftrightarrow{AB}$ that passes through point C is F = (1, 0). Points D, E, and F are the vertices of the inscribed triangle with smallest perimeter.

        b.   DE = $\sqrt{(0-\frac{8}{5})^2 + (2-\frac{6}{5})^2}$ = $\frac{4\sqrt{5}}{5}$, DF = $\sqrt{(0-1)^2 + (2-0)^2}$ = $\sqrt{5}$,

        EF = $\sqrt{(1-\frac{8}{5})^2 + (0-\frac{6}{5})^2}$ = $\frac{3\sqrt{5}}{5}$. So the perimeter of ΔDEF is DE + DF + EF = $\frac{12\sqrt{5}}{5}$.

19.   For an equilateral triangle, the foot of each altitude is the midpoint of each side. From similar triangles, a segment connecting two of these midpoints has half the length of a side of the triangle. Thus the perimeter of the smallest inscribed triangle is 7.5.

Section 8.1.3

1.   The locus of points in 3-space equidistant from two given points is the plane that is the perpendicular bisector of the segment with the two given points as endpoints. The locus of points in 3-space equidistant from two given intersecting lines is the union of two planes that are perpendicular to the plane containing the given lines and bisect the four angles determined by the given lines. The locus of points in 3-space at a fixed distance from a given point is a sphere with center at the given point and radius equal to the fixed distance.

2.   a.   6, 14, 16, 24

        b.   For $0 \le x \le 6$, $A_1(x) = \frac{1}{2}\pi x^2$;

               for $6 < x \le 14$, $A_2(x) = \frac{1}{2}\pi x^2 + \frac{1}{4}\pi(x-6)^2 = \pi(\frac{3}{4}x^2 - 3x + 9)$;

for $14 < x \le 16$, $A_3(x) = \frac{1}{2}\pi x^2 + \frac{1}{4}\pi(x-6)^2 + \frac{1}{4}\pi(x-14)^2$

$= \pi(x^2 - 10x + 58)$;

for $16 < x \le 24$, $A_4(x) = \frac{1}{2}\pi x^2 + \frac{1}{4}\pi(x-6)^2 + \frac{1}{4}\pi(x-14)^2 + \frac{1}{4}\pi(x-16)^2$

$= \pi(\frac{5}{4}x^2 - 18x + 122)$;

for $24 < x \le 30$,

$A_5(x) = \frac{1}{2}\pi x^2 + \frac{1}{4}\pi(x-6)^2 + \frac{1}{4}\pi(x-14)^2 + \frac{1}{4}\pi(x-16)^2 + \frac{1}{4}\pi(x-24)^2$

$= \pi(\frac{3}{2}x^2 - 30x + 266)$

c. The function A is continuous. On the open subintervals, the functions that define A are polynomial functions, which are continuous, and, at the boundary between two subintervals, the polynomial functions on either side of the boundary have the same value.

d. The function A is differentiable. On the open subintervals, the functions that define A are polynomial functions, which are differentiable, and, at the boundary between two subintervals, the polynomial functions on either side of the boundary have the same slope.

e. As $x \to \infty$, the dimensions of the barn become insignificant relative to x, so $A(x) \approx \pi x^2$.

3. a. For $0 \le x \le 10$, $A_1(x) = \frac{3}{4}\pi x^2$; for $10 < x \le 20$, $A_2(x) = \frac{3}{4}\pi x^2 + \frac{1}{4}\pi(x-10)^2 = \pi(x^2 - 5x + 25)$;

for $20 < x \le 30$, $A_3(x) = \frac{3}{4}\pi x^2 + \frac{1}{4}\pi(x-10)^2 + \frac{1}{4}\pi(x-20)^2 = \pi(\frac{5}{4}x^2 - 15x + 125)$;

A is still continuous and differentiable, and, as $x \to \infty$, $A(x) \approx \pi x^2$.

b. Due to the barn's symmetry, A is the same at all four vertices.

4. a. For $0 \le d \le 8$ and $12 \le d \le 20$, $B(d) = 32\pi + \frac{1}{4}\pi(8-d)^2$; for $8 \le d \le 12$, $B(d) = 32\pi$

b. On the intervals $0 \le d \le 8$ and $12 \le d \le 20$, the graph of B is parabolic opening downwards. On the interval $8 \le d \le 12$, the graph is a horizontal line segment.

5. Suppose a leash having length L is tethered to the side of a barn having length s. Consider what happens to the roaming area as the tethering point is moved from a point a distance x $(0 \le x < \frac{s}{2})$ from the closest vertex towards the middle of the side of the barn. If the tethering point moves a small distance Δx, the roaming area in front of the barn will remain a semicircular sector of area $\frac{1}{2}\pi L^2$.

However, the area of the quarter circle on the side of the barn at the near vertex will decrease by approximately $\frac{1}{2}\pi(L-x)\Delta x$, while the area of the quarter circle on the side of the barn at the far vertex will increase by approximately $\frac{1}{2}\pi(L-(s-x))\Delta x$, or 0 if $s - x > L$. Thus the overall change in roaming area will be either $\frac{1}{2}\pi(2x-s)\Delta x$ or $\frac{1}{2}\pi(L-x)\Delta x$, both of which are negative in the interval $0 \le x < \frac{s}{2}$. This means that the area function is monotonically decreasing in this interval. So the roaming area is maximized at the vertex, independent of L or s.

6. The roaming area is determined by the length of the projection of the leash onto the horizontal plane. In this case, this length is $\sqrt{x^2 - 1}$. Thus the solution to this problem is achieved if $\sqrt{x^2 - 1}$ takes the place of x in Problems 1 and 2.

7. Equations for the two lines can be found by applying an appropriate translation $T_{h,k}$ to the line with equation $x + 2y = 5$. The magnitude of this translation is 3, so $\sqrt{h^2 + k^2} = 3$, and the direction is perpendicular to the direction of the line, which has slope $-\frac{1}{2}$, so $\frac{k}{h} = 2$. Thus $h = \frac{3\sqrt{5}}{5}$ and $k = \frac{6\sqrt{5}}{5}$ or $h = -\frac{3\sqrt{5}}{5}$ and $k = -\frac{6\sqrt{5}}{5}$. By the Graph Translation Theorem, equations are $(x - \frac{3\sqrt{5}}{5}) + 2(y - \frac{6\sqrt{5}}{5}) = 5$ and $(x + \frac{3\sqrt{5}}{5}) + 2(y + \frac{6\sqrt{5}}{5}) = 5$.

8.

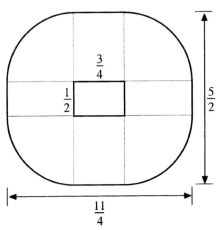

The locus is the union of four segments and four quarter circles, as shown here.

9. Sample: What is the locus of points k units from an angle of measure θ? In the interior of the given angle, the locus is an angle of measure θ whose sides are k units from the given angle and whose vertex is $k \operatorname{cosec} \frac{\theta}{2}$ units from the given angle. In the exterior of the given angle, the locus comprises two rays k units from the given angle joined by a circular arc of radius k and measure $180° - \theta$.

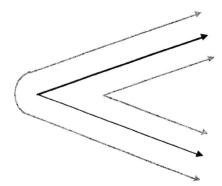

Section 8.1.4

1. Let S be the set of points on a sphere with center O and radius R and M be a plane that contains a point interior to S. First, consider the case in which M contains O. A point P is in S if and only if OP = R. This implies P is in S ∩ M if and only if P is in M and OP = R. Thus S ∩ M is a circle in M. Now, consider the case in which M does not contain O. Let D be the point of intersection of M and the line perpendicular to M through O. Again, a point P is in S ∩ M, if and only if P is in M and OP = R. A line is perpendicular to a plane if and only if it is perpendicular to every line in the plane through the point of intersection. So $\overline{OD} \perp M$ implies $\overline{OD} \perp \overline{DP}$. By the Pythagorean Theorem, $DP = \sqrt{OP^2 - OD^2}$. Thus P is in S ∩ M, if and only if P is in M and $DP = \sqrt{R^2 - OD^2}$. To show that this is a nonempty set, we must show that OD < R. Suppose to the contrary that OD ≥ R. By hypothesis M contains a point X interior to S. Thus OX < R ≤ OD. But this would contradict Theorem 8.3, which states that the perpendicular from a point to a plane is the shortest distance. Thus the intersection of a sphere and a plane through a point interior to the sphere is a circle in M.

2. a. $(x - h)^2 + (y - k)^2 + (z - j)^2 = r^2$

    b. Let C = (x_0, y_0, z_0) be the point of intersection of the plane given by ax + by + cz = d and the line perpendicular to that plane through (0, 0, 0). The normal to the plane is given by the vector A = (a, b, c). So the equation for the line is (x, y, z) = (0, 0, 0) + tA = (at, bt, ct). The point of intersection can then be found by solving for t. Since a(at) + b(bt) + c(ct) = d, $t = \dfrac{d}{a^2 + b^2 + c^2}$.

    Thus $(x_0, y_0, z_0) = \dfrac{d}{a^2 + b^2 + c^2}$ (a, b, c). Now let P = (x, y, z) be any point which lies on both the sphere and the plane. Then $CP^2 = (x - x_0)^2 + (y - y_0)^2 + (z - z_0)^2$
    $= x^2 + y^2 + z^2 - 2(xx_0 + yy_0 + zz_0) + x_0^2 + y_0^2 + z_0^2$. However, $x^2 + y^2 + z^2 = r^2$, since P is on the sphere, and $xx_0 + yy_0 + zz_0 = \dfrac{d}{a^2 + b^2 + c^2}(ax + by + cz) = \dfrac{d^2}{a^2 + b^2 + c^2}$, since P is on the plane. Also $x_0^2 + y_0^2 + z_0^2 = \dfrac{d^2}{a^2 + b^2 + c^2}$. Thus $CP^2 = r^2 - \dfrac{d^2}{a^2 + b^2 + c^2}$. In other words, for all points P in the intersection of the sphere and the plane, CP is a constant. Therefore, the intersection is a circle.

3. Let S be a sphere with center O and radius R and let C_1 and C_2 be two great circles of S. Since two distinct circles with the same center and radius cannot lie in the same plane, C_1 and C_2 must be in different planes M_1 and M_2, but, because these planes have the point O in common, they must intersect in a line ℓ that contains O. Now, there are only two distinct points P_1 and P_2 on ℓ such that $OP_1 = R$ and $OP_2 = R$. Because ℓ lies in both M_1 and M_2, these points must also lie on C_1 and C_2. Therefore C_1 and C_2 intersect in exactly two points that are a distance 2R apart and are thus the endpoints of a diameter of C_1 or C_2.

4. Approximating the Earth's diameter as 7920 miles, its circumference is 7920π miles, and an arc with measure x° is $\dfrac{x}{360}$ • 7920π miles ≈ 22πx miles.

5. a. In the proof, if a = 90°, then m∠COD = 90° and ΔOCD has two right angles, which is not possible. Similarly, if b = 90°, then ΔOCE has two right angles.

    b. Consider spherical triangle ACB, with a = m∠BOC = 90°, b = m∠AOC, and c = m∠AOB. Let points P and Q be in the equatorial plane such that $\overline{AP}$ is perpendicular to the plane and $\overline{AQ}$ is perpendicular to $\overline{OB}$. This means that m∠POQ = m∠C. From the Law of Cosines, then,

$$PQ^2 = OP^2 + OQ^2 - 2OP \cdot OQ \cos C$$
$$= r^2\cos^2(90 - b) + r^2\cos^2 c - 2r^2\sin(90 - b) \cos c \cos C$$
$$= r^2\sin^2 b + r^2\cos^2 c - 2r^2\sin b \cos c \cos C.$$

Since ΔAPQ is a right triangle, we also have

$$PQ^2 = AQ^2 - AP^2$$
$$= r^2\sin^2 c - r^2\cos^2 b.$$

Subtracting the second equation from the first,

$$0 = (r^2\sin^2 b + r^2\cos^2 c - 2r^2\sin b \cos c \cos C) - (r^2\sin^2 c + r^2\cos^2 b).$$
$$= \sin^2 b + \cos^2 c - 2\sin b \cos c \cos C - \sin^2 c - \cos^2 b$$
$$= \sin^2 b + \cos^2 c - 2\sin b \cos c \cos C - (1 - \cos^2 c) + (1 - \sin^2 b)$$
$$= 2\cos^2 c - 2\sin b \cos c \cos C .$$

So cos c = sin b cos C. This is the same result we get from substituting a = 90° into the Spherical Law of Cosines

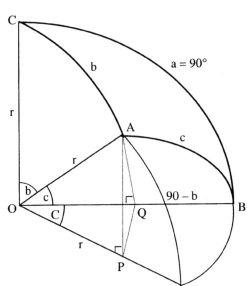

    c. If a = b = 90°, then $\overgroup{AB}$ is in the equatorial plane, so m∠C = m∠c. The Spherical Law of Cosines gives cos c = cos C, which is consistent with m∠C = m∠c.

6. There is only about a 0.2% disparity between the two distances. The figure calculated in the lesson approximates the diameter of the great circle connecting New York and New Delhi by the average diameter of the Earth. The Earth, however, is not a perfect sphere, but roughly an oblate spheroid with an equatorial radius of 3963.19 statute miles and a polar radius of 3949.9 statute miles. The higher

figure given in the almanac could arise from an actual measurement (using the actual airport locations) or from an estimate for the diameter of the great circle that is more accurate than the 7920 miles used in the lesson.

7. We can show that the arc of the great circle from Chicago to Tokyo passes very close to Anchorage by showing that the direct distance is very close to the sum of the distances from Chicago to Anchorage and Anchorage to Tokyo. For the Chicago to Tokyo trip $p = 90° - 41°52'$, $q = 90° - 35°45'$, and

$m\angle PNQ = (180° - 139°45') + (180° - 87°38')$, so n $\approx 91.1°$ and d $\approx \frac{91.1}{360} \cdot 7920\pi \approx 6297$ miles. For the Chicago to Anchorage trip $p = 90° - 41°52'$, $q = 90° - 61°10'$, and $m\angle PNQ = 149°59' - 87°38'$,

so n $\approx 41.3°$ and d $\approx \frac{41.3}{360} \cdot 7920\pi \approx 2854$ miles. For the Anchorage to Tokyo trip $p = 90° - 61°10'$,

$q = 90° - 35°45'$, and $m\angle PNQ = (180° - 139°45') + (180° - 149°59')$, so n $\approx 49.1°$ and

d $\approx \frac{49.1}{360} \cdot 7920\pi \approx 3450$ miles. So the total distance from Tokyo to Chicago through Anchorage is

about 6304 miles, only 7 miles difference. The trip from Chicago to Anchorage is about $\frac{2854}{6304} \approx 45\%$

of the total trip.

8. $a = 90° - 48°50' = 41°10'$; $b = 90° + 22°54' = 112°54'$; $C = 2°20' + 43°13' = 45°33'$

$\cos c = \cos 41°10' \cdot \cos 112°54' + \sin 41°10' \cdot \sin 112°54' \cdot \cos 45°33' \approx .1317$;

$c \approx \cos^{-1}(.1317) \approx 82.4°$; $\frac{82.4}{360} \cdot 7920\pi \approx 5697$ miles

9. a. $\cos c = \cos 50° \cdot \cos 50° + \sin 50° \cdot \sin 50° \cdot \cos 168°23' \approx -.1616$; $\cos^{-1}(-.1616) \approx 99.3°$;

$\frac{99.3}{360} \cdot 7920\pi \approx 6863$ miles.

b. The diameter of the small circle at 40°N latitude is approximately $7920 \cos 40° \approx 6067$ miles.

Flying east from Beijing, the arc measure traveled is $(180° - 116°28') + (180° - 75°9') = 168°23'$.

So the distance traveled is $\frac{168.38}{360} \cdot 6067\pi \approx 8915$ miles.

c. Flying west from Beijing, the arc measure traveled is $116°28' + 75°9' = 191°37'$. So the distance

traveled is $\frac{191.62}{360} \cdot 6067\pi \approx 10145$ miles.

10. a. $c = 7920\pi \cos L°$

b. $x = \frac{d}{360} \cdot 7920\pi \cos L°$

c. $\cos n = \cos^2 (90° - L°) + \sin^2 (90° - L°) \cdot \cos d° = \sin^2 L° + \cos^2 L° \cdot \cos d°$;

$x = \frac{\cos^{-1}(\sin^2 L° + \cos^2 L° \cos d°)}{360°} \cdot 7920\pi = 22\pi \cos^{-1}(\sin^2 L° + \cos^2 L° \cos d°)$

d. Let $\overset{\frown}{ASB}$ be the minor arc connecting points A and B on a circle of latitude with center O that is not the Equator. Let $\overset{\frown}{AGB}$ be the minor arc connecting A and B on the great circle with center C. The chord of each arc is $\overline{AB}$, and $r = OA < CA = R$ because the great circle has the larger radius. So the desired result is a special case of the following more general result. Let $\overline{AB}$ be a chord of a minor arc of two circles with radii r and R, $r < R$. The length of the arc is smaller in the circle with larger radius.

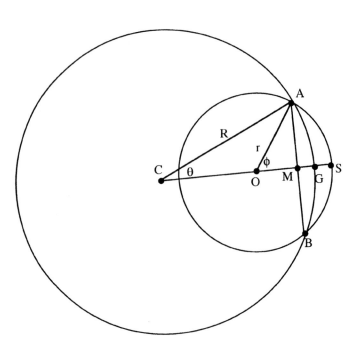

Proof: Let all angles be in radians. The length($\overparen{AGB}$) = 2rϕ and the length($\overparen{ASB}$) = 2rθ. Now r = $\frac{AM}{\sin \phi}$ and R = $\frac{AM}{\sin \theta}$. So length($\overparen{AGB}$) = AB$\frac{\theta}{\sin \theta}$ and length($\overparen{ASB}$) = AB$\frac{\phi}{\sin \phi}$. Since ϕ is an exterior angle of ΔAOC, $\phi > \theta$. So if we can show that the function f: x $\to$ $\frac{x}{\sin x}$ is increasing on the domain $0 < x < \frac{\pi}{2}$, then we will have

shown that the length($\overparen{AGB}$) < length($\overparen{ASB}$). If f(x) = $\frac{x}{\sin x}$, then f'(x) = $\frac{1}{\sin x} - \frac{x \cos x}{\sin^2 x}$

= $\frac{\sin x - x \cos x}{\sin^2 x}$. On this domain, sin x − x cos x > 0 $\Leftrightarrow$ sin x > x cos x $\Leftrightarrow$ tan x > x. A derivation

of this result is in the solution to Problem 3a of Section 10.1.4. Thus f'(x) > 0 for $0 < x < \frac{\pi}{2}$,

which implies that f is increasing. Thus $\frac{\theta}{\sin \theta} < \frac{\phi}{\sin \phi}$, from which length($\overparen{AGB}$) < length($\overparen{ASB}$).

11. a. cos c = cos a • cos b + sin a • sin b • cos 90° = cos a • cos b

b. From the Spherical Law of Cosines, cos a = cos b • cos c + sin b • sin c • cos A. Dividing both sides by cos b • cos c yields $\frac{\cos a}{\cos b \cos c}$ = 1 + tan b • tan c • cos A. Substituting the result from part **a**, $\frac{\cos a}{\cos^2 b \cos c}$ = 1 + tan b • tan c • cos A. Simplifying yields sec^{2}b = 1 + tan b • tan c • cos A. Using the identity sec^{2}b − 1 = tan^{2}b, tan^{2}b = tan b • tan c • cos A. Thus cos A = $\frac{\tan b}{\tan c}$.

c. From part **b**, sin A = $\sqrt{1 - \cos^2 A}$ = $\sqrt{1 - \frac{\tan^2 b}{\tan^2 c}}$. Using the result from part **a**, tan^{2}b = $\frac{\cos^2 a}{\cos^2 c} - 1$. Thus sin A = $\sqrt{1 - \left(\frac{\cos^2 a}{\cos^2 c} - 1\right)\frac{\cos^2 c}{\sin^2 c}}$ = $\sqrt{1 - \frac{\cos^2 a - \cos^2 c}{\sin^2 c}}$ = $\sqrt{\frac{\sin^2 c - (\cos^2 a - \cos^2 c)}{\sin^2 c}}$ = $\frac{\sin a}{\sin c}$.

d. Using the results of parts **a** and **b**, tan A = $\frac{\sin A}{\cos A}$ = $\frac{\sin a}{\sin c} \cdot \frac{\tan c}{\tan b}$ = $\frac{\sin a \cos b}{\cos c \sin b}$. From part **a**, $\frac{\cos b}{\cos c}$ = sec a. So tan A = $\frac{\sin a}{\sin b} \cdot$ sec a = $\frac{\tan a}{\sin b}$.

e. From part **d**, tan A = $\frac{\tan a}{\sin b}$. By symmetry, tan B = $\frac{\tan b}{\sin a}$. Thus, using the result from part **a**, cot A cot B = $\frac{\sin a \sin b}{\tan a \tan b}$ = cos a • cos b = cos c.

f. From part **c**, sin A = $\frac{\sin a}{\sin c}$. By symmetry, sin B = $\frac{\sin b}{\sin c}$. From parts **a** and **b**,

$$\cos a \bullet \sin B = \cos a \bullet \frac{\sin b}{\sin c} = \frac{\cos c}{\cos b} \bullet \frac{\sin b}{\sin c} = \frac{\tan b}{\tan c} = \cos A.$$

12. Let a = m$\widehat{PR}$, b = m$\widehat{QR}$, and c = m$\widehat{PQ}$. We want to show that ra + rb ≥ rc, or, equivalently, a + b ≥ c, where a, b, and c are all in the interval [0, π]. Since the cosine function is monotonically decreasing in the interval [0, π], the inequality is equivalent to cos(a + b) ≤ cos c. From the Spherical Law of Cosines, this becomes cos(a + b) ≤ cos a cos b + sin a sin b cos C, where C is the angle between $\widehat{PR}$ and $\widehat{QR}$. Using the Cosine of a Sum identity, this becomes

cos a cos b – sin a sin b ≤ cos a cos b + sin a sin b cos C.

Simplifying (note that sin a sin b is positive in the interval [0, π]) yields -1 ≤ cos C. The inequality -1 < cos C, or equivalently a + b > c, holds when 0 ≤ C < π. The equality holds when C = π, which is when Q, R, and P lie on the same great circle and P is between Q and R.

13. Since the lengths of all paths from P to Q along the surface are greater or equal to the length of the Euclidean distance, $d_m(P, Q) \geq d_E(P, Q) \geq 0$. Because of this relationship, if $d_m(P, Q) = 0$, then $d_E(P, Q) = 0$, so P = Q. Conversely, if P = Q, then since a Euclidean path of length zero from P to Q also passes along the surface, $d_m(P, Q) = 0$. Because the length of a path is the same whether traversed forward or backward, $d_m(P, Q) = d_m(Q, M)$. Finally, suppose $d_m(P, Q) + d_m(Q, R) < d_m(P, R)$. This is a contradiction, since then the path from P to R through Q would have a smaller length than the path of minimum length from P to R.

Section 8.2.1

1. Suppose ABC and DEF are two triangles with AB = DE, AC = DF, and m∠BAC = m∠EDF. Since $\frac{AB}{DE} = \frac{AC}{DF} = 1$ and the measures of the included angles are equal, by SAS Similarity, ΔABC ~ ΔDEF. Thus m∠ABC = m∠DEF, m∠BCA = m∠EFD, and $\frac{BC}{EF} = 1$.

2. Yes. The condition P′Q′ = k • PQ allows for PQ = 0, or P = Q, whereas $\frac{P'Q'}{PQ} = k$ does not.

3. Though lengths of all corresponding sides of the polygons in Figure 2 are in the ratio $\frac{1}{2}$, other ratios of corresponding distances, such as $\overline{L'I'}$, do not equal $\frac{1}{2}$.

4. Suppose figures α and β are congruent. Then there is a congruence transformation T such that T(α) = β. By the definition of congruence transformation, for any points P and Q in the plane, if T(P) = P′ and T(Q) = Q′, then P′Q′ = PQ, or P′Q′ = 1 • PQ. By definition, then, T is also a similarity transformation with ratio of similitude k = 1. Since T is a similarity transformation and T(α) = β, figures α and β are similar.

5.   a. $k = \frac{11}{5}$

     b.   Consider a photograph with dimensions a × b and a piece of paper with dimensions p × q, where b ≥ a and q ≥ p. The magnitude k of the similarity transformation that would allow you to enlarge the photo as much as possible so that it still fits on the paper is given by $k = \min\{\frac{b}{a}, \frac{q}{p}\}$.

     c. $k = \frac{3}{6} = \frac{1}{2}$

6.   Let P and Q be any two points of the plane. Since T_1 is a similarity transformation, $T_1(P) = P'$ and $T_1(Q) = Q'$, with $P'Q' = k_1 \cdot PQ$. Since T_2 is also a similarity transformation, $T_2(P') = P''$ and $T_2(Q') = Q''$, with $P''Q'' = k_2 \cdot P'Q' = (k_1 k_2) \cdot PQ$. Since $k_1, k_2 \neq 0$, $k_1 k_2 \neq 0$. By definition, then, $T_2 \circ T_1$ is a similarity transformation with ratio of similitude $k_1 k_2$.

7.   If $k - 1 < 0$, then $PP^* = (1 - k)\sqrt{a^2 + b^2} = \sqrt{a^2 + b^2} - k\sqrt{a^2 + b^2} = OP - OP^*$. So $OP = OP^* + PP^*$, which implies P* is between O and P. So P* is on $\overrightarrow{OP}$.

8.   Under a size change with center (5, -7) and magnitude 5, $S_5(a, b) = (5(a - 5), 5(b + 7))$. So $S_5^{-1}(a, b) = (\frac{1}{5}a + 5, \frac{1}{5}b - 7)$.

9.   If (a, b) is on the graph of 3x + 2y = 4, then (100a, 100b) is on the graph of the image of the line 3x + 2y = 4 under S_{100}. Thus the image of 3x + 2y = 4 under S_{100} is $3(\frac{x}{100}) + 2(\frac{y}{100}) = 4$.

10.   Let $P = (x_1, y_1)$ and $Q = (x_2, y_2)$. Then $P' = S_k(P) = (kx_1, ky_1)$ and $Q' = S_k(Q) = (kx_2, ky_2)$, where k > 0. So $P'Q' = \sqrt{(kx_2 - kx_1)^2 + (ky_2 - ky_1)^2} = |k|\sqrt{(x_2 - x_1)^2 + (y_2 - y_1)^2} = k\sqrt{(x_2 - x_1)^2 + (y_2 - y_1)^2} = k \cdot PQ$.

11.   Consider two circles C_1 and C_2, one with center O_1 and radius r_1 and the other with center O_2 and radius r_2. By first applying a translation $T_{\overline{O_1 O_2}}$, the circle C_1 will mapped onto circle C_1' with center O_2 and radius r_1. By then applying a size change with center O_2 and magnitude $k = \frac{r_2}{r_1}$, the circle C_1' will be mapped onto circle C_1'' (Theorem 8.8) which has center O_2 and radius r_2. Thus there is a similarity transformation that maps any circle onto any other circle.

12.   The size change with center O and magnitude k < 0 is the transformation S_k such that for any point P in the plane, $S_k(P)$ is the point P' on the ray *opposite* $\overrightarrow{OP}$ such that $OP' = k \cdot OP$.

a.

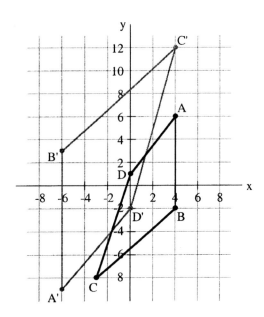

b.   Let O be the centroid of $\triangle$ABC. Since AM = $\frac{1}{2}$AC and AN = $\frac{1}{2}$AB, by SAS Similarity,

$\triangle$MAN ~ $\triangle$CAB. So MN = $\frac{1}{2}$CB, m$\angle$NMA = m$\angle$BCA, and m$\angle$MNA = m$\angle$CBA. Since $\overleftrightarrow{MN}$ //

$\overleftrightarrow{CB}$ and m$\angle$MON = m$\angle$BOC, $\triangle$MON ~ $\triangle$BOC. Thus MO = $\frac{1}{2}$BO with $\overrightarrow{OM}$ opposite $\overrightarrow{OB}$.

Similarly,   NO = $\frac{1}{2}$CO with $\overrightarrow{ON}$ opposite $\overrightarrow{OC}$ and LO = $\frac{1}{2}$AO with $\overrightarrow{OL}$ opposite $\overrightarrow{OA}$. So

$\triangle$LMN is the image of $\triangle$ABC under a size change with center O and magnitude $-\frac{1}{2}$.

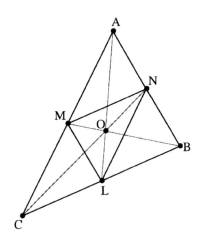

13.   a.   C is the point on $\overrightarrow{AB}$ such that AC = k • AB and E is the point on $\overrightarrow{AD}$ such that

AE = k • AD. If k > 1, then BC = AC – AB and DE = AE – AD. So

$\frac{AB}{BC}$ = $\frac{AB}{AC - AB}$ = $\frac{1}{k-1}$ and $\frac{AD}{DE}$ = $\frac{AD}{AE - AD}$ = $\frac{1}{k-1}$. If 0 < k < 1, then BC = AB – AC and

DE = AD – AE. So $\frac{AB}{BC}$ = $\frac{AB}{AB - AC}$ = $\frac{1}{1-k}$ and $\frac{AD}{DE}$ = $\frac{AD}{AD - AE}$ = $\frac{1}{1-k}$.

b. From part **a**, $\frac{AB}{BC} = \frac{1}{k-1}$, for $k > 1$, or $\frac{AB}{BC} = \frac{1}{1-k}$, for $0 < k < 1$. So either $DE = kAD - AD$ or $DE = AD - kAD$. Since A, D, and E are collinear, $DE = kAD - AD$ implies D is between A and E and $AE = kAD$, and $DE = AD - kAD$ implies E is between A and $AE = kAD$. By SAS Similarity, then, $\triangle BAD \sim \triangle CAE$. So $m\angle DBA = m\angle ECA$, which implies $\overleftrightarrow{BD} \parallel \overleftrightarrow{CE}$.

14. a. If $z = a + bi$, then $S_k(z) = kz = ka + kbi$.

b. In the complex plane, two lines $L = \{z: z = c + mz_0\}$ and $L' = \{z: z = c' + mz_1\}$ are parallel if and only if $z_1 = kz_0$ for some $k \in \mathbf{R}$. Suppose $z \in L$. Then $z' = S_k(z) = kz = kc + kmz_0$. Letting $c' = kc$ and $z_1 = kz_0$, we have $L' = \{z: z \in S_k(L)\} = \{z: z = c' + mz_1\}$, where, since $k > 0$, $z_1 = kz_0$ for some $k \in \mathbf{R}$. Thus $L \parallel L'$.

Section 8.2.2

1. a. If (s, t) is a solution to $y = ax^2$, then (ks, kt) is a solution to $y = bx^2$. So $kt = kas^2 = b(ks)^2$, or $k = \frac{a}{b}$.

b. The graph of $y = \frac{1}{10}x^2$ is flatter than the graph of $y = x^2$, since it grows more slowly. However, the graphs do not appear similar because they are being graphed in the same viewing window. If $y = x^2$ is graphed in the window $-a \le x \le a$, $-b \le y \le b$, then $y = \frac{1}{10}x^2$ should be graphed in the window $-10a \le x \le 10a$, $-10b \le y \le 10b$.

2. $k = \frac{1}{25.4}$, so $y = \frac{1}{25.4}(7.44(25.4x) + 8) = 7.44x + 0.315$.

3. The functions $f(x) = ax^2 + bx$ and $h(x) = x^2 + cx$ are homothetic iff there exists some $k > 0$ such that $k h(\frac{x}{k}) = f(x)$, or $k(\left(\frac{x}{k}\right)^2 + c\frac{x}{k}) = \frac{x^2}{k} + cx = ax^2 + bx$. Thus $f(x)$ and $h(x)$ are homothetic iff $k = \frac{1}{a}$ and $c = b$.

4. Since $y = k\left(\frac{x}{k}\right)^3 = \frac{x^3}{k^2}$, any formula of the form $y = \frac{x^3}{c}$ will have a graph similar to the graph of $y = x^3$.

5. If $g(x) = \frac{1}{x}$, then $\sqrt{c}\, g(\frac{x}{\sqrt{c}}) = \frac{c}{x}$.

6. No. The graph of $f(x) = \sin x$ is similar to the graph of every function g with a formula of the form $g = \frac{1}{b}\cos(bx + c)$.

7. The image of a graph under a size change S_k with $k < 0$ will be congruent to the image under a size change S_{-k} where $-k > 0$: they are related by a rotation of $180°$.

8. The graphs of $y = \log_b x$ and $y = k\log_b \frac{x}{k} = \log_b x^k - \log_b k^k$ are similar, since they are related by a size change. However, since the graphs of $y = \log_b x^k - c$ and $y = \log_b x^k$ are related by a vertical translation, the graph of $y = \log_b x$ is similar to the graph of any equation of the form $y = k\log_b cx$.

9. Sample: If *homothetic* is used to refer to graphs related by a composite of a size change and any congruence transformation, then *homothetic* becomes synonymous with *similar*. Allowing *homothetic*

to refer to graphs related by a composition of a size change and a translation, however, singles out translations as a unique type of congruence transformation. Defining *homothetic* to refer only to graphs related by a size change allows for a simpler and more natural classification of similar graphs; i.e., any two similar graphs are related either by a pure isometry (congruent graphs), a pure size change (homothetic graphs), or a composition of an isometry and a size change.

10. Typically, when a graph is enlarged or reduced using the zoom feature of a graphing utility, the original graph and its "zoomed" image are related by a k-scaling. For example, if we zoom in by a power of 10 on the graph of $y = f(x)$, then the new units on the x- and y-axes, (x', y'), are related to the old units, (x, y), by $(x', y') = (10x, 10y)$. Thus the equation for the "zoomed" graph would be given by $\frac{y'}{10} = f(\frac{x'}{10})$, or $y' = 10f(\frac{x'}{10})$.

Section 8.2.3

1. The SsA condition is sufficient for triangle similarity. In triangles ABC and DEF, suppose $m\angle C = m\angle F$ and that $\frac{AB}{DE} = \frac{BC}{EF}$ with AB > BC and DE > EF. Then if AB = a and BC = b, there is a positive number k with DE = ka and EF = kb. Consequently we apply a size change of magnitude k to $\triangle$ABC. The image $\triangle$A′B′C′ is congruent to $\triangle$DEF by SsA. So $\triangle$ABC can be mapped onto $\triangle$DEF by a size change and an isometry.

2. a. True. All equilateral triangles have two 60° angles, which, by Theorem 8.13(c), is a sufficient condition for the triangles to be similar.

   b. False. Counterexample: $\triangle$ABC with AB = 2, AC = 2, and BC = 2, and $\triangle$DEF with DE = 2, DF = 2, and EF = 1.

   c. False. Counterexample: $\triangle$ABC with AB = 3, AC = 4, and BC = 5, and $\triangle$DEF with DE = 5, DF = 12, and EF = 13.

   d. True. All isosceles right triangles have two 45° angles, which, by Theorem 8.13(c), is a sufficient condition for the triangles to be similar.

   e. False. If the 120° angle is between the sides of length 2 and 3 in the one triangle and opposite the side of 30 in the other triangle, the triangles will not be similar.

3. False. Two isosceles trapezoids with corresponding bases congruent can have different heights.

4. If two triangles are similar, then, by the definition of similarity, the lengths of all corresponding sides must all be proportional and, by Theorem 8.10, the measure of all corresponding angles must be equal.

5. The statement is false. Counterexample: By juxtaposing triangles with sides 3, 4, 5 and 5, 5, 6 along sides of length 5 we get a 3-4-5-6 quadrilateral which is not congruent, and therefore not similar, to a 3-4-5-6 quadrilateral constructed by juxtaposing triangles with sides 3, 4, 4 and 4, 5, 6 along sides of length 4.

6. Because all sides of a regular polygon are of the same length and all interior angles have a measure of $180 - \frac{360}{n}$ degrees, any two regular polygons with the same number of sides will have proportional corresponding sides and congruent corresponding interior angles. Therefore, all regular polygons with the same number of sides are similar to each other.

7. If A, B, C, and D are four distinct points, then $\overleftrightarrow{AB}$ and $\overleftrightarrow{CD}$ are secants of the circle that intersect at point E (point E can be inside, outside, or on the circle), and the product of the lengths of the segments $\overline{AE}$ and $\overline{BE}$ on secant $\overleftrightarrow{AB}$ equals the product of the lengths of the segments $\overline{CE}$ and $\overline{DE}$ on secant $\overleftrightarrow{CD}$. This is sometimes called the Secant Length Theorem. If A = B and C = D, then $\overleftrightarrow{AB}$ and $\overleftrightarrow{CD}$ will be tangents of the circle that intersect at point E, and the square of the length of the segment $\overline{AE}$ on tangent $\overleftrightarrow{AB}$ equals the square of the length of the segments $\overline{CE}$ on tangent $\overleftrightarrow{CD}$. This is sometimes called the Tangent Square Theorem.

8. a. The theorem still holds true, since if B = E, either C = E or D = E. In either case,   AE • BE = CE • DE = 0.

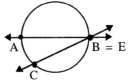

b. The theorem still holds true. We have $m\angle EAC = \frac{1}{2}m\,\widehat{AC}$
    $= m\angle EDB$. So $\triangle ACE \sim \triangle DBE$.

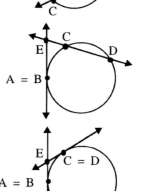

c. The theorem still holds true, since $\triangle ACE$ is isosceles, which
    implies AE = BE = CE = DE.

9. a. Let A = $(\frac{\sqrt{2}r}{2}, \frac{\sqrt{2}r}{2})$ and B = $(\frac{-\sqrt{2}r}{2}, \frac{-\sqrt{2}r}{2})$. Then AE = $2r\sqrt{2} - r$ and BE = $2r\sqrt{2} + r$. Thus AE • BE = $7r^2$.

b. If E = (0, 0), then AE = r and BE = r. Thus AE • BE = r^2.

c. Let A = (0, -r). Then AE = 0. Thus AE • BE = 0.

d. Consider $\overleftrightarrow{AB}$ passing through the circle's center and the point E = (a, b). Let point A be closest to point E. Then AE = $|r - \sqrt{a^2 + b^2}|$ and BE = $r + \sqrt{a^2 + b^2}$. Thus AE • BE = $r^2 - (a^2 + b^2)$, for $\sqrt{a^2 + b^2} \le r$, or AE • BE = $(a^2 + b^2) - r^2$, for $\sqrt{a^2 + b^2} > r$.

10. A circle inscribed in an equilateral triangle is tangent to each side at the side's midpoint. Since the distance from any vertex to the circle is $\frac{s}{2}$, its power is $\frac{s^2}{4}$.

11. a. From Theorem 8.15, we know $EP_1 • EQ_1 = EP_2 • EQ_2$ and $ER_1 • ES_1 = ER_2 • ES_2$. Multiplying the two equations together yields $EP_1 • EQ_1 • ER_1 • ES_1 = EP_2 • EQ_2 • ER_2 • ES_2$.

b. The proof in part **a** makes no assumption about whether or not $Q_1 = R_1$ or $Q_2 = R_2$, so, given the equality, the result still holds.

12. a. Construct midpoint M of segment $\overline{OP}$. Construct circle C′ with center M and radius $\overline{MP}$. This circle will intersect circle C at points T and T′. Lines $\overleftrightarrow{PT}$ and $\overleftrightarrow{PT'}$ will both be tangent to circle C.

b. Since $\overline{OP}$ is a diameter of circle C′ and T is on C′, $m\angle OTP = \frac{1}{2}m\,\widehat{OP} = 90°$. Thus $\overline{OT}$ is perpendicular to $\overline{TP}$. Because T is on circle C, $\overleftrightarrow{PT}$ must be tangent to circle C.

13. a. Draw line $\overleftrightarrow{O_1O_2}$. Pick any point Q_1 on circle C_1 that is not on line $\overleftrightarrow{O_1O_2}$. Construct line m perpendicular to $\overrightarrow{O_1Q_1}$ and then construct line n perpendicular to line m and passing through point O_2. This line will intersect circle C_2 at two points. Let point Q_2 be the point of intersection on the same side of $\overleftrightarrow{O_1O_2}$ as Q_1. Lines $\overleftrightarrow{O_1Q_1}$ and $\overleftrightarrow{O_2Q_2}$ will be parallel and lines $\overleftrightarrow{Q_1Q_2}$ and $\overleftrightarrow{O_1O_2}$ will intersect at a point P. Construct a line through point P tangent to circle C_2 at point T_2, as was done in Problem 12. This line will also be tangent to circle C_1 at a point T_1.

b. Given that $\overleftrightarrow{PT_2}$ is tangent to circle C_2 at T_2, we will show that $\overleftrightarrow{PT_2}$ is also tangent to circle C_1 at a point T_1. First, since $\overline{O_1Q_1}$ is parallel to $\overline{O_2Q_2}$, by AA Similarity, ΔO_1PQ_1 is similar to ΔO_2PQ_2. So $\dfrac{Q_1O_1}{Q_2O_2} = \dfrac{r_1}{r_2} = \dfrac{O_1P}{O_2P}$. Now let T_1 be a point on $\overleftrightarrow{PT_2}$ such that $\overleftrightarrow{O_1T_1}$ is perpendicular to $\overleftrightarrow{PT_2}$. Since $\angle O_2T_2P$ and $\angle O_1T_1P$ are both right angles, by AA Similarity, ΔO_1PT_1 is similar to ΔO_2PT_2. Thus $\dfrac{T_1O_1}{T_2O_2} = \dfrac{O_1P}{O_2P} = \dfrac{r_1}{r_2}$ and since $T_2O_2 = r_2$, $T_1O_1 = r_1$, which means that T_1 is a point on C_1. Because T_1 is on circle C_1 and $\overleftrightarrow{PT_2}$ is perpendicular to $\overleftrightarrow{O_1T_1}$, $\overleftrightarrow{PT_2}$ is tangent to C_1.

c. Perform the same construction as in part **a** except this time let Q_2 be the point of intersection on the side of $\overleftrightarrow{O_1O_2}$ opposite to Q_1.

14. a. P_1, P_2, and P_3 are collinear.

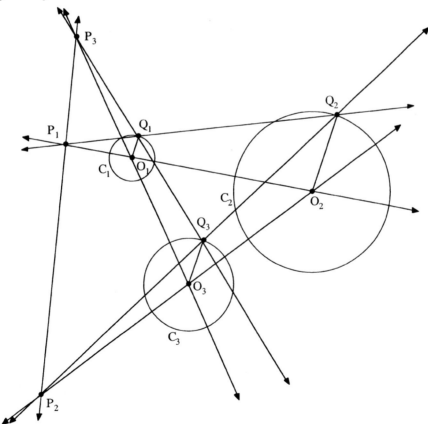

b. Q_1, Q_2, and Q_3 are not collinear.

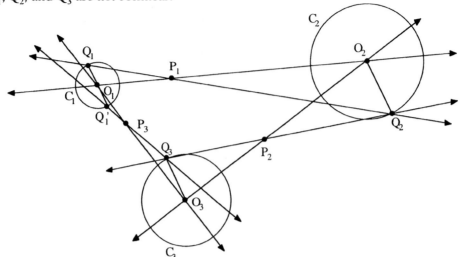

c.   The external center of similitude P_1 of one possible pair of the circles C_1, C_2, and C_3 and the internal centers of similitude P_2 and P_3 of the other two pairs are collinear.

Section 8.2.4

1.   a.   arc length   b.   arc measure   c.   arc measure   d.   arc measure

2.   If the radian measure of the arc equals its length, then the circumference of the circle is 2π, so the radius is 1.

3.   a. $\frac{1}{2\pi}$ of the circle   b. $\frac{r}{2\pi}$

4.   The length of the arc is $\frac{212}{360} \cdot 28\pi \approx 51.8$ units.

5.   a.   Let O be the center of a circle with radius 2 and let $\overline{AB}$ be a chord of length 1. Also let $m\angle AOB = 2\theta$ = measure of minor arc $\overarc{AB}$. Then $2\pi - 2\theta$ = measure of major arc $\overarc{AB}$. Let C be the midpoint of $\overline{AB}$. Then $\overline{OC}$ is the bisector of $\angle AOB$ and $m\angle COB = \theta$. $\sin\theta = \frac{CB}{r} = \frac{\frac{1}{2}}{2} = \frac{1}{4}$, so $\theta = \sin^{-1}\frac{1}{4} \approx .253$ radians. The measure of minor arc $\overarc{AB} = 2\theta \approx .50536$ radians and the measure of major arc $\overarc{AB} = 2\pi - 2\theta \approx 5.778$ radians.

       b.   Let the circle in part a have radius r and let $\overline{AB}$ be any chord of that circle. Then $\sin\theta = \frac{\frac{1}{2}AB}{r}$ implies that $\theta = \sin^{-1}(\frac{\frac{1}{2}AB}{r})$. The measure of minor arc $\overarc{AB} = 2\sin^{-1}(\frac{\frac{1}{2}AB}{r})$ and the measure of major arc $\overarc{AB} = 2\pi - 2\sin^{-1}(\frac{\frac{1}{2}AB}{r})$.

6. For a 45° arc and a 90° arc to have the same length, $\frac{45}{360} \cdot 2\pi r_1 = \frac{90}{360} \cdot 2\pi r_2 \Rightarrow \frac{1}{8} r_1 = \frac{1}{4} r_2 \Rightarrow r_1 = 2r_2$. For example, a 45° arc from a circle with radius 16 will have the same length as a 90° arc from a circle with radius 8 because $\frac{45}{360} \cdot 2\pi(16) = \frac{90}{360} \cdot 2\pi(8) = 4\pi$.

7. Let O be the center of a circle with radius r and let $\overline{AB}$ be a chord of an arc with measure s. Then $m\angle AOB = s$ by the definition of arc measure. If C is the midpoint of $\overline{AB}$, then $\overline{OC}$ is the bisector of $\angle AOB$ and $m\angle COB = \frac{1}{2}s$. Then $\sin \frac{1}{2}s = \frac{\frac{1}{2}AB}{r} \Rightarrow AB = 2r\sin \frac{1}{2}s$.

Section 8.2.5

1. Let $EB = x$ and $EC = y$. Then $x(10 + x) = y(12 + y)$. So $y^2 + 12y - (x^2 + 10x) = 0$, or $y = \frac{-12 + \sqrt{12^2 + 4(x^2 + 10x)}}{2}$. If $x = 1$, then $y = \frac{-12 + \sqrt{12^2 + 44}}{2} \approx 0.86$. Thus $EB = 1$, $AB = 11$, $EC \approx 0.86$, and $BC \approx 12.86$ is one set of possible lengths.

2. Let $EC = x$ and $EB = y$. Then $x(x + 15) = y^2$. For y to be an integer, $x(x + 15)$ must be a perfect square. This will be the case if $x = 1$ or $x = 5$. So two possible triples are (4, 1, 16) and (10, 5, 20).

3. By Theorem 8.18(a), an inscribed angle that intercepts a semicircle has half the measure of the intercepted arc. Since the intercepted arc is π radians, the inscribed angle has a measure of $\frac{\pi}{2}$, which is a right angle.

4. a. $m\angle E = \frac{1}{2}(x - y) = \frac{1}{2}(x - (2\pi - x)) = x - \pi$

   b. $\pi < x \le 2\pi$

5. a. One angle of a regular n-sided polygon inscribed in a circle intercepts an arc of the circle with measure $\frac{2\pi(n-2)}{n}$. By Theorem 8.18(a), this inscribed angle has measure $\frac{\pi(n-2)}{n}$.

   b. One angle of a regular n-sided polygon circumscribed about a circle intercepts arcs of the circle with measures $\frac{2\pi(n-1)}{n}$ and $\frac{2\pi}{n}$. By Theorem 8.18(f), this circumscribed angle will have measure $\frac{1}{2}(\frac{2\pi(n-1)}{n} - \frac{2\pi}{n}) = \frac{\pi(n-2)}{n}$.

Section 8.2.6

1. a. directly similar   b. directly similar   c. directly similar

2. a. $S_5 \circ R_{90°}(0, 0) = S_5(0, 0) = (0, 0)$; $S_5 \circ R_{90°}(1, 0) = S_5(0, 1) = (0, 5)$; $S_5 \circ R_{90°}(0, 2) = S_5(-2, 0) = (-10, 0)$

   b. $S_3 \circ r_{y=x}(0, 0) = S_3(0, 0) = (0, 0)$; $S_3 \circ r_{y=x}(1, 0) = S_3(0, 1) = (0, 3)$; $S_3 \circ r_{y=x}(0, 2) = S_3(2, 0) = (6, 0)$

3.   (There is an error in the first printing. Use A as the center of each spiral similarity.)

a.

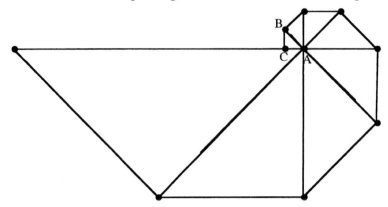

b.   We have for each right triangle $\frac{\text{hypotenuse}}{\text{leg}} = \sqrt{2}$. Thus if AB = x, then the length of the

hypotenuse of the seventh image is $\left(\sqrt{2}\right)^7 x$.

4.   We have m∠PCP′ = m∠QCQ′. So m $\widehat{PP'}$ = m $\widehat{QQ'}$.
This, in turn, implies m∠POP′ = m∠QOQ′. Also,
because m∠OCQ = m∠OCP, m $\widehat{OQ}$ = m $\widehat{OP}$. Thus
m∠OPP′ = m∠OQQ′. So, by AA Similarity,
ΔPOP′ ~ ΔQOQ′. Therefore $\frac{OP'}{OP} = \frac{OQ'}{OQ}$.

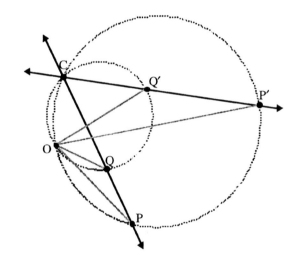

5.   In the drawing below, point O is the center of the spiral similarity.

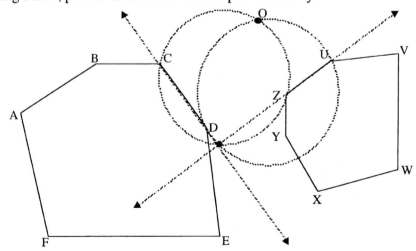

6.　　$S_2(R_{(0,-3),90°}(z)) = 2(i(z - (-3i)) + -3i) = k(z - c) + c = 2i(z - (\frac{6}{5} - \frac{18}{5}i)) + (\frac{6}{5} - \frac{18}{5}i)$. Thus the spiral

similarity has center $(\frac{6}{5}, \frac{18}{5})$ and magnitude 2.

7.　　$S_2(R_{(0,-3),180°}(z)) = 2(-1(z - (-3i)) + -3i) = k(z - c) + c = -2(z - -4i) + -4i$. Thus the spiral similarity has

center $(0, -4)$ and magnitude 2.

8.　　This is an opposite similarity with magnitude $\dfrac{\sqrt{AC^2 + BC^2}}{AC}$.

9.　　$S_{1/2}(r_{x=6}(z)) = \frac{1}{2}(-\overline{(z - 6)} + 6) = k\overline{(z - c)} + c = -\frac{1}{2}\overline{(z - 4)} + 4$. The center of the dilative reflection is

$(4, 0)$ and the reflecting line has equation $x = 4$.

10.　　$S_{C,k}(r_{m,C}(z)) = k((z_\varphi\overline{(z - c)} + c) - c) + c = k((z_\varphi\overline{(z - c)} + c) - c) + c = kz_\varphi\overline{(z - c)} + c$. Since k is real,

$\overline{k} = k$. So $kz_\varphi\overline{(z - c)} + c = z_\varphi\overline{(k(z - c))} + c = z_\varphi\overline{((k(z - c) + c) - c)} + c = r_{m,C}(S_{C,k}(z))$.

11.　　To get $S_{C,k}$, the size change with center C and magnitude k, apply the composite transformation
　　　$T_C \circ S_k \circ T_{-C}$. Thus $S_{C,k}(z) = T_C(S_C(T_{-C}(z))) = k(z - c) + c$.

12.　　a.　　T is of the form $T(z) = a\overline{z} + b$, where $|a| = 1$. So T is an opposite congruence.

　　　b.　　T is of the form $T(z) = az + b$, where $|a| = 1$. So T is a direct congruence.

　　　c.　　T is of the form $T(z) = az + b$, where $|a| = 2\sqrt{2}$. So T is direct similarity with ratio of similitude
　　　　　$2\sqrt{2}$.

　　　d.　　T is of the form $T(z) = a\overline{z} + b$, where $|a| = 2$. So T is an opposite similarity with ratio of
　　　　　similitude 2.

13.　　a.　　Since T is of the form $az + b$, it is a direct similarity with ratio of similitude $|a| = 2$. Thus
　　　　　$T = S_{P,2} \circ D$, where $S_{P,2}$ is a size change with center P and magnitude 2 and D is some direct
　　　　　congruence transformation. To determine D, consider $\triangle ABC$ whose vertices in the complex plane
　　　　　are given by $a = 0$, $b = 1$, and $c = i$. We have $T(a) = 4 + i$, $T(b) = 4 + 3i$, and $T(c) = 2 + i$. By
　　　　　graphing, it can be seen that the transformation D must rotate $\triangle ABC$ by a magnitude of 90°.
　　　　　Therefore $D = R_{P,90°}$, where P, the center of the size change, is also the center of the rotation.
　　　　　Letting p be the number in the complex plane corresponding to point P, we have
　　　　　$S_{P,2} \circ R_{P,90°} = 2(i(z - p) + p - p) + p = 2iz + 4 + i$. Simplifying yields $-2ip + p = 4 + i$, or
　　　　　$p = \frac{2}{5} + \frac{9}{5}i$. Thus $T = S_{(2/5,9/5),2} \circ R_{(2/5,9/5),90°}$, a 90° rotation around the point $(\frac{2}{5}, \frac{9}{5})$ followed by a
　　　　　size change with center $(\frac{2}{5}, \frac{9}{5})$ and magnitude 2.

　　　b.　　The transformation T^{-1} must be a size change with center $(\frac{2}{5}, \frac{9}{5})$ and magnitude $\frac{1}{2}$ followed by a
　　　　　$-90°$ rotation around the point $(\frac{2}{5}, \frac{9}{5})$. Thus
　　　　　$T^{-1}(z) = -i(\frac{1}{2}(z - (\frac{2}{5} + \frac{9}{5}i)) + (\frac{2}{5} + \frac{9}{5}i) - (\frac{2}{5} + \frac{9}{5}i)) + (\frac{2}{5} + \frac{9}{5}i) = -\frac{i}{2}z + \frac{-1 + 4i}{2}$.

14.　　a.　　The direct similarity is of the form $D(z) = az + b$. So we have $a(1 + i) + b = -1 + 2i$ and
　　　　　$a(2 - i) + b = 3 - i$. Solving this system of 2 equations and 2 unknowns yields
　　　　　$D(z) = (2 + i)z + (-2 - i)$. The opposite similarity is of the form $O(z) = c\overline{z} + d$. So we have
　　　　　$c\overline{(1 + i)} + d = c(1 - i) + d = -1 + 2i$ and $c\overline{(2 - i)} + d = c(2 + i) + d = 3 - i$. Solving this system

yields $O(z) = (-\frac{2}{5} - \frac{11}{5}i)\, \bar{z} + \frac{8}{5} + \frac{19}{5}i$.

b. In general, for a direct similarity mapping z_1 onto w_1 and z_2 onto w_2, $a(z_2 - z_1) = w_2 - w_1$. So

$a = \dfrac{w_2 - w_1}{z_2 - z_1}$ and $b = w_1 - \dfrac{w_2 - w_1}{z_2 - z_1} z_1$. For an indirect similarity mapping z_1 onto w_1 and z_2 onto w_2,

$c\overline{(z_2 - z_1)} = w_2 - w_1$. So $c = \dfrac{w_2 - w_1}{\overline{(z_2 - z_1)}}$ and $d = w_1 - \dfrac{w_2 - w_1}{\overline{(z_2 - z_1)}} \bar{z_1}$.

15. Let e be the number in the complex plane corresponding to point E. Then
$S_{D,m}(S_{C,k}(z)) = m(k(z - c) + c - d) + d = kmz - kmc + m(c - d) + d = km(z - e) + e$. Thus

$S_{D,m} \circ S_{C,k} = S_{E,km}$, where $e = \dfrac{-kmc + m(c - d) + d}{1 - km}$. Because

$e = \dfrac{-kmc + m(c - d) + d + c - c}{1 - km} = c + \dfrac{1 - m}{1 - km}(d - c)$, point E is on $\overleftrightarrow{CD}$. The ratio of EC to ED is given by

$\dfrac{|e - c|}{|e - d|} = \dfrac{|-kmc + m(c - d) + d - (1 - km)c|}{|-kmc + m(c - d) + d - (1 - km)d|} = \dfrac{|1 - m|}{|m(1 - k)|}$.

Section 8.3.1

1. a. The tangent is perpendicular to a radius, so $OP = \sqrt{15^2 + 10^2} = 5\sqrt{13}$.

   b. Sample: Let $\overline{PT}$ be a tangent to circle O at T. If circle O has radius r, then $OP = \sqrt{PT^2 + r^2}$.

2. Since $m\angle CDB = m\angle ACB = 90°$ and $m\angle DBC = m\angle CBA$, by AA Similarity, $\triangle CBD \sim \triangle ABC$, with side $\overline{CD}$ corresponding to side $\overline{AC}$, side $\overline{DB}$ corresponding to side $\overline{CB}$, and side $\overline{CB}$ corresponding to side $\overline{AB}$. Similarly, since $m\angle CDA = m\angle ACB = 90°$ and $m\angle CAD = m\angle CAB$, by AA Similarity, $\triangle ACD \sim \triangle ABC$, with side $\overline{AD}$ corresponding to side $\overline{AC}$, side $\overline{DC}$ corresponding to side $\overline{CB}$, and side $\overline{AC}$ corresponding to side $\overline{AB}$. Since similarity is an equivalence relation, $\triangle ACD \sim \triangle CBD$.

3. $x = \sqrt{8^2 - 3^2} = \sqrt{55}; \ 3^2 = \sqrt{55}\,y$, so $y = \dfrac{9}{\sqrt{55}}; \ c = x + y = \sqrt{55} + \dfrac{9}{\sqrt{55}} = \dfrac{64\sqrt{55}}{55};$

   $b = \sqrt{3^2 + \left(\dfrac{9}{\sqrt{55}}\right)^2} = \dfrac{24\sqrt{55}}{55}$

4. a. By Theorem 8.27, $h^2 = 80y$, and by the Pythagorean Theorem, $y^2 = 75 - h^2$. So
   $h^4 = 80^2(75 - h^2)$, or $h^4 + 80^2h^2 - (80^2)(75^2) = 0$. Making the substitution $k = h^2$, the quartic
   equation becomes the quadratic $k^2 + 80^2k - (80^2)(75^2) = 0$. By the Quadratic Formula,

   $k = \dfrac{-80^2 + \sqrt{80^4 + 4(80^2)(75^2)}}{2} = 3600$. So $h = \sqrt{k} = 60$ and $y = \sqrt{75^2 - h^2} = 45$. From this,

   $c = x + y = 125$ and $a = \sqrt{h^2 + x^2} = 100$.

   b. In general, $h = \sqrt{\dfrac{-x^2 + \sqrt{x^4 + 4x^2b^2}}{2}}$. By letting $x = 1$ and $b = 1$, we get $h = \sqrt{\dfrac{-1 + \sqrt{5}}{2}}$, which is not

   rational and so the statement is false.

5.   a.   Since $\triangle BCA \sim \triangle BDC$ by AA Similarity, $\frac{BC}{BA} = \frac{BD}{BC}$. Thus $BC^2 = \sqrt{BD \cdot BA}$. Since

        $\triangle DCA \sim \triangle DBC$ by AA Similarity, $\frac{DC}{DB} = \frac{DA}{DC}$. Thus $DC^2 = \sqrt{DA \cdot DC}$.

    b.   Case 1: Suppose two of a, b, and c are given. Then the Pythagorean Theorem determines the third. Then Theorem 8.27b determines x and Theorem 8.27a determines y, and finally, Theorem 8.27c determines h.

        Case 2: Suppose two of b, h, and y are given. Then the Pythagorean Theorem determines the third. From b and y, x and then c follow using Theorem 8.27a. Since b and c determine a, the rest follows using Case 1.

        Case 3: Suppose two of a, h, and x are given. This is like Case 2.

        Case 4: Suppose two of x, y, and c are given. Then the third is easily found by addition or subtraction and h is determined using Theorem 8.27c. Now we can apply Case 2 to get the result.

        Case 5: Suppose b and x are given. Then, using the solution to Problem 4b, h is found. Now we are again at Case 2. Similarly, if a and y are given, h can be found and we are at Case 3.

        Case 6: Suppose c and h are given. Then $x(c - x) = h^2$ implies $x = \frac{c \pm \sqrt{c^2 - 4h^2}}{2}$. There are two possible solutions because x could refer to either one of the two pieces of c. With the value of x, the situation is reduced to Case 3 or Case 5.

6.   From right angle trigonometry, $\frac{a}{c} = \cos B$ and $\frac{b}{c} = \sin B$, so, if $c = 1$, $a = \cos B$ and $b = \sin B$. We also have $\frac{h}{a} = \sin B$ and $\frac{x}{a} = \cos B$, so $h = \sin B \cos B$ and $x = \cos^2 B$. Finally, $\frac{y}{b} = \sin B$, since $\angle DCA \cong \angle ABC$, so $y = \sin^2 B$.

7.   Let $x = AD$ and $y = DB$. Then, by Theorem 8.28, $CD = \sqrt{xy}$. Since M is the midpoint of AB, $MB = \frac{x + y}{2}$. However, $MB = CM \geq CD$. Thus $\frac{x + y}{2} \geq \sqrt{xy}$. The condition $CM = CD$ only holds when $D = M$, in which case $MB = y = \frac{x + y}{2}$, or $y = x$.

8. $PA = PO - OA$ and $PB = PO + OB$. Since O is the center of the circle, $OA = OB$ and $PA + PB = 2PO$. So PO equals $\frac{PA + PB}{2}$, the arithmetic mean of PA and PB.

9. $PH = PO = PT$, and $H(a, b) = G(a, b) = A(a, b)$.

10. $CP = DP$ and $CP \cdot DP = AP \cdot BP$. Thus $CP^2 = AP \cdot BP$, or $CP = \sqrt{AP \cdot BP}$. That is, CP is the geometric mean of AP and BP.

11.   Proof: P is exterior to $\angle EBC$, so $m\angle PBE = m\angle EBC + m\angle PBC$. Thus $A(\angle PBE, \angle PBC) = \frac{m\angle EBC + 2m\angle PBC}{2} = m\angle CBD + m\angle PBC = m\angle PBD$.

12.   Disproof: Let $RP = y$, $RQ = x$, and $MQ = z$, and suppose $RM = A(RP, RQ) = \frac{y + x}{2}$. Then $x^2 + y^2 = (2z)^2$ and also $\left(\frac{y + x}{2}\right)^2 = z^2$. So and $x^2 + y^2 = 4z^2$ and $(x + y)^2 = 4z^2$. So $x^2 + y^2 = x^2 + 2xy + y^2$. Thus, either $x = 0$ or $y = 0$, which is impossible.

13. $AQ = OA + OQ$ and $BQ = OB - OQ$. So $OP = OA = OB = \frac{AQ + BQ}{2}$ is the arithmetic mean of AQ and BQ. Point Q is the foot of the altitude to the hypotenuse $\overline{AB}$ of right triangle APB. So, by Theorem 8.28(3), PQ is the geometric mean of AQ and BQ. Lastly, $H(AQ, BQ) = \frac{G(AQ,BQ)^2}{A(AQ,BQ)} = \frac{PQ^2}{PO}$ $= PR$, since, by Theorem 8.28(1), PQ is the geometric mean of PR and PO.

Section 8.3.2

1. Since line ℓ is parallel to $\overleftrightarrow{AB}$, $m\angle OCD = m\angle OAB$ and $m\angle ODC = m\angle OBA$. Thus, by AA Similarity, $\triangle COD \sim \triangle AOD$ and $\frac{OC}{OA} = \frac{OD}{OB} = \frac{DC}{AB}$.

2. Since $\overleftrightarrow{B'C'}$ is parallel to $\overleftrightarrow{BC}$, by Theorem 8.29, $\frac{B'A}{BA} = \frac{C'A}{CA}$. So $1 - \frac{B'A}{BA} = 1 - \frac{C'A}{CA}$. Substituting $\frac{AB}{AB}$ and $\frac{AC}{AC}$ for 1, $\frac{AB}{AB} - \frac{B'A}{BA} = \frac{AC}{AC} - \frac{C'A}{CA}$, or $\frac{BB'}{BA} = \frac{CC'}{AC}$. Since M is the midpoint of $\overline{AC}$, $AM = CM$. Since P is the image of C' under a rotation around point M, $MP = MC'$, and since the rotation has magnitude $180°$, C', M, and P are collinear. Thus $AP = AM - MP = CM - MC' = CC'$ and $\frac{BB'}{BA} = \frac{AP}{AC}$.

3. The Multiplication Property of Equality. To get equation (2), both sides of equation (1) are multiplied by $\frac{OA}{OD}$.

4. a. Part c involves part-part ratios on each segment.
    b. Part b involves part-whole ratios on each segment.
    c. Part a involves part-part and whole-whole ratios on different segments.

5. Suppose an object moves at a constant speed from a point D at time T to a point D' at time T'. If the total time interval TT' is partitioned into subintervals t_i, then $\frac{d_i}{t_i}$, the ratio of the distance the object travels in any time subinterval to the duration of that time subinterval, is a constant equal to the object's average speed $\frac{DD'}{TT'}$.

6. We can assume the car and pedestrian are traveling in parallel, but opposite, directions at constant speeds c and p, respectively. The view of the pedestrian is initially blocked by the tree for some small duration of time $\Delta t = t_2 - t_1$. This means the lines of sight at t_2 and t_1 intersect at the position of the tree. Due to similar triangles, then, it must be the case that the ratio of the distances traveled by pedestrian and car is $\frac{p\Delta t}{c\Delta t} = \frac{p}{c} = \frac{5}{25}$. At some later time t_3, the pedestrian has traveled a distance $p(t_3 - t_1)$ and the car has traveled a distance $c(t_3 - t_1)$. The ratio of distances traveled by pedestrian and car does not change, since $\frac{p(t_3 - t_1)}{c(t_3 - t_1)} = \frac{p}{c} = \frac{5}{25}$. Given that the triangles formed by the lines of sight at times t_1 and t_3 are still similar, the altitudes of these triangles must still be in the ratio $\frac{5}{25}$, which means they must continue to intersect at the position of the tree. That is, the ratio of speeds tends to be equal to the ratio of distances, which is why if the tree is blocking the view at one time, it will continue to block the view.

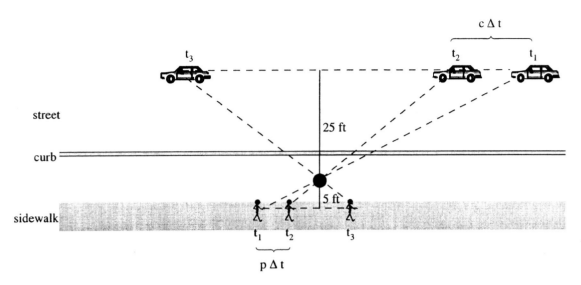

7. In the diagram below, the image of the hallway is projected onto the screen (or camera film). On the photograph the distance from the middle to the ceiling of the near end of the hallway is i_1 and the distance from the middle to the floor of the far end of the hallway is i_2. By similar triangles, $\frac{i_1}{6} = \frac{c}{15}$ and $\frac{i_2}{6} = \frac{c}{15+x}$. Dividing the second equation by the first yields $\frac{i_2}{i_1} = \frac{15}{15+x}$. Measurements on the photograph indicate $\frac{i_2}{i_1} = \frac{1}{3}$. So $\frac{15}{15+x} = \frac{1}{3}$, or x = 30 ft.

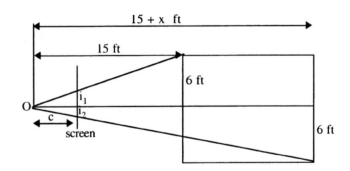

8. a. Consider just the x-z plane, as pictured below. By similar triangles, we have $\frac{x}{c} = \frac{X}{c+Z}$. So $x = \frac{cX}{c+Z}$. Similarly, by looking at the y-z plane, we have $y = \frac{cY}{c+Z}$. Thus $(x, y) = (\frac{cX}{c+Z}, \frac{cY}{c+Z}, Z)$.

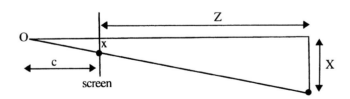

b. Consider any point of the form $(0, 0, Z)$ in the real scene. These will all map onto the point $(0, 0)$ in the perspective scene. Thus the mapping from the perspective scene onto the real scene is not 1-1 and so does not have an inverse.

9. Let h be the height of the observer and t be the length of each pole. Then, in the real scene, the coordinates (X, Y, Z) of the bottom and top of the nth pole are, respectively, $(-w, -h, q + (n-1)s)$ and $(-w, t-h, \ q + (n-1)s)$. Using the results of Problem 8a, the corresponding perspective coordinates are $(x, y) = (\dfrac{-wc}{c+q+(n-1)s}, \dfrac{-hc}{c+q+(n-1)s})$ for the bottom and $(x, y) = (\dfrac{-wc}{c+q+(n-1)s}, \dfrac{(t-h)c}{c+q+(n-1)s})$.

10. a. The right rail will intersect the plane of the screen at $(\frac{w}{2}, -h)$ and the vanishing point of the tracks will have coordinates $(0, 0)$. So $\tan\frac{\alpha}{2} = \frac{w}{2h}$, or $\alpha = 2\tan^{-1}\frac{w}{2h}$.

b. From part **a**, $h = \dfrac{w}{2\tan\frac{\alpha}{2}}$. Measuring the photograph directly gives $\tan\frac{\alpha}{2} = \frac{3}{4}$. So

$h = \dfrac{56.5}{2\left(\frac{3}{4}\right)} \approx 37.7$ inches.

c. Let x and y be the distances from the photograph's vanishing point to the first and second ties, respectively. Then $\frac{x}{y} = \frac{15+1}{15}$, or $y = \frac{15}{16}x$. So the distance from the first to the second tie will be

$x - y = \frac{1}{16}x$

CHAPTER 9 – Trigonometry

Section 9.1.1

1. If the radian measure of the arc equals its length, then the circumference of the circle is 2π, so the radius is 1.

2. The length of the arc is $\frac{212}{360} \cdot 28\pi \approx 51.8$ units.

3. a. Let O be the center of a circle with radius 2 and let $\overline{AB}$ be a chord of length 1. Also let $m\angle AOB = 2\theta$ = measure of minor arc $\overset{\frown}{AB}$. Then $2\pi - 2\theta$ = measure of major arc $\overset{\frown}{AB}$. Let C be the midpoint of $\overline{AB}$. Then $\overline{OC}$ is the bisector of $\angle AOB$ and $m\angle COB = \theta$.

   $\sin\theta = \frac{CB}{r} = \frac{\frac{1}{2}}{2} = \frac{1}{4}$, so $\theta = \sin^{-1}\frac{1}{4} \approx .253$ radians. The measure of minor arc $\overset{\frown}{AB} = 2\theta \approx .50536$ radians and the measure of major arc $\overset{\frown}{AB} = 2\pi - 2\theta \approx 5.778$ radians.

   b. Let the circle in part a have radius r and let $\overline{AB}$ be any chord of that circle. Then $\sin\theta = \frac{AB}{2r}$ implies that $\theta = \sin^{-1}(\frac{AB}{2r})$. The measure of minor arc $\overset{\frown}{AB} = 2\sin^{-1}(\frac{AB}{2r})$ and the measure of major arc $\overset{\frown}{AB} = 2\pi - 2\sin^{-1}(\frac{AB}{2r})$.

4. a. $37°6'52" = (37 + \frac{6}{60} + \frac{52}{3600})° = 37(\frac{412}{3600})° = 37.11\overline{4}°$

   b. $37.11\overline{4}° \cdot \frac{\pi}{180} \approx .6478$ radians

   c. $\sin^{-1}(.4) \approx 23.57818°$. $60(.57818) = 34.6908$ and $60(.6908) = 41.448 \Rightarrow \sin^{-1}(.4) \approx 23°34'41"$.

5. There are 60 seconds in one full revolution of the second hand, so every second the second hand sweeps an arc of $\frac{360°}{60} = 6°$ or $\frac{2\pi}{60} = \frac{\pi}{30}$ radians. In x seconds the second hand will sweep out an arc of $6x°$ or $\frac{\pi x}{30}$ radians. Similarly, since there are 3600 seconds in one full revolution of the minute hand, the minute hand traces an arc of $\frac{360°}{3600}x = \frac{1}{10}x°$ or $\frac{2\pi}{3600}x = \frac{\pi x}{1800}$ radians in x seconds and since there are 43,200 seconds in one full revolution of the hour hand, the hour hand traces an arc of $\frac{360°}{43200}x = \frac{1}{120}x°$ or $\frac{2\pi}{43200}x = \frac{\pi x}{21600}$ radians in x seconds.

6. 1 grad $= \frac{1}{400}$ of a revolution and 1 degree $= \frac{1}{360}$ of a revolution, so $\frac{x°}{360} = \frac{y}{400}$ grad $\Rightarrow \frac{10}{9}x° = y$ grad. Thus $\frac{10}{9}(30°) = 33.\overline{3}$ grads; $\frac{10}{9}(45°) = 50$ grads; and $\frac{10}{9}(60°) = 66.\overline{6}$ grads. Similarly, $\frac{160}{9}x° = y$ mils, so $\frac{160}{9}(30°) = 533.\overline{3}$ mils; $\frac{160}{9}(45°) = 800$ mils; and $\frac{160}{9}(60°) = 1066.\overline{6}$ mils.

7. Since 1 mil $= \frac{1}{6400}$ of a revolution, the arc length subtended by an angle of 1 mil will be $\frac{2\pi r}{6400} \approx \frac{r}{1000}$, where r is the distance from the observer to the object, so the arc length of a 2 mil arc will be about $\frac{r}{500}$.

If we know that the arc length (i.e. height of the tank) is 9 ft, then $\frac{r}{500} \approx 9$ ft $\Rightarrow r \approx 4500$ ft or about $\frac{9}{10}$ of a mile.

8. a. Using the fact that $\theta° = \frac{\pi\theta}{180}$ radians and substituting:

    i. $\frac{d}{d\theta}(\sin(\frac{\pi\theta}{180})) = \frac{\pi}{180}\cos(\frac{\pi\theta}{180})$ which means that $\frac{d}{d\theta}(\sin\theta) = \frac{\pi}{180}\cos\theta$ when θ is in degrees.

    ii. $\lim\limits_{\theta\to 0}\frac{\sin(\frac{\pi\theta}{180})}{\frac{\pi\theta}{180}} = 1 \Rightarrow \frac{180}{\pi}\lim\limits_{\theta\to 0}\frac{\sin(\frac{\pi\theta}{180})}{\theta} = 1 \Rightarrow \lim\limits_{\theta\to 0}\frac{\sin(\frac{\pi\theta}{180})}{\theta} = \frac{\pi}{180}$, so when θ is in degrees,

    $\lim\limits_{\theta\to 0}\frac{\sin\theta}{\theta} = \frac{\pi}{180}$.

    iii. $\sin\theta° = \sin(\frac{\pi\theta}{180}) = \frac{\pi\theta}{180} - \frac{(\frac{\pi\theta}{180})^3}{3!} + \frac{(\frac{\pi\theta}{180})^5}{5!} - \dots + \frac{(-1)^k(\frac{\pi\theta}{180})^{(2k+1)}}{(2k+1)!} + \dots$

    b. Similarly, using θ grads $= \frac{\pi}{200}$ radians and substituting,:

    i. When θ is in grads, $\frac{d}{d\theta}(\sin\theta) = \frac{\pi}{200}\cos\theta$.

    ii. When θ is in grads, $\lim\limits_{\theta\to 0}\frac{\sin\theta}{\theta} = \frac{\pi}{200}$.

    iii. $\sin(\theta \text{ grads}) = \sin(\frac{\pi\theta}{200}) = \frac{\pi\theta}{200} - \frac{(\frac{\pi\theta}{200})^3}{3!} + \frac{(\frac{\pi\theta}{200})^5}{5!} - \dots + \frac{(-1)^k(\frac{\pi\theta}{200})^{(2k+1)}}{(2k+1)!} + \dots$

9. $S_r = \pi r^2 \cdot \frac{\theta}{2\pi}$ where $\theta = m\angle ACB$, so $\frac{2S_r}{r^2} = \frac{2\pi r^2 \cdot \frac{\theta}{2\pi}}{r^2} = \frac{2\pi r \cdot \frac{\theta}{2\pi}}{r} = \frac{2A_r}{r}$ since $A_r = 2\pi r \cdot \frac{\theta}{2\pi}$ in Definition 2. The definitions are equivalent because the ratios are equal.

10. Prove that if $\frac{L_1}{r_1} = \frac{L_2}{r_2}$ then $\overset{\frown}{A_1B_1}$ and $\overset{\frown}{A_2B_2}$ have the same measure. From Theorem 9.2 we know that $L_1 = r_1\theta_1$ and $L_2 = r_2\theta_2$ where θ_1 and θ_2 are the measures of $\overset{\frown}{A_1B_1}$ and $\overset{\frown}{A_2B_2}$ respectively. Substituting, we get $\frac{r_1\theta_1}{r_1} = \frac{r_2\theta_2}{r_2} \Rightarrow \theta_1 = \theta_2$, so $\overset{\frown}{A_1B_1}$ and $\overset{\frown}{A_2B_2}$ have the same measure.

Section 9.1.2

1. Applying the Law of Cosines to a right triangle where c is the hypotenuse, then $c^2 = a^2 + b^2 - 2ab\cos 90° \Rightarrow c^2 = a^2 + b^2$ since $\cos 90° = 0$.

2. ($\Rightarrow$) If C is obtuse, then $0 > \cos C > -1$. Since $\cos C$ is negative, $-2ab\cos C$ is positive, so $c^2 = a^2 + b^2 - 2ab\cos C \Rightarrow c^2 > a^2 + b^2$. ($\Leftarrow$) If $c^2 = a^2 + b^2 - 2ab\cos C$ and $c^2 > a^2 + b^2$, then $-2ab\cos C > 0$. Since both a and b are positive, $\cos C$ must be negative. $0 < m\angle C < 180°$ since C is in a triangle, and in that domain, $\cos C < 0$ only when $90° < m\angle C < 180°$, so C is obtuse.

3. a. Construct the circumcircle S of $\triangle ABC$ and a second triangle $\triangle A'B'C'$, where $A = A'$, so that $\overline{AB'}$ is a diameter of S and $\angle B'AC' \cong \angle BAC$. Then $\angle C'$ is a right angle and $\sin A = \frac{B'C'}{AB'} \Rightarrow AB' = \frac{B'C'}{\sin A}$. Since

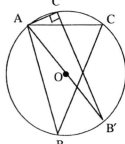

$\angle B'AC' \cong \angle BAC$, $m\overset{\frown}{B'C'} = m\overset{\frown}{BC} \Rightarrow B'C' = BC$.

Substituting BC for B'C', $AB' = \frac{BC}{\sin A}$ where $BC = a$,

since BC is the side opposite of angle A. Thus $\frac{a}{\sin A} = AB' \Rightarrow K = AB'$, the diameter of S.

b.   If $K = 1$, then $\frac{a}{\sin A} = 1 \Rightarrow a = \sin A$. Similarly, $b = \sin B$ and $c = \sin C$.

4.   Let $\angle ACB$ be inscribed in a circle of diameter 1 and center O
and let $m\angle ACB = \theta$. Then the measure of $\overset{\frown}{AB} = 2\theta$
$= m\angle AOB$, since the measure of the arc subtended by an
inscribed angle is twice the measure of the angle. Let D be
the midpoint of $\overline{AB}$. Then $\overline{OD}$ bisects $\angle AOB$, $\overline{OD} \perp \overline{AB}$
and $m\angle DOB = \theta$. Now $\sin\theta = \frac{DB}{OB} = \frac{\frac{1}{2}AB}{\frac{1}{2}}$ because $\overline{OB}$ is
a radius $\Rightarrow \sin\theta = AB$, the length of the chord of the arc
subtended by $\angle ACB$.

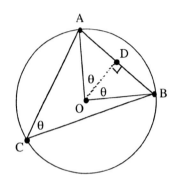

5.   Because $OC = OA$, $\triangle AOC$ is isosceles, with
$m\angle OCA = m\angle OAC$. Thus exterior angle $\angle BOC$ has
measure 2A. Thus chord $\overline{BC}$, which has length L_{2A},
corresponds to the central angle with measure 2A. From
right triangle trigonometry, then, $\sin A = \frac{L_{2A}}{120}$.

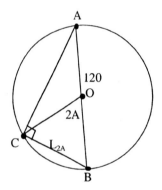

6.   Using the distance formula:
$c^2 = AB^2 = (b\cos C - a)^2 + (b\sin C - 0)^2$
$= b^2\cos^2 C - 2ab\cos C + a^2 + b^2\sin^2 C$
$= a^2 + b^2(\sin^2 C + \cos^2 C) - 2ab\cos C$
$= a^2 + b^2\ 2ab\cos C$.

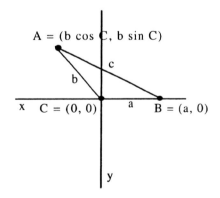

7.   a.   From the figure, $\sin A = \frac{h}{b}$ and $\sin B = \frac{h}{a}$. So $b\sin A = a\sin B = h$, or $\frac{\sin A}{a} = \frac{\sin B}{b}$.

b.   By drawing another altitude h' from vertex A to $\overline{CB}$, we can show that $\sin C = \frac{h'}{b}$ and $\sin B = \frac{h'}{c}$.

Thus $b\sin C = c\sin B = h'$, or $\dfrac{\sin C}{c} = \dfrac{\sin B}{b}$. Using the result from part **a**,

$\dfrac{\sin A}{a} = \dfrac{\sin B}{b} = \dfrac{\sin C}{c}$.

8. a. We know that in any triangle $\dfrac{a}{\sin A} = \dfrac{b}{\sin B} \Rightarrow \sin B = \dfrac{b \sin A}{a}$. If $a \geq b$ then

$m\angle A > m\angle B \Rightarrow 0 < m\angle B < 90°$, so $\sin B = \dfrac{b \sin A}{a}$ has a unique solution and with two sides and two angles the triangle can be solved.

   b. When $a < b$, then $0 < m\angle B < 180°$ and $\sin B = \dfrac{b \sin A}{a}$ has two solutions whenever $a > b \sin A$.

So there are two triangles satisfying the conditions. When $a = b \sin A$, then $\sin B = \dfrac{b \sin A}{a} = 1$ $\Rightarrow m\angle B = 90°$. So there is a unique triangle satisfying the conditions.

   c. When $a < b \sin A$, then $\sin B = \dfrac{b \sin A}{a} > 1$, so there is no solution and therefore no triangle possible.

Section 9.1.3

1. a. Since the pole is vertical, $\gamma = m\angle APQ$. From the Law of Sines, then, $\dfrac{\sin \gamma}{d} = \dfrac{\sin \alpha}{h}$, so $h = d\dfrac{\sin \alpha}{\sin \gamma}$.

   b. It can be seen from the diagram that, even if the flagpole is down in a valley, the formula from part **a** will hold true. As long as $\alpha + \gamma < \pi$, the pole and the lines of sight to the top and bottom of the pole will form a triangle and the Law of Sines will apply. Notice that no matter how long the pole is, the condition $\alpha + \gamma < \pi$ will always be true.

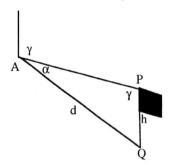

   c. In the case of Question 1, $\gamma = \dfrac{\pi}{2} - \alpha$, so $\sin \gamma = \cos \alpha$ and $h = d\dfrac{\sin \alpha}{\cos \alpha} = d \tan \alpha$.

2. The diagram shows that $m\angle BQT = \dfrac{\pi}{2} - \varepsilon$. By the Exterior Angle Theorem,

$m\angle BPQ = m\angle BQT - \beta = \dfrac{\pi}{2} - (\varepsilon + \beta)$ and $m\angle APQ = \dfrac{\pi}{2} - (\varepsilon + \alpha)$. By the Law of Sines, (1)

$\dfrac{\sin(m\angle BPQ)}{BA} = \dfrac{\sin \beta}{h}$ and (2) $\dfrac{\sin(m\angle APQ)}{AQ} = \dfrac{\sin \alpha}{h}$. From (1), $h = \dfrac{BA \sin \beta}{\cos(\varepsilon + \beta)}$. From (2),

$AQ = \dfrac{h \cos(\varepsilon + \alpha)}{\sin \alpha}$. Since $BA = m + AQ$, $h = (m + \dfrac{h \cos(\varepsilon + \alpha)}{\sin \alpha})\dfrac{\sin \beta}{\cos(\varepsilon + \beta)}$. Solving for h yields

$h = \dfrac{m \sin \alpha \sin \beta}{\sin \alpha \cos(\varepsilon + \beta) - \sin \beta \cos(\varepsilon + \alpha)}$.

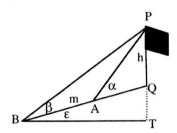

3.　From the Law of Sines, $\dfrac{\sin\beta}{AQ} = \dfrac{\sin(\pi - (\beta + \gamma))}{b}$ and $\dfrac{\sin(\pi - (\alpha + \varepsilon))}{AQ} = \dfrac{\sin\alpha}{h}$. Dividing the first equation

by the second gives $\dfrac{\sin\beta}{\sin(\pi - (\alpha + \varepsilon))} = \dfrac{h\sin(\pi - (\beta + \gamma))}{b\sin\alpha}$. Solving for h and simplifying yields

$h = \dfrac{b\sin\alpha\sin\beta}{\sin(\alpha + \varepsilon)\sin(\beta + \gamma)}$.

4.　a.　From the diagram $m\angle BPA = \pi - (u + t)$ and $m\angle BQA = \pi - (v + s)$. From the Law of Sines,

$\dfrac{\sin u}{AP} = \dfrac{\sin(m\angle BPA)}{b} = \dfrac{\sin(\pi - (u + t))}{b} = \dfrac{\sin(u + t)}{b}$ and

$\dfrac{\sin v}{AQ} = \dfrac{\sin(m\angle BQA)}{b} = \dfrac{\sin(\pi - (v + s))}{b} = \dfrac{\sin(v + s)}{b}$. So $AP = \dfrac{b\sin u}{\sin(u + t)}$ and $AQ = \dfrac{b\sin v}{\sin(v + s)}$.

From the Law of Cosines, $h^2 = AP^2 + AQ^2 - 2(AP)(AQ)\cos r$

$= \dfrac{b^2\sin^2 u}{\sin^2(u + t)} + \dfrac{b^2\sin^2 v}{\sin^2(v + s)} - 2\dfrac{b^2\sin u\sin v}{\sin(u + t)\sin(v + s)}\cos r$.

Thus $h = b\sqrt{\dfrac{\sin^2 u}{\sin^2(u + t)} + \dfrac{\sin^2 v}{\sin^2(v + s)} - 2\dfrac{\sin u\sin v}{\sin(u + t)\sin(v + s)}\cos r}$.

　　b.　As in part **a**, using the Law of Sines, we can find BP and BQ from the relationships

$\dfrac{\sin t}{BP} = \dfrac{\sin(u + t)}{b}$ and $\dfrac{\sin s}{BQ} = \dfrac{\sin(v + s)}{b}$. Since $PQ = h$, from the Law of Cosines,

$w = \cos^{-1}\left(\dfrac{h^2 - \left(BP^2 + BQ^2\right)}{-2(BP)(BQ)}\right)$.

5.　The information is insufficient. Consider the flag positioned closer to the building, as shown. Even though it is taller, it will have the same angles of elevation and depression when viewed from the same two floors of the building.

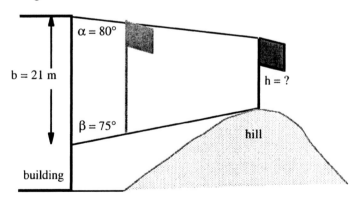

6.   a.   Let $a = 13$, $b = 14$, and $c = 15$. Then $c^2 = a^2 + b^2 - 2ab \cos C \Rightarrow \cos C = \dfrac{c^2 - a^2 - b^2}{-2ab} \Rightarrow$

$\cos C = \dfrac{15^2 - 13^2 - 14^2}{-2(13)(14)} = .\overline{384615} \Rightarrow m\angle C \approx 67.38°$. Similarly,

$\cos A = \dfrac{a^2 - b^2 - c^2}{-2bc} = \dfrac{13^2 - 14^2 - 15^2}{-2(14)(15)} = .6 \Rightarrow m\angle A \approx 53.13°$,

and $\cos B = \dfrac{b^2 - a^2 - c^2}{-2ac} = \dfrac{14^2 - 13^2 - 15^2}{-2(13)(15)} = .5\overline{076923} \Rightarrow m\angle B \approx 59.49°$.

b. $\sin C = \sin 67.38° = .923076$, so $\dfrac{c}{\sin C} = \dfrac{15}{.923076} = 16.25 \Rightarrow \dfrac{a}{\sin A} = 16.25$

and $\dfrac{b}{\sin B} = 16.25 \Rightarrow \sin A = \dfrac{a}{16.25} = \dfrac{13}{16.25} = .8$ and $\sin B = \dfrac{b}{16.25} = \dfrac{14}{16.25} = .861538$.

7.   a.   From the diagram,

$L = 2 \cdot 6 + \dfrac{2\pi \cdot 3}{2} + \dfrac{2\pi \cdot 3}{2} = 12 + 6\pi$.

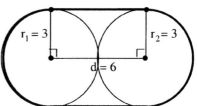

b.   From the diagram,

$L = 2d + \dfrac{2\pi \cdot r_1}{2} + \dfrac{2\pi \cdot r_2}{2}$

$= 2(r_1 + r_2) + \pi(r_1 + r_2)$

$= (2 + \pi)(r_1 + r_2) = (4 + 2\pi)r_1$.

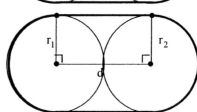

c.

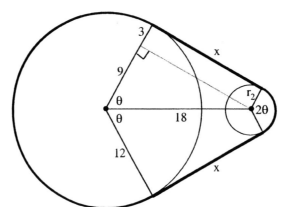

From the diagram, $L = 2x + \dfrac{2\pi - 2\theta}{2\pi} \cdot 2\pi \cdot r_1 + \dfrac{2\theta}{2\pi} \cdot 2\pi \cdot r_2$. We know that

$\cos \theta = \dfrac{9}{18} \Rightarrow \theta = \dfrac{\pi}{3} \Rightarrow x = 9\sqrt{3}$, so we have:

$L = 2(9\sqrt{3}) + \dfrac{2\pi - 2(\frac{\pi}{3})}{2\pi} \cdot 2\pi \cdot 12 + \dfrac{2(\frac{\pi}{3})}{2\pi} \cdot 2\pi \cdot 3 = 18\sqrt{3} + 16\pi + 2\pi = 18(\sqrt{3} + \pi)$.

d.

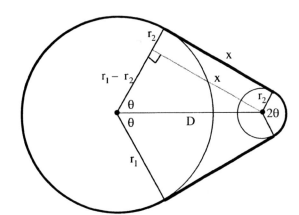

Again, L = 2x + $\frac{2\pi - 2\theta}{2\pi}$ • 2π • r_1 + $\frac{2\theta}{2\pi}$• 2π • r_2. We know that

$\cos \theta = \frac{r_1 - r_2}{D} \Rightarrow \theta = \cos^{-1}(\frac{r_1 - r_2}{D})$ and $x^2 = D^2 + (r_1 - r_2)^2 \Rightarrow x = \sqrt{D^2 - (r_1 - r_2)^2}$. Thus,

$L = 2\sqrt{D^2 - (r_1 - r_2)^2} + (2\pi - 2\cos^{-1}(\frac{r_1 - r_2}{D})) \cdot r_1 + 2r_2 \cos^{-1}(\frac{r_1 - r_2}{D})$

$= 2(\sqrt{D^2 - (r_1 - r_2)^2} + r_1(\pi - \cos^{-1}(\frac{r_1 - r_2}{D})) + r_2 \cos^{-1}(\frac{r_1 - r_2}{D}))$.

8. In the quadrilateral at the left, assume a, b, c, α, and β are given. The figure at the right is formed by drawing $\overline{PC}$ = r.

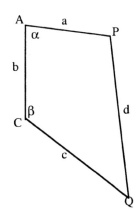 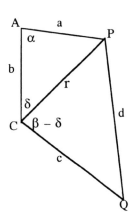

a. From the Law of Cosines in ΔAPC, we can find r. Now with the Law of Sines in ΔAPC, we can find δ, from which we find β – δ. Now in ΔCPQ, we can use the Law of Cosines to find d and the Law of Sines to find m∠Q. m∠P = 360° – m∠Q – α – β, so the quadrilateral is fully determined.

b. From the Law of Cosines in ΔAPC,

$r^2 = a^2 + b^2 - 2ab \cos \alpha$ and $a^2 = b^2 + r^2 - 2br \cos \delta$.

From the latter we solve for cos δ, simplify, and find sin δ:

$\cos \delta = \frac{b - a\cos\alpha}{r}$ and $\sin \delta = \frac{a\sin\alpha}{r}$.

From the Law of Cosines in ΔCPQ,

$$d^2 = c^2 + r^2 - 2cr\cos(\beta - \delta) = c^2 + a^2 + b^2 - 2ab\cos\alpha - 2cr\cos(\beta - \delta)$$
$$= c^2 + a^2 + b^2 - 2ab\cos\alpha - 2cr(\cos\beta\cos\delta + \sin\beta\sin\delta)$$
$$= c^2 + a^2 + b^2 - 2ab\cos\alpha - 2cr(\cos\beta\,\tfrac{b - a\cos\alpha}{r} + \sin\beta\,\tfrac{a\sin\alpha}{r})$$
$$= c^2 + a^2 + b^2 - 2ab\cos\alpha - 2bc\cos\beta + 2ac(\cos\alpha\cos\beta - \sin\alpha\sin\beta)$$
$$= c^2 + a^2 + b^2 - 2ab\cos\alpha - 2bc\cos\beta + 2ac\cos(\alpha + \beta).$$

Hence, a Law of Cosines for a quadrilateral is
$$d^2 = a^2 + b^2 + c^2 - 2ab\cos\alpha - 2bc\cos\beta + 2ac\cos(\alpha + \beta).$$

Section 9.2.1

1. The period of 2π for the sine and cosine functions follows directly from either the wrapping function definition or the unit circle definition in terms of arcs and rotations. The tangent function is defined as a quotient of sine and cosine functions, so its period must be at least the interval between zeroes of the sine function, namely, π. Since $\sin(\theta + \pi) = -\sin\theta$ and $\cos(\theta + \pi) = -\cos\theta$, $\tan(\theta + \pi) = \frac{-\sin\theta}{-\cos\theta}$ $= \frac{\sin\theta}{\cos\theta} = \tan\theta$. Thus the period of the tangent function is π. The cotangent function, being the reciprocal of the tangent function, has the same period as the tangent function.

2.   a.   For an acute angle A, $\sin A = \frac{a}{c}$ and

       $\cos A = \frac{b}{c} \Rightarrow \sin^2 A = \frac{a^2}{c^2}$ and $\cos^2 A = \frac{b^2}{c^2}$.

       We know that $a^2 + b^2 = c^2 \Rightarrow \frac{a^2}{c^2} + \frac{b^2}{c^2} = 1$, so

       substituting, we get $\sin^2 A + \cos^2 A = 1$.

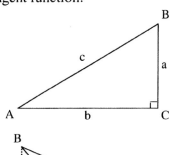

       For an obtuse angle A, $\sin A = \frac{y}{c}$ and $\cos A = \frac{x}{c}$

$\Rightarrow \sin^2 A = \frac{y^2}{c^2}$ and $\cos^2 A = \frac{x^2}{c^2}$.   We know that

$y^2 + x^2 = c^2 \Rightarrow \frac{y^2}{c^2} + \frac{x^2}{c^2} = 1$, so   substituting, we

get $\sin^2 A + \cos^2 A = 1$.

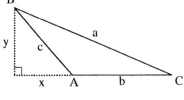

   b.   From the diagram, $\sin x = \frac{a}{1}$ and $\cos x = \frac{b}{1}$ and

       since $a^2 + b^2 = 1$, we have $\sin^2 x + \cos^2 x = 1$.

   c. $\frac{\sin^2 x}{\cos^2 x} + \frac{\cos^2 x}{\cos^2 x} = \frac{1}{\cos^2 x} \Rightarrow \tan^2 x + 1 = \sec^2 x$

       $\frac{\sin^2 x}{\sin^2 x} + \frac{\cos^2 x}{\sin^2 x} = \frac{1}{\sin^2 x} \Rightarrow 1 + \cot^2 x = \csc^2 x$

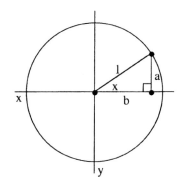

3. The point on the unit circle that corresponds to an angle of -x radians $(\cos(-x), \sin(-x))$ is a reflection over the y-axis of the point corresponding to x radians $(\cos x, \sin x)$. This reflection switches the sign of the y-coordinate, but does not change the x-coordinate. Thus, $\cos x = \cos(-x)$ and $\sin x = -\sin(-x)$.

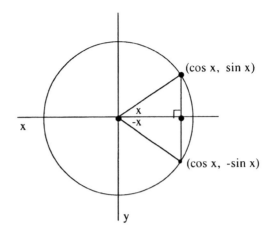

4. a. The point $(-\frac{1}{2}, \frac{\sqrt{3}}{2})$ on the unit circle corresponds to $(1, \frac{2\pi}{3})$ and $(1, \frac{8\pi}{3})$ in the wrapping function.

    b. From this information, we get that $\cos(\frac{2\pi}{3}) = \cos(\frac{8\pi}{3}) = -\frac{1}{2}$ and $\sin(\frac{2\pi}{3}) = \sin(\frac{8\pi}{3}) = \frac{\sqrt{3}}{2}$.

5. From Figure 23, we know that $OS = OP = OU = 1$ and $m\angle SOP = m\angle UTO = t$. From this information we get $\cos t = \frac{OQ}{OP} = OQ$; $\sin t = \frac{PQ}{OP} = PQ$; $\tan t = \frac{RS}{OS} = RS$; $\sec t = \frac{OR}{OS} = OR$; $\csc t = \frac{OT}{OU} = OT$; and $\cot t = \frac{UT}{OU} = UT$.

6. Using Theorem 9.7, for any complex number z, $e^{z+2\pi i} = e^z e^{2\pi i} = e^z(\cos 2\pi + i \sin 2\pi) = e^z$.

7. $e^{i\pi} = \cos \pi + i \sin \pi = -1 + i(0) = -1$

8. $e^{i(\theta+\phi)} = \cos(\theta + \phi) + i \sin(\theta + \phi)$ and $e^{i(\theta+\phi)} = e^{i\theta} e^{i\phi} = (\cos\theta + i\sin\theta)(\cos\phi + i\sin\phi)$
    $= (\cos\theta\cos\phi - \sin\theta\sin\phi) + i(\cos\theta\sin\phi + \sin\theta\cos\phi)$. Thus
    $\cos(\theta + \phi) + i\sin(\theta + \phi) = (\cos\theta\cos\phi - \sin\theta\sin\phi) + i(\cos\theta\sin\phi + \sin\theta\cos\phi)$. Equating the real
    and imaginary parts of this equation, $\cos(\theta + \phi) = \cos\theta\cos\phi - \sin\theta\sin\phi$ and $\sin(\theta + \phi)$
    $= \cos\theta\sin\phi + \sin\theta\cos\phi$.

9. By Theorem 9.7, $e^{i\theta} = \cos\theta + i\sin\theta$ and $e^{i(-\theta)} = \cos(-\theta) + i\sin(-\theta) = \cos\theta - i\sin\theta$. So
    $e^{i\theta} + e^{-i\theta} = (\cos\theta + i\sin\theta) + (\cos\theta - i\sin\theta) = 2\cos\theta$ and $e^{i\theta} - e^{-i\theta} =$
    $(\cos\theta + i\sin\theta) - (\cos\theta - i\sin\theta) = 2i\sin\theta$. Solving for $\cos\theta$ and $\sin\theta$, $\cos\theta = \frac{e^{i\theta} + e^{-i\theta}}{2}$ and
    $\sin\theta = \frac{e^{i\theta} - e^{-i\theta}}{2i}$.

Section 9.2.2

1. The amplitude of $f(x) = 3\sin(4x) + 5$ is 3 and the period $\frac{2\pi}{4} = \frac{\pi}{2}$.

2. Sample: (-C, D)

3. Yes; since $\sin x = \cos(x - \frac{\pi}{2})$, any sine wave of the form $f(x) = A \sin(B(x + C)) + D$ can be written as $f(x) = A \cos(B((x - \frac{\pi}{2}) + C)) + D$.

4. In order to find an equation for L(d) we need to know the length of the equinox day (which gives the amount of the shift in the y-direction), the difference between the longest day (the summer solstice) and the equinox day (which gives the amplitude), the day on which the spring equinox occurs (which gives the amount of the shift in the x-direction), and the length of the year (for the period). From Table 1, the length of the summer solstice at 30° S is 13.93 hours. We can assume that the length of the equinox days will be the same across latitudes, so that will be 12.18 hours. The difference between the lengths of the solstice and the equinox is $13.93 - 12.18 = 1.75$ hours. The spring equinox will occur six months later at 30° S than at 30° N, so the starting day will be day 265 (September 21) and the period (in the year 2000) will be $\frac{2\pi}{366}$. Thus, $L(d) = 12.18 + 1.75 \sin [\frac{2\pi}{366} (d - 265)]$.

5. Let (a, b) be any point on the circle $x^2 + y^2 = r^2$ centered at the origin and let θ be the angle from the positive x-axis to the ray from the origin through (a, b). Then $\cos \theta = \frac{a}{r}$ and $\sin \theta = \frac{b}{r} \Rightarrow a = r \cos \theta$ and $b = r \sin \theta$. If the circle is centered at (h, k), then the point (a + h, b + k) is on the circle and $a + h = h + r \cos \theta$ and $b + k = k + r \sin \theta$, so any point on the circle $(x - h)^2 + (y - k)^2 = r^2$ satisfies the parametric equations $x = h + r \cos \theta$ and $y = k + r \sin \theta$. Any point that satisfies the parametric equations also satisfies the rectangular equation for the circle since substituting yields:
$(x - h)^2 + (y - k)^2 = ((h + r \cos \theta) - h)^2 + ((k + r \sin \theta) - k)^2 = (r \cos \theta)^2 + (r \sin \theta)^2$
$= r^2(\cos^2 \theta + \sin^2 \theta) = r^2$.

6. Any point that satisfies the parametric equations $x = h + a \cos \theta$ and $y = k + b \sin \theta$ also satisfies the rectangular equation for an ellipse since
$$\frac{((h + a\cos\theta) - h)^2}{a^2} + \frac{((k + b\sin\theta) - k)^2}{b^2} = \frac{(a\cos\theta)^2}{a^2} + \frac{(b\sin\theta)^2}{b^2} = \cos^2\theta + \sin^2\theta = 1.$$

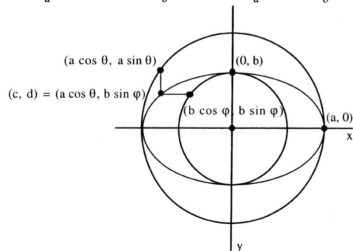

Next we will show that any point on the ellipse satisfies the parametric equations. Let (c, d) be any point on the ellipse centered at the origin and described by $\frac{x^2}{a^2} + \frac{y^2}{b^2} = 1$. Then c can be projected onto the circle centered at the origin with radius a so that c = a cos θ. Similarly, d can be projected onto the circle centered at the origin with radius b so that d = b sin φ. If we can show that θ and φ are the same angle, then we have the parametric equations. We can rewrite the coordinates so that cos θ = $\frac{c}{a}$ and sin φ = $\frac{d}{b}$, and squaring both gives us $\cos^2\theta = \frac{c^2}{a^2}$ and $\sin^2\varphi = \frac{d^2}{b^2}$. Adding the right and left sides of these we get $\cos^2\theta + \sin^2\varphi = \frac{c^2}{a^2} + \frac{d^2}{b^2}$. The point (c, d) satisfies the rectangular equation for the ellipse, so $\frac{c^2}{a^2} + \frac{d^2}{b^2} = 1 \Rightarrow \cos^2\theta + \sin^2\varphi = 1$. Since θ and φ are in the same quadrant, this is only true if θ = φ. Therefore, any point on the ellipse $\frac{x^2}{a^2} + \frac{y^2}{b^2} = 1$ satisfies the parametric equations x = a cos θ and y = sin θ, and so any point on the ellipse $\frac{(x-h)^2}{a^2} + \frac{(y-k)^2}{b^2} = 1$ satisfies the parametric equations x = h + a cos θ and y = k + sin θ.

7.   a.   For $\varphi \neq (2n+1)\frac{\pi}{2}$, where n is an integer,

$$\frac{(a\sec\varphi + h - h)^2}{a^2} - \frac{(b\tan\varphi + k - k)^2}{b^2} = \sec^2\varphi - \tan^2\varphi = \frac{1}{\cos^2\varphi} - \frac{\sin^2\varphi}{\cos^2\varphi} = \frac{\cos^2\varphi}{\cos^2\varphi} = 1.$$

   b.   For φ in the interval $[0, \frac{\pi}{2})$, x = sec φ > 0 and y = tan φ ≥ 0; for φ in the interval $(\frac{\pi}{2}, \pi]$, x = sec φ < 0 and y = tan φ < 0; for φ in the interval $[\pi, \frac{3\pi}{2})$, x = sec φ < 0 and y = tan φ ≥ 0; for φ in the interval $(\frac{3\pi}{2}, 2\pi]$, x = sec φ > 0 and y = tan φ < 0.

8.   Note: There is an error in the first printing. $s(x) = \begin{cases} 1 & \text{if } 2k\pi < x \leq (2k+1)\pi \\ -1 & \text{if } (2k+1)\pi < x \leq (2k+2)\pi \end{cases}$ for any integer k.

   a.   Answers with calculators will vary.

   b.   The graphs are very close. (This indicates the ability of series like Fourier series to approximate two-valued functions.)

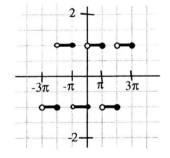

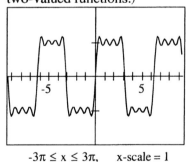

-3π ≤ x ≤ 3π,   x-scale = 1
-2 ≤ y ≤ 2,   y-scale = 1

9. a. The length of arc $\stackrel{\frown}{TP}$ equals the length of arc $\stackrel{\frown}{TA}$, so sb = at, where s = $\angle$TCP. Also,

m$\angle$RCP + $(\frac{\pi}{2} - t)$ + s = π, so m$\angle$RPC = $(\frac{\pi}{2} -$ m$\angle$RCP$)$ = s – t = $\frac{at}{b} - t = \frac{a-b}{b}$t.

b. x = OD + RP = (a – b) cos t + b cos $(\frac{a-b}{b}$t); y = DC – RC = (a – b) sin t – b sin $(\frac{a-b}{b}$t)

c. If b = $\frac{a}{4}$, then $\frac{a-b}{b}$ = 3 and

x = a$(\frac{3}{4}$cos t + $\frac{1}{4}$cos 3t) = a$(\frac{3}{4}$cos t + $\frac{1}{4}$(4 cos^3 t – 3 cos t)) = a cos^{3}t, and

y = a$(\frac{3}{4}$sin t – $\frac{1}{4}$sin 3t) = a$(\frac{3}{4}$sin t – $\frac{1}{4}$(3 sin t – 4 sin^{3}t)) = a sin^{3}t. So

$x^{2/3} + y^{2/3}$ = (a cos^{3}t)$^{2/3}$ + (a sin^{3}t)$^{2/3}$ = a$^{2/3}$(cos^{2}t + sin^{2}t) = a$^{2/3}$.

10.

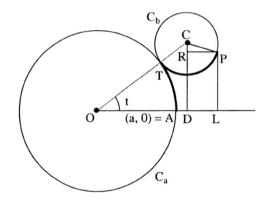

Following the solution to Problem 9, s = $\frac{at}{b}$ and s + t = $\frac{a+b}{b}$t.

x = OD + DL = (a + b)cos t + b sin(s – $(\frac{\pi}{2} -$ t)) = (a + b)cos t – b cos(s + t)

= (a + b)cos t – b cos$(\frac{a+b}{b}$t)

y = CD – RC = (a + b)sin t – b cos(s – $(\frac{\pi}{2} -$ t)) = (a + b)sin t – b sin(s + t)

= (a + b)sin t – b sin$(\frac{a+b}{b}$t)

11. The area under the arch is given by A = $\int$ ydx. Differentiating x with respect to t gives $\frac{dx}{dt}$ = r – r cos t, so

$y\frac{dx}{dt}$ = r(1 – cos t)r(1 – cos t)

= r^2(1 – cos t)^2.

So ydx = r^2(1 – cos t)^{2}dt. The limits of integration for one arch are 0 to 2π. Thus

$$A = \int_0^{2\pi} r^2(1-\cos t)^2 dt$$

$$= r^2 \int_0^{2\pi} \left(1 - 2\cos t + \cos^2 t\right)dt$$

$$= r^2 (\int_0^{2\pi} dt - 2\int_0^{2\pi} \cos t\, dt + \int_0^{2\pi} \cos^2 t\, dt)$$

$$= r^2 (t \big|_0^{2\pi} - 2 \sin t \big|_0^{2\pi} + \int_0^{2\pi} \cos^2 t \, dt)$$

$$= r^2 (2\pi + \int_0^{2\pi} \cos^2 t \, dt)$$

The last integral can be evaluated by rearranging the identity $\cos 2x = \cos^2 x - 1$ to yield $\cos^2 x = \dfrac{\cos(2x) + 1}{2}$. So

$$A = r^2 (2\pi + \int_0^{2\pi} \frac{\cos(2t) + 1}{2} \, dt)$$

$$= r^2 (2\pi + \frac{1}{2} \int_0^{2\pi} \left(\cos(2t) + 1 \right) dt)$$

$$= r^2 (2\pi + \frac{1}{4} \sin(2t) \big|_0^{2\pi} + \frac{1}{2} t \big|_0^{2\pi})$$

$$= 3\pi r^2.$$

The length of the arch is given by $\int_0^{2\pi} ds$, where $ds = \sqrt{(dx)^2 + (dy)^2}$. Differentiating x and y with respect to t gives $\dfrac{dx}{dt} = r - r\cos t$ and $\dfrac{dy}{dt} = r\sin t$. So

$$(\tfrac{ds}{dt})^2 = (\tfrac{dx}{dt})^2 + (\tfrac{dy}{dt})^2 = (r^2 - 2r^2 \cos t + r^2 \cos^2 t) + r^2 \sin^2 t$$
$$= 2r^2 - 2r^2 \cos t. \ ds = \sqrt{2} \, r \sqrt{1 - \cos t} \, dt. \text{ So the length of the arch is given}$$

by $\sqrt{2} \, r \int_0^{2\pi} \sqrt{1 - \cos t} \, dt$. The integral $\int \sqrt{1 - \cos t} \, dt$ can be evaluated by making the substitution

$\sin \tfrac{t}{2} = \sqrt{\dfrac{1 - \cos t}{2}}$. Thus $\sqrt{2} \, r \int_0^{2\pi} \sqrt{1 - \cos t} \, dt = 2r \int_0^{2\pi} \sin \tfrac{t}{2} \, dt = -4r \cos \tfrac{t}{2} \big|_0^{2\pi} = -4r \cos \pi - -4r \cos 0 = 8r.$

Section 9.2.3

1. a. Assume that $\overline{AB}$ is not a diameter and let $m\angle AOB = 2\theta$. The bisector of $\angle AOB$ also bisects $\overline{AB}$. Then

   $$\sin \theta = \sin \tfrac{1}{2}(\angle AOB) = \frac{\frac{1}{2} AB}{1} = \tfrac{1}{2} AB.$$

   If $\overline{AB}$ is a diameter, then
   $m\angle AOB = 180° \Rightarrow m\tfrac{1}{2}(\angle AOB) = 90°$
   and $\sin 90° = 1 = \tfrac{1}{2} AB$.

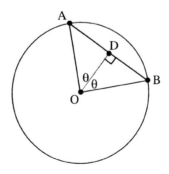

   b. The formula of part **a** works if $\angle AOB$ is measured by its major arc instead of its minor arc since the minor arc measure, 2θ, is between 0 and π (so $0 < \theta < \pi$) and the measure of the major arc is $2\pi - 2\theta$, and $\sin \tfrac{1}{2}(2\pi - 2\theta) = \sin(\pi - \theta) = \sin \theta$ when $0 \le \theta \le \pi$.

2. Choose E on $\overline{AC}$ so that $\angle ABD \cong \angle EBC$.
    Then $\triangle ABD \sim \triangle EBC$ by AA since
    $m\angle BCE = m\angle ADB = 90°$. From this
    similarity we have $\frac{BC}{BD} = \frac{EC}{AD} = \frac{BE}{AB}$. Next,
    $\angle ABE \cong \angle DBC$ because
    $m\angle ABD - m\angle EBD = m\angle ABE$ and
    $m\angle EBC - m\angle EBD = m\angle DBC$ and we
    know already that $m\angle ABD = m\angle EBC$. (If
    the figure is constructed so that E is on the

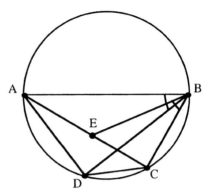

    other side of the intersection of $\overline{AC}$ and $\overline{BD}$, then we still have $m\angle ABE = m\angle DBC$ because
    $m\angle ABD + m\angle DBE = m\angle EBC + m\angle DBE \Rightarrow m\angle ABE = m\angle DBC$.) Also, $m\angle EAB = m\angle BDC$
    since E is on $\overline{AC}$ and $\angle CAB$ and $\angle BDC$ subtend the same arc $\overset{\frown}{BC}$, so $\triangle ABE \sim \triangle DBC$ by AA. From
    this similarity, $\frac{AE}{CD} = \frac{BE}{BC} = \frac{AB}{BD}$. From this set of ratios, $AB \cdot CD = AE \cdot BD$ and from the fist set of
    ratios we get $AD \cdot BC = EC \cdot BD$. Adding the right and left sides of these,
    $AB \cdot CD + AD \cdot BC = AE \cdot BD + EC \cdot BD = (AE + EC) \cdot BD = AC \cdot BD$.

3. a. $\cos 87° = \frac{238,800 \text{ mi}}{d} \Rightarrow d = \frac{238,800 \text{ mi}}{\cos 87°} \approx 4,562,828.6 \text{ mi}.$

    b. $\cos(\angle MES) = \frac{238,800 \text{ mi}}{93,000,000 \text{ mi}} \approx .002567742 \Rightarrow m\angle MES \approx 89.85287906°.$

    c. Small errors in the measurement of $\angle MES$ result in relatively large errors in d because
        $m\angle MES \approx 90° \Rightarrow \cos(\angle MES) \approx 0$ and $\cos(\angle MES)$ is the divisor when d is calculated.

4. a. Measuring that the sun made an angle of 7.2° to the vertical in Alexandria when the sun hit the
        bottom of a deep well in Syene means that the measure of the arc on a great circle of the Earth
        (i.e. circumference) from Syene to Alexandria is $\frac{7.2°}{360°} = \frac{1}{50}$ of the total circle. Thus 50 times the
        distance (arc length) from Syene to Alexandria would be the total distance around the Earth.

    b. $50 \cdot 500 \text{ mi} = 25,000 \text{ mi}$

    c. If Eratosthenes was off by .2° in his measurement of the angle to the vertical in Alexandria, then
        the circumference of the Earth would have been either: $\frac{360°}{7°} \cdot 500 \text{ mi} = 25,714 \text{ mi}$ or
        $\frac{360°}{7.4°} \cdot 500 \text{ mi} = 24,324 \text{ mi}$. (Earth's circumference at the equator is about 24,902 mi.)

Section 9.3.1

1. Using the unit circle definition of the sine and cosine functions, the image of $(x, 0)$ under a rotation of
    magnitude of t around the origin is $R_t(x, 0) = (x \cos t, x \sin t)$. The point $(0, y)$ is the image of $(x, 0)$

under a rotation of magnitude $\frac{\pi}{2}$, so $R_t(0, y) = R_{t + \frac{\pi}{2}}(x, 0) = (x \cos(t + \frac{\pi}{2}), x \sin(t + \frac{\pi}{2}))$

$= (-x \sin t, x \cos t) \Rightarrow R_t(0, y) = (-y \sin t, y \cos t)$.

2.   a. $\cos(2x) = \cos(x + x) = \cos x \cos x - \sin x \sin x = \cos^2 x - \sin^2 x$.

       b. $\cos(2x) = \cos(x + x) = \cos^2 x - \sin^2 x = (1 - \sin^2 x) - \sin^2 x = 1 - 2 \sin^2 x$.

       c. $\cos(2x) = \cos(x + x) = \cos^2 x - \sin^2 x = \cos^2 x - (1 - \cos^2 x) = 2 \cos^2 x - 1$.

       d. $\sin(2x) = \sin(x + x) = \sin x \cos x + \cos x \sin x = 2 \sin x \cos x$.

3.   a.   Using part **c** of Problem 2, $\cos x = \cos(2 (\frac{x}{2})) = 2 \cos^2(\frac{x}{2}) - 1 \Rightarrow \frac{\cos x + 1}{2}$

         $= \cos^2(\frac{x}{2}) \Rightarrow \left| \cos(\frac{x}{2}) \right| = \sqrt{\frac{1 + \cos x}{2}}$.

       b.   Similarly, $\cos x = \cos(2(\frac{x}{2})) = 1 - 2 \sin^2(\frac{x}{2}) \Rightarrow \sin^2(\frac{x}{2}) = \frac{1 - \cos x}{2} \Rightarrow \left| \sin(\frac{x}{2}) \right| = \sqrt{\frac{1 - \cos x}{2}}$.

       c.   There is no formula for $\left| \sin(\frac{x}{2}) \right|$ in terms of only $\sin x$ because the half-angle formulas are derived

         from the double angle formulas which, in turn, are derived from the sum formulas and because

         $\sin(x \pm y) = \sin x \cos y \pm \cos x \sin y$, $\cos x$ is always involved.

4.   a. $\cos(3x) = \cos(2x + x) = \cos(2x) \cos x - \sin(2x) \sin x$

               $= (\cos^2 x - \sin^2 x) \cos x - (2 \sin x \cos x) \sin x$

                $= \cos^3 x - \sin^2 x \cos x - 2 \sin^2 x \cos x$

                $= \cos^3 x - 3 \sin^2 x \cos x$.

         Answers will vary for verification. Sample: Let $x = \frac{\pi}{3}$. Then $\cos(3x) = \cos \pi = -1$, $\cos x = \frac{1}{2}$, and

         $\sin x = \frac{\sqrt{3}}{2}$, so $\cos^3 x - 3 \sin^2 x \cos x = \frac{1}{8} - 3 \cdot \frac{3}{4} \cdot \frac{1}{2} = -1$.

       b. $\cos(3x) = \cos^3 x - 3 \sin^2 x \cos x = \cos^3 x - 3(1 - \cos^2 x) \cos x$

                $= \cos^3 x - 3 \cos x + 3 \cos^3 x$

                $= 4 \cos^3 x - 3 \cos x$.

       c. $\sin(3x) = \sin(2x + x) = \sin(2x) \cos x + \cos(2x) \sin x$

                $= (2 \sin x \cos x) \cos x + (2 \cos^2 x - 1) \sin x$

                $= 2 \sin x \cos^2 x + 2 \cos^2 x \sin x - \sin x$

                $= 4 \cos^2 x \sin x - \sin x$.

         Answers will vary for verification. Sample: Let $x = \frac{\pi}{6}$. Then $\sin(3x) = 1$, $\cos x = \frac{\sqrt{3}}{2}$, and

         $\sin x = \frac{1}{2}$. Also, $4 \cos^2 x \sin x - \sin x = 4 \cdot \frac{3}{4} \cdot \frac{1}{2} - \frac{1}{2} = 1$.

       d. $\cos(4x) = \cos(3x + x) = \cos(3x) \cos x - \sin(3x) \sin x$

                $= (\cos^3 x - 3 \sin^2 x \cos x) \cos x - (4 \cos^2 x \sin x - \sin x) \sin x$

                $= \cos^4 x - 3 \sin^2 x \cos^2 x - 4 \cos^2 x \sin^2 x + \sin^2 x$

                $= \cos^4 x - 7 \cos^2 x \sin^2 x + \sin^2 x$.

       e. $\cos(4x) = \cos^4 x - 7 \cos^2 x \sin^2 x + \sin^2 x$

                $= \cos^4 x - 7 \cos^2 x (1 - \cos^2 x) + (1 - \cos^2 x)$

                $= \cos^4 x - 7 \cos^2 x + 7 \cos^4 x + 1 - \cos^2 x$

                $= 8 \cos^4 x - 8 \cos^2 x + 1$.

       f. $\sin(4x) = \sin(3x + x) = \sin(3x) \cos x + \cos(3x) \sin x$

$$= (4 \cos^2 x \sin x - \sin x) \cos x + (4 \cos^3 x - 3 \cos x) \sin x$$
$$= 4 \cos^3 x \sin x - \sin x \cos x + 4 \cos^3 x \sin x - 3 \cos x \sin x$$
$$= 8 \cos^3 x \sin x - 4 \cos x \sin x.$$

g. We show by induction that for all integers $n > 0$,
$\cos(nx) = a_n \cos^n x + a_{n-1} \cos^{n-1} x + \ldots + a_0$, but we will also need to show that for all integers
$n > 0$, $\sin(nx) = (b_{n-1} \cos^{n-1} x + b_{n-2} \cos^{n-2} x + \ldots + b_0) \sin x$. That is, $\sin(n x)$ is the product of $\sin x$
and a polynomial is $\cos x$.

Basis Step: $\cos(1x) = \cos^1 x$ and $\sin(1x) = \cos^0 x \sin x$.

Inductive Step: Assume for $k < n$, $\cos(kx) = a_k \cos^k x + a_{k-1} \cos^{k-1} x + \ldots + a_0$ and
$\sin(kx) = (b_{k-1} \cos^{k-1} x + b_{k-2} \cos^{k-2} x + \ldots + b_0) \sin x$. Then,
$\cos((k+1)x) = \cos(kx + x) = \cos(kx) \cos x - \sin(kx) \sin x$
$= (a_k \cos^k x + a_{k-1} \cos^{k-1} x + \ldots + a_0) \cos x - (b_{k-1} \cos^{k-1} x + b_{k-2} \cos^{k-2} x + \ldots + b_0) \sin^2 x$
$= (a_k \cos^{k+1} x + a_{k-1} \cos^k x + \ldots + a_0 \cos x) - (b_{k-1} \cos^{k-1} x + b_{k-2} \cos^{k-2} x + \ldots + b_0) \cdot$
$\qquad (1 - \cos^2 x),$

which expresses $\cos((k+1)x)$ in $\cos x$.

Also,
$\sin((k+1)x) = \sin(kx + x) = \sin(kx) \cos x + \cos(kx) \sin x$
$= (b_{k-1} \cos^{k-1} x + b_{k-2} \cos^{k-2} x + \ldots + b_0) \sin x \cos x + (a_k \cos^k x + a_{k-1} \cos^{k-1} x + \ldots + a_0) \sin x$
$= (b_{k-1} \cos^k x + b_{k-2} \cos^k x + \ldots + b_0 \cos x + a_k \cos^k x + a_{k-1} \cos^{k-1} x + \ldots + a_0) \sin x$
$= ((a_k + b_{k-1}) \cos^k x + (a_{k-1} + b_{k-2}) \cos^{k-1} x + \ldots + (a_1 + b_0) \cos x + a_0) \sin x,$

so $\sin((k+1)x)$ is the product of $\sin x$ and a polynomial in $\cos x$.

Thus, by mathematical induction,
$\cos(nx) = a_n \cos^n x + a_{n-1} \cos^{n-1} x + \ldots + a_0$ and
$\sin(nx) = (b_{n-1} \cos^{n-1} x + b_{n-2} \cos^{n-2} x + \ldots + b_0) \sin x$
for all integers $n > 1$.

5. a. $\dfrac{\sin (6x)}{\sin (2x)} = \dfrac{\sin (3 (2x))}{\sin (2x)} = \dfrac{4 \cos^2 (2x) \sin (2x) - \sin (2x)}{\sin (2x)} = 4 \cos^2(2x) - 1$ when $\sin(2x) \neq 0$.

$4 \cos^2(2x) - 1 = 4 (2 \cos^2 x - 1)^2 - 1 = 4 (4 \cos^4 x - 4 \cos^2 x + 1) - 1$
$= 16 \cos^4 x - 16 \cos^2 x + 3$ when $\sin(2x) \neq 0$ or $x \neq 0 + \frac{\pi}{2} k$.

b. Sample: The quotient $\dfrac{\sin(nmx)}{\sin(mx)}$, where n and m are positive integers, can be expressed as a
polynomial of degree $n - 1$ in $\cos x$.

6. Since all the values for x in this problem are in the first quadrant, we can ignore the absolute value sign
in the half-angle formulas from Problem 3.

a. $\sin(\frac{\pi}{8}) = \sin(\frac{\frac{\pi}{4}}{2}) = \sqrt{\dfrac{1 - \cos \frac{\pi}{4}}{2}} = \sqrt{\dfrac{1 - \frac{\sqrt{2}}{2}}{2}} = \sqrt{\dfrac{2 - \sqrt{2}}{4}} = \dfrac{\sqrt{2 - \sqrt{2}}}{2}.$

$\cos(\frac{\pi}{8}) = \cos(\frac{\frac{\pi}{4}}{2}) = \sqrt{\dfrac{1 + \cos \frac{\pi}{4}}{2}} = \sqrt{\dfrac{1 + \frac{\sqrt{2}}{2}}{2}} = \sqrt{\dfrac{2 + \sqrt{2}}{4}} = \dfrac{\sqrt{2 + \sqrt{2}}}{2}.$

b. $\sin(\frac{\pi}{16}) = \sin(\frac{\frac{\pi}{8}}{2}) = \sqrt{\dfrac{1 - \cos \frac{\pi}{8}}{2}} = \sqrt{\dfrac{1 - \frac{\sqrt{2 + \sqrt{2}}}{2}}{2}} = \sqrt{\dfrac{2 - \sqrt{2 + \sqrt{2}}}{4}} = \dfrac{\sqrt{2 - \sqrt{2 + \sqrt{2}}}}{2}.$

$$\cos(\tfrac{\pi}{16}) = \cos(\tfrac{\frac{\pi}{8}}{2}) = \sqrt{\frac{1+\cos\frac{\pi}{8}}{2}} = \sqrt{\frac{1+\frac{\sqrt{2+\sqrt{2}}}{2}}{2}} = \sqrt{\frac{2+\sqrt{2+\sqrt{2}}}{4}} = \frac{\sqrt{2+\sqrt{2+\sqrt{2}}}}{2}.$$

c. $$\sin(\tfrac{\pi}{32}) = \sin(\tfrac{\frac{\pi}{16}}{2}) = \sqrt{\frac{1-\cos\frac{\pi}{16}}{2}} = \sqrt{\frac{1-\frac{\sqrt{2+\sqrt{2+\sqrt{2}}}}{2}}{2}} = \sqrt{\frac{2-\sqrt{2+\sqrt{2+\sqrt{2}}}}{4}} = \frac{\sqrt{2-\sqrt{2+\sqrt{2+\sqrt{2}}}}}{2}.$$

$$\cos(\tfrac{\pi}{32}) = \cos(\tfrac{\frac{\pi}{16}}{2}) = \sqrt{\frac{1+\cos\frac{\pi}{16}}{2}} = \sqrt{\frac{1+\frac{\sqrt{2+\sqrt{2+\sqrt{2}}}}{2}}{2}} = \sqrt{\frac{2+\sqrt{2+\sqrt{2+\sqrt{2}}}}{4}} = \frac{\sqrt{2+\sqrt{2+\sqrt{2+\sqrt{2}}}}}{2}.$$

d. The pattern will persist because, in general, $\sin\frac{\pi}{2n}$ and $\cos\frac{\pi}{2n}$ can be defined recursively as

$$\sin\frac{\pi}{2n} = \sqrt{\frac{1-\cos\frac{\pi}{n}}{2}} = \frac{\sqrt{2-2\cos\frac{\pi}{n}}}{2} \quad\text{and}\quad \cos\frac{\pi}{2n} = \sqrt{\frac{1+\cos\frac{\pi}{n}}{2}} = \frac{\sqrt{2+2\cos\frac{\pi}{n}}}{2}.$$

7. a. The length of a side of the square is $\sqrt{2}$, so the square's area is 2.

b. The area of the regular octagon is 8 times the area of a triangle formed by two radii extending to two of the polygon's consecutive vertices and the side of the polygon connecting those vertices. The area of this triangle is $\frac{1}{2}\sin\frac{2\pi}{8} = \frac{\sqrt{2}}{4}$. So the area of the octagon is

$$8\cdot\frac{\sqrt{2}}{4} = 2\sqrt{2} = 2\frac{1}{\frac{1}{\sqrt{2}}} = \frac{2}{\sqrt{\frac{1}{2}}}.$$

c. The area of a regular n-gon is $\frac{n}{2}\sin\frac{2\pi}{n}$. So the area of a regular 2n-gon is $\frac{2n}{2}\sin\frac{2\pi}{2n} = n\sin\frac{\pi}{n}$. The difference in area is $n\sin\frac{\pi}{n} - \frac{n}{2}\sin\frac{2\pi}{n}$, which can be simplified using the double angle formula for sine: $n\sin\frac{\pi}{n} - \frac{n}{2}\sin\frac{2\pi}{n} = n\sin\frac{\pi}{n} - n\sin\frac{\pi}{n}\cos\frac{\pi}{n} = n\sin\frac{\pi}{n}(1-\cos\frac{\pi}{n})$.

d. The area of a regular 16-gon will be

$$\frac{16}{2}\sin\frac{2\pi}{16} = 4\sqrt{2-\sqrt{2}} = 4\sqrt{2-\sqrt{2}} = 4\sqrt{2-\sqrt{2}}\cdot\frac{\sqrt{2+\sqrt{2}}}{\sqrt{2+\sqrt{2}}} = \frac{4\sqrt{2}}{\sqrt{2+\sqrt{2}}} =$$

$$\frac{2}{\frac{1}{2}\sqrt{\frac{1}{2}\sqrt{2+\sqrt{2}}}} = \frac{2}{\sqrt{\frac{1}{2}}\sqrt{\frac{1}{2}+\frac{1}{2}\sqrt{\frac{1}{2}}}}.$$

e. Looking at the ratio of the area of a regular 2n-gon to the area of an n-gon, we

get $\dfrac{A_{2n}}{A_n} = \dfrac{\frac{2n}{2}\sin\frac{2\pi}{2n}}{\frac{n}{2}\sin\frac{2\pi}{n}} = \dfrac{2\sin\frac{\pi}{n}}{\sin\frac{2\pi}{n}} = \dfrac{1}{\cos\frac{\pi}{n}}$. So, we can generate the recursive relation $A_{2n} = \dfrac{A_n}{\cos\frac{\pi}{n}}$.

Since $A_4 = 2$, $A_{2n} = \dfrac{2}{\cos\frac{\pi}{4}\cos\frac{\pi}{8}\cdot\ldots\cdot\cos\frac{\pi}{n}}$. Using the formulas for $\cos\frac{\pi}{n}$ found in Problem 6, viz.,

$\cos\frac{\pi}{4} = \dfrac{\sqrt{2}}{2} = \sqrt{\frac{1}{2}}$, $\cos\frac{\pi}{8} = \dfrac{\sqrt{2+\sqrt{2}}}{2} = \sqrt{\frac{1}{2}+\frac{1}{2}\sqrt{\frac{1}{2}}}$, etc., we get that

$$A_{2n} = \dfrac{2}{\sqrt{\frac{1}{2}}\cdot\sqrt{\frac{1}{2}+\frac{1}{2}\sqrt{\frac{1}{2}}}\cdot\sqrt{\frac{1}{2}+\frac{1}{2}\sqrt{\frac{1}{2}+\frac{1}{2}\sqrt{\frac{1}{2}}}}\cdot\ldots}.$$

f. In the limit as $n\to\infty$, a regular n-gon will have an area that approaches the area of a unit circle, which is π. Thus $\pi = \dfrac{2}{\sqrt{\frac{1}{2}} \cdot \sqrt{\frac{1}{2} + \frac{1}{2}\sqrt{\frac{1}{2}}} \cdot \sqrt{\frac{1}{2} + \frac{1}{2}\sqrt{\frac{1}{2} + \frac{1}{2}\sqrt{\frac{1}{2}}}} \cdot \dots}$, or

$\dfrac{2}{\pi} = \sqrt{\dfrac{1}{2}} \cdot \sqrt{\dfrac{1}{2} + \dfrac{1}{2}\sqrt{\dfrac{1}{2}}} \cdot \sqrt{\dfrac{1}{2} + \dfrac{1}{2}\sqrt{\dfrac{1}{2} + \dfrac{1}{2}\sqrt{\dfrac{1}{2}}}} \cdot \dots$.

8.　a.　$\frac{1}{2}(\cos(x+y) + \cos(x-y))$

$= \frac{1}{2}(\cos x \cos y - \sin x \sin y + \cos x \cos y + \sin x \sin y) = \frac{1}{2}(2\cos x \cos y) = \cos x \cos y$.

　b.　$x = \cos^{-1}(.95632) \approx 16.99701239°$; $y = \cos^{-1}(.61807) \approx 51.82466778°$.

$\cos(x+y) = \cos 68.82168016° = .361271762$.

$\cos(x-y) = \cos\text{-}34.82765539° = .8208736428$.

$\frac{1}{2}(\cos(x+y) + \cos(x-y)) = \frac{1}{2}(1.182145405) = .5910727024$, so

$.95632 \times .61807 = .5910727024 \Rightarrow 95632 \times 61807 = 5,910,727,024$.

　c.　$\frac{1}{2}(\cos(x-y) - \cos(x+y))$

$= \frac{1}{2}(\cos x \cos y + \sin x \sin y - (\cos x \cos y - \sin x \sin y)) = \frac{1}{2}(2\sin x \sin y) = \sin x \sin y$.

$x = \sin^{-1}(.95632) \approx 73.00298761°$; $y = \sin^{-1}(.61807) \approx 38.17533222°$.

$\cos(x-y) = \cos 34.82765539° = .8208736428$. $\cos(x+y) = \cos 111.1783198°$

$= \text{-}.361271762$.

$\frac{1}{2}(\cos(x-y) - \cos(x+y)) = \frac{1}{2}(1.182145405) = .5910727024$, so

$.95632 \times .61807 = .5910727024 \Rightarrow 95632 \times 61807 = 5,910,727,024$.

9.　a.　$\tan(x \pm y) = \dfrac{\sin(x \pm y)}{\cos(x \pm y)} = \dfrac{\sin x \cos y \pm \cos x \sin y}{\cos x \cos y \mp \sin x \sin y} = \dfrac{\frac{\sin x \cos y \pm \cos x \sin y}{\cos x \cos y}}{\frac{\cos x \cos y \mp \sin x \sin y}{\cos x \cos y}} = \dfrac{\tan x \pm \tan y}{1 \mp \tan x \tan y}$

　b.　$\tan(2x) = \dfrac{\sin(2x)}{\cos(2x)} = \dfrac{2\sin x \cos x}{\cos^2 x - \sin^2 x} = \dfrac{2\sin x \cos x}{\cos^2 x - \sin^2 x} \cdot \dfrac{\frac{1}{\cos^2 x}}{\frac{1}{\cos^2 x}} = \dfrac{\frac{2\sin x}{\cos x}}{1 - \frac{\sin^2 x}{\cos^2 x}} = \dfrac{2\tan x}{1 - \tan^2 x}$.

　c.　$\tan(3x) = \tan(2x + x) = \dfrac{\tan(2x) + \tan x}{1 - \tan(2x)\tan x} = \dfrac{\frac{2\tan x}{1 - \tan^2 x} + \tan x}{1 - \frac{2\tan^2 x}{1 - \tan^2 x}} = \dfrac{\frac{2\tan x + \tan x - \tan^3 x}{1 - \tan^2 x}}{\frac{1 - \tan^2 x - 2\tan^2 x}{1 - \tan^2 x}} = \dfrac{3\tan x - \tan^3 x}{1 - 3\tan^2 x}$.

　d.　$\left|\tan\left(\frac{x}{2}\right)\right| = \dfrac{\left|\sin\frac{x}{2}\right|}{\left|\cos\frac{x}{2}\right|} = \dfrac{\sqrt{\frac{1 - \cos x}{2}}}{\sqrt{\frac{1 + \cos x}{2}}} = \sqrt{\dfrac{1 - \cos x}{1 + \cos x}}$.

　e.　$\left|\tan\left(\frac{x}{2}\right)\right| = \sqrt{\dfrac{1 - \cos x}{1 + \cos x}} = \sqrt{\dfrac{(1 - \cos x)(1 + \cos x)}{(1 + \cos x)(1 + \cos x)}} = \sqrt{\dfrac{1 - \cos^2 x}{(1 + \cos x)^2}} = \sqrt{\dfrac{\sin^2 x}{(1 + \cos x)^2}} = \dfrac{\sin x}{1 + \cos x}$.

10. a. $\cot(2x) = \dfrac{\cos(2x)}{\sin(2x)} = \dfrac{\cos^2 x - \sin^2 x}{2\sin x \cos x} = \dfrac{\cos^2 x - \sin^2 x}{2\sin x \cos x} \cdot \dfrac{\frac{1}{\sin^2 x}}{\frac{1}{\sin^2 x}} = \dfrac{\frac{\cos^2 x}{\sin^2 x} - 1}{\frac{2\cos x}{\sin x}} = \dfrac{\cot^2 x - 1}{2\cot x}.$

   b. $\left|\cot\left(\dfrac{x}{2}\right)\right| = \dfrac{\left|\cos\frac{x}{2}\right|}{\left|\sin\frac{x}{2}\right|} = \dfrac{\sqrt{\frac{1+\cos x}{2}}}{\sqrt{\frac{1-\cos x}{2}}} = \sqrt{\dfrac{1+\cos x}{1-\cos x}} = \sqrt{\dfrac{(1+\cos x)(1-\cos x)}{(1-\cos x)(1-\cos x)}}$

   $= \sqrt{\dfrac{1-\cos^2 x}{(1-\cos x)^2}} = \sqrt{\dfrac{\sin^2 x}{(1-\cos x)^2}} = \dfrac{\sin x}{1-\cos x}.$

11. a. Since $\cos \pi = -1$ and -1 is not irrational, by the contrapositive of the given statement, π is not rational.

   b. $\cos 2x = \cos^2 x - \sin^2 x = (1-\sin^2 x) - \sin^2 x = 1 - 2\sin^2 x$. So $\sin x = \pm\sqrt{\dfrac{1-\cos 2x}{2}}$. Now if x is rational, then 2x is rational, so, by the given statement $\cos 2x$ is irrational. Since the sum and product of a nonzero rational and an irrational is irrational, $\dfrac{1-\cos 2x}{2}$ is irrational, and since the square root of an irrational are irrational , $\sqrt{\dfrac{1-\cos 2x}{2}}$ is irrational. So $\sin x$ is irrational whenever x is a nonzero rational number. $\tan^2 x = \sec^2 x - 1 = \dfrac{1}{\cos^2 x} - 1$ so $\tan x = \sqrt{\dfrac{1}{\cos^2 x} - 1}$. Now $\cos^2 x = \dfrac{\cos 2x + 1}{2}$, $\tan x = \sqrt{\dfrac{2}{\cos 2x + 1} - 1}$. Again, if x is rational, $\cos 2x$ is irrational, and if $\cos 2x$ is irrational, $\sqrt{\dfrac{2}{\cos 2x + 1} - 1}$ is irrational. The functions cot x, sec x, and csc x are the reciprocals of tan x, cos x, and sin x, and the reciprocal of an irrational number is irrational. Thus if x is a nonzero rational number, cot x, sec x, and csc x will all be irrational.

   c. Suppose for x rational $\sin^{-1} x$ is also rational. Then, since $\sin(\sin^{-1} x) = x$, the sine of a rational number is rational, contradicting part **b**. The proof is the same for $\cos^{-1} x$ and $\tan^{-1} x$.

12. Let θ_1 and θ_2 be the angles that each line makes with the positive x-axis. Either θ_1 or θ_2 will be an exterior angle to the triangle formed by the two lines and the x-axis. Without loss of generality, let this be θ_1. Let α be the vertical angle formed by the two lines, that is, an angle of the triangle. By the Exterior Angle Theorem, $\alpha = \theta_1 - \theta_2$, so $\tan \alpha = \tan(\theta_1 - \theta_2) = \dfrac{\tan \theta_1 - \tan \theta_2}{1 + \tan \theta_1 \tan \theta_2} = \dfrac{m_1 - m_2}{1 + m_1 m_2}.$

Section 9.3.2

1. $f(x) = -3\cos(2t) + 4\sin(2t) = 5(-\frac{3}{5}\cos(2t) + \frac{4}{5}\sin(2t))$. Let $\sin \theta = -\frac{3}{5}$ and let $\cos \theta = \frac{4}{5} \Rightarrow \theta \approx 216.87°$. Then $f(x) = 5(\sin \theta \cos(2t) + \cos \theta \sin(2t))$

   $= 5[\sin(\theta + 2t)] = 5[\sin 2(t + \frac{\theta}{2})].$

2. Let $f(x) = a \cos(cx) + b \sin(cx)$ where a, b, and c are real numbers and let $A = \sqrt{a^2 + b^2}$. Multiplying and dividing f by A, we get $f(x) = A(\frac{a}{A} \cos(cx) + \frac{b}{A} \sin(cx))$. But $(\frac{a}{A}, \frac{b}{A})$ is a point on the unit circle since $(\frac{a}{A})^2 + (\frac{b}{A})^2 = \frac{a^2}{A^2} + \frac{b^2}{A^2} = \frac{a^2}{a^2+b^2} + \frac{b^2}{a^2+b^2} = \frac{a^2+b^2}{a^2+b^2} = 1$, so $\frac{a}{A} = \cos\theta$ and $\frac{b}{A} = \sin\theta$ for some $\theta, 0 \le \theta \le 2\pi$. Substituting and simplifying using the sum formulas,

    $f(x) = A(\cos\theta \cos(cx) + \sin\theta \sin(cx)) = A \cos(cx - \theta) = A \cos[c(x - \frac{\theta}{c})]$. Let $B = \frac{\theta}{c}$ and we have

    $f(x) = a \cos(cx) + b \sin(cx) = A \cos[c(x - B)]$.

3. The proof is essentially the same as in Problem 2, except that the coordinates of the point on the unit circle are reversed, $(\frac{b}{A}, \frac{a}{A})$, so that $\frac{b}{A} = \cos\theta$ and $\frac{a}{A} = \sin\theta$ for some $\theta, 0 \le \theta \le 2\pi$. Then

    $f(x) = A(\sin\theta \cos(cx) + \cos\theta \sin(cx)) = A \sin(cx + \theta) = A \sin[c(x + B)]$, where $B = \frac{\theta}{c}$.

4.

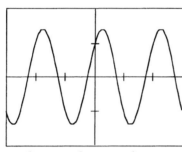

-3π ≤ x ≤ 3π,   x-scale = π
-2 ≤ y ≤ 2,   y-scale = 1

The shape is a sine wave. Applying Theorem 9.11, $g(x) = \sin x + \cos x$ can be expressed in the form $f(x) = A \cos[c(x - B)]$, where $A = \sqrt{1^2 + 1^2} = \sqrt{2}$. Since $c = 1$, $\cos B = \frac{1}{\sqrt{2}} = \frac{\sqrt{2}}{2}$ and $\sin B = \frac{1}{\sqrt{2}} = \frac{\sqrt{2}}{2}$. So $B = \frac{\pi}{4}$ and $f(x) = \sqrt{2} \cos(x - \frac{\pi}{4})$. Thus the graph of $f(x)$ is the same as the graph of a cosine function with amplitude $\sqrt{2}$ and phase shift $\frac{\pi}{4}$.

5.

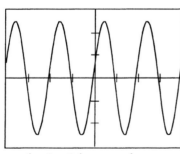

-4π ≤ x ≤ 4π,   x-scale = π
-30 ≤ y ≤ 30,   y-scale = 10

The graph of $g(x) = 7 \cos x - 24 \sin x$ looks like a sine wave with a period of 2π, an amplitude of 25 and shifted to the right by about 3. It looks this way because

$h(x) = 7 \cos x - 24 \sin x = 25(\frac{7}{25} \cos x - \frac{24}{25} \sin x) = 25(\cos \theta \cos x - \sin \theta \sin x) = 25 \cos(x - \theta)$,

where θ is the unique solution between 0 and 2π of $\cos \theta = \frac{7}{25}$ and $\sin \theta = -\frac{24}{25}$ ($\theta \approx 5.0$ radians).

Alternately, $h(x) = 25 \sin(x + \theta)$, where θ is the unique solution between 0 and 2π of $\sin \theta = \frac{7}{25}$ and

$\cos \theta = -\frac{24}{25}$ ($\theta \approx 2.86$ radians).

6.   a.   Applying Theorem 9.11, $f(x) = \sin x - \cos x$ can be
expressed in the form $f(x) = A \cos(x - B)$, where
$A = \sqrt{1^2 + (-1)^2} = \sqrt{2}$, $\cos B = \frac{-1}{\sqrt{2}}$, and $\sin B = \frac{1}{\sqrt{2}}$.
So $B = \frac{3\pi}{4}$ and $f(x) = \sqrt{2} \cos(x - \frac{3\pi}{4})$. Thus the graph
of $f(x)$ should be the same as the graph of a cosine
function with amplitude $\sqrt{2}$ and phase shift $\frac{3\pi}{4}$.

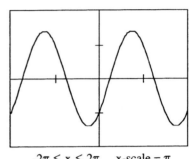

$-2\pi \le x \le 2\pi$,   x-scale = π
$-2 \le y \le 2$,   y-scale = 1

   b.   The function $g(x) = (\sin x - \cos x)e^{-x}$ will oscillate with
the same period as $f(x)$ in part **a**, but its amplitude will
decay exponentially because of the e^{-x} multiplier.

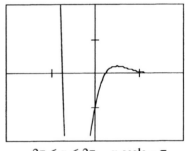

$-2\pi \le x \le 2\pi$,   x-scale = π
$-2 \le y \le 2$,   y-scale = 1

7. $c_1 x = \frac{c_1 + c_2}{2}x + \frac{c_1 - c_2}{2}x$ and $c_2 x = \frac{c_1 + c_2}{2}x - \frac{c_1 - c_2}{2}x$. So

$$f(x) = a[\cos(c_1 x) + \cos(c_2 x)]$$

$$= a[\cos(\frac{c_1 + c_2}{2}x + \frac{c_1 - c_2}{2}x) + \cos(\frac{c_1 + c_2}{2}x - \frac{c_1 - c_2}{2}x)]$$

$$= a[\cos(\frac{c_1 + c_2}{2}x)\cos(\frac{c_1 - c_2}{2}x) - \sin(\frac{c_1 + c_2}{2})\sin(\frac{c_1 - c_2}{2}x)$$

$$+ \cos(\frac{c_1 + c_2}{2}x)\cos(\frac{c_1 - c_2}{2}x) + \sin(\frac{c_1 + c_2}{2})\sin(\frac{c_1 - c_2}{2}x)]$$

$$= 2a\cos(\frac{c_1 + c_2}{2}x)\cos(\frac{c_1 - c_2}{2}x)$$

The $2a\cos(\frac{c_1 + c_2}{2}x)$ term is periodic with period $\frac{4\pi}{c_1 + c_2}$ and amplitude 2a. It is multiplied by

$\cos(\frac{c_1 - c_2}{2}x)$ which has period $\frac{4\pi}{c_1 - c_2}$ and has values ranging from -1 to 1. Since $c_1 + c_2 >> c_1 - c_2$,

$\frac{4\pi}{c_1 - c_2} >> \frac{4\pi}{c_1 + c_2}$. Thus the $\cos(\frac{c_1 - c_2}{2}x)$ will provide an envelope for the graph of $f(x)$. The other

forms are similar.

1. In order to prove theorem 9.12(b), we need to show that $\mathbf{r}_k(t) = R\cos(kt)\mathbf{i} + R\sin(kt)\mathbf{j}$ satisfies the conditions (P*), (V*), and (A*) with $K = kR$ and $M = k^2R$. Let $g(t) = R\cos(kt)$ and let $h(t) = R\sin(kt)$. Condition (P*) is satisfied since (i) $g(t)^2 + h(t)^2 = R^2\cos^2(kt) + R^2\sin^2(kt) = R^2$ for all t and (ii) for any (x, y) that satisfies $x^2 + y^2 = R^2$, $(\frac{x}{R}, \frac{y}{R})$ is a point on the unit circle, so
    $\frac{x}{R} = \cos(kt)$ and $\frac{y}{R} = \sin(kt)$ for some t with $0 \le t \le \frac{2\pi}{k} \Rightarrow x = g(t)$ and $y = h(t)$ for some t. This tells us that the path described by $\mathbf{r}_k(t)$ is a circle centered at the origin of radius R. Condition (V*) is satisfied since g(t) and h(t) are clearly differentiable and $g'(t)^2 + h'(t)^2 = (-kR\sin(kt))^2 + (kR\cos(kt))^2$
    $= (kR)^2$ for all $t \Rightarrow K = kR$, so the speed of the object is constant. Condition (A*) is satisfied since $g''(t) = -k^2R\cos(kt) = -M\,g(t)$ and $h''(t) = -k^2R\sin(kt) = -M\,h(t)$ for all t where $M = k^2$. The magnitude of acceleration is given by $|a_k(t)| = \sqrt{g''(t)^2 + h''(t)^2} = \sqrt{k^4R^2(\cos^2 t + \sin^2 t)} = k^2R$. Thus, since $\mathbf{r}_k(t) = R\cos(kt)\mathbf{i} + R\sin(kt)\mathbf{j}$ satisfies (P*), (V*), and (A*), $\mathbf{r}_k(t)$ describes uniform circular motion on a circle of radius R centered at the origin with a constant speed $K = kR$ and a constant magnitude of acceleration k^2R.

2. With the radius R and the speed s determined, you can find k using the relationship $s = kR$ and once k has been found, the magnitude of acceleration is k^2R.

3. a. In the figure, note that area $\triangle OAB = \frac{1}{2}\sin\theta\cos\theta <$ area sector $OAD = \frac{1}{2}\theta$
        $<$ area triangle with base $\overline{OD} = \frac{1}{2}\tan\theta$. Multiplying this inequality by $\frac{2}{\sin\theta}$ yields
        $\cos\theta < \frac{\theta}{\sin\theta} < \frac{1}{\cos\theta}$. Because $\lim_{\theta\to0^+}\cos\theta = 1 = \lim_{\theta\to0^+}\frac{1}{\cos\theta}$, it follows that $\lim_{\theta\to0^+}\frac{\theta}{\sin\theta} = 1$ and so
        $\lim_{\theta\to0^+}\frac{\sin\theta}{\theta} = 1$. For $0 > \theta > -\frac{\pi}{2}$, it is true that $\frac{\sin\theta}{\theta} = \frac{-\sin(-\theta)}{-(-\theta)} = \frac{\sin(-\theta)}{(-\theta)}$, where $0 < -\theta < \frac{\pi}{2}$, and so
        $\lim_{\theta\to0}\frac{\sin\theta}{\theta} = 1$.

    b. Let $f(x) = \sin x$. Then $\frac{df(x)}{dx} = \lim_{h\to0}\frac{f(x+h)-f(x)}{h} = \lim_{h\to0}\frac{\sin(x+h)-\sin x}{h}$
        $= \lim_{h\to0}\frac{\sin x\cos h + \cos x\sin h - \sin x}{h} = \lim_{h\to0}\left(\frac{\cos x\sin h}{h} + \frac{\sin x(\cos h - 1)}{h}\right)$
        $= \lim_{h\to0}\left(\cos x\frac{\sin h}{h} + \sin x\frac{(\cos h - 1)}{h}\right) = \cos x\lim_{h\to0}\frac{\sin h}{h} + \sin x\lim_{h\to0}\frac{1-\cos h}{h} = \cos x$ since
        $\lim_{h\to0}\frac{\sin h}{h} = 1$ (from part **a**) and $\lim_{h\to0}\frac{1-\cos h}{h} = 0$, because $\frac{1-\cos h}{h} = \frac{(1-\cos h)(1+\cos h)}{h(1+\cos h)}$
        $= \frac{1-\cos^2 h}{h(1+\cos h)} = \frac{\sin^2 h}{h(1+\cos h)} = (\sin h)(\frac{\sin h}{h})(\frac{1}{1+\cos h})$ and the limit of a product is the product of the limits if the limits of each factor exist. Alternately, using the trigonometric identity
        $2\cos A\sin B = \sin(A+B) - \sin(A-B)$ to get
        $\sin(x+h) - \sin x = 2\cos(x + \frac{1}{2}h)\sin(\frac{1}{2}h)$, we obtain

$$\frac{df(x)}{dx} = \lim_{h \to 0} \frac{f(x+h) - f(x)}{h} = \lim_{h \to 0} \frac{\sin(x+h) - \sin x}{h} = \lim_{h \to 0} \frac{2 \cos(x + \frac{1}{2}h) \sin(\frac{1}{2}h)}{h}$$

$$= \lim_{h \to 0} \cos(x + \frac{1}{2}h) \frac{\sin(\frac{1}{2}h)}{\frac{1}{2}h} = \cos x.$$

4. Two nonzero vectors are orthogonal if and only if their dot product is zero.

$\mathbf{r}(t) \cdot \mathbf{v}(t) = (g(t)\mathbf{i} + h(t)\mathbf{j}) \cdot (g'(t)\mathbf{i} + h'(t)\mathbf{j}) = g(t)g'(t)\mathbf{i} \cdot \mathbf{i} + g(t)h'(t)\mathbf{i} \cdot \mathbf{j} + h(t)g'(t)\mathbf{j} \cdot \mathbf{i} + h(t)h'(t)\mathbf{j} \cdot \mathbf{j}$

Since $\mathbf{i} \cdot \mathbf{i} = \mathbf{j} \cdot \mathbf{j} = 1$ and $\mathbf{i} \cdot \mathbf{j} = \mathbf{j} \cdot \mathbf{i} = 0$ (because $\mathbf{i}$ and $\mathbf{j}$ are orthogonal unit vectors),

$\mathbf{r}(t) \cdot \mathbf{v}(t) = g(t)g'(t) + h(t)h'(t)$. Thus $\mathbf{r}(t) \cdot \mathbf{v}(t) = 0$ iff $g(t)g'(t) + h(t)h'(t) = 0$. Note that the radius and velocity vector functions for uniform circular motion are orthogonal since

$\mathbf{r}_k(t) \cdot \mathbf{v}_k(t) = R\cos(kt) \cdot -kR\sin(kt) + R\sin(kt) \cdot kR\cos(kt) = 0$.

5. To establish a stationary orbit, a satellite must make one complete orbit in the same time Earth makes one complete rotation about its axis, viz., 24 h. So, at the equator, the satellite's orbital speed will be

$s = \frac{2\pi r}{24}$, where r is its orbital radius. The satellite's radial acceleration $\frac{s^2}{r} = \frac{4\pi^2 r}{24^2}$ must equal the acceleration due to gravity. However, to assume, as in Example 1, that the acceleration due to gravity is approximately g, the acceleration near the surface of Earth, would be grossly inaccurate. Using this value would give an orbital radius of about 1.2 million miles (more than four times the distance to the moon!). To more accurately estimate the acceleration of gravity, we must use Newton's universal law of gravitation, namely, $a = \frac{GM_E}{r^2}$, where G is the universal gravitational constant ($G \approx \frac{6.672 \cdot 10^{-11} m^3}{kg \cdot s^2}$) and

M_E is the mass of Earth ($M_E \approx 6 \cdot 10^{24}$ kg). In units of $\frac{m}{s}$, $s = \frac{2\pi r}{86400}$, so $\frac{s^2}{r} = \frac{4\pi^2 r}{86400^2}$

$= \frac{6.672 \cdot 10^{-11} \cdot 6 \cdot 10^{24}}{r^2}$. Solving for the orbital radius, $r = \sqrt{\frac{6.672 \cdot 10^{-11} \cdot 6 \cdot 10^{24} \cdot 86400^2}{4\pi^2}} \approx 4.23 \cdot 10^7 m$

≈ 26300 mi. The orbital insertion speed is then $s = \frac{2\pi \cdot 26300}{24} \approx 6885 \frac{mi}{h}$. Notice also that the

acceleration due to gravity at this distance is $\frac{6.672 \cdot 10^{-11} \cdot 6 \cdot 10^{24}}{(4.23 \cdot 10^7)^2} \approx .22 \frac{m}{s^2}$, or about 2% of its value at the surface of Earth.

CHAPTER 10 – Area and Volume

1. We can estimate the area by the number of squares entirely inside the boundary plus half the number crossed by the boundary.

   a. In Figure 1a, there are 14 complete squares and the boundary crosses 20 others. The area estimate is then $(14 + \frac{1}{2}(20))$(area of each square) $= 24 \cdot 1 = 24$.

   b. In Figure 1b, the area estimate is $(76 + \frac{1}{2}(41))$(area of each square) $= 96.5 \cdot \frac{1}{4} = 24.125$.

2. $\alpha(\text{HEAD}) = (7'')^2 = 49$ sq. in. and $\alpha(\text{FIDC}) = (10'')^2 = 100$ sq. in.; $\alpha(\text{ABCD}) = \frac{1}{2}(17^2 - 10^2 - 7^2)$ $= \frac{1}{2}(289 - 100 - 49) = 70$

3. a. Draw rectangle LOCA so that M is the midpoint of $\overline{AB}$ and $\overline{LQ}$, and N is the midpoint of $\overline{QO}$ and $\overline{BC}$. Since $\overline{BP}$ is the altitude to $\overline{AC}$ of $\triangle ABC$, it is perpendicular to $\overline{AC}$. $\overline{BP}$ is also perpendicular to $\overline{LO}$, since opposite sides of a rectangle are parallel. Then $\angle BMQ \cong \angle AML$, LM = MQ, and $\angle ALM \cong \angle BQM$. So $\triangle BMQ \cong \triangle AML$ by SAS congruence and $\alpha(\triangle BMQ) = \alpha(\triangle AML)$. Similarly, $\alpha(\triangle BNQ) = \alpha(\triangle CON)$. From the fact that $\triangle BMQ \sim \triangle ABC$, since $\overline{MN} /\!/ \overline{AC}$, and MN = $\frac{1}{2}$AC, QP = $\frac{1}{2}$BP.

   $\alpha(\triangle ABC) = \alpha(\text{MNCA}) + \alpha(\triangle BMQ) + \alpha(\triangle BNQ) =$

   $\alpha(\text{MNCA}) + \alpha(\triangle AML) + \alpha(\triangle CON) = \alpha(\text{LOCA}) = \frac{1}{2}(BP)(AC) = \frac{1}{2}bh$.

   b.

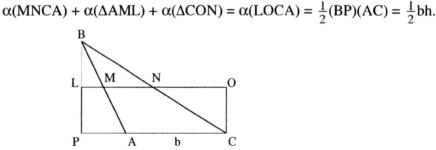

   Using the method of part **a**, we can show for right triangles $\triangle PBA$ and $\triangle PBC$ that

   $\alpha(\triangle PBC) = \frac{1}{2}(BP)(PC) = \frac{1}{2}(BP)(PA + AC)$ and

   $\alpha(\triangle PBA) = \frac{1}{2}(BP)(PA)$. So $\alpha(\triangle ABC) = \alpha(\triangle PBC) - \alpha(\triangle PBC)$

   $= \frac{1}{2}(BP)(PA + AC) - \frac{1}{2}(BP)(PA) = \frac{1}{2}(BP)(AC) = \frac{1}{2}bh$.

4. a. The minimum width $= y$.

   b. The maximum width $= \sqrt{x^2 + y^2}$.

   c. The table top should be passed through so that the plane of table's surface is perpendicular to the plane of the door and the normal to the surface is perpendicular to the diagonal of the door. Then the maximum radius is $\frac{1}{2}\sqrt{x^2 + y^2}$.

5.

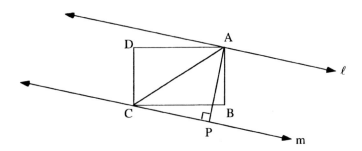

The distance between lines ℓ and m through point A is the length of segment $\overline{AP}$, where P is on m and $\overline{AP}$ is perpendicular to ℓ. By the Pythagorean Theorem, this segment is less than or equal to the length of segment $\overline{AC}$. It will be equal to AC when only when P = C. Thus the distance between lines ℓ and m will be greatest when either line is perpendicular to $\overline{AC}$.

6.

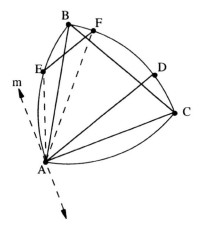

Consider a segment $\overline{EF}$ that connects sides of the Reuleaux Triangle in a direction between $\overrightarrow{AC}$ and $\overrightarrow{AB}$. Let $\overline{AD}$ be a segment connecting vertex A to the opposite arc such that $\overline{AD} /\!/ \overline{EF}$. Segments $\overline{EF}$ and $\overline{AD}$ both lie between $\overrightarrow{AC}$ and the line m which is perpendicular to $\overrightarrow{AC}$ and passes through point A. This means that angle $\angle DAE$ is acute. Because $\overline{EF}$ and $\overline{AD}$ are parallel, $\angle DAE$ and $\angle AEF$ are supplementary, and so $\angle AEF$ is obtuse. Thus, in $\triangle AEF$, AF = AD > EF. But AD = AC, so the longest segment in a direction parallel to $\overline{EF}$ has length AC. If $\overline{EF}$ is in a direction between $\overrightarrow{AC}$ and $\overrightarrow{BC}$ or between $\overrightarrow{AB}$ and $\overrightarrow{BC}$, the argument is the same, and the length of the longest segment will be BC and AB, respectively. Since the triangle is equilateral, AB = AC = BC, so the width in any direction will be the same.

7.   Construct rectangles EBFA, EBGC, EAHD, and EDIC. Then
$\alpha(ABCD) = \frac{1}{2}(EBFA) + \frac{1}{2}(EBGC) + \frac{1}{2}$
$(EAHD) + \frac{1}{2}(EDIC) = \frac{1}{2}(EB)(AE) + \frac{1}{2}(EB \bullet EC) + \frac{1}{2}(EA \bullet ED) + \frac{1}{2}(EC \bullet ED)$
$= \frac{1}{2}(EA + EC)(EB + ED) = \frac{1}{2}(AC)(BD) = \frac{1}{2}d_1 d_2.$

8. Let $\overline{OP}$ be the median of trapezoid ABCD such that $\overline{OP} \perp h$. Then $\overline{OP}$ is parallel to each base $\overline{AB}$ and $\overline{CD}$.

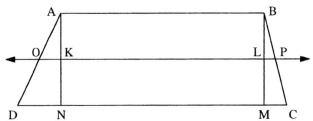

Because $\triangle AOK \sim \triangle ADN$, by AA Similarity, and AD = 2AO, OK $= \frac{1}{2}$DN. Similarly, LP $= \frac{1}{2}$MC. So α(ABCD) = α(ABMN) + α($\triangle$ADN) + α($\triangle$BCM)

$= h(KL) + \frac{1}{2}h(DN) + \frac{1}{2}h(MC) = h(KL + OK + LP) = h(OP)$.

9. For an isosceles trapezoid with sides of length 20, 25, 25, and 28, the two bases must measure 20 and 28. Then by Theorem 10.5, $\alpha = \frac{1}{2}h(b_1 + b_2) = \frac{1}{2}h(20 + 28)$. To find h, consider splitting the trapezoid into a rectangle of length 20 and width h, and two triangles of base 4, height h, and hypotenuse 25. By the Pythagorean Theorem, $h^2 = 25^2 - 4^2$, so h = $\sqrt{609}$. Then $\alpha = \frac{1}{2}(\sqrt{609})(20 + 28) = 24\sqrt{609} \approx 592.27$.

10. Because the trapezoid is circumscribable, the sum of its bases equals the sum of its sides. Since it is isosceles, the sides are equal of length s. Then 9 + 15 = 24 = 2s, so each side is of length 12. Then $h^2 = 12^2 - 3^2 = 135$, and h = $3\sqrt{15}$. By Theorem 10.5, the area of the trapezoid is $\frac{1}{2}(9 + 15)(3\sqrt{15}) = 36\sqrt{15} \approx 139.43$.

11. a. Because trapezoid ABCD is isosceles, $\overline{AD} \cong \overline{BC}$ and $\angle ADC \cong \angle BCD$. Also $\overline{CD} \cong \overline{CD}$. So $\triangle ACD \cong \triangle BDC$, by SAS Congruence, and α($\triangle$BDC) = α($\triangle$ACD). Thus α($\triangle$BEC) = α(ABCD) – α($\triangle$ABE) – α($\triangle$ACD) = (ABCD) – ($\triangle$ABE) – ($\triangle$BDC) = α($\triangle$AED).

   b. Because $\overleftrightarrow{AB} \parallel \overleftrightarrow{DC}$, $\triangle ABE \sim \triangle CDE$. Since AB < DC, the height of $\triangle$ABE is less than the height of $\triangle$CDE. Thus α($\triangle$ABE) = $\frac{1}{2}$(AB)(height of $\triangle$ABE) < $\frac{1}{2}$(AB)(height of $\triangle$CDE) = α($\triangle$CDE).

12. Samples: Let the rhombus be ABCD with sides of length x and point of intersection of diagonals be E.

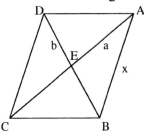

(1) A rhombus, by definition, is a quadrilateral with perpendicular diagonals, so by Theorem 10.4, $\alpha = \frac{1}{2}d_1d_2 = \frac{1}{2}ab$. (2) By the area definition,

$\alpha = \alpha(\Delta ABE) + \alpha(\Delta BEC) + \alpha(\Delta DEC) + \alpha(\Delta AED) = 4 \cdot \frac{1}{2} \cdot \frac{b}{2} \cdot \frac{a}{2} = \frac{1}{2}ab$. (3) A rhombus is a trapezoid so, by definition of trapezoid, $\alpha = \frac{1}{2}h(b_1 + b_2) = \frac{1}{2}h(2x) = xh$. Consider ΔADC. Its area is $\frac{1}{2}xh$, using x as a base, and $\frac{1}{2}a \cdot \frac{1}{2}b = \frac{1}{4}ab$, using a as a base. So $\frac{1}{2}xh = \frac{1}{4}ab$ or $xh = \frac{1}{2}ab$.

13.

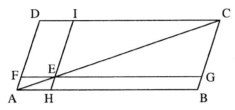

From ASA congruence, $\Delta ABC \cong \Delta ADC$, $\Delta AHE \cong \Delta AFE$, and $\Delta IEC \cong \Delta GEC$, so
$\alpha(\Delta ABC) = \alpha(\Delta ADC)$, $\alpha(\Delta AHE) = \alpha(\Delta AFE)$, and $\alpha(\Delta IEC) = \alpha(\Delta GEC)$.
$\alpha(HEGB) = \alpha(\Delta ABC) - (\alpha(\Delta AHE) + \alpha(\Delta GEC)) = \alpha(\Delta ADC) - (\alpha(\Delta AFE) + \alpha(\Delta IEC)) = \alpha(FDIE)$

14.

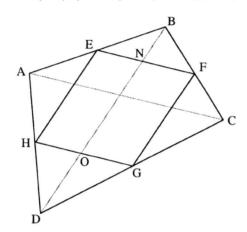

To show that $\alpha(EFGH) = \frac{1}{2}\alpha(ABCD) = \frac{1}{2} \cdot (\frac{1}{2}DB \cdot AC)$, consider the region ΔADB. ΔAHE is similar to ΔADB, with a ratio of similitude 2, so that $AE = \frac{1}{2}AB$, $AH = \frac{1}{2}AD$, and $HE = \frac{1}{2}DB$. Also, the height h_1 of ΔAHE is $\frac{1}{2}$ the height h_2 of ΔADB. Then, $\alpha(\Delta ADB) = \frac{1}{2}DB \cdot h_2$, and $\alpha(\Delta AHE) = \frac{1}{2}HE \cdot h_1 = \frac{1}{2} \cdot \frac{1}{2}DB \cdot \frac{1}{2}h_2 = \frac{1}{8}DB \cdot h_2 = \frac{1}{4}\alpha(\Delta ADB)$. By the area definition, $\alpha(\Delta ADB) = \alpha(\Delta AHE) + \alpha(\text{parallelogram } HONE) + \alpha(\Delta DOH) + \alpha(\Delta BEN)$. Since $\alpha(\Delta AHE) = \frac{1}{4}\alpha(\Delta ADB)$, then $\alpha(HONE) + \alpha(\Delta DOH) + \alpha(\Delta BEN) = \frac{3}{4}\alpha(\Delta ADB)$. $\overline{HE} \parallel \overline{DB}$ so the height of ΔDOH = height of ΔBEN = height $HONE$. Let this be height h, and call $\overline{ON} = \overline{HE} =$ base b, so that $\alpha(HONE) = bh$. Let $DO = x$ so that $NB = b - x$ (since $DB = 2HE$). Then $\alpha(\Delta DOH) = \frac{1}{2}xh$ and $\alpha(\Delta BEN) = \frac{1}{2}(b - x)h$. Then $\frac{3}{4}\alpha(\Delta ADB) = bh + \frac{1}{2}xh + \frac{1}{2}(b - x)h$, which simplifies to $\alpha(\Delta ADB) = 2bh$, or $\alpha(\Delta ADB) = 2\alpha(HONE)$. By a corresponding argument, $\alpha(\Delta CBD) = 2\alpha(GONF)$. By definition, $\alpha(ABCD) = \alpha(\Delta ADB) + \alpha(\Delta CBD)$ and $\alpha(EFGH) =$

α(GONF) + α(HONE). Then α(ABCD) = 2α(HONE) + 2α(GONF) = 2α(EFGH), or α(EFGH) = $\frac{1}{2}$$\alpha$(ABCD).

15.   a.   By HL congruence, α(ΔADF) $\cong$ α(ΔBCE), so α(ABCD) = α(ΔADF) + α(ΔFBC) = α(ΔBCE) + α(ΔFBC) = α(FECD).

       b.   Construct a rectangle AECG. α(AECG) = α(ABCD) + α(ΔADG) + α(ΔBEC).

           ΔADG $\cong$ ΔBEC by HL congruence, so BE = GD. α(AECG) = h(b + DG), so

           h(b + DG) = α(ABCD) + 2α(ΔDGA). But α(ΔDGA) = $\frac{1}{2}$h $\bullet$ DG. So

           hb + h $\bullet$ DG = α(ABCD) + 2 $\bullet$ $\frac{1}{2}$h $\bullet$ DG, from which α(ABCD) = hb.

16.   Consider the triangle formed by the center of the circle and two consecutive vertices of the regular polygon. There are n of these triangles.

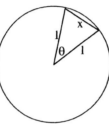

       a.   Let the side of the n-gon be x, so that the perimeter is x $\bullet$ n. Consider one of the n triangles. Since the triangle is isosceles (one side is x, the other two are of length r = 1), the altitude to x bisects the angle θ = $\frac{360^{\circ}}{n}$ and x so that $\sin \frac{\theta}{2} = \frac{\frac{x}{2}}{1}$. Thus, $\sin \frac{180^{\circ}}{n} = \frac{x}{2}$, or x = 2 $\sin \frac{180^{\circ}}{n}$. So the perimeter = 2n $\sin \frac{180^{\circ}}{n}$.

       b.   The area of the polygon = n $\bullet$ (area of each triangle), or nα_t.

           $\alpha_t = \frac{1}{2}$base $\bullet$ height = $\frac{1}{2}$x $\bullet$ h. Also, $\cos \frac{\theta}{2} = \frac{h}{r}$, so r $\cos \frac{180^{\circ}}{n}$ = h. Then

           $\alpha_t = \frac{1}{2}$x $\cos \frac{180^{\circ}}{n} = \frac{1}{2}$(2 $\sin \frac{180^{\circ}}{n}$)($\cos \frac{180^{\circ}}{n}$) = $\sin \frac{180^{\circ}}{n} \cos \frac{180^{\circ}}{n}$. By the identity

           $\sin 2\varphi = 2 \sin\varphi \cos\varphi$, $\alpha_t = \frac{1}{2} \sin \frac{360^{\circ}}{n}$, so that the area of the entire polygon is

           n $\bullet$ $\alpha_t = \frac{n}{2} \sin \frac{360^{\circ}}{n}$.

       c.   If the circle is of radius r, then x = 2r $\sin \frac{180^{\circ}}{n}$ and h = r $\cos \frac{180^{\circ}}{n}$, so that the perimeter is 2nr $\sin \frac{180^{\circ}}{n}$ and the area is $\frac{nr^2}{2} \sin \frac{360^{\circ}}{n}$.

17. For a regular n-gon circumscribed about a circle of radius r, let $\theta = \frac{360°}{n}$. There are again n congruent triangles formed by consecutive vertices of the n-gon and the circle's center. So that the perimeter of the n-gon is $x \cdot n$ and the area is $n \cdot \frac{1}{2}x \cdot r$, where x is the length of the outside edge of the triangle. Let ℓ be the length of each of the other two sides of these isosceles triangles.

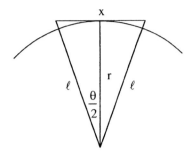

Then $\sin\frac{\theta}{2} = \frac{\frac{x}{2}}{\ell}$ and $\cos\frac{\theta}{2} = \frac{r}{\ell}$, or $\ell = \dfrac{r}{\cos\frac{180°}{n}}$, and $x = 2\ell\sin\frac{180°}{n} = \dfrac{2r\sin\frac{180°}{n}}{\cos\frac{180°}{n}}$

$= 2r\tan\frac{180°}{n}$. Then the perimeter is $2rn\tan\frac{180°}{n}$ and the area is $n \cdot \frac{1}{2} \cdot 2r\tan\frac{180°}{n} \cdot r$

$= nr^2\tan\frac{180°}{n}$.

Section 10.1.2

1. From the proof, we know that $s = AD + BE + CF$. Then $BE = s - AD - CF$. $AD = AF$ because they are tangents from a point to the circle, so $BE = s - AF - CF$. $AF + CF = AC$, so substitution again yields $BE = s - AC$.

2. Because $s = \frac{1}{2}p$, $\sqrt{s(s-a)(s-b)(s-c)} = \sqrt{\frac{p}{2}(\frac{p}{2}-a)(\frac{p}{2}-b)(\frac{p}{2}-c)} = \sqrt{\frac{p}{16}(p-2a)(p-2b)(p-2c)}$

   $= \frac{1}{4}\sqrt{p(p-2a)(p-2b)(p-2c)}$.

3. a. By Theorem 8.18, $m\angle CLB = \frac{1}{2}m\overset{\frown}{BC}$ and $m\angle CGB = \frac{1}{2}(2\pi - m\overset{\frown}{BC})$. So

    $m\angle CLB + m\angle CGB = \frac{1}{2}m\overset{\frown}{BC} + \frac{1}{2}(2\pi - m\overset{\frown}{BC}) = \pi$.

    b. Angles $\angle GKE$ and $\angle LKB$ are vertical angles, so $\angle GKE \cong \angle LKB$. Because circle G is tangent to $\overline{BC}$ at E, $\overline{EG}$ is perpendicular to $\overline{BC}$ and $\angle GEK$ is a right angle. So, by AA Similarity, $\triangle GKE \sim \triangle LKB$.

    c. Because $\triangle GCK$ is a right triangle, $EK \cdot EC = EG^2$ (see Theorem 8.27).

4. a. A 3-4-5 right triangle has perimeter $p = 3 + 4 + 5 = 12$, so that $s = \frac{1}{2}p = 6$. Then, according to Hero's formula, $\alpha = \sqrt{s(s-a)(s-b)(s-c)} = \sqrt{6(3)(2)(1)} = \sqrt{36} = 6$. (You can check this result against that obtained with the formula for the area of a triangle, $\frac{1}{2}bh$. Here, the hypotenuse is 5, so $\alpha = \frac{1}{2} \cdot 3 \cdot 4 = \frac{1}{2}(12) = 6$.)

    b. Perimeter $p = 13 + 14 + 15 = 42$, so that $s = \frac{1}{2}p = 21$. Then $\alpha = \sqrt{21(8)(7)(6)} = \sqrt{7056} = 84$.

    c. The three altitude lengths can be determined using the area from part **b** and the triangle area formula for each base, $\frac{1}{2}$bh. For base 13, $\alpha = 84 = \frac{1}{2}(13)h_1$, so that $h_1 = \frac{168}{13}$. For base 14, $\alpha = 84 = \frac{1}{2}(14)h_2$, so that $h_2 = \frac{168}{14} = 12$. For base 15, $\alpha = 84 = \frac{1}{2}(15)h_3$, so that $h_3 = \frac{168}{15}$.

    d.   A triangle with sides 51, 52, and 53 will have s = 78 in Hero's Formula and an area of 1170 square units (these are the next larger three consecutive integers that will form a triangle with integer area).

5.   Let T_k be a similarity transformation of magnitude k, and $\triangle ABC$ have sides of length a, b, and c. If $T_k(\triangle ABC) = \triangle DEF$, then $T_k(a) = ka = d$, $T_k(b) = kb = e$, and $T_k(c) = kc = f$. Since $s = \frac{a+b+c}{2}$, then the semiperimeter of $\triangle DEF = \frac{d+e+f}{2} = \frac{ka+kb+kc}{2} = ks$.

By Hero's formula, $\alpha(\triangle ABC) = \sqrt{s(s-a)(s-b)(s-c)}$, and

$\alpha(\triangle DEF) = \sqrt{ks(ks-ka)(ks-kb)(ks-kc)} = \sqrt{ks \cdot k(s-a)(s-b)(s-c)} = \sqrt{k^4 \cdot s(s-a)(s-b)(s-c)} = k^2 \cdot \sqrt{s(s-a)(s-b)(s-c)} = k^2 \cdot \alpha(\triangle ABC)$.

6.   There are four cyclic quadrilaterals in Figure 13. LBGC was constructed as such during the synthetic proof of Hero's Formula. BDGE, CEGF, and ADGF are all cyclic quadrilaterals as well since a pair of opposite angles in each are right angles (so the diagonal between the other pair of opposite angles is the diameter of the circle in which it can be inscribed).

7.   a.   Answers will vary.

    b.   Brahmagupta's formula gives the area of a quadrilateral in terms of its sides a, b, c, and d. But two quadrilaterals can have the sides of the same length and not have the same area. So this formula could never work for all quadrilaterals. As a specific example, consider the quadrilateral with vertices (3, 0), (0, 4), (-3, 0), and (0, -4). This is a rhombus with sides of length 5 and diagonals of length 6 and 8. By Theorem 10.4, its area is $\frac{1}{2} \bullet 6 \bullet 8 = 24$. Using Brahmagupta's formula, s = 10, and the area is $\sqrt{(10-5)^4} = 25$.

    c.   Brahmagupta's formula reduces to Hero's formula for the special case in which one side of the quadrilateral has length 0. Taking d = 0, $s = \frac{a+b+c+0}{2} = \frac{a+b+c}{2}$ and $\alpha = \sqrt{(s-0)(s-a)(s-b)(s-c)} = \sqrt{s(s-a)(s-b)(s-c)}$.

8.   Sample: Every square is cyclic inscribable. According to the formula, the area of a square with side s is $\sqrt{s \bullet s \bullet s \bullet s} = s^2$. So the formula works for a square.

9. $\alpha(\triangle ABC) = \frac{1}{2}ab \sin C = \frac{1}{2}ac \sin B = \frac{1}{2}bc \sin A$. Dividing through by the quantity abc gives

$\frac{\sin C}{c} = \frac{\sin B}{b} = \frac{\sin A}{a}$.

10.   Let $\alpha(\triangle ABC) = \alpha$ and side b be fixed. We want to minimize a + c. $\alpha = \frac{1}{2}bh$, or $h = \frac{2\alpha}{b}$. Let h be the altitude to b, with point of intersection Y. The measures of the two sides of b are x and b – x. In $\triangle BCY$, $a^2 = x^2 + h^2$ and $h^2 = \frac{4\alpha^2}{b^2}$. In $\triangle BAY$, $c^2 = h^2 + (b-x)^2$. Then

$a + c = \sqrt{\frac{4\alpha^2}{b^2} + x^2} + \sqrt{\frac{4\alpha^2}{b^2} + (b-x)^2}$. The derivative of (a + c) with respect to x is then

$$\frac{x\sqrt{\frac{4\alpha^2}{b^2}+(b-x)^2}+(x-b)\sqrt{\frac{4\alpha^2}{b^2}+x^2}}{\sqrt{\frac{4\alpha^2}{b^2}+x}\sqrt{\frac{4\alpha^2}{b^2}+(b-x)^2}}$$, which is equal to zero when the numerator is equal to zero, or

when $4\alpha^2 = \frac{8\alpha^2 x}{b}$, or $b = 2x$. Therefore, $a + c$ is minimized when h bisects b, which occurs when $a = c$, or when the triangle is isosceles.

11. Suppose the side known is c, and let $a + b = k$. Then $\frac{a+b+c}{2} = \frac{k+c}{2} = s$. Then by Hero's formula,

$\alpha = \sqrt{s\left(\frac{c+b-a}{2}\right)\left(\frac{c+a-b}{2}\right)\left(\frac{k-c}{2}\right)}$. Since k, c, and s are constant, we only have to look at when

$\left(\frac{c+b-a}{2}\right)\left(\frac{c+a-b}{2}\right)$ is maximized. Since $a = k - b$, this reduces to $\frac{1}{4}(c^2 + 4bk - 4b^2 - k^2)$. With k and

c constant, the area is maximized when $bk - b^2$ is maximized, or when its derivative is zero, $k - 2b = 0$,

$b = \frac{1}{2}k$, or $a = b$. The area is maximized then, when the triangle is isosceles.

12. Let c be the longest side and let P be the perimeter of $\triangle ABC$. From Problem 10, $\alpha(\triangle ABC)$ is greatest

when the other two sides are equal. From this we have $a = b = \frac{P-c}{2}$ and $c \geq \frac{P}{3}$. Using Hero's

Formula, $\alpha(\triangle ABC) = \sqrt{\frac{P}{2}\left(\frac{P}{2} - \frac{P-c}{2}\right)^2\left(\frac{P}{2} - c\right)} = \sqrt{\frac{P^2c^2 - 2Pc^3}{8}}$. This is maximized when $P^2c^2 - 2Pc^3$ is

maximized. Setting its derivative equal to zero gives $2Pc - 6Pc^2 = 0 \Rightarrow c = 0$ or $c = \frac{P}{3}$. Clearly c = 0 is

not a maximum, so $\alpha(\triangle ABC)$ is maximized when $c = \frac{P}{3} \Rightarrow a = b = \frac{P}{3}$ and $\triangle ABC$ is an equilateral

triangle.

13.

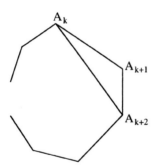

We can prove by contradiction that a polygon of perimeter P with maximal area is equilateral. Suppose, to the contrary, the area of n-gon $A_1A_2...A_kA_{k+1}A_{k+2}...A_n$ is maximal and sides $\overline{A_kA_{k+1}}$ and $\overline{A_{k+1}A_{k+2}}$ of the polygon have lengths s_1 and s_2, where $s_1 \neq s_2$. Construct the segment $\overline{A_kA_{k+2}}$, forming $\triangle A_kA_{k+1}A_{k+2}$. So $\alpha(A_1A_2...A_kA_{k+1}A_{k+2}...A_n) = \alpha(A_1A_2...A_kA_{k+2}...A_n) + \alpha(\triangle A_kA_{k+1}A_{k+2})$.

Now consider a point B on the same side of $\overleftrightarrow{A_kA_{k+2}}$ as A_{k+1} such that $A_kB = BA_{k+2} = \frac{s_1+s_2}{2}$.

By the result of Problem 11, $\alpha(\triangle A_kBA_{k+2}) > \alpha(\triangle A_kA_{k+1}A_{k+2})$, so

$\alpha(A_1A_2...A_kBA_{k+2}...A_n) = \alpha(A_1A_2...A_kA_{k+2}...A_n) + \alpha(\triangle A_kBA_{k+2}) > \alpha(A_1A_2...A_kA_{k+1}A_{k+2}...A_n)$. However,

the perimeter of n-gon $A_1A_2...A_kBA_{k+2}...A_n$ equals $P - (s_1 + s_2) + 2\frac{s_1+s_2}{2} = P$, the perimeter of n-gon

$A_1A_2...A_kA_{k+1}A_{k+2}...A_n$. This contradicts the assumption that n-gon $A_1A_2...A_kA_{k+1}A_{k+2}...A_n$ has maximal area for a given perimeter P.

14. α = bh for a parallelogram. If ϕ is the non-included angle, then the included angle is $180° - \phi$, by the properties of a parallelogram. Then sin $(180° - \phi) = \frac{h}{a}$, or h = a sin $(180° - \phi)$. Then the area is b • a sin $(180° - \phi)$ = ab sin ϕ.

15. a. Let M = (a, b) and N = (c, d). Consider the case where b > d > 0 and c > a > 0. Then the triangle can be inscribed in a rectangle with vertices O = (0, 0), P = (a, 0), Q = (b, d), and R = (0, d). $\alpha(\Delta MNO) = \alpha(OPQR) - \alpha(\Delta OPM) - \alpha(\Delta MNQ) - \alpha(\Delta ONR)$
= ad $- \frac{1}{2}$ab $- \frac{1}{2}$(d – b)(a – c) $- \frac{1}{2}$cd = $\frac{1}{2}$(ad – bc). A similar argument for all other possible positions of M and N shows that $\alpha(\Delta MNO) = \frac{1}{2}|ad - bc|$.

   b. The fourth vertex can be at (c – a, d – b), (a + c, b + d), or (a – c, b – d). Multiplying by 2 the area in part **a** gives the area of each parallelogram as |ad – bc|.

16.

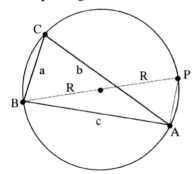 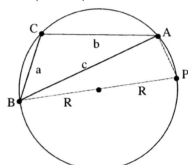

By Theorem 10.8, $\alpha(\Delta ABC) = \frac{1}{2}$ab sin C. Now construct diameter $\overline{BP}$. There are two cases to consider. Either m$\angle$P = m$\angle$C or m$\angle$C = π – m$\angle$P. But, in either case, sin P = sin C. Also note that ΔAPB is a right triangle, so sin P = $\frac{c}{2R}$. Thus $\alpha(\Delta ABC) = \frac{1}{2}$ab sin C = $\frac{1}{2}$ab sin P = $\frac{abc}{4R}$.

Section 10.1.3

1. a. By Theorem 10.8, $\alpha = \frac{1}{2}$ab sin C = $\frac{1}{2}$OA • AB sin θ. As $\theta \to \frac{\pi}{2}$, sin θ approaches 1, OA approaches 5, and OB approaches + ∞. So AB approaches + ∞ and α becomes infinite.

   b. The limit from part **a**, as $\theta \to 0$, also approaches infinity, because $\alpha = \frac{1}{2}$OB • AB cos θ, and OB $\to$ 2, AB $\to \infty$, and cos $\theta \to 1$.

c. Given that the line ℓ has slope tan $(\pi - \theta)$ and passes through the point $(5, 2)$, an equation for the line is $y = x \tan (\pi - \theta) + (2 - 5 \tan (\pi - \theta))$. For $0 < \theta < \frac{\pi}{4}$, $\alpha(\Delta AOB) = \frac{1}{2}(OB)(OA)$. Since $OB = 0 \tan (\pi - \theta) + (2 - 5 \tan (\pi - \theta)) = 2 + 5 \tan \theta$ and $OA = \frac{5 \tan(\pi - \theta) - 2}{\tan(\pi - \theta)} = 5 + 2 \cot \theta$, $\alpha(\Delta AOB) = \frac{1}{2}(2 + 5 \tan \theta)(5 + 2 \cot \theta) = 10 + \frac{25}{2} \tan \theta + 2 \cot \theta$.

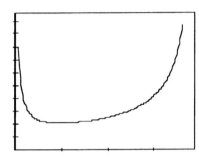

$0 < x < \frac{\pi}{4}$,   x-scale $= \frac{\pi}{8}$

$0 \le y \le 100$,   y-scale $= 10$

2. a. If we know any two of these parameters, we can find the third using the slope-intercept formula $y = mx + b$. So, knowing (1) m and b, we can find $a = -\frac{b}{m}$; (2) m and a, we can find $b = -ma$; and (3) a and b, we can find $m = -\frac{b}{a}$.

b. Given the point $(5, 2)$, if we know any one of the parameters, we can find the other two. (1) Given m and $(5, 2)$, then $2 = 5m + b$, so $a = \frac{5m - 2}{m}$ and $b = 2 - 5m$; (2) Given a and $(5, 2)$, then $m = \frac{2 - 0}{5 - a} = \frac{2}{5 - a}$ and $b = \frac{2a}{a - 5}$; and (3) Given b and $(5, 2)$, then $m = \frac{2 - b}{5}$ and $a = \frac{5b}{b - 2}$.

c. $\alpha = \frac{1}{2} ab = \frac{1}{2}(\frac{5m - 2}{m})(2 - 5m) = \frac{-25m^2 + 20m - 4}{2m}$.

d. $\alpha = \frac{1}{2} ab = \frac{1}{2}(\frac{5b}{b - 2})(b) = \frac{5b^2}{2(b - 2)}$

e. $\alpha = \frac{1}{2} ab = \frac{1}{2}(a)(\frac{2a}{a - 5}) = \frac{a^2}{a - 5}$.

3. a. To show that $f(b) = \frac{5b^2}{2(b - 2)}$ obtains its minimum at $b = 4$, we must show that the derivative $f'(b) = 0$ when $b = 4$ and evaluate $f(4)$. $f'(b) = \frac{10b(2b - 4) - 10b^2}{(2b - 4)^2} = \frac{10b^2 - 40b}{(2b - 4)^2}$, which equals 0 when $10b^2 - 40b = 0$, or $b = 4$. $f(4) = \frac{5(16)}{2(2)} = 20$, so the minimum value of f is 20.

b. To show that $f(b) = \frac{pb^2}{2(b - q)}$ obtains its minimum at $b = 2q$, we must show that the derivative $f'(b) = 0$ when $b = 2q$ and evaluate $f(2q)$ to find the minimum value of f. $f'(b) = \frac{2pb(2b - 2q) - 2pb^2}{(2b - 2q)^2} = \frac{2pb^2 - 4pbq}{(2b - 2q)^2}$, which equals 0 when $2pb^2 - 4pbq = 0$, or $b = 2q$.

$$f(2q) = \frac{p(2q)^2}{2(2q-q)} = 2qp, \text{ so the minimum value of f is 2qp.}$$

c. $\frac{5b^2}{2(b-2)} = \frac{5}{2}b + 5 + \frac{20}{2(b-2)}$. Thus the asymptote has equation $y = \frac{5}{2}x + 5$.

d. $\frac{pb^2}{2(b-q)} = \frac{p}{2}b + \frac{pq}{2} + \frac{pb^2}{2(b-q)}$. Thus the asymptote has equation $y = \frac{p}{2}x + \frac{pq}{2}$.

4. By equating the slopes, we can show that $\frac{v}{5} = \frac{2}{u}$, or $u = \frac{10}{v}$. The area of the triangle is

$A = 5 \cdot 2 + \frac{1}{2}(5v) + \frac{1}{2}(2u) = 10 + \frac{5}{2}v + u = 10 + \frac{5}{2}v + \frac{10}{v}$. Taking the derivative of A with respect to

v gives $A' = \frac{5}{2} - \frac{10}{v^2}$. Setting this equal to zero and solving for v gives $v = 2$ and $A = 20$.

5.   There is an error in the first printing of the statement of this problem. Change 23f to 23e.

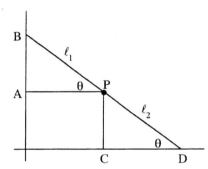

If $\overline{BP} \cong \overline{PD}$, then, by ASA Congruence, $\triangle APB \cong \triangle CDP$. So $\alpha(\triangle APB) = \alpha(\triangle CDP)$. Thus the condition of Figure 23b implies the condition of Figure 23c. Also, $\overline{AP} \cong \overline{CD} \cong \overline{OC}$ and $\overline{AB} \cong \overline{CP} \cong \overline{OA}$. Thus the condition of Figure 23b implies the condition of Figure 23e. Because $OB = 2OA$ and $OD = 2OC$, $\frac{OB}{OD} = \frac{OA}{OC}$ and the slope of $\overline{AC}$ equals the slope of ℓ. Thus the condition of Figure 23e implies the condition of Figure 23d. If $\overline{AC} // \ell$, then ABPC and APDC are parallelograms with $\overline{AC} \cong \overline{BP}$ and $\overline{AC} \cong \overline{PD}$. Thus the condition of Figure 23d implies the condition of Figure 23b. Finally, $\alpha(\triangle APB) = \frac{1}{2}\ell_1^2 \sin\theta \cos\theta$ and $\alpha(\triangle CDP) = \frac{1}{2}\ell_2^2 \sin\theta \cos\theta$. So, if $\alpha(\triangle APB) = \alpha(\triangle CDP)$, then $\ell_1 = \ell_2$ and the condition of Figure 23c implies the condition of Figure 23b.

6. Relationship (3) will hold, since, if (p, q) is in the 2nd quadrant, the slope of the segment that cuts off the triangle of smallest area must be positive, which will be the case for $-\frac{q}{p}$. Relationship (4) will continue to hold, because the slopes will both be negative. It can be seen that Relationship (5) also holds, since $b - q$ and p are both negative.

7. Figure 23g: We can show that when point P bisects ℓ, to achieve minimum area, the length of ℓ is not, in general, minimized. Let $P = (a, b)$. By the condition given in Figure 23e, the length of ℓ is $2\sqrt{a^2 + b^2}$. If $a \neq b$, the line with equation $y = -x + (a + b)$ is a shorter segment through P. To show that it is shorter, note that it will have length $\sqrt{a^2 + a^2} + \sqrt{b^2 + b^2} = \sqrt{2}(a + b)$. Since $(a - b)^2 > 0$, $a^2 + b^2 > 2ab$ and

$4a^2 + 4b^2 = 4(a^2 + b^2) > 2a^2 + 2b^2 + 4ab = 2(a + b)^2$. Thus $2\sqrt{a^2 + b^2} > \sqrt{2}(a + b)$. Figure 23h: We can show that when point P bisects ℓ, to achieve minimum area, the slope of ℓ is not, in general, -1. Let P = (a, b) and suppose the slope of ℓ is -1. Then the equation for the line passing through P is y = -x + (a + b). Then this case reduces to the case of Figure 23g. Figure 23i: By the condition given in Figure 23d, to minimize the triangle's area, ℓ must be parallel to a diagonal of the rectangle. If P = (a, b) and a ≠ b, then the two diagonals of the rectangle will not be perpendicular to each other. Since ℓ is perpendicular to $\overline{OP}$, ℓ will not be parallel to the other diagonal.

8.　　a.　　The minimum value of f(x) occurs where its derivative is zero. If $f(x) = Ax + \frac{B}{x}$, then

$f'(x) = A - \frac{B}{x^2}$, which equals zero when $A = \frac{B}{x^2}$, or, for positive x, $x = \sqrt{\frac{B}{A}}$. Evaluating f(x) at $x = \sqrt{\frac{B}{A}}$ shows that the minimum value of f is $2\sqrt{AB}$.

　　b.　　The graphs of y = Ax and $y = \frac{B}{x}$ intersect when $Ax = \frac{B}{x}$, or $x = \sqrt{\frac{B}{A}}$, which is where the function $f(x) = Ax + \frac{B}{x}$ achieves its minimum value.

　　c.　　From the graphs of y = Ax and $y = \frac{B}{x}$, we can see that y = Ax is increasing, with a constant positive slope A and $y = \frac{B}{x}$ is decreasing, with a slope that is greater than A for $x < \sqrt{\frac{B}{A}}$ and less than A for $x > \sqrt{\frac{B}{A}}$. At $x = \sqrt{\frac{B}{A}}$, $Ax = \frac{B}{x} = \sqrt{AB}$, so $Ax + \frac{B}{x} = 2\sqrt{AB}$. For $x > \sqrt{\frac{B}{A}}$, $Ax > \sqrt{AB}$ and $\frac{B}{x} < \sqrt{AB}$, but since the slope of the graph of $y = \frac{B}{x}$ is less than the slope of y = Ax, $Ax - \sqrt{AB} > \sqrt{AB} - \frac{B}{x}$, so $Ax + \frac{B}{x} > 2\sqrt{AB}$. For $x < \sqrt{\frac{B}{A}}$, $Ax < \sqrt{AB}$ and $\frac{B}{x} > \sqrt{AB}$, but since the slope of the graph of $y = \frac{B}{x}$ is greater than the slope of y = Ax, $\frac{B}{x} - \sqrt{AB} > \sqrt{AB} - Ax$, so, again, $Ax + \frac{B}{x} > 2\sqrt{AB}$. Thus the minimum value of $Ax + \frac{B}{x}$ is $2\sqrt{AB}$ and it occurs at $x = \sqrt{\frac{B}{A}}$.

　　d.　　By the Arithmetic-Geometric Inequality, we know that, for any positive x, $Ax + \frac{B}{x} \geq 2\sqrt{Ax \frac{B}{x}} = 2\sqrt{AB}$. Thus the minimum value is achieved when $Ax + \frac{B}{x} = 2\sqrt{AB}$, or $x = \sqrt{\frac{B}{A}}$.

9.　　Let segment ℓ be partitioned into the two segments ℓ_1 and ℓ_2 by point P. Let θ be the angle between the x-axis and the line ℓ and let P = (a, b). We can write the area of the entire triangular region as $A(\theta) = ab + \frac{1}{2}a^2\tan\theta + \frac{1}{2}\frac{b^2}{\tan\theta}$. When the area is minimized, $\frac{dA}{d\theta} = \frac{1}{2}a^2\sec^2\theta - \frac{1}{2}b^2\csc^2\theta = 0$. This will be true when $a^2\sin^2\theta - b^2\cos^2\theta = a^2 - \cos^2\theta(a^2 + b^2) = 0$,

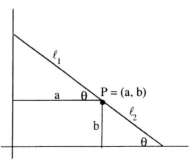

or $\cos\theta = \dfrac{a}{\sqrt{a^2 + b^2}}$. Thus $\ell_1 = \sqrt{a^2 + b^2}$. Similarly, $\sin\theta = \dfrac{b}{\sqrt{a^2 + b^2}}$ and $\ell_2 = \sqrt{a^2 + b^2}$. Therefore $\ell_1 = \ell_2$ and P is the midpoint of ℓ.

10.   a, b. First note that ℓ has equation $y = x\tan\theta + (1 - \tan\theta)$. For $0 \le \theta \le \frac{\pi}{4}$ or $\pi \le \theta \le \frac{5\pi}{4}$, the region bounded by ℓ, $y = 0$, $x = 0$, and $x = 4$ is a trapezoid with height 4 and bases of length $3\tan\theta + 1$ and $1 - \tan\theta$. Thus $A(\theta) = 4 \cdot \dfrac{(3\tan\theta + 1) + (1 - \tan\theta)}{2} = 4\tan\theta + 4$ (see Figure (1) below). For $\frac{\pi}{4} \le \theta < \frac{\pi}{2}$ or $\frac{5\pi}{4} \le \theta < \frac{3\pi}{2}$, the region bounded by ℓ, $y = 0$, and $x = 4$ is a triangle with height $4 - (1 - \cot\theta)$ $= 3 + \cot\theta$ and base of length $3\tan\theta + 1$. Thus $A(\theta) = \frac{1}{2}(3 + \cot\theta)(3\tan\theta + 1)$ $= \frac{9}{2}\tan\theta + \frac{1}{2}\cot\theta + 3$ (see Figure (2) below). For $\frac{\pi}{2} < \theta \le \pi - \tan^{-1}(\frac{1}{3})$ or $\frac{3\pi}{2} < \theta < 2\pi - \tan^{-1}(\frac{1}{3})$, the region bounded by ℓ, $y = 0$, and $x = 0$ is a triangle with height $1 - \cot\theta$ and base of length $1 - \tan\theta$. Thus $A(\theta) = \frac{1}{2}(1 - \cot\theta)(1 - \tan\theta) = 1 - \frac{1}{2}\tan\theta - \frac{1}{2}\cot\theta$ (see Figure (3) below). Finally, for $\pi - \tan^{-1}(\frac{1}{3}) \le \theta \le \pi$ or $2\pi - \tan^{-1}(\frac{1}{3}) \le \theta \le 2\pi$, the region bounded by ℓ, $y = 0$, $x = 0$, and $x = 4$ is a trapezoid with height 4 and bases of length $3\tan\theta + 1$ and $1 - \tan\theta$. Thus

$A(\theta) = 4 \cdot \dfrac{(3\tan\theta + 1) + (1 - \tan\theta)}{2} = 4\tan\theta + 4$ (see Figure (4) below).

(1)
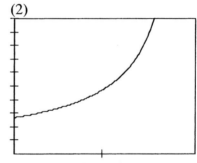
$0 \le x \le \frac{\pi}{4}$,   x-scale $= \frac{\pi}{8}$
$0 \le y \le 10$,   y-scale $= 1$

(2)
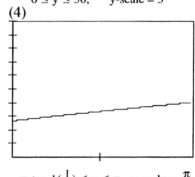
$\frac{\pi}{4} \le x \le \frac{\pi}{2}$,   x-scale $= \frac{\pi}{8}$
$0 \le y \le 30$,   y-scale $= 3$

(3)
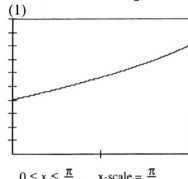
$\frac{\pi}{2} \le x \le \pi - 1(\frac{1}{3})$, x-scale $= \frac{\pi}{8}$
$0 \le y \le 10$,   y-scale $= 1$

(4)
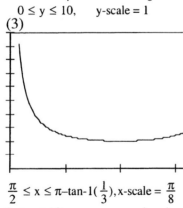
$\pi - \tan-1(\frac{1}{3}) \le x \le \pi$,   x-scale $= \frac{\pi}{8}$
$0 \le y \le 10$,   y-scale $= 1$

11.   a.   Given a convex polygon C, consider a point P inside C, and let L be any line through P. If L is rotated smoothly about P, the portions of L cut off by C vary continuously in length. If at some

11.   a.   Given a convex polygon C, consider a point P inside C, and let L be any line through P. If L is rotated smoothly about P, the portions of L cut off by C vary continuously in length. If at some point the portion between C and P is less than half the length of L inside C, after a half turn this portion will be more than half this length. By this argument, we see that at some point in this rotation L will be P-centered.

       b.   The case of a rectangle with P on a center line shows that the area function may be constant over portions of its domain. This will happen whenever the points where the line through P intersects C lie on parallel sides of C. If the points where the line through P intersects C lie on nonparallel sides of C, the argument based on Figure 22 applies, showing that the area function has either a minimum or a maximum (depending on which side of L the area is being counted.)

12.   a.

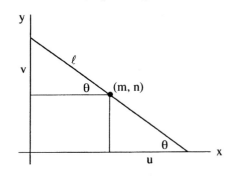

$\ell = \dfrac{m}{\cos\theta} + \dfrac{n}{\sin\theta}$. $\dfrac{d\ell}{d\theta} = \dfrac{m}{\cos^2\theta}\sin\theta - \dfrac{n}{\sin^2\theta}\cos\theta$. Setting $\dfrac{d\ell}{d\theta} = 0$, $\dfrac{m}{\cos^2\theta}\sin\theta = \dfrac{n}{\sin^2\theta}\cos\theta$, or $\dfrac{n}{m} = \dfrac{\sin^3\theta}{\cos^3\theta} = \tan^3\theta$. Thus the shortest line through (m, n) has slope $\tan\theta = \sqrt[3]{\dfrac{n}{m}}$.

       b.   In the diagram of part **a**, let the x-axis be the floor, the y-axis be the wall, and the rectangle with corner (0, 0), (m, 0), (0, n), and (m, n) be the box.

       c.

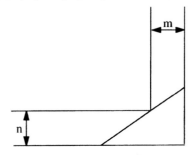

             Note that only a ladder that is not long enough to make contact with a wall of each hallway and the corner where the hallways meet will be able to turn the corner. The longest ladder for which this will be true is slightly shorter than the shortest ladder that can make contact with all three points.

       d.   Suppose line ℓ has the shortest length in the first quadrant of all lines through (m, n). See the diagram. Let θ_s be the angle that ℓ makes with the horizontal. We show that θ_s depends on m and n.

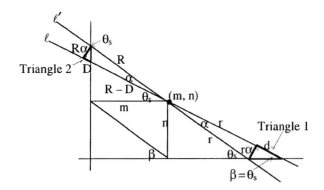

Represent the length of the portions of ℓ on each side of (m, n) as R and r, as shown. Consider another line segment ℓ' that also passes through point (m, n), where ℓ' makes a small angle α with the line ℓ. Line segment ℓ' is longer than ℓ by an amount d on the right, but shorter than ℓ by an amount D on the left.

Mark off segments of length r and R along ℓ' from (m, n) as shown. For small values of the angle α, the indicated line segments between ℓ and ℓ' have the approximate lengths $r\alpha$ and $R\alpha$. (These segments are chords of circle sectors of small angle, and hence approximately equal to arcs.) These segments are part of Triangle 1 and Triangle 2, respectively. One of the angles in Triangle 2 is exactly θ_s, as shown, and, in Triangle 1, we have $\beta = \theta_s - \alpha$.

One angle of each of these triangles is approximately a right angle, for small α. Hence, Triangles 1 and 2 are approximately similar for small α. (In the limit as α approaches 0, they are precisely similar.) From the similarity, we conclude $\frac{D}{r\alpha} \approx \frac{r\alpha}{d}$.

Since from Triangle 1, $\tan \beta \approx \frac{r\alpha}{d} \approx \tan \theta_s$, we have $\alpha \approx \frac{d \tan \theta_s}{r}$, or $\tan^2 \theta_s \approx \frac{Dr}{dR} = \frac{D}{d} \bullet \frac{n}{m \tan \theta_s}$. Hence, $\tan^3 \theta_s \approx \frac{D}{d} \bullet \frac{n}{m}$.

Now, if line _ is indeed the shortest line through (m, n) then, for small values of α, the lengths D and d are approximately equal, since these are the increments by which _ is lengthened and shortened, respectively, when it is rotated by a small amount. Assuming $D \approx d$, we have

$$\tan^3 \theta_s \approx \frac{n}{m}, \text{ or } \tan \theta_s \approx \sqrt[3]{\frac{n}{m}}.$$

The argument used here can be called the "equal increments principle". It says that if a function f obtains a maximum or minimum at a point x = a, then the increments $|f(a + \Delta) - f(a)|$ and $|f(a - \Delta) - f(a)|$ are approximately equal for small Δ (and precisely equal in the limit as Δ goes to 0). An instance of this principle is applied in the argument based on Figure 22. There the quantity being minimized was area, and the equal increments principle says that the increments of area (the areas of the pairs of small triangles) are approximately equal. The principle can be justified by a simple analytic argument.

13. The position of the line in which it is bisected by the parabola will minimize the enclosed area. This can be seen by an argument similar to the one based on Figure 22, since, for small deviations of the line from this bisected position, the nearby portions of the parabola are nearly straight lines.

14.   Investigations may take different forms. Here is one way to describe the desired line ℓ. Let $O = (0, 0)$. The key to the solution is to realize that, if a circle with center (r, r) is tangent to the two axes at $A = (r, 0)$ and $B = (0, r)$, then the tangent to the circle at a point P on the minor arc $\overset{\frown}{AB}$ forms a triangle $\Delta A'OB'$ whose perimeter is $2r$, independent of the location of P. (A' and B' are the points of intersection of the tangent and the x- and y-axis, respectively.) This follows since $A'P = A'A$ and $B'B = B'P$, because tangents to a circle from a point outside have equal lengths. Consequently, the smaller the circle, the smaller the perimeter of the triangle.

Suppose now we are given a point P in the first quadrant. Construct the circle that is tangent to the axes and that contains P. Suppose it has radius r. The desired line ℓ is the tangent to this circle at P. For given any other line through P, a circle tangent to this line and to the two axes will have radius larger than r, and hence by the above argument will form a triangle with larger perimeter.

For an extended discussion, see George Polya (1968), *Mathematics and Plausible Reasoning*, Volume II, Second Edition, Princeton University Press, page 205.

Section 10.1.4

1. a. A regular hexagon, circumscribed about a circle of radius r, can be divided into 6 congruent triangles, each of area α_t. Each of these triangles has interior angle $\theta = \frac{360^{\circ}}{n} = \frac{360^{\circ}}{6} = 60^{\circ}$. Since the triangle is isosceles with the angle 60°, the triangles are equilateral. Because the hexagon is circumscribed, the height $h = r$. Let x be the measure of one side, so that tan

$30^{\circ} = \dfrac{\frac{1}{2}x}{r}$, or $x = \dfrac{2r\sqrt{3}}{3}$. Then $\alpha_t = \frac{1}{2}x \cdot r = \dfrac{r^2\sqrt{3}}{3}$, and $\alpha(\text{hexagon}) = 6 \cdot \alpha_t = 2r^2\sqrt{3}$.

A regular hexagon, inscribed in a circle of radius r, can be divided into 6 congruent triangles, each of area α_t. Each of these triangles has interior angle $\theta = \frac{360^{\circ}}{n} = \frac{360^{\circ}}{6} = 60^{\circ}$. Since the triangle is isosceles with the angle 60°, the triangles are equilateral. Because the hexagon is inscribed each side is of length r, and $\cos 30^{\circ} = \frac{h}{r}$, or $h = \dfrac{r\sqrt{3}}{2}$. Then $\alpha_t = \frac{1}{2}r \cdot h = \dfrac{r^2\sqrt{3}}{4}$, and

$\alpha(\text{hexagon}) = 6 \cdot \alpha_t = \dfrac{3r^2\sqrt{3}}{2}$.

  b. Let x be the side length of the regular n-gon and y the side length of the regular 2n-gon. Then

$y^2 = \left(\dfrac{x}{2}\right)^2 + \left(r - \sqrt{r^2 - \dfrac{x^2}{4}}\right)^2 = 2r^2 - 2r\sqrt{r^2 - \dfrac{x^2}{4}}$, so that $y = \sqrt{2r^2 - 2r\sqrt{r^2 - \dfrac{x^2}{4}}}$. With $r = 1$,

$y = \sqrt{2 - 2\sqrt{1 - \dfrac{x^2}{4}}} = \sqrt{2 - \sqrt{4 - x^2}}$.

c. If $r = \frac{1}{2}$, then $x = \frac{\sqrt{3}}{2}$ when $n = 3$ and $y = \sqrt{\frac{1}{2} - \sqrt{\frac{1}{4} - \frac{x^2}{4}}} = \sqrt{\frac{1}{2}(1 - \sqrt{1 - x^2})}$. From this, we can calculate the side length for each n and multiply by n to obtain the perimeter. If $n = 3$, $x = \frac{\sqrt{3}}{2}$, and $p = \frac{3\sqrt{3}}{2}$. If $n = 6$, $y = \frac{1}{2}$, and $p = 3$. If $n = 12$, $y = \sqrt{\frac{1}{2}\left(1 - \sqrt{\frac{3}{4}}\right)} \approx 0.2588$, and $p \approx 3.1058$. If $n = 24$, $y \approx 0.1305$, and $p \approx 3.1327$. If $n = 48$, $y \approx 0.6540$, and $p \approx 3.1392$. If $n = 96$, $y \approx 0.0327$, and $p \approx 3.1411$. If $n = 192$, $y \approx 0.0164$, and $p \approx 3.1415$.

2. We know that the area of the circle is πr^2. Since the arc measure of the entire circle is 2π, then the arc of measure θ accounts for $\frac{\theta}{2\pi}$ of the circle. The area of the sector is similarly proportional to the area of the circle. Then, $\frac{\theta}{2\pi} = \frac{A}{\pi r^2} \Rightarrow A = \frac{\theta}{2\pi} \cdot \pi r^2 = \frac{r^2 \theta}{2}$.

3. a. In Figure 34, $m\widehat{BD} = \theta$, $BC = \sin\theta$, and $ED = \tan\theta$. Then, since BC is the shortest distance from B to $\overline{AD}$, $BC < m\widehat{BD} \Rightarrow \sin\theta < \theta$. Then, using the result from Problem 2 and the fact that $\alpha(\Delta EDA) > \alpha(\text{sector BDA})$, we get $\frac{1}{2}ED \cdot 1 > \frac{1}{2}\theta \Rightarrow \tan\theta > \theta$. Therefore, $\sin\theta < \theta < \tan\theta$.

   b. As θ goes to 0, AC goes to 1, so $\sin\theta = \frac{BC}{AC}$ approaches BC. We also have $\theta = \widehat{BD}$ approaching BC as θ goes to 0, so $\frac{\sin\theta}{\theta}$ approaches $\frac{BC}{BC} = 1$ as θ goes to 0. Similarly, as θ goes to 0, $\tan\theta = ED$ approaches BC, so $\frac{\tan\theta}{\theta}$ approaches $\frac{BC}{BC} = 1$ as θ goes to 0. This is why $\lim\limits_{\theta \to 0} \frac{\sin\theta}{\theta} = \lim\limits_{\theta \to 0} \frac{\tan\theta}{\theta} = 1$.

4. The perimeter of a Reuleaux triangle of width w is 3(length of a 60° arc of a circle with radius w) $= 3(\frac{2\pi w}{6}) = \pi w$. The area of the Reuleaux triangle with width w is 3(area of a 60° sector of a circle with radius w) – 2(area of an equilateral triangle with side w) $= 3\left(\frac{w^2(\frac{\pi}{3})}{2}\right) - 2\left(\frac{w^2\sqrt{3}}{4}\right) = \frac{w^2(\pi - \sqrt{3})}{2}$.

5. a. Let the side of JKLM = s, so that $\alpha(JKLM) = s \cdot s = s^2$. Let T(JKLM) = J'K'L'M', and J = (x, y), K = (x + s, y), L = (x + s, y – s), and M = (x, y – s). Then J' = T(J) = (ax, by); K' = T(K) = (ax + as, by); L' = T(L) = (ax + as, by – bs); and M' = T(M) = (ax, by – bs). So J'K'L'M' has sides of length as and bs, and $\alpha(J'K'L'M') = as \cdot bs = abs^2 = ab \cdot \alpha(JKLM)$.

   b. Let (x_1, y_1) be any point on the unit circle. Then $T(x_1, y_1) = (ax_1, by_1)$ will be a point that satisfies the image of the unit circle under T. By the Graph Transformation Theorem (Section 7.2.6), an equation for the image can be found by replacing x by $\frac{x}{a}$ and y by $\frac{y}{b}$. So the ellipse with the equation $\left(\frac{x}{a}\right)^2 + \left(\frac{y}{b}\right)^2 = 1$ is the image of the unit circle under T.

   c. Since each square unit of area becomes ab square units under the transformation T(x, y), then the area of the image of a unit circle becomes $ab\pi$ under the same T.

6.   a. $L = \sum_{i=0}^{9} i^2 = 0 + 1 + 4 + 9 + \ldots + 81 = 285.$

$U = \sum_{i=1}^{10} i^2 = 1 + 4 + 9 + \ldots + 81 + 100 = 385.$

$L < \alpha(R) < U$ because both L and U use the sum of areas of rectangles to estimate $\alpha(R)$ and the rectangles used in L are always underestimates while the rectangles used in U are always overestimates.

   b.   If we cut the width of the rectangles used in L and U in half, we get:

$L' = \sum_{i=0}^{19} \tfrac{1}{2}(\tfrac{1}{2}i)^2 = \tfrac{1}{8}\sum_{i=0}^{19} i^2 = 308.75$ and $U' = \sum_{i=1}^{20} \tfrac{1}{2}(\tfrac{1}{2}i)^2 = \tfrac{1}{8}\sum_{i=1}^{20} i^2 = 358.75.$

   c. $\int_{0}^{10} x^2 dx = \tfrac{1}{3}x^3 \Big|_{0}^{10} = 333.\overline{3}.$

7.   a.   For n = 4, the inscribed polygon is a square with a diagonal of length 1 and a perimeter of $2\sqrt{2}$. The circumscribed polygon is a square with a side of length 1 and a perimeter of 4.

   b.   Approximate values for the successive perimeters of the inscribed n-gons:

(n = 4) $2\sqrt{2} \approx 2.8284271247461903$, (n = 8) 3.0614674589207187, (n = 16)

3.121445152258053, (n =32) 3.1365484905459398, (n = 64) 3.1403311569547534, (n = 128)

3.1412772509327733, (n = 256) 3.141513801144302, (n = 512) 3.141572940367092,

(n = 1024) 3.14158772527716, (n = 2048) 3.1415914215112, (n = 4096) 3.141592345570118,

(n = 8192) 3.141592576584873.

Approximate values for the successive perimeters of the circumscribed n-gons:

(n = 4) 4, (n = 8) 3.3137084989847607, (n = 16) 3.1825978780745285, (n = 32)

3.151724907429257, (n = 64) 3.144118385245905, (n = 128) 3.1422236299424577, (n = 256)

3.1417503691689674, (n = 512) 3.1416320807031823, (n = 1024) 3.1416025102568095,

(n = 2048) 3.1415951177495893, (n = 4096) 3.1415932696293076, (n = 8192)

3.141592807599645.

   c.   i. $\dfrac{P}{p} = \dfrac{n \cdot CD}{n \cdot AB} = \dfrac{CE}{AH} = \dfrac{OE}{OH} = \dfrac{OA}{OH}$. By AA Similarity, $\triangle AHO \sim \triangle CAF$, so $\dfrac{OA}{OH} = \dfrac{CF}{AF}$. Finally,

AF = FE, so $\dfrac{CF}{AF} = \dfrac{CF}{CE} = \dfrac{P}{p}$.

   ii. $\dfrac{P+p}{2p} = \tfrac{1}{2}(\dfrac{P}{p} + 1) = \tfrac{1}{2}(\dfrac{CF}{FE} + 1) = \tfrac{1}{2}(\dfrac{CF}{FE} + \dfrac{FE}{FE}) = \dfrac{CF+FE}{2FE} = \dfrac{CE}{FG}$

   iii. $\dfrac{P}{P'} = \dfrac{n \cdot CD}{2n \cdot FG} = \dfrac{2n \cdot CE}{2n \cdot FG} = \dfrac{CE}{FG}$

   iv. $\dfrac{P+p}{2p} = \dfrac{CE}{FG} = \dfrac{P}{P'}$

   v. $\dfrac{P}{p'} = \dfrac{n \cdot AB}{2n \cdot AE} = \dfrac{2n \cdot AH}{2n \cdot AE} = \dfrac{AH}{AE}$

   vi. $\dfrac{P}{p'} = \dfrac{2n \cdot AE}{2n \cdot FG} = \dfrac{AE}{FG} = \dfrac{2 \cdot EN}{2 \cdot EF} = \dfrac{EN}{EF}$

   vii. $\overline{FE} // \overline{AH}$, so $\angle FEN \cong \angle EAH$, and $\angle AHE$ and $\angle ENF$ are both right angles. So, by AA

Similarity, $\Delta ENF \sim \Delta AHE$ and $\dfrac{AH}{AE} = \dfrac{EN}{EF}$.

viii. $\quad \dfrac{P}{p'} = \dfrac{AH}{AE} = \dfrac{EN}{EF} = \dfrac{p'}{P'}$

Section 10.1.5

1. Let ABCD be the given rectangle. Construct a circle with diameter $\overline{BE}$ equal to AB + AD and containing A. Construct the perpendicular to $\overline{BE}$ at A, intersecting the circle at G. $\overline{AG}$ is a side of the desired square, as shown below.

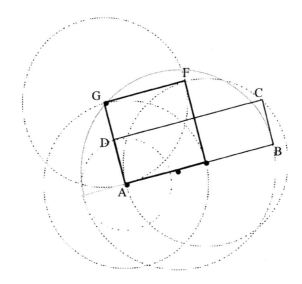

2. For a triangle with vertices at (0, 0), (5, 0), and (-6, 7), using the side from (0, 0) to (5, 0) as the base, then the base = 5 and the height = 7, so that the area of the triangle is $\frac{1}{2}bh = \frac{35}{2}$. A square with side length $\sqrt{\dfrac{35}{2}}$ will have the same area as the triangle.

3. By Theorem 10.5, the area of the trapezoid is $\frac{1}{2}h(b_1 + b_2)$. In the trapezoid with given vertices, then the $\alpha = \frac{1}{2}c(a + (b - d)) = \frac{1}{2}c(a + b - d)$.

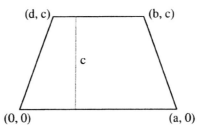

For the area of a square to equal this, then the side of the square must be of length $\sqrt{\dfrac{c}{2}(a + b - c)}$.

4.   The corollary to Theorem 10.13 can be proven by induction on n. The basis step, $n = 2$, is proven in Theorem 10.13. The inductive step remains. Let Σ_{n+1} be the union of $n + 1$ triangular regions. Then the area of $\Sigma_{n+1} = \alpha(\Sigma_n) + \alpha(\Delta_{n+1}) = \alpha(square_n) + \alpha(\Delta_{n+1})$. By Theorems 10.12 and 10.11, we can find a square with the same area as Δ_{n+1}, so that $\alpha(\Sigma_{n+1}) = \alpha(square_n) + \alpha(square_{n+1})$. If the side length of each are x and y, respectively, then let a new square have side of length $(x + y)$. Then this square has the same area as Σ_{n+1}.

5.   a.   From Section 10.1.1, problems 14 and 15, the area of a circumscribed regular n-gon is $nr^2 \tan \frac{180}{n}$, and the area of an inscribed regular n-gon is $\frac{nr^2}{2} \sin \frac{360}{n}$. For $n = 4$, then $\alpha_c = 4r^2 \tan 45 = 4r^2$ and $\alpha_i = \frac{4r^2}{2} \sin 90 = 2r^2$ and the area of the circle is πr^2. Then the side of the circumscribed square measures 2r and the side of the inscribed square measures $r\sqrt{2}$, so that their average side length is $\frac{2r + r\sqrt{2}}{2} = r + \frac{r}{\sqrt{2}}$. Then the area of the third square with side of this length is $\left(\sqrt{2} + \frac{3}{2}\right)r^2 \approx 2.914r^2$, while the area of the circle $\pi r^2 \approx 3.1416r^2$.

   b.   This is a worse approximation of the area of the circle than averaging the areas of the squares. Averaging the areas of the squares would give an estimate of $3r^2$ for the area of the circle.

6.   Let the parabola be the graph of $y = x^2$ and the line parallel to the directrix be the graph of $y = k$, where $k > 0$. Then the area between the two graphs will be the difference between the area of the rectangle bounded by $y = 0$, $y = k$, $x = -\sqrt{k}$, and $x = \sqrt{k}$ and the area under the parabola bounded by $y = 0$, $y = x^2$, $x = -\sqrt{k}$, and $x = \sqrt{k}$. The area between the graphs is thus $2k\sqrt{k} - \int_{-\sqrt{k}}^{\sqrt{k}} x^2 dx = 2k\sqrt{k} - \frac{x^3}{3}\Big|_{-\sqrt{k}}^{\sqrt{k}}$

$= 2k\sqrt{k} - \frac{2}{3}k\sqrt{k} = \frac{4}{3}k\sqrt{k}$. A square with the same area would therefore have sides of length $s = \sqrt{\frac{4}{3}k\sqrt{k}}$. So s is the solution to the algebraic equation $9s^4 - 16k^3 = 0$.

Section 10.1.6

1.   Answers will vary.

2.   The 16 scenarios occur with symmetry, so that $p(3) = p(18) = \frac{1}{216}$; $p(4) = p(17) = 3 \cdot \frac{1}{216} = \frac{1}{72}$; $p(5) = p(16) = 6 \cdot \frac{1}{216} = \frac{1}{36}$; $p(6) = p(15) = 10 \cdot \frac{1}{216} = \frac{5}{108}$; $p(7) = p(14) = 15 \cdot \frac{1}{216} = \frac{5}{72}$; $p(8) = p(13) = 21 \cdot \frac{1}{216} = \frac{7}{72}$; $p(9) = p(12) = 25 \cdot \frac{1}{216} = \frac{25}{216}$; and $p(10) = p(11) = 27 \cdot \frac{1}{216} = \frac{1}{8}$.

3.   The normal curve in Figure 41 has $\mu = 500$ and $\sigma = 100$. The specific formula then for the normal curve is $y = \frac{1}{\sqrt{2\pi}\sigma}e^{\frac{-(x-\mu)^2}{2\sigma^2}} = \frac{1}{\sqrt{200\pi}}e^{\frac{-(x-500)^2}{20000}}$.

4.   If the experiment is performed 100 times, and the point was inside the circle 78 times, then an estimation for π is $\frac{4 \cdot 78}{100} = 3.12$. If the point was inside the circle 79 times, then an estimation for π is $\frac{4 \cdot 79}{100} = 3.16$.

5. Any result between 240 and 260 would be within 2% of the actual situation. Given this, a series of 20 such experiments that we conducted (with results 249, 229, 245, 257, 253, 230, 251, 238, 235, 258, 240, 273, 244, 254, 242, 267, 261, 232, 238, 245) would suggest that there is a 50% chance of falling within 2%.

6. Consider the quarter falling within any region that is 2 squares by 2 squares. If the squares have sides of length s, then the area of this region is $4s^2$. In order for the quarter to cover the central lattice point of this region, it must fall within a circle with the lattice point as the center and a radius equal to s. Since the area of this circle is πs^2, the probability that the quarter lands in this region is $\frac{\pi s^2}{4s^2} = \frac{\pi}{4}$.

Section 10.2.1

1. For a solid to be convex, the segment connecting any two points on the surface of the solid must be entirely contained by the solid. Then, since any solid must have at least four faces, one can choose a point on each of any four distinct faces of the solid. These four points describe a tetrahedron entirely contained by the solid because the solid is convex.

2. Two.

3. Four.

4. Part three: The volume of a solid is equivalent to the number of cubic units it displaces.

5. a. If Σ and a shape S lie between parallel lines a and b, and for each line c between a and b, $c \cap S$ is a known length, and the length of $c \cap \Sigma$ = the length of $c \cap S$, then $\alpha(\Sigma) = \alpha(S)$.

   b. Let $T(x, y) \to (x + ky, y)$ and let S be a shape such that $\alpha(S) = A$ and $T(S) = \Sigma$. Also let a and b be lines parallel to the x-axis with S between a and b. Then for any line $y = c$ between a and b, we have to show that the length $c \cap S$ = length $c \cap \Sigma$ (or $c \cap T(S)$ since $T(S) = \Sigma$).

   There are four cases:

   (1) If $c \cap S = \varnothing$, then $c \cap T(S) = \varnothing$ as well, since T does not change y. Then the length of $c \cap S$ = length $c \cap T(S)$.

   (2) If $c \cap S$ is a point, then $c \cap T(S)$ will also be a point since T does not change y. Then the length of $c \cap S$ = length $c \cap T(S)$.

   (3) If $c \cap S$ is a segment, then let (x_1, y_1) and (x_2, y_2) be the endpoints of it. Since T preserves betweenness and any point on c in S will also have its image on c in Σ, we only have to show $d((x_1, y_1), (x_2, y_2)) = d(T(x_1, y_1), T(x_2, y_2)) = |(x_2 + kc) - (x_1 + kc)| = |x_2 - x_1|$, so the length of $c \cap S$ = length $c \cap T(S)$.

   (4) If $c \cap S$ is a combination of points and segments, then each point in $c \cap S$ is mapped to a point in $c \cap T(S)$, by case (2), and each segment in $c \cap S$ is mapped to a segment of equal length in $c \cap T(S)$, by case (3), so that the total length of $c \cap S$ = total length of $c \cap T(S)$ and T preserves area.

   c. Let $k = \frac{b-c}{h}$. Then $T(x, y) = (x + \frac{b-c}{h}y, y)$. So $T(0, 0) = (0, 0)$, $T(b, 0) = (b, 0)$,

$T(c, h) = (c + \frac{b-c}{h}h, h) = (b, h)$, and $T(c - b, h) = (c - b + \frac{b-c}{h}h, h) = (0, h)$.

d. Let $T_1(x, y) = (x + k_1y, y)$ and $T_2(x, y) = (x + k_2y, y)$, then
$T_1 \circ T_2(x, y) = (x + k_2y + k_1y, y) = (x + (k_2 + k_1)y, y)$. So the set of shears is closed under composition. Let $T_e(x, y) = (x + 0y, y) = (x, y)$. Then T_e is a member of the set of shears and T_e is the identity transformation. Then Let $T_1^{-1}(x, y) = (x - k_1y, y)$. Then $T_1 \circ T_1^{-1}(x, y)$
$= T_1^{-1} \circ T_1(x, y) = (x, y) = T_e(x, y)$. Thus the set together with the operation of composition satisfies all the properties of a group. (An analytic proof is to represent T_e by the matrix $\begin{bmatrix} 1 & k \\ 0 & 1 \end{bmatrix}$ and use matrix multiplication to establish the group.

6. a. Consider the points $(1, 1, 0)$ and $(0, 0, 0)$. The distance between these points is $\sqrt{(1-0)^2 + (1-0)^2 + (0-0)^2} = \sqrt{2}$. These points map to the points $(1 + k, 1, 0)$ and $(0, 0, 0)$, respectively. The distance between these points is $\sqrt{(1+k-0)^2 + (1-0)^2 + (0-0)^2} = \sqrt{k^2 + 2k + 2}$, which is not equal to $\sqrt{2}$ for $k \neq 0$.

b. Let Σ be a solid object and $T(\Sigma)$ be its image under the shear transformation T. Let c be a cross-sectional plane parallel to the x-y plane. Then c has the equation $z = m$, for some constant m. For any point $P = (x, y, z)$ in Σ such that $P \in c \cap \Sigma$, $P = (x, y, m)$ and $T(P) = (x + ky, y, m)$. So $T(P) \in c \cap T(\Sigma)$. Using the result of Problem 5b, we can show that $\alpha(c \cap \Sigma) = \alpha(c \cap T(\Sigma))$. So, by applying Cavalieri's Principle to these cross-sectional areas, $v(\Sigma) = v(T(\Sigma))$.

7. a. Let the plane intersect the cube only at a vertex.
   b. Let the plane intersect the cube only along one edge.
   c. Let the plane intersect the cube through three sides, cutting off a corner.
   d. Let the plane intersect the cube through parallel diagonals on opposite sides.
   e. Let the plane intersect the cube so that it is perpendicular to four faces and parallel to the other two.
   f. Let the plane intersect the cube through the top and four sides, cutting off the upper corner where it intersects the top face.

   g. Let the plane intersect the cube through the top, bottom, and four sides, cutting off the upper corner where it intersects the top face, and the lower corner where it intersects the bottom face.

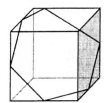

1. A cube with edges 1 mile long has edges 5280 feet long, so its volume would be 5280^3 ft^3, or $1.47198 \cdot 10^{11}$ ft^3. A conservative estimate for the population of Earth is 7 billion, taking each person to be a 7 ft tall square prism with base 2 ft by 1 ft. Then the volume of each person is 14 ft^3. For 7 billion people, the total volume is $7 \cdot 10^9 \cdot 14 = 9.8 \cdot 10^{10}$ ft^3. Since we overestimated both the average size and population, the actual population of Earth would fit inside the cube.

2. a. The equations relating the lengths of the three sides of the box, $x^2 + y^2 = 3^2$, $x^2 + z^2 = 4^2$, and $y^2 + z^2 = 6^2$, have no real solutions for x, y, and z. Thus the box cannot exist.

   b. Let a, b, and c be the lengths of the diagonals, so that x, y, and z are the lengths of the sides of the box. Then without loss of generality, $b^2 = y^2 + x^2$;
   $a^2 = z^2 + x^2$; and $c^2 = z^2 + y^2$, so that $y = \sqrt{\dfrac{c^2 + b^2 - a^2}{2}}$; $x = \sqrt{\dfrac{a^2 + b^2 - c^2}{2}}$; and
   $z = \sqrt{\dfrac{a^2 + c^2 - b^2}{2}}$. Then the volume of the box is
   $$xyz = \sqrt{\left(\dfrac{c^2 + b^2 - a^2}{2}\right)\left(\dfrac{a^2 + b^2 - c^2}{2}\right)\left(\dfrac{a^2 + c^2 - b^2}{2}\right)} =$$
   $$\tfrac{1}{2}\sqrt{\tfrac{1}{2}(c^2 + b^2 - a^2)(a^2 + b^2 - c^2)(a^2 + c^2 - b^2)}$$

3. Suppose P is a parallelepiped with bases parallelograms ABCD and EFGH, with equal areas, and perpendicular height H. Then its volume is $\alpha(ABCD) \cdot H$. Consider $\alpha(ABCD)$, which is equal to the length of a base multiplied by its perpendicular distance to the opposite base. Call the base AB and the distance h, so that $\alpha(ABCD) = h \cdot AB$. Construct a rectangular parallelepiped with base WXYZ such that WX = AB and XY = h. Then $\alpha(WXYZ) = \alpha(ABCD)$. Let the distance between WXYZ and its opposite base be H. Then the rectangular parallelepiped has the same volume as P, their bases have the same area, and their heights are the same, so that the two parallelepipeds are equivalent.

4. Any plane passing through a median of a tetrahedron and another vertex splits the original tetrahedron into two smaller tetrahedrons with the same height. Since the volume of a tetrahedron is one third of the product of the area of the base and the height, and since the plane contains the median of the triangular face (which is the base of the two smaller tetrahedrons) opposite the vertex of the median of the tetrahedron, we just have to show that the median of a triangle bisects the area. This is clearly true since a median of a triangle splits the triangle into two smaller ones with the same height and one half of the original. Therefore, since a median of a triangle bisects the area of the triangle, a plane containing the median of a tetrahedron and another vertex of the tetrahedron, bisects the volume of the tetrahedron.

5. The tetrahedron OACB makes up $\frac{1}{6}$ of the cube so the volume of the cube is 6V.

6. The volume of a regular octahedron with edge e is twice the volume of a regular square pyramid with edge e. The volume of the pyramid is $\frac{1}{3}e^2 \cdot h$, where h is the altitude of the pyramid. h is also the altitude of the triangle formed by two opposite slant edges of the pyramid and a diagonal of the square

base. The length of the diagonal is $\sqrt{2} \cdot e$ and the slant edges are both e, so $e^2 = (\frac{\sqrt{2}}{2}e)^2 + h^2$

$\Rightarrow h = \frac{1}{\sqrt{2}}e.$ Therefore, the volume of the regular octahedron with edge e is $2 \cdot \frac{1}{3}e^2 \cdot h = \frac{\sqrt{2}}{3}e^3.$

7. a.   The volume of a square pyramid, from Theorem 10.18, is
         $\frac{1}{3}(\alpha \text{ of base})(\text{altitude}) = \frac{1}{3}(230)^2(147) = 2,592,100 \text{ m}^3.$

    b.   With the new altitude, the volume is $\frac{1}{3}(230)^2(137) \approx 2,415,767 \text{ m}^3.$

    c.   The volume of each block is equal to the total volume of the pyramid divided by the number of blocks. Assuming the original height, the volume of each block is about 1.127 m^3. Assuming the current height, the volume of each block is approximately 1.05 m^3.

8. An equilateral tetrahedron ABCD with spherical ΔABC centered at D, spherical ΔBCD centered at A, spherical ΔCDA centered at B, and spherical ΔDAB centered at C will serve as a three-dimensional analogue to the Reuleaux triangle. A plane tangent to any point in the interior of the spherical triangles will be parallel to the plane through the opposite vertex and will therefore have constant width. There will be no planes tangent to the sides of the spherical triangles.

Section 10.2.3

1.

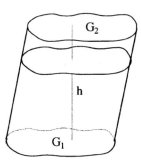
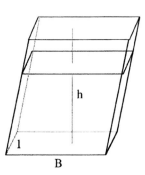

2. a.   If the cylinder has height 2r and base radius r, then the inscribed cone has volume $\frac{2}{3}\pi r^3$ and the cylinder has volume $2\pi r^3$. So the ratio of the volume of the cone to the volume of the cylinder is $\frac{1}{3}$.

    b.   An inscribed sphere will have volume $\frac{4}{3}\pi r^3$, so the ratio of the volume of an inscribed cone to the volume of the inscribed sphere is $\frac{1}{2}$.

3. A hemisphere has base area $B = \pi r^2$ and height $h = r$. The volume of a hemisphere is $\frac{2}{3}\pi r^3 = \frac{2}{3}hB$.

4. a. Suppose the heights of the rain water collected by the two gauges are h_1 and h_2, respectively. If the cone radius associated with h_1 is R_1 and with h_2 is R_2, then the gauges collected water volumes $V_1 = \frac{1}{3}\pi R_1^2 h_1$ and $V_2 = \frac{1}{3}\pi R_2^2 h_2$, respectively. By similar triangles, $\frac{R_1}{r_1} = \frac{h_1}{H}$ and $\frac{R_2}{r_2} = \frac{h_2}{H}$. So $V_1 = \frac{1}{3}\pi r_1^2 \frac{h_1^3}{H^2}$ and $V_2 = \frac{1}{3}\pi r_2^2 \frac{h_2^3}{H^2}$. However, since the volume of water collected by a gauge is proportional to the area of the gauge's opening, $\frac{V_1}{V_2} = \frac{\pi r_1^2}{\pi r_2^2}$. Thus $h_1^3 = h_2^3$, or $h_1 = h_2$.

   b. From the volume expression in part **a**, we can see that $d = kh^3$, where $k = \frac{1}{3}\pi \frac{r^2}{H^2}$. Thus $h = \sqrt[3]{\frac{d}{k}}$. So the volume varies directly as the cube root of the amount of rainfall.

5. The volume of a 400-foot cube will be 400^3 cubic feet, or 64 million cubic feet. A sphere of 400 cubic feet has the same amount of space as a $\sqrt[3]{400}$-foot cube.

6. Let P be a point on the middle cross section of the prismatoid. The two pyramids with P as apex and the bases of the prismatoid as their bases have volumes $\frac{1}{3}B\frac{h}{2}$ and $\frac{1}{3}B'\frac{h}{2}$. Now partition the rest of the prismatoid into triangular pyramids with bases lying in the lateral faces. Suppose there are n of these triangular pyramids. The volume of each of these triangular pyramids is 4 times the volume of the triangular pyramid formed by taking its cross section at $\frac{h}{2}$. Thus the total volume of the triangular pyramids is $4 \cdot \frac{1}{3} \cdot \frac{h}{2}(M_1 + M_2 + ... + M_n)$. But $M_1 + M_2 + ... + M_n$ is just M, the area of the cross section of the prismatoid. Therefore, the volume of the prismatoid is $\frac{1}{6}(B + B' + 4M)h$.

7. Theorem 10.14 (volume of a rectangular parallelepiped): $B = xy, B' = xy, M = xy, h = z$; $V = \frac{1}{6}(xy + xy + 4xy)z = xyz$. Theorem 10.15 (volume of a prism): $B = B, B' = B, M = B, h = h$; $V = \frac{1}{6}(B + B + 4B)h = Bh$. Theorem 10.17 (volume of a tetrahedron): $B = B, B' = 0$, $M = B \cdot \left(\frac{\frac{h}{2}}{h}\right)^2 = \frac{B}{4}, h = h$; $V = \frac{1}{6}(B + 0 + 4 \cdot \frac{B}{4})h = \frac{1}{3}Bh$. Theorem 10.18 (volume of a pyramid): $B = B, B' = 0, M = B \cdot \left(\frac{\frac{h}{2}}{h}\right)^2 = \frac{B}{4}, h = h$; $V = \frac{1}{6}(B + 0 + 4 \cdot \frac{B}{4})h = \frac{1}{3}Bh$. If we relax the condition that the prismatoid be a polyhedron, then also Theorem 10.19 (volume of a cylinder): $B = B, B' = B$, $M = B, h = h$; $V = \frac{1}{6}(B + B + 4B)h = Bh$. Theorem 10.20 (volume of a cone): $B = B, B' = 0$, $M = B \cdot \left(\frac{\frac{h}{2}}{h}\right)^2 = \frac{B}{4}, h = h$; $V = \frac{1}{6}(B + 0 + 4 \cdot \frac{B}{4})h = \frac{1}{3}Bh$. Theorem 10.21 (volume of a sphere): $B = 0, B' = 0, M = \pi r^2, h = 2r$; $V = \frac{1}{6}(0 + 0 + 4\pi r^2)(2r) = \frac{4}{3}\pi r^3$.

8. As the height of the cone h approaches 10, the radius of the cone's base will go to infinity. Thus there is no upper bound for the volume of the cone.

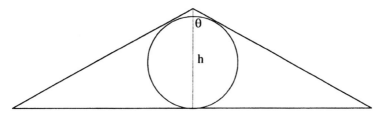

9. We can think of the volume of a cone of height h and base radius r as the sum of the volumes of infinitesimal cylinders of base area πy^2 and height dx, where y is the distance from the cone's axis of symmetry, the x-axis, to the lateral edge. Thus. $V = \int_0^h \pi y^2 dx$. Since $y = -\frac{r}{h}x + r$,

$$V = \int_0^h \pi\left(-\frac{r}{h}x + r\right)^2 dx = \int_0^h \pi\left(\frac{r^2}{h^2}x^2 - 2\frac{r^2}{h}x + r^2\right)dx = \frac{r^2 x^3}{3h^2}\bigg|_0^h - \frac{r^2 x^2}{h}\bigg|_0^h + r^2 x\bigg|_0^h = \frac{1}{3}\pi r^2 h.$$

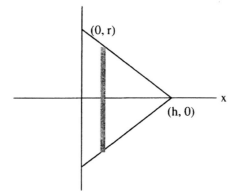

10. We can think of the volume of a hemisphere of radius R as the sum of the volumes of infinitesimal cylinders of base area πy^2 and height dx, where y is the distance from the hemisphere's axis of symmetry, the x-axis, to the hemisphere's surface. Thus $V = \int_0^R \pi y^2 dx$. Since $x^2 + y^2 = R^2$,

$$\int_0^R \pi(R^2 - x^2)dx = \pi R^2 x\bigg|_0^R - \pi\frac{x^3}{3}\bigg|_0^R = \frac{2}{3}\pi R^3.$$ The volume of a sphere or radius R is twice the volume of a hemisphere of radius R, or $\frac{4}{3}\pi R^3$

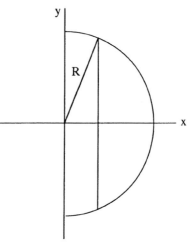

11. Let X be a point belonging to a line ℓ that is perpendicular to the plane of $\triangle ABC$ and passes through point E, the circumcenter of $\triangle ABC$. By the Pythagorean Theorem, $AX = \sqrt{AE^2 + EX^2}$, $BX = \sqrt{BE^2 + EX^2}$, and $CX = \sqrt{CE^2 + EX^2}$. But because E is the circumcenter of $\triangle ABC$, $AE = BE = CE$. Thus $AX = BX = CX$. Now, let Y be a point that is equidistant from A, B, and C. In 3

dimensions, the set of points equidistant from two points is a plane that is perpendicular to and bisects the segment joining the two points. Let p be the plane equidistant from points A and B, and q be the plane equidistant from points A and C. Planes p and q will both be perpendicular to the plane of $\triangle ABC$, so their intersection, line ℓ, will also be perpendicular to the plane of $\triangle ABC$. Since ℓ is the set of points equidistant from points A, B, and C, point Y will be on ℓ. Therefore, a point is equidistant from points A, B, and C if and only if it lies on a line perpendicular to the plane of $\triangle ABC$ and passing through the circumcenter of $\triangle ABC$. Now, by the same argument, a point will be equidistant from points A, B, and D if and only if it lies on a line m that is perpendicular to the plane of $\triangle ABD$ and passes through the circumcenter of $\triangle ABD$. Because ABCD is a tetrahedron, planes containing $\triangle ABC$ and $\triangle ABD$ are not parallel, and so lines ℓ and m intersect at a unique point G. Point G is therefore the unique point equidistant from points A, B, C, and D, and the sphere with center G and radius AG = BG = CG = DG is the only sphere that contains the vertices of tetrahedron ABCD.

12. The volume of a spherical cap of depth h for a sphere of radius r will equal the difference in volumes of the cylinder and the cone of Figure 66 above a height r – h. The volume of the cylinder above a height r – h is $\pi r^2 h$. The volume of the cone above a height r – h is the difference in volumes of the cones of height r and of height (r – h), that is, $\frac{1}{3}\pi r^3 - \frac{1}{3}\pi r^2(r-h)\frac{(r-h)^2}{r^2} = \pi(hr^2 - h^2r + \frac{h^3}{3})$. Thus

$$V = \pi r^2 h - \pi(hr^2 - h^2r + \frac{h^3}{3}) = \pi h^2(r - \frac{h^3}{3}).$$

Section 10.3.1

1. When $\phi = 90°$, $\sin \phi = 1$, so that the lateral area formula reduces to $\pi\ell^2$, the area of a circle.

2. Let r be the radius of the base, ϕ the angle measuring the opening of the cone, and θ the angle between a lateral edge and the plane of the base. Since lateral area is equal to $\pi r\ell$, and $\ell = \frac{r}{\cos\theta}$, then lateral area is equal to $\frac{\pi r^2}{\cos\theta}$.

3. a. Let ℓ be the slant height and ϕ the angle measuring the opening. The volume of a cone is equal to $\frac{1}{3}hB$, where h is the height and B is the area of the base. The area of the base is then πr^2, with $h = \ell\cos\phi$. Since $r = \ell\sin\phi$, the formula for volume becomes

$$V = \frac{1}{3}\ell\cos\phi \cdot \pi(\ell^2\sin^2\phi) = \frac{\pi}{3}\ell^3\sin^2\phi\cos\phi.$$

  b. Since 2ϕ is the measure of the angle between slant heights on opposite sides of the cone, $2\phi = \frac{1}{2}\theta$, where θ is the measure of the central angle of the removed sector.

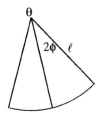

Thus $4\phi = \theta$. We can then find the maximum of the volume function for ϕ and find θ. Since ℓ is constant, consider $A = \sin^2\phi \cos \phi$. Then the derivative of A is

$A' = (2 \sin \phi \cos \phi)\cos \phi + \sin^2\phi(-\sin \phi) = 2 \sin\phi - 3\sin^3\phi$. This is equal to zero when

$\sin \phi = \sqrt{\frac{2}{3}}$. Then ϕ is approximately $54.7356°$, or 0.3041 radians, and θ is approximately

$218.9424°$, or 1.2163 radians.

4.   a.   The volume of a cylinder is a product of its height h and the area of the base B. One way of rolling the cylinder has b as the circumference of the base and a as its height, so that the radius of

the base is $r_b = \frac{b}{2\pi}$. The volume is then $\pi\left(\frac{b}{2\pi}\right)^2 a = \frac{ab^2}{4\pi}$. The other way, with a as the

circumference and b as the height has a base radius of $r_a = \frac{a}{2\pi}$, and a volume of $\pi\left(\frac{a}{2\pi}\right)^2 b = \frac{a^2b}{4\pi}$.

    b.   The larger volume will result from having the longer side cubed in the equation, so that the circumference of the base should be the longer 11" side, and the height should be the 8.5" side. The resulting volume will be approximately 81.85 cubic inches.

5.   a.   Let the equilateral triangle T_r have sides of length x. Then the radii to the vertices of the triangle split it into three congruent isosceles triangles with sides r, base x, and center angle

$\theta = \frac{360°}{3} = 120°$. For each of these triangles then, $h = r \cos 60° = \frac{r}{2}$ and $x = 2r \sin 60° = r\sqrt{3}$.

Then the area of each of these smaller triangles is $\frac{r^2\sqrt{3}}{4}$, so that $A(r) = \frac{3r^2\sqrt{3}}{4}$ and $A'(r) = \frac{3r\sqrt{3}}{2}$.

The perimeter is $3 \cdot x$, so $P(r) = 3r\sqrt{3}$, which is not equal to $A'(r)$. For the square, S_r, let each side be length x. Then the radii to the vertices of the square split the square into four congruent right triangles with legs r and hypotenuse x. By the Pythagorean Theorem, $x^2 = 2r^2$, or $x = r\sqrt{2}$.

Since the area of the square is x^2, $A(r) = 2r^2$ and $A'(r) = 4r$. The perimeter is $4 \cdot x$, so $P(r) = 4r\sqrt{2}$, which is not equal to $A'(r)$.

    b.   For an equilateral triangle circumscribed about a circle, the area is given by $A(r) = 6 \cdot \frac{r}{2} \cdot \frac{s}{2}$,

where s is the length of a side of the triangle. Since $\frac{r}{\frac{s}{2}} = \tan 30°$, $s = \frac{2r}{\tan 30°} = 2\sqrt{3}r$. So

$A(r) = 3\sqrt{3}r^2$ and $P(r) = 3s = 6\sqrt{3}r$. Thus $P(r) = A'(r)$. For a square circumscribed about a circle, the area is given by $A(r) = (2r)^2 = 4r^2$ and $P(r) = 4(2r) = 8r$. So, again, $P(r) = A'(r)$.

6. We know that $A_n = \frac{nr^2}{2}\sin\frac{2\pi}{n}$ (see Section 10.1.1, Problem 16c) and $P_n = 2rn\sin\frac{\pi}{n}$. Then the derivative of A_n, $A_n'(r) = rn\sin\frac{2\pi}{n}$. Letting $k = \frac{2\pi}{n}$, $\lim\limits_{n\to\infty} A_n'(r) = \lim\limits_{n\to\infty} rn\sin\frac{2\pi}{n} = \lim\limits_{k\to 0} 2\pi r\frac{\sin k}{k} = 2\pi r$.
Letting $k = \frac{\pi}{n}$, $\lim\limits_{n\to\infty} P_n(r) = \lim\limits_{n\to\infty} 2rn\sin\frac{\pi}{n} = \lim\limits_{k\to 0} 2\pi r\frac{\sin k}{k} = 2\pi r$. Thus $\lim\limits_{n\to\infty} A_n'(r) = \lim\limits_{n\to\infty} P_n(r)$.

7. Let B be the area of the base of the cylinder. As a great circle of a sphere of radius r, then $B = \pi r^2$. Let h be the height of the cylinder, and as the diameter of the sphere, $h = 2r$. Finally, let C be the circumference of the base, which will be $2\pi r$, as the base is a great circle of the sphere. Then the surface area of the cylinder is $2B + h \cdot C = 2\pi r^2 + 4\pi r^2 = 6\pi r^2$. The surface area of the sphere, from Theorem 10.22, is $4\pi r^2$, so that $\frac{3}{2}$ this value equals the surface area of the cylinder.

8. Partition the hemisphere into "almost pyramids" as was done in the proof to Theorem 10.22. In the limit as the base areas go to zero, the sum of the volumes of those pyramids with bases on the spherical cap will equal the volume of the spherical cap, $V_{h,r} = \pi h^2(r - \frac{h}{3})$, plus the volume of a cone with height $r - h$ and base area $(r^2 - (r - h)^2)\pi = (2hr - h^2)\pi$. Equating these volumes gives $\frac{1}{3}r$S.A. $= \pi h^2(r - \frac{h}{3}) + \frac{1}{3}(2hr - h^2)\pi(r - h) = \frac{2}{3}\pi h^2 r$. Thus S.A. $= 2\pi rh$.

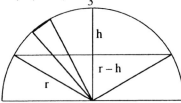

9. a. $\triangle PAO$ and $\triangle AHO$ are similar by AA similarity, so $\frac{OH}{r} = \frac{r}{r + a}$, or $OH = \frac{r^2}{r + a}$. Then $d = r - OH = r - \frac{r^2}{r + a} = \frac{r^2 + ra}{r + a} - \frac{r^2}{r + a} = \frac{ra}{r + a}$.

   b. From Problem 8, we know that the surface area of a spherical cap, which is the visible area here, with depth d is $S_{d,r} = 2\pi rd$. Let S_r be the surface area of the sphere, so that the fraction of the sphere visible from a point P that is a units away is $F_{a,r} = \frac{S_{d,r}}{S_r} = \frac{2\pi rd}{4\pi r^2} = \frac{d}{2r} = \frac{a}{2(r + a)}$.

   c. Let $a = 1000$ miles and $r = 3960$ miles. Then $F_{a,r} = \frac{1000}{2(3960 + 1000)} = \frac{1000}{9920} \approx 0.1008$, which is approximately 10.08%.

   d. At 20,000 miles above the earth, a satellite is able to see $\frac{20,000}{2(3960 + 20,000)}$, or 41.74% of the earth. If all three satellites were in orbit above the equator, however, most of the overlap would occur near the equator and both poles would not be covered. The north-south distance covered is indicated by $\angle POA$: $\cos\theta = \frac{r}{r + a}$, so that θ is approximately 80.57°. If the satellites were at the equator, anything above or below 80°N or 80°S would not be covered.

   e. As a increases without bound, $F_{a,r}$ approaches $\frac{1}{2}$ since the far side of the earth would never be visible: $\lim\limits_{a\to\infty}\frac{a}{2(r + a)} = \frac{a}{2a} = \frac{1}{2}$.

Section 10.3.2

1.   a.   The equilateral triangle has side of length b = $\frac{p}{3}$, and area of $\frac{1}{2}$bh, where h = $\frac{p}{3}$ sin 60° = $\frac{p\sqrt{3}}{6}$, so that its area is $\frac{p^2\sqrt{3}}{36}$. The square has side of length $\frac{p}{4}$, and its area is the square of a side, $\frac{p^2}{16}$. The regular hexagon contains six equilateral triangles of base $\frac{p}{6}$, so that the area of the hexagon is $\frac{p^2\sqrt{3}}{24}$. A circle with circumference of p = $2\pi r$, has radius of $\frac{p}{2\pi}$, so its area is $\frac{p^2}{4\pi}$. Each figure has area of p^2 multiplied by a different value; the values are approximately: 0.048 (triangle), 0.063 (square), 0.072 (hexagon), and 0.080 (circle).

     b.   Since the circle has the least perimeter of all figures with the same area, the minimum length of the lake will occur if the lake is a circle. If α = 1000, then r ≈ 17.84, so that the circumference is $2\pi r$ ≈ 112.1 km. The maximum length of beach will occur by minimizing the width of a rectangular lake. For example, if α = length • width = 1000 and length is 1000, width = 1, then the perimeter will be 2002 km.

2.   An equilateral triangle with area A = $\frac{1}{2}$bh has perimeter 3b. With h = b cos 30 = $\frac{b\sqrt{3}}{2}$, then 2A = $\frac{b^2\sqrt{3}}{2}$, so that b = $\frac{2\sqrt{A}}{\sqrt[4]{3}}$. Then the perimeter = 3b = $\frac{6\sqrt{A}}{\sqrt[4]{3}}$ ≈ $4.559\sqrt{A}$. A square with area A = s^2 has perimeter 4s. With s = $\sqrt{A}$, the perimeter = $4\sqrt{A}$. A regular hexagon with area A = 3bh has perimeter 6b. With h = b cos 30 = $\frac{b\sqrt{3}}{2}$, then A = $\frac{3\sqrt{3}b^2}{2}$, so that b = $\frac{\sqrt{2A}}{\sqrt{3}\sqrt[4]{3}}$. Then perimeter = 6b = $2\sqrt{2}\sqrt[4]{3}\sqrt{A}$ ≈ $3.722\sqrt{A}$. Finally, a circle with area A = πr^2 has perimeter $2\pi r$. Then r = $\sqrt{\frac{A}{\pi}}$, so that perimeter = $2\sqrt{A\pi}$ ≈ $3.545\sqrt{A}$. By comparing 4.559, 4, 3.722, and 3.545, the circle's perimeter is the smallest.

3.   We can use Hero's formula for the area of a triangle: A = $\sqrt{s(s-a)(s-b)(s-c)}$. Here the semiperimeter is fixed, since a + b is fixed and c is fixed. Also, b = k − a, so A = $\sqrt{s(s-a)(s-(k-a))(s-c)}$ = $m\sqrt{-a^2 + ka - ks + s^2}$, where m is the constant $\sqrt{s(s-c)}$. Setting $\frac{dA}{da}$ = 0 yields $m\frac{-2a + k}{\sqrt{-a^2 + ka - ks + s^2}}$ = 0, which only holds if -2a + k = 0. Thus a = $\frac{k}{2}$ and b = $\frac{k}{2}$ and the triangle is isosceles.

4.   Many solutions are possible. One possibility that is used for some arenas is to have seats in large concentric circles (broken only by aisles along diameters) whose common center is the center of the ring. Suppose a circle has radius r. This maximizes the number of seats closer than a given distance to the center of the ring. Near the square ring, we would have (ringside) seats that are parallel to the sides of the ring. If we assume that a seat is 22" wide (quite ample, but chosen to simplify computations with $\pi \approx \frac{22}{7}$), then each circle can include about $\frac{2\pi r}{22}$, or about $\frac{2r}{7}$, seats, if r is measured in inches, or $\frac{24r}{7}$ seats, if r is measured in feet. So, at a distance of 50 feet from the center of the ring, there would be

about $\frac{1200}{7} \approx 172$ seats less those taken out for the aisles. Perhaps take out a couple of seats for every 15 seats of circumference, leaving about 150 seats at this distance. A complete plan would have a certain distance between rows, deal with the seats near the ring, and also deal with seats farther away.

5. With a given area, the shape that minimizes perimeter (and thus the cost of the walls) will be a circle. With area 600 ft^2, the circle's radius is approximately 13.82 ft, so the perimeter is approximately 86.83 ft.

6. a. Here $2\ell + 3w = 300$ and $\ell w = A$. So $A = (150 - \frac{3}{2}w)w = 150w - \frac{3}{2}w^2$. Setting $\frac{dA}{dw} = 0$ yields $150 - 3w = 0$, or $w = 50$ and $\ell = 75$. So the maximum area is 3750 sq yd.

    b. If the pen has a square shape divided into two rectangular halves, then $4s + s = 300$, so $s = 60$ and $A = s^2 = 3600$ sq. yds. If the pen has a rectangular shape divided into two square halves, then $7w = 300$, so $w = \frac{300}{7}$ and $A = 2w^2 \approx 3673$ sq yd. So neither of these gives as much room as the rectangle in part **a**. However, if the pen has a circular shape and is divided in half along a diameter, then $2\pi r + 2r = 300$, so $r = \frac{300}{2\pi + 2}$, and $A = \pi r^2 = \pi \left(\frac{300}{2\pi + 2} \right)^2 \approx 4121$ sq. yds.

7. The rectangular pen will have area $A = \ell w$. For a fixed length of fencing P, $\ell + 2w = P$. Thus $A = (P - 2w)w = Pw - 2w^2$. Setting $\frac{dA}{dw} = 0$ yields $P - 4w = 0$, or $w = \frac{P}{4}$ and $\ell = \frac{P}{2}$. Thus the pen has a length twice its width.

8. In the sphere with surface area A, $A = 4\pi r^2$, so $r = \sqrt{\frac{A}{4\pi}}$. Since the volume of a sphere is $\frac{4}{3}\pi r^3$, $V = \frac{4}{3}\pi \left(\sqrt{\frac{A}{4\pi}} \right)^3 = \frac{A^{\frac{3}{2}}}{6\sqrt{\pi}}$. By Theorem 10.24, the sphere has the largest volume with a given surface area, so any other shape has a volume $V \le \frac{A^{\frac{3}{2}}}{6\sqrt{\pi}}$, or equivalently $A \ge (6V\sqrt{\pi})^{\frac{2}{3}}$.

9. Let r be the radius of the original sphere and R the radius of the hemisphere. The volume of the soap bubble, $\frac{4}{3}\pi r^3$, remains constant as its shape changes. The surface area of the hemisphere is $4\pi R^2 = 8\pi r^2$, so that $R = r\sqrt{2}$.

10. a. For a circular cylinder, $V = \pi r^2 h$ and $S = 2\pi r^2 + 2\pi rh$. We can rewrite these expressions as $V = \pi r^3(\frac{h}{r})$ and $S = 2\pi r^2(1 + \frac{h}{r})$. Solving for r in the surface area formula yields $r = \sqrt{\dfrac{S}{2\pi\left(1 + \frac{h}{r}\right)}}$.

    Substituting this expression for r in the volume formula gives $V = \pi \left(\dfrac{S}{2\pi\left(1 + \frac{h}{r}\right)} \right)^{3/2} (\frac{h}{r})$. To find the maximum volume for constant S, let $x = \frac{h}{r}$, $k = \pi \left(\frac{S}{2\pi} \right)^{3/2}$, and set $\frac{dV}{dx} = 0$. So $V = kx\left(\frac{1}{1+x} \right)^{3/2}$ and $\frac{dV}{dx} = k\left(\frac{1}{1+x} \right)^{3/2} + \frac{3}{2}kx\left(\frac{1}{1+x} \right)^{1/2} \frac{-1}{(1+x)^2} = 0$. So $\left(\frac{1}{1+x} \right)^{3/2} = \frac{3}{2}x\left(\frac{1}{1+x} \right)^{5/2}$, or $1 + x = \frac{3}{2}x$. Thus $x = \frac{h}{r} = 2$.

b.   The volume V of a circular cylinder with height h and base radius r is $\pi r^2 h$ and the surface area is given by $S = 2\pi r(r + h)$. So $S = 2V \frac{r+h}{r}$, from which $V = \frac{1}{2}S \frac{rh}{r+h}$. Now suppose S is constant.

Section 10.3.3

1.   a.   Let the first figurine have height h and weight w. Then, with k = 2, the second figurine has weight w_2 and height 2h. By Theorem 10.25, $w_2 = k^3 \cdot w = 8w$.

      b.   Let the first pail have height h and weight 5 lb. Then, with k = 2, the second pail has weight w_2 and height 2h. By Theorem 10.25, $w_2 = k^3 \cdot w = 8 \cdot 5 = 40$ lb.

      c.   For a size transformation of magnitude k, multiplying dimensions by k results in a weight that is k^3 times the original weight.

2.   Given that a height of 6 feet corresponds to a weight of 158 lb.

      a.   With a height of 7 feet, $k = \frac{7}{6}$, so the corresponding weight is $(158)\left(\frac{7}{6}\right)^3 \approx 250.9$ lb.

      b.   With a height of 5 feet, $k = \frac{5}{6}$, so the corresponding weight is $(158)\left(\frac{5}{6}\right)^3 \approx 91.43$ lb.

      c.   With a height of h feet, $k = \frac{h}{6}$, so the corresponding weight is $(158)\left(\frac{h}{6}\right)^3 \approx 0.73h^3$ lb.

3.   Since $r = \frac{1}{2}d$, then the area is $\pi r^2 = \pi\left(\frac{1}{2}d\right)^2 = \frac{\pi}{4}$. By Theorem 10.26, $A(d) = A(1) \cdot d^2$. So the area of a circle with diameter d is $d^2 \frac{\pi}{4}$.

4.   Let the side of the hexagon be 1. Then we can split the hexagon into six equilateral triangles of side 1, so that $h = 1 \cos 30 = \frac{\sqrt{3}}{2}$. Then the area of each triangle is $\frac{\sqrt{3}}{4}$, and the area of the hexagon is $6 \cdot \frac{\sqrt{3}}{4} = \frac{3\sqrt{3}}{2}$. Thus if a side of the hexagon is s, its area will be $\frac{3s^2\sqrt{3}}{2}$.

5.   Let the side of the n-gon be s. Then we can split the n-gon into n isosceles triangles of side r and angle $\theta = \frac{360°}{n}$. Then $s = 2r \sin \frac{180°}{n}$ and $h = r \cos \frac{180°}{n}$. The area of each triangle then, is $\frac{1}{2}s \cdot h = \frac{1}{2}(2r \sin \frac{180°}{n})(r \cos \frac{180°}{n}) = r^2 \sin \frac{180°}{n} \cos \frac{180°}{n}$. So the area of the entire n-gon is $nr^2 \sin \frac{180°}{n} \cos \frac{180°}{n}$. Since $r = \frac{s}{2\sin \frac{180°}{n}}$, the area is $\frac{ns^2}{4} \cot \frac{180°}{n}$.

6.   Let $g = \alpha(\text{circle}) = \pi r^2$, and the perimeter of the circle $= p = 2\pi r$. Then let $a = \alpha(\text{n-gon X})$ with perimeter p, and $b = \alpha(\text{circumscribed n-gon Y})$. We know that X has side of length $\frac{2\pi r}{n}$, so from problem 5, its area is $\frac{\pi^2 r^2}{2n}\left(\frac{\sin \frac{360°}{n}}{\sin^2 \frac{180°}{n}}\right)$. We also know that Y can be divided into n isosceles triangles of height r, so that the area of $Y = nr^2 \tan \frac{180°}{n}$.

      a.   Sample: If n = 6, then $g = \pi r^2$, $a = \frac{\pi^2 r^2 \sqrt{3}}{6}$, and $b = 2r^2\sqrt{3}$. Show that g is a geometric mean between a and b by proving that $g^2 = ab$. Multiplying a and b yields $\frac{\pi^2 r^2 \sqrt{3}}{6} \cdot 2r^2 \sqrt{3} = \pi^2 r^4 = g^2$.

b.   To prove the general theorem, we need to show that $g^2 = ab$. Multiplying a and b yields

$$\left(nr^2 \tan \frac{180°}{n} \right)\left(\frac{\pi^2 r^2}{2n} \right)\left(\frac{\sin \frac{360°}{n}}{\sin^2 \frac{180°}{n}} \right),$$ so that we need to prove that $\dfrac{\tan \frac{180°}{n} \sin \frac{360°}{n}}{2 \sin^2 \frac{180°}{n}} = 1$. Using

trigonometric identities shows that the equality holds, and the theorem is true.

7.   Yes. Suppose the figures in the set of similar figures $\{F_1, F_2, ..., F_m\}$ have n surfaces $S_1, S_2, ..., S_n$. Let $\alpha(S_{ij})$) designate the area of surface j of figure i and $\alpha(F_i) = \alpha(S_{i1}) + \alpha(S_{i2}) + ... + \alpha(S_{im})$ designate the total surface area of figure i. By Theorem 10.26, for each surface S_j of a particular figure F_i, there is an area formula $\alpha(S_{ij}) = k_j L_{ij}^2$, where L_{ij} is a corresponding length on surface j of figure i. Thus $\alpha(F_i) = k_1 L_{i1}^2 + k_2 L_{i2}^2 + ... + k_n L_{in}^2$. We are free to choose all L_{ij} such that $L_{i1} = L_{i2} = ... = L_{in} = L_i$. Thus $\alpha(F_i) = L_i^2 (k_1 + k_2 + ... + k_n) = L_i^2 k$.

8.   Let L be the length of a segment in figure F(L) of volume V(L). The figure F(1), where L = 1, becomes F(L) by a similarity transformation of magnitude L. By Theorem 10.25, $V(L) = V(1) \cdot L^3$. Since V(1) is constant, $V(L) = k \cdot L^3$.

9.   The volume of a sphere is $\frac{4}{3}\pi r^3$, and $r = \frac{d}{2}$. Then $V = \frac{4}{3}\pi \left(\frac{d}{2}\right)^3 = \frac{\pi}{6}d^3$.

OR

Since all spheres are similar, there is a volume formula $V = kd^3$, where d is the diameter and k is the volume of a sphere with diameter 1. In that case, $r = \frac{1}{2}$ and $V = \frac{4}{3}\pi \left(\frac{1}{2}\right)^3 = \frac{\pi}{6}$. Thus $V = \frac{\pi}{6}d^3$.

10.   The volume of a regular square pyramid is $\frac{1}{3}Bh$, and $B = s^2$. Then $V = \frac{1}{3}s^2 h$.

11.   The volume of a cone is $\frac{1}{3}Bh$, and $B = \frac{\pi ab}{4}$. Then $V = \frac{\pi abh}{12}$.

12.   Those figures whose volume formulas involve two variables, such as a square pyramid, have fewer independent dimensions than those whose volume formulas involve three variables, such as a right cone with an elliptical base. A sphere has one independent dimension, a square pyramid has two, and a cone with an elliptical base has three. Cross sections of figures with fewer independent dimensions will have greater symmetry than those with more independent dimensions.

Section 10.3.4

1.   a.   By the construction of S_{n+1} from S_n, S_{n+1} has four times as many sides as S_n and each side is $\frac{1}{3}$ the length of a side of S_n. Let S_n have k sides of length s, so that the perimeter of $S_n = ks$. Then S_{n+1} has 4k sides, each of length $\frac{1}{3}s$, so that the perimeter of $S_{n+1} = \frac{4ks}{3} = \frac{4}{3} \cdot$ perimeter of S_n.

b.   The formula only works for $n \geq 2$. The number of sides of S_n is equal to the number of new triangles added on. There are $3 \cdot 4^{n-1}$ sides of S_n and the side length of these triangles are $\frac{1}{3}$ the side lengths of S_n. If we start with sides of length 1, then the side lengths of S_n are $\left(\frac{1}{3}\right)^{n-1}$, so the side length of the triangles added is $\frac{1}{3} \cdot \left(\frac{1}{3}\right)^{n-1} = \left(\frac{1}{3}\right)^n$. The area of each of the equilateral triangles added is $\alpha = \frac{s^2 \sqrt{3}}{4}$, with $s = \left(\frac{1}{3}\right)^n$ and $3 \cdot 4^{n-1}$ total triangles. The area added on then is

$$3 \cdot 4^{n-1} \cdot \frac{\left(\frac{1}{3}\right)^{2n} \sqrt{3}}{4} = \left(\frac{4}{9}\right)^n \cdot \frac{3\sqrt{3}}{16}.$$ Then $\alpha(S_{n+1}) = \alpha(S_n) + \left(\frac{4}{9}\right)^n \cdot \frac{3\sqrt{3}}{16}$. Then $\lim_{n \to \infty} \alpha(S_n)$ is the sum

of a geometric series, $a + ar + ar^2 + \ldots + ar^n + \ldots = \frac{a}{1-r}$ with $r = \frac{4}{9}$, $\alpha(S_1) = \frac{\sqrt{3}}{4}$, and

$$\alpha(S_2) = \frac{\sqrt{3}}{12} = a. \text{ Then } \alpha = \frac{\sqrt{3}}{4} + \frac{\frac{\sqrt{3}}{12}}{\frac{5}{9}} = \frac{2\sqrt{3}}{5}.$$

2. S_{n+1} has 9 times as many edges as S_n, with each edge having $\frac{1}{5}$ the length of an edge of S_n. Let $E(S_n)$ and $e(S_n)$ be the number of edges and the length of each edge of S_n, respectively. Then

$E(S_n) = 9E(S_{n-1}) = S_1 9^{n-1} = 4(9^{n-1})$ and $e(S_n) = \frac{e(S_{n-1})}{5} = \frac{e(S_1)}{5^{n-1}} = \frac{s}{5^{n-1}}$, where s is the length of a side of

the original square.

a. The perimeter of S_n will be $E(S_n) \cdot e(S_n) = 4(9^{n-1}) \cdot \frac{s}{5^{n-1}} = 4s \cdot \left(\frac{9}{5}\right)^{n-1}$. Thus

the $\lim_{n \to \infty} (\text{perimeter } S_n) = \lim_{n \to \infty} 4s \cdot \left(\frac{9}{5}\right)^{n-1} = \infty.$

b. For each edge of S_n, there will be 2 new squares in S_{n+1}, each having area $(e(S_{n+1}))^2 = \left(\frac{s}{5^n}\right)^2$. So

$$\alpha(S_{n+1}) = \alpha(S_n) + 2E(S_n) \cdot (e(S_{n+1}))^2$$

$$= \alpha(S_n) + 8(9^{n-1})\left(\frac{s}{5^n}\right)^2 = \alpha(S_n) + 8s^2 \cdot \frac{9^{n-1}}{25^n} = \alpha(S_n) + \frac{8}{9}s^2\left(\frac{9}{25}\right)^n. \text{ Since } S_1 = s^2, \text{ this is}$$

equivalent to $\alpha(S_{n+1}) = \frac{1}{9}s^2 + \frac{8}{9}s^2\left(1 + \left(\frac{9}{25}\right) + \left(\frac{9}{25}\right)^2 + \ldots + \left(\frac{9}{25}\right)^n\right)$, so that

$$\lim_{n \to \infty} \alpha(S_n) = s^2\left(\frac{1}{9} + \frac{\frac{8}{9}}{1 - \frac{9}{25}}\right) = 1.5s^2.$$

c. The dimension of S_n is the solution to the equation $5^d = 9$, so $d = \frac{\log 9}{\log 5} \approx 1.365$.

CHAPTER 11 – Axiomatics and Euclidean Geometry

Section 11.1.1

1. Let the set of points be {A, B, C} and let the set of lines be {{A, B}, {A, C}, {C, B}}. This model clearly satisfies Axioms I-1 to I-4.

2. a. Sample: Let the model consist of two distinct points {A, B} and one line {{A, B}}. This model satisfies Axioms I-2 and I-3, but it violates Axioms I-1 and I-4.

    b. Sample: Let the model consist of three distinct points {A, B, C} and one line {ABC}. This model satisfies Axioms I-1, I-2, and I-3, but it violates I-4.

3. a. Let m and n be two distinct lines that intersect. Then there is at least one point P on both m and n. Suppose there exists a point Q distinct from P on both m and n. Then, by I-2, m = n. This would contradict the hypothesis that lines m and n are distinct. Therefore there is exactly one point of intersection of two intersecting distinct lines.

    b. By I-1, there exist distinct points A and B. By I-2, $\overleftrightarrow{AB}$ exists. By I-4, there exists a point P not on $\overleftrightarrow{AB}$, and, by I-2, $\overleftrightarrow{PA}$ and $\overleftrightarrow{PB}$ exist. Because point P is not on $\overleftrightarrow{AB}$, $\overleftrightarrow{AB}$ and $\overleftrightarrow{PA}$ are distinct, as are $\overleftrightarrow{AB}$ and $\overleftrightarrow{PB}$. By part **a**, then, $\overleftrightarrow{AB}$ and $\overleftrightarrow{PA}$ can only intersect at point A and $\overleftrightarrow{AB}$ and $\overleftrightarrow{PB}$ can only intersect at point B. Since A and B are distinct, $\overleftrightarrow{AB}$, $\overleftrightarrow{PA}$, and $\overleftrightarrow{PB}$ must be non-concurrent.

    c. Let m be a line. By I-1, at least three distinct points exist and, by I-4, not all of them can lie on the same line. So there must be at least one point that does not lie on m.

4. a. Let m be a line on distinct points B and C, and A be a point not on m. Since B and C are distinct, by I-2, m is the only line on both of them. Since A is not on m, there is no line containing all three points.

    b. Suppose there is no line on A, B, and C. Assume A = B = C. By I-1, there exists a point D distinct from A, and by I-2, there exists a line on A and D. Thus there exists a line on A = B = C, contradicting the hypothesis. Therefore, at least one of A, B, and C is distinct from the other two. Suppose, then, that A = B and A and C are distinct. Again, by I-2, there exists a line on A = B and C, contradicting the hypothesis. Thus A, B, and C must all be distinct.

5. Choose any of the 7 lines in Fano's geometry to verify F-1. F-2 is verified by observation of the defined set of lines. We have shown that Fano's geometry satisfies the incidence axioms, so F-3 and F-2 are verified, since they are I-1 and I-2, respectively. F-5 is verified by taking all pairwise intersections of lines: ABC ∩ ADE = A, ABC ∩ AFG = A, ABC ∩ BDF = B, ABC ∩ BEG = B, ABC ∩ CDG = C, ABC ∩ CEF = C, ADE ∩ AFG = A, ADE ∩ BDF = D, ADE ∩ BEG = E, ADE ∩ CDG = D, ADE ∩ CEF = E, AFG ∩ BDF = F, AFG ∩ BEG = G, AFG ∩ CDG = G, AFG ∩ CEF = F, BDF ∩ BEG = B, BDF ∩ CDG = D, BDF ∩ CEF = F, BEG ∩ CDG = G, BEG ∩ CEF = E, CDG ∩ CEF = C.

6.   (1) There exists at least one point. (2) There are exactly three lines on every point. (3) Not all lines are on the same point. (4) There exists exactly one point on any two distinct lines. (5) There exists at least one line on any two distinct points. Sample model: Fano's 7-point geometry.

7.   a. Sample: Let the set of points be {A, B, C} and the set of lines be {{A, B, C}}. Then there are exactly three points (F-2) and one line (F-1). But F-3 is not satisfied, since all points are on the same line.

    b. Sample: Let the set of points be {A, B, C} and the set of lines be {{A, B}}. Then there is exactly one line (F-1) and a point C not on it (F-3). But F-2 is not satisfied, since there are only two points on the line.

    c. Sample: The model in part **a** cannot be a model of incidence geometry, since F-3 is the same as I-4, This model in part **b** is not a model of the incidence axioms, since it does not satisfy I-2.

8.   a. Let P be an arbitrary point. By F-1, there exists at least one line m. P either is or is not on m. Assume P is on m. By F-2, there exists at least one point Q on m distinct from P, and by F-3, there exists a point S not on m. S ≠ P and S ≠ Q, since S is not on m. By F-4, there is exactly one line m′ on P and S, and one line n on Q and S. m′ ≠ n, since otherwise, Q would be on m′ and, by F-4, m′ would not be distinct from m. But m′ must be distinct from m, since S is not on m and S is on m′. So m, m′, and n are distinct lines. Let R be a point on n distinct from Q. R exists by F-2. R is not on m, since if it were, there would be two distinct lines m and n on Q and R, violating F-4. R ≠ P, since R is not on m. By F-4, let m″ be the unique line on P and R. m″ ≠ m′, since otherwise, R would be on m′ and, by F-4, m′ would not be distinct from n. So there are at least three distinct lines on P: m, m′, and m″. Now assume P is on a fourth line n′ ≠ m, n′ ≠ m′, and n′ ≠ m″. By F-5, there is at least on point T on n and n′. T ≠ Q, T ≠ S, and T ≠ R, for if not, n′ would not be distinct from m, m′, and m″, respectively. But then there are four points S, Q, R, and T on n, contradicting F-2. Thus n′ cannot be a fourth line containing P and P is on exactly three lines. For the case where P is not on m, choose a point P′ on m and construct line p on P and P′. The proof follows as above, substituting p for m everywhere.

    b. In Fano's axioms, if we interpret "point" to be "new member," "line" to be "meeting," and "on" to be "attend," then we have the conditions for the Rotary club's meetings. (Axioms F-1, F-3, and F-5 are stated implicitly.) Since a geometry with 7 points on 7 lines provides a model for Fano's axioms, we know that a model with 7 new members attending 7 meetings will satisfy our reinterpreted axiom set. Reinterpreting the result from part **a**, we can show that each new member must attend exactly three meetings.

9.   I-1: There are 9 points. I-2: By inspection, for each two distinct points there exists a unique line on both of them:

A, B ABC	B, C ABC	C, D CDH	D, F DEF	E, I AEI	H, I GHI
A, C ABC	B, D BDI	C, E CEG	D, G ADG		
A, D ADG	B, E BEH	C, F CFI	D, H CDH	F, G BFG	
A, E AEI	B, F BFG	C, G CEG	D, I BDI	F, H AFH	
A, F AFH	B, G BFG	C, H CDH		F, I CFI	
A, G ADG	B, H BEH	C, I CFI	E, F DEF		

A, H AFH	B, I BDI		E, G CEG	G, H GHI
A, I AEI		D, E DEF	E, H BEH	G, I GHI

I-3: Every line has three distinct points. I-4: There are 9 points and only three points are on any line, so not all points are on the same line.

10. Verification of the incidence axioms relies on the Euclidean properties of points and lines. In the presence of Euclid's definitions 4, 14, 15, and 17, and Postulates 1, 2, and 3, verify I-1 and I-4 by choosing a diameter of the circle (without its endpoints) and any open chord that is not a diameter. I-2 and I-3 follow immediately from the postulates, but note that Euclid does not explicitly postulate the uniqueness of a line. He tacitly assumes it.

11. Verification of the incidence axioms relies on the Euclidean properties of points and lines. In the presence of Euclid's definitions 4, 8, 14, 19, and 21, and Postulates 1, and 2, verify I-1 and I-4 by choosing two bisectors of any two of the angles of the triangle (Proposition 9). I-2 and I-3 follow as in Problem 10.

12. Points: {A, B, C, D}. Lines: {AB, AC, AD, BC, BD, CD}. Sample theorem: For every line m and every point not on m, there is exactly one line on that point parallel to m.

Proof: Without loss of generality, let be the line on A and B, and let C be the chosen point not on m. By Axiom 2, there is a unique line on C and D. Call it n. A and B are not on n since, by Axiom 3, there are only two points on a line. Similarly, D cannot be on m. So n is a line on C parallel to m. Assume there exists another line n′ ≠ n on C parallel to m. By Axiom 3, there is another point on n′. But it cannot be D, since n′ ≠ n. It cannot be A or B, since n′ would intersect m. Since there are no other points in the geometry, the theorem is proved.

13. a. Sample:

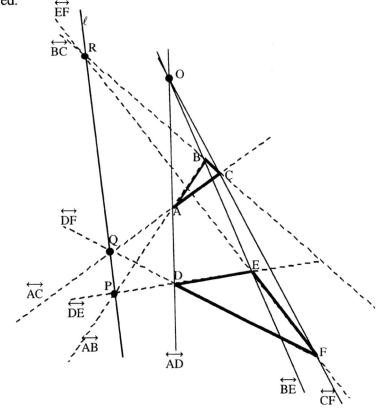

b. In the geometric model of Fano's geometry, consider two triangles that satisfy the hypothesis of Desargues' Theorem, such as ∆ADG and ∆FCB. The three lines on A and F, D and C, and G and B all contain G, satisfying the hypothesis of the theorem. Sides AD and FC contain E, sides DG and CB contain C, and sides AG and FB contain F. The conclusion holds since E, F, and C are all on the same line.

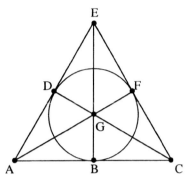

Section 11.1.2

1. a. By the definition of line segment, $\overline{AB}$ includes its endpoints A and B. So $\overline{AB}$ has at least two points. By B-1, there exists a point between A and B, and, by, B-2, this point must be distinct from A and B. Since, by definition, $\overline{AB}$ also contains all points between A and B, there are at least three points on $\overline{AB}$.

    b. Let P be on $\overline{AB}$. Show P is on $\overline{BA}$. By definition of $\overline{AB}$, either P = A, P = B, or P is between A and B. By definition, $\overline{BA}$ consists of B, A, and all the points between B and A. So, if P = A, or P = B, P belongs to $\overleftrightarrow{BA}$. If P is between A and B, by Axiom B-3, P is between B and A. Thus, in every case, P is on $\overline{BA}$. Interchanging A and B, the same argument shows that P is on $\overline{BA}$ implies P is on $\overline{AB}$. So $\overline{AB} = \overline{BA}$.

2. B-1: Let A and B be two distinct points. There exist points C, D, and E on line $\overleftrightarrow{AB}$ such that A-B-C, A-B-D, and E-A-B. B-2: If A, B, and C are points such that A-B-C, then A, B, and C are distinct and on the same line. B-3: If A, B, and C are points such that A-B-C, then C-A-B. B-4: If A, B, and C are three distinct points on the same line, then exactly one of the following is true: A-B-C, A-C-B, or C-A-B.

3. By I-4, there exists a point E not on ℓ. Let m = $\overleftrightarrow{EB}$. Then m ≠ ℓ (because E is on m and not on ℓ) and A, C, and D are not on m (because otherwise m = ℓ). So, by I-2. Since A-B-C, $\overline{AC}$ intersects m at B. Consequently, A and C are on opposite sides of m. Now since B-C-D (from the first part of the proof), $\overline{CD}$ does not intersect m (otherwise B is between C and D). Thus, by Axiom B-5 (Plane Separation), C and D are on the same side of m. Consequently, again by Axiom B-5, A and D are on opposite sides of m, and since $\overline{AD}$ intersects m at B, A-B-D.

4. Part (1): Let A, B, C, and D be four distinct points on ℓ such that A-B-C and B-C-D. Show A-B-D and A-C-D. By Axiom I-4, there exists a point E not on ℓ. Let m = $\overleftrightarrow{BE}$. Then, because E is on m and not on ℓ, m ≠ ℓ and A, B, and C are not on m. So $\overleftrightarrow{AD}$ ≠ m. Since A-B-C, $\overline{AC}$ intersects m at B. Consequently, A and C are on opposite sides of m. Now, since B-C-D, $\overline{CD}$ does not intersect m (otherwise, B is

between C and D). Thus, by Axiom 5 (Plane Separation), C and D are on the same side of m. Consequently, again by Axiom 5, D and A are on opposite sides of m, and since $\overline{AD}$ intersects m at B, A-B-D. Now let m = $\overleftrightarrow{CE}$. Since B-C-D, $\overline{BD}$ intersects m at C. Consequently, B and D are on opposite sides of m. Now, since A-B-C, $\overline{AB}$ does not intersect m (otherwise, C is between A and B). Thus, by Axiom 5, A and B are on the same side of m. Consequently, again by Plane Separation, A and D are on opposite sides of m, and since $\overline{AD}$ intersects m at C, A-C-D.

Part (2): Assume A-B-D and B-C-D, and show A-B-C and A-C-D. Since A-B-D and B-C-D, by Axiom B-3, D-B-A and D-C-B. By Theorem 11.3, D-B-A and D-C-B imply D-C-A and C-B-A. So, by Axiom B-3, A-B-C and A-C-D.

5. The incidence and betweenness axioms are valid in Euclidean geometry and we use this fact, as well as the well-known properties of segments and circles due to Euclid's postulates and propositions to solve this problem. In particular, Euclid's propositions 1 and 5 of Book IV and proposition 2 of Book 3 guarantee, respectively, that a given segment can be inscribed in a circle, that a circle can be circumscribed about a triangle, and that any segment joining two points of a circle lies in the circle Let A and B be any two distinct points on circle C. I-2: The incidence axioms guarantee a unique line on A and B, and the definition of segment and the betweenness axioms to guarantee the uniqueness of segment $\overline{AB}$. Hence the open chord determined by $\overline{AB}$, i.e., the Beltrami-Cayley-Klein line $\overleftrightarrow{AB}$, is uniquely determined by A and B. I-3 and I-1: The betweenness axioms guarantee an infinite number of points on the Euclidean segment $\overline{AB}$, and hence on open chord $\overline{AB}$. Therefore, there are at least two points on any Beltrami-Cayley-Klein line and three points in the plane model (i.e., the interior of circle C). I-4: Circumscribe a circle about a triangle ΔABD. Since D cannot be on $\overleftrightarrow{AB}$, construct the Euclidean line $\overleftrightarrow{AD}$. Euclidean lines $\overleftrightarrow{AB}$ and $\overleftrightarrow{AD}$ can only intersect at point A (see 11.1.1, Problem 3). Thus open chords AB and AD have no points in common. Since there are at least two points on the open chord AD that are not on open chord AB, not all the points of the plane model are on the same line.

6. Define betweenness in the Beltrami-Cayley-Klein plane as follows: Given any three collinear points $A = (x_1, y_1)$, $B = (x_2, y_2)$, and $C = (x_3, y_3)$ in the model, C is between A and B if and only if there exists a real number t, where $0 < t < 1$, C, such that $C = ((1-t)(x_2 - x_1) + x_1, (1-t)(y_2 - y_1) + y_1)$. Now we need to show that if $x_1^2 + y_1^2 < 1$ and $x_2^2 + y_2^2 < 1$, then $x_3^2 + y_3^2 < 1$, that is, if A and B are interior to the circle, then C is interior to the circle. $x_3^2 + y_3^2 = ((1-t)(x_2 - x_1) + x_1)^2 + ((1-t)(y_2 - y_1) + y_1)^2$
$= (1-t)^2(x_2 - x_1)^2 + 2(1-t)(x_2 - x_1)x_1 + x_1^2 + (1-t)^2(y_2 - y_1)^2 + 2(1-t)(y_2 - y_1)y_1 + y_1^2$
$= t^2(x_1^2 + y_1^2) + (1-t)^2(x_2^2 + y_2^2) + 2t(1-t)(x_1x_2 + y_1y_2)$.
Let $D = t^2(x_1^2 + y_1^2)$, $E = (1-t)^2(x_2^2 + y_2^2)$, and $F = 2t(1-t)(x_1x_2 + y_1y_2)$. Then $D < t^2$, since $x_1^2 + y_1^2 < 1$; $E < (1-t)^2$, since $x_2^2 + y_2^2 < 1$. Now we show that $x_1x_2 + y_1y_2 > 1$.

$x_1^2 + y_1^2 < 1$ and $x_2^2 + y_2^2 < 1$ $\Rightarrow x_1^2 + x_2^2 + y_1^2 + y_2^2 < 2$

But $(x_1 - x_2)^2 + (y_1 - y_2)^2 > 0$ $\Rightarrow x_1^2 + x_2^2 - 2x_1x_2 + y_1^2 + y_2^2 - 2y_1y_2 > 0$

$\Rightarrow x_1^2 + x_2^2 + y_1^2 + y_2^2 > 2x_1x_2 + 2y_1y_2$

$\Rightarrow 2x_1x_2 + 2y_1y_2 < 2$

$\Rightarrow x_1x_2 + y_1y_2 < 1$

Thus $0 < F < 2t - 2t^2$.

So $D + E + F < t^2 + (1 - t)^2 + (2t - 2t^2) = 1$. Consequently, each point between (x_1, y_1) and (x_2, y_2) lies inside the unit circle.

B-2: Let C be between $A = (x_1, y_1)$ and $B = (x_2, y_2)$, where $A \neq B$. Then for any t such that $0 < t < 1$, $C = ((1 - t)(x_2 - x_1) + x_1, (1 - t)(y_2 - y_1) + y_1)$. Suppose $C = A$. Then $((1 - t)(x_2 - x_1) + x_1, (1 - t)(y_2 - y_1) + y_1) = (x_1, y_1)$ or $t = 0$, which contradicts $0 < t$. So $C \neq A$. Similarly, $C \neq B$. Thus A, B, and C are distinct. Points A and B determine the line given by the equation $ax + by + c = -(y_1 - y_2)x + (x_1 - x_2)y + (y_1 x_2 - x_1 y_2) = 0$. Point C satisfies this equation, since $-(y_1 - y_2)((1 - t)(x_2 - x_1) + x_1) + (x_1 - x_2)((1 - t)(y_2 - y_1) + y_1) + (y_1 x_2 - x_1 y_2) = 0$, and thus falls on the same line.

B-3: Let C be between $A = (x_1, y_1)$ and $B = (x_2, y_2)$. Then there exists t such that $0 < t < 1$ and $C = ((1 - t)(x_2 - x_1) + x_1, (1 - t)(y_2 - y_1) + y_1)$. Let $t' = 1 - t$. Then $0 < t' < 1$ and $C = (t'(x_2 - x_1) + x_1, t'(y_2 - y_1) + y_1) = ((1 - t')(x_1 - x_2) + x_2, (1 - t')(y_1 - y_2) + y_2)$. Thus C is between B and A.

B-4: To verify this axiom, we assume one betweenness relation and show that the other two betweenness relations fail. Without loss of generality, let C be between A and B. That is, let $A = (x_1, y_1)$ and $B = (x_2, y_2)$, where $A \neq B$, and $C = (x_3, y_3) = ((1 - t)(x_2 - x_1) + x_1, (1 - t)(y_2 - y_1) + y_1)$ for some $0 < t < 1$. We first show by contradiction that A cannot be between C and B. Assume that A is between C and B. Then, for some $0 < t' < 1$, $A = (x_1, y_1) = ((1 - t')(x_2 - x_3) + x_3, (1 - t')(y_2 - y_3) + y_3)$. Substituting $(1 - t)(x_2 - x_1) + x_1$ for x_3 and $(1 - t)(y_2 - y_1) + y_1$ for y_3, $x_1 = (1 - t')(x_2 - ((1 - t)(x_2 - x_1) + x_1)) + (1 - t)(x_2 - x_1) + x_1, = (1 - tt')(x_2 - x_1) + x_1$ and $y_1 = (1 - t')(y_2 - ((1 - t)(y_2 - y_1) + y_1)) + (1 - t)(y_2 - y_1) + y_1 = (1 - tt')(y_2 - y_1) + y_1$. However, $0 < t < 1$ and $0 < t' < 1$ implies $0 < tt' < 1$ and $0 < 1 - tt' < 1$. Let $t'' = 1 - tt'$. Then $(x_1, y_1) = ((1 - t'')(x_2 - x_1) + x_1, (1 - t'')(y_2 - y_1) + y_1)$, where $0 < t'' < 1$. This implies A is between A and B. By part **b** (B-2), this would imply A is distinct from A, which is clearly a contradiction. In a similar manner we can show that B cannot be between A and C.

B-5: The two sides of the line $\ell = \{(x, y): ax + by + c = 0, x^2 + y^2 < 1\}$ in the Beltrami-Cayley-Klein model are $S_1 = \{(x, y): ax + by + c < 0, x^2 + y^2 < 1\}$ and $S_2 = \{(x, y): ax + by + c > 0, x^2 + y^2 < 1\}$. Suppose $(x_1, y_1) \in S_1$ and $(x_2, y_2) \in S_1$. Then $ax_1 + by_1 < -c$ and $ax_2 + by_2 < -c$. Now a point between (x_1, y_1) and (x_2, y_2) has coordinates $((1 - t)(x_2 - x_1) + x_1, (1 - t)(y_2 - y_1) + y_1)$, where $0 < t < 1$. Since $0 < t$, $atx_1 + bty_1 < -c$. Since $t < 1$, $a(1 - t)x_2 + b(1 - t)y_2 < -(1 - t)c$. So $a((1 - t)(x_2 - x_1) + x_1) + b((1 - t)(y_2 - y_1) + y_1)$ $= t(ax_1 + by_1) + (1 - t)(ax_2 + by_2) < -tc - (1 - t)c = -c$. So any point between (x_1, y_1) and (x_2, y_2) is in S_1. So S_1 is convex. A similar proof shows that S_2 is convex. Now suppose $(x_1, y_1) \in S_1$ and $(x_2, y_2) \in S_2$. Then $ax_1 + by_1 < -c$ and $ax_2 + by_2 > -c$. We want to show that there exists a point between these two on ℓ. When $((1 - t)(x_2 - x_1) + x_1, (1 - t)(y_2 - y_1) + y_1)$, $0 < t < 1$, is on ℓ, then $a((1 - t)(x_2 - x_1) + x_1) + b((1 - t)(y_2 - y_1) + y_1) = -c$. So $(ax_1 - ax_2 + by_1 - by_2)t = -c - ax_2 - aby_2$. Thus $t = \dfrac{-c - ax_2 - by_2}{ax_1 + by_1 - (ax_2 + by_2)}$. The numerator $-c - ax_2 - aby_2 < 0$, and the denominator

$ax_1 + by_1 - (ax_2 + by_2)$ is less than the numerator (since $ax_1 + by_1 < -c$). So $t > 0$. Also, since

$t = \dfrac{-c - ax_2 - by_2}{ax_1 + by_1 - (ax_2 + by_2)}$, and $ax_1 + by_1 < -c$, $t < 1$. Thus a point between (x_1, y_1) and (x_2, y_2) lies on ℓ.

7. Let ℓ be any line. By B-5 (Plane Separation), every line ℓ partitions the plane into ℓ itself and two convex sets S_1 and S_2. We must show that S_1 and S_2 are nonempty. By I-4, there exists a point P not on ℓ. P must be in either S_1 or S_2, which are disjoint. Without loss of generality, let P be in S_1. By I-3, there exists a point A on ℓ, by I-2, there exists a line $\overleftrightarrow{PA}$ and, by B-1, there exists a point Q on $\overleftrightarrow{PA}$ such that A is between P and Q. $\overleftrightarrow{PA} \neq \ell$, since P is not on ℓ. Q cannot be on ℓ (otherwise, by I-2, $\overrightarrow{PA} = \ell$). Suppose Q is in S_1. Then, because S_1 is convex, $\overline{PQ}$ is in S_1. However, this leads to a contradiction, since A is on $\overline{PQ}$ and A is on ℓ, and therefore not in S_1. Thus Q must be in S_2, which means S_1 and S_2 are nonempty and there are exactly two half-planes.

8. In Proposition 21, Euclid assumes that a line which contains the vertex of a triangle and an interior point must intersect the opposite side. To make this statement he needs Pasch's Postulate (Theorem 11.2) or one equivalent to it.

9. a. B1: Let A and B be any two real numbers such that $A \neq B$. Then, by Theorem 2.12, there exists a real number C such that $A < C < B$ or $B < C < A$. Thus there exists a point C that is between A and B. Let $D = B + 1$. Then $A < B < D$. Let $E = A - 1$. Then $E < A < B$. Thus there exist points D and E such that B is between A and D and A is between E and B.

   B2: Let A, B, and C be real numbers such that B is between A and C. Then $A < B < C$. By the Trichotomy Property of ordering, $A \neq B$, $B \neq C$ and $A \neq C$. Thus A, B and C are distinct and since $A, B, C \in \mathbf{R}$, they are all on the same line. $\{A, B, C\}$

   B3: If B is between A and C, then, by definition, $A < B < C$ or $C < B < A$. Thus $C < B < A$ or $A < B < C$, which implies B is between A and C.

   B4: Let A, B, and C be three distinct points on the same line. Then A, B, and C are real numbers such that $A \neq B$, $A \neq C$, and $B \neq C$. By Trichotomy, $A < B$ or $B < A$, $A < C$ or $C < A$, and $B < C$ or $C < B$. This gives rise to the following 6 possibilities: $A < B < C$, $A < C < B$, $B < A < C$, $B < C < A$, $C < A < B$, and $C < B < A$.

   b. B1: Let A and B be any two real numbers such that $A \neq B$. Let $x = .5$ and $y = .5$ and $C = .5A + .5B$. Thus C is between A and B. Let $D = 2B - A$. Then $B = .5A + .5D$, so B is between A and D. Let $E = 2A - B$. Then $A = .5E + .5B$, so A is between E and B.

   B2: Let A, B and C be points such that B is between A and C. If B is between A and C, then $A \neq C$ and $B = Ax + Cy$, where x and y are positive real numbers such that $x + y = 1$. Thus $B = Ax + C(1 - x) = x(A - C) + C$. Since $x > 0$ and $A \neq C$, $x(A - C) \neq 0$ and $B \neq C$. Similarly. $B = A(1 - y) + Cy = A + y(C - A)$. Since $y > 0$ and $A \neq C$, $y(A - C) \neq 0$ and $B \neq A$. Thus A, B, and C are distinct.

   B3: By definition B is between A and C if and only if B is between C and A.

   B4: Let A, B and C be three distinct points. Then A, B and C are all real numbers such that $A \neq C$, $A \neq B$, and $B \neq C$. Without loss of generality, assume $A < B < C$. Let $x = \dfrac{C - B}{C - A}$ and $y = \dfrac{B - A}{C - A}$.

Since B – A, C – B, and C – A are all positive, x and y are positive, and
$Ax + Cy = A\frac{C-B}{C-A} + C\frac{B-A}{C-A} = B$. So B is between A and C.

10.   They do not because betweenness guarantees an infinity of points in the presence of the incidence axioms, which hold in any incidence geometry: I-1 guarantees that there exist at least two points A and B. Then, by B-1 and B-2, between A and B there must exist a distinct point C. Again, by B-1, there exists another point between A and C. By B-2, this point cannot be A or C, and, by B-4, this point cannot be B. So their must be a fourth point D. Continuing in this way, we can see that a geometry which satisfies the incidence and betweenness axioms cannot be finite.

Section 11.1.3

1.   a.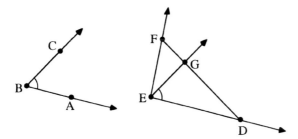

      b.

      c.

2.   a.   Two angles are complementary and each is a complement of the other if they are respectively congruent to adjacent angles that form a right angle.

      b.   An obtuse angle is one that is greater than a right angle.

3.   Euclid's definition includes the interior points, whereas the definition given in this section does not.

4.   a.   Let O and A be distinct points. The set of all points B such that the distance OB equals the distance OA is a circle with center O.

      b.   Two angles are supplementary if their angle measures sum to 180°.

      c.   An angle is a right angle if its angle measure equals 90°.

5.   a.   A point X is interior to a circle with center O if and only if X = O or there exists a point Y on the circle such that X is on ray $\overrightarrow{OY}$ and X is between O and Y. The interior of the circle is then the set of all such interior points. A point Z is exterior to a circle with center O if and only if there exists a point Y on the circle such that Z is on ray $\overrightarrow{OY}$ and Y is between O and Z. The exterior of the circle is the set of all such exterior points.

b. Suppose A is a point on a circle C with center O. By I-2, $\overleftrightarrow{AO}$ exists. By B-1, there exists a distinct point Z on $\overleftrightarrow{AO}$ such that A-O-Z. By C-1, there exists a point B distinct from O on $\overrightarrow{OZ}$ such that $\overline{OA} \cong \overline{OB}$. So, by definition of circle, B is also on C. Now, we can show that A and B are distinct. Suppose, to the contrary, that A = B. Because B is on $\overrightarrow{OZ}$, exactly one of three cases must hold: either B = Z, O-Z-B, or O-B-Z. Then we would have, respectively, A-O-A, O-Z-A, or O-A-Z. The case A-O-A would violate B-2, and, since A-O-Z, the cases O-Z-A and O-A-Z would each violate B-4. So A and B are distinct points on $\overleftrightarrow{OZ}$. We show that A-O-B. If B = Z, then A-O-B. By the corollary to Theorem 11.3, the other two cases also yield A-O-B. (If A-O-Z and O-B-Z, then A-O-B. If O-Z-B and A-O-Z, then A-O-B.) Now, by B-1, there exist points X and Y such that A-X-O and O-Y-B. Since A and B are on circle C and X is between A and O and Y is between B and O, by the definition of circle interior, X and Y are in the interior of circle C. Finally, we show O is between X and Y. By Theorem 11.3, A-O-B and A-X-O guarantees X-O-B, and X-O-B and O-Y-B guarantees X-O-Y. Thus there are two points X and Y in the interior of circle C with O between X and Y.

6. Suppose a line ℓ contains a point on side $\overline{AB}$ of ΔABC but does not contain a vertex. Since ℓ does not contain points A or B, by the Postulate of Pasch, either ℓ contains C, ℓ contains a point on $\overline{AC}$ between A and C, or ℓ contains a point on $\overline{BC}$ between B and C, and no two of these. By hypothesis, however, ℓ does not contain C, so ℓ either contains a point between A and C or a point between B and C, but not both. Thus ℓ cannot contain points on all three sides of ΔABC if it does not contain a vertex. If it does contain a vertex and a point between the other two vertices, then it will contain points on all three sides, since the vertex is on two sides.

7. There is an error in the first printing. C-7 should be C-6.
Let ΔABC be an isosceles triangle with $\overline{AB} \cong \overline{AC}$. Consider the correspondence of vertices A $\leftrightarrow$ A, B $\leftrightarrow$ C, and C $\leftrightarrow$ B. By C-5, $\angle ABC \cong \angle CBA$. So two sides and an included angle of ΔABC are congruent respectively to two sides and an included angle of ΔACB, and, by C-7, $\angle CAB \cong \angle ACB$.

8. First, suppose P is on $\overrightarrow{AB} \cap \overrightarrow{BA}$. Then P is on $\overrightarrow{AB}$ (since $\overrightarrow{AB} \cap \overrightarrow{BA}$ is a subset of $\overrightarrow{AB}$), and, by definition of ray, P is on $\overline{AB}$. Assume P is on $\overline{AB}$, then P is on $\overrightarrow{AB}$ by definition of ray. Since $\overline{AB} = \overline{BA}$ (see Section 11.1.2, Problem 1), P is on $\overrightarrow{BA}$, again by definition of ray.

9. Sample: The converted Plane Separation Axiom the student suggests and the line separation property are not equivalent. In the converted Plane Separation Axiom, a point would partition a line $\overleftrightarrow{AB}$ into three sets: the point itself and two convex sets that are disjoint open sets. The two convex sets are open sets whose intersection is the empty set. On the other hand, the line separation property says that any point P on a line separates the line into two convex closed sets whose intersection is the point P.

10. Let E be a point on $\overline{AB}$ between A and B. Since A and E are distinct, by C-1, there exists a unique point F on $\overrightarrow{CD}$ such that F is distinct from C and $\overline{AE} \cong \overline{CF}$. It remains to be shown that F is between C and D. Suppose, to the contrary, F is not between C and D. Then, by the definition of $\overrightarrow{CD}$, either F = D or C-D-F. We can show by contradiction that neither of these cases can hold. First, if F = D,

then $\overline{AE} \cong \overline{CD}$ and $\overline{AB} \cong \overline{CD}$, so, by C-2, $\overline{AE} \cong \overline{AB}$. Then B and E are two distinct points on $\overrightarrow{AB}$ such that $\overline{AE} \cong \overline{AB}$, contradicting C-1. If D is between C and F, then, by C-1, there is a point G on the ray opposite $\overrightarrow{BA}$ such that $\overline{BG} \cong \overline{DF}$. Thus A-B-G, C-D-F, $\overline{AB} \cong \overline{CD}$, and $\overline{BG} \cong \overline{DF}$. So, by C-3, $\overline{AG} \cong \overline{CF}$. Since $\overline{AE} \cong \overline{CF}$, by C-2, $\overline{AG} \cong \overline{AE}$. But G and E are distinct points on $\overrightarrow{AB}$. This again violates C-1. So F must be between C and D.

11.   a.   By C-1, there exists a unique point E on $\overrightarrow{CD}$, distinct from C, such that $\overline{AB} \cong \overline{CE}$. By the definition of ray, either E = D, C-E-D, or C-D-E. If E = D, then $\overline{AB} \cong \overline{CD}$. If C-E-D, then, by definition, $\overline{CD} > \overline{AB}$. Finally, if $\overline{AB} \cong \overline{CE}$ and C-D-E, then there exists a point F between A and B such that $\overline{AF} \cong \overline{CD}$ (see Problem 10). By definition, then, $\overline{AB} > \overline{CD}$.

       b.   Let $\overline{AB} > \overline{CD}$ and $\overline{CD} > \overline{EF}$. By definition, there exists a point X between A and B such that $\overline{AX} \cong \overline{CD}$. By part **a**, $\overline{AX} > \overline{EF}$, $\overline{AX} \cong \overline{EF}$, or $\overline{EF} > \overline{AX}$. If $\overline{AX} \cong \overline{EF}$, then, by Theorem 11.5 and the given $\overline{CD} > \overline{EF}$, $\overline{CD} > \overline{AX}$, which contradicts $\overline{AX} \cong \overline{CD}$. If $\overline{EF} > \overline{AX}$, then, by Theorem 11.5, $\overline{EF} > \overline{CD}$, which contradicts the given $\overline{CD} > \overline{EF}$. Thus $\overline{AX} > \overline{EF}$. By definition, then, there exists a point Y between A and X such that $\overline{AY} \cong \overline{EF}$. By Theorem 11.3, if A-Y-X and A-X-B, then A-Y-B, so $\overline{AB} > \overline{AY}$. Finally, by Theorem 11.5, if $\overline{AB} > \overline{AY}$ and $\overline{AY} \cong \overline{EF}$, then $\overline{AB} > \overline{EF}$.

12.   Given $\angle DBC$ and ray $\overrightarrow{HE}$, by Axiom C-4, there exists a unique ray $\overrightarrow{HP}$ on the same side of $\overleftrightarrow{HE}$ as $\overrightarrow{HI}$ such that $\angle DBC \cong \angle EHP$. By Axiom C-6, since $\angle ABD \cong \angle GHE$ and $\angle DBC \cong \angle EHP$, $\angle ABC \cong \angle GHP$. By Axiom C-5, then $\angle GHP \cong \angle GHI$. But by Axiom C-4, given $\angle ABC$ and ray $\overrightarrow{HG}$, there exists a unique ray on the same side of $\overleftrightarrow{HG}$ as $\overrightarrow{HI}$ such that $\angle ABC \cong \angle GHI$. Thus point P must be on ray $\overrightarrow{HI}$ and $\angle EHP = \angle EHI$. Thus $\angle DBC \cong \angle EHI$.

13.   a.   By Axiom B-1, there exists a point Q between A and P. Consider $\triangle APC$. Line $\overleftrightarrow{BQ}$ intersects $\overline{AP}$ between A and P. Thus, by the Postulate of Pasch, $\overleftrightarrow{BQ}$ either (1a) contains the point C, (2a) contains a point X between A and C, or (3a) contains a point X between P and C. If case (1) is true, then $\overleftrightarrow{BQ} = \overleftrightarrow{BC}$. Thus $\overleftrightarrow{AP}$ intersects $\overleftrightarrow{BC}$ at Q and the theorem is proved. Otherwise, either case (2a) or case (3a) is true. Now construct $\triangle BXC$. We know that $\overleftrightarrow{AP}$ intersects $\overline{BX}$ at Q. Thus, again by Pasch, $\overleftrightarrow{AP}$ either (1b) contains point C, (2b) contains a point Y between X and C, or (3b) contains a point Y between B and C. If case (1b) were to hold, then points A, P, and C would be collinear, and P would not be interior to $\triangle ABC$, which is a contradiction. Now, suppose case (2b) is true, so that Y is on $\overleftrightarrow{XC}$. If, by case (2a), X is on $\overleftrightarrow{AC}$, then Y is on $\overleftrightarrow{AC}$, which means P is on $\overleftrightarrow{AC}$. If, by case (3a), X is on $\overleftrightarrow{PC}$, then Y is on $\overleftrightarrow{PC}$, which means $\overleftrightarrow{AP} = \overleftrightarrow{PC}$ and P is on $\overleftrightarrow{AC}$. Again, this would imply that P is not interior to $\triangle ABC$, which is a contradiction. Since cases (1b) and (2b) cannot hold, case (3b) must hold. Therefore, $\overleftrightarrow{AP}$ intersects $\triangle ABC$ between points B and C.

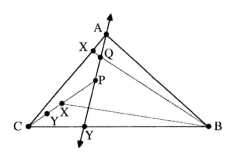

b. Let line ℓ be a line through point P. By Axiom I-3, there must be another point Q on ℓ. Point Q must be either interior, exterior, or on $\triangle$ABC. Case 1: consider the case in which Q is on $\triangle$ABC. Then Q is either on a vertex or on a side of the triangle. If it is on a side of the triangle, then, by the Postulate of Pasch, ℓ must intersect $\triangle$ABC either at the opposite vertex or on a second side. If Q is on a vertex of the triangle, then ℓ already intersects two sides of the triangle. Case 2: consider the case in which Q is interior to the triangle. Construct the three triangles $\triangle$APC, $\triangle$APB, and $\triangle$BPC. If Q is on either $\overline{AP}$, $\overline{BP}$, or $\overline{CP}$, then ℓ intersects either A, B, or C, respectively, and we are done. Now suppose Q is interior to one of these three triangles. Without loss of generality, assume Q is interior to $\triangle$APC. Then by the result of part **a**, ℓ must intersect $\overline{AC}$ and then, by Pasch, ℓ must intersect at least one other side of $\triangle$ABC. Case 3: assume Q is exterior to $\triangle$ABC. Then Q and P will be on opposite sides of at most two of the lines $\overleftrightarrow{AB}$, $\overleftrightarrow{AC}$, or $\overleftrightarrow{BC}$. Suppose, for example, P and Q are on opposite sides of line $\overleftrightarrow{AB}$. By the Plane Separation Postulate, $\overline{PQ}$ must intersect $\overleftrightarrow{AB}$ at some point R. Let Q′ be between R and P. Then Q′ and R are on the same side of $\overleftrightarrow{AB}$. In this way, we can find a second point P′ ≠ P on line ℓ that is also interior to $\triangle$ABC. Thus case 3 will reduce to case 2.

14. Proof: Since angles are determined by rays, not individual points, by C-1, we are free to choose points D and F such that $\overline{BA} \cong \overline{ED}$ and $\overline{BC} \cong \overline{EF}$. By Axiom C-7 (SAS Congruence), then, $\overline{AC} \cong \overline{DF}$, and $\angle$CAB $\cong \angle$FDE. By the theorem in Problem 10, since $\overline{AC} \cong \overline{DF}$, there exists a unique point Y between D and F such that $\overline{AX} \cong \overline{DY}$. By Axiom C-7, $\angle$ABX $\cong \angle$DEY.

15. a.

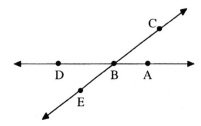

Let $\angle$ABC and $\angle$DBE be vertical angles. Then they are each a supplement of $\angle$DBC. By C-5, $\angle$DBC $\cong \angle$DBC. By Theorem 11.7, supplements of congruent angles are congruent, so

$\angle ABC \cong \angle DBE$.

b.

Let $\angle ABC$ be a right angle and let $\angle EFG \cong \angle ABC$. Suppose $\angle DBC$ is a supplement of $\angle ABC$ and $\angle HFG$ is a supplement of $\angle EFG$. By the definition of a right angle, $\angle ABC \cong \angle DBC$. Since, by part **a**, supplements of congruent angles are congruent, $\angle HFG \cong \angle DBC$. By C-5, $\angle EFG \cong \angle HFG$. Thus, by the definition, $\angle EFG$ is a right angle.

16.   Theorem 1: If $\angle ABC > \angle DEF$ and $\angle DEF \cong \angle GHI$, then $\angle ABC > \angle GHI$.

Proof: Since $\angle ABC > \angle DEF$, by definition, there exists $\overrightarrow{BP}$ such that $\angle DEF \cong \angle ABP$ and P is interior to $\angle ABC$. By C-5, $\angle DEF \cong \angle GHI$ and $\angle DEF \cong \angle ABP$ implies $\angle GHI \cong \angle ABP$. Thus $\angle GHI \cong \angle ABP$, so, by definition, $\angle ABC > \angle GHI$.

Theorem 2: Exactly one of the following conditions holds: $\angle ABC > \angle DEF$, $\angle ABC \cong \angle DEF$, or $\angle DEF > \angle ABC$.

Proof: Given $\angle DEF$, by C-4, there exists point X such that $\overrightarrow{BX}$ is on the same side of $\overleftrightarrow{AB}$ as $\overrightarrow{BC}$ and $\angle DEF \cong \angle ABX$. By B-5 (the Plane Separation Axiom), either point X is on $\overleftrightarrow{BC}$, or on the same side of $\overleftrightarrow{BC}$ as A, or on the side of $\overleftrightarrow{BC}$ opposite A, and no two of these can hold. Suppose X is on $\overleftrightarrow{BC}$ and on the same side of $\overleftrightarrow{AB}$ as C. Then $\overrightarrow{BX} = \overrightarrow{BC}$ and $\angle DEF \cong \angle ABC$. Next, suppose X is on the same side of $\overleftrightarrow{AB}$ as C and on the same side of $\overleftrightarrow{BC}$ as A. Then X is in the interior of $\angle ABC$. By definition, then, $\angle ABC > \angle DEF$. Finally, suppose X is on the same side of $\overleftrightarrow{AB}$ as C and on the side of $\overleftrightarrow{BC}$ opposite A. Then, by B-5, $\overline{XA}$ intersects $\overleftrightarrow{BC}$ at some point Y. Because $Y \neq X$ and $Y \neq A$ (otherwise, $\overrightarrow{BX} = \overrightarrow{BA}$ or $\overrightarrow{BC} = \overrightarrow{BA}$), Y is between X and A. By B-4, then, X is not between Y and A, so $\overline{YA}$ does not intersect $\overleftrightarrow{BX}$ and, by B-5, Y and A are on the same side of $\overleftrightarrow{BX}$. Similarly, X and Y are on the same side of $\overleftrightarrow{BA}$. Thus Y is interior to $\angle ABX$. So there exists $\overrightarrow{BY}$ such that $\angle ABY = \angle ABC$ and Y is interior to $\angle ABX$. By definition, then, $\angle ABX > \angle ABY$. Since $\angle DEF \cong \angle ABX$ and Y is between X and A, by the theorem of Problem 14, there exists a unique point G between D and F such that $\angle DEG \cong \angle ABY$. Since G is interior to $\angle DEF$, $\angle DEF > \angle DEG$. By Theorem 1 above, $\angle DEF > \angle DEG$ and $\angle DEG \cong \angle ABY$ implies $\angle DEF > \angle ABY$. But $\angle ABY = \angle ABC$, so $\angle DEF > \angle ABC$.

Section 11.1.4

1. Given $\triangle ABC$ and $\triangle DEF$ with $\angle CAB \cong \angle FDE$, $\angle ACB \cong \angle DFE$, and $\overline{AB} \cong \overline{DE}$, show $\triangle ABC \cong \triangle DEF$. If $\overline{AC} \cong \overline{DF}$, the triangles would be congruent by Axiom C-7 (SAS) and the definition of triangle congruence. Our method of proof is to assume these segments are not congruent, and derive a contradiction. Assume $\overline{AC}$ is not congruent to $\overline{DF}$. Without loss of generality, assume that $\overline{AC} > \overline{DF}$. Then, by definition of greater than, we can find a point C′ on $\overleftrightarrow{AC}$ such that A-C′-C and $\overline{AC'} \cong \overline{DF}$. Construct $\overline{BC'}$. So, by Axiom C-7, $\angle AC'B$ is congruent to $\angle DFE$, which is congruent to $\angle ACB$ by hypothesis. By Axiom C-5, $\angle AC'B \cong \angle ACB$. We show this congruence is impossible. Consider $\triangle AC'B$. Choose V on $\overrightarrow{BC'}$ such that V- C′-B. Find points P and Q such that C′-P-C, B-P-Q, $\overline{C'P} \cong \overline{PC}$, and $\overline{BP} \cong \overline{PQ}$ so that Q lies in the interior of $\angle VC'C$. (The justification for the existence of these points can be secured using Pasch's postulate and the congruence postulates. Their existence can also be obtained by assuming the existence of a midpoint (Theorem 11.11).) Then $\angle VC'C$ and $\angle AC'B$ are vertical angles, and so, by Problem 15a of Section 11.1.3, are congruent. By the same reasoning, $\angle QPC'P \cong \angle CPB$ and, by C-7 and triangle congruence, $\triangle C'PQ \cong \triangle CPB$. $\angle PCB = \angle C'CB = \angle ACB$ is congruent to $\angle PC'Q = \angle CC'Q = \angle QC'C$. $\angle AC'B \cong \angle VC'C$, which is the union of $\angle VC'Q$ and $\angle QC'C$. So $\angle ACB$ and $\angle AC'B$ cannot be congruent. Therefore, $\overline{AC} \cong \overline{DF}$ and $\triangle ACB \cong \triangle DFE$.

2. Suppose M_1 and M_2 are distinct midpoints of $\overline{AB}$. By the definition of midpoint, A-M_1-B, A-M_2-B, $\overline{BM_1} \cong \overline{AM_1}$, and $\overline{BM_2} \cong \overline{AM_2}$. By Problem 11 of Section 11.1.3, we have either $\overline{AM_1} \cong \overline{AM_2}$, $\overline{AM_1} > \overline{AM_2}$, or $\overline{AM_2} > \overline{AM_1}$. We cannot have $\overline{AM_1} \cong \overline{AM_2}$, since then there would exist two distinct points on $\overrightarrow{AB}$ producing two segments congruent to $\overline{AM_1}$, violating Axiom C-1. Suppose, then, $\overline{AM_1} > \overline{AM_2}$. Then A-$M_2$-$M_1$. By Theorem 11.3, A-$M_2$-$M_1$ and A-M_1-B together imply, M_2-M_1-B, which, in turn, implies $\overline{BM_2} > \overline{BM_1}$. By Theorem 11.5, $\overline{BM_1} \cong \overline{AM_1}$ and $\overline{BM_2} > \overline{BM_1}$ imply $\overline{BM_2} > \overline{AM_1}$. By Problem 11 of Section 11.1.3, $\overline{BM_2} > \overline{AM_1}$ and $\overline{BM_2} \cong \overline{AM_2}$ imply $\overline{AM_2} > \overline{AM_1}$, contradicting $\overline{AM_1} > \overline{AM_2}$. Similarly, $\overline{AM_2} > \overline{AM_1}$ leads to a contradiction. Thus the midpoint must be unique.

3. Suppose in triangles $\triangle ABC$ and $\triangle DEF$, $\overline{AB} \cong \overline{DE}$, $\angle BAC \cong \angle EDF$, and $\angle ABC \cong \angle DEF$. By Problem 11 of Section 11.1.3, either $\overline{AC} \cong \overline{DF}$, $\overline{AC} > \overline{DF}$, or $\overline{DF} > \overline{AC}$. If $\overline{AC} > \overline{DF}$, then there exists a point X between A and C such that $\overline{AX} \cong \overline{DF}$. By SAS Congruence, $\angle AXB \cong \angle DFE$, so $\angle ABX \cong \angle DEF$. By Axiom C-5, then, $\angle ABX \cong \angle ABC$. However, ray $\overrightarrow{BX}$ is between rays $\overrightarrow{BA}$ and $\overrightarrow{BC}$, so $\angle ABC > \angle AXB$. This leads to a contradiction (see Section 11.1.3, Problem 16). Thus $\overline{AC} \not> \overline{DF}$. A similar argument can be used to show that $\overline{DF} \not> \overline{AC}$. Therefore, $\overline{AC} \cong \overline{DF}$ and, by SAS Congruence, $\overline{AC} \cong \overline{DF}$.

4.

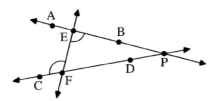

Suppose $\overleftrightarrow{AB}$ and $\overleftrightarrow{CD}$ intersect at point P. Without loss of generality, assume P is on the same side of $\overleftrightarrow{EF}$ as point B. Then ∠CFE is an exterior angle of ΔFEP. Since P is on $\overrightarrow{EB}$, ∠PEF = ∠BEF. Thus ∠CFE is congruent to interior angle ∠PEF. This contradicts Theorem 11.12.

5.   a.   Let ℓ be an arbitrary line and P be an arbitrary point. There are two cases to consider: Case 1: P does not lie on ℓ and Case 2: P lies on ℓ.

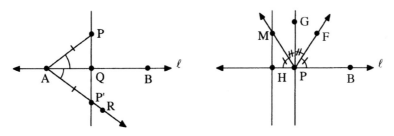

Case 1: Assume first that that P does not lie on ℓ. By I-3, there exist distinct points A and B on ℓ. By C-4, there exists $\overrightarrow{AR}$ on the side of ℓ opposite to P such that ∠BAR ≅ ∠BAP. By C-1, there exists P′ on $\overrightarrow{AR}$ such that $\overline{AP} ≅ \overline{AP'}$. By the definition of opposite sides, $\overline{PP'}$ intersects ℓ at some point Q. If Q ≠ A, then, by C-7, ∠PQA ≅ ∠P′QA. Since these two angles form a linear pair, they are supplementary and therefore each is a right angle. So, by definition of perpendicular, $\overleftrightarrow{PP'} \perp ℓ$. If Q = A, then ∠BQP = ∠BAP and ∠BQP′ = ∠BAP′. Therefore, ∠PQB ≅ ∠P′QB, and it follows as before that $\overleftrightarrow{PP'} \perp ℓ$.

Case 2: Assume now that P lies on ℓ. By I-4, there exists a point M not on ℓ. Use the above method to construct a perpendicular to ℓ through M. Let H be the point of intersection of the perpendicular and ℓ. If H = P, then $\overleftrightarrow{MH} = ℓ$ and the theorem is proved. If H ≠ P, first find a point B on ℓ such that H-P-B (B-1), then find a ray $\overrightarrow{PF}$ on the same side of ℓ as M such that ∠MPH ≅ ∠FPB (C-4). Bisect ∠MPF by $\overleftrightarrow{PG}$ (see below for proof of the existence of an angle bisector). Since ∠MPG ≅ ∠FPG and ∠MPH ≅ ∠FPB, ∠HPG and ∠BPG are a congruent linear pair (C-6), and so are right angles. Thus $\overleftrightarrow{PG}$ is perpendicular to ℓ.

Proof of the existence of an angle bisector: Let ∠AOB be any angle. Find C and C′ on rays $\overrightarrow{OA}$ and $\overrightarrow{OB}$, respectively, with segment $\overline{OC} ≅ \overline{OC'}$ (C-1). Let D be the midpoint of $\overline{CC'}$ (Theorem 11.11). Then D is in the interior of ∠AOB, and ΔODC ≅ ΔODC′ (Theorem 11.9). Therefore, ∠AOD ≅ ∠BOD and $\overleftrightarrow{OD}$ bisects ∠AOB

b.   Let ℓ be a line and P a point not on ℓ. By part **a**, there exists a line n (the transversal) on P perpendicular to ℓ. Again by part **a**, there exists a line m on P perpendicular to n. Since m and ℓ are intersected by n such that alternate interior angles are right angles, assuming all right angles are congruent, by Theorem 11.13, m is parallel to ℓ.

c.

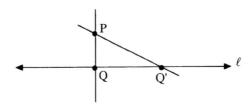

Let Q and Q′ be distinct points on ℓ and suppose $\overleftrightarrow{PQ}$ and $\overrightarrow{PQ'}$ are both perpendicular to ℓ. Then $\angle PQQ'$ and $\angle PQ'Q$ are both right angles, which contradicts Theorem 11.12.

6.   We need to prove that if ℓ is any line and P is any point on ℓ, there exists at least one line through P parallel to ℓ. By Problem 5a, there exists a line g on P perpendicular to ℓ. And, again by Problem 5a, there exists a line h on P perpendicular to g. So ℓ and h are both perpendicular to g. By assuming the given corollary to the alternate interior angle theorem (two lines perpendicular to the same line are parallel to each other), ℓ and h are parallel. Since P belongs to ℓ and h, the theorem is proved.

7.   The purpose of this problem is to help students understand that the existence of parallel lines can be deduced without Euclid's parallel postulate and that the proof is primarily due to the alternate interior angles theorem, which uses the congruence axioms and the existence of an infinity of points on a line, which, in turn, appeals to the incidence and betweenness axioms. In Problem 5, students have constructed a parallel line. So the "proof" here follows from that solution.
Axioms I-1 and I-2 guarantee the existence of at least one line ℓ. Axiom I-4 guarantees that there is a point P not on ℓ. Using the arguments of Problem 5, we can show that there exists at least one line m through P parallel to ℓ.

Section 11.1.5

1.   P-E $\Rightarrow$ statement: Suppose lines m and n are parallel, and line ℓ is perpendicular to line n. We show ℓ is perpendicular to m. Line ℓ intersects m at a point P. If not, ℓ is parallel to m and m is parallel to n, so by Theorem 11.14, ℓ would be parallel to n, contrary to the hypothesis. Let ℓ intersect m at point P. By Problem 5 of Section 11.1.4, there exists a unique line k on P perpendicular to n. So k intersects both m and n. By the parallel postulate, k must be perpendicular to m. If k were not perpendicular to both n and m, then k falling on m and n would make the interior angles on the same side less than two right angles, and m and n would intersect, which is a contradiction. Since, by Problem 5 of Section 11.1.4, the line on P perpendicular to m is unique, k = ℓ.

2.

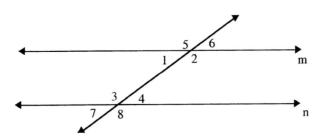

We have already shown that Euclid's parallel postulate is equivalent to the statement: If two parallel lines are cut by a transversal, then the interior angles on the same of the transversal are supplementary. So we only need to show that interior angles on the same side of a transversal are supplementary if and only if corresponding angles are congruent. Suppose $\angle 1$ is the supplement of $\angle 3$. Then m // n by P-E. Now $\angle 7$ is the supplement of $\angle 3$. Since supplements of congruent angles are congruent (Theorem 11.7), $\angle 1 \cong \angle 7$. The same can be shown for other pairs of corresponding angles. Conversely, if $\angle 1 \cong \angle 7$, since $\angle 7$ is the supplement of $\angle 3$, then $\angle 1$ and $\angle 3$ are supplementary.

3. $(1) \Rightarrow (2)$: Let m and n be parallel lines. Let line t, distinct from m, intersect m at point P. We show t intersects n. If not intersect n, then t and m would be two distinct lines through point P parallel to n. This would contradict (1).

    $(2) \Rightarrow (1)$: Suppose line m is a line on a point P and m is parallel to line n. If a line t distinct from m is on P and is parallel to n, then t intersects m. But by (2), t must also intersect line n. This contradicts the hypothesis that t is parallel to n. Thus there is at most one parallel to a given line through a point not on that line.

4. Proof by contradiction: Suppose parallel lines $\overleftrightarrow{AB}$ and $\overleftrightarrow{CD}$ are cut by a transversal $\overleftrightarrow{AD}$ such that alternate interior angles $\angle BAD$ and $\angle ADC$ are not congruent. Without loss of generality, let $\angle BAD > \angle ADC$. By Axiom C-4, there exists a ray $\overrightarrow{AX}$ such that $\angle XAD \cong \angle ADC$. By Theorem 11.13 (alternate interior angles theorem), $\overleftrightarrow{AX}$ is parallel to $\overleftrightarrow{CD}$. Since $\overleftrightarrow{AX}$ is distinct from $\overleftrightarrow{AB}$, we have two lines through A parallel to $\overleftrightarrow{CD}$, which contradicts (1).

5. a. The parallel postulate does not hold in Fano's geometry. Consider line ABC. There is no line passing through point E that does not intersect ABC.

    b. The parallel postulate does hold in Young's geometry. Consider, for example, line ABC. Through point D there is only one line that does not intersect ABC, namely DEF.

    c. The parallel postulate does not hold in three-point geometry. All the lines in this geometry intersect.

    d. The parallel postulate does hold in the four-point geometry. Proof: Let m be a line and P a point not on m. By Axiom 3, there are exactly two points on m. By Axiom 1, there are exactly four points. Thus there exists exactly one point Q other than P not on m. By Axiom 2 there exists exactly one line on Q and P, and, by Axiom 3, there are no other points on this line. Thus there is at least one line on P parallel to m. Suppose there were a second line on P parallel to m. Then, by Axiom 3, there would be a point other than P on this line. This point cannot be Q, since that would violate Axiom 2, and it cannot be either point on m, or the lines would intersect. Thus there is exactly one line on P parallel to m.

6. a. The Euclidean parallel postulate does not hold since, for example, there is more than one line parallel to ABC through point D (DHI, DJK, DLM).

    b. Axiom I-1 is satisfied since there are 13 points. Axiom I-3 is satisfied since there are three distinct points on every line. Axiom I-4 is satisfied since point D does not lie on line ABC. By inspection, we can see that for each two points, there exists exactly one line, so Axiom I-2 is satisfied.

    c. Sample: Each point is on exactly six lines.

    d. Betweenness is not a feature of this geometry, so the postulate of Pasch, as stated in Theorem 11.2, does not apply.

7. a. The Euclidean parallel postulate does not hold since, for example, there are no lines parallel to ABCD through point E.

    b. Axiom I-1 is satisfied since there are 13 points. Axiom I-3 is satisfied since there are four distinct points on every line. Axiom I-4 is satisfied since point E does not lie on line ABCD. By inspection, we can see that for each two points, there exists exactly one line, so Axiom I-2 is satisfied.

    c. Sample: Each point is on exactly four lines.

    d. Betweenness is not a feature of this geometry, so the postulate of Pasch, as stated in Theorem 11.2, does not apply.

8. a. Consider $\triangle ABC$. Using the idea of Theorem 11.11, we can find the midpoints of segments $\overline{AB}$ and $\overline{BC}$. Using the idea of Problem 5 of Section 11.1.4, we can construct the unique perpendicular lines m and n through the midpoints of these two segments. Suppose lines m and n intersect at a point P. Again, using the idea of Problem 5 of Section 11.1.4, we can construct the unique line ℓ through point P perpendicular to $\overleftrightarrow{AC}$. Let ℓ intersect $\overleftrightarrow{AC}$ at Q. Since $\overline{AP} \cong \overline{BP}$ and $\overline{BP} \cong \overline{CP}$, by Axiom C-2, $\overline{AP} \cong \overline{CP}$. From HL congruence for a triangle, then, $\triangle APQ \cong \triangle CPQ$. Thus $\overline{AQ} \cong \overline{CQ}$ and ℓ is the perpendicular bisector of $\overline{AC}$. Therefore, the perpendicular bisectors of the three sides of a triangle have the point P in common.

    b. The only unjustified step in part **a** was the supposition that lines m and n, the perpendicular bisectors of $\overline{AB}$ and $\overline{BC}$, respectively, intersect. In order to prove that they do in fact intersect, we need the parallel postulate. Suppose to the contrary that they did not intersect. Then m and n would be parallel. Consequently, by an equivalent to Euclid's parallel postulate (see Problem 1), $\overleftrightarrow{AB}$ would also be perpendicular to n. Thus, by the Alternate Interior Angle Theorem (Theorem 11.13), $\overleftrightarrow{AB} \mathbin{/\!/} \overleftrightarrow{BC}$, which contradicts the hypothesis that $\overleftrightarrow{AB}$ and $\overleftrightarrow{BC}$ are distinct lines that intersect at B.

Section 11.2.1

1. For $A = 0$, $B \neq 0$, the set of all solutions is $\{(x, -\frac{C}{B}): x \in \mathbf{R}\}$. For $B = 0$, $A \neq 0$, the set of all solutions is $\{(-\frac{C}{A}, y): y \in \mathbf{R}\}$. For $A \neq 0$, $B \neq 0$, the set of all solutions is $\{(x, -\frac{Ax + C}{B}): x \in \mathbf{R}\}$.

2.
   a. $-(b - d)x + (a - c)y + (bc - ad) = 0$
   b. $x_0 y - y_0 x = 0$
   c. $ay + bx - ab = 0$
   d. $x - x_1 = 0$
   e. $y + x = 0$

3. Sample: First explanation: An equation for line containing the two points $(1, 1)$ and $(0, -4)$ is $-5x + y + 4 = 0$. The point $(\frac{3}{8}, 7)$ is not a solution to this equation and therefore not on the same line.

   Second explanation. The slope of the line containing the two points $(1, 1)$ and $(0, -4)$ is 5. The slope of the line containing the two points $(\frac{3}{8}, 7)$ and $(1, 1)$ is $-\frac{48}{5}$. Since two points determine a unique line, and the same line cannot have two different slopes, the points $(1, 1)$, $(0, -4)$ and $(\frac{3}{8}, 7)$ cannot be on the same line.

4.
   a. $\{(x, y): Ax + By = 0\}$
   b. $\{(x, y): x = 2\}$
   c. $\{(x, y): ax + by = ac\}$
   d. $\{(x, y): -2x + 4y = \frac{1}{3}\}$

5. The circle with center $(0, 0)$ and radius b has equation $x^2 + y^2 = b^2$ and the circle with center $(b, 0)$ and radius b has equation $(x - b)^2 + y^2 = b^2$. These circles intersect when $(x - b)^2 + y^2 = x^2 + y^2$, or when $x = \frac{b}{2}$ and $y = -\frac{b\sqrt{3}}{2}$. Let $C = (\frac{b}{2}, \frac{b\sqrt{3}}{2})$. Then $AB = AC = BC = b$ and $\triangle ABC$ is equilateral.

6.
   a. B-1: Let $A = (x_1, y_1)$ and $B = (x_2, y_2)$, where $A \neq B$. We demonstrate the existence of the required points C, D, and E by finding a value for t that will ensure the betweenness relations. Let $t = .5$. Then $C = (.5x_1 + .5x_2, .5y_1 + .5y_2)$ is between A and B. Let $D = (2x_2 - x_1, 2y_2 - y_1)$. Then $B = (x_2, y_2) = (.5x_1 + .5(2x_2 - x_1), .5y_1 + .5(2y_2 - y_1))$ is between A and D. Let $E = (2x_1 - x_2, 2y_1 - y_2)$. Then $A = (x_1, y_1) = (.5(2x_1 - x_2) + .5x_2, .5(2y_1 - y_2) + .5y_2)$ is between E and B.

   b. B-2: Let C be between $A = (x_1, y_1)$ and $B = (x_2, y_2)$, where $A \neq B$. Then for any t such that $0 < t < 1$, $C = ((1 - t)x_1 + tx_2, (1 - t)y_1 + ty_2)$. Suppose $C = A$. Then $((1 - t)x_1 + tx_2, (1 - t)y_1 + ty_2) = (x_1, y_1)$ or $(x_1, y_1) = (x_2, y_2)$, which contradicts $A \neq B$. So $C \neq A$. Similarly, $C \neq B$. Thus A, B, and C are distinct. Points A and B determine the line given by the equation $-(y_1 - y_2)x + (x_1 - x_2)y + (y_1 x_2 - x_1 y_2) = 0$. Point C satisfies this equation, since $-(y_1 - y_2)((1 - t)x_1 + tx_2) + (x_1 - x_2)((1 - t)y_1 + ty_2) + (y_1 x_2 - x_1 y_2) = 0$, and thus falls on the same line.

   c. B-3: Let C be between $A = (x_1, y_1)$ and $B = (x_2, y_2)$. Then there exists t such that $0 < t < 1$ and

$C = ((1 - t)x_1 + tx_2, (1 - t)y_1 + ty_2)$. Let $t' = 1 - t$. Then $0 < t' < 1$ and
$C = (t'x_1 + (1 - t')x_2, t'y_1 + (1 - t')y_2) = ((1 - t')x_2 + tx_1, (1 - t')y_2 + t'y_1)$. Thus C is between B and A.

d.   B-4: To verify this axiom, we assume one betweenness relation and show that the other two betweenness relations fail. Without loss of generality, let C be between A and B. That is, let $A = (x_1, y_1)$ and $B = (x_2, y_2)$, where $A \neq B$, and $C = ((1 - t)x_1 + tx_2, (1 - t)y_1 + ty_2)$ for some $0 < t < 1$. We first show by contradiction that A cannot be between C and B. Assume that A is between C and B. Then, for some $0 < t' < 1$,

$A = (x_1, y_1) = ((1 - t')((1 - t)x_1 + tx_2) + t'x_2, (1 - t')((1 - t)y_1 + ty_2) + t'y_2)$. Thus
$(x_1, y_1) = ((1 - t')(1 - t)x_1 + (1 - (1 - t')(1 - t))x_2), (1 - t')(1 - t)y_1 + (1 - (1 - t')(1 - t))y_2)$.
However, $0 < t < 1$ and $0 < t' < 1$ imply $0 < 1 - t < 1$ and $0 < 1 - t' < 1$ and therefore
$0 < (1 - t')(1 - t) < 1$ and $0 < 1 - (1 - t')(1 - t) < 1$. Let $t'' = 1 - (1 - t')(1 - t)$. Then
$(x_1, y_1) = ((1 - t'')x_1 + t''x_2, (1 - t'')y_1 + t''y_2)$, where $0 < t'' < 1$. This implies A is between A and B. By part **b** (B-2), this would imply A is distinct from A, which is clearly a contradiction. In a similar manner we can show that B cannot be between A and C.

7.   Idea of proof: Let P be a point distinct from the origin O. Then a point X lies on $\overleftrightarrow{OP}$ if and only if $X = Pt$ for some real number t. We represent a system of linear equations in the parameter t by $X = Pt + Q$, for Cartesian points P and Q, and real number t. If P is distinct from Q, then $X = P + (Q - P)t$ is a system of equations for the line $\overleftrightarrow{PQ}$. If $0 < t < 1$, the X lies on segment $\overline{PQ}$. Construct ΔPOQ with sides $\overline{PQ}$ $(X = P + (Q - P)t)$, $\overline{OP}$ $(X = O + (O - P)t)$, and $\overline{QO}$ $(X = Q + (O - Q)t)$, and use the results of Problem 6 to demonstrate Pasch's Theorem.
Proof: Given ΔPOQ and line ℓ intersecting $\overline{OP}$ at X in the interior of segment $\overline{OP}$, show that only one of the following can occur: ℓ contains Q, ℓ intersects the interior of $\overline{PQ}$, or ℓ intersects the interior of $\overline{QO}$. Coordinatize ΔPOQ as follows: $O = (0, 0)$, $P = (p, 0)$, and $Q = (q, r)$, where p, q, and r are greater than 0. X is interior to $\overline{OP}$, so P-X-O, and there exists a t such that $X = (tp, 0)$ for $0 < t < 1$. Assume ℓ contains Q. So we can write the equation $\ell = XQ$ as $y = \frac{r}{q - tp}(x - tp)$. We show that ℓ cannot intersect the interiors of segments $\overline{PQ}$ or $\overline{QO}$. Assume ℓ intersects the interior of $\overline{PQ}$ at Y. Then Y is interior to $\overline{PQ}$, so P-Y-Q and there exists a t' such that $Y = ((1 - t')p + t'q, t'r)$ for $0 < t' < 1$. So Y belongs to ℓ and so must satisfy its equation, $y = \frac{r}{q - tp}(x - tp)$. Thus $t'r = \frac{r}{q - tp}(((1 - t')p + t'q) - tp)$, or $qt'r - tt'pr = pr - t'pr + t'qr - tpr$. Since $r > 0$, we can divide this equation by r to get $-ptt' = p - t'p - tp$. Since $p > 0$, we divide by p to get $-tt' = 1 - t' - t$, or $t'(1 - t) = (1 - t)$. Because $t < 1$, we can divide by $1 - t$ to get $t' = 1$. This is a contradiction since $t < 1$. The proof that ℓ cannot intersect the interior of $\overline{QO}$ proceeds in the same manner.

8.   We show that given a point, there exists at least two distinct lines on it. Let $P = (x_1, y_1)$ be a point in the Cartesian plane. Consider points $Q = (x_1 + 1, y_1)$ and $R = (x_1, y_1 + 1)$. The horizontal line $\overleftrightarrow{PQ}$ with equation $y + -y_1 = 0$ passes through P, as does the vertical line $\overleftrightarrow{PR}$ with equation $x + -x_1 = 0$. Solving

these equations simultaneously, we determine that P is the only point that satisfies both, so the two lines must be distinct.

9. The coordinate system for Young's geometry based on the system of integers modulo 3 is the set of points $\{(0, 0), (0, 1), (0, 2), (1, 0), (1, 1), (1, 2), (2, 0), (2, 1), (2, 2)\}$. A line in this system is the set of points that satisfy an equation equivalent to a linear equation of the form $Ax + By + C = 0$, where A, B, and C are 0, 1, or 2 and A and B are not both 0. Just as for equations of lines in the Cartesian plane, all multiples $kAx + kBy + kC = 0$, where k is non-zero, represent the same line. Thus, for example, the equations $x + 2y = 0$ and $2x + y = 0$ are equivalent. The equations for the 12 lines in Young's geometry and their associated solution sets are as follows: $x = 0$, $\{(0, 0), (0, 1), (0, 2)\}$; $x + 1 = 0$, $\{(2, 0), (2, 1), (2, 2)\}$, $x + 2 = 0$; $\{(1, 0), (1, 1), (1, 2)\}$; $y = 0$, $\{(0, 0), (1, 0), (2, 0)\}$; $y + 1 = 0$, $\{(0, 2), (1, 2), (2, 2)\}$; $y + 2 = 0$, $\{(0, 1), (1, 1), (2, 1)\}$; $x + y = 0$, $\{(0, 0), (1, 2), (2, 1)\}$; $x + y + 1 = 0$, $\{(0, 2), (1, 1), (2, 0)\}$; $x + y + 2 = 0$, $\{(0, 1), (1, 0), (2, 2)\}$; $x + 2y = 0$, $\{(0, 0), (1, 1), (2, 2)\}$; $x + 2y + 1 = 0$, $\{(0, 1), (1, 2), (2, 0)\}$; $x + 2y + 2 = 0$, $\{(0, 2), (1, 0), (2, 1)\}$. Each line has exactly three points.

10. By I-1 and I-2, there exist two distinct points $P_{0,0}$ and $P_{1,0}$ and $\overleftrightarrow{P_{0,0}P_{1,0}}$. Call point $P_{0,0}$ the origin, $\overleftrightarrow{P_{0,0}P_{1,0}}$ the x-axis, $\overrightarrow{P_{0,0}P_{1,0}}$ the positive x direction, and $\overline{P_{0,0}P_{1,0}}$ the unit length. By B-1, there exists a point R on $\overleftrightarrow{P_{0,0}P_{1,0}}$ such that $P_{0,0}$-$P_{1,0}$-R. By C-1, there exists a point $P_{2,0}$ on $\overrightarrow{P_{1,0}R}$ such $\overline{P_{0,0}P_{1,0}} \cong \overline{P_{1,0}P_{2,0}}$. Proceeding inductively, we can establish an infinite sequence of points $P_{j,0}$, where $j \in \mathbf{Z}$, in the positive and negative x directions such that $P_{k-1,0}$-$P_{k,0}$-$P_{k+1,0}$ and $\overline{P_{0,0}P_{1,0}} \cong \overline{P_{j-1,0}P_{j,0}}$. There exists a line ℓ perpendicular to $\overleftrightarrow{P_{0,0}P_{1,0}}$ through $P_{0,0}$ (see Section 11.1.4, Problem 5). By I-3, there exists a point Y distinct from $P_{0,0}$ on ℓ. Call ℓ the y-axis and $\overrightarrow{P_{0,0}Y}$ the positive y direction. By C-1, there exists a point $P_{0,1}$ on $\overrightarrow{P_{0,0}Y}$ such that $\overline{P_{0,0}P_{1,0}} \cong \overline{P_{0,0}P_{0,1}}$. Reasoning as above, we can establish an infinite sequence of points $P_{0,k}$, where $k \in \mathbf{Z}$, in the positive and negative y directions such that $P_{0,k-1}$-$P_{0,k}$-$P_{0,k+1}$ and $\overline{P_{0,0}P_{1,0}} \cong \overline{P_{0,k-1}P_{0,k}}$. We can further construct unique lines through points $P_{k,0}$ and $P_{0,j}$ and perpendicular to the x-axis and y-axis, respectively. By the parallel postulate, these lines are guaranteed to intersect at a point $P_{k,j}$.

Section 11.2.2

1. Sample synthetic proof: Consider parallelogram ABCD.

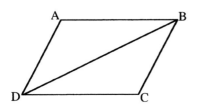

Construct $\overline{BD}$ (Axiom I-2). By definition of parallelogram, $\overleftrightarrow{AD}$ // $\overleftrightarrow{BC}$ and $\overleftrightarrow{AB}$ // $\overleftrightarrow{DC}$. So, by the parallel postulate, $\angle ADB \cong \angle CBD$ and $\angle ABD \cong \angle CDB$. Also, $\overline{BD} \cong \overline{BD}$ (Axiom C-2). So, by ASA congruence, $\overline{AD} \cong \overline{BC}$ and $\overline{AB} \cong \overline{DC}$.

2. Sample analytic proof: Consider $\triangle ABC$.

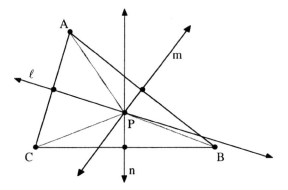

Let lines ℓ, m, and n be the perpendicular bisectors of $\overline{AC}$, $\overline{AB}$, and $\overline{BC}$, respectively. Because these lines are not parallel, they intersect at some point P. (Note that P does not have to be interior to the triangle.) Because P is on the perpendicular bisector of $\overline{AB}$, $\overline{PB} \cong \overline{PA}$, and because P is on the perpendicular bisector of $\overline{AC}$, $\overline{PA} \cong \overline{PC}$. By the transitivity of congruence (Axiom C-2), $\overline{PB} \cong \overline{PC}$. Thus P is on line n and the three perpendicular bisectors are concurrent. Sample analytic proof: Consider $\triangle ABC$ in the Cartesian plane with vertices A = (a, 0), B = (b, 0), and C = (0, c). The perpendicular bisector of $\overline{AB}$ will have equation $x = \frac{a+b}{2}$. An equation for $\overleftrightarrow{AC}$ is $y = -\frac{c}{a}x + c$ and the midpoint of $\overline{AC}$ has coordinates $(\frac{a}{2}, \frac{c}{2})$. So an equation for the perpendicular bisector of $\overline{AC}$ is $y = \frac{a}{c}x + \frac{c^2-a^2}{2c}$. Similarly, the perpendicular bisector of $\overline{BC}$ has equation $y = \frac{b}{c}x + \frac{c^2-b^2}{2c}$. Thus the perpendicular bisectors of $\overline{AB}$ and $\overline{AC}$ intersect at the point $(\frac{a+b}{2}, \frac{ab+c^2}{2c})$. The perpendicular bisectors of $\overline{AB}$ and $\overline{BC}$ also intersect at the point $(\frac{a+b}{2}, \frac{ab+c^2}{2c})$. Thus the three perpendicular bisectors of $\triangle ABC$ are concurrent.

3. Let $\triangle ABC$ have centroid K. Apply the size transformation $S_{K,-2}$ applied to $\triangle ABC$ to produce $\triangle A'B'C'$. Since under a size change the image of a line is one parallel to it (Theorem 8.10), $\overleftrightarrow{A'B'}$ // $\overleftrightarrow{AB}$, $\overleftrightarrow{B'C'}$ // $\overleftrightarrow{BC}$, and $\overleftrightarrow{A'C'}$ // $\overleftrightarrow{AC}$. Also, since CK = 2KM, $S_{K,-2}(M) = C$, and since M is the midpoint of $\overleftrightarrow{AB}$, C is the midpoint of $\overleftrightarrow{A'B'}$. Similarly, B is the midpoint of $\overleftrightarrow{A'C'}$ and A is the midpoint of $\overleftrightarrow{B'C'}$. Thus the altitudes of $\triangle ABC$ will be perpendicular bisectors of $\triangle A'B'C'$, which, by Lemma 2, are concurrent. Thus the altitudes of $\triangle ABC$ are concurrent.

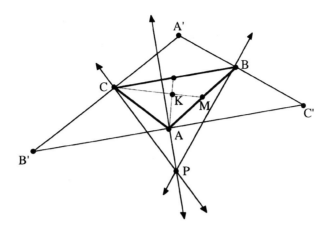

4.   Sample synthetic proof: Consider parallelogram ABCD with diagonals $\overline{AC}$ and $\overline{BD}$ that intersect at P.

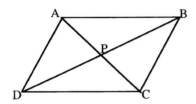

We have already shown (Problem 1) that $\angle ADB \cong \angle CBD$ and $\overline{AD} \cong \overline{BC}$. Since vertical angles are congruent (Problem 15, Section 11.1.3), we also know that $\angle APD \cong \angle BPC$. Thus by AAS Congruence (Theorem 11.7), $\overline{DP} \cong \overline{BP}$ and $\overline{AP} \cong \overline{CP}$.

Sample analytic proof: Let A = (a, 0), B = (b, 0), C = (b – a, d), and D = (0, d). Then an equation for $\overleftrightarrow{AC}$ is $y = \frac{d}{b-2a}x + \frac{-ad}{b-2a}$ and an equation for $\overleftrightarrow{BD}$ is $y = \frac{-d}{b}x + d$. These two lines intersect at the

point P = $(\frac{b}{2}, \frac{d}{2})$. So AP = CP = $\frac{\sqrt{b^2 - 4ab + 4a^2 + d^2}}{2}$ and BP = DP = $\frac{\sqrt{b^2 + d^2}}{2}$.

5.   Sample synthetic proof: Consider three non-collinear points A, B, and C. Form $\triangle ABC$. As in Problem 2 (synthetic), find the circumcenter P of $\triangle ABC$. Construct circle M with center P and radius $\overline{PA}$. Because $\overline{PB} \cong \overline{PA}$ and $\overline{PC} \cong \overline{PA}$, points A, B, and C will all fall on circle M.

Sample analytic proof: Consider three non-collinear points A, B, and C. Form $\triangle ABC$. As in Problem 2 (analytic), locate a coordinate system so that A = (a, 0), B = (b, 0), and C = (0, c). Let the point

P = $(\frac{a+b}{2}, \frac{ab+c^2}{2c})$. Using the distance formula, PA = PB = PC = $\frac{\sqrt{(a^2 + b^2 + c^2)c^2 + a^2b^2}}{|2c|}$. So the points A, B, and C all lie on a circle with center P and radius PA.

6.   Let S be a categorical axiom set. Suppose S is not complete. Then there exists an axiom A that is independent of the axioms of S and can be added to them. Let $S_1 = S \cup \{A\}$. If M_1 is a model of S_1, then M_1 is necessarily a model of S. However, since A is independent of the axioms of S, we can also construct another axiom set $S_2 = S \cup \{not\text{-}A\}$. If M_2 is a model of S_2, then M_2 is necessarily a model

of S. However, M_1 and M_2 cannot be isomorphic, since the axiom A is true in M_1 and the axiom not-A is true in M_2. Thus S would not be categorical, which is a contradiction.

7.   a.   By F-1 and F-2, there exists at least one line m on exactly three points, A, B, and C. Using the results of Problem 7a of Section 11.1.1, we know point A is on exactly two more distinct lines and, by F-2, there exist two points other than A on each of these lines. The four additional points on the two additional lines must all be distinct, since no two of the lines on A can have a point other than A in common (otherwise, two distinct would have more than one line on them, contradicting F-4). Thus there exist at least seven distinct points (A, B, C, D, E, F, G) and three distinct lines (ABC, DAE, FAG). Now suppose there exists an eighth point H. By F-4, there must be a line on H and A that is distinct from the other three lines on A. This would mean that A is on four distinct lines, which contradicts the fact that A is on exactly three distinct lines.

    b.   Sample: Interpret "point" to mean any binary string of seven digits with exactly one 1 digit. Then the set of points in our model is
P = {0000001, 0000010, 0000100, 0001000, 0010000, 0100000, 1000000}. Interpret "line" to mean any binary string of seven digits with at least two 1 digits. Interpret "point p on line ℓ" to mean p & ℓ = p, where & is the bitwise AND operator. By restricting our set of lines to
L = {1011000, 0101100, 0010110, 0001011, 1000101, 1100010, 0110001}, we have a model that satisfies all five axioms of Fano's 7-point geometry. Note that this model is isomorphic to the model given in Section 11.1.1.

    c.   Let the set of points be {A, B, C, D, E, F, G} and the set of lines be {ABC, DEF, AGF, BGE, CGD}. This is a 7-point geometry that satisfies Axioms F-1 through F-4. It does not satisfy F-5, however, since there is no point that is on both lines ABC and DEF.

    d.   Sample: It is likely that all models of Fano's geometry are isomorphic, since they all must have exactly 7 points and 7 lines.